Public Speaking in the Age of Diversity

Second Edition

Public Speaking in the Age of Diversity

Teri Kwal Gamble
College of New Rochelle

Michael W. Gamble
New York Institute of Technology

Allyn and Bacon
Boston London Toronto Sydney Tokyo Singapore

We dedicate this book with love to our two children, Matthew Jon and Lindsay Michele, our favorite communicators, who make our lives complete.

Vice President, Humanities: Paul Smith
Series Editor: Karon Bowers
Development Editor: Carol Alper
Editorial Assistant: Kathy Rubino
Marketing Manager: Kris Farnsworth
Sr. Editorial Production Administrator: Susan McIntyre
Editorial Production Service: Ruttle, Shaw & Wetherill, Inc.
Photo Researcher: Laurie Frankenthaler
Composition Buyer: Linda Cox
Manufacturing Buyer: Megan Cochran
Cover Administrator: Linda Knowles
Text Designer: Glenna Collett
Electronic Composition: TC Systems, Inc.

A Viacom Company
160 Gould Street
Needham Heights, MA 02194

Internet: www.abacon.com
America Online: keyword: College Online

Library of Congress Cataloging-in-Publication Data
Gamble, Teri Kwal.
Public speaking in the age of diversity / Teri Gamble, Michael Gamble. — 2nd ed.
p. cm.
Includes bibliographical references and index.
ISBN 0-205-27559-1
1. Public speaking. 2. Critical thinking. 3. Ethics. 4. Pluralism (Social sciences) I. Gamble, Michael. II. Title.
PN4121.G253 1998 97-25533
808.5'1—DC21 CIP

Printed in the United States of America
10 9 8 7 6 5 4 3 COU 04 03 02 01 00

Brief Contents

Contents

Chapter Seven
The Speaker's Search for Materials
How to Research Your Topic 125

Chapter Eight
Supporting What You Say
How to Integrate Supporting Materials into Your Speech 157

Part Three Putting It Together: The Plan Takes Shape

Chapter Thirteen
The Speaker's Delivery
Style, Voice, and Body Language 265

Chapter Fourteen
Speaking with Visual Aids 288

Part Five At the Speaker's Stand: Speaking for an Array of Purposes

Chapter Fifteen Speaking to Inform 316

Chapter Sixteen Speaking to Persuade 342

Preface

Why did we write *Public Speaking in the Age of Diversity?* We wrote this book because we wanted to create a text that would positively influence the perceptions students have regarding the importance of public speaking in their lives. We wrote it because we aspired to create a public speaking text that would function as a bridge to change—in knowledge, in attitudes and beliefs, and in values and behavior.

As our world becomes more complex and technologically sophisticated, the ability to create, deliver, and process the messages of public speakers becomes increasingly important. Both speakers and receivers can benefit by learning to think more critically about the multitude of messages competing for attention in the public arena. What is more, we are convinced that it is becoming increasingly necessary for each of us to examine our ethical values and cultural sensitivities and biases so that we may acquire the depth of understanding and conceptual framework needed to share knowledge; defend diverse points of view; and persuade others to accept, support, or serve as advocates for our beliefs or for changes we would like to see occur.

Public Speaking in the Age of Diversity reflects our conviction that students learn best when actively involved in their learning and perform best when actively challenged to explore the interplay between ideas, society, and themselves. It is only after carefully considering how speechmaking and speech receiving personally affect them and only after speculating about the significance and impact of a speechmaker's efforts that students can be expected to evaluate the outcomes of speechmaking and become more adept speechmakers and listeners themselves. With this in mind, we sought to:

familiarize students with both the theory and the practice of public speaking;

help students internalize key public speaking principles and skills; and

give students the opportunity and the confidence to become more adept thinkers, creators, speech practitioners, and evaluators.

Although this text explores all the major content areas of public speaking, it distinguishes itself from the competition by offering a truly unique and timely learning package. *Public Speaking in the Age of Diversity* presents its content in a clear, easily comprehensible manner and format, and offers numerous features designed to enhance and maintain reader interest.

FEATURES OF THIS BOOK

Considering Diversity

The students of today and tomorrow will inhabit a society that is increasingly multicultural. *Public Speaking in the Age of Diversity* is the first public speaking text to incorporate one or more sections on cultural diversity in every chapter in addition to providing boxes containing cultural issues, controversies, and readings for students to consider, evaluate, and act on.

Professional Insights

This boxed series includes discussions on the public speaking process by a variety of professionals. We hear from well-known individuals including Dr. Ruth Westheimer as well as from public speaking trainers who work for major public relations companies. Also included are insights gleaned from the experiences of speechwriters for corporate executives and politicians. But the insights do not stand alone; rather, students are prompted to make connections between the insights offered by the professionals and their own speechmaking activities.

Speaking of Ethics

An entire chapter and a boxed series both consider the numerous ethical issues that challenge today's public speakers. Documentation of source material is one such issue students will wrestle with; speaking about a topic with which they are unfamiliar and advocating a position they do not support are others.

Speaking of Critical Thinking

Chapters in *Public Speaking in the Age of Diversity* contain critical thinking queries—questions and dilemmas that put students' minds to work as they explore, analyze, critique, and personalize the public speaking process. The disciplined thinking of the critical mind is central to the practice of effective public communication.

Speaking of Skillbuilding

A number of exercises and activities designed to help students focus their attention on particular aspects of public speaking are integrated into each chapter. Each skillbuilding experience further helps make the study of public speaking active, experiential, and exciting for students.

Case Studies

Every chapter opens with an introductory case study that is designed to introduce students to a key public speaking concept explored in that chapter. By putting students in the midst of a chapter-related problem they must resolve, each case study also helps demonstrate the relevance of the public speaking–related dilemma to students' lives and involves students in brainstorming possible solutions to the highlighted problem.

Speech Texts with Commentaries

Public Speaking in the Age of Diversity contains an array of speech texts that feature annotations and probes designed to help students analyze and evaluate the effectiveness of speeches. By reading and/or viewing, as well as critiquing, these sample speeches, students become more adept at processing and preparing speeches themselves.

The Speaker's Stand

A variety of end-of-chapter assignments designed to promote speechmaking mastery are interspersed throughout the text. These assignments provide students with repeated opportunities to apply the principles discussed to actual speechmaking challenges and situations. These application exercises can also be used to spur class discussion and more active student participation.

Student Focus Group Reports

Public Speaking in the Age of Diversity encourages students to pool the understandings and insights they gain from studying and experiencing the concepts, principles, and applications contained in a unit into a group report, analysis, or critique delivered to the class. In addition to allowing students to summarize the new knowledge they have acquired, this feature gives students the opportunity to revisit the case studies at the beginnings of chapters to see how, after reading the material, they would refine or revise their initial reactions. These focus group reports also provide students with a number of opportunities to vent their feelings and share their perceptions.

NEW TO THIS EDITION

WE HAVE ADDED TWO new chapters to this edition: Chapter 2 addresses strategies students can use to handle speech apprehension and stress, and Chapter 3 focuses on the important subject of ethics in public speaking. In addition, we have greatly enhanced our coverage of diversity and critical thinking in every chapter, added a case study to every chapter, introduced a plethora of new speech examples, included many new exercises, and significantly updated the coverage of all content areas.

To summarize, *Public Speaking in the Age of Diversity* is the first public speaking text to cover the basic ground traversed by traditional public speaking texts at the same time that it provides a *total instructional and motivational package* to help students think critically about professional speaking situations, focus on issues of cultural diversity and ethics, and learn from public speaking solutions developed by both professionals and other students. We hope you enjoy reading *Public Speaking in the Age of Diversity* as much as we enjoyed writing it! You can reach us with your feedback by e-mailing us at SpchCommAB@aol.com or writing to us in care of Allyn & Bacon.

ACKNOWLEDGMENTS

WE WANT TO THANK OUR EDITOR, Paul Smith, whose belief in and commitment to this book made the second edition fun to work on. We also want to thank our project editor, Carol Alper, for her careful reading, creative suggestions, and ability to think in sync with us. She worked tirelessly to help us meet all deadlines. Kudos to the designer and photo research team, who gave the work a look and feel that supports the content.

We also want to thank the following reviewers who so generously offered suggestions and whose insights and expertise we continue to value: Linda Anthon, Valencia Community College; Marion Boyer, Kalamazoo Valley Community College; Stanley R. Crane, Hartnell Community College; Terrence Doyle, Northern Virginia Community College; Betsy Gordon, McKendree College; Nina-Jo Moore, Appalachian State University; Bill Poschman, Diablo Valley College; Susan Richardson, Prince George's Community College; Jay Ver Linden, Humboldt State University; Chérie C. White, Muskingum Area Technical College.

Our heartfelt thanks also go out to our students, students across the country, and our colleagues for testing the ideas contained in this book and for contributing video speeches, sample speeches, and invaluable feedback.

Finally, we want to thank our children, Matthew and Lindsay, who endured life with us during the revision of this book.

Chapter One

Public Speaking

An Introduction

After reading this chapter, you should be able to:

- Describe how public speaking can help you realize personal, professional, and societal goals.
- Explain why making the decision to respect diversity, speak ethically, and think critically will enhance your effectiveness as both speechmaker and speech receiver.
- Compare and contrast types of communication.
- List and explain the essential elements of communication.

CASE STUDY

Welcome to Public Speaking

"Welcome to public speaking," said the instructor. "By enrolling in this course you are giving yourself not one but three golden opportunities. First, the opportunity to grow personally; second, the opportunity to excel in your career; and third, the opportunity to practice communication skills essential to the survival of a democracy."

Dana heard everything the instructor was saying, but the words just bounced around in her head. Public speaking. Public speaking. Public speaking. Not only did Dana have to give presentations at work, but now, to earn her degree, she was going to have to give speeches in class too. That was all she could think about. Give speeches. Give speeches. Give speeches.

Giving presentations at work was easy because her topics were always chosen for her. The audience was one Dana knew and interacted with daily. She made an effort because the outcomes were important to her personal well-being and financial stability. But this was different. Here she was facing a group of students with whom she had never interacted previously, a group of students who were not joined by a loyalty to some corporate being, and who had no stake in her success or failure. What would she talk to these people about? What would she have in common with them?

As Dana pondered these questions, the instructor continued: "Public speaking is more important today than ever before. With the advent of the information explosion, society's burdens fall on those who, of necessity, need to be able to make sense of and give order to this wealth of new information. In addition, you will need to be able to speak to a society in which diversity is now a fact of life. At colleges across the country," the instructor said, now quoting from an article in the *New York Times*, "'Student bodies are not only more diverse in terms of ethnicity, income and age; they are also more heterogeneous in terms of preparation and aptitude. Today's students do not all have the same interests, nor do they wish to learn the same things. In the typical college classroom, the social, cultural and intellectual differences among individual students are immediately and persistently in evidence.'"[1] The instructor put the newspaper down and, looking straight at the students, continued, "Thus, the need to develop effective speaking skills that enable you to adapt to such differences will almost certainly affect you in the very near future. Indeed, I am willing to go so far as to say that the amount of success you experience in the future will relate directly to your ability to speak effectively before different publics. With that in mind, your first assignment is to identify how public speaking can enable you to make a difference in the new world in which we live."

Dana stared silently at the professor and nodded her head. She and the other students were facing a new world. Her experiences mirrored the changing experiences of students across the country.

- Put yourself in Dana's situation.
  1. What would you say to fulfill the assignment? Explain in detail.
  2. How might the skills you develop in this class better prepare you to speak confidently in a variety of contexts? Be specific.

S WE FACE THE TWENTY-FIRST CENTURY, we are heading straight into an age that is certain to be characterized by rapid change. The continued explosion in information will be accompanied by a continued explosion in issues—issues that generate public concern, controversy, and the need for creative and reasoned thought. What are some of the issues we will need to face in the days and years ahead? Surf the Internet, open a newspaper, or turn on a television and you soon come face-to-face with an array of them. Issues from A to Z: affirmative action, battered children and women, crime, disappearing families, educational inequities, freedom of speech, genetic engineering, honesty at work, illegal immigration, juvenile justice, knowledge level required for citizenship, liquor advertising, media fairness, Native American rights, opinion poll democracy, product safety, quality of life, rhetorical sensitivity, sound-bite news reporting, technological innovations, universal language, values, women and leadership, xenophobia, youth culture, and Zionism, just for starters.

We'd like you to think of this book as a guide in beginning your journey into the territory of public speaking. We will point you in certain directions, illuminate key issues, warn of dangers, and highlight the use of public speaking by others. As you begin this public speaking journey, you have a special opportunity to empower yourself by learning how to communicate more effectively to others. As you develop this skill, however, you will also face a number of challenges that will test your sense of ethics, show why it is important for you to be able to think about and evaluate what you hear critically, and spark your desire to share your information and convictions with audiences like you and different from you, culturally similar and culturally diverse.

The world of the public speaker is changing rapidly. As our society becomes increasingly culturally diverse and the media hold up to us a plethora of speakers in whom ethical fairness seems to be lacking, as we consider the consequences that uncritical acceptance of a speaker and a message present for us, we begin to comprehend why public speakers possess a unique power in their ability to influence our society, for better or for worse.

Throughout history, public speaking has been a bridge to new things. Public speakers have produced in their audiences changes in knowledge, attitudes, beliefs,

You can empower yourself to make a difference by learning how to communicate your ideas effectively.

Figure 1.1

The choice is yours.

You can cling to the: or	*Enter the:*
Age of ethnocentrism	Age of diversity
Age of propaganda	Age of ethical communication
Age of uncritical acceptance	Age of critical thought

values, and behavior. For example, they have changed the way some people think about the role of government, caused others to revise their feelings about affirmative action programs, and helped still others to reconsider their roles and responsibilities as citizens. Learning not only to bring about but also to process such changes is what this book is about. It is our goal to help you learn to analyze public discourse in an age in which professional persuaders are paid very well to do what they can to discourage such critical analysis. We hope to help you learn to understand culture's influence in an age in which many people still cling to their own group or culture as the center of the universe. All over the world today, speakers are going to find themselves increasing their contacts with members of diverse cultures, and they do not necessarily possess the insights and skills needed to make those contacts meaningful and/or respectful. In other words, if we cling to the notion of a "homogeneous melting pot"[2] in lieu of taking cultural differences into account, if we cling to the age of ethnocentrism when the age of multiculturalism is upon us,[3] we will not be as prepared as we must be to meet the challenges of tomorrow. It is also our goal to help you develop the ability to make good ethical choices—even in what has been referred to as the "age of propaganda."[4] If we can help you resist manipulating others and show you how to avoid being manipulated by others, if we can help you learn how to be a savvy speaker and a savvy consumer of speech, then you will be equipped with assets you can use not only on your campus but well beyond it (see Figure 1.1). Let's get started.

THE PUBLIC SPEAKER'S ROLE: REALIZING PERSONAL, PROFESSIONAL, AND SOCIETAL BENEFITS

CAN YOU SEE YOURSELF in any of these situations?

Your best friend just got married. As a member of the wedding party, you are asked to deliver the toast at the reception. Two hundred and fifty guests are in attendance. You prepare and deliver a two-minute speech that brings tears to the bride's eyes, touches the groom, and moves everyone in the room deeply. At the end of your toast the bride and groom kiss and embrace you, and the guests cheer.

You are the parent of two children, one of whom has Tourette's Syndrome, an affliction characterized by uncontrolled cursing and involuntary gesturing. Congress is holding a hearing on the disease, and you have been asked to testify. At the hearing you deliver a thoughtful, forceful, and emotional appeal for increased federal funding for drug research to help allay the disease's debilitating effects. The bill passes.

You and five others are finalists competing for a single opening as a sales representative for a national computer firm. During the final interview each of you is asked to deliver a presentation before the firm's regional sales managers on the merits of the product. One by one you are called into the room to make your speeches. The others competing for the position have not studied public speaking and are uneasy, disorganized, and uninspiring. You, however, have studied public speaking, and thus understand the importance of organization, motivation, and delivery. You have mastered the art of creating and then filling an information hunger in receivers. Because you have learned how to harness anxiety and exude communication confidence, and because you have discovered how important it is to buttress ideas with a variety of support, you deliver a speech that is informative, persuasive, and credible. You are hired for the position.

People place a high value on public speaking ability because the art of public speaking is such a vital means of communication. Ideas are shared, influence exerted, and behavior changed by the public speeches of both famous and lesser-known men and women. Each of these names—big and small—communicated a message important to him or her by speaking in public: Susan B. Anthony (a leader in the women's suffrage movement), Winston Churchill (prime minister of Great Britain during World War II), Rev. Martin Luther King, Jr., and Rev. Jesse Jackson (leaders in the U.S. civil rights movement), Bill Gates (chair and CEO of Microsoft), Bill Clinton (president of the United States), Gen. Colin Powell (former chairman of the Joint Chiefs of Staff), C. DeLores Tucker (chair of the National Political Congress of Black Women), Madeleine Albright (the first woman U.S. Secretary of State), Cesar Chavez (founder of the National Farm Workers Association), Eleanor Smeal (former president of the National Organization of Women), Jeanne Kirkpatrick (former U.S. ambassador to the United Nations), Janice Payan (vice president of U.S. West Communications), Sada Ko Ogata (U.N. High Commissioner for Refugees), Mary Matalin and James Carville (political spokespersons) and, of course, you. The list, to be sure, could go on and on. The point is that all of these people had the opportunity to use their brains to get their ideas across to others . . . and most of them did. What will you do? As former Chrysler chair Lee Iacocca so aptly noted, "You can have brilliant ideas, but if you can't get them across, your brains won't get you anywhere."[5]

Throughout history, the delivery of public speeches has benefited individuals personally and professionally, as well as contributed to the betterment of society. If you open yourself to the possibility, this course will also contribute in important ways to you and your world. For example, developing greater skill in public speaking will enable you to inform people about things they don't know but you feel they should know; it will help you educate others so they can perhaps make better-informed decisions about a variety of perplexing issues; it will help you persuade people to do something you believe ought to be done; and it can also help you motivate people, reward them, or simply make them feel good about themselves. In addition, by knowing how to relate who you are, what you stand for, what you know, and what you believe to others, you also benefit yourself personally and professionally. In fact, skill in public speaking is one asset job recruiters look for when choosing among potential hirees.[6] Articulate spokespersons, people who have the ability to communicate their thoughts and feelings effectively to others, are in demand—not only by employers, but by society at large.

The Personal Benefits of Speechmaking

Public speaking skills and personal satisfaction and success go hand-in-hand. As a public speaker you are expected to reflect on your own interests, to explore where you stand on controversial issues, and to consider the needs and concerns of others. Preparing to speak in public often precipitates self-discovery at the same time it affords you the opportunity to practice the art of creative self-expression.

Becoming a more confident speaker will make you a more confident student. By developing the ability to speak in public, you develop your ability to speak up in class—any class. By learning how to speak publicly, you become better able to verbally demonstrate your mastery of content and better able to convey your thoughts regarding key course ideas and concepts to your peers and instructors.

Having an idea to express and the ability to express it can empower you intellectually and socially. As the Greek statesman Pericles noted 25 centuries ago: "One who forms a judgment on any point but cannot explain himself clearly . . . might as well never have thought at all on the subject."[7] The same is true today. By mastering the ability of communicating your ideas in public, you harness the power of speech. By being better able to control yourself and your ideas, you enhance your ability to control your environment. By being better able to manage the impression you leave others with, you promote continued communication. As your public speaking competence grows, so do your confidence and self-esteem. As your self-esteem grows you will feel better able to communicate your ideas, others will be more accepting of the ideas you communicate, and instead of shirking from sharing your thoughts you will openly seek such opportunities. Public speaking is a bridge to personal satisfaction and success.

The Professional Benefits of Speechmaking

Education in public speaking can also help you grow professionally. In many instances your ability to attain professional success is related to your ability to communicate effectively what you think, know, and can do. In addition to improving your chances for securing a job, your climb up the corporate ladder of success can also be advanced by effective public speaking. In fact, how far you go in your career may well depend on how capable you are at addressing, impressing, and influencing others. Thus, as you develop your speaking ability you also develop a brighter career outlook. Effective speakers are perceived to be more powerful than ineffective speakers; for that reason, those who cannot communicate their ideas clearly are often limited in the ability to control their careers. As you will see in the "Professional Insight" box, the corporate executives of tomorrow will need to be skilled public speakers who have mastered the art of speaking before groups of all sizes, including the news media.[8] As the number of business conferences increases and the demand for competent speakers rises, it becomes increasingly difficult to imagine a job totally devoid of public speaking responsibilities. In truth, avoiding public speaking on the job is no longer a viable option for those who aspire to advance in their careers. Public speaking is a bridge to career success.

Public Speaking and Your Career

Patricia Ward Brash is director of communications for the Miller Brewing Company. These remarks are excerpted from a speech she delivered to a meeting of Women in Communication in Milwaukee, Wisconsin.

. . . All of us in communications recognize that the further we advance in our profession, the greater our opportunities and requirements for giving presentations. We also recognize that it's wise to get experience: as *much* . . . *as soon* . . . *as often* as possible.

. . . We can all benefit throughout our careers from taking public speaking courses and studying to improve our presentation skills. . . . We should learn to tailor every presentation to the *audience,* to the *occasion* and to the *theme* of the meeting. . . .

A classic example of someone who tailored his message to the audience and the occasion was *Christopher Columbus.*

Before Columbus met the King and Queen of Spain, navigational experts in both Portugal and Spain had already recommended against backing his rather unusual proposal to reach the Far East by sailing in the opposite direction—*westward.*

But Columbus understood the art of persuading, of tailoring the message to the audience, and he knew how to put together an effective presentation. He knew, for example, that the Queen had a fervent desire to win more *converts* to her religion. So he made frequent references to the teeming masses of the Orient, just waiting to be converted. . . .

He knew the *King* wanted to expand Spain's commercial power, so he made frequent references to gold, spices, and other fabulous riches of the East.

All these points were worked into his presentation, which won the backing that resulted in discovery of the new world.

While few of us are called on to make presentations where the stakes are quite that high, many of us *do* make presentations where a critical contract, approval of a major marketing program, or the fate of our own careers can hinge on the outcome.

. . . Television has helped create an impatient society, where audiences expect us to make our point simply and quickly. . . . What they want is a comprehensive picture. If we can present it with clarity and enthusiasm, it will be more memorable and more likely to persuade them. . . .

. . . We should write each presentation with the adrenalin pumping, with a high degree of excitement about the message we are sharing with the audience. The audience should feel that we cared enough to prepare the talk just for them. They must feel that our presentaion is like a tailor-made suit, not one taken off the rack. . . .

. . . Becoming a poised, polished presenter is a journey of a lifetime, and each time we do a presentation, we should learn something more about ourselves and our subject that will enable us to improve our performance the next time.[9]

- Consider these questions:
  1. When was the last time you were called on to make a presentation? Describe the situation.
  2. What was at stake?
  3. What was the outcome?
  4. What did you learn about yourself during the experience?

The Societal Benefits of Public Speaking

Education in public speaking can also help you develop skills to make you a better citizen. Without the effective and responsible participation of citizens, democracy cannot survive or flourish. Thus freedom of speech has always been viewed as an essential ingredient in a democracy. What does freedom of speech mean? It means:

1. You can speak freely without fear of retaliation.
2. You can expose yourself freely to all sides of a controversial issue.
3. You can debate freely all disputable questions of fact, value, or policy.
4. You can make decisions freely based on your evaluation of the choices confronting you.

Without these abilities you would not be able to add to individual or group knowledge, or bring about individual or group change peaceably.

Freedom of speech in the United States was guaranteed by the nation's founders when they authored the First Amendment to the Constitution. In it they ensured that:

> Congress shall make no law respecting an establishment of religion, or prohibiting the free exercise thereof; or abridging the freedom of speech, or of the press, or the right of the people peaceably to assemble, and to petition the government for a redress of grievances.

The U.S. political system depends on a commitment by U.S. citizens to speak openly and honestly and to listen freely and carefully to all sides of an issue. It depends on our ability to think critically about what we listen to so that we are able to accept or reject the speaker's goal and, in so doing, make informed decisions about our future. It depends on our willingness to understand and respond to expressions of opinion, belief, and value different from our own. It depends on how we choose to act when speaking in public and when listening to public speech. As you study public speaking, your ability to be an effective participant in the democratic process will grow.

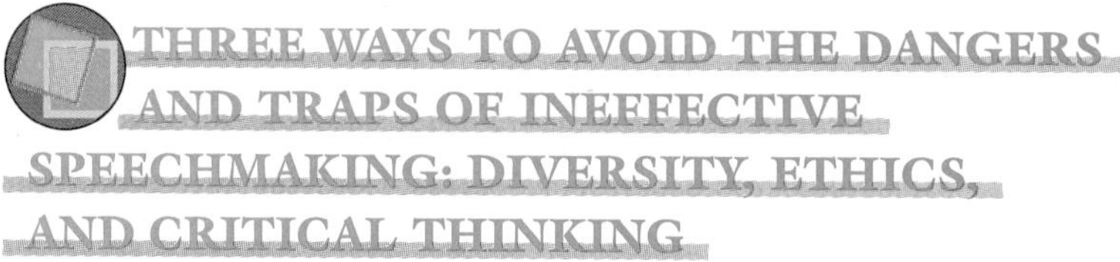

THREE WAYS TO AVOID THE DANGERS AND TRAPS OF INEFFECTIVE SPEECHMAKING: DIVERSITY, ETHICS, AND CRITICAL THINKING

ALTHOUGH THERE IS NO simple formula that will ensure you become an effective public speaker, there are decisions you can make that will help pave your way. Each speech you give tells those who hear it what you are like, what you value, how much importance you place on your role as a speaker, and how much respect you have for the intelligence and needs of your receivers. Although you may speak for personal benefit, professional growth, or society's gain, the questions you need to answer are:

1. Does the way you speak to your audience acknowledge your respect for and understanding of cultural diversity?
2. Are you acknowledging that diversity in an ethical manner?
3. Does your manner reflect and encourage critical thinking?

Throughout this text we will look at these issues and how they relate to the various aspects of public speaking.

Deciding to Respect Diversity

As you can see in the "Considering Diversity" box, in today's world, virtually all of us find ourselves in situations that require us to communicate with, inform, or per-

CONSIDERING DIVERSITY

Today and Tomorrow

According to the United States Census Bureau the demographics of the United States are changing. Research indicates that Hispanics are rapidly becoming the biggest minority group, followed by African Americans, Asian Pacific Islanders, and American Indians. According to Greg Schmidt, a senior researcher at the Institute for the Future: "Sixty years from now, we won't know what a minority is. It could be that a Hispanic will be the same as we think of an Italian today. . . . In a crowd, in the workplace, it will be hard to tell the difference."[10]

A more diverse society lies ahead; what implications does this have for public speakers? for audiences? In your opinion, will the speaker's task become more or less complex in a more diverse society? What about the tasks of receivers? To what extent, if any, do you believe that increases in diversity will result in decreases in discrimination by both speakers and receivers?

Imagine it is 20 years from now and you are part of a team of communication specialists who suggest to the Commander of a U.S. Army post that an information/facilitation program aimed at increasing awareness of the disruptive effects of sexual harrassment be conducted. How would the ethnic make-up of your audience affect the way your group pitched its proposal? You would need to consider the sex of the post commander and the sexual composition of the troops. You would want to identify the minority cultures represented among the soldiers. You would be wise, for instance, if the troops were Hispanic, to consider how culturally conditioned attitudes toward women and gender roles might predispose them to have a particular response.

suade audiences that are likely to be, at least in part, culturally different from us. Although we cannot insulate ourselves from such occurrences, we can prepare for them.[11] This realization alone can help force us into an even more rigorous process of audience analysis every time we address a group, whether large or small. Otherwise we may fail not only to communicate but to understand why we are not able to communicate.

Our speeches reveal what we stand for and demonstrate by their content, structure, language, and conclusions whether we respect differences and whether we are tolerant of dissent. Even beyond mutual respect and democratic values, however, lies our self-interest in "global competitiveness," at which we will not succeed if we fail to understand, respect, and persuade culturally diverse audiences. As a public speaker you can choose to use rhetorical tools that help hold society together—tools that are inclusive of difference and rely on logical proof, effective reasoning, and ethical persuasive strategies—or you can choose to use rhetorical tools that help drive societies and their groups farther apart—tools that are exclusive of difference and rely on questionable strategies that defy logic, manipulate reason, and exploit emotion. The choice of whether you will acknowledge cultural differences in the selection and development of your speeches or ignore such differences is yours. By taking the time to learn how to deliver speeches that take into consideration the cultures of others, you also come to understand how culture

Figure 1.2

Public speaking diversity continuum

Speaker Who Respects Cultural Diversity	*Speaker Who Neglects Cultural Diversity*
1. Develops a complex view of issues	1. Develops a simplistic view of issues
2. Demonstrates a decreased use of stereotypes, and avoids their consequences	2. Uses stereotypes and frequently has to confront their negative consequences
3. Is able to see from the viewpoints of others—is able to empathize with them	3. Sees only from his or her perspective; assumes that his or her values are shared by everyone, and fails to communicate as a result
4. Is no more anxious when speaking before diverse audiences	4. Experiences greater anxiety when speaking before culturally diverse audiences
5. Does not impose his or her views on others	5. Imposes his or her views on others; fails to be persuasive and risks open hostility from his or her audience

affects behavior and you improve your ability to have people from diverse cultures accept your ideas as worthy of their time, attention, and consideration. Increased intercultural contact is becoming the norm rather than the exception. In the years ahead, it will become increasingly difficult to avoid speaking before audiences that include culturally diverse receivers. To make democracy work, people from different cultures must be able to speak to and understand each other. A speaker who is sensitive to cultural differences does not think of his or her culture as superior to others, and therefore will be less apt to exhibit signs of racism or sexism (see Figure 1.2).

Speakers who respect cultural diversity are better able to communicate, better able to make themselves understood, and better able to elicit desired responses from receivers. By recognizing that speakers from diverse cultures may display different amounts of expressiveness in their communication styles, by paying attention to the ways people think and how they feel, you can become a more culturally flexible speaker.

Deciding to Speak Ethically

The actions of the Hill and Knowlton public relations firm (see the "Speaking of Ethics" box) caused a public debate regarding ethical concerns. One of the first choices you need to make as a public speaker is to decide on the ethical standards to which you will adhere. In other words, what "I wills," and "I won'ts" will you use as guides when speaking in public? What will you do, and what will you refrain from doing in order to impress an audience and make your point? For example, would you sacrifice or insist on achieving your goal if it turned out to not contribute to the overall well-being of others? If, for example, your aim was to gain

SPEAKING of ETHICS

Who Is Responsible for a Speaker's Words, Actions, and Effects?

In the early 1990s Kuwait hired a major communications and public relations firm, Hill and Knowlton, to help rally support for United States military intervention prior to the Gulf War. In conducting a campaign to get the Kuwaiti story out to the American people, Hill and Knowlton coached a young Kuwaiti woman named Nayirah in the art of public presentation. As it turned out, the presentation she made caused a nationwide debate on the ethics of public communication.

In an appearance before the Human Rights Caucus of Congress, Nayirah, who was introduced as a 15-year-old Kuwaiti escapee, spoke movingly of 312 babies in Kuwait having been pulled mercilessly from their incubators by Iraqi soldiers and left to die. This supposed occurrence was quoted by the media, referred to in speeches by President Bush and a number of U.S. senators who advocated war against Iraq, and even held up for a time by Amnesty International as an example of Iraqi atrocities. Nayirah's story, however, could not be confirmed; in time it was shown to be a hoax. It also turned out that Nayirah was no ordinary Kuwaiti citizen, but a member of the Kuwaiti royal family; her father was also Kuwait's ambassador to the United States, Sheik Saud Nasir Al Sabeh. This fact was concealed from Americans, and was not revealed to them even when the cochair of the congressional caucus became aware of it. Not until the publisher of *Harper's* magazine, John R. McArther, uncovered it was Nayirah's true identity brought to light. Although a broad debate on the war issue was already finished by the time the revelations were made, many people in and out of government were disturbed that such a questionable presentation had gained so much attention.

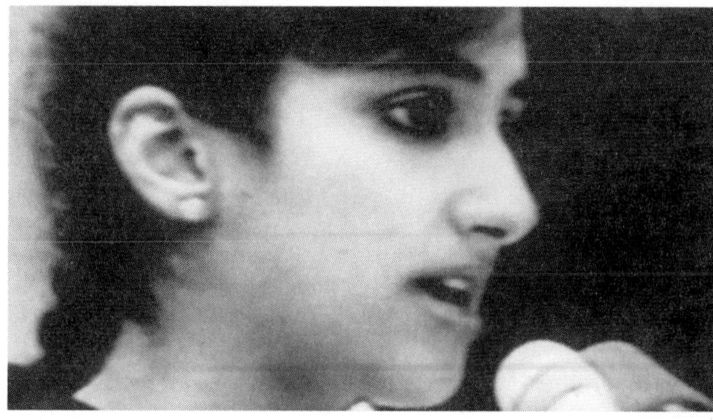

Why do you think so many people were concerned about Nayirah's testimony about atrocities in Kuwait?

- What are the ethical implications of a speaker concealing his or her true identity from receivers?
- What are the ethical implications of a speaker using inaccurate or fabricated evidence to achieve a desired effect?

(continued)

Speaking of Ethics *(continued)*

- Would the fact that Nayirah was the daughter of the ambassador have affected you as a receiver?
- Does the desire to hit a responsive chord in receivers free a speaker from ethical obligations?

These questions and more were raised in Congress and in the media, clearly indicating that many people felt important ethical considerations in public communication had not been adequately considered.

planning board approval for the building of low- and middle-income single-family homes in an upscale residential neighborhood, and you knew that doing so would substantially reduce the property values of present area residents, in presenting the plan would you be honest and apprise them of the potential impact of the project, or would you instead attempt to conceal any adverse effects from them in an effort to push your program through? Ethical speakers treat receivers as they would want a speaker to treat them; they do not intentionally deceive them just to attain their objectives. If you reveal everything your listeners need to know to be able to fairly assess both you and your message, then you don't cover up, lie, distort, or exaggerate your information to win their approval and support. When you make your real intentions clear to your receivers, you do not attempt to manipulate their reactions by keeping from them information that would cause your speech to have a lesser impact than if they were aware of it.[12] By using valid evidence and by refusing to substitute only emotion-arousing materials in their place, you encourage the audience to critically evaluate your speech's content. As an ethical speaker you need to inform your audience that you are an advocate on behalf of a particular group or individual, and not knowingly misrepresent to them who you represent when speaking. As an ethical speaker you need to document the sources of your ideas, not steal the ideas of another (plagiarize) and pass them off as your own. As an ethical speaker you prepare your speech carefully; you do not knowingly waste your audience's time and energy by delivering an ill-prepared, poorly researched, unrehearsed presentation.

Democracy depends on your behaving ethically; it depends on your making moral choices regarding how you, the speaker, will behave toward your receivers. The moral choices you make should not be turned on and off at whim. As a partner in democracy you have ethical responsibilities and need to concern yourself with the consequences of your speaking (see Figure 1.3). We will explore the question of ethics in greater depth in Chapter 3.

Deciding to Think Critically

You choose both how you will process material to be incorporated into a speech and how you will act when on the receiving end of such material. As you can see from the "Speaking of Critical Thinking" box on pages 14–15, it is up to you as both public speaker and public listener to take an active role in the speechmaking and speech

The Ethical Speaker	*The Unethical Speaker*
1. Intends to contribute to the well-being of receivers	1. Is intent only on achieving his or her goal, no matter what the cost
2. Respects receivers and treats them as he or she would like to be treated by a speaker	2. Treats receivers strictly in terms of his or her own needs, ignoring their needs
3. Reveals everything listeners need to know to fairly assess the speaker and the message	3. Conceals, lies, distorts, or exaggerates information to win listener approval and support
4. Encourages critical evaluation by relying on valid evidence	4. Discourages critical evaluation by deliberately overwhelming critical evidence with appeals to emotion
5. Informs receivers who, if anyone, he or she represents	5. Conceals the fact he or she is speaking for another person or interest group
6. Carefully documents all sources	6. Plagiarizes the ideas of others or exhibits reckless disregard for sources of ideas or information
7. Painstakingly prepares and rehearses all speeches	7. Exhibits disdain for receivers by delivering unprepared or unrehearsed speeches
8. Makes good use of the audience's time	8. Wastes the audience's time

Figure 1.3

Public speaking ethics continuum

evaluation process so that you practice critical thinking rather than subvert its use. It is up to you to be sure that there is a logical connection between ideas and feelings, rather than swaying or being swayed by strong emotional appeals that are devoid of logic. It is up to you to know your subject and examine the evidence on which conclusions are based to be sure they are valid and sound, to spot weaknesses in arguments, and to judge the credibility of statements.

As a speaker it is up to you to think not only critically, but also creatively—to be able to play with existing ideas to yield new insights, and to see clearly the interconnectedness among ideas. It is also up to you to avoid presenting bad arguments.

As a listener, it is up to you to avoid accepting bad arguments and to search for a healthy voicing of differences of opinion before making a final judgment. It is your job to look for differences or inconsistencies in various parts of a message, to ask questions about or raise challenges about unsupported content, so that you are able to form an opinion about the message that you can support with evidence. You need to listen between the lines; you need to decide whether conclusions are convincing or unconvincing, and ultimately you need to decide whether what you are listening to makes sense and is worth retaining or acting on (see Figure 1.4 on page 15).

SPEAKING of CRITICAL THINKING

Sense or Nonsense

Speeches can be persuasive, sometimes dangerously so. It's important for both listeners and speakers to be alert to the potential distortions or perversions of democratic values that can occur when a speaker "gets carried away" with the urgency of his or her cause.

A keen desire to persuade-or to be persuaded—can lead speakers and listeners to believe that false or dangerous ideas have been made to look reasonable. In the chapters that follow you will discover that it's important to stay alert, to be ready to challenge and raise reasonable questions about the grounds for the claims that are made in a speech.

As an example, consider the following speech, made by a dictator famous for riding roughshod over the values of democratically elected governments. He delivered the speech to defend the slaughter of hundreds of his own citizens, asserting that those killed were plotting against him and the country. Can you discover points in the speech when dangerous leaps in logic are made?

> If people bring against me the objection that only a judicial procedure could precisely weigh the measure of the guilt and of its expiation, then against this view I lodge my most solemn protest. He who rises against [our nation] is a traitor to his country: and the traitor to his country is not to be punished according to the range and the extent of his act, but according to the purpose that that act has revealed. He who in his heart proposes to raise a mutiny and thereby breaks loyalty, breaks faith, breaks sacred pledges, he can expect nothing else than that he himself will be the first sacrifice. I have no intention to have the little culprits shot and to spare the great criminals. It is not my duty to inquire whether it was too hard a lot that was inflicted on these conspirators, these agitators and destroyers, these poisoners of the wellsprings of [our nation's] public opinion and in a wider sense of world opinion. It is not mine to consider which of them suffered too severely: I have only to see to it that [our nation's] lot should not be intolerable.[13]

- How does the speaker define "traitor?" What jump in logic does this definition permit him to make?
- What assumptions does the speaker encourage receivers to make? Are these assumptions reasonable or unreasonable based on the facts given? Explain.
- To what extent do the speaker's appeals to emotion discourage critical thinking? Explain.
- In your opinion, is the speaker's view of the situation simplistic or complex? In what ways does his perception of the situation limit his receivers' options?

This speech was delivered by Adolf Hitler to his fellow Germans over half a century ago—and in hindsight we can see how the disastrous worldwide turmoil followed from Hitler's famous contempt for democratic values. We could analyze how a Germany desperate to regain its earlier power and success might blindly accept this speech's false conclusions. Yet it is difficult to avoid wondering whether more people had been asking and answering some hard questions and been thinking for themselves about communications like this, the outcome could have been different.

In your opinion, could equally dangerous consequences result from this kind of speaking in our own time? Why or why not?

The future of our world depends, in part, on our ability to process public speech critically. To what extent do you find yourself an able judge of the merits of public discourse?

Figure 1.4

The public speaking critical thinking continuum

The Critical Thinker	*The Uncritical Thinker*
1. Recognizes what he or she does not know	1. Thinks he or she knows everything
2. Is open-minded and takes time to reflect on ideas	2. Is closed-minded and impulsive; jumps to unwarranted conclusions
3. Pays attention to both those who agree and those who disagree with him or her	3. Pays attention only to those who agree with him or her
4. Looks for good reasons to accept or reject expert opinion	4. Disregards evidence of legitimate authority
5. Is concerned with unstated as well as stated assumptions	5. Is concerned only with what is stated, not with what is implied
6. Insists on getting the best evidence	6. Ignores sources of evidence
7. Reflects on how well conclusions fit premises and vice versa	7. Disregards the connection or lack of connection between evidence and conclusions

Speaking of skillbuilding Self-Evaluation

Identify a recent speechmaking experience you participated in as a speaker that required you to consider the diversity of your audience, caused you to consider the ethical implications of your message, and challenged you to find creative ways to help your receivers think critically about your topic.

1. On a scale of 1 to 5, with 1 representing extremely ineffective and 5 representing extremely effective, rate yourself on the extent to which you demonstrated the ability to respect diversity, speak ethically, and encourage critical inquiry.
2. Provide a rationale for each rating.
3. Finally, describe how you would replay the speech event, were you to give the speech again.

You can discern from Figure 1.4 that the speaker who is a critical thinker presents his or her audience with ideas that are logically developed and supported. By choosing to not share information that adds nothing new to the understanding of receivers and thus wastes their time, speakers who are critical thinkers demonstrate their commitment to expanding the knowledge of their receivers; to introducing them to new ideas and new ways of perceiving; and to challenging them to open themselves up to reexamine their beliefs, values, and behaviors. Similarly, the listener who is a critical thinker does not judge a speaker or the speaker's remarks prematurely, is willing to challenge him- or herself to reexamine his or her ideas and beliefs, and refuses to use shoddy thinking habits to substantiate invalid conclusions. Speakers and listeners have a right to hold each other accountable for both truth and accuracy.

At this point, take some time to assess your own ability to consider diversity, speak ethically, and encourage critical thinking when speaking in public (see the "Speaking of Skillbuilding" box above).

WHO IS THE SPEAKER'S PUBLIC? COMPARING AND CONTRASTING TYPES OF COMMUNICATION

COMMUNICATION INVOLVES FIVE DIFFERENT TYPES: intrapersonal, interpersonal, group, public, and mass. Although each form of communication involves the deliberate or accidental transfer of meaning, one is distinguished from another by the number of persons involved in it, the formality of the interaction they share, and the opportunity offered to give and receive feedback.

- **Intrapersonal communication** requires only a single communicator. When you engage in this type of communication you communicate with yourself. We practice intrapersonal communication continuously: every time we worry about something we said or didn't say; daydream about what we have done, need to do, want to do, or should do; or engage in any kind of self-talk.

- **Interpersonal communication** occurs when we interact with another person to form a dyad (two people communicating). Any time we communicate with another, whether a friend, coworker, parent, or stranger, we are communicating interpersonally.
- When we find ourselves interacting with three or more people to accomplish a definite task or attain a specific goal, we are engaging in **group communication.** Although researchers differ on the number of people who may make up a group, it is accepted that the group must have some means of group identity. As part of a group we have the opportunity to both influence and be influenced by the other members of the group. Just as we share many dyadic relationships daily, we also participate in many friendship or work groups daily.
- When, instead of interacting in a group, we find ourselves either facing or acting as a member of an audience, we are engaging in **public communication.** Public communication is communication in a one-to-many-people setting, and the number of the "many" involved can vary greatly. The number in the public speaker's audience may be as small as a class or as large as there is room in a concert hall or stadium. As audience size increases, the opportunity for speaker and listeners to interact informally with each other decreases; one person assumes the primary responsibility of speaking while all others involved function primarily as listeners. For this reason, public communication is usually more highly structured than the other types of communication, as is the message the speaker delivers and the time limit during which the message is shared.
- In contrast to public communication, **mass communication** is characterized by the placement of a print or an electronic medium (a radio, television, newspaper, or magazine, for example) between the source and the receivers. Unlike other types of communication, the mass communication audience rarely exists in a single location. With call-in shows and interactive television the exceptions, speakers and listeners usually have little chance for direct and immediate interaction with each other; therefore feedback is usually more limited and delayed. It is becoming increasingly common for today's public speakers to use the mass media to get their message across to the public. Thus training in speaking to reporters, a radio or talk-show host, or a commentator is becoming an important part of the required preparation for public speakers.

Although the abilities to (1) organize ideas logically, (2) encode ideas clearly, and (3) analyze and adapt to listeners readily are skills needed in all types of communication, they are particularly important for the public communicator. Receivers usually have higher expectations for public speakers than for other types of communicators with whom they interact. When functioning as a public speaker you are expected to adhere to more formal standards of grammar and usage, pay careful attention to your style of presentation and appearance, accomplish your goals within a specific time frame, and anticipate and respond to questions that will be posed by your listeners (because unlike in more casual types of communication your receivers are expected to not interrupt you). Thus, as a public speaker you polish, formalize, and apply your basic conversational skills to help you achieve a specific communication goal in a somewhat more structured setting. Public speaking makes the primary focus of the communication the public. Whether you succeed in realizing your objective or fall short of achieving it depends on how well receivers respond to the choices you make during your time together.

THE COMMUNICATION PROCESS AT WORK

WHEN YOU COMMUNICATE YOUR GOAL is to share meaning with others, that is, to ensure that your messages—the thoughts and feelings-being sent and received reflect each other's as closely as possible. In many ways communication is a match game that involves a circle of give and take between speaker and listener. As linguist Deborah Tannen explained, "it . . . is a continuous stream in which everything is simultaneously a reaction and an instigation, an instigation and a reaction."[14]

The better your understanding of how communication works, the better your ability to make it work for you. No matter the type of communication involved, no matter the different cultural groups involved, the following elements are an integral part of the process: the source, the receiver, the message, the channel, noise, feedback, and the situational and cultural contexts. One way to study the interactions of these elements is to explore a model of the communication process in action (see Figure 1.5).

Let us look more closely at the variables depicted in the model in Figure 1.5 to identify how they relate dynamically to each other during public speaking. The model shows us that both the speaker, or **source,** and listener, or **receiver,** are involved in communication. Each party performs both sending (giving out messages) and receiving (taking in messages) functions, sometimes simultaneously, so that the sending and receiving processes are continuously reversed, making neither function the exclusive property of any interactant. The irregular area on the left represents you, the speaker, and the irregular area on the right represents your receivers. The areas have an irregular border to indicate that both source and receiver are in a process of constant change and development; every experience we have influences us in some way, making us at least a little bit different (not necessarily better or worse) than we were before we experienced it.

Figure 1.5

Communication is a dynamic process involving constant change and development with respect to source and receiver.

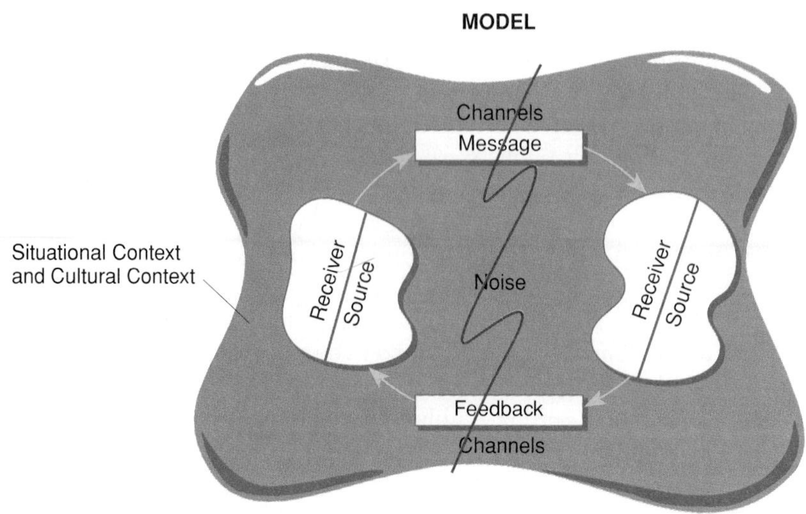

During the communication encounter we send and receive **messages**—both verbal and nonverbal. What we choose to speak about, the words and visuals we use to express our ideas and feelings, the sounds of our voices, and our body language together comprise the content of our communication and communicate information to others. Everything we do as senders and receivers has potential message value for those observing us.

Channels are pathways or media through which messages are carried; thus, every **channel** we use is a means of transportation for a message. The auditory channel carries our spoken words, the visual channel carries our kinesics cues (gestures, facial expressions, and postural moves), and the vocal channel carries our paralinguistic cues (rate quality, volume, and pitch). Communication is usually a multichannel event.

Noise is anything that interferes with or impedes our ability to send or receive a message. Noise can be created by physical discomfort, a psychological state, intellectual ability, or the environment. Noise need not contain sound, but it sometimes does. As the model shows, noise can enter the communication event at any point; it can be found in or caused by the context, the channel, the message, or the interactants themselves.

The **situational/cultural context** is the setting or environment in which the communication event occurs. Because every communicative act occurs in a situation that has particular cultural and social meanings, conditions of place and time influence both the way we behave and the outcome of a transaction. The context in which communication occurs is also depicted as irregular in shape to indicate that it too is constantly changing and evolving rather than static or fixed. To be effective at communicating, we must also adapt to it.

Feedback is information we receive in return for messages we have sent. Feedback tells us how we are doing—how our message is being responded to. Positive feedback serves a reinforcing function and causes us to continue behaving as we are, whereas negative feedback serves a corrective function and leads us to extinguish or reduce one or more ineffective behaviors. Because we constantly communicate with ourselves, even when we are communicating with others, feedback emanates from both internal and external sources. Internal feedback is that which you give yourself; external feedback comes from others who are party to the communicative event. Which kinds of feedback do you think are most important to each type of communication?

All parts of the communicative act continuously interact with and affect each other. They are interconnected and interdependent. When something happens to one variable, it affects all the other variables in the process. Communication is a moving experience, constantly in flux. It is accumulative; the communicative experiences we have add up and have the potential to alter our perceptions and behaviors. The **effects** of communication cannot be erased, but become part of the total field of experience we bring to every communication event. Ultimately, our **field of experience** influences our attitudes toward ourselves, our receivers, and our desire to communicate, in addition to the way we communicate. Your success as a source ultimately depends on you—your abilities to encode a message effectively, establish common ground with your receivers, adapt to cultural and situational differences, alleviate the effects of noise, and understand and respond to the reactions of those with whom you are interacting. The essence of your communicative effectiveness depends not only on what you intend to communicate, but also on the meanings given to that message by your receivers. A communicator who is too self-centered is insensitive to the needs of

Speaker Evaluation

Use the following scale to evaluate:

A. your current speechmaking effectiveness;
B. the speechmaking effectiveness of the best speaker you have heard; and
C. the speechmaking effectiveness of the worst speaker you have heard.

1. Identify the characteristics and skills that you believe distinguish the most effective from the least effective speaker.
2. Set a goal to improve your speechmaking effectiveness by specifying what you intend to do to become more like the best speaker.

Totally Ineffective	0	10	20	30	40	50	60	70	80	90	100	Totally Effective

receivers and thereby limits his or her own effectiveness. If you keep your eyes on your communication goal, you'll keep them off yourself; instead of focusing on you, remember to focus on your receivers.

SUMMARY

PUBLIC SPEAKING IS A BRIDGE TO CHANGE. By learning how to deliver and analyze public discourse you enhance your ability to be a changemaker.

Unlike other forms of communication, public speaking occurs in a somewhat more formal setting and requires the communicator to be well prepared. Although there is no simple formula you can follow to ensure you become an effective public speaker, there are three decisions you can make to help pave the way: to speak ethically, think critically, and respect diversity.

THE SPEAKER'S STAND

Choose one of the following assignments or an assignment of your instructor's choosing and share your thoughts with your peers in a two- to three-minute presentation.

A. Interview another member of the class to identify a number of unique facts about that person that others in your class would find interesting. When your research is complete, be as creative as possible in organizing and sharing what you discovered about your partner and what it has taught you about diversity.

B. Describe a significant personal experience that challenged either your sense of ethics or your ability to think critically.

C. Based on a review of recent news stories, share a concern you have regarding the ability of members of your society to respect diversity, act ethically, or think critically.

D. Bring to class a picture, object, or brief literary or nonfiction selection that helps you express your feelings about diversity, personal ethics, or the need for critical thinking. During your presentation share the selection with the class, discuss why you selected what you did, and explain how it helps you better understand yourself, others, or your relation to the subject.

Whatever your topic for this preliminary presentation, be sure you structure your presentation so it has a clear introduction, definite body, and strong conclusion.

STUDENT FOCUS GROUP REPORT

Now that you have had the opportunity to consider the nature, functions, and responsibilities of public speaking, in groups composed of five to seven students take a few minutes to answer the following questions:

1. To what extent, if any, would you now change your responses to the questions asked of you in the initial case study? Why?
2. What personal, professional, and societal benefits of public speaking do you aspire to realize?
3. How can you use critical thinking, diversity, and ethics to fulfill your unique responsibilities?
4. Why is public speaking a vital means of communication?
5. What kinds of problems might be precipitated by speakers and/or receivers who think uncritically, are insensitive to the diversity inherent in society, and/or behave unethically?
6. What key characteristics does the model of the communication process at work (Figure 1.5) reveal to you?
7. Summarize the most important information you have learned thus far about speaking in public.

Chapter Two

Understanding and Handling Speech Anxiety and Stress

Getting Ready for Your First Speech

After reading this chapter, you should be able to:

- Assess the amount of speech apprehension you experience.
- Identify the sources of your speechmaking anxiety.
- Use neurolinguistic programming, systematic desensitization, cognitive restructuring, and skills training to alleviate the symptoms of speech apprehension.
- Explain the characteristics shared by effective speakers.
- Enumerate and demonstrate the steps to be taken in approaching a first speech.

CASE STUDY

The Effects of Apprehension

Ned was a wreck. His knees buckled. His throat felt like he had swallowed a piece of chalk. His stomach was one big knot. His heart seemed ready to leap from his chest. Little beads of sweat formed on his forehead. With clammy hands, he gripped the sides of the podium and held on for dear life. As he attempted to steady his stance, Ned looked out at the faces before him, felt the room begin to spin, and fainted.

Ever since Ned found out that, as luck would have it, he had drawn the number one position in round one of the speeches in his public speaking class, this daydream played itself out in his mind. There was no doubt about it. Speechmaking anxiety had taken hold of him and was unwilling to let go. Ned gazed at his reflection in the mirror. Who was this shell of a person looking back at him?

Nothing had made Ned this apprehensive before. Normally he was confident, relaxed, even happy-go-lucky. Now, however, just the mere thought of having to give a speech caused him to experience palpitations. What made him feel this way?

At that moment, Ned's friend Sara entered the room and caught him staring at himself in the mirror. "You look like you just saw a ghost!" she laughed. "You can't be that scared of your appearance."

Ned realized that Sara had just seen him grimacing at his own reflection. "I can't do it," he whined, nearly falling into a chair.

"Can't do what?" she asked.

"Can't give the speech," he said, sounding truly traumatized.

"Sure you can, Ned," she reassured him. "You just need to harness that nervous energy you're feeling and make it work *for* you instead of *against* you."

"That's easy for you to say," Ned groaned. "You're not me. I'd rather have my tooth drilled than give this speech."

Sara laughed. "Ned, stop thinking about the worst things that can happen, and start preparing yourself to speak by talking more positively to yourself. Can't you see yourself succeeding instead of failing?"

Ned turned to answer . . . .

- Put yourself in Ned's shoes. How would you respond to Sara's question?
- Put yourself in Sara's place. What steps could you suggest Ned take to help him overcome his anxieties?
- Describe how you feel when it is your turn to speak and your professor calls you to the front of the room.

FORMER PRESIDENTIAL PRESS SECRETARY and White House spokesperson Marlin Fitzwater, clearly an experienced speaker, once commented that each of the 700 press briefings he delivered was a "fearful prospect." Not only was the president listening to him, but Fitzwater was aware that the words he spoke could make "whole nations go crazy."[1] Thus, you are in good company if the thought of speaking in public causes you some concern. Exactly how much concern does it cause you? To find out, complete the self-survey in the "Speaking of Skillbuilding" box on page 24.

Speech Fright versus Speech Flight

For each of the following statements, select the number that best represents your feelings.

1. I am afraid I will forget what I plan to say.
   Not at all afraid 1 2 3 4 5 Terrified
2. I am afraid my thoughts will confuse listeners.
   Not at all afraid 1 2 3 4 5 Terrified
3. I am afraid the words I use will offend listeners.
   Not at all afraid 1 2 3 4 5 Terrified
4. I am afraid my receivers will laugh at me when I don't mean to be funny.
   Not at all afraid 1 2 3 4 5 Terrified
5. I am afraid that I'm going to be embarrassed.
   Not at all afraid 1 2 3 4 5 Terrified
6. I am afraid my ideas will have no impact.
   Not at all afraid 1 2 3 4 5 Terrified
7. I am afraid I will look foolish in front of my audience because I won't be able to look them in the eye and I won't know what to do with my hands.
   Not at all afraid 1 2 3 4 5 Terrified
8. I am afraid that my voice and body will shake uncontrollably.
   Not at all afraid 1 2 3 4 5 Terrified
9. I am afraid I will bore my audience.
   Not at all afraid 1 2 3 4 5 Terrified
10. I am afraid everyone will just stare at me unresponsively.
    Not at all afraid 1 2 3 4 5 Terrified

Now add the numbers you circled, and score yourself as follows:

41–50	You are terrified.
31–40	You are very apprehensive.
21–30	You are concerned to a normal extent.
10–20	You are very confident.

Although this self-survey may not be a scientific indicator of your oral communication apprehension, it can help you face exactly what it is you fear. That is the first step you need to take to harness the excess energy that accompanies anxiety.

THE SOURCES OF SPEECHMAKING ANXIETY

WHY ARE WE AFRAID to speak in public? Why do many of us, like Ned in the chapter-opening case study, fear speaking before a group more than we fear heights, snakes, bee stings, or death?[2] There are a number of reasons.

Fear of Failure

We all fear failure. The idea of speaking in public often precipitates feelings of personal inadequacy, which in turn cause us to conclude that we are unable to cope with the speechmaking situation. Consequently, we find it preferable to "play it safe" and keep quiet.[3] If you choose not to take risks because you visualize yourself failing rather than succeeding, if you disagree with what you hear or read but choose to keep your thoughts to yourself rather than share them, then you are probably letting your feelings of inferiority and your fear of being judged incapable limit you. If you feel that others are more competent than you are, you put yourself at a disadvantage, and your anxiety naturally increases.

To reduce your speech anxiety, visualize yourself succeeding.

Fear of the Unknown

Many of us fear what we do not know or have not had successful experience with. The unknown, the unfamiliar, and the undiscovered leave much to the imagination—and far too frequently, we irrationally choose to imagine the worst. If you are one of the many comfortable traveling familiar roads, happier doing what you have always done, and content with the tried and true, then you probably fear the unknown and the idea of change.

Fear of Evaluation

We fear being evaluated by others. We are afraid others will not like what we say, how we sound, how we look, or what we do. We fear that the judgments they make will damage our self-concept. Thus, when faced with the option, we would rather avoid altogether being judged. We tell ourselves that if others do not judge us, they cannot reject us, dismiss our ideas, or consider us foolish.

Fear of Being the Center of Attention

We also fear being conspicuous or singled out by others. Typically, when we give a speech, the eyes of all receivers are focused on us. Some of us turn this positive focus into negative feedback, however, by interpreting the gazes of audience members as scrutinizing, hostile stares. That is, we further fuel our fears by convincing ourselves that the eyes of our receivers are sending us messages filled with hostile intentions rather than messages that reveal a genuine interest in us.

Fear of Difference

Feelings of ethnocentrism often lead to a fear of speaking to audiences composed of people from different cultural, ethnic, or racial backgrounds. When we are **ethnocentric,** we display cultural arrogance. We believe that our own group or culture is better than other groups or cultures. We believe that the values, beliefs, and customs of the group to which we belong or with which we identify are superior to those held by other groups. To be an effective speaker in an increasingly diverse world, you need to work to alleviate such fears of difference and eliminate such ways of thinking.

When we fear that we share nothing in common with our receivers, our feelings of anxiousness increase even more. Feelings of difference make it harder for us to find common ground, cause us to develop irrational beliefs regarding how receivers will react to us, and conjure up images of what could be a very unpleasant experience in our minds.

Most of us find it easier to talk to people who are similar to us than to interact with those we perceive to be unlike us or who we believe hold attitudes significantly different from our own. Because of this, culturally different or diverse audiences may enhance our feelings of apprehension. Yet, as a direct result of the increased diversity of our lives, it is quite likely that the vast majority of audiences you will address will include people of different cultural backgrounds.

Fear Imposed by Culture

Culture is known to correlate with the amount of fear we experience about communicating in public. For example, many Japanese and Taiwanese are more apprehensive about communicating in public than are Americans. In contrast, Puerto Ricans, Filipinos, and Israelis and other Middle Eastern peoples are typically less apprehensive than Americans.[4] Similarly, African Americans, who report some apprehension, in general have lower levels of communication apprehension than do White Americans.[5]

Why do these cultural differences exist? According to some researchers, one reason is that in some cultures, among them the Japanese and the Taiwanese, the parents, rather than the child, receive credit for each child's success and are blamed for each child's failure. As a result, when a child does not perform well, both the child and his or her family may suffer a loss of face. Such actions may well precipitate increased communication apprehension. In contrast, in cultures in which children are rewarded for merely trying, such as in Israel, communication apprehension appears to be less intrusive. No matter what causes our fears, we can work toward understanding them. (See the "Considering Diversity" box.)

COMBATING THE ADVERSE PHYSICAL EFFECTS OF SPEECH APPREHENSION

WHATEVER YOU CALL YOUR FEAR, whether the term you apply to it is apprehension, shyness, speech fright, reticence, stage fright, or something else, its impact causes you to experience anxiety about speaking in public. The discomfort you actually experience is usually the result of either a trait or a state. An **apprehension trait** is an ongoing individual characteristic; an **apprehension state** is a state of mind that an individual experiences for a period of time. For instance, if you are fearful of

CONSIDERING DIVERSITY

Imagine the Possibility

Visualize yourself in a specific speechmaking situation during which you are speaking to an audience composed of people from a cultural background different from your own.

- How will the anxiety factors discussed thus far come into play?
- To what extent, if any, do you think the cultural differences between you can be mitigated? For example, what adaptations, if any, should you make? What adaptations, if any, would you expect your receivers to make?
- To what extent would you experience a different level of anxiety if asked to speak before an audience composed primarily of Asian Americans, African Americans, Hispanic Americans, Middle Easterners, Native Americans, White Americans, or another cultural group? Explain.
- In your opinion, are you more apt to experience anxiety when speaking before an audience comprised primarily of men or before one comprised of women? Explain.

any kind of communication, or if your fear is triggered by all communication events, your apprehension would be a trait—innate to you. You would probably hesitate to engage in conversation, group discussions, or public discourse. Some 20 percent of Americans suffer from trait communication apprehension.[6] On the other hand, speechmaking apprehension is a state when it is related only to public speaking situations. Thus, people who experience no fear interacting one on one, whether with a friend, a stranger, or a supervisor, may experience considerable discomfort when faced with having to address an audience. Remember, if you experience such apprehension you are not alone. A large percentage of the U.S. public suffers the same affliction.

Learning how to deal with apprehension and manage your fear is important if you are to realize your speaking potential. You need to be able to manage both the physical (nonverbally displayed) and the mental (cognitive) manifestations of speech fright, as well as make a commitment to improving your skill level.

When you experience anxiety, adrenalin is released into your system and your respiration rate and heart rate increase. In effect, anxiety prepares you for either "fight," by giving you extra energy to meet the fear-producing situation head on, or "flight," by giving you extra energy to remove yourself from the situation quickly. These benefits of speech anxiety can help you perform your best. When the anxiety levels get too high, you may need to manage the physical effects of speech fright. Try the following exercise.

> Find a ball, tennis ball size or smaller. Stand up. Close your eyes and begin gently to toss the ball back and forth from hand to hand. Continue doing this with your eyes shut for at least five minutes, or until the physical sensations produced by your anxiety begin to subside.

Research in neurolinguistic programming suggests that such an activity helps restore a sense of balance to your nervous system, making you feel more comfortable and confident about facing a specific situation.[7]

There are a number of techniques speakers can use to lessen the physical symptoms of apprehension. Which of them do you use?

Another strategy, **systematic desensitization,** is also known to be a successful means of eliminating the physical responses of apprehension.[8] Systematic desensitization works by focusing on the physical responses to apprehension. By reducing the muscle tension that commonly accompanies fear and anxiety and substituting an alternative response that alleviates such stress, systematic desensitization helps individuals handle anxiety-producing situations such as public speaking. Tightening your muscles when you become frightened is an involuntary response; deep muscle relaxation forces you to reverse this behavior. Systematic desensitization relies on the knowledge that if an alternative response—muscle relaxation—can be substituted in place of muscle tension and tightening, then those who experience the response can learn to cope with it. The principle behind this technique is that after being tensed, a muscle relaxes. Try the following exercise.

> Tense your neck and shoulders. Count to ten. Relax. What feelings did you experience? Continue by tensing and relaxing other parts of your body including your hands, arms, legs, and feet. As you continue this process, you will find yourself growing calmer and gaining control of the jitters that once controlled you.

Systematic desensitization programs *teach* us how to relax. By learning to control the reactions of our bodies, we thereby learn to control and better handle anxiety-producing situations.

COMBATTING THE ADVERSE MENTAL
EFFECTS OF SPEECH APPREHENSION

FAR TOO OFTEN, our **self-talk**—our internal communication—fans the flames of our fears instead of extinguishing them.[9] Every time you find yourself thinking an upsetting or anxiety-producing thought, every time you visualize yourself experiencing failure instead of success, say to yourself: "Stop!" and follow that self-order with the instruction "calm." This technique is an example of **cognitive restructuring;** it differs from systematic desensitization by focusing on our thoughts rather than on our bodily reactions.

Cognitive restructuring works by altering the beliefs people have about themselves and their abilities. When irrational beliefs such as "I am incapable," "I am a failure," or "No one cares about what I have to say," interfere with a person's ability to express him- or herself, they need to be brought to the person's attention, unlearned, and replaced with ideas and behaviors that are growth supportive rather than growth inhibitive.

SKILLS TRAINING COMBATS APPREHENSION

YOU CAN ALSO COMBAT the adverse physical and mental effects of speech apprehension by making a conscious effort to:

1. speak on a topic about which you truly care;
2. prepare thoroughly for the speechmaking event; and
3. keep in mind that your listeners are much less likely than you to perceive your signs of anxiety.

By keeping your eyes and your thoughts focused on your receivers, and by believing in your ability to develop the skills you need to communicate successfully, you will be less apt to focus on yourself.

Limited speechmaking ability is a primary cause of speechmaking anxiety. The lower the skill level at which you perceive yourself, the greater the level of apprehension you experience. Because you have not been trained to speak in public, it is reasonable to expect you will feel anxious about doing so—it's like undertaking any activity at which you are a novice. However, as you increase your skill level and become accustomed to preparing and delivering speeches, the idea of doing so actually becomes less threatening.[10] Thus by learning the process of speechmaking—by mastering topic selection; formulating a purpose statement; developing your abilities to gather

SPEAKING of ETHICS

Should We Be Forced to Face Fear?

Confronting an innermost fear is not something we all do equally well. Some of us tend to repress fear, preferring to bury it rather than confront it. When we act in this way, however, it becomes even more difficult for us to handle or overcome that which we fear.

- In your opinion, should all students who suffer from speech anxiety have to try and overcome the fear of speaking in public? Why or why not?
- What if that anxiety is culturally conditioned? In your opinion, is it ethical to compel those whose cultures discourage making overt statements of individual opinion because they might offend others to speak in public?

appropriate materials, organize your ideas into an effective introduction, body, and conclusion, and choose the right words in which to dress those ideas, you can help yourself increase your speechmaking stamina and reduce your speechmaking reticence.

Remember the fears you had going out on your first date? Remember the anxiety you felt entering a new school or moving to a new town? Once you learned to perform effectively in those situations, you were able to conquer those fears, weren't you? Similarly, with training and practice, you can learn to channel and control your fear of public speaking. Increased experience and practice are the keys to your success. By making your fear work for you, by converting your fear into positive energy, you learn to fear fear less, and you learn to like public speaking more. Let's begin together to manage your speech fright. Over time you will learn to face the speechmaker's challenge competently and confidently.

LEARNING TO MANAGE YOUR SPEECH FRIGHT

CONTRARY TO WHAT YOU MAY THINK, we do not think you can or *should* rid yourself of all speech fright. Rather, we want you to learn to use your anxiety to motivate yourself to perform even more effectively than you would if you experienced no fear at all. What follows are some suggestions you can use as you harness the constructive energies that are a key part of the anxieties you may be feeling.

1. **Visualize a positive experience.** Very few people suffer really debilitating fear. So instead of focusing on your negative thoughts and fears, focus on the potential positives of your performance. By not allowing yourself to become hypersensitive to the physical side effects of fear, you can alleviate some of the anxiety you are actually feeling.

It is important that you work to visualize yourself being successful from start to finish. If, prior to speaking, you are able to visualize yourself approaching the front of the room confidently, imagine the introduction coming off without a hitch, and actually see yourself successfully delivering each part of your speech right down to its conclusion, you can then also visualize yourself receiving the congratulations of your audience. As the maxim goes: *Think you can. Think you can't. Either way you are right.*

2. **Remind yourself that receivers cannot usually see or hear your fear.** Receivers have come to listen to you, not to observe and focus on the signs of nervousness you may display. Thus, audience members are probably unaware of the manifestations of nervousness you think are visible to all. Although you may feel the flutters that fear causes, the audience generally cannot detect these flutters in your performance. In fact, observers usually underestimate rather than overestimate the amount of apprehension they believe a speaker is experiencing.[11] What receivers do not detect, what remains invisible to them does not exist for them, and does not detract from your performance. What can't be seen or heard can't hurt you!

3. **Choose a topic you care about and are comfortable with.** One of the best means of controlling your fear and laying the groundwork for a successful speech is to choose a topic that is important to you, one you know something about, and about which you yearn to find out even more. Highly apprehensive speakers rarely do this. As a result, they spend far too much preparation time trying to interest themselves in or master a subject, and far too little time rehearsing the presentation itself.[12]

4. **Focus on your receivers, not on yourself.** Highly anxious speakers tend to be self-obsessed, but more effective speakers focus their attention on their receivers rather

than on themselves. When you avoid focusing on your fear responses and concentrate on your receivers instead, you shine the communication spotlight on those you are speaking to and minimize your nervousness.

5. **Prepare thoroughly and rehearse.** Preparation helps instill confidence. It includes everything you do between thinking up a topic and speech delivery. Prepared speakers are competent speakers. Rehearsal is part of this preparation. It is essential to rehearse your speech many times if you are to increase your self-confidence. Rehearsed speakers are more confident speakers.

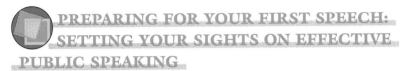

PREPARING FOR YOUR FIRST SPEECH: SETTING YOUR SIGHTS ON EFFECTIVE PUBLIC SPEAKING

NOW THAT YOU HAVE looked closely at how to handle public speaking anxiety, it's time to set your sights on becoming an effective public speaker. It's time to explore the characteristics shared by effective speakers and to start to learn the steps you can follow to help ensure that you are included in that group. Most likely you will be asked to deliver your first speech before you have had the opportunity to finish reading and applying all the relevant information contained in subsequent chapters; for that reason, in this section we offer a brief preview of the speech preparation information you need to keep in mind as you get ready to speak before your class for the first time. Each of the elements we mention now will be discussed in greater depth in future chapters.

Characteristics of Effective Speakers: Keep Your Eyes on the Prize

When you are a member of an audience, what expectations do you have for the person who will address you? How do you expect him or her to act? What do you expect him or her to do? When you are the public speaker, if you think about the answers to those questions you will be better prepared to keep your eyes on your listeners and to focus your attention on their perception of you and your message. You will be able to keep your eyes on the prize: effective public speaking.

Effective Speakers Are Insightful. Effective speakers recognize their strengths and their limitations and are in touch with the personal reservoir of experiences, interests, and concerns available for them to draw on. Based on an understanding of themselves and their resources, they discover ideas that result in new insights for their receivers. We discuss specific techniques to use when choosing a topic in greater detail in Chapter 6.

Effective Speakers Analyze Their Receivers. Effective speakers take the time required to analyze their audience, that is, to understand and tap into the interests, needs, and concerns of their receivers. By considering the topic from their listeners' perspective, by standing in their listeners' collective shoes and contemplating their receivers' perceptions of them, effective speakers discover what they need to do to be able to share ideas and feelings of value with their receivers. This topic is covered in more detail in Chapter 5.

Effective Speakers Practice Critical Thinking. Effective speakers think clearly and critically. They are adept at selecting and narrowing a topic, formulating a specific purpose for speaking, organizing their main and subpoints so that they support that purpose, and testing and assessing whether the conclusions they draw are justified and logical. They know that emotion can augment reason but never replace it, that their supporting materials must be current and relevant, and that if they impartially evaluate the substance of their presentation prior to sharing it with receivers, then they are better able to assist their listeners in becoming better receivers. Information about using critical thinking throughout the speechmaking process is covered in the "Speaking of Critical Thinking" boxes in most chapters.

Effective Speakers Are Culturally Sensitive. Effective listeners are sensitive to the myriad ways that both situation and culture can influence encoding and decoding processes. Because they have the urge to communicate, they also have the urge to ensure that receivers understand their message as they intend them to, and they research their topic, the situation that brought about the speech, and the cultures they are communicating with in an effort to devise creative means to develop that understanding. Information about diversity and public speaking is covered in the "Considering Diversity" boxes found in each chapter.

Effective Speakers Act Ethically. Effective speakers do not lie or dissemble, conceal facts, or feign feelings. They are true to their values, recognize that informed participation is key in a democratic society, are tolerant of disagreement, and believe they will fail or succeed through their own efforts. We look at ethical issues in Chapter 3, as well as in the "Speaking of Ethics" boxes found in most chapters.

Effective Speakers Are Well Prepared. Effective speakers prepare fully and conduct ample rehearsals. By conducting a number of presentation dry runs, they are able to identify and correct message and delivery weaknesses, integrate changes that enhance their performances, and do what they can to ensure that the delivery of the speech is pleasurable for both themselves and their receivers. We look at effective delivery more fully in Chapter 13.

Effective Speakers Conduct a Postpresentation Analysis. Effective speakers critique their performances. They know that they and their receivers will be changed in some way by every speech event; they know that their words, once uttered, leave an indelible impression, and they want to be certain that they learn as much as possible from this experience so that they can apply the lessons learned to the next experience. The effective speaker always has his or her eyes on the prize.

How to Prepare an Effective Speech the Very First Time

The speechmaking wheel reveals a systemic process that encourages you to develop both your creative and your critical thinking abilities. If you work your way through the **speechmaking wheel** (see Figure 2.1) in advance of each time you step up to speak, you will increase your chances of being a successful speaker.

Before we look at the individual phases of the wheel, however, let us remind you throughout the process to consider the hub of the wheel. Are you handling your topic as *ethically* as possible? Are you applying principles of *critical thinking*? Are you

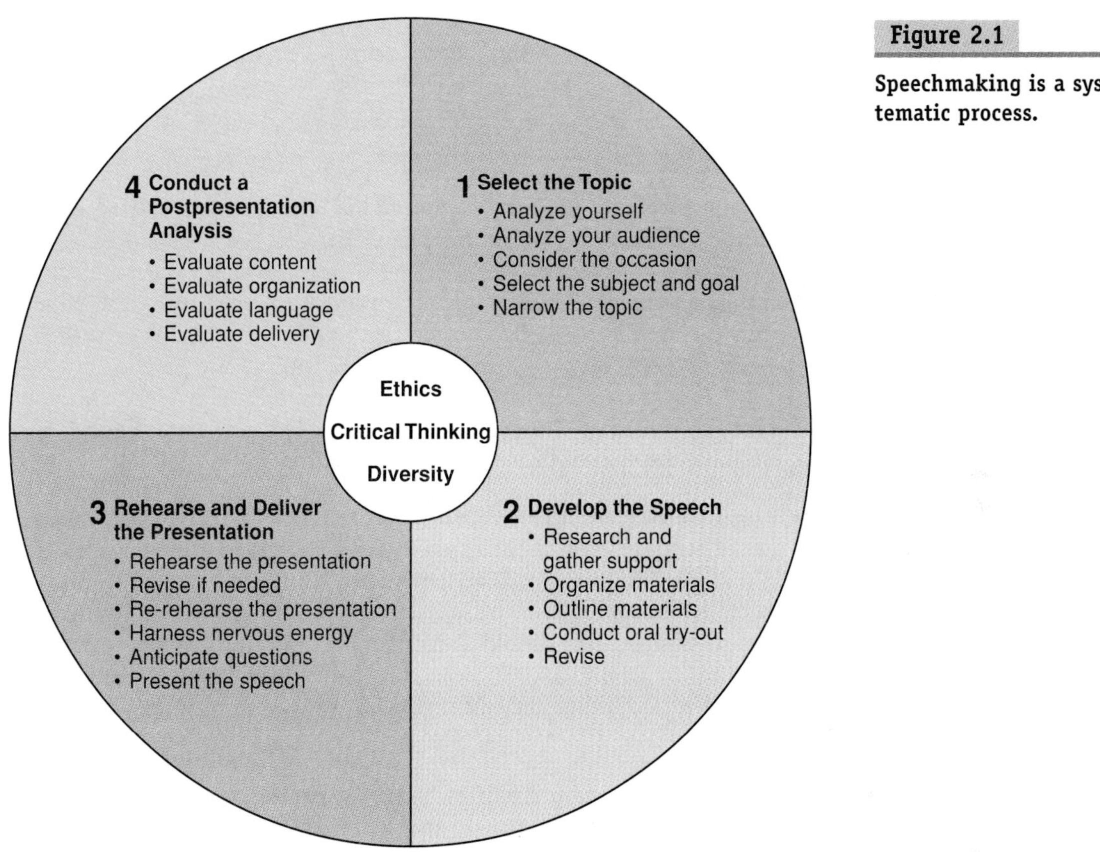

Figure 2.1

Speechmaking is a systematic process.

as sensitive as you can be to the challenges posed by the *diversity* inherent in your receivers?

Select the Topic. During the first phase of speech preparation you focus on topic selection. To choose an appropriate topic, you:

1. analyze yourself to identify your interests, concerns, and areas of special knowledge;
2. analyze your audience to identify ways in which their interests, needs, and knowledge could affect your selection;

SPEAKING of CRITICAL THINKING

It's Your Call

The audience is central to any speaker's being judged effective.

- If an audience does not agree with the position you are taking, can they still judge you an effective speaker?
- What steps would you need to take to ensure that this is feasible?
- Would you be willing to take those steps? Why or why not?

3. identify the occasion for speaking, including any special requirements assigned by your instructor, or the nature of the event that precipitated the speech;
4. choose a general subject area; and
5. concentrate on making that subject increasingly specific, narrowing its scope so you can cover it in the time allotted.

Develop the Speech. During the second phase of speech preparation you focus on developing the speech. It is during this phase that you research and gather supporting materials that will facilitate your realizing your purpose for speaking. Once this is done, you organize the materials you have gathered into a clear logical sequence that facilitates the communication of your message; you then outline your speech's introduction, body, and conclusion. By examining your outline and practicing it aloud you can assess whether your speech will achieve the response you seek from your audience, whether your main points support your central idea or proposition, and whether your subpoints explain or prove your main points.

Rehearse and Deliver the Presentation. During the third phase of speech preparation you concentrate on presentation—making every effort to ensure you deliver your speech as effectively as possible. Toward this end, you rehearse your presentation, revise it, rerehearse it, and revise it until it flows, has maximum impact, and is readily comprehensible. You should also anticipate questions audience members may ask and reactions they may have. You can then focus the energy produced by any anxiety you may be experiencing and put it to work for you during the actual delivery of your speech.

Conduct a Postpresentation Analysis. After delivering your speech, you enter the last phase of the speech wheel, the postpresentation analysis. During this phase you

By spending sufficient time rehearsing your speech, you allow yourself to get comfortable with your material. Does rehearsing in front of a mirror work for you? Does it help you visualize yourself succeeding?

compare and contrast your expectations of your content, organization, language, and delivery to what you actually realized.

As you turn the speech wheel, systematically working your way around it, as you move from one speech experience to the next, in time you will master the ins and outs of public speaking. What you will discover is that not every turn of the wheel will consume the same amount of time for every speech. For some speeches you will need to spend more time than usual analyzing your audience, identifying its needs, and adapting your speech and its contents. For others you may be quite familiar with your audience, but the nature of your topic may require that you spend a great deal of time researching, gathering materials, and organizing what you have gathered. Some lengthier speeches may require significantly more rehearsal time than briefer speeches, but all speeches require that you spend some time assessing their effectiveness. Take your eyes off the wheel, skip a turn and fail to consider something important, or turn the wheel too quickly and fail to consider something adequately, and you run the risk of having a rather bumpy speechmaking ride. But keep your eyes on the wheel, learn how to handle each phase of it, and you will realize the prize—a speech well made and well received.

Subsequent chapters will thoroughly consider each component introduced in the speechmaking wheel. This is merely an overview of the process that you can use to guide you through your first speechmaking assignment. In later chapters we will add to and refine that understanding.

A Sample First Speech

Now that we have seen the phases of the speechmaking wheel, let's look at one student's first attempt at speechmaking.

For his first assignment, student Chris Hornung strove to:

1. tailor his topic to suit both the needs and interests of his audience;
2. develop and organize his ideas so they were easy for his receivers to follow; and
3. use language and adopt a delivery style that facilitated communication between Chris and his listeners.

After his speech was over Chris thought about how he had done and whether he had fulfilled his objectives. He also considered whether he had handled the topic ethically, applied principles of critical thinking, and been sensitive to the challenges posed by audience diversity.

Following is a transcript of his presentation. Do you think Chris succeeds in attaining his speechmaking goals?

MY HOMETOWN

For the past couple of weeks, I've been listening to each of you give your speeches about your hometowns and all the different places you've lived. At first I was kind of envious, but when I sat and thought about it, even though I've never moved, I've actually lived in three different places. I live in Stafford County, Virginia, which today looks like a suburb of Washington, D.C., but it didn't always used to be that way. When I was little, Stafford County was like a wilderness. There were all kinds of trails and woods everywhere. You could see deer in my backyard, and to me it was just a . . . it was just a wilderness.

In his opening statement, the speaker relates his speech to the presentations of students who preceded him. Do you find this effective?

Why do you think that the speaker reveals his private thoughts to his receivers? Does doing so help the speaker build rapport with receivers?

My favorite place when I was growing up was this tree of mine in the back . . . in the middle of the woods. It really was my tree fort, but it wasn't a tree fort in the . . . the typical sense. It was just a tree with a bunch of boards nailed to it so you could climb up it. It was very special to me because I was the only kid in the neighborhood who could climb up to the top to the special point where you could see the entire neighborhood. And it was my special little place, my special paradise where I could go and just think.

The use of a narrative based on the speaker's personal experiences should help the speaker draw the audience into the body of the presentation. Did it succeed?

Perhaps the biggest impact on me when I was a little kid was this one day I was walking through the woods, and I came across this little rock in the ground. And I looked at it, and I realized what it was. It was a little Indian arrowhead, and I was really amazed by it to think that hundreds of years ago somebody sat and made this little rock. And, you know, I was just thinking what was he thinking when he made it, you know, and to me it was very special. So every afternoon I'd go back in the woods, and I'd look around for these arrowheads. And I would find a few, and to me it . . . it was amazing. I used to see Indians in my sleep. I used to see them in the woods. When I was, you know, out playing I'd . . . I'd see them hiding behind trees, and, you know, I really just got involved into Indians. So every afternoon I'd go and look for them.

The disjointed prose and occasional questionable word choice reveal the speaker's deep emotional connection to the topic. How did they affect you?

One afternoon in particular, I remember I came across this little yellow marker in the woods on one of these trees, and I thought it was, you know, some Indians coming across and claiming my territory, my little hometown. But when I finally got to the woods and realized what it was, it was a development company coming in and putting a house right where my special little spot was. When I walked around and realized they had also put in some steps from the . . . from the road up to the property, and it was kind of scary to me because somebody was coming in and . . . and taking over my . . . my own little special place. They had knocked off all the little wooden slats on my tree as well. And so it was kind of scary to me because they were taking away my paradise, and I could no longer climb up to the top of the hill . . . up to the top of the tree. So I did what I thought was right. I ran home and grabbed my dad's hammer and started pulling up the . . . the steps that the . . . the construction men had come and put down, and so, you know, I was furious. I was ripping them up. And in my haste I didn't realize that I had hit myself in the ankle with the back of the hammer, and so I had to go and get stitches. But, despite the stitches, I was happy because I thought that I had, you know, saved my paradise and saved my little home, my little secret place.

Needless to say, a couple of days later the . . . the developers came back and put in some houses—put in a house. And, you know, my paradise to me was gone. This kind of signified a change in Stafford County to me; everything was . . . was changing. They started putting in new malls, new shopping . . . shopping centers. Instead of going thirty-five minutes to the grocery store, it now took five. I could go and buy new clothes; my mom didn't go and get me Toughskins from Sears anymore. I . . . I actually had to go and do my own shopping and fashion started becoming more important to me and a lot of other things. I got to go to movies on the weekends, and you know, it . . . it was really nice. The only bad part about it was I lived next to Quantico Marine Corps base, which meant all my friends would come and go, and, you know, they were never there for a long period of time. And so I didn't learn . . . I learned not to . . . not to rely on friends and that they weren't going to be there for me. And it was kind of sad, but it was just a fact of life.

The speaker reiterates the sense of loss he feels. Are you able to share his feelings?

I didn't realize what was changing in Stafford, all the houses, until one day I went with my friend. It was my sophomore year of high school, and I decided to go and look once again to see if I could find any arrowheads. After looking for a while in this site where they were building a house, I came across this other rock. It was an Indian axe head, and it dated back to 3000 B.C. And it was then that I realized that all of this stuff was getting covered up, everything that I was looking for and was important to me was being lost. My trails were getting covered up, my . . . the arrowheads that were there for all those years were getting covered up with houses, and they would never be found again. And it made me really sad because I thought that other little boys, when they were growing up, wouldn't have the chance to find arrowheads and that kind of stuff that was so important to me, that they wouldn't have that opportunity.

So today when I go home, I drive down the road, and there are houses upon houses right there where all my woods were. There are no more trails; there are shopping centers everywhere. It's completely developed. Stafford in the last ten years has grown; fifty . . . the population has grown 51.3 percent. My subdivision went from 70 homes to 200 . . . 2,000 . . . 2,100 homes. so there's really no place to run and play like I used to. There's no wildlife, nothing.

With the last paragraph, the speaker ends the speech on a more upbeat tone. What is the speech's effect on you?

I went home this past weekend and I looked at . . . went . . . took my little sister out looking for arrowheads, just to . . . see if maybe I could find them again. We looked in the only place we could find to look in for about, I don't know—about two hours, and we didn't find anything. I was really sad. You know. I started walking home thinking that, you know, all this stuff was gone. And my whole home was gone. There was nothing left of it, and just when I rounded the corner to my house to go home, I came across this . . . this property. There was a big . . . big house with a big tree in the backyard. When I looked at the tree, I realized it was my tree, the tree that I had when I was growing up. And when I squinted and looked up the top far enough I could see my initials that I carved in the tree. That, you know, showed me that even though my home was gone, my little piece of paradise was still there.

HOW EFFECTIVE A PUBLIC SPEAKER ARE YOU PREPARED TO BECOME?

THIS CLASS IS YOUR LABORATORY. It is here you train for and take your speechmaking road test. It is here you experiment with, learn, practice, and develop skills. To be sure, there is no such thing as becoming too effective at public speaking; there is no such thing as being too good at establishing your credibility, too good at developing a logical argument, or too good at creating emotional involvement. What is essential is that you take advantage of the opportunities this class offers you to assess and enhance your speechmaking competence, and that you use it as a means to position yourself as a speaker who is a critical thinker, attuned to the challenges of diversity, and ethical in mind and manner.

With this in mind, how many of the following commitments are you willing to make?

- ❑ I am committed to using this public speaking lab to develop my critical thinking abilities.
- ❑ I am committed to using this public speaking lab to sensitize myself to the challenges presented by cultural diversity.
- ❑ I am committed to using this public speaking lab to discover how I can achieve desired outcomes yet remain true to high ethical standards.

If, in addition, you are interested in issues, in sharing ideas and concepts, in people, and in results, this course presents you with the opportunity of a lifetime—the op-

The Speechmaker's Feelings

1. How do you feel reading or hearing this next sentence?

   "It's your turn to give a speech."

2. As you read the sentence, what thoughts traveled through your mind? What sensations traveled through your body?

portunity to start wherever you are, to step to the "Speech Wheel of Fortune" and take turn after turn after turn, developing and refining skills you will use your whole life. Are you ready for the first turn of the wheel? Warm yourself up for it by exploring how you now feel about speaking in public by answering the questions in the "Speaking of Skillbuilding" box above.

Experiencing some speechmaking apprehension is normal. It is not something you necessarily can get rid of, but it is something you can learn to cope with.[13] Instead of expecting to fail at speaking in public, allow yourself to expect to succeed. Rather than trying to avoid public speaking, allow yourself to seek out such opportunities. Rather than allowing your apprehension to work against you, use your apprehension as an energy source. If harnessed, your apprehension can help motivate you to work harder to succeed as a public speaker.

SUMMARY

MOST PUBLIC SPEAKERS EXPERIENCE some form of speech anxiety. By analyzing exactly what it is that frightens you about speaking in public and using a number of simple techniques, you can harness the excess energy that accompanies speechmaking anxiety and make it work for you.

The public speaking process contains four key stages (exhibited in the speechmaking wheel) that describe the steps to follow whenever you are asked to deliver a speech. By working your way systematically through the (1) topic selection, (2) speech development, (3) rehearsal and delivery, and (4) postpresentation phases of speechmaking you improve your chances of delivering a well-made and well received speech.

THE SPEAKER'S STAND

It's your turn to prepare and deliver a three- to four-minute speech! Either select and customize one of the following topics, choose another topic, or follow the instructions of your teacher. Optional topics are: What Is Unique about Me; A Difficult Choice I Had to Make; How Discrimination Affects Me; Why I Want to Become a ______.

When choosing the subject for your speech, consider both your interests and the interests of your audience. What topics that interest you do you imagine other students would like to hear you speak about? What topics that interest you do you think they would have little or no desire to hear about? How do you account for your perceptions?

STUDENT FOCUS GROUP REPORT

Now that you have had the opportunity to consider how to handle anxiety and prepare for your first speech, take a few minutes and in groups composed of five to seven students each, answer the following questions:

1. Revisit the case study at the beginning of this chapter. To what extent, if any, have your initial reactions to it changed?
2. What role does speech anxiety play in the development of an effective speaker?
3. What is it that most speakers fear?
4. How can speakers make their fear work in their favor?
5. What key characteristics does the model of the speech wheel reveal to us?
6. What qualities distinguish effective and ineffective speakers?
7. Summarize the most important information you have learned about handling speech apprehension.

Chapter Three

The Role of Ethics in Public Speaking

After reading this chapter, you should be able to:

- Define *ethics.*
- Describe how Plato, Aristotle, Cicero, and Quintilian contributed to our understanding of ethics.
- Discuss the ethical obligations of speakers and receivers.
- Describe how you would act when faced with specific ethical dilemmas.
- Identify the kinds of decisions speakers and receivers make about being ethical.
- Define *plagiarism.*
- Describe the relationship among ethics, critical thinking, and multiculturalism/cultural understanding.

CASE STUDY: The Substitute

Shoshanah was stumped. She had agreed to substitute for her boss and be the speaker of honor at the local Rotary Club dinner scheduled for two days from now. That meant that she had to spend all her time trying to come up with a speech that would involve and interest the club members. Her boss had been slated to speak on the future of work. He was an expert on that subject. But a pending merger necessitated that he take a business trip . . . and so the burden fell to her.

Shoshanah knew nothing about the future of work. It was all she could do to complete the week's work, let alone think about what future work life would be like. Yet here she was trying to educate herself about the topic with just two days. As she sifted through pages of reports, yahooed on the Internet, and made frantic phone calls to the corporate librarian, suddenly she saw the answer to her prayers. In the May 1, 1996, issue of *Vital Speeches of the Day,* Eugene I. Lehrmann, president of the American Association of Retired Persons, had delivered a speech to the Economic Club of Detroit on just that topic. She read the speech. The ideas Lehrmann shared with his audience sounded right to her. It would save her so much time and allow her to get on to her other assignments if she could simply use his speech and pass it off as her own. Ordinarily such an idea wouldn't even have occurred to her. It was just that this was her company's busy time of year, and she had so many other responsibilities to fulfill. Who would know that the ideas being expressed were not actually her own. Probably no one, she rationalized. Shoshanah went to make a copy of the speech.

- You see Shoshanah at the copy machine. Knowing her situation, what advice would you give her and why?

Do we have a moral obligation to behave ethically when speaking in public? Do we commit an ethical breach when we speak on a subject about which we do not personally care? Do we err when, in order to increase our personal persuasiveness, we include a fabricated illustration but fail to tell our receivers that the story is merely hypothetical? Do we have the duty to let a speaker know when we do not find him or her a credible source? Is it just for us to attempt to convince others to believe what we do not ourselves believe? Is it ethical for us to refuse to listen to speakers we find offensive? These are just a few of the many questions that today's speakers and receivers need to be able to answer.

ETHICS AND PUBLIC SPEAKING

ETHICS INVOLVES AN EXPLORATION of how our values help us decide what is right and wrong. When we come face to face with a dilemma or a potentially compromising or self-incriminating situation, our definition of ethical conduct is supposed to guide us in making an appropriate choice. Ethics "reflects a society's notions about the rightness or wrongness of an act and the distinctions between virtue and vice."[1] In public speaking questions of ethics arise over whether a suggested course

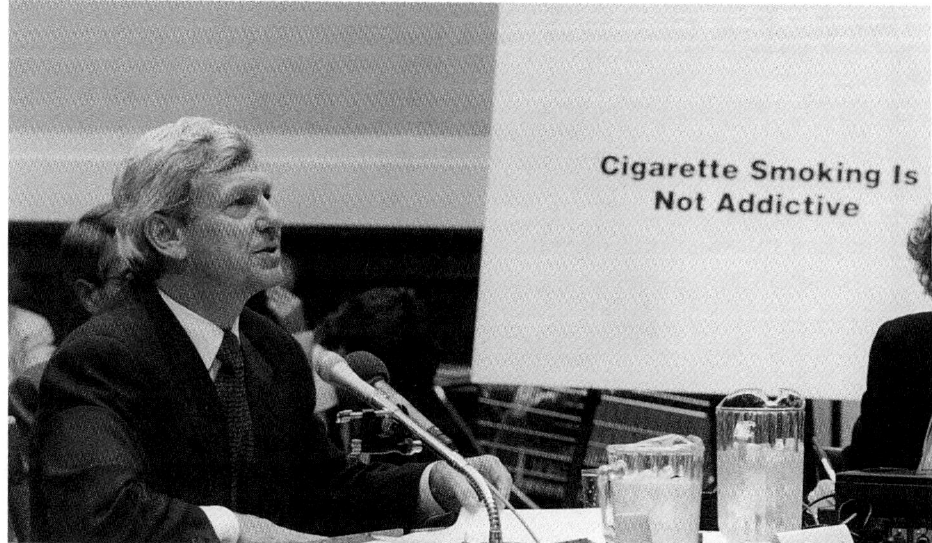

Information revealed in the Congressional hearings on the tobacco industry has sparked a national debate over the ethical practices of some tobacco manufacturers.

of action is fair or unfair, an uttered statement is just or unjust, a speaker is honest or dishonest.

To be sure, communicating ethically is not a new idea. In the fourth century B.C. the Athenian philosopher Plato admonished those who condoned using any means to win the support of receivers. Plato argued against using word tricks or other devious means to accomplish a goal. For Plato, "the first goal of the speaker is to know the truth." Aristotle, a student of Plato, carried on Plato's work by affirming that knowledge could only be gained by logic and reason. Like the Greeks, the Romans were concerned about ethics, as reflected in Cicero's belief that "Wisdom without eloquence has been of little help . . . but eloquence without wisdom has often been a great obstacle and never an advantage."[2] This concern is also evident in Quintilian's position that for a person to be a great orator, that individual must be "a good man, skilled in speaking,"[3] that is, morally upright as well as eloquent. Quintilian cautioned that speech should not be used as an accomplice to crime, serve as the foe to innocence, or act as the enemy of truth. Since childhood many of us have been repeatedly cautioned with similarly sounding warnings such as: "Don't lie," "Don't cheat," "Don't steal."

Just as ethics plays a role in all forms of communication today—from intrapersonal to interpersonal, from group to organizational—our personal codes of ethics also play a key role in public communication.[4] In fact, questions of ethics may arise every time a speaker and his or her receivers interact. What may we question? We may question the speaker's goals. We may question the tactics used. We may question whether facts are being twisted. We may question the speaker's motives. We may question the audience's interest. We may question whether the minds of receivers are open or closed. We may question whether receivers share our values.

What are the ethical obligations of speakers and receivers? How do we decide right and wrong in public speaking? Do speakers and receivers always have to agree on what is and is not ethical?

Respond honestly to each of the following questions:

If you were running for office, would you ever tell people what they wanted to hear just to get them to vote for you? Why or why not?

If you were a highly paid lobbyist for a foreign government, would you work to convince legislators in the United States to provide funding for an administration that you knew to be repressive? Why or why not?

If you were the spokesperson for a major company, would you use emotional appeals, falsified statistics, or doctored evidence to convince the public of something you knew to be untrue? Why or why not?

If you were addressing members of an ethnic group different from your own, would you adopt the speaking style favored by members of that group in order to build rapport with your receivers, even if that style did not feel natural to you?

How you answer each of these questions reveals whether you are willing to tell the truth and risk being perceived less positively than you might otherwise be if you lied. Your answers reveal whether you feel a need to dissemble or conceal information in an effort to enhance your chances of accomplishing a personal objective at your receivers' expense.

Unfortunately, opinion polls continue to indicate an erosion of credibility and confidence in those who lead us and address us about important issues.[5] Today an increasingly large number of Americans expect our leaders and speakers to behave unethically. Some have become cynical about the truthfulness of politicians and public figures. Others have become callous, doubting that anyone in the public arena is able to distinguish truth from self-serving falsehood. Others comment that the goal of too many of today's speakers is to move receivers toward a desired position or point of view rather than to inform or enlighten them.[6]

Our society is becoming increasingly message driven. Politicians, corporations, and special interest groups hire consultants and public relations and advertising firms to provide expert advice on how to influence the public. For better or worse, we live in an era that uses symbols and slogans to affect change. Yet in public speaking as in life, there are standards for ethical communication. It is important for you to clarify your position about what ethical communication really is.

One of our goals in this book is to help you enhance your **ethical awareness.** When speakers and receivers practice **ethical communication,** critical thinking replaces cynicism and callousness, the careful processing and evaluation of ideas replaces the careless handling of ideas, and cultural understanding replaces cultural disregard. When speakers and receivers practice ethical communication their communication with each other is honest, accurate, and reflective of the best interests of the receivers, not just those of the source.

THE ETHICAL OBLIGATIONS OF SPEAKERS AND RECEIVERS

IT IS IMPORTANT TO note that it is ethical to honestly disagree with the ideas or beliefs of another. There is a distinct difference between disagreeing with others about a controversial issue and deliberately lying, falsifying information, or otherwise misrepresenting data in an effort to get others to accept a particular point of view.

How do speakers and listeners decide what is appropriate behavior? What principles of conduct can speakers and listeners use to help them ensure that the public

SPEAKING of ETHICS

Is It Ethical for a Speaker to Use Words Just Because Opinion Polls Reveal That They Resonate with Receivers?

Prior to his reelection to a second term as president, Bill Clinton addressed an audience with the following words:

> We have to think anew about what our basic values are, what kind of people we are.

Soon after, he addressed another audience, saying:

> I hope we can balance the budget in a way that is true to our fundamental values.

Later he noted:

> Peace in Bosnia is important to America, both our values and our interests.

And on a trip to Germany, he intoned:

> It is in our nation's interest and consistent with our values to see that this peace endures.

Although Clinton may believe in the values he speaks about, according to journalist Alison Mitchell, he repeatedly incorporated the word *values* into his remarks because it "resonates in a Pavlovian way with the American public, causing the same kinds of good feelings as words like patriotism or family."[7]

Mitchell indicates that there now exists a plethora of consultants in both political parties who use focus groups and polls to test market concepts, moods, and even individual words.

- Is it morally right for a speaker to formulate his or her message based on such tests of public sentiment?
- To what degree, if any, do you believe that the speaker's own beliefs, rather than polls and focus groups, should guide message construction? Explain.

speaking behaviors they exhibit will be judged by others as responsible, respectful, and in keeping with the public interest rather than irresponsible, insensitive, and self-serving?

Because ethical behavior is so vital to our future, we need to understand what constitutes ethical speechmaking. **Ethical speechmaking** is based on trust in and respect for participants—both speaker and receivers—the responsible handling of information, and an awareness of and concern for speechmaking outcomes or consequences.

The Ethical Speaker: Receiver Expectations

Receivers have certain expectations of speakers. Among these are that the speaker is honest and trustworthy. The amount of trust receivers place in a speaker is to a large extent based on their perception of that individual's character. In other words, when receivers judge a speaker to be of good character they are more likely to trust the speaker's integrity, his or her motives, the consistency of his or her behavior, and his or her discretion. When receivers trust a speaker's **integrity,** they believe that the speaker possesses a basic honesty that permeates the bond between them. They trust his or her **motives** and **intentions**—that is, they do not think the speaker would exhibit malevolent behavior toward them. When receivers trust the speaker on the basis of the **consistency of his or her behavior,** they feel that they know that person well enough to be able to predict his or her actions in future presentations—that is, that the speaker has "positive" predictability. Finally, when they trust the speaker on the basis of his or her **ability to be discrete** they conclude that the speaker will not take any action that would bring them harm. When receivers discover that speakers are being less than candid, they lose faith in the speaker's trustworthiness, integrity, credibility, and sincerity. Once receivers doubt a speaker, his or her words soon fall on deaf ears. Consequently, speakers who want to be perceived as ethical should adhere to a series of guidelines.

When Functioning as a Speaker, You Should Share only What You Know to Be True. Receivers have a right to expect you to be honest with them. They have a right to believe that you will not:

- misrepresent your purpose for speaking;
- distort information to make it more useful; or
- deceive them regarding the credentials of a source.

Nothing is more important to ethical speaking than the integrity of the speaker. When receivers doubt the veracity of your words, they also doubt you.[8] Deliberately lying by distorting facts (commiting an **overt lie**) or concealing sensitive information (commiting a **covert lie**) is a violation of the unspoken bond between speaker and receivers. Whenever we hope to convey a false impression or convince another individual to believe something about us, someone else, or something else that we ourselves do not believe, we are lying. Whether or not we want to admit it, our goal is to intentionally deceive the receivers into accepting what we know to be untrue. In other words, our verbal and nonverbal communicative intent is to mislead receivers either

Do you believe Oliver North had an ethical responsibility to speak the truth when he was questioned by Congress?

by providing them with false information or by purposefully failing to provide them with the information they need to make choices.[9] Once a speaker loses the trust of his or her receivers, it is extremely difficult to restore it. If a speaker exhibits a total lack of concern for the truth by distorting facts, reframing statistics, misquoting a source, taking a quotation out of context, omitting important information, using atypical examples and illustrations as support, or otherwise working to deceive receivers, the speaker has violated an ethical guideline.

When Functioning as a Speaker, You Should Fully Prepare Yourself to Present. Receivers have a right to expect you to be thoroughly informed and knowledgeable about your topic. They have a right to believe that they will be able to use the information you share with them to make decisions that could affect their lives. They have a right to know that you will:

- present them with correct information;
- present them with more than one side to an issue; and
- not knowingly mislead them.

The speaker who presents receivers with erroneous information, one side of an issue, or misleading advice runs the risk of hurting his or her receivers rather than helping them make better-informed decisions or preparing them to act.

When Functioning as a Speaker, You Should Consider the Best Interests of Your Receivers. Receivers have a right to expect that you will neither manipulate nor exploit them. They have a right to believe that you will not ask them to commit an illegal act or do anything that poses a danger to them or is destructive of their welfare. They have a right to expect that you will not use any means to secure desired ends. They have a right to expect that you share their concern for the consequences of your message.

When Functioning as a Speaker, You Should Consider Whether You Have Made It Easy for Your Receivers to Understand You. Receivers have a right to expect that you will talk at rather than below or above their level. Receivers have a right to believe that they will be able to derive information from your presentation so that they will come away from it feeling they have a grasp of the content and are able to make informed choices.

When Functioning as a Speaker, You Should Refrain from Using Words as Weapons. Language used inappropriately is a weapon that can maim. Although the words you use may not literally wound others, they can inflict psychological damage. Speakers who use language to abuse, defame, or degrade others display a shallowness and a lack of sensitivity for the needs or feelings of others. Willfully making false statements about another, engaging in name calling or other personal attacks, or using language to inflame or insight panic is unethical. Remember, it is hard to earn the respect of those you fail to respect.

When Functioning as a Speaker, You Should Not Wrap Information in a Positive Spin Just to Succeed. Receivers have a right to expect that you will not ma-

CONSIDERING DIVERSITY

The Texaco Tapes

The setting was a meeting room at Texaco. The topic was diversifying the management ranks of Texaco. The speakers were four white men.

In the course of presenting their ideas the four executives made racial slurs about African Americans, suggested intolerance of Jews, and spoke of obliterating or changing company records that indicated a deep racial bias.

The chairman of Texaco later noted, "This alleged behavior violates our code of conduct, our core values, and the law."[11]

- Have you ever used or heard slurs that demeaned or were offensive to others?
- How did others respond?
- To what extent, if any, does admitting wrong-doing and pledging to do what's right in the future correct the wrong?

nipulate their reactions by providing half-truths or failing to share with them information that proves you wrong. A speaker who knowingly suppresses information that contradicts his or her position destroys whatever bond of trust existed with his or her audience.

When Functioning as a Speaker, You Should Respect the Cultural Diversity of Receivers. Different audiences have different ideas about what constitutes an interesting topic, proper language, appropriate structure, and effective delivery. For example, a speech that may hold the attention and arouse the fervor of a Middle Eastern audience may have a very different effect on an audience composed primarily of North Americans. Similarly, whereas members of some cultural groups—Africans, for example—expect to participate overtly in a speech event, even to the point of helping to co-create it, members of other cultural groups find such participation to be disruptive and disrespectful of the speaker.[10]

In like fashion, a presentation that is straightforward in its detailing of information and blunt in its revelation of speaker attitude may be found acceptable and perhaps even preferable by American receivers while judged rude or insensitive by Asian audiences.

Whatever their cultural backgrounds, receivers have a right to hold their assumptions. They have a right to hold any attitudes and beliefs, including that you do not possess the absolute truth. They have a right to expect that you will acknowledge their right to disagree with you and, although they may disagree, that you will still treat them with respect.

When Functioning as a Speaker, You Are Accountable for What You Say. Receivers have a right to expect that you are responsible for your message, and not merely its messenger. They have a right to expect you to be morally responsible for your speech's content and to distinguish your personal opinions from other factual information. They also have a right to believe that when you do not credit other sources of information, the words you are using are your own. Were you to present the ideas and words of others as if they were your own, you would be guilty of plagiarism.

Plagiarism involves both mispresentation and lying. The word itself is derived from the Latin word *plagiarius,* meaning "kidnapper." Thus, when you plagiarize, you kidnap or steal the ideas and words of another and claim them as your own. In effect, you carry on a speechmaking masquerade or deception by dressing your speech in the thoughts and word choices of another. There is a series of simple steps you can follow to avoid passing off someone else's ideas or words as your own.

1. Attribute the source of every piece of evidence you cite. Never borrow the words or thoughts of someone else without acknowledging that you have done so.
2. Either indicate when you are quoting a statement or paraphrase it.
3. Use and credit a multiplicity of sources.

When you fail to adhere to these guidelines, in addition to demonstrating your lack of respect for your receivers, you also expose yourself to serious personal consequences. For example, at one time U.S. Senator Joseph Biden was a promising candidate for nomination to the presidency by the Democratic party. His supporters believed him to be an effective and articulate speaker. Then the press reported that a speech Biden had recently delivered was plagiarized from an address given by a British political figure, Neil Kinnock. Subsequently it was discovered that in another speech Biden had used the words of U.S. Senator Robert Kennedy without crediting him. It was also noted that years earlier, while still a law student, Biden had been found to have committed plagiarism. These disclosures harmed Biden's reputation and ended his dreams of becoming president.

However, receivers are not alone in having expectations regarding the kind of behavior that is desirable during public speaking encounters. Speakers also have beliefs regarding desirable behavior in receivers.

The Ethical Receiver: Speaker Expectations

Receivers who make a sincere effort to conduct themselves ethically when listening to a speaker enrich the meaningfulness, significance, and effectiveness of the speaking situation itself. Ethical receivers contribute greatly to the speaker's ability to deliver an effective presentation. What ethical guidelines can receivers use to ensure that they function to facilitate speechmaking effectiveness?

When Functioning as a Listener, You Need to Give the Speaker a Fair Hearing. Speakers have a right to expect that receivers will not prejudge them but instead will fairly evaluate what they have to say. They have a right to expect that receivers will try to understand the message, see it from their perspective, and honestly assess their speech's content based on what they share, and not on any preconceptions or personal biases receivers may have.

Receivers who act ethically process the speaker's words before deciding whether to accept or reject the speaker's ideas. They do not jump to conclusions and blindly

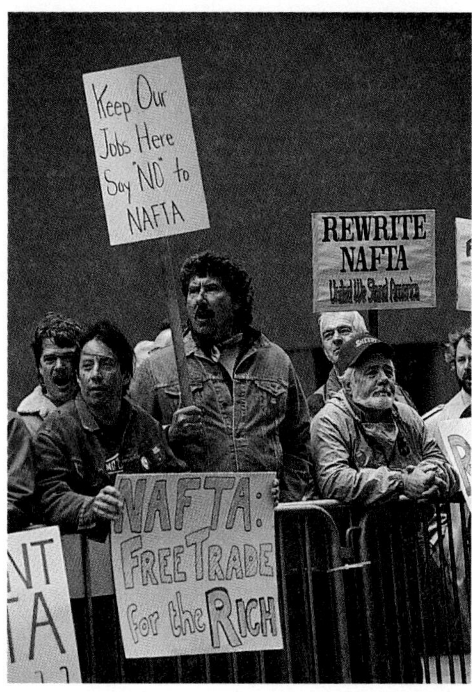

Do you believe speakers have a right to expect that receivers will give their speech a fair hearing? Do you think these receivers are giving that fair hearing?

accept or reject the speaker's ideas on the basis of the speaker's reputation, appearance, opening statements, or manner of delivery.

When Functioning as a Listener, You Need to Be Courteous, Attentive, and Honest with the Speaker. Speakers have a right to expect that receivers will listen and respond honestly and critically, not merely politely or blindly, to a presentation. They have a right to believe that receivers will put other concerns aside during a speech so that they are able to focus fully on the ideas being presented. Although ethical receivers need not agree with everything a speaker says, they do need to provide speakers with accurate and thoughtful feedback that indicates what they have understood and how they feel about the message.

When Functioning as a Listener, You Need to Be Speaker-Centered, Not Self-Centered. Speakers have a right to expect that receivers will listen to them whether they are older or younger, of the same or a different culture, of the same or a different religion, of the same or a different nationality, of the same or a different class, of the same or a different sex, of the same or a different educational background. The ethical listener recognizes that not all speakers share their perspective. Above all else, the behavior of ethical listeners does nothing to undermine a speaker's right to be heard.

Based on these expectations, speakers and receivers enter into informal agreements with each other. They need to be able to trust each other to keep those agreements if public confidence in the values of free expression and rational deliberation of the issues are to flourish.

Did an Ethical Lapse Occur?

As you read the following examples, decide whether a lapse in ethics occurred. If you think not, explain why you feel this way. If you think a lapse did occur, identify the nature of the lapse and note what the speaker might have said instead to avoid creating a problem.

1. Richard Jewell is the Atlanta security guard wrongly implicated in the Olympic Park bombing during the summer of 1996. NBC News anchor Tom Brokaw announced on the air that authorities "probably have enough to arrest [Jewell] right now [and] probably enough to prosecute him." As a result of that statement, NBC reportedly paid more than $500,000 to Richard Jewell to compensate him for damage to his reputation.
2. In 1993, while speaking at a New Jersey college, Nation of Islam leader Khalid Abdul Muhammad criticized the roles of whites and Jews in American society. Muhammad began his speech: "To the whites who are in the audience, let me say to you before we even get started, it's going to be a rough ride, buddy! It's going to be a rough ride. You better buckle in, buckle up, guys. I didn't come to Kean College to tiptoe through the tulips. I didn't come to Kean College to pussyfoot. I didn't come to Kean College to dilly-dally or beat around the bush. I didn't come to pin the tail on the donkey. I came to pin the tail on the honky!"[12]

   During his campus visit, Muhammad verbally attacked a number of people, including Pope John Paul II: "You know that cracker," he said. "Somebody need to raise that dress up and see what's really under there." He also attacked Spike Lee: "It was the Jews, the so-called Jews that financed Spike Lee . . . bubble-eyed, pigeon-toed, Jimmy-the-cricket, grasshopperlooking Spook Lee."[13]

   Although the event was not well attended, the speech captured national attention when the Anti-Defamation League of B'nai B'rith took out a full-page ad in the *New York Times* to denounce Muhammad's remarks.

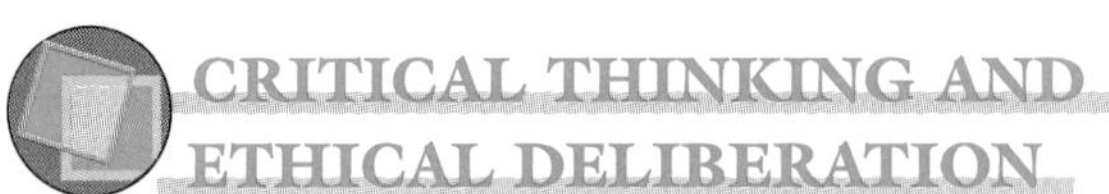

CRITICAL THINKING AND ETHICAL DELIBERATION

CRITICAL THINKING, THE ABILITY to explore an issue or situation, integrate all the available information about it, arrive at a conclusion, and validate a position, plays a key role in public speaking.[14] In public speaking, critical thinking begins with both the speakers and the receivers thinking critically about themselves and each other. Both speakers and receivers need to consider exactly what to question.

Speakers and Receivers Need to Define the Speechmaking Situation

Defining what you expect from either a speaker or receivers is a precurser to speechmaking. You should also be able to identify the motivations of parties to the event. To what degree is the speaker speaking to serve the interests of others or him- or herself? To what degree are receivers open to the speaker's ideas?

Speakers and Receivers Need to Analyze the Speechmaking Situation

A thoughtful analysis is the real heart of critical thinking. You should be able to identify the extent to which the parties to the speechmaking event performed their respective roles to the best of their abilities. In this stage, speakers and receivers use all the information available to evaluate their own behavior, the behaviors of others, and the likely consequences of those behaviors.

During this phase you also assess the ethicality of the behaviors exhibited by both the presenter and the evaluators. Included in this evaluation would be an assessment of your personal behavior during the presentation, not just what you observed about the behaviors of others. For example, you might ask:

Were the presenter and his or her evaluators honest with each other?

Did either party withold information?

Did either party sacrifice convictions in order to pander to or cater to the needs of the other?

Were rational claims backed up with logical evidence?

Were emotional appeals used to buttress or conceal the truth?

Was each party's performance motivated by what was in the best interests of the other party rather than by self-interest?

Speakers and Receivers Need to Make a Decision about the Outcomes/Effects of the Speechmaking Event

The foregoing analysis should lead you to formulate an opinion regarding the extent to which the speechmaking event was a success or a failure and your reasons for this perception. When evaluating a presentation, it is helpful to locate the presentation on an effectiveness continuum and think in terms of how effective the speechmaker was, rather than whether he or she was *absolutely* effective or ineffective.

SPEAKING of CRITICAL THINKING

The Spin Is In

Myriad individuals and groups are competing for a piece of your mind. Each wants to convince you to hold a point of view in line with his or her own. How good are you at evaluating the effectiveness of a stated position?

- Tape any news segment or speech that focuses on a social issue. Possible issues include nicotine addiction, liquor advertising on television, affirmative action programs, the welfare system, racism, or sexism.
- Discuss the extent to which you find the speaker(s) to be responsible and effective in getting points across.
- Identify the criteria you used to make your judgments.

Holger Kluge

Holger Kluge is president of the personal and commercial bank Canadian Imperial Bank of Commerce. He delivered a speech including the following remarks to the Diversity Network Calgary, Alberta, Canada, on October 28, 1996. As you read his words, consider these questions:

- What has Holger Kluge learned about diversity?
- How can you apply the lessons he learned to public speaking?

I'd like to begin my remarks with a story. A number of years ago we hired an employee as a teller in one of our branches. A few weeks after this individual began work, he was called into the branch manager's office for a discussion.

The manager was a good boss and a good mentor; and he wanted to tell the employee the facts of life about working for the bank.

He told him not to expect to rise too far in the organization.

When the young man asked why, the manager replied:

"You've got an accent. You weren't born in Canada. And you're not Anglo-Saxon. Basically, you've got the wrong name and the wrong background for advancement." He went on to say that the best the employee could hope for was to someday become a branch manager.

I was that young employee.

The irony is, that at the time I was considered an example of the bank's progressive hiring practices.

Somehow, the significance of this honor eluded me. In the space of a few moments, I had been ban-

MULTICULTURALISM AND ETHICAL DELIBERATION

SPEAKERS AND RECEIVERS NEED to understand that no individual can be reduced to a formula of understanding based on his or her race, gender, or disability or any other personal characteristic. At the same time, each one of us needs to gain insights into group identity to develop the awareness necessary to process the information needed to exist in an increasingly diverse society. If we are to understand the diversity of ideas that motivate speakers and receivers to interact with each other and move toward or away from each other, we also need to better understand the diversity in people. Diverse groups bring different expectations. We need to learn to do more than be sensitive to difference. We need to know what it is we do that offends or is insensitive to the feelings others have or the values others hold.[15]

Our expectations and predictions regarding how members of various cultural groups will communicate with us can facilitate or impede the development of trust when we actually address or listen to a member of that group. Some of us are much less apt to trust someone we perceive to be different from us than someone we perceive to be similar to us.

As noted in Chapter 1, the presence of **ethnocentrism** can impede the development of a trusting speaker–receiver relationship with people from cultural groups dif-

ished to a wilderness of diminished expectations all because of my name, the way I spoke, and my country of origin. . . .

That's one experience that shaped my views on diversity, knowing what it's like to be on the outside, having to overcome obstacles which others don't, simply because you're different.

My second experience took place in the early 1970s.

I had just been assigned to the Far East and was in Japan with my wife. One day we decided to see a movie. Since neither of us were fluent in Japanese, we chose a film in English, with Japanese subtitles. There was a long line-up at the theater, but eventually we got to the cashier and I asked for two tickets. She refused to sell them to me and motioned for us to step aside. I repeated my request, and again she refused.

I was furious at what seemed to be a clear case of discrimination, aimed at us because we were foreigners.

At this point a young Japanese man, who spoke English, approached us to explain what was going on. He said it was common in his country for people to stand in theaters once all the seats had been sold out. The cashier knew this wasn't the custom in the West. So she was telling us to wait and she'd provide tickets for a later showing with available seating.

Naturally, I was embarrassed. I had rashly attributed mean motives to someone who was trying to treat us with empathy and respect. But my Western culture and upbringing prevented me from seeing that.

This time, I was the problem.

That one incident taught me how deeply embedded, in all of us, our cultural assumptions are, and how easily they can distort perception and become barriers to communication. As Anais Nin has observed, "We don't see things as they are; we see things as we are."[17]

ferent from our own. Feelings of ethnocentrism can make it difficult for individuals to dispel preconceptions, impede the personalizing of communication, limit the acceptance of "outsiders," and, consequently, hinder the development of a trusting relationship between speaker and receiver.

The more ethnocentric one is, the more anxious he or she is when listening to persons from other cultures. When we are fearful, we are less likely to expect a positive outcome from such presentations and less willing to trust the speaker. If relationships between people from diverse cultures are to thrive, then the parties involved at least "need to act as if a sense of trust were justified, and set their doubts aside."[16]

Thus, public speakers and receivers need information about the perspectives that different groups of people bring to any speechmaking event. Although many of us may find it uncomfortable to even acknowledge that there are differences between people, it is just such an understanding that can unite us in the effort to improve our public communication efforts. Developing public speaking skills can help us learn to appreciate each other as individuals as well as members of a group.

SUMMARY

ETHICS, WHICH REFLECTS a society's feelings about right and wrong, plays an important role in speechmaking. While not a new idea, questions of ethics do arise when speakers and audiences interact.

In public speaking as in life, there are standards for ethical communication. Both speakers and receivers expect each other to behave in certain ways. Receivers expect speakers to share only what they know to be true, to be fully prepared to present a speech, to consider what is in the best interests of receivers, to make it easy for others to understand them, to refrain from using words inappropriately, to refrain from putting either a positive or a negative spin on information just to win a point, to respect cultural diversity, and to be accountable for the message. Speakers expect receivers to give them a fair hearing; to be courteous, attentive, and honest about their responses; and to be speaker-centered rather than self-centered. In addition, both critical thinking and respect for multiculturalism play key roles in ethical speechmaking.

THE SPEAKER'S STAND

Although many believe that speakers should educate receivers rather than merely tell them what they want to hear or serve their personal self-interests, politicians, public relations practitioners, advertisers, talk show hosts, and other public figures often seem to violate this advice. Indeed, the use of deception by those in the public arena is not new. Choose one of the following three- to four-minute assignments or an assignment of your instructor's choosing.

1. Identify a public figure who you believe deliberately deceived the public, describe the alleged deception, and identify whether you agree with the speaker's behavior and why.
2. Describe an ethical choice that you had to make, how you decided what to do, and why you believe your decision was right or wrong.
3. Prepare an ethical analysis of a recent speech, commercial, tabloid news report, or infomercial.

STUDENT FOCUS GROUP REPORT

Now that you have considered the role of ethics in public speaking, in a group of five to seven students, answer the following questions.

1. To what extent, if any, would your answers to the questions following the introductory case study change now that you have completed this chapter? Explain.
2. What role does your personal code of ethics play in speechmaking?
3. Can the expectations that speakers and receivers have for each other be fully realized? Explain.
4. To what extent, if any, does the ability to think critically affect one's ability to act ethically?
5. In what ways, if at all, is sensitivity to cultural diversity a prerequisite for ethical speechmaking?
6. Summarize the most important information you have learned about the role ethics plays in public speaking.

Chapter Four

Listening Critically

What Is the Speaker Really Saying?

After reading this chapter, you should be able to:

- Explain why the ability to listen critically is essential in a free society.
- Define *listening.*
- Describe the components of the listening cycle.
- Evaluate and improve your listening ability.
- Discuss the benefits derived from effective listening.
- Explain the various types of listening.
- Describe how cultural diversity can affect the listening process.
- Explain why failing to listen is unethical.
- Use critical listening skills to analyze speeches.

CASE STUDY

Are You Listening?

Jana couldn't believe it. Somehow she found herself in the middle of a rally that was organized to demonstrate support for Proposition 209, the voter initiative approved in 1996 that would end her state's affirmative action programs. Jana directly benefited from such programs and couldn't understand why anyone would want to eliminate them. After all, she reminded herself, there were real college admission and corporate hiring inequities that society had to correct and affirmative action was the only fair way to accomplish it. Now, however, people were yelling that admitting individuals to college or hiring them for work on the basis of sex or race was discriminatory.

The governor, a politician who vehemently supported the demise of affirmative action, moved forward to address the crowd. "We must not retreat back to a state of preferential treatment," he intoned. "The will of the majority must be served."

Who is the governor kidding? Jana asked herself, not hearing a thing he said after that remark. It's his position that is turning everything upside down. I'm the one being discriminated against here. Her mind raced ahead. All he wants is to protect the wealthy and the privileged, she thought. They're the ones who are receiving all the preferential treatment. Sensing that there was no reason for her to listen to anything else the governor had to say, Jana started to walk away from the demonstration.

- Have you ever found yourself in a position similar to Jana's?
- If you answered yes to 1, did you, too, seek to remove yourself from the situation? If you answered no, how would you imagine you would respond?
- Is avoiding listening to a message with which you do not agree an effective strategy? an ethical strategy? Explain.

IF YOU WERE AGAINST GUN CONTROL could you listen—really listen—to a speech that advocated strict gun control? If you were a fervent antiabortion activist, would you work hard to ensure that a speaker who supported a woman's right to choose was given a fair hearing before your group? Is there any topic you find so objectionable that you do not believe it should be provided a forum?

The First Amendment to the U.S. Constitution protects the citizens' right to speak freely. Unless others listen to what is being said, however, that right becomes an empty right. After all, what good is it to safeguard free speech if it falls only on deaf ears or closed minds? In effect, for the First Amendment to be fully realized, we must also demonstrate a willingness to listen freely to the expression of all ideas, whether they are popular or unpopular, ideas we support or oppose, ideas we feel deeply committed to or don't care much about, or ideas we judge to be abhorent or we believe must be accepted. If we "walk out" on our need to listen, if we are unwilling to pay attention when attention must be paid, then we must be prepared to pay a terrible price—freedom. The right to freedom of expression requires that we exercise our ears and listen carefully and critically to what others have to say.

Our Constitutional freedom of expression is dependent on the people's willingness to listen to the ideas of all of us.

The question is, can we afford not to improve our listening ability when faced with facts like these?

FACT 1. We are exposed to millions of words every year.

FACT 2. We spend a much larger percentage of our waking time listening than we do speaking, writing, or reading.[1]

FACT 3. On average, we listen at only 25 percent efficiency; that is, instead of retaining most of what we hear, we lose approximately 75 percent of it over a very short period of time.[2]

FACT 4. Errors in listening are very common; although listening is our most frequent activity, it is also our least developed skill.

FACT 5. Whether we want to gain knowledge or critically evaluate a message or its messenger, listening requires active participation. Passive recipients are not really listening.

FACT 6. If we don't give people who speak to us honest feedback, we forfeit our right to complain about them.

FACT 7. The purpose of this course is not just to develop speaking skills, but to develop listening skills as well.

FACT 8. You will spend more time listening in this course than you will speaking.

FACT 9. It pays to listen. Listening mistakes carry both a personal and a monetary cost. In fact, if each U.S. citizen made just one ten-dollar listening mistake a year, the total national cost would come to more than two billion dollars annually.

FACT 10. Our very existence depends on our ability to listen and respond appropriately. Listening is the primary process through which we make sense out of what we hear. It is through listening that we gather the information we need to (a) develop relationships, (b) make personal and professional decisions, (c) formulate attitudes and opinions, (d) mentally store data for later use, and (e) provide feedback to others.

It is because of the many ways that listening affects us that we will take the time to explore not only what you can do to enhance your listening abilities, but also how you can help others to listen more effectively. It is essential to develop your abilities to understand and critically evaluate what you hear, but it is equally essential that you recognize those factors that cause you to tune out when this is that last thing you should be doing.

WHAT LISTENING IS AND IS NOT

EFFECTIVE LISTENERS do not use only their ears to listen. Effective listeners also rely on their minds. If you listen well, you also think well. Listening and hearing are very different processes. **Listening** is a voluntary psychological process. **Hearing** is an involuntary physiological process. In other words, just as we do not need to think to breathe, so do we not need to think to hear. As long as our eardrums are functional, when sound waves hit them, the subsequent vibrations cause the hammer, anvil, and stirrup, located in the middle ear, to vibrate and produce sound. Once these vibrations reach our auditory nerves they are transformed into electrical impulses and are automatically processed by the brain, and we hear. However, it is what we do with these impulses once we have received them that takes us into the complex arena of listening. If we do not function well as listeners, we likely will not understand what we hear and we may communicate misinformation to others. For this reason, the best listeners often make the best speakers. In fact, we can learn a lot about speaking just by critically listening to the speeches of others. Far too often, however, instead of critically listening to the speeches of others, we only hear them. The mind is asleep rather than alert, and thus we passively receive, rather than actively process, the speaker's message. When we listen, however, we not only hear the message, but we also try to make sense out of it.

Listening involves a number of stages: sensing, attending, understanding and interpreting, evaluating, responding, and remembering. In each stage we are offered choices and we make conscious decisions. Let us examine each in turn.

Stage One—Sensing

During the **sensing** stage we receive aural stimuli. We exist in a world filled with sounds. Sounds surround us and compete to be noticed by us. Some sounds we choose to ignore, others we focus on. Eugene Raudsepp of Princeton Creative Research explains the sensing process by telling the story of a zoologist who was walking with a friend down a busy street filled with the sounds of honking horns and screeching tires. Turning to his friend, the zoologist says, "Listen to that cricket!" The friend, astonished, replies, "You hear a cricket in the middle of all this noise?" The zoologist takes out a coin and flips it in the air. As the coin falls to the sidewalk, a dozen heads turn in response to its *clink*. The zoologist responds, "We hear what we listen for."[3] We all sense and take in some sounds and block out others.

Stage Two—Attending

Attending involves our willingness to select and focus on particular stimuli. Once we select a sound, we have the opportunity to attend to it and concentrate on it. Of course, here again, we have a choice. Although our attention may have been captured, it may have been captured only momentarily. Unless it is held, we will soon choose to focus on something else. Our attention will simply drift away. For this reason, speakers quickly learn that it is not enough to capture a listener's attention, they must also continually work to maintain that attention.

To promote and maintain the attention of receivers, speakers use a number of techniques designed to facilitate listening. For example, speakers may:

- focus on subjects of particular interest to receivers; topics that are timely; topics with which the receivers are either familiar or would like to be familiar; and topics that affect them directly;
- use words and images that evoke pictures in the minds of receivers;
- incorporate activity and movement into presentations; or
- integrate human interest into presentations by telling stories that create suspense, describe conflict, or evoke humor.

Maintaining receiver attention also requires that speakers develop a sensitivity to how cultural background or diversity can affect the interests of audience members.

Stage Three—Understanding and Interpreting

During the **understanding and interpreting** stage receivers attempt to give meaning to what the speaker is communicating. If we only sense and attend, but fail to comprehend and derive meaning, we are not really listening.[4] To figure out what the speaker really means we consider the speaker's words, emotional tone, and general demeanor. We may relate what the speaker says to what we already know, compile questions to ask the speaker in an effort to clarify things in our minds, or restate or paraphrase the speaker's thoughts in our own words.

Stage Four—Evaluating

Once we fully understand the speaker's position we are ready to evaluate the message and the speaker's intent. During the **evaluating** stage we weigh what has been communicated; we appraise or critically evaluate what we have heard and understood. We decide whether we accept the speaker's point of view, whether his or her message has relevance for us, whether it is valid and well intentioned, based on what we know.

Stage Five—Responding

During the **responding** stage we react and provide feedback. We communicate our thoughts and feelings about the message we've received. Of course, we do not react only when the speaker is finished speaking. We also react during the course of the speaker's presentation. Both during and after a speech, we let the speaker know if we thought the message was successful or flawed, if it was "on target" or "missed its mark." During this stage we are in essence the speaker's radar.[5]

Stage Six—Remembering

During the **remembering** stage we mentally save what we've gained from the speaker's message for further use. Here again, we make choices as we decide what has value and is worth storing in memory and what we can discard. Of course, if a speaker builds redundancy into his or her message, our chances of remembering it and of being able to reconstruct it increase. Sometimes we may also take notes or, if permit-

Figure 4.1

The Listening Process

Affectors

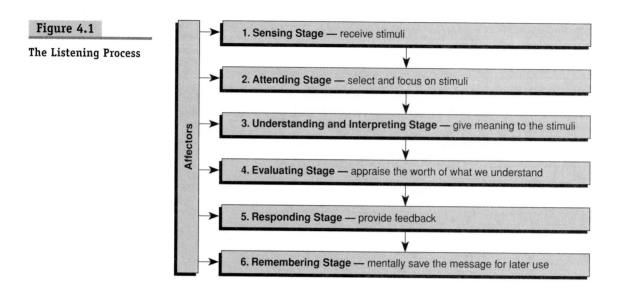

1. **Sensing Stage** — receive stimuli
2. **Attending Stage** — select and focus on stimuli
3. **Understanding and Interpreting Stage** — give meaning to the stimuli
4. **Evaluating Stage** — appraise the worth of what we understand
5. **Responding Stage** — provide feedback
6. **Remembering Stage** — mentally save the message for later use

ted, record the speaker's remarks to have a more accurate record of what the speaker has said.

It is noteworthy that each of the six stages of listening we have just explored may be influenced by **affectors,** emotional and intellectual selectivities that can impede us from processing the speaker's message in an impartial way. At any point during the communication we may either stop paying attention, misinterpret what is sent, or judge it to be of little—if any—value (see Figure 4.1).

CULTURAL DIVERSITY AND LISTENING

FOR EACH OF US, culture, lifestyle, attitudes, and values influence and help determine:

1. what we sense;
2. what we attend to;
3. what we comprehend;
4. how we evaluate communication; and ultimately,
5. what we retain.

Cultural Preferences and Listening Behavior

Ethnocentrism, the tendency to assess the values, beliefs, and behaviors of our own culture as better than those of other cultures, can hinder effective listening. We all tend to process the speech of others through personal filters. The amount of ethnocentrism we exhibit depends on who we are listening to or interacting with. For example, were we Turkish American we might exhibit a low degree of ethnocentrism when listening to an Italian American, but a significantly higher degree of ethnocentrism when processing the speech of Japanese Americans because they are less like us.

Effective listeners recognize the tendency of audiences to be ethnocentric and work to resist the temptation to evaluate what is shared with them only through their own cultural affectors—especially when participating in a public speaking situation that is intercultural in context.

Just as evaluating a speech solely on the basis of the speaker's culture can be a problem, so can evaluating a speech solely on the basis of the speaker's race, sex, or sexual/affectional choices. It is important that we develop the ability to listen to what the speaker is saying, no matter who is the speaker.

There are stimuli that a number of us cannot hear or see because our culture puts no value on them. For instance, many of us will fail to listen effectively to statements that contradict our own beliefs. But we cannot afford *not* to try and suspend our opinions so that we can more fully open our minds to experience. If we succeed, we eliminate a number of major roadblocks to both effective listening and critical thinking.

Even if we speak the same language, we may have different accents or certainly have had different experiences that may cause us to give different meanings to words. For example, the meaning a person from a high socioeconomic group gives to the word "education" may be different than the meaning understood by another person whose socioeconomic group is lower.

In addition, some cultures exhibit a more direct communication style. Cultures such as those in Western Europe and the United States, for example, tend to prefer a "tell it like it is" approach to spoken discourse. Many Asian cultures, in contrast, exhibit a more indirect style. They prefer to practice politeness, accommodation, and the maintenance of face.[6] To that end, they would rather help preserve the positive public image of another person than be direct and absolutely truthful in what they say in public. Effective listeners are sensitive to such cultural differences and learn to listen between the lines and to communicate across differences.

Cultural Background and Listening Style

Although the generalizations do not always hold true, people from different cultural backgrounds may have learned different ways of demonstrating their readiness to listen to a speaker. White Americans, African American, Latino, and Middle Eastern American audiences, for example, are comfortable using their eyes and bodies to communicate their listening receptivity. They have learned to lean forward when interested, fix their eyes on the speaker, and indicate agreement or disagreement with nonverbal cues such as head nods.

In contrast, others, including Native Americans and Asian Americans, are more likely to indicate their listening receptivity in a somewhat more restrained manner. Most Native Americans, for instance, demonstrate their respect for a speaker by avoiding sustained and direct eye contact with him or her. Many Asian Americans have also been taught to avoid making direct eye contact with a speaker and to display little if any overt expression in either their faces or their bodies in response to what a speaker says.

Although the generalizations do not hold true for all people, research shows that males and females also tend to listen differently. Women are more apt to communicate supportiveness. Thus women are more likely than men to be overtly expressive and exhibit explicit listening cues such as nodding in agreement and smiling at the speaker. In contrast, men are more apt to play up their personal knowledge and ex-

What can speakers and listeners do to bridge the differences among members of various cultures?

pertise. Unlike women, men exhibit a posture that is more argumentative in style, as if they were getting ready to disagree with or challenge the speaker in an effort to demonstrate their own expertise.

Becoming attuned to the differences between cultures can help us become more effective listeners as well as free us to think critically and evaluate competing ideas more rigorously. By taking steps to become more effective listeners, we also help ourselves eliminate the prejudices, biases, and misconceptions we have established over the years.[7]

WHY LISTENING IS IMPORTANT

THINK OF THE VERY WORST LISTENERS YOU KNOW. What words would you use to describe their behavior? Most people choose words like "inattentive," "close-minded," "daydreamer," "bored," "impatient," "nonresponsive," and "rude." Now do the same with the best listeners you know. Probably among the words you've chosen are "concerned," "open-minded," "intelligent," "attentive," "interested," and "respectful." Compare and contrast the words you selected to describe the best and worst listeners. Which descriptive words would you prefer to have applied to you by speakers? Which would you prefer to use to describe the members of your listening audience? Very few, if any, of us would actually prefer to interact with people who display the attributes of poor listeners. Most of us would opt instead to interact with more effective listeners. The responsibility for effective listening, however, is shared by both speakers and listeners. Speakers must do their part in making it easy for those with whom they communicate to listen to them, and listeners must monitor their listening behaviors so that they facilitate rather than impede speakers' efforts (see the "Speaking of Critical Thinking" box). Both speakers and listeners need to establish acceptable performance standards in their own minds—standards they should attempt to surpass as they communicate with each other.

Speaking of Critical Thinking

Listening between the Lines

Effective listeners are able to listen both to gain knowledge and to analyze and evaluate a message's validity, worth, or potential value. Effective listeners have learned to suspend judgment so they do not merely accept a message at face value. Instead, they think critically about the message. They distinguish between main and minor points, differentiate facts from opinions, assess the evidence provided, and identify errors or weaknesses in reasoning. They also work actively to overcome those barriers that stand in the way of their accurate reception. Thus, they do much more than "hear" the speech. Accomplishing all this, of course, requires real effort. Effective listeners must prepare themselves to listen to a speech by asking themselves questions such as:

- How familiar am I with this topic?
- What do I know of the speaker's credentials or authority?
- Do I believe the speaker is a biased or an unbiased source?
- How would an opponent on the issue perceive the same evidence or examples offered by the speaker?

Consider each of these questions as you read or view on videotape a speech assigned you by your instructor or one you select.

We all know that we stand to lose by listening poorly and that we stand to gain by listening well. But what exactly is it that we stand to lose or gain? To find out, refer to Figure 4.2 on page 64 and ask and answer the questions there. Then ask them of two other people as well.

Listening increases satisfaction. Speakers are satisfied when listened to because they have been given a fair hearing, and successful listeners are satisfied because they have heard, understood, and responded appropriately to the message delivered to them.

The responsibility for effective listening is shared by speakers and receivers. In your opinion, are any of the receivers in this picture involved in listening to the speaker?

Figure 4.2

Rating Listening

The Losses	*The Gains*
1. What consequences have you suffered when you showed a lack of respect for the person speaking to you? 2. What problems have you encountered when you lost your temper while someone was explaining something to you? 3. What challenges have you faced when you failed to comprehend what someone told you? 4. How has jumping to a wrong conclusion caused difficulties for you? 5. What transpired after you missed a key segment of a speaker's message because you were distracted? 6. How did others respond to you when they were cognizant of the fact that you had failed to respond appropriately?	1. What benefits have you derived from showing real interest in what a speaker wants to share with you? 2. What benefits have you derived from maintaining control of your emotions when someone was relaying to you something you really didn't want to hear? 3. What benefits have you derived from correctly understanding instructions given you? 4. What benefits have you derived from concentrating on what the speaker was saying instead of giving in to distractions? 5. How has patience aided you as a listener? 6. How has responding appropriately to a speaker helped facilitate communication between you?

When receivers fail to listen, the speaker is doomed to failure too. Consider this tragic example reported by listening researchers:

> On March 27, at 5 P.M., a Boeing 747 carrying 248 passengers was beginning its take off on Runway 12 of the Tenerife Airport in Spain. As the plane gained speed, a second Boeing 747, Pan Am Flight 1736, also waiting to take off on Runway 12, emerged from the fog; this plane had 335 people aboard. The two planes crashed in one of the worst accidents in airline history. The cost? 583 human lives, two destroyed multi-million dollar planes, hundreds of millions of dollars in damages, and incalculable grief and suffering experienced by those who lost loved ones and friends.
>
> *The question:* What was the crash attributed to?
>
> *The answer:* Poor listening. The pilots misinterpreted control tower communications and failed to respond properly to instructions. The official accident report read as follows:
>
>> The fundamental cause of this accident was the fact that the KLM Captain (1) took off without clearance, (2) did not obey or misinterpreted the "Stand by for take off," from the tower, (3) did not interrupt take off on learning the Pan Am flight was still on the runway.[8]

Poor listening can also have humorous consequences at times. Of course, the person guilty of the poor listening may not join in the laughter. Some years ago, Joseph Montoya, a member of the U.S. Senate, was to speak at a national legistlative conference held in Albuquerque, New Mexico. Shortly before he approached the podium to speak, Senator Montoya's press aide handed him a press release. When the senator rose to address the crowd, to the horror of his press aide but to the great amusement of his audience, Montoya delivered the press release just handed him instead of his prepared speech. The senator intoned: "For immediate release. Senator Joseph M. Montoya, Democrat of New Mexico, last night told the National Legislative Conference at Albuquerque. . . ." Unfortunately, the senator didn't stop there. He wasn't even listening to himself. Montoya read the entire release, concluding with the words: "Senator Montoya was repeatedly interrupted by applause."

Failing to listen to yourself can hurt just as much as failing to listen to others. In contrast, there are many advantages you can derive from effective listening.

Listening Can Facilitate the Elimination of Stress in Both the Speaker and the Listener. The listener's stress level is reduced as information is communicated, complex data are simplified, and objectives are clarified. The speaker's stress level is reduced as she or he is provided a forum to speak his or her mind and fulfill a communicative need.

Listening Lets Both Speaker and Listener Learn. Listeners learn more about the speaker and the speaker's subject. Speakers learn more about what listeners respond to, and how listeners react to their ideas.

Listening Cements the Relationship between the Speaker and the Listener. We all need someone to listen to us. We appreciate those who listen to us much more than those who ignore us. In fact, we do not like to be around those who do not listen to us for very long. We also tend to listen more to people who listen to us. Listening can create bonds between people from diverse backgrounds.

Listening Improves Decision Making. Given a variety of speakers opportunities to share their information, attitudes, and beliefs with you provides you with the kind of input you need to develop better judgment.

Listening Can Improve the Speaker. When speakers perceive themselves to have the rapt attention of their listeners and when they perceive their listeners to be open, alert, and active, then they are more comfortable in the speaking role and able to do an even better job of communicating their ideas.

Listening Can Improve the Listener. As a college student, you spend approximately 60 percent of each class day listening.[9] Listening more effectively will increase both your personal confidence and your grades. Because you understand what has been said, you gain confidence in your ability to express yourself and your opinions.

Listening Can Protect Both the Listener and Society. People who listen critically to the messages of others and do not just accept what is presented to them can spot faulty reasoning, invalid arguments, and gross appeals to prejudice. In this way they protect themselves against irresponsible speakers. It is the uncritical listener who pays the price charged by the unscrupulous speaker. If we are not adept at analyzing and evaluating the messages of others, we may end up accepting the unacceptable.

Charles Osgood

Charles Osgood, a two-time Peabody Award winner, wrote and anchored The Osgood File *over the CBS radio network. In 1990 he was inducted into the National Association of Broadcasters' Broadcasting Hall of Fame.*

As somebody who spends a fair amount of his time talking into television cameras and radio microphones, I can tell you that we broadcasters have certain illusions about you viewers and listeners. For openers, we expect you listeners to listen and you viewers to view.

Anybody in a room with a television set on is by definition a viewer, and anybody in a room or car with a radio that's on is by definition a listener, although this does not always reflect the truth. A person in the same room with a book is not necessarily a reader, even if the book is open.

It is probably a good thing that those of us who are jabbering away at these inanimate objects in our studios cannot see what is happening at the receiving end. We imagine, of course, that we are talking to a real person, but that's not always the case. Sometimes you get up and walk right out of the room while I'm in the middle of a sentence, I'll bet, without so much as an "excuse me" or "by your leave" or "I'll be right back," or anything.

And sometimes, I'm sure, just when I'm getting to what I think is the good part of whatever it is I'm telling you about, you and somebody else start talking to each other as if I weren't there. This would be a bit disconcerting to me if I knew it, but mercifully I don't. Oblivious to the fact that you are not paying attention any more, I keep going.

So there I am, all dressed up in my bow tie, with my hair slicked down and everything, assuming that

TYPES OF LISTENING

LISTENING THEORISTS identify four different types of listening.

Type One: Listening for Pleasure—Appreciative Listening

How recently have you listened to music, taken in a movie, or spent an evening at the local comedy club? What was your main reason for doing so? Probably because you wanted to have a good time. You wanted to be entertained. Often we listen simply because doing so enables us to unwind, relax, or escape. When we listen to music, a comedy routine, an after-dinner speech, a humorous roast, or a television show, we are listening because it gives us pleasure.

Type Two: Listening to Provide Emotional Support—Empathic Listening

Other times we listen simply because another person needs us to understand his or her feelings and point of view. For example, when was the last time you called a friend because you needed a sounding board—someone to whom you could tell your troubles? When was the last time you helped someone else work through a problem by

I have your rapt, undivided attention, while you are actually wrapping a package, looking at your mail, fixing a sandwich, or eating one, or dressing or undressing, or Lord knows what. If I actually could "see you on the radio," you could have me arrested for being a Peeping Tom.

I do not mean to suggest that this is all your fault. It is your living room and your television set, your car and your car radio, after all. And if we news people were half as fascinating as so many of us think we are, you'd listen to more of what we have to say.

John Robinson and Mark Levy of the University of Maryland have done some scholarly studies of how network television news reports are being taken in on the receiving end. According to them, most people miss about two-thirds of the main points of most stories. In other words, we network news people are batting about .333. That would be excellent if we were playing baseball. But this is another game altogether.

The late E. B. White warned writers that the average reader is in trouble about half the time. If Messrs. Robinson and Levy are right, the average TV news viewer is in trouble about two-thirds of the time. This is slightly discouraging if you happen to be in my line of work.

Sometimes you will lose your audience no matter what you do. The phone rings, or the doorbell, or there's an urgent call of nature. Calls of nature always seem to the callee to be more urgent than anything the President or Congress have been up to on a given day.

Robinson and Levy suggest, among other things, that news broadcasters stop assuming total concentration on the part of the audience. They think we should repeat important information in case the listener/viewer happens to be distracted the first time around. They think we should stop trying to pack so much information into so little airtime, and concentrate instead on making more sense. Too often, I'm afraid, we think we're making sense, but from the audience's point of view, we're not. The idea of making sense certainly makes sense to me. I wish I had thought of it before.[10]

offering a listening ear so he or she could share a dilemma with you? Empathic listening serves a therapeutic function. It helps speakers come to terms with problems and develop clearer perspectives of the situations they face, and aids them in restoring emotional balance to their lives. When you listen empathically, you understand a speaker's plight from his or her perspective rather than your own.

Type Three: Listening to Derive Information—Comprehensive Listening

When you are lost and ask another person for directions, when you attend a presentation and seek to comprehend the speaker's message, when you sit in class and listen to a lecture, you are listening with the objective of gaining knowledge. That is the purpose of comprehensive listening.

Type Four: Listening to Make an Evaluation—Critical Listening

After listening to a speech or a testimonial, have you ever doubted the truth of a message, the usefulness of the information, or the reliability of a source? Frequently, in addition to working to understand the content of a message, we must also make judgments about its worth, validity, and soundness, and ultimately whether we accept or reject it. We perform these functions when we listen critically.

Each of these types of listening is of value not just to the speaker but to the listener as well. Listening for pleasure can provide us with insights on how we can enhance our own presentations. We can experience new ways of capturing an audience's attention, and we can study techniques used to sustain audience interest. Listening to empathize can help us understand what we need to do to help an audience see things through our eyes, what we need to do to enable our receivers to appreciate our perspective. By listening to derive information, we can sensitize ourselves to the ways we should transmit information to others if we want to simplify the comprehension process for them. And by listening to evaluate information we will realize that just as we evaluate the speeches of others, so, too, others will evaluate our speeches. It is good for us to recognize the impact that sound evidence, valid reasoning, and proper emotional support have on an audience.

CONSIDERING DIVERSITY

Do We Listen for Different Things?

Listening patterns and behaviors are influenced by specific cultural contexts. For example, what if in the future you have to do business with Japanese individuals? How would knowing about their listening habits and preferences make it possible for you to facilitate communicating with them?

In an article in the *Harvard Business Review,* management expert Peter Drucker comments on the listening practices of Japanese CEOs (corporate executive officers):

> Very few CEOs of large Japanese companies have *any* time available for managing their companies.
>
> All their time is spent on relations, even the time spent on internal company business. They keep control of things by giving careful attention to personnel decisions in the upper ranks and by requiring meticulous financial and planning reports. But they do not "manage"—that is left to lower levels.
>
> The top people spend their time sitting, sipping cups of green tea, listening, asking a few questions, then sitting some more, sipping more cups of green tea, listening, asking a few more questions. They sit with the people from their own industries, with suppliers, with the trading company people, with the managers of subsidiaries. They sit with top people from other companies in their groups—as, for instance, in the famous five-hour luncheons in which the presidents of all companies in the Mitsubishi group come together once a week. They sit with people from the banks, with senior bureaucrats from the various ministries, with people from their own companies in after-hours parties in Ginza bars. They sit on half a dozen committees in half a dozen economic and industry federations. They sit and sit and sit.
>
> In all these sittings they do not necessarily discuss business, surely not their own business. Indeed, to a Westerner their conversation at times appears quite pointless. It ranges far afield, or so it seems, moving from issues of economic policy to personal concerns, from the other fellow's questions and problems to the topics of the day, from expectations for the future to reappraisals of the past.
>
> The aim, of course, is not to solve anything but to establish mutual understanding. When there is a problem, one knows where to go. One knows what the other person and his institution expect, what they can and will do, and what they

cannot or will not do. When either crisis or opportunity arrives, these immobile sitters are able to act with amazing speed, decisiveness, and at times ruthlessness, for the purpose of all this sitting is not to produce mutual liking, agreement, or trust. It is to produce an understanding of why one does not like another, does not agree, does not trust.[11]

Imagine a situation in which an American businessperson must negotiate with a Japanese executive. What questions must he or she ask him- or herself in anticipation of the executives questions? How will time-processing expectations be influenced? Will it still be okay to disagree with or dislike each other?

THE NONLISTENERS VERSUS THE LISTENERS: THE ETHICS OF LISTENING

IN THE UNITED STATES citizens are privileged to be guaranteed free speech. But that's as far as the First Amendment goes. It doesn't guarantee listeners. Yet the freedom to listen is equally precious as the freedom to speak. Far too often, listening problems interfere with the ability or desire of audience members to listen, forcing us to speak to "unlisteners" rather than listeners. For this reason, to become more effective at both speaking and listening, you need to recognize those internal and external factors that contribute to deficient listening—or nonlistening—and then take steps to eliminate them.

How exactly do nonlisteners behave? What kinds of listening problems do they experience?

Nonlisteners Tune Out

Nonlisteners have the ability to tune out what is said to them. They simply do not pay attention to the speaker. While someone is trying to share information with them, influence them, or establish common ground with them, it seems as if their ears and minds are "out to lunch" or "on vacation." Words bounce off them. Nothing penetrates. Nonlisteners are too busy thinking about something else.

This kind of behavior is all too common. At one time or another we have all committed an unlistening act, preferring to pursue our private thoughts, reminisce, worry about something personal, or make silent plans for an event rather than concentrate on a speaker. In fact, as far as nonlisteners are concerned, their own thoughts are more worthy of their attention than anyone else's. Consequently, when you function as a speaker, the thoughts of audience members compete with your own for their attention; only the most effective speakers win this nonlistening battle.

Nonlisteners Fake Attention

Nonlisteners know how to fake attention. They pretend they are listening when nothing could be further from the truth. How do they do this? They look at the speaker, smile or frown appropriately, nod their heads approvingly or disapprovingly, and even utter remarks like "ah" or "uh-huh." All the external cues tell the speaker they are listening. But nonlisteners only pretend to listen.

You do it yourself. Think of the last time you pretended to listen to an instructor, a friend, or a coworker when you actually heard little, if anything, being said to you. What did you miss in the process? How can you possibly answer that question? You weren't listening.

Nonlisteners Prejudge the Speaker and/or the Topic

Before even giving the speaker a fair hearing, nonlisteners decide that the speaker looks uninteresting or sounds boring, or that his or her ideas will be useless and thus nothing he or she says will be of any real value. By prejudging the speaker and his or her presentation, the nonlistener puts an unfair burden on the speaker and usually misses any of the real value inherent in the speaker's remarks. Prejudgment, whether positive or negative, seriously impedes understanding. It causes you to uncritically accept or unfairly reject speakers and their ideas.

Nonlisteners React Too Emotionally

Sometimes nonlisteners let their disagreement with the speaker's poistion get in the way of listening. Nonlisteners go out of their way to avoid listening to anything with which they do not agree, that they believe has little relevance to their lives, or that they feel will be too difficult for them to comprehend. Instead of hearing what the speaker says as he or she actually utters it, nonlisteners hear it the way they *wish* the speaker would say it. When was the last time you distorted a speaker's comments because you wanted to hear something else? Nonlisteners manufacture rather than process information. Personally threatened by a speaker's position, they do not really listen to it, preferring to work instead on defending their own.

We listen selectively. Primarily, we expose ourselves to opinions that agree with our own. We interpret these opinions however we like, often making them fit our preconceptions. We retain those ideas that support our personal points of view, forgetting those that do not.

Nonlisteners also allow particular words uttered by a speaker to interfere with their ability to listen. These words, referred to by listening pioneer Ralph Nichols as "red-flag words," trigger an emotional deafness among nonlisteners, causing listening efficiency to drop to zero as they go off on an emotional side trip, as it were. Among the words contributing to a nonlistener's emotional deafness are words like *taxes, Nazi, AIDS,* and *welfare*. Are you aware of any specific words or phrases that cause you to erupt emotionally, thereby disrupting your ability to process a speaker's remarks accurately?

Nonlisteners Seek the Easy Way Out

Listening is voluntary; unfortunately, nonlisteners do not usually volunteer to listen to material that is challenging. Believing they won't comprehend it anyway, they fail to even give themselves a chance to exercise their minds.

When was the last time you dismissed a topic as unimportant because you told yourself "I won't understand it anyway." Would you willingly attend to a speech on thermonuclear engineering, geophysics, hydropower, molecular biology and gene therapy, or privatization of industry, or would you turn off because you would have to work too hard? Oliver Wendell Holmes once noted: "The mind, once expanded to the dimension of larger ideas, never returns to its original size." Nonlisteners, however, refuse to stretch their minds; they won't work at listening.

Nonlisteners Are Egocentric

When was the last time you tuned out a speaker because you felt his or her topic was irrelevant to you? Would you listen—really listen—to a speech on retirement, life in the Dominican Republic, or the ramifications of a cut in the capital gains tax? Nonlisteners would not, unless the topic had some particular relevance to them. They are egocentric; they view themselves as the center of the universe, and they dismiss as unimportant speeches that might be relevant to society but not to them personally. Seeking only self-satisfaction, the nonlistener is so wrapped up in him- or herself that he or she fails to realize the interconnectedness of all human beings.

Nonlisteners Are Overly Sensitive to Setting

Think of the story of Goldilocks and the three bears. For Momma, Pappa, and Baby Bear things were either too cold or too hot, too big or too small, too high or too low. If we let them—and nonlisteners do—physical factors can function as attention distractors. Nonlisteners let themselves be distracted by the temperature, the arrangement of seats, and the acoustics of the room. Instead of working to overcome any such difficulties, they give in to them and use them as nonlistening excuses. Once they succumb to external distractions, they are unlikely to listen to what the speaker is saying.

Nonlisteners Waste Time

The average speaker speaks at a rate of 150 to 175 words per minute. The average listener, however, comprehends at about 400 to 500 words per minute. The difference between the two is referred to as the **speech–thought differential.** Nonlisteners waste this extra time by daydreaming instead of focusing on, summarizing, and asking themselves questions about the substance of a speaker's remarks.

HOW TO ENHANCE YOUR LISTENING EFFECTIVENESS

LISTENING IS HARD WORK. When you listen actively your body temperature rises, your palms become moist, and your adrenalin flow increases. Your body actually prepares itself to listen. You are the catalyst in this operation; you set the listening process in motion. Making a conscious effort to listen has its benefits; refusing to listen has its costs. Take a moment and calculate both in the "Speaking of Skillbuilding" box on page 72.

As you work to improve your listening, keep the following facts in mind:

FACT 1. Listening is a conscious process. It requires your full attention. You can't half-listen; the half you miss could be critical.

FACT 2. Evaluation should follow, not precede reception. Effective listening takes both time and patience. Effective listeners withold evaluation until they are certain they have understood the entire message. Anger and hostility, like rapture and worship, can impede understanding. A heightened emotional response, either positive or negative, can decrease your ability

Speaking of skillbuilding: The Costs and Benefits of Not Listening

Costs:

Identify five or more problems that you might experience or have experienced as a result of ineffective listening.

Benefits:

Identify five or more benefits that you could realize or have realized as a result of effective listening.

Analyze your listening behavior by responding "yes" or "no" to each of the following questions:

	Yes	No
1. Do you ever find yourself thinking either a speaker or the speaker's subject uninteresting?	❑	❑
2. Do you ever find yourself getting overstimulated by what a speaker says?	❑	❑
3. Do you ever jump ahead of a speaker?	❑	❑
4. Do you ever fake paying attention to a speaker?	❑	❑
5. Do you ever try to avoid listening to difficult material?	❑	❑
6. Do you ever daydream when you should be listening to a speaker?	❑	❑
7. Do you ever try to process every word a speaker says?	❑	❑
8. Do you ever let the speaker's delivery or mannerisms interfere with your reception of his or her remarks?	❑	❑
9. Do you ever let the environment or personal factors distract you from paying attention to the speaker?	❑	❑
10. Are there some topics you refuse to listen to?	❑	❑

Every "yes" is a listening behavior that merits additional work on your part.

to comprehend. Never allow what the speaker says or how he or she says it to close your mind.

FACT 3. Neither appearance nor delivery is a "not listening alibi." Focus on the speaker as a potential source of information. Every speaker presents you with the opportunity to learn something new. Use, don't abuse, that opportunity. At times you might need to overlook a speaker's monotone or lack of eye contact. Instead of being distracted by a speaker's rough or unpolished demeanor, try to concentrate on the message. Try not to kill the message because of the messenger. Realize that ineffective delivery is not the only detractor you need to be aware of. A very smooth, effective delivery can be equally as harmful if you let it blind you to an absence of substance. Again, focus on the message, not just on the messenger. If you are too quick to praise or criticize the speaker's presentation, you could miss the message.

FACT 4. Negative or positive prejudices toward either a speaker or a topic can cause you unconsciously or consciously to judge either quickly. Either you will be too busy arguing against the speaker or too quickly impressed by what he or she is saying to listen accurately to the message.

FACT 5. Good listeners listen for major ideas and principles. Effective listeners focus their listening efforts; rather than working to absorb every isolated fact, they concentrate on identifying the main points and the evidence used to support them.

FACT 6. Become a better notetaker, and your listening ability will improve. Become a better listener and your notetaking ability will improve. Your job is to look for relationships among a speaker's ideas, not to jot down or retain every word the speaker says.[12] Learning to take notes effectively will help you listen effectively, and vice versa. The following suggestions will help you improve both your notetaking and your listening abilities:

A. Divide a piece of paper in half. At the top of the left column write "Facts and Evidence." At the top of the right column write "My Questions and Reactions."
B. Jot down key words, but not a verbatim transcript of the speaker's ideas. You are attempting to summarize and then evaluate the speaker's message, not reproduce it.
C. Use your extra thinking time to analyze whether the speaker answers the questions you noted in the right column, and determine whether your responses to the message are favorable, unfavorable, or mixed.
D. Finally, decide on the extent to which you agree with the ideas and point of view expressed by the speaker, and evaluate the speaker's presentation.

FACT 7. If you seek opportunities to practice skillful listening you will become a more skillful listener. As much fun as it might be to listen just to be entertained, it is important to insure that you listen to more demanding content as well. Recognize that not every speaker is funny, action-oriented, or likeable. Work to increase your attention span, and you'll find quite a lot worthy of attending to. By challenging yourself to listen to difficult material, you will also prepare yourself to meet the speaker's challenge. Recreational listening is more like dessert, whereas being comfortable listening to difficult material is like the main meal.

The following is a four-step program you can use to ensure you become a better listener. By following these guidelines you can take concrete steps toward becoming an effective listener.

STEP ONE. Catch yourself performing a bad habit. Recognition of a fault precedes correction of the fault. If you monitor your listening behavior, you can catch yourself before you exhibit an undesirable behavior. That's the first step toward positive change.

STEP TWO. Substitute a new, good habit in place of the old, bad habit. Think about the new listening habits you would like to make your own. For example, if you are a daydreamer and mentally wander off while others are speaking to you, discipline yourself to exhibit greater attentiveness and concentration. Visualize yourself attending to a presentation. Imagine the positive impact your new behavior will have on a speaker.

STEP THREE. Use your whole body to listen. Take steps to ensure that your physical mannerisms do not distract or confuse a speaker. Instead of fidgeting or looking repeatedly at your watch, make a commitment to convey a more positive listening demeanor. Sit with an attentive posture, make good eye contact with the speaker, and acknowledge the speaker's words with appropriate facial expressions. Look more like a listener and you will behave more like a listener.

STEP FOUR. Use an evaluation form like the one shown in Figure 4.3 on page 74 to help you assess a speaker's effectiveness.

Figure 4.3

Speech Checklist

Name ______________________ *Speech* ______________

Specific Purpose ______________________________

1. Content

____ Was based on accurate analysis of speaking situation
____ Specific goal of speech was apparent
____ Subject appropriate, relevant, and interesting to intended audience
____ All material clearly contributed to purpose
____ Had specific facts and opinions to support and explain statements
____ Support was logical
____ Handled material ethically
____ Used audiovisual aids when appropriate
____ Included a variety of data—statistics, quotations, etc.
____ Moved from point to point with smooth transitions

2. Organization

____ Began with effective attention-getter
____ Main points were clear statements that proved or explained specific goals
____ Points were arranged in logical order
____ Each point was adequately supported
____ Concluded with memorable statement that tied speech together

3. Language

____ Ideas were clear
____ Ideas were presented vividly
____ Ideas were presented emphatically
____ Language was appropriate for intended audience

4. Delivery

____ Got set before speaking
____ Stepped up to speak with confidence
____ Maintained contact with audience
____ Sounded extemporaneous, not read or memorized
____ Referred to notes only occasionally
____ Sounded enthusiastic
____ Maintained good posture
____ Used vocal variety, pitch, emphasis, and rate effectively
____ Gestured effectively
____ Used face to add interest
____ Articulation was satisfactory
____ On finishing, moved out with confidence
____ Fit time allotted

Additional Comments:

Put these four steps into action as you process student Paul Higday's speech on ferrofluids.[13]

FERROFLUIDS

Twenty-five-year-old Anton Mesmer had women slipping into his cellar by the dozens and then stripping down to a single silk stocking. Quite a guy. Once they had placed one foot into an iron urn and the other into a bucket filled with water, Mesmer slowly ran his iron wand up and down the body of the unrequited lovers. The process, according to Mesmer, used the animal magnetism present in every woman to take away the pain and heal that broken heart. But after three centuries of research we know the only thing that can heal a broken heart is time and quite possibly chocolate and roses.

Do you know who Mesmer was? Do you find the introduction effective? Did it make you want to learn more?

Today, however, the simple combination of magnets and liquids, which Mesmer hypothesized, now called ferrofluids, have catapulted out of the cellar, to be christened by *Process Engineering* in October 1994, as the key to overcoming problems ranging from dishwashing to disease. And the *PR Newswire* of September 15, 1995, jumps on the same bandwagon when it points out that soon, ferrofluids will be christened the largest medical marvel since the introduction of penicillin.

Do you understand what a ferrofluid is yet?

The simple combination of magnets and water is representative of scientists' return to effective simplicity. Though we are usually on the receiving end of such benefits, developing a deeper understanding of ferrofluids will enable us to peer into the future of magnetic science and solutions. In order to do so, we must first open the ferrofluids history book. Second, we'll be seduced by the current applications of ferrofluids, so that finally, we can look at the future of these magnetic liquids and discover why it looks very attractive.

Do you find the speech preview helpful?

The January 15, 1995 edition of *Scotland on Sunday* explains that nineteenth-century doctors followed in Mesmer's footsteps by routinely performing an operation called "gaz plucking," which used strong magnets to pull harmful metals from the body's intestines. As the popularity of this process caught on, something I suppose you'd have to experience to understand, so did scientists' fascination with Mesmer's basic theories. According to *Machine Design* of January 26, 1995, a ferrofluid is a synthetic liquid which holds magnetic particles in suspension. In other words, it's a mix between billions of tiny magnets and a simple liquid like water. However, when the liquid is placed into a magnetic field the magnetic particles will then align in one direction, literally pulling the liquid toward the magnet.

The speaker introduces his first main point.

What is the function of this definition?

Ferrofluid research didn't become attractive, however, until inventor John Ramirez placed a small quantity of ferrofluid inside of an electric motor and turned it on. He quickly realized that the magnetic field created by the motor's electricity pulled the tiny particles into tiny deficiencies in the motor's shaft, in effect, providing a liquid Band-Aid that covered up the motor's problems before they could get worse. Since Ramirez's initial discovery, scientists have used ferrofluids in everything from capping oil wells to capping teeth. But the current uses of ferrofluids far exceed Ramirez's initial speculations. Today, the three most common uses of these magnetic liquids are cleaning our dishes, operating our audio equipment, and protecting our environment.

Does this figure of speech work for you?

The speaker explores the second main point.

While you may not have realized it, more than one third of all the illnesses Americans contract come from bacteria that's left over on dirty dishes, even after they're cleaned. According to *The Guardian* of May 18, 1995, an ominous-sounding company named Dreadco has currently manufactured a new type of ferrofluid called dry water. This oxymoronic compound uses magnetic particles to form a

How many different kinds of research does the speaker cite? Which did you find most valuable?

trong flexible skin around each molecule of lard. Drop a few drops on a wet plate and the molecules bond together, carrying the leftover food and bacteria with them. As *The Guardian* concludes, "As long as dry water isn't used on anything magnetic, it will leave almost any surface completely dry and bacteria free."

Yet ferrofluids aren't just doing our dinner dishes. They're providing the after-dinner music as well. According to *HFD* of May 2, 1994, a home furnishings newspaper, the more audio speakers are used, the hotter they become and consequently the more likely they are to break down. So it becomes a race to see which is going to die first, the speaker or the teenager's eardrums. However, according to the *PR Newswire* of August 21, 1995, the audio industry now places a small quantity of ferrofluid in the gap between the voice coil, which resonates to provide the sound, and a magnet, which causes the voice coil to vibrate. The benefit is that ferrofluids not only dissipate heat faster than air, but they also dampen the voice coil vibration, providing for a much crisper, cleaner sound. So while we may not think it's possible to make would-be musicians like David Hasselhoff sound any better, you have to admit that ferrofluids make the quality of their sound close to perfect.

Finally, environmentalists and scientists alike have known for decades that drilling for oil damages the environment. The July 30, 1995, edition of *The Dallas Morning News* explains that as oil comes up through a well, dangerous chemicals such as paraffin build up within, not only shutting the well down, but damaging the environment around it. Fortunately, according to the February 26, 1996, edition of the *Engineering News Record,* by placing a strong magnet around the exterior of the well and then moving it rapidly up and down, it becomes impossible for magnetic particles to stick to the side of the well. An added benefit is that most of the impurities found in oil are magnetic anyway, so that magnetic scrubbing removes them before the oil even leaves the well, decreasing your gasoline costs.

The speaker introduces the third main point of the speech.

The seductive appeal of ferrofluids is so attractive that many of us can't help but be drawn into a closer look at its future applications. Fortunately, ferrofluids will continue to entertain us with new applications that not only unravel our medical mysteries, but provide us with the first smart materials. As Mesmer learned almost 200 years ago, almost every cell in the human body contains magnetic particles. However, the more diseased the cell is, the more magnetic particles it has within it. And scientists can use this idea to identify hundreds of different diseases. The June 4, 1994, edition of *AIDS Weekly* explains that by placing a small quantity of biological ferrofluid inside a blood sample, scientists will soon be able to place the sample into a magnetic field and then use the magnetic potential of the diseased cells to separate them from the healthy ones, allowing them to identify viruses like AIDS in less than 30 minutes, at a cost of under $10 dollars, with 100 percent accuracy. An added benefit is that the technique works very early in virus and disease stages, and consequently will get us valuable information for the scheme of the disease before it becomes too late.

Yet, ferrofluids' detective abilities extend to the pharmaceutical industry as well. According to a spring 1995 Application Note by the Ferrofluidics Corporation, by placing a small quantity of biological ferrofluid inside a pill and then using the magnetic field created by a magnetic resonance image, or MRI, it becomes possible to direct the pill to a specific portion of the body. Most importantly, this will allow scientists to deliver drugs directly to where the illness resides, such as the common cold or cancer, enabling scientists for the first time not to have to use invasive techniques that usually hit more than just the illness.

But despite all the benefits, there is one drawback to ferrofluids. Because they're liquid, they only work on applications where liquids are allowed, such as the medical industry. But when you're building an electrical circuit, water is the last thing you want to have around. Fortunately, *Machine Design* of August 8, 1955, points out that the industry is hard at work on a new type of ferrofluid that changes to a solid when electricity passes through it. These smart materials will therefore react to small changes in their environment, allowing us to create the first airplane wings that change their shape based on the airflow going around them. Or a chair, which uses our magnetic potential within our human body to conform the chair to our own shape, keeping us awake during those long informative rounds.

You may think that knowledge of ferrofluids lies in the realm of the esoteric. But there isn't a more practical substance known to man. If it wasn't for these magnetic liquids, mankind could never have entered space, created the first robots or the first X-ray machines. In fact, you could claim that ferrofluids are the reason you're alive today, since blood, the most basic of all ferrofluids uses its magnetic potential to transport iron throughout the body, keeping us alive.

So when Anton Mesmer dreamed up this idea of animal magnetism, he may have thought it was nothing more than a high-tech pickup line. But after taking a decent look at a couple of ferrofluids applications, we can see it's not a pickup line—well, unless it's picking us up and taking us into the future. Most importantly, however, it shows us something very critical, the naked truth.

How did the speaker tie his conclusion to his introduction? Did you find the conclusion effective?

SUMMARY

LISTENING IS AS IMPORTANT in communication as speaking. Unless we are effective at listening, the right to speak becomes an empty right. Unfortunately, the average person listens at only 25 percent efficiency, losing 75 percent of what he or she hears. Various ineffective listening behaviors contribute to this. By taking the time to understand the listening process and practicing effective listening habits, this deficiency can be alleviated.

An understanding of both the listening cycle, which describes the components at work during the listening process, and the types of listening we engage in can help sensitize us to the importance of effective listening. They reveal to us that our culture and our values both affect our listening ability. In order to become better listeners we need to work to eliminate the prejudices, biases, and misconceptions we have erected. Although this is not easy, it is essential if we are to listen critically as well as ethically.

Whereas ineffective listening can precipitate serious consequences, effective listening can turn us into winners. Effective listeners experience less stress, learn more, develop better relationships, make better decisions, and are able to contribute more to society.

THE SPEAKER'S STAND

Determine how many students in your class support the following controversial positions:

	Agree	Disagree
1. Abortion should be legal.	❑	❑
2. Capital punishment should be abolished.	❑	❑
3. Condoms should be distributed in all public high schools.	❑	❑
4. Americans should buy only American products.	❑	❑

	Agree	Disagree
5. Welfare recipients should be required to perform civic services for their weekly checks.	❑	❑
6. The rich should pay less tax to fuel the economy.	❑	❑
7. College tuition must be raised to increase teachers' salaries.	❑	❑
8. Ebonics (Black English/African Language System) should be considered a language.	❑	❑
9. Gambling should be legal in all major U.S. cities.	❑	❑
10. Prayer should be permitted in public schools.	❑	❑

Working with a partner, select a position diametrically opposed to the position held by the majority of your fellow students. For example, if most students are against capital punishment, present a speech advocating capital punishment. At the end of your presentation discuss the following questions with your audience members:

1. To what extent, if any, were their opinions altered by your speech?
2. What problems did they experience in listening to you?
3. How did they work to overcome initial prejudices toward you or your position?
4. At what points did they tune you out and tune in to their own counterarguments?
5. What did they do to handle their emotions?
6. To what degree, if any, would their responses have been different if the speaker had been a public figure who genuinely supported the unpopular position?

STUDENT FOCUS GROUP REPORT

Now that you've had the opportunity to consider the behaviors exhibited by proficient and deficient listeners, in a group of five to seven students, answer the following questions.

1. Revisit the case study at the beginning of the chapter. What advice would you now offer Jana?
2. What are the greatest challenges facing you as listeners? How do these compare with the greatest challenges facing you as speakers?
3. How can the way audience members listen facilitate or impede a speaker's performance?
4. How can the speaker faciliate or impede the listeners' performances?
5. What kinds of questions should listeners ask themselves when preparing to listen to a speaker?
6. How might cultural or ethical sensitivities affect the ability to listen accurately?
7. Summarize the most significant information you have learned about listening.

Choose a team member to report your conclusions to the class.

Chapter Five

Analyzing the Audience

Focusing on Your Listeners

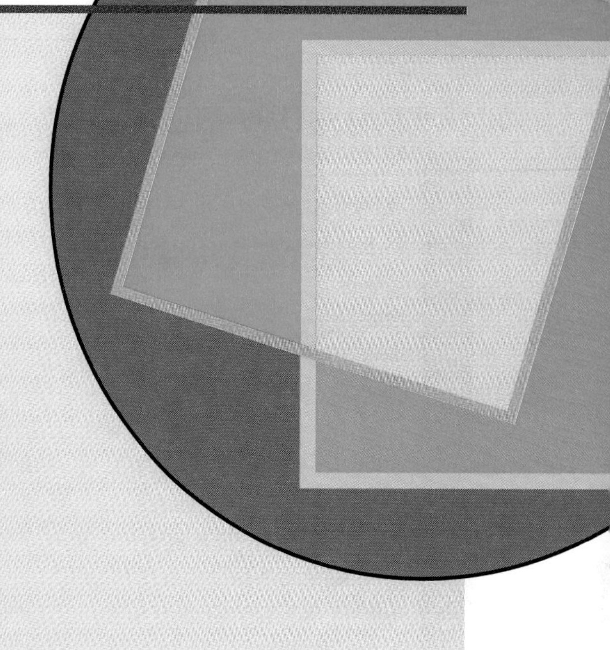

After reading this chapter, you should be able to:

- Explain why audience analysis is so important.
- Discuss how speechmakers can overcome the challenge posed by audience diversity.
- Plan your speech to reflect audience demographics.
- Plan your speech to reflect audience psychographics.
- Plan your speech to reflect the nature of the environment.
- Describe and employ a number of tools to help you conduct informal and formal audience analyses.

CASE STUDY

Meet the Audience

Rafael gazed at the sea of faces before him. Here he was standing before his team, and as their coach it was his job to energize them to victory. This was the most important game they would play—the game that would decide which team left the field number one—undefeated and victorious. Though he had never given the team a pre-game pep talk before, he decided this game warranted it. It was that important.

He began: "Guys, we've worked hard to get where we are. We've made sacrifices. We've worked and trained when we would have rather played or gone out. We've stretched ourselves. When we didn't think we could win, we dug deep inside and found the strength to persevere. We need to do that one more time.

"Your families have sacrificed too. They've cheered you from the sidelines. They have helped you maintain yourselves in top physical condition, ensured that you followed your exercise regimen, nursed your aches and pains after a game, and did whatever was necessary to see that you were prepared to meet the challenges ahead of you.

"We've now arrived at the moment of truth. We're facing a team every bit as good as we are. Our records to this point in time are identical. Only one of us can emerge from this field number one. Who will it be? I believe it will be us. I've watched you all season, and I have come to believe in each and every one of you. I believe in your integrity. I believe in your ability to persevere. I believe in the spirit of commitment you have shown yourselves to have. I believe in your readiness to bury your desire to shine as an individual in order to elevate your potential to function as a team. The whole has always been greater than the sum of its parts. We all know that. So today, as you take your positions on the field of life, remember everything we have been through, and let's win one more for the Gipper!"

The players stared in disbelief. Who was this person standing before them? What was he saying? All they wanted to do was go out and play the game.

Just then, to their relief, the refs called the team to centerfield to make sure they were wearing the right kind of cleats. Lila and Mary, the team captains, led the group of five- and six-year-old soccer players out to meet the refs. The game would start soon. When it was over they would have ice cream. They couldn't wait.

- To what extent did the coach succeed in adapting his remarks to his audience?
- What errors, if any, did the coach commit?
- In what ways, if at all, would you change the speech to enhance its effectiveness? Be specific.

THE PROFESSOR WHO TEACHES his class on German playwright Bertold Brecht in German because he thinks the sound of the language helps him sound more authoritative; *unfortunately, not one of his students speaks or understands German.* The lecturer who walks four miles through a blizzard to deliver a talk entitled "Entrepreneurship: The World of Work after Welfare Reform" to the local chapter of Rotarians; *unfortunately, no one else dared brave the weather.* The doctor who uses words like *cephalgia* and *kwashiorkor*[1] when addressing a meeting of the local PTA; *unfortunately, no one has a clue what he is talking about.* Each of these speakers may know his or her material inside and out and care deeply about the subject. But all forgot a cardinal rule. Speeches are not meant to be delivered in a vacuum.

Most speakers do not speak to inform, convince, motivate, or entertain themselves. Rather, the goal of most public speakers is to gain and maintain an attentive hearing from members of an audience. It is the audience that should be at the heart of the public speaking process, and it is the audience that should control the beat of the public speaker's performance. We cannot say it more directly than this: *Speeches are made for audiences.* The audience is the speaker's compass. The audience directs the speaker on how best to get from point A—the speech's introduction—to point B—the speech's conclusion.

Your achievement as a speaker depends on how well you are able to reach everyone in your audience and how well you are able to communicate your ideas to them. It is the relationship that you build between yourself and your audience that determines your success as a public speaker. And it is for this reason that you need to make a commitment to learn as much as possible about the diverse groups of listeners who come to hear you each time you speak. Only if you do will you be able to speak each time so they really listen. You, your message, and your audience are inextricably linked. Audience analysis is essential to successful public speaking.

What do you think accounted for Dr. Martin Luther King Jr.'s ability to spellbind audiences?

TO WHOM ARE YOU SPEAKING? ARE YOU FULLY PREPARED TO BECOME AN AUDIENCE-CENTERED SPEAKER?

MOST OF US MEET AND TALK TO many different individuals every day. Some of the people we interact with are old friends; others are new acquaintances. Some have higher status than we do; others report to us. Some we seek to impress; others seek to impress us. Some we hope to inform or persuade; others hope to inform or persuade us. Some we know a lot about; others are virtual strangers. If we are to communicate with the strangers as easily as we communicate with people we feel we know well, if we are to inform or persuade the strangers as adroitly as we inform or persuade friends, then we must focus the communicator's spotlight not just on ourselves, but also on the target of our communication efforts. As we discover as much as we can about the "strangers," we also discover how best to communicate with them, and by doing so we improve our chances of relating to them more effectively.

CULTURAL DIVERSITY AND THE ADAPTATION CHALLENGE

AS A RESULT OF THE EXPERIENCES we each have had with speaking, some of us have been encouraged and feel empowered to speak, while others of us may been discouraged or feel that we lack the power to speak. For example, survivors of sexual abuse tend to suffer from a speechlessness that frequently renders them unable to talk about the trauma they have suffered. Some gays, lesbians, and members of other disenfranchised groups have similarly chosen to live in a closet of speechlessness. Some of us may feel ill-equipped to speak using "standard" English, while others of us simply feel excluded from its use.[2] When this happens, socially imposed silence becomes a measure of perceived powerlessness. For those of you who feel this way, it is time for you to have the opportunity to speak about your own lives to others who are now ready to listen. It is time to communicate across differences.

To this end, let us enlarge our sights. Instead of considering the different individuals with whom you interact daily, identify the possible audiences you might find yourself addressing during the coming years. For example, you might find yourself speaking before a group of students; a civic club; the members of a political organization; a parents' club; the members of a temple, church, or mosque; a teachers' organization; women in communication; coworkers; a board of directors; a sales force; members of a union; members of a community group; a fraternity, sorority, or alumni group; or a stockholders' meeting. The list of possibilities is virtually endless. Would you know all the members of each of these audiences equally well? Probably not. Would you speak to each audience about the same topic in the same way? Probably not. Your knowledge of your audience would influence your choice of topic and the way you approached it. Your goal, just as when you seek to find out more about a stranger, is to find out as much as you can about the members of your audience so you can understand them better and determine how best to reach, influence, motivate, or entertain them. This is not a new idea. Over two millenia ago, writing in his

Rhetoric, Aristotle noted: "Of the three elements in speechmaking—speaker, subject, and person addressed—it is the last one, the listener, that determines the speech's end and object."[3]

Acknowledging Diversity

To demonstrate your sensitivity to audience diversity and your respect for receiver differences, you may want to work to adapt your speech to reflect the makeup of a specific audience. This may require you to learn more about the particular group you will be addressing so that you are able to adjust your speech's topic, specific purpose, language, and style of speaking to reflect the group's unique practices, beliefs, interests, and concerns. In other words, you have to educate yourself to understand the differences created by the inclusion of multicultural perspectives and how these differences may ultimately affect the speech you give.

What you need to keep in mind as you do this, however, is that members of every racial group differ in their life experiences, and it may well be that it turns out to be the range of similarities and differences *within* different groups that you, the speaker, must acknowledge. Not all African Americans, Hispanics, or Asians, for example, think alike. Thus, in addition to learning about differences, it is also helpful for you to discover just how much you may have in common with each other.[4] Doing this will ensure that you do not stereotype people because of a group to which they belong.

Centering on the Audience

Speakers who are unaware with whom they are interacting and are not conscious of their audiences usually display a similar ignorance when selecting topics, wording speeches, or organizing ideas. Speakers who do not take the time to understand their audiences are normally the ones audiences do not understand. Speakers who do not let their audiences know that they care about them are most frequently the ones audiences do not end up caring about. However, if you center your attention on your audience, your audience will let you take center stage in their minds. If you are mind-

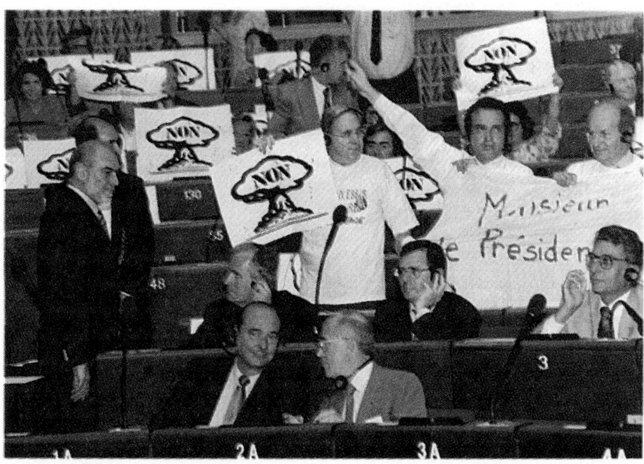

When a speaker fails to take audience composition into account, the result may be unanticipated confrontation, such as this demonstration by opponents of President Chirac's nuclear testing program.

ful of your audience members, your audience members will more readily let your words and ideas penetrate.

Your desire to use communication to share what is important to you with an audience is your reason for public speaking. Only if the speeches you deliver mean something to your audience will receivers respond to both them and you as you hope they will. Of course, unlike the individuals with whom you communicate daily, you can't expect to interact separately with each member of your audience. The more you find out about audience members, however, the more adept you become at adapting your presentation to them. Your reward is reception. Your listeners' reward is understanding.

To whom do speakers speak, then? Effective speakers speak to audiences. They speak not to hear themselves, but to empower others to understand them.

What do speakers speak about? Effective speakers select their topics based on both their desire to articulate their own life experiences publicly together with an understanding of what members of their audience need or want to listen to. They have progressed to the point that they are able to select their topics based not merely on what they alone want to talk about. The **audience-centered speaker** is not a self-centered speaker. The audience-centered speaker is directed in how to frame a topic, present views, and maintain attention by a real understanding of the individuals who comprise the speaker's audience.

Peggy Noonan

Peggy Noonan served as a speechwriter for Presidents Ronald Reagan and George Bush. How can you put to use the advice and insights she offers in "Speech, Speech," a segment from her book What I Saw at the Revolution?

(The use of *man* here is generic; I mean *man* and *woman; he* also means *she*.)

A speech is a soliloquy—one man on a bare stage with a big spotlight. He will tell us who he is and what he wants and how he will get it and what it means that he wants it and what it will mean when he does or does not get it, and . . .

And he looks up at us in the balconies and clears his throat. "Ladies and gentlemen. . . ." We lean forward, hungry to hear. Now it will be said, now we will hear the thing we long for.

A speech is part theater and part political declaration; it is a personal communication between a leader and his people; it is art, and all art is a paradox, being at once a thing of great power and great delicacy.

A speech is poetry: cadence, rhythm, imagery, sweep! A speech reminds us that words, like children, have the power to make dance the dullest beanbag of a heart.

Speeches are not significant because we have the technological ability to make them heard by every member of our huge nation simultaneously. Speeches are important because they are one of the great constants of our political history. For two hundred years, from "Give me liberty or give me death" to "Ask not what your country can do for you," they have been not only the way we measure public men, they have been how we tell each other who we are. For two hundred years they have been changing—making, forcing—history: Lincoln, Bryan and the cross of gold, FDR's first inaugural, Kennedy's, Martin Luther King in '63, Reagan and the Speech in '64. They count. They more than count, they shape what happens. (An irony: You know who doesn't really know this? Political professionals. The men who do politics as a

AUDIENCE ANALYSIS: WHAT TO LOOK FOR AND HOW TO LOOK FOR IT

THE MEMBERS OF AN AUDIENCE, like many of us, like to tune into station **WIIFM**—the **"What's In It For Me"** station. We pay closest attention to those messages we perceive to be meaningful to us, and we fail to notice or we ignore competing communication. Auditory reception, like its counterpart visual perception, is highly selective. Thus, in order for a speaker to penetrate the invisible shield we use to protect ourselves from information overload, he or she needs to relate his or her message to our values, beliefs, needs, and wants. Many of us exhibit an egocentric approach to life, so it is incumbent upon a speaker to convince us that his or her message is relevant to us. If the speaker fails to adjust or adapt the message so that our favorite station (you remember, WIIFM) receives it, he or she will miss a very important communication opportunity. Miss too many opportunities, and you become a **missed communicator**—a speaker who is unable to convince an audience to pay attention.

How can you persuade your audience to tune into and stay tuned for your communicative efforts rather than miss or avoid them? The answer lies in your ability to relate your message to your listeners. If you are able to demonstrate how your mes-

business in America are bored by speeches. They call them "the rah rah." They prefer commercials).

Another reason speeches are important: because the biggest problem in America, the biggest problem in any modern industrialized society, is loneliness. A great speech from a leader to the people eases our isolation, breaks down the walls, includes people: It takes them inside a spinning thing and makes them part of the gravity.

All speechwriters have things they think of when they write. I think of being a child in my family at the dinner table, with seven kids and hubbub and parents distracted by worries and responsibilities. Before I would say anything at the table, before I would approach my parents, I would plan what I would say. I would map out the narrative, sharpen the details, add color, plan momentum. This way I could hold their attention. This way I became a writer.

The American people too are distracted by worries and responsibilities and the demands of daily life, and you have to know that and respect it—and plan the narrative, sharpen the details, add color and momentum.

I work with an image: the child in the mall. When candidates for president are on the campaign trail they always go by a mall and walk through followed by a pack of minicams and reporters. They go by Colonel Sanders and have their picture taken eating a piece of chicken, they josh around with the lady in the mall information booth, they shake hands with the shopper. But watch: Always there is a child, a ten-year-old girl, perhaps, in an inexpensive, tired-looking jacket. Perhaps she is by herself, perhaps with a friend. But she stands back, afraid of the lights, and as the candidate comes she runs away. She is afraid of his fame, afraid of the way the lights make his wire-rim glasses shine, afraid of dramatic moments, tense moments. When you are a speechwriter you should think of her when you write, and of her parents. They are Americans. They are good people for whom life has not been easy. Show them respect and be honest and logical in your approach and they will understand every word you say and hear—and know—that you thought of them.[5]

sage pertains to them, if you are able to explain why they should care about what you have to share with them as much as you do, and if you are able to convey the favorable outcomes they will receive as a result of listening to you, then you will be better prepared to meet the speechmaker's challenge. How can you deliver a speech that fulfills these requirements? You can do so in part by learning as much as possible about your audience so you are better equipped to make accurate decisions regarding how you can make ideas clear and meaningful to them. If you analyze your audience—that is, if you draw as complete a profile or picture of your listeners as possible—then you will have discovered the fuel you need to empower the speaker-audience connection. You will have tuned into their frequency—WIIFM—and you will have improved your chances of having them respond as you desire.

To what extent is student Lawrence Mandes successful at tuning into a favorite frequency of his receivers when he shared the following introductory thoughts with them?

FROM "HOW TO FIND AN APARTMENT"

The speaker voices the issue in a series of lively questions that helps the audience identify with the situation.

Arthur Anderson Company would like to extend to you an offer of employment—starting salary, $28,000. This was a beginning of an actual letter that my good friend John received back in March. There was more to it, and he read on. We want you to begin work on June 12th, and you'll be located in our Washington, D.C. office. Immediately, John's face drew a blank. "Washington, D.C." he stated. "Where am I going to live? I'm from Charleston, South Carolina, and the only time I've been to Washington was in sixth grade on a field trip to visit the monuments and museums. Where am I going to live?"

The speaker switches to a direct statement identifying his topic with the interests of his audience.

This is not only a viable question for John, but for all of us sitting in this room. Unless we're professional students, all of us will be graduating soon, and, thus, we need to relocate after graduation. This is what I want to talk to you about. I want to talk to you about relocating and how to find an apartment in a large metropolitan area.

Answering several general questions can help you identify how to best relate to each audience:

- To whom am I speaking?
- What would they like me to share with them?
- What kind of presentation do they expect me to deliver?
- What do I hope to accomplish?
- How important is my presentation to them?
- What do they know, want to know, and need to know about my subject?
- How do they feel about me?
- How do they feel about my topic?
- What problems or goals do the members of the audience have?
- What should I do to gain and maintain their interest and attention?

The better you become at answering each of these questions, the better you will be able to adapt your presentation to the needs and interests of your listeners. In order to discover as much as possible about your audience, you will want to draw three key audience analysis profiles:

1. Demographic profile
2. Psychographic profile
3. Environmental/situational profile

Once you analyze each of these profiles you will be in the best position to uncover the most effective means of presenting your ideas to a particular audience. Doing this is not always easy; however, it is always worthwhile. As you begin, keep this quotation from Abraham Lincoln in mind: "When I get ready to talk to people, I spend two thirds of the time thinking what they want to hear and one third thinking about what I want to say."

Taking the Demographic Picture: Focusing on Diversity

Developing a picture of your audience starts with drawing a demographic profile of them. The **demographic profile** of your audience is composed of an amalgam of characteristics including age; gender; educational level; racial, ethnic or cultural ties; group affiliations; and socioeconomic background. For example, imagine that you have been asked to give a speech on the use of ebonics to two different audiences. (The word *ebonics,* meaning Black English, was created by combining *ebony* and *phonics.*) Your first audience is composed primarily of middle-aged, well-educated, weathy African Americans who are employed in white-collar jobs. Your second audience is composed primarily of middle-aged, high-school educated African Americans who live in the inner city, work in blue-collar jobs, and occupy the lower or lower-middle rungs on the socioeconomic ladder. Which group do you believe would be more sympathetic to using ebonics to teach? Why? In your opinion, would you succeed as a speaker if you gave the same speech to both groups? Why or why not? Without sacrificing your own stand on the issue, how could you adapt your message to these and other groups? Let's next consider how the demographic data you derive can help you enhance communication with an audience.

Age. How old or young are the members of your audience? Do you expect to speak before an audience of senior citizens, middle-aged business executives and community leaders, newly hired college graduates, or teenagers? Whatever your response, one of your key goals is to diminish the age deficit or surplus that exists between you and the people you hope to reach. To accomplish this you need to be sensitive to the references you employ and the language you use. Ask yourself questions like:

- Will we give the same meanings to the words I use?
- Will they be able to identify with my examples and illustrations?
- Are they old (or young) enough to be familiar with persons and events I refer to?

For example, when delivering a speech entitled "Freedom to Speak and Write" before the First Amendment Congress in Richmond Virginia, Jean Otto, the founder of the First Amendment Congress and associate editor of the *Rocky Mountain News* was careful in selecting her initial references and examples. Notice how she chose to use references and examples that were age neutral, linked the past with the present, and helped her establish common ground with her receivers:

It is a tribute to our Bill of Rights that all of you have gathered here in Richmond, where its protections of individual liberty became the law of the land almost 200 years ago. It is a document, no—a way of life—that deserves to be celebrated. But none of us here, I think, is so naive or out of touch with today's reality as to believe that these protections are necessarily forever.

Yet, almost 200 years ago, these bulwarks of liberty were considered so essential that a bill of rights was required to secure ratification of our Constitution. Today, uncompromising support for individual freedoms has become a sometime thing. It is, indeed, a time for choices.

Many of you knew, or knew of, John Henry Faulk, a broadcaster who was targeted by the House Un-American Activities Committee and Joe McCarthy. He lost his job. He was blacklisted. He sued. And he won, though he never collected a dime. Although he lost his career, he became a scholar of the First Amendment, a folklorist who talked to groups, mostly young people, all around the country about what the First Amendment means in our lives.

John Henry told the story of growing up in rural Texas, where one summer he and a young friend agreed to help his Mama by gathering eggs from the chicken house. One day, clad in overalls, barefooted, Johnny put his hand into a nest to get an egg and it was followed out by a chicken snake.

The two boys cut a new door in the chicken house. They ran to Johnny's mama, their courage draining down their legs, and with great excitement told her what had happened. Mama said, "Lawsy, John Henry, don't you know a chicken snake can't hurt you?" "Yes'm," he answered, "but it can scare you so bad you hurt yourself."

A key question at this meeting may be: Are Americans today running scared?[6]

Often you will not be speaking to a **homogeneous audience**—an audience whose members are similar in age, have similar characteristics, attitudes, values, and knowledge—instead you will speak before a **heterogeneous audience**—that is, an audience composed of persons of diverse ages with different characteristics, attitudes, values, and knowledge. When this is the situation your goal is to be sure you include, rather than exclude, any and all groups. Speaking before an audience of students, professors, and administrators at Princeton University, former Secretary of State James A. Baker III closed the age gap this way:

Forty-one years ago this week, while I was in my junior year here at Princeton and reading the great authors, William Faulkner was already accepting the Nobel Prize for Literature. In his acceptance speech, he said the tragedy of the day—indeed, one might say the challenge of the generation—was "a general and universal physical fear" and that this fear was so great as to extinguish problems of the spirit. As he put it, "There is only one question: When will I be blown up?"

For my generation, Faulkner surely posed the right question. . . .

History has now answered Faulkner's question: We will not be blown up in a war with the Soviet Union.[7]

When speaking before attendees at a leadership conference, James R. Houghton, chairman and CEO of Corning, used a series of historical references, which he fully explained to establish common ground with his audience:

As we stand at the door to a new century, it's useful to look back and check the century we're leaving. One hundred years ago, the United States was primarily rural and agrarian. People lived on farms. They worked the fields or toiled in small workshops. Markets were local and the workforce was largely homogeneous. Formal education was pretty informal. It usually ended at an early age.

By the start of the 1900s, the Industrial Revolution had changed all that. The body and the soul of America were transformed. Millions of workers and their families migrated to our shores—attracted by opportunity, by jobs. These workers brought a tremendous capacity for work. They helped this country grow great. However, many of them did not know the language; few had any education. These factors—combined with the prevailing psychology of the day—resulted in the creation of large, hierarchial organizations. Workers were considered little more than cogs. Leaders were expected to be commanding and authoritative, armed with all the answers.

But of course, all of that has changed with the advent of the Information Age.[8]

What other adaptations might a speaker make after analyzing the age of his or her listeners? Because research tells us that children are more susceptible to persuasion than adults and that youth are more open to new ideas whereas older people are less receptive to change, we can also gauge how difficult it will be for us to attain our speaking objectives.[9]

Similarly, as people grow older, their responsibilities and their interests change. Recognition of this could be helpful to you as you choose a topic and an approach. Because age is a prime determiner of life experience, when you have drawn as accurate a profile of the "average" age of audience members as you possibly can, you will also be better able to select supporting materials appropriate to that age.

Of course, age is more relevant to the development of some topics than to others. For example, the age of listeners might be terribly significant if you were speaking on life after retirement, but it could be less important if your topic was taking care of planet earth. The relevance of age is linked to the goals of the speaker. So ask yourself this question:

> Could the age of audience members influence the way they respond to my presentation and to me?

Gender. Another key variable to consider when analyzing your audience is the ratio of males to females. For example, in a speech delivered during the Seventeenth Annual Professional Development Conference for Women, Nancy W. Dickey, MD, chair of the American Medical Association, acknowledged that her audience was composed primarily of women by beginning this way:

Good morning. How many of you had one of these dolls when you were growing up? Or if you have children—I know you recognize this bright pink package from Mattel.

But this particular toy is special, because she . . . is Dr. Barbie.

And if I had room up here, I suppose I could also show you Air Force Pilot Barbie, Business Suit Barbie, Broker Barbie and . . . Ken.

Now I'm not sure all of those dolls really exist—but they do make a point: That even in the merchandise-driven world of Mattel, what a woman chooses to be when she grows up is a decision that is formed while she is growing up.

And if we're talking about where all of this growth and input leads us, as women, into the next millennium . . . then this doll has grown up from the toy box as a symbol of what women can be today, in the same way that the issues of women's health—and women patients—have grown in social importance and ethical conscience, right alongside the issues of women physicians.

And that's what I'm going to talk about this afternoon: How we are all in this together. Not as dolls or icons or bathing beauties—but real-life women, facing real-life issues of women's health and well-being.[10]

Contemporary research reveals a number of differences in the ways males and females listen and respond to messages. According to sociolinguist Deborah Tannen, whereas "women speak and hear a language of connection and intimacy . . . men speak and hear a language of status and independence."[11] Whether you are a male or a female speaker addressing a predominantly male, female, or mixed sex audience, this finding could affect the amount of time you spend building rapport with your listeners, and could alter the approach you select to deliver your information and ideas to them. To be sure, both men and women can enhance their speechmaking abilities by understanding the gender styles of the opposite sex; doing so will let you cross the gender gap, much as being senstive to age helps you close the age gap.

Research suggests that women are perceived to be more highly persuasible than are men. However, research also indicates that this finding is muted when the speaker is a woman.[12] Of course, the opinion that women tend to be prejudiced against women is a controversial one, and research does support the fact that for a number of topics, such as fashion, females prefer to listen to other females.[13] In addition, the belief that women are more readily persuaded than men could simply be reflective of a preferred response style. After listening to a message, women may appear more accommodating because they tend to take more time thinking through what they've internalized than do men. Ultimately, women may reject as many messages as men, but it probably takes them longer to do so.[14]

Another research finding is that male speakers are usually judged more dynamic than females;[15] this tells us that females will need to work especially hard to ensure that their word choice and delivery techniques support their objectives. Yet a woman speaker who is competent and develops strong evidence supporting her central idea may still fail to communicate effectively because of poor word choice, speech nonfluencies, or a low-power presentation style.

The key to males' and females' communicating equally well to audiences composed of either or both sexes is flexibility. Although gender differences are less pronounced than they were in the past and although men and women display greater role versatility today, males and females still bring different perspectives to many issues. Women tend to be more interested in people-related issues, whereas men usually show more interest in sports, conflicts, and controversies. Adept speakers are able to tie their ideas to the interests of the group they are addressing. Speakers of both sexes need to work to ensure that gender does not get in the way of communicating with their receivers. In order to ensure gender does not impede communication, ask yourself this question:

> Could the sexual makeup of my audience influence members' responses to my speech and to me?

Educational Level. Knowing the level of education that the average listener in your audience has attained will help you make choices regarding vocabulary, language style, and supporting materials. Your goal is to adapt your remarks to your listeners' knowledge. If you miss your mark and speak above their knowledge level, they will not understand you; if you speak below their knowledge level, you will insult and bore them. An audience that knows either more or less than you think they do is an audience that could stop listening to you at any moment. And that's the last thing a speaker wants an audience to do.

Audience interests tend to correlate with educational level. The better educated your audience members, the more likely they are to be concerned about contemporary issues like gun control, depletion of the ozone layer, equal rights, and balance of trade, and the more active they are apt to be in politics. In addition, the higher the education level of the audience members, the more tolerant they usually are to a speaker's call for social change.

More highly educated audiences are also more discriminating. Thus, when speaking before an educated audience, you will want to deliver a **two-sided presentation,** that is a presentation that allows audience members to consider alternative perspectives, rather than a **one-sided presentation,** which offers a single side or perspective only.[16] Also, when addressing an audience of well-educated individuals, keep in mind that they will be more accepting of your ideas if you present them with strong evidence to back them up and include arguments that are logically sound. In addition, better educated audiences are more apt to be able to process more complex communication and to distinguish between a variety of positions and options. Such an audience is also better able to pay attention and comprehend your message; in general, they are more sophisticated receivers.[17] In order to be certain you pay education level its due, ask yourself this question:

> How could the educational level of audience members influence the way they respond to my speech and to me?

Racial, Ethnic, Religious, or Cultural Ties

U.S. society is becoming increasingly multiracial and multicultural.[18] Speakers need to be attuned to the traditions and beliefs of members of their correspondingly diverse audiences. As you prepare your presentation, keep in the front of your mind any potential misunderstandings that racial, ethnic, religious, or cultural differences could precipitate. Your appreciation of the makeup of your audience could well affect the kinds of material you use to illustrate or support your ideas and provide a benchmark for predicting where audience members might position themselves on an issue. For example, a predominantly Catholic or Orthodox Jewish audience is likely to support the abolition of abortion on demand. An audience composed of mostly minority students is likely to favor the continuation of affirmative action programs. An audience composed of recent immigrants is likely to oppose the reduction of immigration quotas. An audience composed primarily of Japanese individuals will not support a program calling for organ donation because most Japanese do not believe in organ transplants.

In addition, there are a number of other ways that an understanding of cultural differences can make it easier for you to adapt to an audience. Among these are a determination of whether your receivers belong to a culture that is predominately individualist or collectivist, high or low context, tolerant of uncertainty or in need of certainty, and high or low power.

In **individualist cultures** such as in most Western European countries, Australia, Canada, and the United States, the "I" predominates over the "we." Individual identity is paramount, and speaking one's mind is a sign of honesty. Thus, conflict is seen as inevitable. In **collectivist cultures** such as in most Asian, Arab, and Latin American countries, identity is derived from the social group to which one belongs and harmony, rather than speaking one's mind, is a key value. As a result, conflict is perceived to be a negative force. In addition, persuasive appeals directed at individual achievement would be more effective when addressing members of individualist cultures than when addressing members of collectivist cultures. The opposite would be true for persuasive appeals directed at group/team benefits.

Members of **high-context cultures** (Asian, Latin American, and Middle Eastern countries), expect verbal messages to be implicit in nature because they prefer to rely on other cues such as voice tone, body language, facial expressions, and even silence to derive meaning—for them, communication is contextual and an art form. In contrast, members of **low-context cultures** (among them the United States and Germany) rely more on the words spoken than on the nonverbal cues used to derive meaning; they are more comfortable when meaning is explicitly expressed.

Cultures also differ in the extent to which they are able to adapt to change and cope with uncertainties or ambiguities. Cultures that have a **high tolerance for uncertainty and ambiguity** include Singapore, Jamaica, Great Britain, and the United States. Members of such cultures accept and encourage dissent. Conversely, members of Asian, Latin American, and Arab cultures prefer to **avoid uncertainty and ambiguity,** tend to demand consensus about goals, and are apt not to tolerate individual dissent.

When it comes to power, **high-power cultures** such as Mexico, India, most Arab countries, and the Philippines, prefer clearly defined lines of authority and responsibility, whereas **low-power cultures** including Austria, Israel, Denmark, and the United States are more at home with less formalized and more egalitarian lines of authority.[19]

It is up to you to acknowledge that some of your listeners may disagree with your stand or point; because we all inhabit a common "village," it is also up to you to find ways to encourage them to explore and consider different ideas. To what extent, if any, do you believe that Ray Halbritter, Nation Representative of the Oneida Indian Nation succeeded in accomplishing that goal with this excerpt from his speech on "Indian Economic Futures," delivered at Cornell University for its American Indian Program.

There's an old Indian joke about the race to the moon being started because white men believed there was Indian land there. I have often said that Indian people never have anything for very long before the white man tries to take it away. That is the situation confronting us today. . . .

It is important to remember that only a small percentage of Indian nations have achieved tangible improvement in their economic welfare over the past twenty years. The vast majority of tribes still find their members living in conditions of poverty. Statistics show that almost 32 percent of Indian people live in poverty. That compares to 13 percent of the general population in the United States. Nearly 15 percent of Indian people are unemployed. Our people still suffer from higher rates of liver disease, diabetes, alcoholism, suicide, homicide and accidental death, all signs of a society in stress, a culture endangered and a species nearly extinct. Sometimes it seems as if society is more concerned about spending dollars to save eagles from extinction than it is about saving indigenous peoples. . . .

Reduced to simple terms, this is what today's clash between Indian nations and other governments is all about, our struggle, their greed.[20]

Whatever the group's makeup, it is up to you to do your best to ensure that you open the door to all in your audience and bridge racial, ethnic, religious, or cultural differences rather than permit them to impede effective communication. Speakers who suffer from **ethnocentrism**—the belief that the racial, ethnic, religious, or cultural groups to which they belong are superior to all others—will find it increasingly difficult to be effective public communicators. It is important to acknowledge that the diversity inherent in audiences makes it all the more important for speakers to explore diverse ideas and seek commonalities. Although it is enlightening to recognize that "an American child sticks out a tongue to show defiance, a Tibetan to show courtesy to a stranger, and a Chinese to express wonderment," it is equally enlightening to communicate the universalities that help unite them.[21] As anthropologist Laura Nader notes, "Diversity is rich."[22]

In order to reflect fully on the richness inherent in diversity, ask yourself this question:

How might the diversity or lack of diversity in my audience influence the members' responses to my speech and to me?

SPEAKING of ETHICS

Across Cultures

If acknowledging and sensitizing ourselves to diversity is the watchword for communicators today and in the future, how will our ethical obligations as speakers be affected? How can we reconcile the urge to take a strong moral position with the need to recognize diversity? Consider the following.

Speaking about U.S. economic problems, the Japanese House Speaker Yoshio Sakurauchi said the following: "American workers don't work hard enough. They don't work but demand high pay."[23] Echoing this perception some days later, then Japanese Prime Minister Kitchi Miyazawa added that America "may lack a work ethic," and that some of the country's economic problems are due to the fact that too many American college graduates headed to Wall Street during the last decade rather than spend time "producing things of value."[24] Reinforcing the prime minister's words were those of Japanese conservative lawmaker and former Minister of Information, Trade, and Industry, Kabun Muto, who noted that Americans were too preoccupied with the weekend to work wholeheartedly on Fridays, and then too exhausted to work properly on Mondays.[25]

In your opinion, is it ethical for individuals to speak about the work habits of citizens of another country? To what extent, if any, should "moral outbursts" be restrained or encouraged? And how should Americans respond to such criticism? Does it matter to you if the above comments were made for Japan's ears only, rather than foreign and American consumption, or is a distinction between the two meaningless?

How do you think most Americans would react if similar criticisms were leveled at them by U.S. politicians? As a speaker, it is important for you to consider how your words will be perceived by your receivers. Speakers who insult their listeners are more likely to alienate them and create hostile reactions than are those who choose their words carefully, anticipating a divergence of opinion among receivers from foreign cultures. What people of one culture can say to and of others from that culture often contrasts with what is considered acceptable for someone who is perceived to be an outsider to say.

Group Affiliations. Often memberships in occupational, political, civic, and social groups also provide speakers with a pretty accurate prediction of the way audience members will react to a topic. Group affiliations serve as a bond. Workers who belong to the same union, hunters who belong to the National Rifle Association, citizens who support a political candidate, parents who are active in the PTA, and environmentalists who attend or support Greenpeace demonstrations probably also share a number of key interests, attitudes, and values with others in the group. Members embrace and endorse a number of their organization's stances on major issues; otherwise they would not be willing to identify themselves with the group. Thus, the political party we belong to, the professional organizations we are part of, the social groups we attend, or the cultural or entertainment groups we take part in will all strongly influence our approach to an audience and to the message we send. For example, some years ago when Vice President Dan Quayle, a Republican, attacked fictional television character Murphy Brown for having a child out of wedlock, he precipitated a whirlwind of reactions. Quayle stated:

> It doesn't help matters when prime time TV has Murphy Brown—a character who supposedly epitomizes today's intelligent, highly paid, professional woman—mocking the importance of fathers by bearing a child alone and calling it just another "lifestyle choice." It's time to talk again about family, hard work, integrity and personal responsibility. We cannot be embarrassed out of our belief that two parents, married to each other, are better in most cases for children than one.[26]

Some weeks later, Bill Clinton said during his acceptance speech at the Democratic Convention:

> And, I want to say something to every child who is trying to grow up without a father or a mother: I know how you feel. You're special, too. You matter. And don't let anyone ever tell you you can't become whatever you want to be. If the politicians who are lecturing you don't want you to be part of their families, you can be part of ours.[27]

Others, including journalist Kenneth L. Woodward, countered that perhaps the people who make TV shows are really different and quoted a study of the Center for Media and Public Affairs: "The Center found that on issues of sexual morality, abortion and religion, the people at the top in television and moviemaking were far more liberal than the rest of the country."[28]

Whenever you function as a speaker, you need to consider how the various affiliations of audience members could influence both your topic and your approach. Remember, your goal is to identify clues regarding how listeners will respond to your presentation, so the question you ask yourself is:

> Do audience members belong to any groups that might affect the way they respond to my speech and to me?

Socioeconomic Background. People from different socioeconomic backgrounds naturally look at situations, events, and issues from very different perspectives. A wealthy, upscale audience might not appreciate what it means to grow up in poverty. It is up to you to find the common denominator you can use to increase audience understanding of, and audience identification with, your subject.

Writing about this issue, journalist Anthony Lewis noted: "Upper-income Americans generally, whether in public or private employment, live not just a better life but

Does the speaker appear to be adapting to the needs of the children in his audience?

one quite removed from that of ordinary families. They hardly experience the problems that weigh so heavily today on American society. . . . The top 20 percent of Americans now get 47 percent of the country's total income. The bottom fifth get 3.9 percent."[29] It is up to you, the speaker, to close the perceptual gap created by this disparity. You can start to do that by asking this question:

> How will the socioeconomic backgrounds of the audience members influence the way they respond to my speech and to me?

To learn about your audience, you need to draw a second kind of audience picture—an attitudinal or psychographic profile.

Assessing Psychographics

Drawing a demographic profile allows you to make a number of useful predictions about your audience and the way they will probably respond to you and your presentation; learning even more about audience member **psychographics**—that is, what's

Speaking of skillbuilding: Are Strangers Stranger?

Work with a partner. Go to a location such as a shopping center or a mall. Pick out five people who are different from you—either older, younger, from another cultural group, or of the opposite gender.

Walk up to one such person together and explain that you are conducting a survey for your class in public speaking. Ask if he or she would mind answering two quick questions:

> Can you identify a public figure or personality you think is an effective speaker?
>
> To what qualities or traits do you attribute that person's effectiveness?

Make a note of each interviewee's age, gender, cultural background, and answers.

To what extent, if any, were the answers provided by interviewees of similar ages, genders, and cultures similar? To what extent, if any, were they different? Did any of the responses surprise you? Why? How could such information better prepare you to speak in public?

going on in the minds of receivers, including how they see themselves; their attitudes toward various issues; their motives in being there; and how they feel about your topic, you, and the occasion or event may provide additional clues to their likely reactions. In order to draw this kind of audience profile, you need to uncover the beliefs and values that support audience members' attitudes. Let us begin by clarifying the relationship that exists among the attitudes, beliefs, and values of listeners.

Attitudes are the favorable or unfavorable predispositions or mental sets that we carry with us everywhere we go. The attitudes we hold help direct our responses to everything, including a speech. Attitudes are evaluative in nature and are measured on a continuum that ranges from favorable to unfavorable, pro to con, for to against. Our attitudes reflect our likes and our dislikes and are shaped by myriad influences including family, education, culture, and the media.

Beliefs are what we hold to be true and false. They are also the building blocks of our attitudes, and they can be used to help explain them. Because our belief systems are composites of everything we hold to be true and untrue, they influence the way we process messages. Some beliefs that we hold are more important to us than are others. The more important our beliefs, the harder we work to keep them alive and the less willing we are to alter them.

Values are the anchors to which our attitudes and beliefs are attached. Our values illustrate what is important to us; they indicate what we judge to be good and bad, ethical or unethical, worthwhile or worthless. Our values represent our conception of morality. They are the standards against which we measure right and wrong.

How might the attitudes, beliefs, and values of audience members influence the way they respond to a topic, a speaker, and a particular speaking occasion?

The Audience and Your Topic. Knowing how your audience feels about your topic can help you determine how to handle your material. If you can estimate your audience's predisposition to respond favorably or unfavorably in advance, you can adapt your approach so that you address their beliefs and reflect their values. If you are able to relate your ideas to their needs and wants, as well as to use their individual motivations to impel them to listen to your speech, then you can improve the chances of your message receiving a fair hearing.

Once you understand what listeners believe about a topic, you can more readily identify the kind of information you need to add, or the misconceptions you need to correct. And if you can demonstrate for them how your message supports values they already hold dear, you are much more likely to succeed. However, only if you are able to uncover why audience members feel the way they do about your topic will you possess the clues you need either to reinforce or to alter their attitudes.

Thus, if you plan to talk about gender bias in schools, you might first want to identify how your listeners feel about equal treatment for males and females, teacher training, gender stereotyping in textbooks, formal policies against sexual harassment, and special programs in math and science for women. Do they feel the topic is an important one?

If, on the other hand, you were going to give a speech on what constitutes mutual respect in a relationship, you might explore how audience members feel about sex, the images of relationships portrayed in popular culture, and the concept of commitment.

Knowing such information could help you plan and present your message. Being able to acknowledge audience member attitudes, beliefs, and values is a very significant part of the adaptation process.

How might you use audience feelings about your topic to guide your speechmaking approach?

The Audience and You. How the audience feels toward you, the speaker, can also affect their reaction to your speech. No matter how audience members feel about your topic, if they assess you to be a credible source, they are much more apt to listen to what you have to say. In other words, the way your audience perceives you directly influences the way they hear your speech: Perception colors conception. If listeners truly believe you have their best interests at heart, then they will be more likely to give your speech a positive reception.

What if you know audience members don't look favorably on you? First, you need to ask yourself if this is because they lack information, have received misinformation, or have a legitimate reason for holding that judgment. Then you need to identify what you can do to unfreeze their feelings and influence them to view you more favorably. For example, if they don't believe you are an authority on your subject, you can work experiences you've had that qualify you to speak on the topic into your presentation. One speaker gained instant credibility when addressing her audience about how to get out of an abusive relationship by allowing them to share the personal experience she had with the topic: she had been an abused wife. Another student who asked his audience to accept that the U.S. government should significantly increase social services to the homeless made his message more appealing by telling them about his own experiences as a homeless person some years earlier. Attempting to establish common ground and credibility with his audience, Al Gore, then Democratic candidate for vice president, told delegates to the Democratic National Convention:

> Three years ago, my son Albert was struck by a car crossing the street after watching a baseball game in Baltimore. He was thrown 30 feet in the air on impact and scraped along another 20 feet on the pavement after he hit the ground.
>
> I ran to his side and held him and called his name, but he was limp and still, without a breath or pulse. His eyes were open only with the empty stare of death and we prayed, the two of us, there in the gutter, with only my voice.
>
> Albert is plenty brave and strong, and with the support of three wonderful sisters, Karenna, Kristen, and Sarah, and two loving parents who helped him with his exercises every day and prayed for him every night, he pulled through. And now, thank God, he has fully recovered and he runs and plays and torments his older sisters like any little boy.
>
> But that experience changed me forever. When you've seen your 6 year old son fighting for his life, you realize that some things matter more than winning, and you lose patience with the lazy assumption of so many in politics: that we can always just muddle through. When you've seen your reflection in the empty stare of a boy waiting for a second breath of life, you realize that we weren't put here on earth to look out for our needs alone; we're part of something much larger than ourselves.[30]

What your audience thinks of you could change the way they respond to your message. Your credentials and your reputation accompany you to the podium.

How might what the audience thinks of you influence the reaction to your speech?

The Audience and the Occasion. Is your audience attending the speech voluntarily, or are they a captive audience? Are those in attendance members of your audience

Considering Diversity

Lessons for Today

Are there some messages that would be better received if communicated to the public by a member of a specific cultural group or do some messages need a more specific link to the speaker than cultural identity is able to provide? Consider the following.

In 1991, NBA superstar Earvin "Magic" Johnson tested positive for HIV. It was noted that his candor was needed most sorely among African Americans, among whom the deadly disease is spreading fastest.[31]

According to Dr. Ernest Dricker, director of the Division of Community Health at Montefiore Hospital in New York City, "Among blacks, there is a tremendous distrust of AIDS prevention messages coming from public health officials who are mostly white. . . . The importance of Johnson's revalations is that there is suddenly a messenger who has impeccable credentials to that group."[32] In addition, it was noted that in the current state of an American culture, so dominated by athletes and its heroes, Magic Johnson "may well be the ultimate spokesman for all groups in the battle against the dread disease."[33]

But perhaps the message about AIDS goes beyond simple cultural identity. Would a popular African American who was not HIV positive, such as Eddie Murphy, be as effective with this audience as Johnson? Would an African American athlete with a different personality, such as Dennis Rodman, have been more or less effective than Johnson? How and why is this particular messenger a factor in the message?[34]

because they have chosen that role or because they have been coerced or cajoled into functioning that way?

If you know in advance the reasons why people are present for your speech, you can adjust your remarks accordingly.

When thinking about the occasion, you need also to consider the kind of speech audience members are expecting you to deliver. If, for example, you are to speak after dinner, they probably expect to listen to an "after-dinner speech." If you are speaking to commemorate someone who has passed away, they have a right to expect you deliver a euology. If you are speaking at a rally to encourage fund raisers, listeners might well anticipate a motivational speech.

Whenever possible, it is wise for you to try to fulfill audience expectations. Thus, be sure you can answer these questions:

1. What is the nature of the group you are to address?
2. What is your reason for speaking?
3. What is the length of time allotted for your presentation?

Considering the Speaking Environment

In addition to demographic and psychographic issues, an important component of audience analysis is the environmental/situational profile—the "where and when" of your presentation. It is up to you, the speaker, to take as much control over the speech setting as possible; lose control of the setting, and you could lose control of the audience and the speech.

Too many speakers pay little, if any, attention to environmenal variables like place, time, and audience size. Yet these variables affect the audience and ultimately influence audience reaction to you and your presentation. By paying attention to the physical and temporal settings for your speech and by considering how audience size could affect your style, language, and manner of delivery, you take steps to ensure that "little things" don't stand in the way of communication—because when they do, little things have a way of becoming big things, and big things can get you!

The Physical Setting. Will you deliver your speech indoors or outside? Is the space well lit or dim? airy or a hot box? noisy or quiet? attractive or ugly? Will audience members be sitting or standing? Will the speaker's area include a lectern and microphone, or will it be less traditional and allow you more intimate contact with the audience? Your answers to these questions could have an impact on the nature of your speechmaking, could influence the audience's response to you, and, ultimately, could affect the outcome of your presentation.

Consider some of the ways that physical setting could affect the receptivity of listeners by answering these questions:

- Why do we find it difficult to concentrate when we're too hot or too cold?
- Why do we find it tough to focus on or pay attention to a speaker when a room is poorly lit or too noisy?
- Why might an environment that is unattractive, or too attractive adversely affect audience response?

The physical setting becomes part of the message, and unless you understand its potential impact, you won't be prepared to adjust to it. It is up to you to adapt your presentation to allay listener discomfort and promote listener understanding and acceptance. That could mean talking louder or more softly, turning a thermostat down or up, bringing extra lights, or working extra hard to attract and maintain audience interest.

The Temporal Setting. Speeches are given at different times of the day, the week, and the year. Time can make a difference. If you are giving a speech early in the morning, right after lunch, later in the evening, or late in the week, you probably will have to wake up members of your audience by doing something unusual or by including some intriguing or startling example or illustration that compels their attention. Your goal is to keep your listeners from drifting off into daydream land, and time is of the essence.

Just as time of day or week can affect listener receptivity, so can time of year. Rainy, gloomy, or cold weather can make listeners less receptive to ideas, as can hot, steamy, humid weather. Are you prepared to meet another speechmaking challenge by using specific words and techniques to put audience members in a more receptive mindset? Consider how you might change your speech to overcome the winter doldrums or the summer sweats.

Time has another aspect worthy of your attention: the length of time you are to speak. If you go over the time allotted, don't expect audience members to necessarily listen. If you greatly short circuit your speaking time, don't expect that audience members will necessarily be pleased. Instead, find out the amount of time you are given, and work to fill that time with as stimulating and informative a presentation as you possibly can.

Another consideration is the number of speakers sharing the program with you. Will you speak first, last, or somewhere in between? Will you be flexible enough to tie your remarks to the remarks of those who precede you? Will you be sensitive to the lethargy that could affect your audience after a long evening of virtually uninterrupted listening? Communication consultant Roger Ailes describes it:

> I've seen speakers get up at the end of a long evening, after the emcee has read the treasurer's report and has introduced everybody in the room. By then the members of the audience are thinking about their baby sitters and whether the hubcaps have been stolen off their cars in the parking lot. What you really need to do at that point is lighten it up, let them know that you're aware of how they feel. Tell them that you recognize the hour is late and you're not going to keep them too long. You want to move immediately into the text and relax them. If the time is short, don't talk *faster.* Talk *less.* Edit your text."[35]

Then, exemplifying with an experience that directly involved him, Ailes adds:

> A couple of years ago, I was the last speaker at a particularly long dinner where more than fifty people had received awards. The entire audience was thinking the same thing: "When will this be over? How many more of these can there be?" I got up and said, "Before I actually start my speech, I'd like each of you who got awards to stand up again one at a time so that we can recognize you."
>
> Of course, the place broke up in laughter because everyone in the audience felt that the evening had gone on too long. By kidding about the situation, I became one of them and they became more receptive to the rest of my speech.[36]

Speakers need to empathize with what the audience is feeling and decide how best to communicate that empathy. Accurate perception can eliminate audience rejection.

How could time affect your presentation?

Audience Size. How many people will be in your audience: 10, 50, 100, 1,000, tens of thousands, or millions? Audience size and formality are directly related. As audience size increases, speaker formality increases. As audience size decreases, so should the speaker's formality.

Audience size is related to style of delivery in other ways as well. It directly influences the amount of interaction you are able to have with members of your audience, the kinds of visual aids you use, and whether you will use an amplification system and a podium. Adept speakers are ready to adapt their presentations to meet the requirements of different audience sizes. In fact, audience size is one of those variables that helps make every speech situation different. When you are sensitive to it, you increase your chances for success. An effective speaker is like a thermostat. After surveying the situation, he or she sets the right temperature level for that presentation.

How could audience size affect your delivery?

TOOLS YOU CAN USE TO GATHER INFORMATION ABOUT YOUR AUDIENCE: HOW TO FIND OUT WHAT YOU NEED TO KNOW

BY NOW YOU SHOULD RECOGNIZE the kind of information it would benefit you to have about your audience. The next question to answer is: How can you gather this information? Who do you ask, where do you go, and what kinds of tools can you use to gain insight into the audience you will address?

Query Contacts

A sensible starting point is the person who invites you to speak. Ask that individual about the group he or she represents. Questions such as the following will yield valuable information:

- Why does the group exist?
- What goals does the group hope to fulfill?
- What is the nature of the occasion at which I will speak?
- How many people do you anticipate will be in attendance?
- Can you share any insights about the composition of the audience?
- What expectations do you believe audience members will bring with them to the presentation?
- Are you aware of any attitudes held by audience members on the whole that could positively or negatively affect how they receive to my presentation?
- How much time will be allotted for the presentation?
- Will any other speakers be sharing the program with me?
- At what point in the program will I speak?
- What will the physical setting be like?
- How will I be introduced?

You can obtain this information by phone, mail, e-mail, fax, or in person. Of course, your sponsor is not the only person you might query. If you know anyone who has spoken to the group before, or if you know members of the group, you might also ask them similar questions.

Your Personal Knowledge and Observations

If you'll be speaking before a group that you belong to such as a class, club, or civic organization, you can make decisions regarding your presentation based, at least in part, on prior conversations you have had with audience members, your perceptions of their opinions of you, and insights you have gained from hearing many of them voice personal opinions. Don't be afraid to watch people in action prior to the speech and to make educated guesses regarding ages, education and income levels, and cultural background.

Research Attitudes of People Similar to the Group You Will Address

The library and the Internet hold clues to the attitudes of audience members. By researching what local, regional, and national opinion polls reveal about the attitudes of various groups on a variety of social and political issues such as abortion, the death penalty, the AIDS epidemic, and health care, you might be able to make a number of assumptions regarding the attitudes of those before whom you will speak. Among those newspapers and magazines that regularly report the results of opinion polls are the *New York Times,* the *Washington Post,* the *Wall Street Journal, USA Today, Time,* and *Newsweek.*

To increase specificity and add to the knowledge you are gathering about the group you will address, you can also use a questionnaire.

The Questionnaire. A well thought-out questionnaire helps you approximate the amount of knowledge your listeners already possess about your subject and their attitudes toward it. Questionnaires generally contain three different kinds of questions: close-ended questions, scaled questions, and open-ended questions.

Close-ended questions are highly structured, only requiring that the respondent indicate which of the provided responses most accurately reflects his or her answer to a question. The following are examples of close-ended questions:

Please indicate your marital status.
❑ married ❑ single ❑ divorced
❑ widowed ❑ separated

Do you think prayer should be permitted in public schools?
❑ yes ❑ no ❑ undecided

Should pregnant teenagers be allowed to attend public schools?
❑ yes ❑ no ❑ undecided

Questions like these usually generate clear, unambiguous answers.

In contrast, **scaled questions** make it possible for a respondent to indicate his or her view along a continuum or scale that ranges by degree from polar extremes such as *strongly agree* to *strongly disagree, extremely important* to *extremely unimportant,* and *extremely committed* to *extremely uncommitted,* thereby allowing the respondent more leeway than close-ended questions. The following are scaled questions:

How important is it for Congress to reduce the capital gains tax?

Extremely Important	Somewhat	Neutral	Unimportant	Extremely Unimportant

To what extent do you agree or disagree with the following statement? Condoms should be dispensed in public high schools.

Strongly Agree	Agree	Neutral	Disagree	Strongly Disagree

Scaled questions better enable the speaker to estimate the strength, and not just the direction, of each respondent's feelings.

Open-ended questions allow a respondent even greater freedom in answering questions. For example:

- What would you do if you found out a teammate on the baseball team had AIDS?
- How do you feel about libraries that ban books such as *Catcher in the Rye* and *Huckleberry Finn?*
- Respond to this statement: A politician's private life is not the public's business.

Because open-ended questions invite participants to answer in their own words, they produce more detailed and personal responses; however, they are also harder to interpret and may not even deliver the desired information.

Because each kind of question can aid you in drawing a profile of your audience, you would be wise to use a mix in any questionnaire you design. For every question you incorporate, ask yourself: Will answers to this question provide me with the kind of information I need? If the answer is no, don't use it (see the sample questionnaire in Figure 5.1).

Figure 5.1

Sample Questionnaire on Abortion

1. Age:
2. Sex: ❑ Male ❑ Female
3. Race: ❑ White ❑ African American ❑ Hispanic ❑ Native American ❑ Asian ❑ Other
4. Religion: ❑ Catholic ❑ Protestant ❑ Jewish ❑ Muslim ❑ Buddhist ❑ Atheist ❑ Other
5. Highest educational level attained: ❑ High school ❑ College ❑ Graduate school
6. Occupation:
7. Organizational memberships:
8. Income:
9. Marital Status: ❑ Married ❑ Single ❑ Widowed ❑ Divorced ❑ Separated
10. Political Affiliation: ❑ Democrat ❑ Republican ❑ Independent
11. Have you or your significant other ever had an abortion?
    ❑ Yes ❑ No
12. Do you know anyone who has had an abortion?
    ❑ Yes ❑ No
13. How many persons would you estimate have abortions in the United States every week?
    ❑ 100 ❑ 500 ❑ 1,000 ❑ 10,000
14. Which answer best reflects your opinion of the following statement: "Abortion should be prohibited."
    ❑ Strongly Agree ❑ Agree ❑ Neutral ❑ Disagree ❑ Strongly Disagree
15. Explain your response to question 14.

HOW TO USE WHAT YOU'VE DISCOVERED: ADAPTING TO YOUR AUDIENCE

IT IS APPARENT THAT THE DEMOGRAPHIC, attitudinal, and environmental profiles you draw will have profound effects on your speechmaking. Each profile should exert an influence on what you decide to say. There is no way around it. The words you use, the support you include, and your manner of presentation will all be affected. Only if you use the information you've gathered, only if you are able to step out of your frame of reference and see things as your audience members are likely to will you have prepared yourself to meet the speechmaker's challenge.

As you prepare and plan your speech you need to keep in mind everything you have learned about your audience and the speaking situation. You need to:

- Phrase your topic in such a way that audience members will not be turned off by it or tune it out.
- Resist the urge to concentrate exclusively on what you want to say; spend more time understanding what the audience wants to hear.
- Find ways to convince audience members early in your presentation that what you are communicating will solve a problem they have, help them reach their goals, or otherwise enrich their lives.
- Use your creative powers to encourage your listeners to care about your subject.
- Uncover ways to build on whatever common ground exists between you and your audience; make a personal connection with them.
- Always refer first to areas of agreement before speaking about areas of disagreement.
- Demonstrate that you repsect your listeners; if they sense that you think you're superior to them, chances are they won't listen to you. If you communicate to them in words they don't comprehend, it won't even matter that they're not listening.
- Hear your speech and see yourself and the environment through the ears and eyes of the members of your audience. Put yourself in their place and they will more readily give you their attention. Adjust your message to meet their level of understanding, needs, and interests, and they will be more likely to adapt to you.

SUMMARY

BECAUSE THE GOAL OF MOST public speakers is to gain and maintain an attentive hearing from members of an audience, it is the audience that should be at the heart of the public speaking process. Speeches are made for audiences, and your effectiveness as a speaker depends on how well you communicate your ideas to your receivers. Audience analysis is thus a central concern.

The audience-centered speaker works to adjust his or her message to reflect the demographics of the audience. By considering such variables as age, gender, education level, racial, ethnic, religious, or cultural ties, group affiliations, and socioeconomic factors, the speaker is better able to customize his or her message. In addition to drawing demographic profiles, audience-centered speakers complete psychographic and situational profiles. After assessing how the audience feels about the speaker, the topic, the occasion, and the speaking environment, the speechmaker has more knowledge he or she needs to fine-tune the presentation.

Speakers use a variety of tools to help them derive information about their audiences. Among the most widely used are personal observation, interviews, and questionnaires.

THE SPEAKER'S STAND

Develop a survey to analyze an audience on an issue of your choice; your survey should contain close-ended, scaled, and open-ended questions. Once you are sure your survey's questions are clear and unambiguous, have class members complete it. Then, based on what survey results and personal knowledge tell you about your listeners' knowledge of and attitudes toward your chosen issue, develop a presentation that takes those findings into account.

In a three- to four-page paper accompanying your speech, explain how you used the insights you gained about your listeners to guide you in:

- formulating your objective;
- creating an introduction and a conclusion;
- organizing your main points; and
- wording your speech.

Explain how your analysis of your audience helped you address both the needs and interests of your listeners.

After your presentation, ask your classmates to rate your speech on a five-point scale indicating:

1. how relevant it was to them and
2. how interesting it was to them.

If the outcome is not what you anticipated, discuss steps you might have taken to increase receptivity and interest.

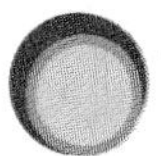

STUDENT FOCUS GROUP REPORT

Now that you have had the opportunity to explore the audience analysis and adaptation process, in a group of five to seven students, respond to the following questions:

1. Reread the case study at the beginning of the chapter. Would you change any of your answers now? Why or why not?
2. What challenges have you faced or can you see yourself facing as you sought and/or seek to adapt a speech to the needs and interests of a particular audience?
3. Which kind of information do you believe is of more value: demographic, attitudinal, or situational?
4. Are there any sources of information about an audience that a speaker should refrain from using? Why or why not?
5. How were you able to use the information you learned about your audience while at the same time maintaining the integrity of your own ideas?
6. Summarize the most important information you have learned about audience analysis and the adaptation process.

Select a team member to share your conclusions with the class.

Chapter Six

Analyzing Your Purpose

Selecting a Topic

After reading this chapter, you should be able to:

- Use a variety of approaches to help you choose a topic appropriate for you, your audience, and the occasion.
- Develop an effective general purpose statement for a speech.
- Develop an effective specific purpose statement for a speech.
- Formulate a behavioral objective for audience members.
- Create an effective central idea/proposition for a speech.
- Use criteria to help you evaluate the effectiveness of your general and specific purpose statements as well as your central idea.

CASE STUDY

The Quandary

Young Sub Kim was in a panic. The instructor had just told Young Sub's public speaking class that in one week students had to be prepared to give a five- to six-minute informative speech on a topic of their choice. Young Sub had never given a speech. His family had come to the United States from South Korea five years earlier. Aside from attending school, much of his time in the United States had been spent helping his family make ends meet and learning English. What would he talk about?

His instructor had given the class some advice, telling them to talk about a topic with which they had some personal experience and about which they cared. Young Sub had many interests, including Confucianism, the challenge of keeping *kibun*[1] in good order, and the problems of learning English as a second language. Who in this class would be interested in hearing about such topics? he thought. As far as Young Sub could tell, kids his age cared most about their looks, clothes, and sports, and he had no desire to speak on those subjects. Finally he decided that Americans needed to know about *kibun*. That would be his topic. He approached a number of his fellow students. "What would you like to know about *kibun*?" he asked each one. No student was able to supply an answer; however, each did reply with the same question: "What's *kibun*?"

- Based on the fact that no one in his class knew what *kibun* was, was Young Sub's choice of topic appropriate? Why or why not?
- Assuming that Young Sub stays with the topic, what advice can you offer him about how to develop it?

SO YOU'RE GOING TO give a speech. In public. And because of that, you are now confronting the dilemma faced by many speakers as you ask yourself: "What am I going to speak about?"

Choosing your topic is an integral part of the speechmaking process. In fact, it is a major step on your way to speechmaking success. Choose the right topic—one that is appropriate for you, your audience, and the occasion—and your chances of delivering a "total quality speech" are enhanced. Choose the wrong topic—one that you really do not care about, one your audience cares even less about, and one totally inappropriate to the speaking situation—and you'll probably find yourself unable to maintain your own interest, let alone the interest of those who must listen to you.

It's true, there is an infinite number of topics for you to choose among.[2] But before you choose one, let's explore approaches you can use to help ensure you select a good topic, one that will enable you to fulfill your general and specific purposes for speaking, and thus help you accomplish your goal. Learning how to select and narrow a topic, identify your general purpose, formulate your specific purpose, and state your central idea are essential components in speech preparation that are inseparably related to each other. You can master this phase of speechcrafting if you approach it both systematically and creatively—that is, if you work within a format but allow yourself to think creatively every step of the way. Once you combine a tried-and-true system with a spirit of innovation, no speaking hurdle will be insurmountable. Becoming a "total quality speaker" is within your reach.

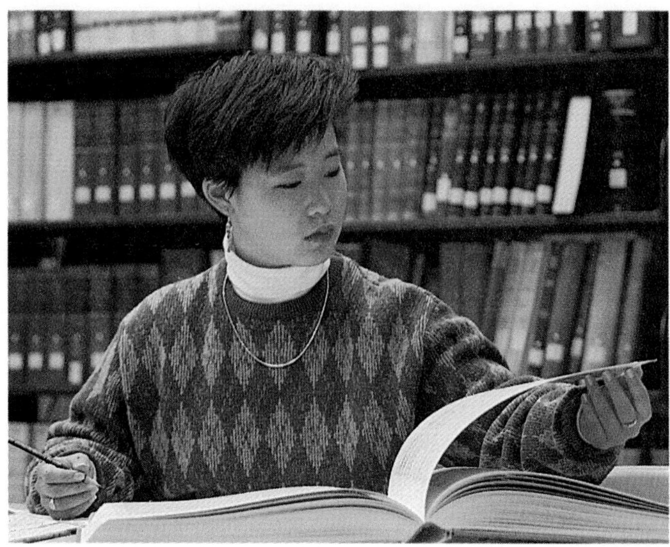

Although there are seemingly endless possibilities for speech topics, you can learn how to select and narrow a topic that's right for you.

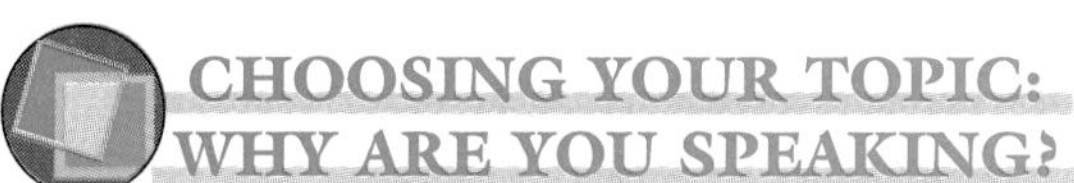

CHOOSING YOUR TOPIC: WHY ARE YOU SPEAKING?

WHY DO YOU TALK to your friends? If you're like most people, you talk because you are stimulated by your interests and your desires to establish contacts and cement relationships, as well as by the urge to share information, opinions, and feelings. We talk because talk helps us begin relationships as well as develop and control them. We talk because doing so helps us understand ourselves and other people, because it helps us feel an integral part of any relationship, and because it helps us influence others. What's noteworthy is that similar statements may be made about why we engage in public speaking. So if you know what to talk about when conversing with your friends, you already hold the key to discovering a good topic for a speech: You are going to talk about a topic you are familiar with or would like to know more about, one that reflects your personal concerns and convictions and that you believe listeners will be interested in and gain something from as well. To reach this point, some self-analysis is in order.

Idea Generation: Who Are You and What Do You Know?

The best way to begin your topic search is to examine your personal behaviors and interests. We all have experienced or know things that could be developed into a speech. In fact, by now you've accumulated a wealth of information and a variety of experiences you can draw on to create an intensely interesting and involving presentation. All you need to do is identify them. We have included suggested idea-generation exercises to help you accomplish just that. Before tackling any of the exercises, however, consider this. Whichever of the suggested exercises you choose to use, keep the following idea-generation guidelines in mind.

1. *Brainstorm ideas.* Initially your objective is to **brainstorm** to get every possible idea down on paper.[3] No idea should be ruled out until you have had a chance to think more critically about and evaluate it. But that occurs only after the idea-generation phase is completed, not during the brainstorming session itself.
2. *Piggyback ideas.* Try to **piggyback** the ideas you come up with—that is, see if there are different ways various ideas may be combined to produce a novel, even more interesting idea. Mix and match ideas you've generated to form interesting combinations.
3. *Don't censor ideas.* At this point, feel free to be as **wild** as you want. You'll have ample opportunity to tame an idea once you evaluate it for usefulness and appropriateness to the speaking situation.

Exercise One: Brainstorm to Develop a Personal Inventory of Subjects That Interest You. For the next few moments think about subjects you either have some knowledge of or would like to learn more about. The subjects may relate to something you have experienced personally, like a hobby, or something you would like to explore, like tornadoes. It could involve an issue you care deeply about, such as conservation; or local, national, or international concerns, such as a workers' strike, national health insurance, or terrorism. What is important is that you not censor your ideas and instead write down everything that comes to mind. From the array of ideas you generate may surface a general topic area you can then develop in a more specific speech topic.

Exercise Two: Brainstorm Using Categories as a Stimulus. Divide a sheet of paper into eight columns. At the top of each column list one of the following words: *people, processes, problems, phenomena, procedures, possessions, products,* and *programs.*[4] Then devote the next 40 minutes (five minutes per category) to writing down every word you associate with each category, in turn. For example, in the *people* column you might list the following: the president, Jonas Salk, Jesse Jackson, your mother, and so forth. The word *processes* might prompt you to jot down photosynthesis, recycling, an assembly line, computer operations, and so forth. Under *problems* you might write alcoholism, the federal deficit, drug abuse, racism, downsizing, and homelessness. The word *phenomena* might elicit associations such as icebergs, earthquakes, tsunamis, and comets. *Procedures* could prompt you to write heart transplants, dialysis, registration, and fire evacuation. Under *possessions* you might list words such as home, car, jewelry, CD player, bank book. Under the *profession* column you could generate words like medicine, law, teaching, finance, and so forth. The *products* category could give rise to soda, Nutrasweet, cereals, tennis rackets, and gold. Finally, the word *programs* could spark associations such as after school, food stamps, welfare, or workfare. There are no right or wrong answers—remember, you're brainstorming.

Review your lists of responses and see which, if any, of the general subject areas you might develop into a specific topic.

Exercise Three: Brainstorm Using the "ABC" Approach. The "ABC" approach uses the alphabet to help find a potential topic. We provide you with one potential topic idea for each alphabet letter; your task is to generate at least two more on your own.

Don Aslett

What do you do once you have selected a topic? You need to prepare your presentation as well as consider why your audience should consider your choice a good one. Professional speaker and writer Don Aslett has delivered more than 8,000 public speeches. In these excerpts from his book Is There a Speech Inside You? *he offers advice on both speech preparation and subject justification. After reading his advice, explain how you can put his ideas into practice during the development of your next speech.*

Aslett on Speech Preparations

Be prepared. If you had to choose the most important message in this book, this would surely be it, because most of what makes a good speech is done before you ever stand up in front of an audience and open your mouth. . . .

When should you start preparing your speech?

About four seconds after you've been asked to present it—even if your speaking date is nine months from now. Trust me, your best ideas, the fastest pace and the most progress will be made on your speech right when you are asked to do it—that's when your enthusiasm is at its peak.

Aslett on Subject Justification

A simple explanation is a great tool of communication, in ordinary conversation or public speaking. Everyone subconsciously has to have a reason to be sitting there watching your mouth move and words come out. They don't and won't wait until the middle of your speech to find out if the message is important to them or not. They rightfully want to know your reason for using their time (and it bet-

A	Autoimmune diseases	______	______
B	Black holes	______	______
C	Credit cards	______	______
D	Date rape	______	______
E	Earthquakes	______	______
F	Fire safety	______	______
G	Gun control	______	______
H	Hazardous waste	______	______
I	IQ tests	______	______
J	Justice system	______	______
K	Ku Klux Klan	______	______
L	Law and order	______	______
M	Music	______	______
N	Nervous disorders	______	______
O	Occult	______	______
P	Paper	______	______
Q	Quarantining	______	______
R	Rabies	______	______
S	Shyness	______	______

ter be good!) Justifying a subject is nothing more than convincing the audience of its importance. Let me give you three examples of this:

1. You're giving a presentation on "How to Pack Your Own Parachute."

Standard opening: "Today we're going to learn how to pack our own chutes. I'll give you the 1-2-3-4 instructions and then all of you can pack your own chutes."

Justifying the subject: "When you jump out of the plane next week your chute will do one of two things—open or not open. If it opens, that means you probably listened to me today. If it doesn't open you won't have to repeat this class, and that's a promise. Now for the instructions. . . ."

2. You're giving a presentation on the assigned subject of "Respecting the Flag."

Standard opening: "True and loyal citizens respect their flag because it represents a great heritage of a great nation."

Justifying the subject: "How many of you have ever been on a trip to a foreign country? How many of you gained from that trip a deeper appreciation for the place you live? How many of you would like to keep the freedoms you have now? It's up to all of us to make sure we keep them, and our reminder of this is our flag. Its job is not just waving . . ."

3. You're giving a speech on how to find work.

Standard opening: "Government statistics show that 8 percent of our citizens at any given point are unemployed and looking for work. Just where and how do you look for work?"

Justifying the subject: "You've been fired. Everyone in here is fired as of right now; you have no job. You are unemployed! Some of you are smiling comfortably and saying to yourself, 'It can't happen to me.' Did you know that last month 28,000 people, secure in their jobs and positions for sixteen years or more, were told to go with not much more than 'thanks' and a good record?"[5]

T	Terrorism	______	______
U	UFOs	______	______
V	Volcanoes	______	______
W	Wilderness	______	______
X	X rays	______	______
Y	Yoga	______	______
Z	Zoos	______	______

This technique is particularly useful in helping prevent "idea paralysis." The real work begins when you survey the resulting lists and explore which of the potential topics you would like to further refine.

Exercise Four: Scan the Media. Each of us can look, listen, and read to discover a topic idea. Newspaper and magazine headlines and articles, books, advertisements, films, broadcast news, and sitcoms, as well as the Internet might just provide the spark that lights our fire on a particular subject. Browsing through sources like those identified as well as listening to or watching specialized programs could result in a list of possible topics like the following:

Copyright protection and the Internet
Neighborhood crime

The electric chair
Train safety
Diversity and the corporation
Volunteerism
Spanglish
The woman as global leader
The food pyramid
Job security
Airline deregulation
Right to privacy
Fertility clinics
Television rating system
Depression and holidays
Airbags
AIDS
School buses
Organ donation
Laser surgery
Sexual harassment
Prison conditions
Job hunting

Exercise Five: Survey Reference Books and Indexes. You can browse through reference books such as an encyclopedia, the *Reader's Guide to Periodical Literature,* or *Education Index* to help stimulate your idea search. Simply open one of these sources at random and compile a list of words and phrases that interest you. Once you have a list of a page or so, reexamine it to determine which words strike you as fuel for a potential speech.

Exercise Six: What's Taboo to Whom? Consult a resource such as *Do's and Taboos around the World* to determine speech topics that specific groups of people might find offensive or inappropriate for public discussion.[6] For example, although residents of the Middle East enjoy talking about horses, they are not likely to discuss religion or politics in public. Similarly in many Arab, Asian, and African cultures, talking about sex to audiences made up of both men and women is likely to be judged offensive.[7]

On a smaller scale, be careful not to assume that because you are interested in a topic, others in your class will automatically be interested in that topic as well. Culture plays a role in how we assess the appropriateness of a topic.

After completing these exercises and compiling an extensive list of possible topics, you are ready to continue assessing each topic's viability. As you review the possibilities, remember that the one topic you ultimately select should:

- Interest and concern you.
- Be adaptable to the increasingly diverse interests and concerns of your receivers.
- Be significant to you and your receivers.
- Allow you to add to or acquire information about it.

Considering Diversity

The I behind the Eye

To what extent, if any, should the cultural, social, and educational backgrounds of both the speaker and the audience influence the choice of a topic? Are there some speech topics you would be unable to speak on because of the cultural, ethnic, or social class makeup of your audience? In his article "Culture: A Perceptual Approach," author Marshall R. Singer notes the following:

> When the physicist talks to his barber in the U.S., he knows that he is expected to discuss baseball, the weather, and women. He also knows that it would be futile for him to attempt to discuss quantum physics. Thus he adjusts his communication expectations accordingly and leaves the barber shop a little wiser about the league standing of the home team, a little apprehensive about the impending winter. . . . But he certainly has no feeling of frustration at not having been able to discuss physics. He knows his own society well enough to know with whom he may discuss baseball and with whom he may discuss physics.[8]

How much do the differences and similarities between speaker and audience affect the kind of topic they can share? With certain audiences we may feel a limitation on the topics we can discuss—or at least in the ways we can approach a topic. Is there any way, for example, the physicist could talk about his work on some level so as to interest the barber? Why would that discussion differ from one with a fellow physicist? On the other hand, if the barber and the physicist chose baseball as a topic of discussion, what were the qualities that made that the right topic? What do the similarities and differences between these two tell us about choosing a topic when social class, cultural differences, or general interests are apparent?

Selecting your topic is one of the most crucial decisions you will make as a speaker. Only if you choose an idea that both you and your receivers believe is consequential and interesting will you be in a position to break the boredom barrier.

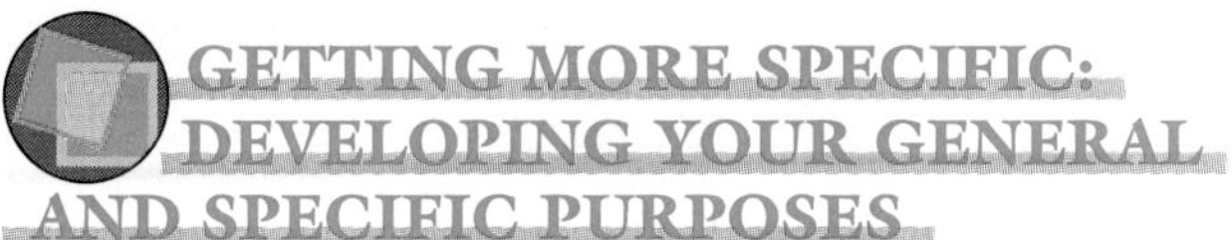

GETTING MORE SPECIFIC: DEVELOPING YOUR GENERAL AND SPECIFIC PURPOSES

ONCE YOU CHOOSE A general topic area for your speech, selection number one is completed. However, there are more selections for you to make. In fact, selectivity will characterize your work from now on. As you pare away the nonessentials and narrow down your subject, you take a giant step forward in the speech preparation process. The next challenge is to select a general purpose that either reflects your assignment or facilitates the attainment of your primary objective, or both. In effect, you are now answering the question "What purpose do I want to fulfill by speaking on this topic?"

Speaking of General Purposes

Virtually all speeches fulfill one of three general purposes: to inform, to persuade, or to entertain. Let us examine each in turn.

Speaking to Inform. The speech to inform is designed primarily to teach. Thus an informative speaker resembles a teacher, and his or her primary goal is to communicate and share knowledge with an audience—to give listeners information not in their possession prior to the presentation. Speakers deliver informative speeches when they want to explain a process, procedure, organization, or function; when they describe a person, place, or thing; or when they define a word or concept.

Most informative speeches are not controversial, but they are prevalent in our lives. Informative speaking occurs in virtually all classes you take, and is equally common in work and community settings. Because of the contributions made by informative speakers, we are better able to appreciate and understand a wide variety of topics. The following are examples of informative speech topics:

the meaning of friendship;
how a nuclear reaction occurs;
the appearance of Stonehenge;
the nature of sickle cell anemia;
what is stuttering;
the effects of a computer virus;
the meaning of success;
the causes of sudden infant death syndrome; or
how to dress for a job interview.

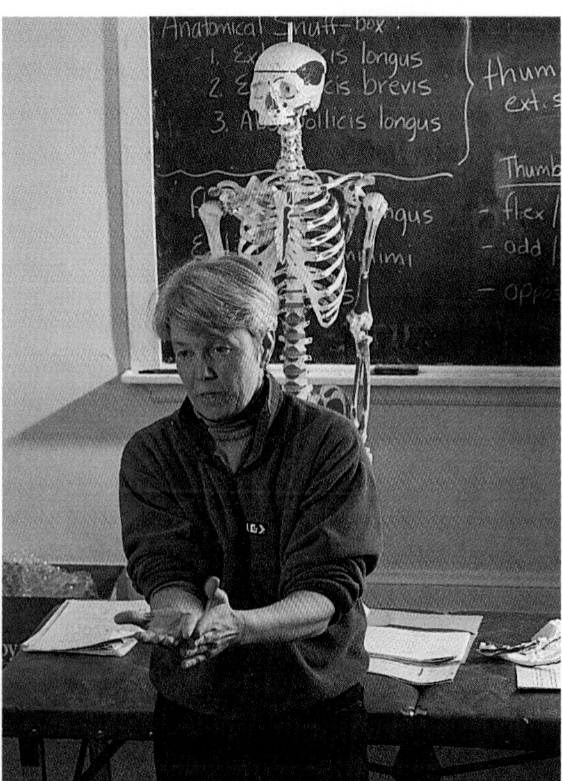

Informative speaking occurs in most college classes.

Speaking to Persuade. The speech to persuade is designed primarily to change the thoughts and/or the behaviors of receivers. The persuasive speaker hopes to alter not only what the audience members know, but also how they feel and/or act. Persuasive speakers want to convince their receivers that something is or is not so or to adopt or discontinue some behavior.

Persuasive speech topics are usually more controversial than informative speech topics because there are frequently others who oppose what the speaker advocates. Thus, while a speaker may deliver a speech supporting organ donation, a number of audience members may hold very different opinions about the subject. Just because a speaker wants audience members to support prochoice candidates does not guarantee acceptance of the idea by listeners. The following are examples of persuasive speech topics:

televised ads for alcohol should be prohibited;
Nutrasweet is hazardous to your health;
book censorship is a contemporary problem;
the tax burden placed on the middle class is unfair;
caffeine should be kept out of soda;
lifesaving should be a required course;
Caesarean deliveries are performed unnecessarily;
the U.S. space program has failed;
Indian sovereignty should be respected;
mandatory recycling should be enforced; or
fad diets are dangerous.

Speaking to Entertain. The speech to entertain is designed to amuse an audience. The speaker's goal is to ensure that the audience is put at ease and enjoys the speech. If, as a result of the speaker's efforts, audience members smile, laugh, and generally feel good or have a good time, the speech is a success.

You might be called on to deliver a speech to entertain when serving as an after-breakfast, luncheon, or dinner speaker, or when delivering a comic monologue at a comedy club, for example. Humor is usually an essential ingredient in the speech to entertain; thus, skill in using humor is necessary. The following are examples of topics of speeches to entertain:

how to fail a course;
famous sports bloopers;
the part of the city I wouldn't show a tourist;
pet idiosyncrasies;
different walks; or
handshakes I have experienced.

In this text we will touch on the value of integrating humor when appropriate into both informative and persuasive presentations, and we will discuss using speech to entertain again in Chapter 17, but in this chapter more emphasis will be placed on speaking to inform and speaking to persuade.

The general purpose of your speech, then, is the overall effect you hope to have on your audience. Unless you become a humorist, most of the speeches you deliver during your lifetime will probably be designed to inform or persuade.

The next step is to make your general purpose more specific.

Speaking of Specific Purposes

The **specific purpose** of a speech is your personal statement of the speech's main objective. The specific purpose identifies the particular response you seek from your audience as a result of your speech. It summarizes what you want from your listeners or what you hope to accomplish by speaking. Consequently, your specific purpose describes exactly what you would like audience members to understand, believe, value, or do after hearing your presentation. Although in this class the general purpose of your speech may be assigned to you by your instructor, it is otherwise usually left to you to develop a specific purpose that reflects how you want to shape your audience's reaction. The following are examples of specific purposes for informative speeches:

to inform my audience about the effects of Down Syndrome;
to explain to my audience the signs of dyslexia;
to explain the role of cultural sensitivity in health care communication;
to report to audience members about IRS rules that directly affect them; or
to describe for audience members how decreases in state funding will affect them.

Whereas words like *inform, explain, report,* and *describe* commonly turn up in the specific purposes of informative speeches, words like *persuade, motivate, convince,* and *act* are characteristic of specific purposes for persuasive speeches, as in the following examples:

to persuade listeners to resist book censorship efforts in our community;
to persuade audience members to refrain from purchasing products containing Nutrasweet;
to motivate listeners to contribute money to the Make a Wish Foundation;
to convince audience members to act to increase their personal safety in case of fire; or
to persuade listeners that sleep deprivation is a pervasive health problem.

What do you notice about each of these specific purposes? Though formulated for very different topics, they share at least five characteristics.

1. The specific purpose is stated as an infinitive phrase, that is, *to explain* or *to convince.*
2. The specific purpose is for your personal use and is written from your perspective; as such, it identifies your concrete goal and can be used to guide your research and the direction of your speech.
3. The specific purpose focuses on a single, distinct idea.
4. The specific purpose relates your topic to your audience by specifying what you want the audience to know, think, or do as a result of your speech.
5. The specific purpose is clear and concise, not muddled or unfocused.

While a good specific purpose is ambitious rather than trivial, it does not overreach. You need to be able to manage it in the time given you to speak. If you're unable to develop a speech reflective of your specific purpose in the time available, then you need to narrow your specific purpose even more. Formulating a specific purpose you could not possibly cover in your presentation means you have not made it specific enough; it is still too general. Delivering a speech that is too general makes it harder for you to offer listeners new information or novel perspectives. Remember, you keep the purpose specific by limiting its scope. If it is too broad, it is probably also ill-defined.

Speaking of skillbuilding ***Narrow the Topic***

Generate at least ten specific purpose statements on the subject toys. Once your list is complete ask yourself if each purpose statement is as limited in scope for an informative speech as the following: "To inform my audience how to choose a safe toy for a toddler," or, for a persuasive speech: "To persuade my audience to buy toddlers nonsexist toys."

Once you are able to answer affirmatively, brainstorm two to three main points to make during a seven-minute speech. Also brainstorm the types of support you would look for to buttress each main point, as well as possible visuals to use during the speech.

The sharper your specific purpose, the easier you will find it to develop your speech. So while formulating your specific purpose, ask yourself these questions:

- Does my specific purpose reflect the assignment or speech situation?
- Will I be able to obtain my specific goal in the speaking time allotted me?
- Will I be able to prepare a speech that fulfills my specific purpose in a manner my listeners will be able to understand and respond to?
- Will my audience assess my goal to be relevant to their needs and reflective of their interests?
- Will my audience judge my purpose to be significant and worthy of their attention?

Each of these questions must be answered with a "yes" and a "because . . ." before you can proceed.

Speaking of the Audience's Perspective

In addition to formulating a specific purpose that is written from your perspective, it is also helpful to "change chairs" and assess the speech from the audience's perspective. To facilitate this, you might find it useful to compose a desired behavioral objective. A behavioral objective begins with seven words: "After experiencing my speech audience members will" and then describes the response you want audience members to experience.

The following are sample behavioral objectives for informative and persuasive speeches:

Sample Behavioral Objectives for Informative Speeches. After experiencing my speech, audience members will:

List three symptoms of premenstrual syndrome.
Name four causes of global warming.
Explain how depletion of the ozone layer will affect them.

Sample Behavioral Objectives for Persuasive Speeches. After experiencing my speech, audience members will:

Contribute money to fund bulletproof vests for city police officers.

Sign a card specifying their willingness to serve as organ donors.

Sign a petition advocating that the U.S. government regulate the airlines.

Writing a behavioral objective like these will help ensure that you focus the content of your speech on those aspects that audience members will find most interesting or appropriate. By identifying an observable, measurable audience response, you position the audience and its behavior in the forefront of your mind. By keeping the audience at the center of your focus, you help guarantee that the members will pay attention to you. Goal articulation is a key part of effective speech preparation.

SPEAKING of ETHICS

The Purpose behind the Purpose

What kind of an obligation do you owe your listeners in selecting a topic? If, in a democratic situation, you want to respect your audience and treat them as your equals in their concern for social issues, how does this affect the topic you select and your approach to it? Is the U.S. government, also a democracy, a good model for the way social or public issues are selected?

According to political scientist Roger Hart, contemporary U.S. presidents deliver public speeches an average of 25 times per month.[9] It is as a result of speaking frequently on specific issues that the president paints a picture of society in keeping with the social policies he favors. In fact, according to psychologists and authors Anthony Pratkanis and Eliot Aronson, the job of presidential advisors such as pollster Robert Teeter is to inform the president what Americans are thinking about and what issues should be topics of his speeches. They believe that it is the president's ability to choose the ideas on which he will speak and to set the

Through the speeches he delivers, the President helps set the national agenda.

national agenda that determines what will be discussed, what is viewed as most pressing by Americans, and what will be selectively ignored.[10]

Does it seem that the U.S. president is regularly treating his fellow citizens as equals when picking his topics to address? To what extent is he exercising his own agenda-setting power over others, and to what extent do they set the agenda or select the topics? How can you, as a speaker, strike a balance between your own "power" to select a topic and your listeners' right to hear—and possibly respond to—a topic of concern to them? To what extent can you do your own "polling" of an audience, and to what extent should you speak on topics they want to hear?

It is important for you to focus on the relationship between speaker and audience and on your need (like the president's) to make a decision and take action to address topics that will be responded to. Too much focus on your own agenda may alienate the audience (or electorate); too much focus on what "they" want will mean that you as the speaker don't make any real decision or take responsibility for what is said.

FORMULATING YOUR CENTRAL IDEA: MAKING YOUR WORDS WORK

WHEREAS YOUR GENERAL and specific purpose and your statement of desired audience response establish the goals of your speech, the **central idea** identifies exactly what you want to communicate. The central idea, sometimes referred to as a subject sentence, thesis statement, theme, claim, or proposition, is one declarative sentence that summarizes your presentation. For all practical purposes, the central idea is the essence of your speech. Because the central idea is the core of the message you want to share with receivers, it functions as the controlling force in your speech. It brings the heart of your speech into focus, identifies your major thrust, and thus influences the development of your entire presentation.

Frequently, the central idea appears in the introduction to your speech. It previews what you will cover and forecasts your main points and content for your audience. Because everything you include in the speech should be clearly related to the central idea, the central idea also helps you identify what content is relevant to your speech.

Observe the following rules when wording your central idea:

1. Express your central idea as a single declarative sentence. Neither infinitive phrases nor questions make effective central ideas.
2. Your central idea should make one major point about your topic.
3. Your central idea should forecast the development or organization of your speech.
4. Phrase your central idea diplomatically. Figurative language that is apt to inflame has no place in a central idea.
5. Because the central idea will guide the audience members as they process your speech, it should be as specific as possible.

When listeners are asked what your speech was about, they should be able to respond by offering your central idea. At the least, it is the central idea you hope listeners retain after you have given your speech.

SPEAKING of CRITICAL THINKING

Making Your Purpose Clear

Before you formulate a general purpose, specific purpose, and central idea for a speech of your own, read the accompanying transcript and/or view on videotape student Patricia Ann Compos's speech on tissue engineering. Once you have read or viewed the speech, evaluate the extent to which you believe Compos succeeds in making clear for receivers the general purpose, specific purpose, and central idea of her speech by formulating and examining each in your own words.

To show how this works, let us examine two of the examples we used earlier, one for an informative speech and one for a persuasive speech, and develop them into usable central ideas.

Specific purpose: To describe for audience members how decreases in state funding to colleges will affect them

Central idea: Decreases in state funding to colleges will result in cuts in educational programs, extracurricular offerings, and financial aid.

From this central idea we can say that the speaker will explore three main points or ideas in his or her speech, each point corresponding to one of the three effects resulting from diminished state aid to colleges.

Specific purpose: To persuade listeners to resist book censorship efforts in our community

Central idea: Community efforts to censor the books we read is an infringement of our individual right of freedom of expression and will result in limiting our ability to think critically about important issues.

From this central idea we are able to determine that the speaker will treat two main points or ideas in his or her speech: (1) we have a right to freedom of expression; and (2) if that right is limited, we will not be able to think critically about important issues.

Unlike the specific purpose, the central idea is usually delivered directly to your audience. Thus, a well-phrased central idea not only helps you divide your presentation into its major components, it helps your listeners follow your speech's progression more easily. Phrasing your central idea brings you a step closer to the structure of the speech itself—a subject we will cover in Chapters 7 and 9. Are the specific purpose and central idea clear in the following speech?

TISSUE ENGINEERING

The speaker begins with a startling example.

The analogy the speaker makes helps her define a key term.

Scientists recently made national headlines after growing a human ear on the back of a mouse. Although it may resemble a bizarre carnival attraction, this rising star is allowing researchers to refine the technology that will forever change the medical landscape. A marriage of biology and chemistry has given birth to a new branch of medicine known as tissue engineering.

The *Annals of Biomedical Engineering* of April 1995 explain that the idea is to use our own living cells to grow new tissue. According to *Scientific American* of

September 1995, tissue engineering will not only regenerate body parts for the millions of Americans who have lost organs to injury or disease, but will also provide less costly therapy that can save lives.

The speaker uses a variety of support to build credibility.

The *Congressional Task Force on Organ and Tissue Donation* revealed on February 23, 1996, that each day eight people die waiting for an organ. In an age when the waiting list is becoming longer and transplants are plagued with problems of availability and staggering costs, a new treatment is desperately needed. Fortunately, this procedure will also help treat degenerative and neurological diseases and provide a safe haven for premature babies.

Her use of statistics adds to the sense of urgency.

The impacts are far reaching, so to better understand this "grow-your-own-organ" approach, we will first examine the history of tissue engineering and how it works. Second, we will focus on its benefits and present applications. And finally, we will discuss the future implications of this young medical field.

The speaker previews the speech for receivers.

Today, scientists correct tissue damage by transplanting synthetic parts or organs from humans or animals. However, the risk has left the medical community searching for new alternatives. Born only twelve years ago, tissue engineering is the most viable option. The November 6, 1995, issue of *Blood Weekly* describes how Dr. Robert Langer envisions ways to grow new cells for sick children. After collaborating with Dr. Joseph Vancati of MIT, the duo successfully developed a biodegradable scaffold to grow healthy cells into permanent issue. Recently, the November 4, 1995, *British Medical Journal* professes that the duo has successfully grown skin, heart valves, and even liver tissue. The process involved is relatively simple.

She introduces the first main point.

The speaker incorporates an array of research findings.

Chemical and Engineering News of March 13, 1995, points out that first, porous, biodegradable materials are sculpted into three-dimensional scaffolds. These scaffolds will resemble the organs and will help guide the growing tissues. Next, the 1995 *American Chemical Society* states that doctors remove the living cells from the patients and seed them into the porous materials. The cells will be fed oxygen and blood. As the cells multiply they begin to take the shape of the scaffold and the organ. The scaffolds eventually dissolve. Finally, permanent healthy tissues will form bone, skin, muscles, and even full-fledged organs that may be transplanted back into the body.

The speaker explains the central process succinctly and clearly.

Although tissue engineering may seem as easy as growing a Chia pet it is a highly sophisticated technology with practical benefits. It eliminates the risk of rejection and will not deteriorate in the body. But first, unlike current transplants, engineered organs will not be rejected by our immune systems. Our bodies recognize and reject foreign objects. As a result, patients must be administered immunosuppressant drugs. The *Washington Post* of January 16, 1996, contends that our bodies attack transplanted organs so viciously that they may be destroyed within minutes, and the drugs only leave our bodies vulnerable to disease. However, the May 15, 1995, *Journal of Transplantation* asserts that with this technology the issue is not strange to the body. Maintenance drugs become unnecessary and rejection becomes irrelevant.

The speaker uses an analogy receivers will comprehend. She also easily segues into her second main point.

Again, support helps the speaker demonstrate the benefits of the process.

Next, fabricated tissue will not deteriorate in the body. Over time, manmade parts such as hips and knees must be replaced again. For example, artificial arteries will function as blood vessels for a while. But the blood soon realizes that it's been deceived and begins to clog the tube. Yet a length of artery grown from the patient's own tissue would be genetically the same. *Scientific American* of September 1995 alleges that these living implants will merge easily with surrounding tissue, eliminating deterioration and repeated operations.

While it may not be readily apparent, engineered skin and cartilage have already improved our medical services. Scientists have grown skin which is treating burn victims and diabetic patients. The *Economist* of January 6, 1996, estimates that 800,000 Americans suffer from chronic diabetic foot ulcers. 75,000 will have to undergo amputations. And the patients can expect to pay more than $60,000 a year in treatment. Because of this technology we'll be able to help these individuals. Additionally, this therapy will also allow us to help the one million Americans who suffer from torn knee cartilage. According to the *Sunday Advocate* of October 22, 1995, more than one million Americans have torn knee cartilage. Until recently, patients could only have the cartilage removed and then remove stress to the area. Now an actual cure has been found, restoring active lifestyles to patients everywhere.

The speaker introduces the third main point.

There is no doubt that tissue engineering will provide life-saving therapies now and in the future. But before we reach these future possibilities we must overcome two obstacles. First, natural proteins often interfere with developing tissue. According to *Science* of October 13, 1995, the growing cells secrete protein, which prevents the tissue from precisely taking the shape of the scaffold. The answer may be implants and chemicals that attract the growth cells and push away the proteins. However, more time is needed to perfect this procedure.

The speaker uses research in supporting her argument.

The second, new advanced scaffolds will have to be designed before complex organs may be grown. Current scaffolds can only shape simple tissues such as skin, and do not have the ability to attract nerve endings into tissue. However, the *National Academy of Science* in August of 1995 revealed that new polymers may be the key to engineering full-fledged livers, pancreases, hearts, and even arms and legs by the turn of the century. After overcoming these obstacles, tissue engineering will move to the future quickly. It will help millions of people suffering from various diseases, such as cancer, arthritis, and osteoporosis. The *Daily Mail Healthcare Forum* of November–December 1994 states that two million diabetic patients could soon receive implants of encapsulated insulin-producing cells, reducing daily shots to once every three years. Additionally, the *American Chemical Society* announced in April of 1995 that engineered heart valves will soon restore rhythmic heartbeats to 60,000 Americans.

In less dire situations, tissue engineering will also revolutionize the cosmetic and obstetric industries. The *Daily Mail* of March 11, 1996, mentions that Americans pay billions of dollars each year for cosmetic surgery. This research makes it possible to customize noses, chins, and even breasts.

Finally, premature infants will be nurtured in an artificial womb until its second birth. By 2020 babies may be grown from removed embryos, and women may opt for painless pregnancies. But a roomful of developing babies and engineered limbs raises chilling ethical and moral questions. The *National Times* of April 1996 argues that while scientists could engineer vital organs and limbs, they could possibly couple this with artificial intelligence, to build the Frankenstein of the twenty-first century. While this technology promises to save lives, we must be aware of its future implications on our society.

The speaker summarizes the speech and prepares receivers for its conclusion.

The speaker refers to the example she used in the introduction as a means of achieving closure.

After examining the history of tissue engineering and how it works, its benefits and important applications, and its future, we can now appreciate this method. Tissue engineering has the capacity to remove many Americans from a long, daunting waiting list and give them the gift of life. Additionally, it will help millions who struggle from genetic and degenerative diseases. The mouse with a human ear on its back may have made national headlines, but tissue engineering, the heartbeat of the medical industry, is a constant reminder that we are living in a remarkable age.[11]

EVALUATING YOUR CHOICES

AS YOU CHOOSE a topic, develop your general and specific purposes, and phrase the central idea of your speech, consider a number of important questions. If you are unable to answer these questions with a "yes," you still have more thinking and refining ahead of you:

	Yes	*No*
1. Am I genuinely interested in my topic?	❑	❑
2. Am I willing to research the topic to enhance my knowledge of it?	❑	❑
3. Will an exploration of this topic benefit my listeners?	❑	❑
4. Is my topic suitable for this particular speaking situation?	❑	❑
5. Will my listeners find a discussion of my topic worthwhile, important, and interesting?	❑	❑
6. Have I narrowed my topic sufficiently to fit the speaking time allotted me?	❑	❑
7. Have I identified a general speech purpose appropriate to the assignment or speaking situation?	❑	❑
8. Have I formulated a clear specific purpose?	❑	❑
9. Have I composed a behavioral objective that identifies the specific response I desire from audience members?	❑	❑
10. Have I phrased my central idea so that it helps me control the development of my speech?	❑	❑

Effective speaking begins with effective planning. At this point in your speech preparation you know yourself and your relationship to your audience better, and you have a better handle on your speech topic. By becoming selective and making careful choices, you have begun to focus your efforts to focus your content. Just doing this will help you communicate more *clearly,* more *concisely,* and more *confidently.* Concentrating your focus will better enable you to get your message across, and of course that's what speechmaking is all about.

SUMMARY

SELECTING A TOPIC is a key step in the speechmaking process. A good topic is one that is appropriate for the speaker, the audience, and the occasion.

Speakers use a number of techniques to help them select good topics. They use various idea-generation exercises to help examine their personal behaviors and interests, they scan the media, and they survey reference books and indexes.

Selectivity characterizes the work of speakers during the topic-identification process. Speakers must select both general and specific purposes for their speeches. The general purpose describes the overall effect a speaker hopes to have on an audience; the specific purpose describes the particular response the speaker seeks from an audience after the speech. In addition to formulating general and specific purposes, speakers also find it useful to compose desired behavioral objectives for receivers.

Once the speaker has identified the general and specific purpose of his or her speech and created a statement describing the desired audience response, he or she then needs to formulate a central idea or proposition for the speech. The central idea or proposition summarizes the speech in a single declarative sentence. Because everything the speaker includes in the speech should be clearly related to the speech's central idea or proposition, the central idea or proposition also helps the speaker identify relevant content.

THE SPEAKER'S STAND

While sculpting a bird from a block of marble, a sculptor was asked by a naive observer, "How can you create such a beautiful bird?" The sculptor replied: "I just cut away from the marble what isn't a bird." Similar advice could be offered to a novice speaker by a more experienced one: "Cut away the excess from your general subject until you are left with a more specific topic. Only then will you succeed in narrowing your focus to a suitable central idea."

Understanding and sharing the steps you took to formulate your specific purpose and central idea from a general topic can help others. In a presentation not to exceed two minutes, trace for your peers the progression of thought you used to move from a broad subject to your much more specific and focused central idea.

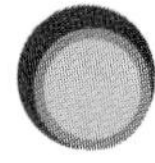

STUDENT FOCUS GROUP REPORT

Now that you have had the opportunity to immerse yourself in topic selection and refinement, in a group of five to seven students, respond to the following questions:

1. Think again about this chapter's introductory case study. Would your advice to Young Sub change at all based on what you have now learned? Why or why not?
2. What thoughts went through your mind after you were told to select a topic for a speech?
3. Was there any particular idea-generation strategy that worked better for you than others? Which was it, and why did you find it more useful?
4. What criteria did you use to make your ultimate topic selection?
5. Which posed greater problems for you and why: the selection of your subject, the selection of your specific purpose, or the phrasing of your central idea?
6. Summarize the most important information you have learned about the selection and refinement of speech topics, specific purposes, behavioral objectives, and central ideas.
7. Take a single topic and create three purpose statements that show how you might approach the topic as an informative speech, pursuasive speech, and speech to entertain. Then formulate a central idea for each version.

Chapter Seven

The Speaker's Search for Materials

How to Research Your Topic

After reading this chapter, you should be able to:

- Identify the kinds of research speakers need to conduct.
- Draw raw material for a speech from your personal knowledge and experience.
- Plan and conduct an interview with a person who possesses special knowledge related to your topic.
- Discover and use information available to you from an array of relevant associations and governmental organizations.
- Use the library's resources to find, retrieve, and evaluate needed information.
- Conduct computer-assisted research.

CASE STUDY

Behind the Scenes

Eric and Lindsay were sitting at the computer on Eric's desk. They worked for a major computer company and had just been assigned the task of researching handling information anxiety in the Information Age. Their boss, Arlene, would use what they found in preparing the speech she was scheduled to deliver before an audience of college students.

Eric sighed. "What a dumb topic. I find it impossible to conceive of the fact that anyone alive today would be scared of information. It's information that drives our world. It's information that let's us progress. Who picked this topic?"

Lindsay answered, "Arlene did. But she had her reasons. People who don't know how to find information are afraid of information. People who don't know how to process information are afraid of it. People who don't know how to use information are afraid of it. Unfortunately, we're talking about a lot of people."

Eric suddenly sat up. "Well, why don't I go and interview some college students and their profs regarding how they feel about information. You know—get their thoughts on information overload, what they're doing to cope with the information explosion, how they're attempting to keep current—things like that. Then I'll go speak to some people who are in the information business and interview them regarding how they're trying to facilitate the transference and understanding of new information. I'll also talk to some people involved in designing the computer technology that made the information explosion possible in the first place."

"Good idea," Lindsay offered. "While you do that I'll access the on-line encyclopedia and then some data bases so that I can pursue the references they lead me to and develop a preliminary bibliography for us to use."

"Don't forget to define key terms," Eric added. "And be sure to get us a bunch of meaningful statistics and examples."

"Sure thing," Lindsay agreed. You take care of the opinions and narratives, and I'll take care of the descriptions and facts."

- Have Eric and Lindsay covered all the key research bases?
- If you were one of the students Eric interviewed, how would you respond to his queries?

HAVE YOU EVER ASKED ANOTHER PERSON questions such as these: "What would you like to do tonight?" "Do you want to go out to see a movie?" "Would you rather go out to dinner?" "Why don't we do something different?" When faced with choices regarding how to spend your free time, how do you make decisions? If you are like most people and wanted to see a movie or try a new restaurant, you would probably start by checking the movie listings of your local newspaper or driving by a theater to see which films are listed on the marquee. Perhaps you would ask your friends for their advice regarding new restaurants you might like. You'd probably also peruse the various restaurant guides or home pages that exist on the Internet. In addition, because films and restaurants are reviewed in local newspapers as well as on local radio and TV news

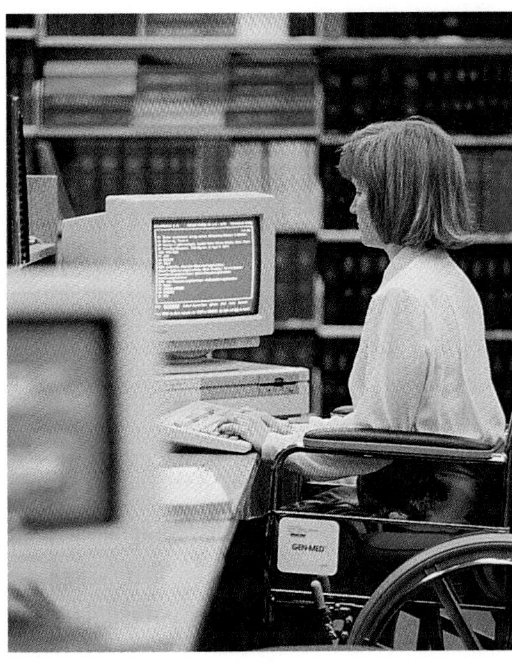

Have you checked out the Internet as one way to begin your research for a speech?

programs, you might also check those sources for recent reviews. Eventually, based on your experiences and those of people whose advice you trust, you would make a decision.

What does all of this have to do with public speaking? The research we do when preparing to speak in public is very much like the personal research we conduct daily. However, because a speech is apt to be shared with others in a somewhat more formal setting, we use a somewhat more formal approach to research it. Let's explore this approach.

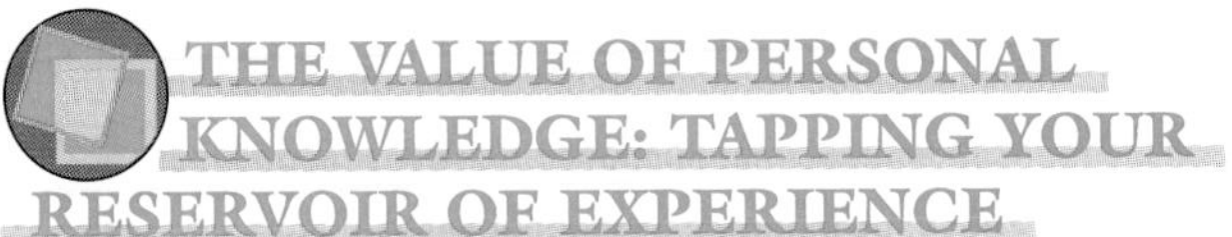

THE VALUE OF PERSONAL KNOWLEDGE: TAPPING YOUR RESERVOIR OF EXPERIENCE

FOR SOME REASON, the public speaking student frequently overlooks a most valuable primary research resource—him- or herself. Let's face it—you have been alive for a number of years. You probably have some job experience to your credit, and have certainly been in school studying a wide variety of subjects for several years. During this time you have probably also read a vast number of newspaper and magazine articles, watched countless hours of television, written papers, and talked with an array of individuals—many more knowledgeable than yourself. Just going about the business of living provides you with a plethora of experiences from which to draw raw material for a speech. For starters, did you grow up in a lower- or middle-class family or was your family well off? In any case, you have fuel for a speech. Yet many college students often discount the value of their own lives when they begin to research a topic. Interestingly, college students are not alone in this. Corporate and gov-

SPEAKING of ETHICS

Embellishing the Message

Tom decided to speak about the problem of unemployment in this country. He began researching the topic and found many interesting statistics about the unemployment rates both in his state and within his own community. He needed an attention-getting aspect, so he began to think back over his own life. He had never really been unemployed. That is, although he had quit a number of jobs because they were too much to handle with his course load, he never knew personally what it meant to be laid off or unable to find work. He did, however, have a number of friends who had been unemployed. In fact, now that he thought about it, he had not only accompanied one of his friends down to the unemployment office, he had waited in line and walked through the entire process with her.

Tom jotted down all of his recollections about this experience and worked them into the introduction of a speech. As he rehearsed his presentation, however, he found that it did not have the impact that he really wanted it to. So he began adjusting his introductory illustration. It would sound much better, he reasoned to himself, if I were the person who was unemployed and a friend of mine had accompanied me to the unemployment office. He told himself that the change he was making was minor—but an important one. The story itself was absolutely true. All of the details were correct. All he had done was modify the person who was actually unemployed.

- What do you think about Tom's actions? Is it unethical to tell a "white lie" during a speech? Could stretching the truth cause problems? What would you have done if you were Tom?

ernment speakers suffer the same nearsightedness, setting their sights on something distant while rejecting what is available at hand.

Of course, not every one of your experiences can be transformed into an effective speech topic or be used to embellish a speech. While personal experience is often a starting point for speech research, rarely will it be sufficient to serve as your main point. To be certain you deliver ample information to receivers, you need to augment your personal experience and knowledge with library research.

No one has had exactly the same personal experiences as you. For that reason, we all have a lot to learn from each other. Once we write down our experiences, they serve as a form of personal research. They also enhance our credibility as speakers. That is not to suggest that you can't speak about a topic unless you have lived it. Of course you can. For example, you can talk about poverty without actually having been impoverished by researching the subject. You can talk about high school drop-outs without having been one yourself. You can talk about the future of genetic research without ever having conducted any. However, if you have experience with a particular topic that is important to you, that experience—when supplemented with additional outside research—will greatly increase your credibility with your audience. Thus, to the extent you can, capitalize on your own experience and firsthand knowledge by using both to provide effective explanations, examples, or definitions.

For instance, one student, a survivor of Hodgkin's disease, chose to explain to his class how he coped with the impact of the illness. He described first discovering that he had Hodgkin's, its symptoms, his treatment, and survival rates. He buttressed his message by revealing his personal fears in depth.

Being a cancer survivor is a gift. My disease helped me to realize before most of us our age do, just how vulnerable each of us is. You can worry about small stuff—what your hair looks like, if you're wearing a name brand shirt, or if your face has an unseemly pimple, or you can concentrate on what really matters—how good you are inside, and whether you'll make someone's life better just by being there. Small stuff means nothing to me anymore. The small stuff is even more transitory than I am—than we all are. What matters to me is living each day like it could be my last—because the gift of life doesn't last forever.

The speaker's simple words conveyed his message more meaningfully and eloquently than if he had quoted another source. Even if your experiences are not as dramatic or as emotionally powerful as this speaker's, you can still use them to your advantage. Think over your life and consider how you could integrate one or more experiences into a speech to add a sense of freshness and authenticity to your message.

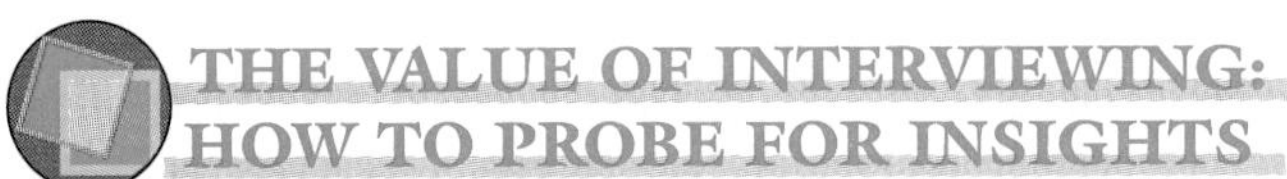

THE VALUE OF INTERVIEWING: HOW TO PROBE FOR INSIGHTS

INTERVIEWING PEOPLE with special knowledge is another way of acquiring both information about and insight into a topic, and can be used either to supplement or to substitute for personal experience. In fact, few—if any—student speakers have enough material from their own lives on which to base an entire speech. Ordinarily, audiences expect and usually want more from a speech than just "you." Therefore, you will need to go beyond yourself and consult other sources as well. One possibility is to talk to others who are experts on the topic you have selected. For example, if you want to give a speech on college admissions criteria, you would probably want to speak to your school's admission director, as well as the admission directors from a number of other area colleges. If you want to speak on the advantages and disadvantages of IQ tests you might speak to a representative from an educational testing service or a member of your college's education department. If you wanted to explore why mandatory drug testing is required to be considered for employment by a municipal organization, you might consult members of the human resources division of the organization in question.

Be aware, however, that seeking an interview with such persons most likely does not eliminate your need to conduct research, such as examining newspaper and magazine articles or looking at relevant books on the subject. Questioning experts, however, can help you structure your research and provide you with ideas and information that are not readily available to you but that can benefit you as you seek to bring your speech alive. For example, if you plan to talk about the current housing market, you might interview homeowners or perhaps individuals who are having problems purchasing a home. If you plan to talk about nuclear energy, a phone call to the public relations department of the local power company might produce someone who could discuss with you the need for nuclear energy in your area. If your goal is to speak about the dangers of nuclear power plants, a call to a nuclear physicist at the Nuclear Regulatory Agency in Washington, D.C., could help bring you up to date on the issues you plan to discuss in your speech.

Whenever the news media need information about a variety of subjects they call on college professors. Yet for some reason, when college students need information they tend to forget that they are surrounded by a wide array of experts from a variety of fields. Think for a minute about the faculty who teach and conduct research at your own college. What subjects do they teach? In what kinds of research are they engaged? Most likely there are professors of chemistry, computer science, engineering, languages, history, marine biology, marketing, sociology, math, sciences, advertising, international affairs, law, and journalism—just to name a few—all waiting for you to interview them about a topic related to their area of expertise.

When you interview experts on your campus you might need to set aside some time so you can sit down face to face with them to discuss the questions you would like them to answer in depth. However, for those interviewees who are not nearby you can also rely on two tools—one traditional, the other more recent—that have served journalistic researchers quite well: the telephone and the Internet. A few well-placed calls or a few on-line chats, coupled with a little creativity and perseverance, can provide you with a great deal of new information to incorporate into your presentation. However, you can't just pick up the phone and start calling or go on-line and start chatting. You must begin by doing some preliminary research that will enable you to formulate the particular questions for which you need an expert's answers.

Preinterview Preparation

Your first task is to determine why you are interviewing someone. What qualifies him or her as an expert? For example, one student decided to talk about significant road construction that was scheduled to begin near his campus and that would likely seriously disrupt access to the college and its nearby business district. He was interested in detailing exactly what was being done, why it was necessary, and what was the source of financing. He began his research by reading recently published news reports on the topic and discovered that the construction project itself was quite controversial. In fact, many area shopkeepers believed that there was no reason to widen the existing bridge or move the adjacent highway entrance to a new location. The federal government insisted, however, that doing so would relieve the traffic congestion around the campus. During his research, the student found that one particular shopkeeper had surfaced as the voice of the opposition and was thus often quoted in local articles. A look in the phone book turned up the individual's address and phone number. Sure enough, one phone call produced specific insights about the building project that the student was able to use in his speech. Because he wanted to be sure to inform his audience about both perspectives, the student also interviewed a government official and incorporated the results of that interview into his speech.

To set up an interview, all you need to do is pick up the phone and ask permission. You might use the following dialogue:

> Hello, Mr./Ms. ________________. My name is ____________________, from ________________ College/University. I am researching a presentation for my public speaking class on the subject of ________________. I understand that you are well versed in this field and I wondered if it would be possible for us to talk about it now or in the near future?

If you aren't successful reaching the person you want to interview by phone, if time allows you could send a letter or e-mail to the desired source. You might begin a letter like this:

> Dear Mr./Ms. ______________ :
>
> I am a student at ________________ and am currently working on a speech on the topic of ________________________. It is my understanding that you are an expert in this field, and I was wondering if it would be possible for us to get together either in person or over the phone to discuss it.
>
> I would only need a few minutes of your time to answer some basic questions about ________________ . My peers would really enjoy hearing your views.
>
> Please contact me at ____________ so we can work out the details of such a meeting. Thank you for your help. I look forward to meeting you.
>
> Sincerely,
>
> ________________

Before you make that phone call or actually start to conduct that in-person or e-mail interview, be certain that you have a series of questions to ask your interviewee. Most interviewees will become impatient and cut the interview short if you simply ramble on without displaying any real sense of purpose, direction, or familiarity with the subject. After all, the interviewees are giving you their time and doing you a favor. You will rarely be given a second chance if you don't impress them the first time.

Here are some sample questions you might use if you were interviewing a source from the Communication Fraud Control Association regarding the problem of people stealing calling card numbers and using them to make long distance calls.

Preliminary Questions for the Communication Fraud Control Association Representative

1. How extensive is calling card fraud?
2. How do people obtain calling card numbers?
3. How can you tell if your card number is being used illegally?
4. What recourse do people have when they find out that others have made calls using their cards without their permission?
5. How do so called "card surfers" record card numbers?
6. How are such numbers sold? Who purchases them?
7. What can be done to reduce card number theft?
8. What laws have been proposed?
9. Are men or women more likely targets of card theft?
10. What can we do to protect ourselves from calling card fraud?

Whenever you conduct an interview, it is important for you to decide how you are going to preserve the results of your conversation. If the interviewee grants you permission, for example, you may decide to tape record your conversation with him or her. When you have such permission, you will find that using a small microcassette recorder is most appropriate. Such a machine is unobtrusive and thus will not serve as a distraction. If permission to tape is not granted, you can simply decide to take notes. If you do so, be prepared to sit down by yourself *immediately* after the discussion and go over and clarify your notes so that you do not run the risk of misquoting your expert.

Speaking of skillbuilding: Plan the Interview

1. Working in groups of three to five students, select an issue facing the United States today that especially concerns you. Though locating the right person to interview is often challenging, for purposes of this exercise assume that you can reach any public figure you believe possesses information relevant to your chosen issue.
2. Identify the desired interviewee and his or her position, and explain why you consider him or her an expert. Then compile a list of at least ten specific questions you would like to ask the expert—either in person, via e-mail, or by phone.
3. Give examples of how you could use the information derived from the interview to encourage your audience members to pay attention and become involved in the topic.

Conducting the Interview

You now have an interviewee all lined up and you are ready to talk to him or her. How do you proceed? You have your questions ready, you have a notebook with you, and you have a tape recorder also ready to use, should permission to tape be granted. Adhering to a number of other guidelines will facilitate your task as well.

First, arrive on time. You are imposing on the interviewee by taking up his or her time, so it is inappropriate to be late. It is better to find yourself waiting for the interviewee and using the extra thinking time to plan strategy than it is to make the interviewee wait for you. In fact, if you arrive early you may find that the interviewee is more willing to talk to you and will actually give you a few extra minutes of his or her time.

Second, explain your reasons for the interview right away. You know why it was important to interview the subject, but your interviewee may not be so sure of your reasons. Therefore, begin by describing your objectives for the interview. If you need to set up a tape recorder, you can use that time to establish some common ground with the interviewee and give him or her a few extra seconds to focus on your topic.

Once you ask your questions, you will probably discover in short order that the person you are interviewing may take your discussion into other areas as well. Should that occur, you have a decision to make. If the tangents are adding material to the interview that you never considered but that is relevant to your objectives, by all means let the interviewee pursue the area. You may, however, be dismayed to find that the informational detour, while interesting, is irrelevant to your purpose; if this is the case, gently guide the interviewee back by returning to your prepared list of questions. For example, if you were interviewing a Vietnam veteran specifically about the war, and the interviewee began explaining how difficult it was for him to adjust to civilian life after returning from the war, you would probably try to bring the interviewee back to answering questions on your list. However, if your concern was for how the individual, as a veteran, was treated by society both during and after the war, such a discussion would be entirely appropriate and relevant.

During the interview process take advantage of every opportunity to ask questions that probe for additional information. That is, ask questions that follow up on answers provided by the interviewee or make comments that mirror supplied responses in an effort to verify your understanding of what the interviewee has said. For example, as you listen carefully to interviewee answers to your primary questions, you will find that some points he or she makes need further clarification. Asking probing questions such as "Why did you make that decision?" or "What caused you to take that action at that time?" in addition to providing needed clarification also let the interviewee know that you have a keen interest in the topic and that you are carefully listening to what is being said.

Also remember to give the interviewee feedback. Here using the paraphrase will serve you well. You want to be able to let your interviewee know the extent to which you understand the responses he or she is offering. For example, you may want to say, "So, what you are saying is . . ." or "What I hear you telling me is. . . ." Asking mirroring questions that reflect a response offered by an interviewee such as "You said attitude is more important than aptitude?" also encourages discussion at the same time that it elicits a verification of perceived meaning. An even more effective approach is to combine a mirroring response with a probing question: " So you are suggesting that emotional intelligence is equally as important as IQ. Are you implying that schools should be teaching this as well?" Techniques like these help ensure that you have accurately processed and understood the information that the interviewee is giving you, and also shows the interviewee that you really care about what he or she is sharing.

Cultural Diversity and Interviewing

Conducting an informational interview is hard enough when you and the interviewee are from the same culture and speak the same language. Imagine the problems presented when the interviewee is a person from another culture for whom English is a second language.

If you are confused about what the interviewee says, you must take a moment to ask clarifying questions or paraphrase a response: "So you believe that we should . . . ." Make an effort, too, to seek definitions of what the person means when he or she uses a particular term. You might, for example, suggest a synonym for the word being used

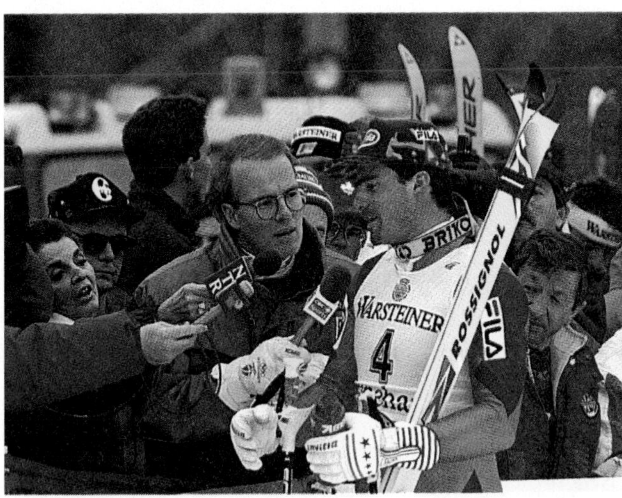

Interviewer and interviewee may come from different cultures. When this occurs, what kinds of problems might this present for both parties?

Considering Diversity

Who Are You Prepared to Interview?

Think of a specific cultural or ethnic group other than your own. Use the following series of questions to help you evaluate your ability to understand members of that group. Respond to each statement by noting the extent to which you are able to agree with it; answer each question with either "fully" (award yourself 5 points), "somewhat" (award yourself 2.5 points), or "not at all" (award yourself 0 points).

- I understand the communication rules of ______.
- I understand the language or dialect of ______.
- I understand the values of ______.
- I understand the customs of ______.

Tally your points. Scores will range from 0 to 20. The higher your score, the better equipped you believe you are to communicate with and understand members of that cultural or ethnic group. Also, the greater your knowledge of other peoples, the less likely it is that you will misinterpret the messages people in that group encode.

in an effort to determine whether your perception of its meaning coincides with the interviewee's perception.

If you were in a foreign land in which another language was being spoken you would want people to treat you with respect and make every attempt to understand you. The same is true for people who were not born in this country. Take the time to show that you are concerned about them and that you genuinely want to understand what they are sharing with you.

Finally, remember that your interviewee has probably not decided to devote his or her entire day to being interviewed. If you are reaching the end of your allotted time and he or she begins to give signals to end the meeting, be courteous. Review your list of questions and make certain that you have covered all of the major ones. If not, move right to the important questions so that you do cover them—however briefly. At the conclusion of the interview be certain to thank the person for seeing you. Summarize how he or she has helped you and assure the person that you will use the information he or she has provided you fairly and accurately. Shake hands warmly, and depart.

The Postinterview Review

Whether you have taken notes or taped the interview, you should review the information you have gathered soon after holding the interview. Concentrate on the main points that came out of the interview. Be especially watchful for specific examples and information provided by the interviewee that you can incorporate into your presentation.

Compile a list of key ideas covered during the interview. Having such a list will make it easier to determine which pieces of information are relevant to your speech

Raymond Robinson, Mayor of Ourtown, NJ

"During the storm, many people had to be evacuated. Otherwise they would have been caught in grave danger. This was a storm that caught us completely by surprise."

Interview 1/16/97, 4 p.m.

Figure 7.1

Notecard derived from an interview

and which can be discarded. Transcribe or rewrite your notes, being certain to spend the largest percentage of your time on the most relevant material. Stories, analogies, and statistical information provided by the interviewee will be particularly helpful to you as you prepare your speech. You may want to write each piece of information on an individual index card so it will be easier to organize your presentation. For example, suppose you were talking about property damage caused by a recent hurricane; you might record information resulting from your interview as shown in Figure 7.1.

THE VALUE OF ORDERING MATERIAL BY MAIL OR FAX: WRITING AWAY FOR DATA

THERE IS A GREAT DEAL OF INFORMATION out there waiting to be discovered. Though much of it is not in your library, if you give yourself ample preparation time (that means you *don't* wait until the night before your presentation) you may be able to use information provided by government, business, industrial, professional, and lobbying organizations—often at little or no cost to you.

Discovering the Information Available

How do you discover what information is available? Many organizations are in business just to promote ideas or policies. A number of these groups are located in Washington, D.C., but some are situated in various locations across the country. In your library you will find a book called the *Encyclopedia of Associations*—a resource that contains a listing of worldwide groups interested in your topic. For example, the National Rifle Association promotes ownership of guns. The American Medical Association lobbies on behalf of physicians and other health professionals. The National Association of Realtors promotes the value of private property ownership. The American Association of University Professors lobbies in behalf of higher education. Organizations like these have a wealth of information you could use to your advantage when preparing a speech.

You must keep in mind, however, that if you use materials that are sent to you from groups like those identified above, the information they provide is designed to present a very positive view of whichever industry or organization they represent. Thus, you and your audience will probably want to look very carefully at who did the study or prepared the report and how they are issuing the results. Despite this, such material can still be worthy of inclusion in speeches.

Using Government Resources

The U.S. government is a major producer of materials on just about every topic imaginable. By using its resources, including the *Monthly Catalog of U.S. Government,* published by the U.S. Government Printing Office, you can find data on such diverse subjects as biofeedback, interferon, contraception, aspirin, baldness, lasers, packaging, tranquilizers, building construction, small business techniques, real estate, and a variety of farming techniques. Each department of the U.S. government prints materials that relate specifically to that department's mission. Most of the material is available to you at minimal or no cost. You can obtain a listing of such materials from the U.S. Government Printing Office, Washington, DC 20401. You will also find it of value to obtain the *Consumer Information Catalogue* by writing to New Catalogue, Pueblo, CO 81009. If your topic depends on information supplied by the government for its development you should begin your research gathering early, since several weeks may go by before the materials you request are delivered to you. (You will also want to check your library. Some college and public libraries are designated government depositories and contain some of the materials that are printed by the government agencies.) Try to formulate topics early in the semester that you may want to discuss later in the term; doing so will enable you to order materials on those subjects early. It will do you little good if the booklets you need arrive two weeks after you present your speech.

THE VALUE OF LIBRARY RESEARCH: THE SOURCE SEARCH[1]

HOW OFTEN DO YOU USE YOUR SCHOOL LIBRARY? Many students go out of their way to avoid the library, much as they would a deadly virus. The library is deadly, however, only if you do not use it. In fact, the majority of the sources you use to prepare your speech will be derived from library research. By serving as a depository for a wide variety of research materials the library is a public speaker's ally. The information sources contained in your library are organized in a way that allow you to use it with relative ease. Advances in technology provide you with access to computers, microfilm, and copy machines to help you do your work. If you are familiar with your library this section will simply be a quick review. If your library is still a mystery to you, this is your opportunity to get to know it better.

Libraries are masterfully organized. Years of refinement have transformed library catalogue and reference systems into easy-to-use sources of information. If you have not yet used your school library it is a good idea to arrange to take the "tour" that librarians frequently make available to students. You may want to ask your professor to make arrangements for your class to take such a tour if one has not yet been scheduled.

Suggestions for Library Use: How to Find Out Anything about Everything

Do not wait until the night before a speech is due to start your library research. Not only is it too late for you to be able to really internalize the material at that point, but the evening is usually the busiest time for most college libraries. You will do much better to start gathering materials well in advance of the scheduled date for your presentation.

Do not be nervous about asking for help. Librarians are trained to be excellent researchers and they can provide you with a great deal of assistance. However, you must do the preliminary work first and then turn to them when a particular problem arises. Also, be certain to take the materials you need to do your investigative work with you to the library. Having sufficient pens, paper, note cards, and even change for the copy machine can save you inordinate amounts of wasted library time.

Undertaking Your Investigation: Conducting Research in the Library

Starting to research a topic is very much like conducting an investigation. Fox Mulder, Dana Scully, Andy Sipowicz, and thousands of other real and fictional investigators show us that investigative research can be exciting and interesting. Yet college students often approach the task with trepidation. With the materials available to you today, this should not be so. More information is available today through our library systems than at any other time in history. Though this plethora of information makes research a real challenge, it also makes it exciting. To be an effective investigator today you must be familiar with some of the resources available to you through your library.

The Computerized Catalogue. You are fortunate that computer or on-line catalogues are used in most libraries today. When using these you can conduct a Boolean search. This means that you do not need to know a specific author or title to find resource materials. All you need to do is enter two or three key words into the computer and it will search the library's collection for you. On-line systems save you hours of racing from card catalogue drawer to card catalogue drawer looking for information. Now you can locate needed information much more efficiently (see Figure 7.2 on page 138).

The Card Catalogue System. If your library still uses a card catalogue system, the cards in it are organized alphabetically under three headings: author, title, and subject. You will find the call number in the upper-left corner of each card. That is your key to locating and retrieving a book from the stacks, or library shelves. Of course, no one expects you to read every library book available on your topic. However, you should be sure that you do selective reading from the books you find. Periodicals are also listed by title in the card catalogue, which also reveals which issues are available. (See Figure 7.3 on page 139 for samples of the three types of cards.)

Most libraries have a separate room or area in which they store recent issues of periodicals. Bound volumes of back issues may also be kept there.

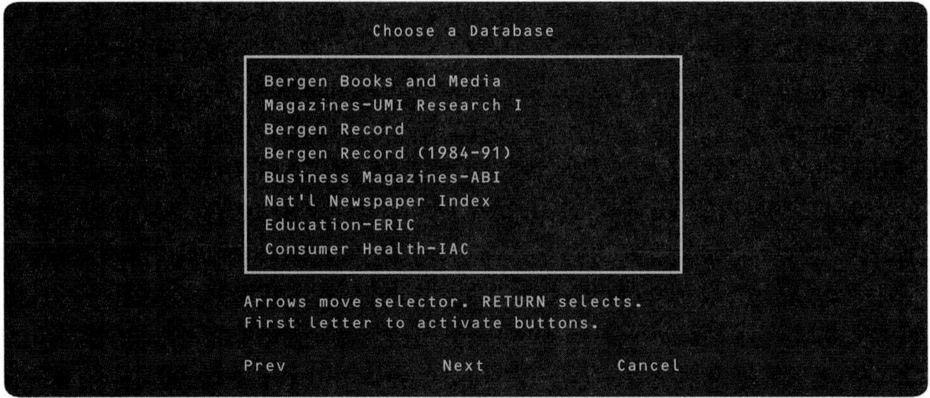

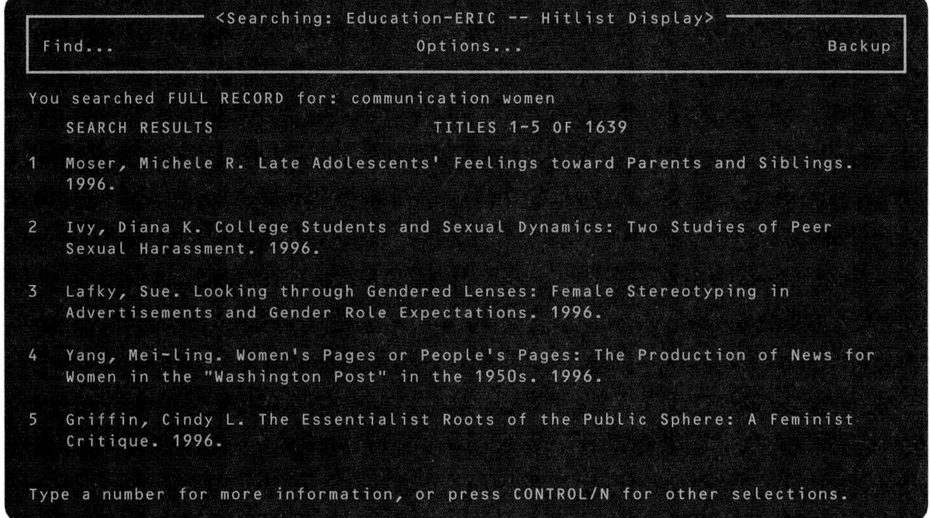

Figure 7.2

Screens from a computerized catalogue system

Dual Systems. A number of libraries have dual systems in place. Newer materials are on the computer systems and older books are still listed in the card catalogue. There are so many systems available today that it is a good idea to work with your librarian to determine exactly how your college library is organized.

Browsing. Even though catalogue systems are available to you, sometimes libraries have open stacks through which you can browse. Make it your business, therefore, to learn the art of creative browsing. As you attempt to locate on the shelves materials that you discovered in the card or on-line catalogue, keep your eyes open for additional titles that you may have missed. Often the title of a book is not an accurate description of what the book is about. In addition, the book next to the one you have been looking for may also contain information related to your topic, but you may have overlooked it during your preliminary research.

E
872
J67

United States — Politics and Government

Jordan Hamilton

Crisis: the last year of the Carter presidency/Hamilton Jordan. — New York: G. Putnam's Sons, c. 1982.

431 p.
Includes indexes
ISBN 0-399-12738-0
1. United States — Politics and government — 1977–1981;
2. United States — Foreign Relations — 1977–1981;
3. Carter, Jimmy, 1924–; 4. Iran Hostage Crisis, 1979–1981.

E
872
J67

Jordan Hamilton

Jordan Hamilton

Crisis: the last year of the Carter presidency/Hamilton Jordan. — New York: G. Putnam's Sons, c. 1982.

431 p.
Includes indexes
ISBN 0-399-12738-0
1. United States — Politics and government — 1977–1981;
2. United States — Foreign Relations — 1977–1981;
3. Carter, Jimmy, 1924–; 4. Iran Hostage Crisis, 1979–1981.

E
872
J67

Crisis: the last year of the Carter presidency

Jordan Hamilton

Crisis: the last year of the Carter presidency/Hamilton Jordan. — New York: G. Putnam's Sons, c. 1982.

431 p.
Includes indexes
ISBN 0-399-12738-0
1. United States — Politics and government — 1977–1981;
2. United States — Foreign Relations — 1977–1981;
3. Carter, Jimmy, 1924–; 4. Iran Hostage Crisis, 1979–1981.

Figure 7.3

Sample subject, author, and title cards. If your library still uses the card catalogue, the cards will look like these.

Investigating Your Library's Reference Room

The catalogues are only one stop along your investigatory road. As you think through your chosen topic you may discover, for example, that you need to find the total number of people who died from heart attacks last year, or the size of Somalia. You could read scores of newspapers and magazine articles hoping to run across such information, or you could employ a more efficient approach: Take your investigation to the reference section of the library, where you will find an incredible amount of

An incredible amount of information awaits you in the reference room of a library.

data waiting for you. Your job is to locate that information that will be of most use to you and that your audience will find most interesting.

Among the resources included in your library's research room are encyclopedias, yearbooks, dictionaries, biographical aids, atlases, and an array of indexes. Let's examine each of these categories.

Encyclopedias. When we think of encyclopedias several may come to mind: *Encyclopedia Britannica, Encyclopedia Americana, Compton's Encyclopedia,* or one of the many other general encyclopedias available in most libraries. General encyclopedias are good sources of background or historical information on a plethora of topics. You will probably want to photocopy some appropriate articles from one or more encyclopedias to help you acquire the general background information you need to set your topic in perspective. If you let them, however, general encyclopedias can also trap you. Too many investigators stop their library research at the shelves on which they are located. However, encyclopedias are not designed to provide you with all the information you need for a speech. They are simply too general to be of that much value. Thus, your job is to use them merely as a starting point for research.

Consulting more subject-specific or specialized encyclopedias can also provide you with valuable information. Sometimes called dictionaries, these one-volume encylopedias include:

Encyclopedia of Banking and Finance
Encyclopedia of Associations
Dictionary of American History
Encyclopedia of Religion
Encyclopedia of Education
McGraw-Hill Encyclopedia of Science and Technology

Take a pad and pencil with you to the reference section of your library. Compile a list of fifteen encyclopedias you find there. Include both general and specialized publications. Put the library reference number next to each so that you will have easy access to it the next time you work on a speech.

Yearbooks. Audiences like speakers to present them with up-to-date information. Providing your receivers with ten-year-old data on drunk driving or conditions in prisons, for example, is not nearly as effective as offering them the latest data on these subjects. Where can you find such data? Yearbooks may well be the best place. Published annually, yearbooks provide what is often the most current information on specific topics. Perhaps the most widely consulted yearbook is the *Statistical Abstract of the United States.* The Census Bureau has produced this reference source since the nineteenth century; it includes an incredible array of facts about American life. For example, by consulting it you can find statistical information about death rates, birth rates, family income, production figures, employment data, and hundreds of other topics. Take time to flip through the *Statistical Abstract* and become familiar with it so you will know how to use it when you are researching a speech.

Another commonly referred-to yearbook is the *World Almanac and Book of Facts.* Unlike the *Statistical Abstract,* this reference contains more than statistical information and is not limited to the United States. Included in it are lists of award recipients, sports record holders, natural resources in various countries, and so on. You will be spending your time well if you thumb through the latest *World Almanac* to become familiar with this incredible one-volume source.

A third source is *Facts on File,* a relative newcomer to the reference sections of most libraries. Included in it are news articles on major topics like science, sports, medicine, crime, economics, and the arts. It is a valuable compendium of national and foreign current events. If you know an event happened last year, *Facts on File* will be a great quick reference source for you. Published weekly, issues are bound together in a yearbook version at the end of every twelve-month period.

Biographical Sources. In addition to yearbooks, you will want to consult a number of biographical reference guides. Whenever information about noteworthy persons, past or present, can be of use, one of the following biographical resources may hold the key.

Established in 1940, *Current Biography* is an interesting monthly magazine that provides complete articles about newsworthy people from around the world. Major names in areas such as politics, sports, and the arts are covered. At the end of every year, three- to four-page articles on each individual are edited and published in one volume, making it a convenient source. If the person you are investigating is in the news, *Current Biography* will be one source you will definitely want to consult for up-to-date information.

The *Who's Who* references, including *Who's Who in America,* are valuable biographical resources. If your speech topic requires that you have some biographical information about a particular individual, then you will certainly want to check *Who's Who.* If you do not find the individual in the general reference, there are *Who's Who* publications for a number of more specific fields including business, science, math, engineering, and so on. *Who's Who of American Women* and *International Who's Who* can be helpful to you as well.

Dictionaries. When preparing a speech, if you are interested in the history of a word or its meaning, you could consult a standard collegiate dictionary like *Webster's* or the *Random House Dictionary.* By using a thesaurus you will find effective synonyms and antonyms for the words in question. In addition, sometimes the meaning of a particular term becomes important because you need to precisely define a specific term. A look at *Black's Law Dictionary,* for example, could help you define legal terms, and *Black's Medical Dictionary* could help you explain the meaning of some particular medical jargon. The detailed history of a specific word can be found in the *Oxford English Dictionary.* William Safire's *Political Dictionary,* the *Dictionary of Americanisms,* and the *Dictionary of Word and Phrase Origins* are interesting and useful as well. Investigate the dictionaries in your library's reference section.

Quotations. What if you want to begin or end your speech with a quotation? You could spend years digging through literature or speeches in an effort to discover appropriate material. Or you could use a book of quotations to find hundreds of potentially useful quotations at one sitting. The best-known such book is *Bartlett's Familiar Quotations,* a resource containing more than 20,000 quotations. There are also other books of quotations that contain interesting material for your speeches. Some are particularly useful for speeches made to certain audiences, such as businesspeople. Others provide examples of humor or are from the mouths or pens of contemporary writers. Examine an array of the quotation books available to you. Be particularly observant of the categories into which the quotations are divided. In fact, you might jot down one or two that you like as you thumb through the book.

Atlases and Gazetteers. Where can you look for the latest information about developing countries around the world? How many people live in the country on which you are focusing? What can you discover about that country's climate? its population? its politics? Atlases and gazetteers can help you discover the answers to such questions. The *Rand-McNally Cosmopolitan World Atlas* contains maps of the entire world. It also gives specific information about each region and country. *Webster's New Geographical Dictionary* is a gazetteer, in alphabetical order, that gives specific facts about nearly 50,000 locations around the world. If you plan to deliver a speech about any particular geographical location in the world, you should check these or other atlases and gazetteers as part of your preparation.

Periodical Indexes. Magazines, professional journals, and newspapers are referenced in their own indexes. In essence, each index functions like a card catalogue for periodicals. Let's explore a number of key indexes with which you will want to become more familiar.

Reader's Guide to Periodical Literature. What is the "greenhouse effect" and how serious a problem is it? How popular is soccer worldwide? The answers to these questions may lie in the *Reader's Guide to Periodical Literature,* a general index of periodicals. Articles that appeared in more than 180 major magazines including *Time, Newsweek, US News and World Report, Scientific American, Consumer Reports, Vital Speeches, Ms,* and *Ebony* are referenced in it and cited by author, title, and subject. The *Reader's Guide* program is also available on computer by using Wilson Disc Information Retrieval System for issues dating back as far as 1983. Figure 7.4 contains a

Figure 7.4

***Reader's Guide* listings**

READER'S GUIDE TO PERIODICAL LITERATURE

COMPUTERS—*cont.*

Financial Services use

Programs

See also

Andrew Tobias' Managing Your Money (Computer program)

Government use

Anecdotes, facetiae, satire, etc.

Rapid Robyn drives a point home [using R. Allan's black box driving monitor to control behavior of politicians] A. Fotheringham, il *Maclean's* 106:60 F 15 '93

Handbooks, manuals, etc.

The tech–writing biz, K. Jacobs, il *Home Office Computing* 11:34 Ja '93

Home use

See also

Smart houses

Compute your way to cash [making money with a personal computer] M. Levin, il *Career World* 21:21 Ja '93

Image Processing use

See Image processing

Input–output equipment

See Computer input–output equipment

Maintenance and repair

See also

Computer diagnostic programs

Computer maintenance made easy, il *Home Office Computing* 11:67 F '93

When bad things happen to good PCs, il por *PC World* 11:35–6 Ja '93

Map making use

See Computers—Cartographic use

Memory Systems

See also

Backup storage (Computers)
Data tapes
Flash memories
Floppy disk storage
Hard disk drives
Memory cards

Motion picture use

Cinema by computer, R. Ebert, il *Byte* 18:334 Ja '93

Musical use

Programs

See also

Finale (Computer program)

Periodicals

See also

Byte (Periodical)
Compute (Periodical)
Home Office computing

Speed

Making Windows rock and roll [Windows accelerators] R. Grehan, il *Byte* 18:202–6 Ja '93

Study and teaching

Ramping up to Windows. A. LaPlante, il *PC World* 11:189–90+ Ja '93

Testing

25 new 486s: the quest for the best PC [cover story] il *PC World* 11:116–23+ F '93

The 1992 Byte Awards [cover story] M. E. Nadeau, il *Byte* 18:116–19+ Ja '93

1992 editors' picks [cover story] il *Home Office Computing* 11:40–3+ Ja '93

AST's PowerExec goes modular. R. L. Mitchell, il *Byte* 18:209–10+ Ja '93

Big Blue, less green [IBM PS/1 Essential] J. Nimersheim, il *Home Office Computing* 11:80+ Ja '93

Commodore gets tough [Amiga 3000T–040/200 and 4000–040/120] T. Yager, il *Byte* 18:239–40 Ja '93

The Compute Choice Awards [cover story; with editorial comment by Clifton Karnes] R. Bixby, il *Compute* 15:65–6+ Ja '93

Epson Progression: born to run Windows. S. Apiki, il *Byte* 18:60 Ja '93

Hewlett–Packard launches network–ready Vectra 486N line. J. Forbes, il *PC World* 11:68 Ja '93

A higher end for Compaq notebooks [LTE Lite 4/25C and 25E] E. Perratore, il *Byte* 18:47 Ja '93

Hyundai and Gecco roll out local–bus PCs. M. Desmond, il *PC World* 11:84 F '93

NCR System 3200 Model 3220. J. Sides, *Compute* 15:140+ Ja '93

NEC's Ready Systems offer rapid setup. L. McLaughlin, il *PC World* 11:86 F '93

New Dell PCs speed graphics [486 systems] J. Bertolucci, il *PC World* 11:62–5 F '93

Tandy 3820 SL [notebook] T. Benford, il *Compute* 15:129–30 Ja '93

Test lab: 486 SX desktop systems, il *Compute* 15:6–8+ Ja '93

Two Toshiba systems to go [T4500 notebook series and Dynapad T100X] G. Smarte, il *Byte* 18:46+ Ja '93

What's wrong with this picture? [Tandy 3800HD notebook computer] H. F. Beechhold, il *Home Office Computing* 11:94+ F '93

The world's best $2500 Windows PCs [cover story] R. Farrance and M. Goodwin, il *PC World* 11:98–104+ Ja '93

Zeos and Gateway VL–bus PCs offer speed and performance for Windows [Gateway 486DX2–66V and Zeos Upgradeable 486DX2–66] M. Hogan, o; *PC World* 11:65 Ja '93 sample of a page from the *Reader's Guide*. Notice that each listing gives you information on the date, author, title, name of the magazine, volume number, and page number. All the data you need to locate a particular information source are provided.

Special Indexes to Periodicals. If you decide to research a topic that is more specialized and/or more esoteric than the information to be found in general newspapers or magazines, you may also need to consult a more field specific index. Among the more specialized indexes available to you are:

Art Index
Applied Science and Technology Index
Business Periodicals Index
Education Index
Engineering Index
Index to Journals in Communication Studies
Index to Legal Periodicals
Music Index
Public Affairs Information Index
Social Sciences Index

Most—if not all—of these indexes are now computerized. We will discuss computer research in a later section.

Newspaper Indexes. With regard to newspaper indexes, there is both bad news and good news. The bad news is that most local newspapers in the United States are not indexed. If you see an article in a local paper that would be appropriate for your speech, clip it out and save it. Although a library might hold back issues of some papers, you would probably need to be able to provide at least an approximate date of when the article you are looking for appeared before you would be able to find it.

The good news, however, is that a number of the major U.S. newspapers are indexed. The most recent issues may be available in the original format, but the size and quality of the newsprint make it necessary for back issues to be preserved on microfilm. Your librarian can easily help you set up the required film on the reader. Newspapers that are indexed include:

New York Times
Los Angeles Times
Washington Post
Wall Street Journal
Christian Science Monitor
Chicago Tribune

Check with your librarian about the indexes and microfilm available.

Using Electronic Resources

We are all the beneficiaries of the electronic age. We have access to a wealth of material that is stored electronically on CDs and CD-ROM, film, audiotapes, videotapes, and computer data banks. For example, in addition to recording excerpts from news magazine shows such as *20/20* or *60 Minutes,* we can now also access CD-ROM re-

InfoTrac – Magazine

Heading: Jogging
-Health aspects

Running away from diabetes, (jogging to control diabetes) v8 The University of California, Berkeley Wellness Letter Jan '92 p6 (1)
ABSTRACT AVAILABLE
ABSTRACT
Studies conducted at the University of California (Berkeley), Stanford University and elsewhere offer direct evidence that physical activity may help prevent noninsulin–dependent diabetes.
--- end ---

Bad vibes: jarring aerobic exercise can have deep reaching impact, by Donald D. Aspergren il v53 Muscle & Fitness June '92 p52 (1)
ABSTRACT AVAILABLE
ABSTRACT
Some aerobic exercises, such as jogging, can cause back problems because vibrations radiate to the low back region. Joggers should avoid hard running surfaces, wear good shoes and use proper running form.
--- end ---

Figure 7.5

Sample InfoTrac Entry. InfoTrac is a magazine index that is available in many libraries. Here is a sample entry on "Jogging."

sources such as Microsoft's *Encarta,* Grolier's *Encyclopedia,* and Compton's *Multimedia Encyclopedia.* CD-ROM encyclopedias let you access information simply by typing in the topic you want to explore. Video illustrations and audio enhancement often accompany the article, and hypertext capabilities enable you to obtain more detailed or in-depth information on highlighted items.

We have already seen that a variety of sources including the *Reader's Guide to Periodical Literature, Facts on File,* and a number of encyclopedias are available for you to research via computers. Similarily, *Magazine Index* (a database that indexes more than five hundred American and Canadian magazines), and *Infotrac* (a resource covering general publications and government documents) are available on laser discs (see Figure 7.5). *Business Index,* another computerized resource, indexes the *New York Times* financial section and the *Wall Street Journal.*

Computer Databases

There are even more sophisticated databases available for you to consult via computer. ERIC is a comprehensive research database that provides you with published and unpublished materials on a wide array of educational topics. ASI (American Statistics Index) offers a comprehensive guide to statistical information that has been compiled since 1973.

Fortunately, most computer-aided research does not require sophisticated computer knowledge. However, the more complex databases will require that you seek help from librarians. The more complex your topic, the greater the chances you will

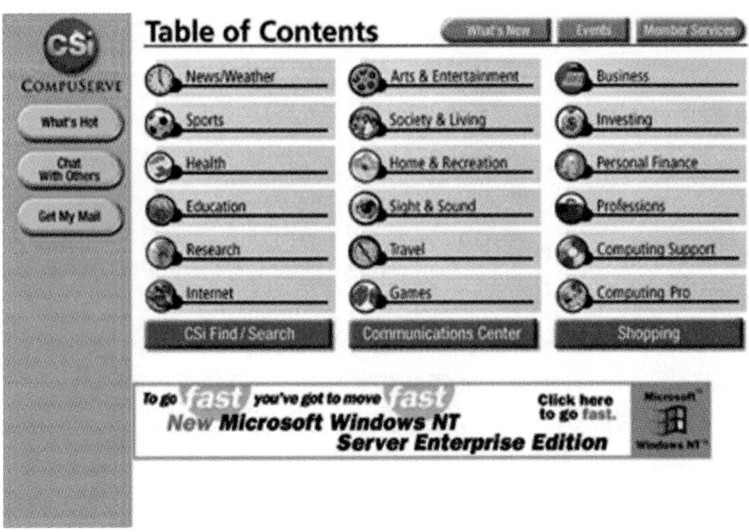

Figure 7.6

Sample materials from CSI (CompuServ®)

need to conduct a computer search and consult a database. The search of databases, however, should be your last research stop. There is no reason to invest the time—and often the money—in computer searches when the hard copy information in the library will be more sufficient in providing you the information for your presentation. However, as you work on specific topics you may find you need one or two very specialized bits of information. When this occurs, conducting a computerized search may be your best answer. Librarians will help you select key words to enter into the databases and help you make decisions about the number of citations you can use. If you find that there are hundreds of citations available on your topic, you will want to find ways to delimit their use before you print the bibliographic resources offered. On the other hand, if the search finds no information about your topic, you need to consider changing the key words used to conduct the search or expanding your topic. You may find that some popular consumer on-line services such as America Online and CSI (CompuServ®) can also provide you with useful information (see Figure 7.6).

Computer databases are coming into their own. Just as you can now read books entirely on laptop computers, you are now able to do much of your research from a computer. Computers save you time and save library systems an enormous amount of space.

In addition to the indexes and abstracts that are now available on CD-ROM or on-line, your college library may offer the following databases: *Psychlit* and *Sociofile*, each containing citiations from more than one thousand journals in the subject area and related fields; *Medline,* including the *Index to Dental Literature* and the *International Nursing Index;* and the *New York Times.*

World Wide Web

By connecting to the Internet you are now able to use the resources found on the World Wide Web's "information superhighway," as well as other Internet services. While some people have to go to a college or public library to access the Internet, others can access it from personal computers. The Web now functions as "an international library of information resources as well as a communications medium for conducting business, instruction, entertainment, politics, and social discourse."[2] Research is no longer limited by one's college library or the physical constraints of one's campus. We all now have access to information on every continent.[3]

In many ways the Web resembles a well-equipped library. The information on it is available to anyone who can access it. Almost any kind of content you can find in print is available on the Web. While much of what you can find on the web consists of plain text, the Web also offers an array of multimedia content including pictures and photographs, CD-quality sound, video, and animation.

As with a library, you can divide the content found on the Web into categories such as "books," "periodicals," "news," and other reference materials. You can subscribe to various newsgroups devoted to specific interests such as social issues, science, or ethics; once in a newsgroup you can save news items for future use, as well as ask questions and solicit the opinions of others who participate in that newsgroup. You can also search Web catalogues or use a virtual library or search engine such as Yahoo, Lycos, or Excite to browse the net. Simply type in the keywords you are interested in and it searches millions of pages for those words, providing you with the results ordered according to the likelihood that selected pages match your search criteria. While browsing you might also access news and information from CNN or the Associated Press, visit the *Congressional Record* or *Federal Register*, obtain copies of historical documents and speeches, review Supreme Court decisions, or obtain information on a broad range of subjects and issues. Some Web sites are free, but others charge for their content.

The amount of information that on-line electronic resources can provide you with can be overwhelming. It is up to you to separate relevant from irrelevant information.

Using Your Critical Thinking Skills to Evaluate Your Research

It is unlikely that you can cover everything there is to know about a topic in one brief speech. Consequently, it is your task to sift through materials you locate in an effort to identify those that are the most valuable, the most interesting, the most unusual, or the most relevant. You simply will not have the luxury of reading every book you find from cover to cover. Therefore, check the table of contents in each and select those chapters that highlight the most important information. Similarly, you will probably not be able to read every piece of material identifed by the various search engines used to find material on the Web. You will want to examine those that are most relevant, however. Honing your ability to think critically will be extremely important to you as you conduct research. Keep in mind that you have a finite amount of time to prepare and present any speech. If you find yourself bogged down in a pile of material, sit back for a minute and remind yourself of your speech goals. Then return to the material and begin to prioritize it by analyzing how helpful each item will be to you in reaching your goals.

Of course, research often leads to unplanned discoveries. At times you may encounter an entirely new topical path to follow—one that had not occurred to you. If this happens, you may want to allow yourself some time to explore what has been written in that area to see whether a revision of your topic is called for. If not, it may simply be an area that you will want to research on your own another time or use for a subsequent project or class. As you work, keep asking yourself, "How does this relate to the goal of my presentation?" If the answer is that it does not, do not become bogged down in it.

Recording Information

Most good researchers or investigators realize that research itself can change the way they view a topic. As you conduct research, some topic facets will take on more importance; some become less important. As you work your way through your research materials you will find yourself adjusting and limiting the information that you actually plan to present to your audience. While you do this, keep your mind open: new and exciting roads for inquiry will surface only if you are willing to explore them. If your explorations are to be meaningful, you will need to decide how to chart or record your discoveries—that is, the information you hope to use. When gathering information, for example, Detective Columbo always carried a small notebook. Real-life officers of the law carry similar notebooks. What will you carry with you?

Many researchers record their notes in a notebook, allocating a new page for every source they use; for you this makes it easier to organize and document your work once it is time to construct your speech. Others suggest that you record your notes on 4 X 6 cards instead, which allows you to literally shuffle the cards into the order in which you will use the information in your presentation. Try this approach.

- Use a bibliography card for each basic article you reference.
- Record the title, author, and subject on the top of each card.
- Record one bit of information per card.

For examples of what note cards look like, see Figure 7.7. Notice how each card contains a direct quotation from the material or paraphrased information.

Using a laptop computer can also facilitate taking notes. By entering your research into a word processor or a database, all the information you need to complete your speech is at your fingertips. What is more significant, you are easily able to move information around to wherever you need it or want to use it in the speech itself. You will want to treat each computer page as you would a note card. If you are computer literate and extremely comfortable with a portable computer, you may want to try this approach. However, if you are not particularly proficient, you may want to leave the computer at home and stay with the hard copy notes for now.

Whose Words Are You Using, Anyway?

As you take notes, be sure to give each source correct attribution to avoid the potential appearance of plagiarism. Giving sources the credit due them not only protects you but also increases your credibility. When you cite, quote, or paraphrase another source, it lets the audience know that you have taken the time to prepare and research the speech. Let your research show. Do not ever cover it up or try to claim ideas that belong to someone else as your own.

Credit must be given where credit is due. When you use the work of another, note it. Audiences do not expect you to have developed all of the ideas contained in your speech. Thus, during the presentation you will need to provide oral citations or

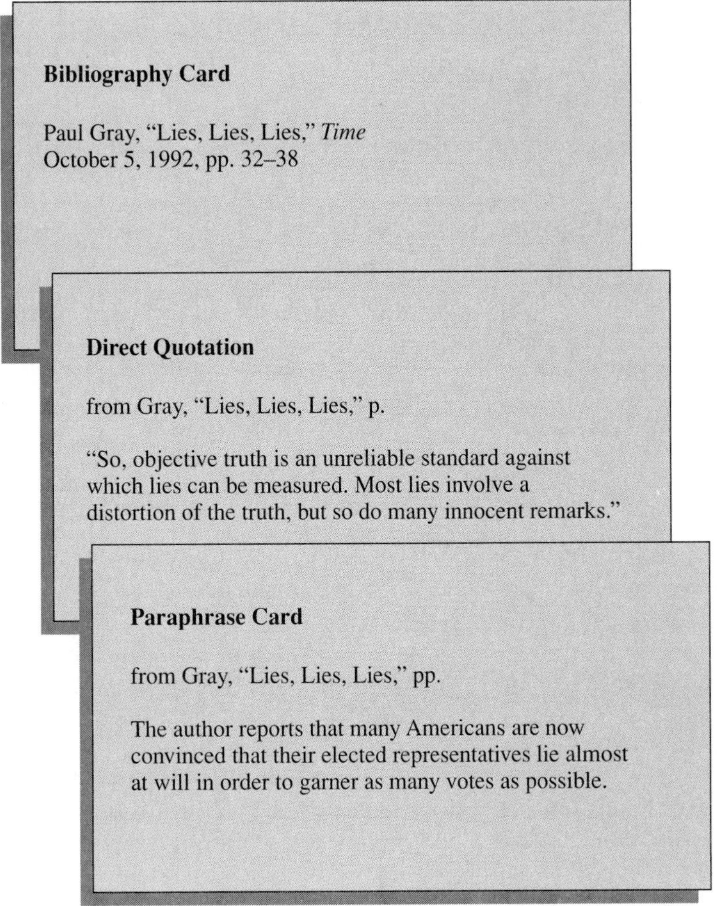

Figure 7.7

Sample note cards. Using bibliography, direct quotation, and paraphrase cards will greatly increase the speed and accuracy of your information gathering for presentations.

footnotes. Such citations are not difficult to include as long as you have done your research and recorded your information carefully. What do you say in an oral citation? Here are some samples.

If you are citing a speech or article, you might say:

> "In his January speech on economic indicators, President Bill Clinton told a Washington audience. . . ."
>
> "According to the World Almanac last year. . . ."

If you are using a direct quotation, state the name of the author and the source:

> "In her book *You Just Don't Understand,* researcher Deborah Tannen tells her readers. . . ."

If you are paraphrasing a book or article, you might tell your audience:

> "Harvey Mackay, corporate president and author of the best seller Beware the Naked Man Who Offers You His Shirt feels that most Americans are simply too gullible for their own good."

As you build your speech you bring experts onto your team in order to gain credibility and give your message the maximum impact.

Demographic Research Team

Some people conduct research for a living. Connie and Jim Hughes are two such people. Working in New Jersey, they conduct research for both the U.S. government and academic audiences. The following commentary explores their work.[4]

In her role as keeper of New Jersey's vital statistics, Connie O. Hughes offers an example of the questions posed to her every day: "Parents of single women frequently ask, 'Can you tell me where there is a high concentration of young men?'"

Her answer: Rahway—home of the state prison.

With one-liners like that, Connie Hughes might be a tough act to follow. So, for a headliner at her annual conference on how to get and use information from the U.S. Census, she turned for the second year in a row to a proven crowd pleaser: her husband James Hughes.

Tracing the state's changing income patterns, he addressed the common perception that people are either poor and happy or rich and miserable: "Most New Jerseyans wisely ask, 'Couldn't we be moderately wealthy and just moody?'"

Meet Jim and Connie Hughes, the first couple of demography. He's a tweedy professor. She's a government official in a business suit. He can be wry. She can be witty. They can get very esoteric, but they prefer to keep it light.

"If you need to know the latest scoop on something, call Jim or Connie," says Judy McKinney-Cherry, a friend who lives in Delaware. "Jim just sort of has a knack for knowing what is *avant garde*." McKinney-Cherry recently sought his opinion on what's hot in men's briefcases.

When Jim's phone rings on the Rutgers University campus in New Brunswick, it's often a reporter seeking a pithy interpretation of the latest figures on home-building or employment. He rarely disappoints, which is why he may be the most quoted "expert" in the state.

He makes about 30 major speeches a year, before groups ranging from realtors and builders to professors of what he calls "pure demographics"—theorists who study subjects such as "fertility patterns in Punjab from 1850 to 1870," he says. "Some academics only like to speak in front of academic audiences at traditional academic conferences," Jim says. He adds that he feels an obligation to serve the community by sharing his views with other groups, even though some can be hostile.

How Many Sources Should You Use?

After all of this research has been done, the question that invariably is asked is, "How many sources do I really need?" Of course the topic and the available material will be a major part of that answer. However, if you are looking for a guideline you can keep the "rule of three" in mind. It is sometimes suggested that when you are looking for material you should aim for three sources for every minute of the presentation. So if you need to prepare a five-minute speech, you would start with a goal of fifteen sources. As you work, however, you will quickly find that many of those sources are not appropriate to the presentation, and you can then refine the materials to the "rule of one." That is, you will probably want to refer to at least one source for every minute of your presentation.

Do not become too hung up on these rules. They are just rules of thumb or guidelines to let you know when you are in the ballpark. If you selected eighty sources for your five-minute presentation you would know that you have probably located far more information than you could use and thus you would need to narrow them down to the most important sources available to you. If, on the other hand, you

"You tell the builders in 1989–1990 that every industry in America has been restructured and housing most likely is next on the list—that's not a pleasant message," he says, recounting experiences.

"If I say that the '81 tax act was the cause of the overbuilding and a lot of the excess problems we have today, like the S&L crisis, that's not a pleasant message to all bodies out there. . . ." Jim has written or co-written 32 books, many of them in collaboration with his mentor, George Sternlieb. Together they tackled some of the thorniest issues with brutal frankness. In *The Atlantic City Gamble,* a 1983 analysis of why legalized gaming didn't fulfill its promise of reviving the seaside resort, they concluded: "The costs of New Jersey's style of casino gambling as a means of revitalization far outweigh its virtues."

Sternlieb gave Jim his first assignment as a demographer. In 1968 he sent him out in the middle of winter to interview marina owners along the shore for a state-sponsored study of waterfront land use.

Jim survived that task and went on to team up with Sternlieb as national experts on housing trends and the effect of population changes on housing demand. In the Eighties, when the study of demographics—previously known as population characteristics—came into vogue, the pair contributed articles to *American Demographics* magazine. Sternlieb also hired Connie at Rutgers, after she found teaching high school math in Elizabeth less than challenging. . . . As director of the State Data Center for the past 12 years, Connie's primary responsibility has been to serve as a conduit of statistical information. She is the first to receive information from the U.S. Census Bureau, the agency in Washington that regularly attempts to define America by the characteristics of its population. Jim is usually the second.

"When the unemployment rate comes out, Connie's able to get me that stuff by 8:30 A.M.," says Jim, "so by a quarter of nine, we've had a discussion on why did the unemployment rate go up or down, what does it signify."

Jim actually confesses to waiting "with bated breath" for the data on median annual incomes that are released every 10 years. "That's when it's sort of anxious time. . . . You're anxious to see what happened up or down."

After more than a dozen years in their respective positions, can these two really get worked up about one more set of numbers?

"We're boring," Connie says. To hear them tell it, the Hugheses are just a couple of dull workaholics, ruled by their work. But McKinney-Cherry disputes that. She sees them as hip and funny, despite their reputations for analytical number-crunching.

could find only one source of information for your speech, the "rule of three" tells you that you have far too little material and that you need to go back to the purpose of the speech to see if you can adjust it so that other materials that are available can also be used. For example, if you want to talk about the current effect of AIDS on your hometown and you find only one newspaper article, you would need to return to your investigation and broaden the scope of your work to include the surrounding county or even your state.

DRY CLEANING

In the early 1700's a mistake molded into what many believed to have been magic. After turpentine was accidentally spilled on a dirty table cloth, well, the cloth was then meticulously clean. Soon after, this amazing discovery transpired into a scientific method of removing dirt from fabrics. Well, today we call this process dry

Does the speaker's introduction set the right tone?

Are the speaker's definitions of terms clear?

Why does the speaker cite this source?

cleaning. Actually, the term "dry cleaning" is a misnomer. The process merely does not use water. The clothes themselves are soaked in a toxic solvent called perchlorothalene, otherwise known as perc, which substitutes for turpentine and revolutionized the dry cleaning industry as well as our health. According to the Galveston/Houston Association for Smog Prevention home page, last updated on January 28, 1996, perc is a chemical that is listed under the Clean Air Act as a hazardous air pollutant and carcinogen. Its residue is even considered a hazardous waste. Yet today more than 80 percent of U.S. dry cleaners rely on this toxic solvent. In the past, clothes made of such fine fabrics needed to be worn until they become so filthy they needed to be thrown away. Well, clothes continue to be a luxury and in a world that demands such fine fabrics to fulfill so many needs, we can no longer afford to throw away our lives and our health, with perc prevalent in our threats.

Evaluate the speech preview. Does it prepare you for what is to come?

Therefore, to best combat the threat of perc we must first understand the negative ramifications of dry cleaning that affect our health, then reveal some of the ineffective measures of governmental and industrial control of this toxic process, and finally learn some of the realistic measures we can adopt to keep our clothes and our health clean.

Can you follow the speaker's point easily?

Do you recognize this source?

Dry cleaning has turned itself into an art and a science. We incorporate the cleaning into high, fast style. However, the history of dry cleaning . . . well, it's really quite humble. The process has gone from petroleum solvents that burst into flame into what many have believed to have been a safe solvent—perc. So finally the *World and I* on November 5, 1995, reveals that up to 40 to 50 percent of the five hundred million pounds of perc produced annually is by dry cleaners.

Will receivers respond to the speaker's use of this source?

Of what value are these examples?

Do you find this source credibile? Why or why not?

The main route for human exposure is via inhalation, but this chemical has also been known to be passed through skin and mouth contact. It is extremely soluble when in blood. According to the Information Ventures home page, last updated on March 3, 1996, this chemical has also been known to be spread through blood, water, and other toxic solvents. In a study done at the University of California of individuals who frequented dry cleaning establishments at least three times a month, there were found decreased fertility and misshapen sperm in men, and pregnant women experienced nearly five times the rate of spontaneous abortions. In other studies, individuals were found to have a high incidence of pelvic cancer. And children who were exposed to perc solvent through water had an unusually high incidence of leukemia. New York City apartment owner Sue Kassier, well, she's living proof of these studies. After experiencing a toxic odor coming from her bedroom vent, Kassier was later diagnosed with upper respiratory problems and retinal nerve destruction. These enhanced perc levels are due largely to the emissions from the clothing of dry cleaning workers. And according to the November 1995 issue of *The Archives of Environmental Health,* the exhalations from the lungs of dry cleaning workers are actually toxic. Perc is not particular in choosing its victims but finds it easiest to attack individuals who live in neighborhoods near dry cleaning establishments.

Furthermore, perc is passed even easier through water than air. This toxic solvent has a capability of seeping into water systems at all different levels. According to the *University of California at Berkeley Wellness Letter* of October 1995, this chemical is extremely dangerous when in water because of its density. Well, this becomes even more dangerous to us because perc is colorless and odorless when in water. But unfortunately, our problem does not stop at perc itself, but also is a result of the feeble attempts at governmental and industrial control which have left us with hazardous conditions. Yet the Clean Air Act was enacted in 1990. Measures taken to lower levels of perc required dry cleaning establishments to utilize upscale machinery. However, dry cleaning establishments like Robert Geruso's found many drawbacks. According to *Dateline News,* which aired on October 11, 1995, Geruso found that the cost of this machinery would be nearly a quarter of a million dollars—money that Geruso cannot afford. The unfortunate news goes on. The cost of this machinery will then fall to the customer.

How do you feel about the speaker using popular media as support?

Other industrial alternatives have left both customers and dry cleaners unhappy. Such is a process called eco-clean. Oh, what a brilliant idea in theory. However, it has failed us both on our clothes and our budgets. According to the *London Business Monthly Magazine* of January 1996, the British described eco-clean as gentle hand scrubbing which relies solely upon water and soap. However, dry cleaning establishments and consumers found this to be both labor intensive and unsatisfactory with heavily soiled garments. The government is not solely to blame for our problems with perc. Many of the measures taken thus far have been with good intention; however, perc is still surrounding us. We may think we are doomed and we are. We seem to bring contamination home with us.

Does the use of information derived from another country add credibility?

In a personal interview with Maureen Carney, head of the biology department at the University of Wisconsin at Madison, conducted on February 17, 1996, she explained that most dry cleaning establishments have failed to identify the problem. For example, among the tests that are run before the purchase of a new home, perc levels are not tested like radon, lead, or carbon dioxide. She went on to explain that any level of perchlorothalene exceeding a hundred and twenty micrograms was reason enough to worry and get out. The power of Carney's words was illustrated in a study done by Dr. Donna Felkner. Felkner placed four freshly dry cleaned suits in nine different homes. She later discovered that seven of the nine homes were heavily contaminated with the perc solvent, enough to have adversely affected the health of a young baby or child.

Was the speaker's use of this source a wise choice?

Fortunately, there are steps we can initiate on our own. Examining clothing well is perhaps our first step in cutting down our costs and perc. Many of us take our clothing to the dry cleaners when there is very little to actually clean. Occasional spotting can be taken care of at home with a gentle sponge and Ivory soap. Other simple steps can save lives, including selecting darker color dress clothing. Timothy Raymond of Pendleton Wool explains most men's and women's suits if dark can withstand five to six wearings before true dry cleaning is needed. If dry cleaning is imperative in your life, chemist Bonnie Pereria has now created the home dry cleaning kit. This kit includes a glycerol ether solvent bag made from 90 percent seaweed and carrageen. The process is simple, effective, but most importantly, it is safe. Perhaps, most important, are the plastic bags in which we bring our clothing home. According to the aforementioned *Dateline News* these garments should be placed outside on a porch or deck for ten to fifteen minutes. If a toxic odor continues to come from that garment after three hours you should no longer have your clothing dry cleaned at that certain establishment. If you live near a dry cleaning facility you may be exposed to high levels of perc. According to the aforementioned Galveston/Houston Association for Smog Prevention home page, in a study done in New York City of seventeen apartments above dry cleaning establishments, the air was found to be one thousand times the level considered safe. By informing your local EPA office you can have a free perc test done on your dwelling and quite possibly have that dry cleaning establishment shut down.

How do you evaluate the use of this source?

Does the word "aforementioned" bother you?

Dry cleaning at this point may sound like a pretty dry idea. Having fresh, clean clothes doesn't have to be. Having first understood the negative ramifications of cleaning that affect our health, then having revealed some of the ineffective measures of governmental and industrial control, and finally learning some of the real-

Does the conclusion fulfill its purpose?

istic measures we can adopt to keep our clothes and our house clean, hopefully we can end this mystery to science. In the eighteenth century turpentine was merely a mystery to scientists, however, if we can open up our lives and make today's new discovery . . . this new toxic solvent . . . perc, too, will be part of our past.

Research calls on you to make judgment calls—just like coaches are expected to do in sports. Every coach makes judgment calls every game. She or he must decide whether to have the team run or pass (football), whether to use a zone or one-on-one defense (basketball), whether to try for the spike or merely make an attempt to return the serve (volleyball), or whether to walk or pitch to the best batter (baseball/softball).

As a researcher you do exactly the same thing. You decide which materials will be of the most interest to your audience, which materials will help you make the best case, and which visuals can bring your presentation to life. These are all judgment calls similar to those made by athletic coaches. Of course, immediately after the game and on into the next day the audience members will "Monday morning quarterback" your calls. That is, audience members—whether student peers or business associates—will decide whether you have selected information that is relevant and important to them. It is amazing that when things work well, the coach gets little credit for making the right calls. Every fan claims he or she would have made the same decisions! The same is true of a speech. If the presentation is well researched, your audience members will not even notice it. They will remember the important information. It will almost seem to them as if the presentation developed itself naturally. When they begin to notice the speech and its lack of appropriate information, then you have to worry about the judgment calls you have made while conducting your research. Being an athletic coach is not an easy job. Neither is researching a speech.

SPEAKING of CRITICAL THINKING

How Sound Is the Research?

In her speech on dry cleaning (page 151) student Suzi Kim drew on personal experience, interviews, home pages, and published articles as she researched her presentation on the use of the chemical perc in dry cleaning. After reading the transcript and/or viewing her speech on videotape, answer these questions:

- Did the speaker interview the best people? Why or why not?
- How many different sources did the speaker use? Were they equally effective? Explain.
- How do you feel about Suzi's use of home pages as sources? How else might she have used the Internet?
- What additional kinds of source materials, if any, might the speaker have benefited from using?
- Did any speechmaking errors impede the speaker's effectiveness? Explain.
- To what degree was the speaker able to realize her speaking goal?

SUMMARY

AN EFFECTIVE SPEAKER KNOWS WHERE and how to locate information to use in a speech; thus the speaker makes a concerted effort to gather as much relevant information as he or she can when preparing to speak. The information a speaker uses is typically derived from various sources including personal experience, interviews, private and government organizations and associations, the library, and computer-assisted searches.

By using personal experience, a speaker enhances his or her credibility and adds believability to his or her presentation. By conducting interviews with authorities on a subject, the speaker comes into direct contact with recognized experts and invests the presentation with even greater validity and relevance. Library and computer-assisted research further enhances the information storehouse of the speaker by enabling him or her to discover and integrate the latest in objective, authoritative information into the speeches.

Once a speaker has gathered as much relevant information as possible in the time available to him or her, he or she then needs to evaluate the materials amassed and take notes from those he or she will use. Once this is done, the speaker will be better prepared to meet the speechmaker's challenge.

THE SPEAKER'S STAND

Select a topic that interests you. Go to the library and locate as much information as possible related to the topic. Classify the material that you find into appropriate groups such as scholarly, professional, or popular. Determine whom you might interview for such a project.

The following checklist can help you as you begin your research.

RESEARCH CHECKLIST

- _____Preliminary purpose
- _____Card catalogue (if applicable)
- _____Computerized catalogue
- _____Periodical indexes
- _____Newspaper indexes
- _____Research room
  - _____General encyclopedias
  - _____Specialized encyclopedias
  - _____Yearbooks
  - _____Biographical references
  - _____Dictionaries
  - _____Quotation books
  - _____Atlases and gazetteers
- _____Computerized sources and databases
  - _____Library databases (if necessary)
  - _____Consumer databases (AOL, Compu-Serv, etc.)
  - _____World Wide Web
- _____Potential interviewees selected
  - _____Interview times determined (by phone or in person)
- _____Materials ordered
  - _____Government sources
  - _____Appropriate special interest groups
- _____Additional research materials

Bring the material you gather to class and discuss the research procedures you used with your class or your group.

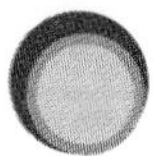

STUDENT FOCUS GROUP REPORT

Take some time to consider what you have learned about researching a speech. In a group of five to seven students, answer these questions:

1. Revisit the case study and questions at the beginning of this chapter. To what extent, if any, would you change your answers?
2. How much of your preparation time should you devote to conducting research? Why?
3. What kinds of challenges do you anticipate facing during various phases of the research process?
4. What specific areas of the library do you now understand better than you did before reading this chapter?
5. How important is it to conduct interviews as part of your research? What do you do if you do not know anyone who is an expert in a particular subject area?
6. How important is it to use the Internet when conducting research?
7. What are the key lessons you have learned about conducting research?

Chapter Eight

Supporting What You Say

How to Integrate Supporting Materials into Your Speech

After reading this chapter, you should be able to:

- Explain why supporting materials are important for effective speechmaking.
- Identify and define the following types of support available to speakers: specific instances and illustrations, explanations and descriptions, definitions and analogies, statistics, and testimony.
- Employ specific criteria to evaluate the effectiveness of supporting materials.
- Select and integrate an array of supporting materials into a speech.

CASE STUDY

The Sleeper

Salima had to develop a research-based oral presentation on sleep deprivation for her psychology class. She had chosen her topic because she believed that her personal experiences qualified her as an expert on the subject.

Salima sat down at the word processor and wrote page after page describing her personal experiences with sleep deprivation. She talked about the number of all nighters she had pulled when studying for midterms; the countless late-night hours she had spent conversing via the Internet with friends around the world; the people she had played interactive video games with, often well into the wee hours of the morning; the fun she had had club hopping; and the effects that such habits had on her behavior both inside and outside the classroom, including instances when she nodded off during lectures, failed pop quizzes, forgot to go to class, or fell asleep during a meal or when driving.

Upon finishing what she thought was an excellent overview of the current sleep deprivation crisis in America, Salima pushed "print" and left the dorm for another night of revelry. On her way out, she bumped into her friend Carla, who was also in her psychology class. Carla was loaded down with an array of books, magazines, xeroxes of journal articles, and a tape recorder.

"What's all that for?" Salima asked.

"For my presentation on the effects of designer drugs," answered Carla.

"Oh!" noted Salima. "Obviously you don't have personal experience with your topic like I have with mine. Poor you—having to do all that research just to come up with supporting materials. You should have selected an easier subject. Well, good luck! See you in the morning." And with that, Salima was gone.

- Who is likely to be better prepared to give a good presentation, Salima or Carla? Explain.
- What specific advice would you give Salima prior to the presentation of her project?

WHAT DISTINGUISHES EFFECTIVE SPEECHES from ineffective speeches? What distinguishes good speakers from poor ones? First, effective speeches contain an array of relevant materials that help support the speechmaker's point of view. Second, good speakers know how to evaluate and select those materials that will add force to their ideas and help build a case. When you use them wisely, supporting materials provide the substance, believability, and impact your speech needs if audience members are to understand it clearly, judge its contents to be credible, and assess you to be an appealing and competent spokesperson.

Consider the questions you ask yourself when listening to a speaker. If you are a conscientious receiver you listen critically; you're not interested in puffery, unsubstantiated generalizations, or hot air. Instead, you relish concrete support. Thus, in your search for understanding you wage a mental battle with the speaker:

What do you mean? you inquire silently.
Why should I accept what you say?
Why should I care?

Effective speakers like the Reverend Jesse Jackson know how to provide the substance that audience members need to understand a speech.

If the speech is well developed, the answers to each of these questions will surface clearly and creatively. If, on the other hand, the speech fails to supply answers to these questions, it most likely will fail to capture and sustain your interest. More than likely, it will fail to give you the justification and information you need to keep you from dismissing it as unworthy of your time and attention.

THE CRITICALLY THINKING AUDIENCE

AS YOU LOOK CAREFULLY at your audience members, you will find that they have their own criteria for evaluating your claims, your authority and credibility, and the evidence you show them. As you bring evidence to bear, you must think critically about what evidence your audience can accept as authoritative. Later we will explore in more detail the "credibility factor" as it relates to both testimony and the speechmaker.

Speeches are much like hot air balloons. When they are filled with support that amplifies, clarifies, and sustains the ideas contained in them, speeches are fed with the fuel that allows them to take off and reach their destination successfully. When the right mixture of fuel is missing, however, they are carried aimlessly by the wind of a voice filled, as William Shakespeare said, "with sound and fury signifying nothing," and they are left to fall flat on deaf ears. Thus, it is essential for speechmakers to search diligently for materials that bolster their ideas. As you fuel your speech with support ask yourself these questions:

1. Do the materials I am using help me communicate my ideas more clearly and creatively?
2. Are the examples I am including useful and representative?
3. Am I incorporating relevant, reliable, and solid statistics?

4. Am I referring to the testimony of qualified unbiased sources?
5. Am I using support that is relevant and appropriate to my audience?
6. Am I using support that audience members will find moving and memorable?
7. Am I using a variety of supporting materials to build my speech?

The types of support discussed in this chapter will serve you well as you prepare to meet the speechmaker's challenge. As we explore each of the main kinds of supporting materials, we'll examine its use, how it can add substance and interest to your message, and how it can help you build a body of content that stands firm and strong when critically evaluated by your listeners.

THE POWER OF EXAMPLES AND ILLUSTRATIONS

WHEN YOU TAKE A VAGUE, lifeless, impersonal idea and fuse it with an effective example or illustration, you end up with a piece of vivid, concrete, and personal support that influences listeners' beliefs and behaviors more than any other kind of supporting material.[1] Examples and illustrations turn the general into the specific, the unfocused into the focused, and the dull into the interesting. As social psychologist Eliot Aronson notes, "Most people are more deeply influenced by one clear, vivid personal example than by an abundance of statistical data."[2] Because everyone likes to hear stories, it is examples that can breathe life into a speech.

Kinds of Examples

Speakers use different kinds of examples in order to fulfill specific speechmaking needs. Among the many kinds are *specific instances, illustrations,* and *hypothetical examples.*

Specific Instances. Brief examples, also known as **specific instances,** are referred to by speakers to support points they are trying to make. Although brief examples are typically no longer than a sentence or two, when you use them in a series (that is, when you pile one on top of another) they gain power and help you create a desired impression. Why do speakers pile brief example on top of brief example rather than simply offer their listeners a single example? Simply because skeptical audience members might dismiss a single example as unrepresentative of the situation being considered or atypical. In contrast, when linked in a series, examples help demonstrate a message's validity more forcefully.

In her speech "Let's Stop Fooling Ourselves," Claudette Mackay-Lassonde, chairman and CEO of Enghouse Systems Limited, uses a series of brief examples to convince her audience that her more general statement—that no person can have it all—is true.

> Look at the media images of modern-day success. When we read about someone famous, the overall tone is one of aggressive, hyped-up success. This month's *Vanity Fair* magazine has Sharon Stone on the cover with the headline "She wants it all." A while back, a business magazine cover asked "What does Bill Gates really want?" Inside, we find out there are few things that Bill Gates doesn't want. *Working Woman* magazine last summer profiled Martha Stewart. We learn from the article that "whatever Martha wants, Martha gets." . . .
>
> One survey found that more than half of the men polled said they would give up as much as a quarter of their salary to have more family or personal time. . . .

Another survey, this one by the Families and Work Institute in New York, looked at what factors influence people to take a particular job. One of the most important was "the job's effect on family and personal life." . . .

There was an interesting piece in the *Wall Street Journal* late last year that looked at the aspirations of the daughters of some successful career women. In every case, these young women opted for a greater role in the family rather than the fast track.[3]

In addition to providing proof and clarifying a speaker's position, specific instances help involve audience members in the speaker's topic by adding human interest to the speech.

Illustrations. Extended examples are also known as **illustrations,** narratives, or anecdotes. More detailed and vivid than brief examples, extended examples are built very much like a story: they open, reveal a complication, contain a climax, and describe a resolution. Though extended examples are longer, and thus consume more of the speechmaker's speaking time, when well planned and placed they are also more emotionally compelling and add a real sense of drama to the speech.

Kellie Rider used an extended example to introduce her speech "Happily Ever After?" to convince audience members that marital rape should be a crime.

Jane was just an average girl from an average town. She met Bill at a high school dance. They dated for three years, went on to college together and soon were married. Two years later, little Patricia was born. Sounds like a storybook romance doesn't it? Boy meets girl, boy and girl fall in love, get married and live happily ever after. In Jane's case happily ever after never came. You see, Jane is a woman I've counseled for almost a year. Because Bill began to take his frustrations out on Jane, by beating her violently, and demanding sex on call. One time, Jane refused his demands, Bill threw her to the bed, with a gun to her head, and tied her up. When she began to scream and fight he wrapped the phone cord around and around her neck to keep her quiet; she almost couldn't breathe. While she lay there, helpless, with the gun on the night stand, he repeatedly raped and sodomized her. When he was finished he just left her there. Sometime later, she got herself loose. She had bruises on her wrists, ankles, throat, inner thighs, breasts, and vaginal areas.

Jane was terrified for her life and the life of her baby, so she decided to report the rape to the police. But they told her she had brought it on herself and couldn't prosecute Bill. You see, in forty-five states, a man cannot be prosecuted for raping his wife.[4]

In like fashion, Brian Swenson used an extended example to involve listeners in his speech, "Gun Safety and Children."

Kunkleton, PA—At first, police feared a sniper was loose. It was March 6 and, up on Hideaway Hill, 7 year old Jessica Ann Carr had been shot once in the back as she and a friend rode a snowmobile. Terrified neighbors screamed for other children to come inside, then cried and prayed as ambulance workers tried in vain to save the little girl. That night, police officers found a suspect with a bloody, crescent-shaped gash on his forehead. It matched the telescopic sight of a Marlin .35 caliber hunting rifle found in an upstairs bedroom. Soon, the suspect confessed that he had fired the gun.

But tragedy is still tearing at this tiny Poconos Mountain community. Police say the killer is Cameron R. Kocher, a 9 year old Cub Scout, Bible class leader, and honor-roll student. And if prosecutors have their way, Kocher may be the youngest person ever tried for murder in a U.S. adult court.[5]

By touching audience members in the way a generalization never could, this example helps the speaker pull listeners into his speech and focuses their attention on the issue at hand.

Hypothetical Examples. The examples cited in the preceding sections were factual. Sometimes, however, you will find it useful to refer to examples that describe imaginary situations. When you integrate brief or extended examples that have not actually occurred into your speeches, you are using **hypothetical examples.** In order for these examples to fulfill their purpose, audiences must accept that the hypothetical scenarios you create could really happen. The function of hypothetical examples is not to trick your listeners into believing something that is not true. Rather, you use hypothetical examples when either you are unable to find a factual example, whether brief or extended, that suits your purpose; you want to exaggerate your point; or you want to encourage your audience members to suspend disbelief and imagine themselves facing a particular scenario. Sometimes, rather than being totally contrived, the hypothetical situations you cite will really be a synthesis of actual situations, people, or events. But be careful. If you use hypothetical examples that are too far-fetched, audience members won't judge the example credible and thus your example will fail to fulfill its prime purpose of support.

As you read the following hypothetical examples used by students Kurstin Finch and Pam Espinosa, respectively, ask yourself which sets the scene most effectively:

Congratuations! You have all been invited to play "Choose Your Own Personality," and take a spin at the Prozac wheel. What will you win? A legitimate cure to chronic depression? A chance at one of a dozen annoying and dangerous side effects? Or maybe a whole new personality! It could be worse. You could win a date with Pat Sajak.[6]

I'd like you to imagine you're working in a laboratory. It's long past quitting time and you're fighting the intense desire to say, "to heck with it all," and go home. But you're paid by how many slides you process, and, as of right now, you haven't met your quota. So, it's back to work, no matter how tired you are or what you may miss.[7]

The next hypothetical example is an amalgam, or composite, of actual people and their situations. Notice how the speaker lets you know that the example described did not actually occur.

An elderly man, we'll call him Sam, enjoys a relatively healthy lifestyle. He is taking Tenormen for moderate high blood pressure and has developed a nagging wheeze. Sam decides to go to his doctor to see about alleviating the problem. Instead of switching Sam's medication, his doctor prescribes Theophylline, an asthma medication which upsets Sam's stomach and makes him so jittery he can't sleep. To treat his stomach his doctor prescribes Tagamet, which makes Sam confused and disoriented. To treat the jitteriness and the insomnia, his doctor prescribes Valium. In addition to causing mental confusion, Tagamet also increases the level of Valium in Sam's blood system thus making the drug more toxic. So Sam has Tagamet causing confusion, and higher levels of Valium causing disorientation. His condition continues to deteriorate and he is eventually diagnosed as having senile dementia: senility. Feeling at the end of his rope, Sam decides to go to another doctor and inquires if his medication could have anything to do with his problem. Absolutely.[8]

Culture and Gender Factors in Examples

As we search for supporting materials we open ourselves to learn about others and where cultures intersect. We can use support to question our assumptions and expectations, connect ouselves to our receivers, and bridge whatever differences may exist. As a result we may discover what is taboo or accepted in various cultures, as well as the extent to which persons are defined by gender, class, or ethnic affiliation.

Every speaking situation requires you to think about how your examples and evidence will affect your listeners. In particular, you need to be alert to your own assumptions, which are sometimes hidden, about the relevance and value of the example. If you are a male athlete and you concentrate most of your examples on football stories, you may be likely to lose the half of your audience that is female. If you are a native speaker of English and tell a number of stories involving subtle understanding of American idiom, you may lose much of your audience if a larger number of them are recent immigrants. Again, you must evaluate not only the beliefs and values of your audience, but your own beliefs and attitudes toward examples that may not be particularly pertinent to those you are addressing.

Take the time to think critically about the nature of the support being used when assessing its value. Ask yourself about the distinguishing characteristics of the support, if a particular group is excluded as a result of the kind of support selected, if the support used implies that the audience is characterized by homogeneity or diversity, and if cultures other than White Americans would find the support acceptable. For example, although White Americans in general, and males in particular, tend to rely heavily on data when evaluating information, they still appreciate the inclusion of illustrations rich in human interest. Female White Americans, as well as other groups including Native Americans, Latinos, African Americans, and Asian Americans, are also apt to judge examples and illustrations drawn from real life as valuable forms of support.[9]

CONSIDERING DIVERSITY

It's in the Example

What role does cultural diversity play in a speaker's choice of examples? Speakers define their attitudes toward their subject, at least in part, by the examples and illustrations they share with their receivers. If a person is addressing an audience, how might culture and gender affect the kind of examples chosen or the way the examples will be received? For instance, how would you feel about speakers who used examples that implied that all African Americans are athletically gifted, all homosexuals are effeminate, all Arabs want revolutionary change, or all men keep women from achieving their rightful places in corporations?

First, consider this: How do you think audiences of mostly women, mostly men, or mixed genders would react to the examples used in this excerpt from a speech by Sheila Wellington, president of Catalyst, an organization that believes gender should not be a factor in the workplace?

> . . . [W]e asked, "What holds women back from the highest ranks?" CEOs in the survey said that women "lack management experience," and "haven't been in the pipeline long enough." The women, in concert with the CEOs, pointed to lack of line experience as holding them back, but listed it third. The biggest barriers to their advancement, the women said, were "male stereotyping" and "exclusion from informal networks." Not sexism. Not misogynism, but informal exclusion. Stereotypes, those unexamined assumptions, those outdated practices,

(continued)

Considering Diversity *(continued)*

To what extent, if any, does the gender of the audience affect the speaker's choice of supporting materials?

> those undone programs and policies that are keeping our nation's talent pool from virtually doubling with ease. Thus, the women were more than twice as likely as CEOs to consider factors in the work environment, in the culture of the job, as barriers to advancement. CEOs were more than twice as likely as the women to fault "not being in the pipeline long enough."
>
> Clearly, most women respondents do not agree with CEOs that it's simply a matter of time until they catch up with men.[10]

Next, consider the following hypothetical illustration a male speaker used in a speech he delivered on the spread of the AIDS epidemic.

> A recently divorced man went to a singles bar where he met a very pretty woman. They drank, chatted, and danced for a while, shared a mutual physical attraction, and ended the evening by going to his apartment where they made love a number of times before falling asleep. When the man awoke the following morning, the woman had already departed. Rising, he went into his bathroom, only to be startled by what he saw written on the bathroom mirror: Written in bright red lipstick, the message left by the woman read: "Welcome to the world of AIDS."

The speaker went on to tell his audience members that the woman had contracted AIDS from a former male lover and, filled with anger, she sought to avenge her affliction by infecting as many men as she could. The speaker revealed that while there was no evidence for the story's truth and no reason to believe it actually happened, it served a purpose in warning that AIDS is a sexually transmitted disease that is spread not only through drug injection and homosexual sex, but also through heterosexual sex.

Evaluate the use of the preceding example in light of this information: There is more evidence of men infecting women with the AIDS virus than there is of women infecting men. Given this statistical reality, and the fact that the story was hypothetical, should the speaker have made the vindictive spreader of the disease male rather than female? Would a woman delivering the speech have reversed the roles?

Finally, consider the effects achieved by both of these speakers. What does each speaker's use of examples or hypothetical illustration reveal about culture, our attitudes toward sex, and men and women? To what extent, if any, do you think speakers should adjust the presentation of their supporting materials to consider the reactions caused by cultural and/or gender differences in their audiences?

Putting Power in the Examples You Use

Whether you use real or hypothetical, brief or extended examples, what matters most is that the examples you do use reinforce, clarify, and personalize your ideas, as well as relate directly to your listeners. If you think of yourself as a storyteller, and each example used as a key part of your story, then you'll be better able to use your words, your voice, and your body to paint mental pictures that involve, touch, and bring your listeners into the center of your story's plot. To do this successfully, you need to search for and/or create examples that your listeners can readily get excited about and identify with. Use the following checklist to gauge the power of your examples.

	Yes	No
1. Are the examples you cite typical?	❑	❑
2. Do the examples you cite involve people?	❑	❑
3. Do the examples you cite make abstract ideas more concrete?	❑	❑
4. Do the examples you cite clarify your message?	❑	❑
5. Are the examples you cite directly relevant to your message?	❑	❑
6. Are the examples you cite vivid—that is, are they filled with details?	❑	❑
7. Can you relate your examples to your audience without relying excessively on your notes?	❑	❑
8. Can you use speaking rate and volume to increase the impact of your examples?	❑	❑
9. Will your listeners readily identify with your examples?	❑	❑
10. Are your listeners able to accept your examples as credible without straining to do so?	❑	❑

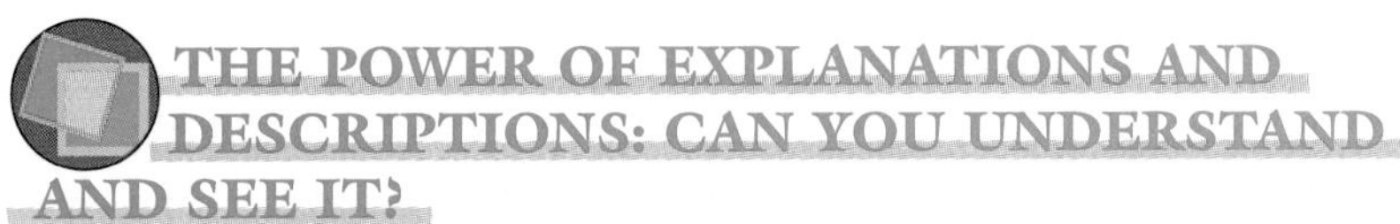

THE POWER OF EXPLANATIONS AND DESCRIPTIONS: CAN YOU UNDERSTAND AND SEE IT?

WE USE EXPLANATIONS and descriptions frequently when talking to others. We use explanations to clarify what we have said, and we use descriptions to help those we interact with imagine they can see, hear, smell, touch, taste, or feel what we do. Public speakers use explanations and descriptions similarly. If you believe your audience might be unfamiliar with your topic or could be confused by information you are about to share, then you might choose to head off audience members' questions before the fact by including an explanation. Likewise, if you want to be certain to arouse the senses of your receivers, you will make it your business to include language rich in sensory detail. The better you are at anticipating an audience's questions, the better you are at explaining your ideas to your listeners. The better you are at awakening sensory responses in audience members, the better you are at description.

Explanations

Both Terrika Scott and Ann Lorentson, college students, anticipated a lack of subject familiarity on the part of their audiences, and so used **explanations.** In Terrika's case, that information was how education during early U.S. colonial times was modeled on a paradigm derived from the African philosophy of community; in Ann's case it was why we are facing an ever-increasing amount of plastic refuse. As you read excerpts from their speeches, ask yourself if you believe an audience of college students would have lacked such knowledge, if either speaker was guilty of overexplaining or underexplaining and would be viewed as condescending or inadequate by listeners, or if either speaker's explanation facilitated understanding.

Terrika's excerpt:

Education during early U.S. colonial times also modeled the African paradigm. There were strict religious constraints, but there was also continuity among children, families and neighbors. Each had a common thread, woven of the same cloth. Philip Greven, a historian of the colonial era, called these common threads "kinship networks" and indeed they were. The social ills we see today—illiteracy, gang violence, child abduction—were not issues. In this system, multitudes of children didn't fall through the cracks. They had safety nets, networks, kinship networks—collaborative efforts by community members to build their future. So what happened?[11]

Ann's excerpt:

According to the ICPB (the Iowa Corn Promotion Board), 50 million pounds of plastic products are currently being used in the U.S. In 1985, manufactured plastic was double the production of aluminum, copper and steel. The result? The plastic will remain in a landfill for 300 to 400 years before it decomposes. Plastics whose only purpose is to cover a hamburger for 60 seconds are the cause for such landfill explosions along with garbage bags, disposable diaper liners, styrofoam cups, and so on.

The reason why plastics take so long to break down, says the December, 1987 issue of the *Wall Street Journal,* is due to repeating hydrocarbon molecules, called polymers, which are derived from petroleum. These chains or polymers are too long for microorganisms to eat and that is why they are so resistent to decay.[12]

Greg Robinson, another student, uses explanation to help his audience understand how the pit bull terrier came to be thought of as a canine Frankenstein.

Historically, pit bulls were developed in Great Britain over 150 years ago, when English Terriers were bred with bull dogs in order to create a vicious breed of dog that would attack bulls for sport. Today, these dogs are typically used to compete in illegal fight-to-the-death gambling events and they've been made more vicious by being bred in what are referred to as "puppy mills," in which the most mentally unstable pit bulls are often bred together, to create the most violent and aggressive offspring possible.[13]

Speakers commonly use explanations not only to tell *why* something is so, but also to relate *how* something occurred. Luther Lasure used an explanation to explain how the brain may be injured during a motor vehicle accident.

Damage to the brain is a result of the brain's bouncing around inside the skull. When the head is at rest, the brain floats in the center. When the head is suddenly pushed forward, the brain will hit the back of the skull. When the head's movement is stopped, the brain will continue forward until it is stopped by the front of the skull. This movement continues until the brain once again comes to rest in the center. But the damage has been done.[14]

Descriptions

In contrast to explanations, **descriptions** produce fresh and striking word pictures that are designed to create sensory reactions in audience members and to ensure greater message vividness and clarity. Novelist, essayist, and screenwriter Joan Didion relied heavily on description in a speech entitled "Why I Write."

I was in this airport only once, on a plane to Bogota that stopped for an hour to refuel, but the way it looked that morning remained superimposed on everything I saw until the day I finished *A Book of Common Prayer.* I lived in that airport for several years. I can still feel the hot air when I step off the plane, can see the heat already rising off the tarmac at 6 A.M. I can feel my skirt damp and wrinkled on my legs. I can feel the asphalt stick to my sandals. I remember the big tail of a Pan American plane floating motionless down at the end of the tarmac.[15]

Renowned broadcaster Edward R. Murrow relied heavily on description rich in specific details to communicate to his listeners some of what it was like for him to view the crematorium of the Buchenwald concentration camp near the end of World War II:

The wall was about eight feet high; it adjoined what had been a stable or garage. We entered. It was floored with concrete. There were two rows of bodies stacked up like cordwood. They were thin and very white. Some of the bodies were terribly bruised, though there seemed to be little flesh to bruise. . . . I tried to count them as best I could and arrived at the conclusion that all that was mortal of more than five hundred men and boys lay there in two neat piles.[16]

Putting Power into the Explanations and Descriptions You Use

What matters most about the explanations and descriptions you develop to facilitate the communication of your ideas is your ability to predict how your audience will respond to them. If one of your goals is to share how something is done, or why it exists in its present form, then explanations will be a valuable resource. If you don't merely want your audience to understand, but also want them to be able to experience more fully the subject of your speech, then description will also be a tool you'll want to master. Use the following checklist to gauge the power of the explantions and/or descriptions you use.

	Yes	No
1. Am I using explanations to deliver information audience members clearly do not know?	❑	❑
2. Have I avoided overexplaining or underexplaining?	❑	❑
3. Are my descriptions rich in specific detail?	❑	❑
4. As a result of the descriptions I employ, will the subject or object of my description come more alive for my listeners?	❑	❑
5. Have I been appropriately selective in choosing what I explain and/or describe?	❑	❑

THE POWER OF DEFINITIONS AND ANALOGIES: FURTHER INCREASING AUDIENCE UNDERSTANDING

DEFINITIONS AND ANALOGIES are two more forms of support that are designed to bridge cultural diversity, enhance audience understanding, and facilitate audience acceptance of a speaker's ideas.

Definitions

In addition to clarifying what particular words or concepts mean, **definitions** indicate how you hope your audience members will interpret the words or concepts you use. Definitions are especially useful when your audience members are unfamiliar with the way you are using key terms, or when they might have associations for words or concepts that differ from the ones you have. Consequently, as with other forms of support, definitions are designed to enhance audience understanding.

Which Kinds of Words Should You Define? When speaking you need to define words that are technical in nature, that have specialized meanings, that are rarely used, that you are using in unique or unusual ways, or that have two or more meanings. That is, if a word's context fails to make the meaning of the word you are using immediately apparent to your listeners, then it is up to you to define the word in such a way that its intended meaning becomes clear.

How Do You Define a Word? Speakers sometimes use a dictionary definition to clarify meaning, while other times they make up or explain their own meaning or even choose to share the meanings others (usually recognized experts) have given the word. When you take your definition for a word from a dictionary you invest the meaning you cite with a degree of authority and credibility. On the other hand, using an original definition could help audience members share your personal meaning for a word and could help make the speaker–audience connection more intense. Of course, using definitions supplied by experts also could help precipitate audience understanding and acceptance.

When student Jocelyn So delivered a speech entitled "Liquid Bone," she used a definition to be certain her audience would both understand what liquid bone was and develop an appreciation for its significance.

The April 10, 1995, edition of Forbes describes liquid bone as a gap filling glue, much like the epoxy used to mend broken china. And for physicians, Little League players, and all the other Humpty-Dumptys out there who have been searching for an alternative to the bulky casts, invasive surgery and metal implants, it is currently the only remedy for the 1.5 million fractures suffered each year in the United States. Liquid bone really is something of a super glue.[17]

Similarly, student Laura K. Oster used a definition in her speech entitled "Deforestation: A Time for Action" to ensure that her audience would understand both what a rain forest is and the seriousness of the deforestation issue.

Rain forests are lush tropical forests, existing primarily in the rich Amazonian River Basin and covering 2.7 million square miles—an area equal to the size of the continental United States. The forests have a delicately balanced eco-system, which when disturbed, or even partially altered, becomes unable to sustain life.[18]

Lori M. Hawkins relied on an array of definitions supplied by experts in her speech, "Critical Thinking: An Ancient Philosophy for Modern Times."

Exactly what does it mean to be a critical thinker? What traits are present in a critical thinker? Dr. Robert Ennis of the University of Illinois describes critical thinking as reasonable and reflective thinking that is focused on what to believe and do. Barry Beyer described critical thinking as assessing the authenticity, worth, and accuracy of knowledge, beliefs, claims and arguments. Ralph Johnson and Anthony Blair, two leaders in the critical thinking movement from the University of Windsor, Canada, say that a critical thinker is disposed to asking the following questions: What evidence is there for this? What evidence is there against this? What are the unstated assumptions here? What are the consequences? In short, a critical thinker must interrogate the obvious. He or she must be willing to question their deepest beliefs and prejudices. Critical thinkers cannot rely on traditional solutions for problems.[19]

Similarly, student Lisa Reinhack used both a personal defintion and a definition by an expert to define "cultural illiteracy" in her speech, "In Pursuit of the Not So Trivial."

Cultural illiteracy. It is not illiteracy, which is not being able to read or write. It is not alliteracy, which is not having the desire to read. Rather it is lacking the background information necessary to understand a concept after knowing how to read the word.

As defined by E. D. Hirsch, author of the 1987 bestseller, *Cultural Literacy,* to be culturally literate means "to be capable of using and understanding a vocabulary that we use through our shared associations with others in our society."[20]

But it is the personal definition of "whistleblower" supplied by student Shannon Dyer in her speech "The Dilemma of Whistleblowers" that really helps intensify the speaker–audience relationship at the same time that it pinpoints exactly how Shannon perceives her subject.

Whistleblowers are simply employees who object in a situation they feel is dangerous or illegal. They are social workers such as Irvin Levin of the Brooklyn Office of Special Services for Children who reported that serious cases of child abuse and even death were not being properly investigated. They are medical personnel, such as Dr. Grace Pierce of a New Jersey pharmaceutical company, who protested the production of a new drug for infants which she believed would have dangerous—even fatal—side effects. They are security officers such as John Berter of the Veterans Administration Hospital in Cincinnati who following his conscience exposed two of his superiors for repeatedly beating patients. But whistleblowers are also you and I when we see something illegal or dangerous going on in our professions and we just can't look the other way.

Inevitably, these reports aren't always welcome to employers; thus, whistleblowers become "troublemakers" and "traitors."[21]

Analogies

Sometimes the most effective kind of support available to a speaker is an **analogy.** Although related to the definition, the analogy is used somewhat differently. Like the definition, the analogy functions to increase understanding, but unlike the definition, it does so through comparison and contrast.

There are two main types of analogies: *literal* and *figurative.* A **literal analogy** compares like things from similar classes; for example, two viruses, two novels, or two crises. A **figurative analogy** compares two things that are distinctively dissimilar and that at first appear to have little in common with each other—a war and a dragon, or mad cow disease and an alien. Whatever type of analogy you use, your primary purpose is to explain the unfamiliar by relating it to something the audience is more familiar with. Thus, whether you are pointing out the similarities between two basically unlike things or clarifying what two basically similar things have in common, you can use analogies to enhance your audience's understanding and acceptance of your ideas.

Speakers often use literal analogies to point out the similarities between two policies or two programs. For example, if the points of similarity outweigh the points of difference, then audience members might be persuaded that what worked before might also work now. Speakers use figurative analogies to awaken the collective imagination of listeners, to prod listeners into accepting that two things that appear to have little, if anything, in common, actually share one or more vital similarities.

It is important that the essential similarities inherent in the analogies you use be readily apparent. If you strain to create analogies, audience members may conclude that your analogies are far-fetched, inappropriate, unbelievable, or unpersuasive.

Kelly Campbell used a figurative analogy to help listeners understand the nature of a decoy virus vaccine.

The ploy in duck hunting goes something like this. A wooden decoy, artfully painted, is used to fool real ducks into thinking it's a fellow feathered friend. Now following this lead, Structure Biologicals, a biotechnology firm, has taken that same deception out of the pond and into the medical lab. Before you think these scientists are a bunch of quacks, the *South China Morning Post* on January 6, 1996, explains that Structure Biologicals, a company comprised of 35 scientists from UCLA, the Morehouse School of Medicine, and the Centers for Disease Control and Prevention have almost perfected their own decoy, a decoy virus vaccine, which will revolutionize medical technology as we know it.

Like the traditional concept, the decoy virus masquerades as a real virus, tricking our body's immune systems into action.[22]

Student Doug Wehage used a literal analogy to compare fire deaths in American and foreign cities.

Philip Schanman, President of Tri-Data, a Virginia-based fire consulting firm, reports that Chicago, although half the size of Hong Kong, has three times as many fire deaths. Baltimore, while about the size of Amsterdam, has 13 times as many fire deaths each year.[23]

Analogies

1. Work with a partner to create figurative and literal analogies for the following:

   Public speaking course
   Your instructor
   Your job
   Your love life

2. Select a speech from a recent issue of *Vital Speeches of the Day* that incorporates analogies. What kinds of analogies did the speaker use? Were they used effectively? To what extent, if any, could you improve them?

Similarly, student Tracy A. Schario used a literal analogy to argue against discrimination in the military.

> In 1941, the Navy Department issued the following statement: There is "the necessity for the highest degree of unity and morale. . . . Demanding participation . . . disrupts present working organizations."
>
> In 1981, the Defense Department issued the following statement: "The presence of such members adversely affects the ability of the armed forces to maintain discipline, good order and morale. . . ."
>
> Both statements, issued 40 years apart, are strikingly similar. The 1941 statement was used to justify that blacks should not serve among whites in the armed forces. The 1981 statement refers to gay men and lesbians in the military.[24]

Putting Power into the Definitions and Analogies You Use

Definitions and analogies are designed to clarify intended meanings or concepts. Once you are convinced they will increase listener understanding or acceptance of your ideas, there is sufficient reason to use them. By helping you explain the nature of a term or situation to your audience members, a definition or analogy may also help you inform and persuade them. You can use the following checklist to gauge the power of the definitions and analogies you employ.

	Yes	No
1. Do I use a definition or analogy only when needed?	❑	❑
2. Are my definitions or analogies easily understood?	❑	❑
3. Am I consistent in the way I define or explain a term or problem?	❑	❑
4. Have I avoided using too many definitions or analogies?	❑	❑
5. Will audience members readily accept my definitions or analogies?	❑	❑

The Power of Statistics: The Purpose behind Numbers

Numbers. Numbers. Numbers. We live in an age that seems to worship numbers. There is something comforting in the fact that we can express what we know with numbers. Like the other forms of support we have examined, we use numerical shorthand—**statistics**—to clarify and strengthen our ideas and claims. Thus, we use statistics to express the seriousness of a situation, the magnitude of a problem. We use statistics to express the relationship that exists between a part and the whole, and to predict future patterns. We use statistics to compare and contrast different points, and to heighten the impact of a message.

There is a lot more to statistics than meets the eye. Statistics can be worked with until they create the kind of impression the speaker desires. It is critical, however, that you neither distort statistics nor lie with them.[25] It is your reponsibility to ensure that the statistics you use represent what you claim to be measuring, that you obtain them from a reliable source, that you use them correctly, and that you interpret them accurately. If you follow these precepts, then your statistical support will help you make your speech both more understandable and more memorable.

What Statistics Mean

It is essential that you understand what the statistics you are using mean. While statistics may be used to impress an audience, if you use them inappropriately, rather than enhance your speech's overall impact, they will weaken it. Because statistics are no more nor less trustworthy than the people who create them, your goal is not only to cite reputable, authoritative, and unbiased sources, but also to be sure that the measure you are using is the one you intend to, and that your audience understands that as well.

For example, you need to be able to distinguish among the following statistical measures: the range, the mean, the median, the mode, and the percentage. The **range** is the difference between the highest and the lowest numbers in a series. The **mean** is the number obtained from adding all the numbers in the series and dividing that by the number of items. The **median** is the middle number in a group of numbers arranged in order from highest to lowest. The **mode** is the number that occurs most commonly in a group of numbers, and the **percentage** is the number expressed as a part of 100.

Statistical Sources

There are a variety of statistical sources available to you. You can consult any reputable publication including scholarly journals, newspapers and news magazines, and books. The *World Almanac* can be a valuable source, as can the annual edition of *Statistical Abstract of the United States* and the U.N.'s *Statistical Yearbook. The Guinness Book of Records* is a source of unusual statistics that you might also find useful.

Incorporating Statistics into Speeches

In a speech entitled "Capital Punishment from a Global Perspective: The Death Penalty: Right or Wrong?" University of Cincinnati Professor of Law Emeritus Jorge L. Carro used statistical support to quantify his ideas and show the existence of a perplexing situation:

According to statistics compiled by the human rights group Amnesty International, on June 30, 1995, 55 countries have abolished the capital punishment for all crimes, 15 countries have abolished the death penalty for all but exceptional crimes such as wartime crimes, and 27 countries have de facto abolished the death penalty. These countries retain the death penalty in their codes but they have not carried out any execution during the past ten years or more.

Furthermore, an average of two countries per year have abolished the death penalty since 1976, and 21 countries have abolished it since 1989. As you will notice, the trend

SPEAKING of ETHICS

Working with Statistics

- Examine the following two groups of numbers.

Group One	*Group Two*
12,000	16,000
10,000	15,000
8,400	9,500
7,000	8,400
5,000	5,000
4,000	4,200
4,000	4,000
4,000	3,000
2,500	3,000
56,900	68,100

- Determine the range, mean, median, and mode for each group and a percentage measure for the first number in each group. Check your answers by comparing them with these:

  The range is 9,500 for Group One and 13,000 for Group Two.
  The mean for Group One is 6,322.The mean for Group Two is 7,567.
  The median is the same for both Groups One and Two. It is 5,000.
  The mode is 4,000 for Group One, and 3,000 for Group Two.
  The first number is 21 percent of Group One and 23 percent of Group Two.

- Now imagine that these figures were the monthly salaries of salespeople employed by the Triple X Corporation (Group One), and the Triple Y Corporation (Group Two). How might the sales manager of either corporation use these figures to convince someone choosing between jobs with Triple X and Triple Y to work for his or her company?

How would you feel if the sales manager of Triple X cited the median salary ($5,000) to show that the "average" earnings of sales representatives in both corporations were identical; whereas, in contrast, the sales manager of Triple Y cited the mean salary of his or her sales representatives ($7,567) and the mean salary of Triple X representatives ($6,322) to demonstrate that Triple Y sales representatives earned on the "average" $1,200 a month more than Triple X sales representatives?

Although both sales managers would be telling the truth, only if the sales representative who was considering the job offer understood how the sales manager was using the statistics to make a point would it be really fair. Because the results obtained depend on the statistical measure used, it is important that you fully explain your statistics to your audience.

George Will

Consider what writer and speaker George Will says about the use of "nutty numbers." Do you believe his warnings will be acknowledged? Why or why not?

To the untrained eye, it was just another of the numbing numbers by which journalism calls attention to this or that crisis: "Every year, the World Health Organization estimates, 220,000 people die from pesticide poisoning." To the trained eye of Richard McGuire, New York's Commissioner of Agriculture and Markets, that assertion in an upstate New York newspaper's editorial looked implausible.

It was. Follow the slithering number to a lesson about the strange life led by some statistics and the terrible data on which government often bases decisions.

A call from McGuire's office to the upstate editor revealed that he had received the editorial from a California syndicate. A call there revealed that the 220,000 number was from information supporting Patrick Leahy's (D-Vt.) bill to prohibit U.S. companies from exporting pesticides whose use is banned in America. Leahy was concerned about America importing foods containing residues of chemicals banned here.

Leahy's office directed McGuire to the WHO, which directed him to a WHO report McGuire wrote to the author in Switzerland, who wrote back to say the figure of 220,000 deaths came from another WHO publication.

The author had warned readers that "reliable data on pesticide poisonings are not available and the figures given are derived from various estimates." Unfortunately, he said, quoted figures often acquire misplaced momentum because they are shorn of their tentativeness.

Here is what the WHO publication the author relied on actually said: "Of the more than 220,000 intentional or unintentional deaths from acute (pesticide) poisoning, suicides account for approximately 91 percent, occupational exposure for 6 percent, and other causes, including food contamination, for 3 percent." Of the 3 percent (itself a guess), we are left to guess what portion involved food contamination.

in the international organizations as well as individual countries is towards abolition. This trend places us in an awkward position. The United States is now the only Western industrialized country that retains the death penalty.[26]

Similarly, student Nancy Shaver used statsitics to make it easier for her audience members to comprehend the enormity of a challenge facing them. Because she expressed the statistics she cited in units that were readily understandable, she also increased their memorability.

Lola Davidson of the National Council on Alcoholism says, the "alcoholic affects the lives of at least four other people." Currently, there are 10,000,000 alcoholics in the United States who are affecting the lives of 40,000,000 people. It is a statistical fact that you or someone you know is suffering from familial alcoholism.[27]

In the next example, student Bob Moore used a percentage measure to increase the impact of his statistical citations. Notice how the statistics he uses are rounded off to aid comprehension, and how comparison and contrast are used to heighten the meaning of the numbers.

In a personal interview on March 16, 1995, with Dr. Emily Greene of the National Institutes of Health, she explained that of the approximately 9 million emergency room patients each year, almost 1 of every 9 are mistreated by inadequately trained emergency

WHO's basic message was that there were actually 20,000 deaths from unintentional pesticide poisoning in a world population of five billion. And U.S. Food and Drug Administration tests on imported foods reveal no significant problem with chemical residues on food imports.

The use of nutty numbers to advance political agendas may result from cynicism or from confusions borne of carelessness. The result can be foolish public policies, feeding on and fed by the journalism of apocalypse.

Twenty years ago, *The Public Interest* published "The Vitality of Mythical Numbers," by Max Singer, then president of the Hudson Institute. He dissected a then commonly cited number, that New York City's "100,000-plus" heroin addicts were stealing upwards of $5 billion worth of property a year.

The assumptions behind the numbers were: 100,000 addicts were each spending an average of $30 a day on their habits, or $1.1 billion a year (100,000 × 365 × $30). Stolen property is fenced for about one-quarter of its value, so addicts must steal upwards of 45 billion worth.

Singer was skeptical.

Most stealing by addicts then was by shoplifting and burglary. All retail sales in the city then totaled $15 billion (including cars, carpets, diamonds, and other goods not susceptible to shoplifting). All losses from all forms of theft and embezzlement were about 2 percent. Even if shoplifters accounted for half of that (they don't; employees steal much more), and if all shoplifters were addicts (they aren't), the addicts' shoplifting total would be $150 million.

Burglary? Even if one-fifth of the city's $2.5 million households had been burglarized each year (they weren't), and accepting the police estimate that the average loss from a burglary was property worth $200, the burglary total ($200 × 500,000) was $100 million.

So even with inflating assumption, the burglary and shoplifting sum was a quarter of a billion dollars worth of property. That is not chopped liver. But it is one-twentieth of $5 billion.

Probably the "100,000-plus" number of addicts was inflated. A pertinent question about such numbers is: Whose interests are served by numerical exaggeration? The answer often is: The people whose funding or political importance varies directly with the perceived severity of a particular problem.

room physicians. So from misdiagnosis to mistreatment, over 1,000,000 Americans will be affected this year alone. To compound the problem even further, Dr. Thompson Bowles, president of the National Board of Medical Examiners, notes in a Josiah Macy Jr. Foundation report on American medical care published in September 1994, that of the nation's 25,000 jobs in emergency care, only 50% are staffed with professionals specifically certified in emergency medicine. But perhaps most alarming is that an estimated 43% of these so called professionals are not even certified in basic first aid and CPR. The bottom line is that many emergency room physicians are inadequately trained and their patients are suffering the consequences.[28]

Speakers frequently find it useful to employ visual aids to help communicate the meaning of their statistics to audience members. The right visual aid will save you time as well as make it easier for your listeners to understand the significance of the statistical evidence you cite. Suppose, for example, you chose to speak on the relationship between vitamin D and breast cancer. In the course of your presentation you might well include a number of these findings: the breast cancer death rate was lowest in the sunny South and West and highest in the Northeast; breast cancer rates were more than 1.5 times as high in New York and Boston as in Phoenix or Honolulu; and breast cancer is more prevalent in communities with the most light-blocking air pollution and less prevalent where more solar radiation is received by resi-

Figure 8.1

Graphs help speakers communicate complex statistical data.

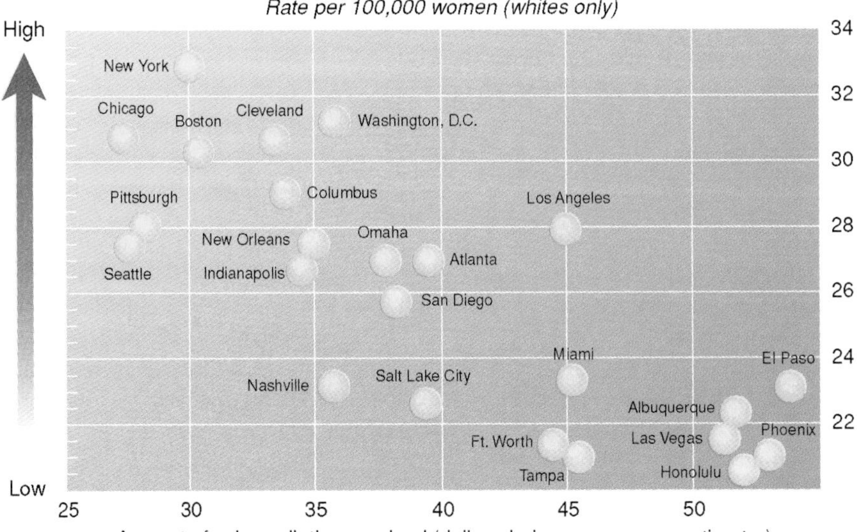

dents.[29] These are interesting findings, but they probably would be even more effective if shown on a simple graph as in Figure 8.1.

We will discuss visual aids in greater detail in Chapter 14, but for now keep in mind that you can use them to help you communicate complex statistical data with ease.

Putting Power into the Statistics You Use

If used so that they do not overwhelm your listeners, statistics can aid you in adding impact to your speech. In fact, research tells us that the impact of examples is strengthened when they are followed by statistics that demonstrate their representativeness. But before you integrate any statistics into your speech, you need to use your critical thinking skills to evaluate their usefulness. Use the following checklist to gauge the effectiveness of your statistics.

	Yes	No
1. Are the statistics I am using representative of what I claim they measure?	❑	❑
2. Am I being totally honest in my use of these statistics?	❑	❑
3. Have I obtained my statistics from a reliable source who has no vested interest in the figures?	❑	❑
4. Have I interpreted the statistics correctly?	❑	❑
5. Have I used statistics sparingly?	❑	❑
6. Have I explained my statistics creatively?	❑	❑
7. Have I rounded off my statistics to facilitate understanding?	❑	❑
8. Have I used a visual aid to increase the memorability of my statistics?	❑	❑

9. Have I provided a context for my statistics? ❑ ❑
10. Have I used my statistics to clarify and enlighten rather than confound and confuse? ❑ ❑

The Power of Testimony: Who Says So?

When speakers use the opinions of others either to support positions they are taking or to reinforce claims they are making, they are using testimony. Though, of course, your own opinions do count, you will find that audiences, in general, are more influenced when you supplement your personal opinions with expert testimony. In fact, if you think about it, the testimony of other people affects us daily. When we are called on to make an important decision, we are apt to look to persons who possess more knowledge or experience than we do to help us evaluate the strengths and weaknesses inherent in each of our opinions. Of course, we do not rely exclusively on the testimony of "experts"; our decision making is also influenced by our peers who have had firsthand experience with a situation, by literature, and by the media. Thus, while speakers integrate quotations or paraphrase the opinions of experts in their speeches, they also integrate literary quotations, and peer or lay testimony as well. For example, Terrika Scott used "The Real," a poem by Johari Kungufu, as testimony and a means to share her thoughts with receivers in her speech "Curing Crisis with Community":

> Sisters, Men
>
> What are we doin?
>
> What about the babies, our children?
>
> When we was real we never had orphans or children in joints.
>
> Come spirits
>
> drive out the nonsense from our minds and the crap from our dreams
>
> make us remember what we need, that children are the next life.
>
> bring us back to the real
>
> bring us back to the real
>
> "The Real." Johari Kungufu, in her poem, specifically alludes to a time in African history when children were not confused about who they were. A time when fathers and mothers and grandmas and grandpas and uncles and aunts and cousins and . . . neighbors raised a child; a time when the community and the education process were inseparable and complacency towards children and their learning was far from their minds.[30]

What determines whether you paraphrase an opinion or quote it directly? You would opt to paraphrase an opinion—that is, restate it in your own words—if your doing so would increase audience members' understanding of and response to it. If the quotation is neither too long nor too difficult for audience members to comprehend, if it is phrased in language that is easy for audience members to listen to and process, and if you believe it has sufficient force and clarity the way it is, then direct quotations—stated in the exact same words used by the source—are generally preferred.

Expert testimony helps you establish the validity of your message. Because expert testimony is provided by sources who are recognized authorities on your topic, it helps to enhance your speech's credibility.[31]

Student Ben Lohman used the testimony of an expert to help communicate his ideas to his audience and to strengthen the position he was advocating—that fiberglass insulation is dangerous to the human body.

Former long distance runner Dean Lavery began waking up with his face covered in blood from nighttime nose bleeds. Lavery's job in the automotive industry required him to work extensively with fiberglass. But after suffering lung damage and asthma, Lavery sued. He settled out of court and cannot discuss his case. However, Dr. Peter Infante, a scientist with the Occupational Safety and Health Administration summarized his findings in the 1994 *American Journal of Industrial Medicine.* He wrote, "On a fiber per fiber basis, glass fibers may be just as potent, or even more deadly than asbestos. A candid disclosure about the risk of lung cancer is warranted."[32]

Similarly, student Theresa McGuiness used expert testimony to try to convince her receivers that fraternities should be abolished.

Andrew Merton, Associate Professor of English at the University of New Hampshire and acknowledged scholar on the issue of fraternities and sexism, says: "Studies have shown that men who join fraternities have a much greater need to dominate than those who don't." He adds, "I think these men are scared of women, scared of dealing with them in any way approaching a basis of equality. They see women only in a sexual context, in a context where men are rule-makers. And there's a tremendous pressure to drink in fraternities. Drinking allows the guys to act upon the sexual stereotypes in their heads and then say, "Oh, it wasn't really my fault. I didn't know what I was doing."

Bernice Sandler, Executive Director of the Project on the Status and Education of Women at the Association of American Colleges, said that 90 percent of the gang rapes reported to her office involved fraternity members. According to Sandler, fraternity members have a word for gang rape: they call it "pulling train." She adds that charts of how many beers it took to seduce sorority women are common in fraternity houses. And if a woman actually does press charges against a fraternity, Sandler says, "Their excuse is, 'she asked for it'—even if she was unconscious."[33]

Notice how Theresa used a direct quotation in her first paragraph but relied predominately on paraphrases in the second paragraph.

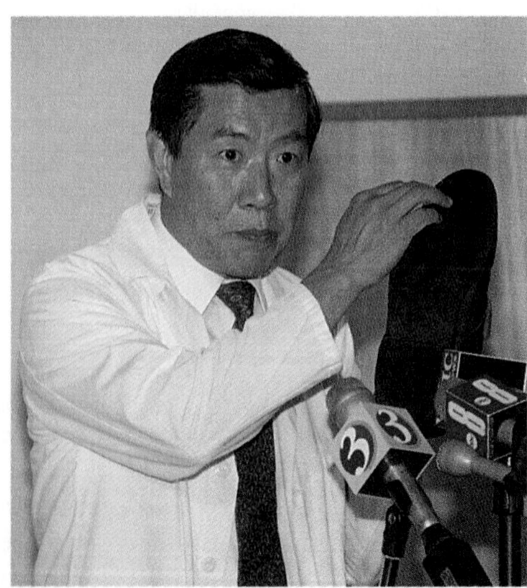

Connecticut's forensic scientist Henry Lee is a source of expert testimony.

SPEAKING of CRITICAL THINKING

Who Do You Trust?

Supporting materials are evaluated two times: first by the speaker, and then by the receivers. Speakers and receivers who are well trained to think critically are able to spot the strengths and the weaknesses in the messages they deliver to others or that others deliver to them. Among the responsibilities critical thinkers perform are assessing the credibility of the speaker's statements and judging the validity of the evidence supplied by the speaker. Consider the following.

The federal government has contemplated a moratorium, if not an outright ban, of silicone-filled breast implants. The *New York Times* reported that both advocates and critics of implants have swamped the Food and Drug Administration and Congress with letters and telephone calls. Those who had serious health problems as a result of receiving implants urged recall of the devices, while those who suffered no adverse effects contended that women should have the right to make their own decisions.

Following is a sample of the testimony offered by three implant recipients. Use your critical thinking skills to judge the effectiveness of the support offered by Darcy Sixt, mastectomy survivor, implant recipient, and paid spokesperson for the Dow Corning Corporation, once the nation's largest manufacturer of silicone breast implants; Kali Korn, who had breast implants to enlarge small breasts and suffered severe immune reactions as a result; and Sybil Goldrich, mastectomy survivor, aggrieved implant recipient, and leader of an advocacy group for other aggrieved implant patients.

> I lost my hair; I lost my ability to have children and I still fear I'll lose my life. The implant is the one positive thing that has happened to me.
>
> *Darcy Sixt*

> I'm angry that I was told, "Enjoy them," rather than being told that somewhere down the line they might wreck my life. And I'm angry at myself for thinking implants would change my life and there wouldn't be a price.
>
> *Kali Korn*

> We've had a lifetime of insidious indoctrination. We have been sold a dream: breasts as fashion accessories.
>
> *Sybil Goldrich*

To what extent, if any, do the credentials of any of the individuals who offered testimony affect your judgment of their credibility? Explain.

In contrast to expert testimony, peer or lay testimony involves citing the opinions of people who are not necessarily recognized authorities, but "ordinary people" who have firsthand experience with the subject. Peer or lay testimony provides audience members with more personal insights; the speaker shares the feelings, the reactions, and the knowledge of individuals who have "been there" with audience members.

In her speech "Homeless Children: A National Crisis," student Becky McKay used the testimony of Sherry, a homeless girl. By using Sherry's own words, Becky was able to convey Sherry's innermost feelings to her audience.

I Want to Live in a House

I saw them at their house today.
They had new coats and mittens.
I don't have a house like that,
I don't have a coat or mittens.
Things will change; Mommy said they will
As she buttoned my cotton blouse.
I sure hope it's true, you know,
'Cause I really want to live in a house![34]

Putting Power into the Testimony You Use

Testimony works because it lets you borrow someone else's credibility. In effect, testimony enables you to associate your ideas with the knowledge, experience, qualifications, and reputation of another. But before you integrate testimony into your speech, you need to know that the person or source you are citing is recognized in the specific area you are discussing. It will do you no good to associate yourself with someone who is not an authority on your topic, is not highly regarded by others, or does not have firsthand experience with your subject. Use the following checklist to gauge the effectiveness of the testimony you cite.

	Yes	No
1. Have I clearly identified the source of each piece of testimony?	❑	❑
2. Is the source I cite recognizable and credible?	❑	❑
3. Is the testimony I am using absolutely relevant to my presentation?	❑	❑
4. Have I quoted or paraphrased the source accurately and used his or her words in proper context?	❑	❑
5. Am I certain that I neither twisted nor distorted testimony just to make a point?	❑	❑
6. Have I cited an objective, unbiased expert?	❑	❑
7. Have I used verbatim quotations whenever possible?	❑	❑
8. Have I used lay or peer testimony to enhance the audience's ability to identify with my topic?	❑	❑
9. Did I use the most up-to-date testimony available?	❑	❑
10. Have I stressed each of my sources' qualifications so audience members will not have to strain to find statements credible?	❑	❑

SUMMARY

THE USE OF APPROPRIATE supporting materials distinguishes effective speeches from ineffective speeches. Among the kinds of supporting materials a speaker can include are specific instances and illustrations, explanations and descriptions, definitions and analogies, statistics, and testimony. Each, when used correctly, can help add substance and interest to a speaker's message as well as help build a body of content that will hold up well when critically evaluated by an audience.

Specific instances and illustrations (both real and hypothetical) fulfill specific speechmaking roles. Specific instances are brief examples, but when piled one on top of another, they gain power. Illustrations, more detailed and vivid than specific instances, function to involve receivers by adding a sense of drama to a speech. Like brief examples and illustrations, explanations and descriptions are also the speechmaker's allies. By explaining the unfamiliar and using language rich in sensory detail, a speaker improves his or her listeners' comprehension and facilitates the communication of his or her message. Similarly, definitions and analogies are used to enhance audience understanding. When a speaker uses words that are technical, words that have specialized meanings, or words that are apt to be misinterpreted, a definition is in order. Like definitions, analogies are used by a speaker to clarify intended meaning. A speaker uses statistics to clarify and strengthen an idea or claim. Statistics heighten the impact of a message by communicating the magnitude of a problem and by demonstrating the representativeness of an example. Whenever a speaker uses the opinion of others as support, he or she is using testimony. By integrating expert and lay testimony into a speech, a speaker can help establish the validity of his or her message.

In addition to being able to integrate these forms of support into a speech, a speaker also needs to be adept at evaluating their usefulness.

THE SPEAKER'S STAND

1. Select a topic that concerns or interests you.
2. Formulate a statement related to the topic that you are prepared to support. Your statement should begin "I think that . . ." or "I believe that. . . ."
3. Locate two types of support from two different sources that you can use to make your point.
4. Develop a 60-second presentation.

For example, one student developed his idea this way:

> I believe that we must increase the number of long-term shelters that are available for homeless people to use.
>
> Long-term shelters are effective in helping people return to productive lives. San Francisco Judge Robert Coates states in his book *A Street Is Not a Home* that "Recovery is a long-term process that long-term shelters can address." According to Coates, in one such shelter studied, 83 percent of the residents were able to obtain permanent housing after thirty days in the shelter.
>
> Unfortunately, the availability of long-term shelters for the homeless is grossly inadequate. According to David Schwartz, professor of Political Science at Rutgers University, "In some localities, the shortage of shelter beds is simply stupefying. Los Angeles County alone has a bed to need ratio of one to fifteen."
>
> Thus, we see that while long-term shelters help reduce homelessness, the number of such facilities is inadequate.

Speaking on this same subject, another student used testimony obtained from a journalist and information derived from an interview with a former homeless person. Her presentation began with the following:

> I believe that care for the homeless is an urgent issue facing Americans.
>
> In an article entitled "Prosperity Lost," journalist Phillip Mattera notes, "A survey by the U.S. Conference of Mayors found that in most cities, emergency shelter and food facilities were being overwhelmed by the rising number of homeless persons, many of whom had to be turned away."
>
> Unfortunately, even when allowed into a shelter, it is not an appropriate place for our citizens. A former homeless man I interviewed told me: "A fire in my apartment forced me into homelessness. The shelters I lived in in New York City were unsanitary and unsafe. I had my personal be-

longings stolen and I personally witnessed several stabbings in the shelter. There were sadistic and brutal security guards there as well."

Yes, this is America—land of opportunity—unless you are homeless.

5. Once you select your issue, ask yourself these questions:

Have I selected an issue that I can support?

What types of support should I use?

Does each potential piece of support back up my claim?

How can I use other forms of support to further enhance the impact of my remarks?

STUDENT FOCUS GROUP REPORT

Now that you have had the opportunity to locate and use a variety of supporting materials, in a group of five to seven students, answer the following questions:

1. Reread the chapter's case study. In what ways, if any, would you now change your assessment of Salima's readiness to present her speech?
2. What problems did you encounter as you looked for appropriate supporting materials for your own presentation? How did you meet each challenge?
3. What techniques can you use to successfully adapt supporting materials to meet the needs of a specific speaking situation?
4. How do supporting materials make the public speaker's task easier or more difficult?
5. What kinds of questions should speakers ask themselves when selecting supporting materials?
6. Are there any kinds of supporting materials a speaker should refrain from using because of potential ethical or cultural sensitivities? Explain.
7. Summarize the most significant information you have learned about the use of supporting materials.

Select a group member to give a brief report of your findings to the class.

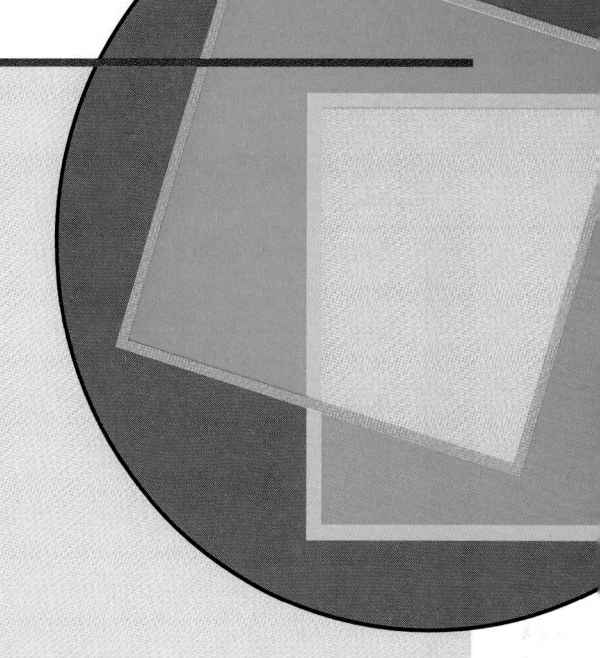

Chapter Nine

Order Please!

How to Organize the Body of Your Speech

After reading this chapter, you should be able to:

- Explain how structure and order help us make sense out of experience.
- Compare and contrast speech preparation with essay writing.
- Explain what is meant by the "skeleton" of a speech.
- Define and describe the following organization structures: time order; spatial order, cause-and-effect order, problem-solution order, and topical order.
- Identify and use the following kinds of speech connectors: transitions, internal previews, and internal summaries.
- Discuss how culture influences organizational preferences.

CASE STUDY

Order, Order

Tamiko stared in horror at the chaos on her desk. Hundreds of note cards stared back at her. A molecular biology major, Tamiko had spent hours researching the topic of genetic engineering. She had read countless articles, examined many books, examined a number of Internet sites, and interviewed several professors. Now, as she surveyed the piles of research she had gathered, Tamiko realized that she had no idea how to put her speech together so that it would make sense to an audience potentially unschooled in her subject. How am I ever going to pull this off? she wondered. I feel like I need the speech equivalent of a closet organizer.

No sooner had that thought entered Tamiko's mind when, seemingly out of nowhere, a strong breeze blew through the open window, scattering her note cards all over the floor. Tamiko fell to her knees, her hands struggling to regather the cards that, in the wind, appeared to take on a life of their own, randomly changing and rearranging their order themselves. As she simultaneously observed and participated in this hectic scene, Tamiko remembered a saying: "Even in chaos, one can find order."

With the wind now quieted, Tamiko finished picking up the cards that remained on the floor. As she placed them on her desk, an idea occurred to her. She would find the order in the chaos. She would look at each of the cards with a fresh eye. She would find the organizational pattern best suited for her presentation. Tamiko began sorting the cards into two piles: genetic dreams and genetic nightmares.

- At one time or another, we have all been organizationally challenged. Like Tamiko, we possessed a wealth of information but lacked a clear vision of what to do with it. Identify the last time you faced such a challenge and the factors you considered as you decided how to respond to it.
- What specific strategies did you use to reconfigure and shape your information to create order out of disorder? Were the strategies you used successful? If so, why? If not, why not?

WE ALL WANT TO PUT THINGS IN ORDER. We organize our closets, our books, our papers, our lives. Today we even use computers to help organize our time. We want others to be organized as well. For instance, we want our teachers to be organized. Would you want to attend a course in which the professor rambled aimlessly because he had no idea what he was going to cover during most classes? Of course not. It would be difficult—if not impossible—for you to understand him, and there would be even less of a chance that you would learn from him. Disorder is discomforting. It scrambles our brains.

We often evaluate the people we know according to how organized they are. Gestalt psychologists have long asserted that the concept of organization is basic to our mental activities. Our desire for structure and orderliness helps us make sense out of experience.

If organization is so important, is there any reason why a speaker would stand in front of a group of people without striving to deliver a carefully organized speech unless the goal was to disappoint rather than enlighten receivers? The ability to organize ideas is an intrinsic component of effective speaking. Unless audience members can follow and understand your message, they might as well not waste their time listen-

Disorder is uncomfortable. Putting things in order helps us make sense of experiences.

ing to it. In this chapter we will explore how you can put your speech together—how you can organize and structure your ideas to achieve coherence and attain your desired speechmaking results.

WHY ORGANIZATION COUNTS

WHY IS ORGANIZATION SUCH A CRITICAL FACTOR? Why do we relish order rather than disorder? For one thing, though at times it may seem chaotic, our world is actually quite an orderly place.[1] Can you imagine attending a college where there were no scheduled meeting times for classes? How would you know when your next math class would start? How would you find out when and where your English seminar was to meet? Most work days are characterized by tight rather than haphazard schedules. We work certain days of the week and take others off.

It is only natural that as we organize our lives, we want speakers we hear to be organized as well. Research supports what we know intuitively—that listeners learn more from an organized speech than from a disorganized one.[2] There seems to be little doubt that organization helps audience members attend to ideas.

In 1988, when he was still governor of Arkansas, Bill Clinton delivered a long, disorganized presentation to the Democratic national convention; needless to say, the speech was the target of a great deal of criticism. Audience members simply stopped listening to him. Four years later, Clinton returned to the convention as its presidential nominee. But this time, however, he delivered a much more concise and better organized presentation. And for his second inaugural address, Clinton's speech was a tightly packed 22 minutes.[3] You, too, can learn to develop your ability to better organize your speech so that your ideas don't ramble around uncontrollably, and so they have the impact that only compactness and compression can deliver.

ORAL VERSUS WRITTEN ORGANIZATION

PREPARING A SPEECH IS OFTEN COMPARED TO writing an essay. Yet in some ways they are very different experiences. A speech is generally heard only once, whereas a reader is able to read a passage again and again. Speakers normally use shorter sentences than writers, and they also repeat the main ideas of their work more frequently than writers. Writers can use heads and subheads in preparing texts; as a

SPEAKING of CRITICAL THINKING

Should Speakers Build Speeches around Myths?

The myth is a common form of narrative. *Star Wars, Raiders of the Lost Ark,* and *Star Trek* are just a few of the hero, heroine, and villain mythic stories that have become a part of our popular culture. Do myth and narrative have a place in spoken discourse as well? In other words, is it possible for a speaker to use a myth as the basis of a speech to make a point—even if the point made by the myth is not necessarily true? According to Janice Hocker Rushing, former President Ronald Reagan did just that when he introduced his Strategic Defense Initiative.[4]

Reagan's calling his plan the "Star Wars initiative" and his integration in his remarks of stories about missiles shooting down other missiles, made great copy. However, according to Rushing, the story offered did not reflect the technological reality the president asserted it had.[5]

Others have used myth and narrative. Basically, human beings are storytellers. Thus, speakers of all kinds use myth and narrative to share their stories, define themselves, solve their problems, and communicate their visions of a good society to others. Native Americans, for example, have a strong mythic and narrative tradition to draw on.

Coaches use narratives to motivate their teams. Parents use narratives to teach their children lessons. Religious leaders use narratives when addressing the members of their congregations. Politicians use narratives to persuade voters to support them. At various times throughout our lives, we all share the myths of our culture. We all act as narrators. We all tell a story.

What functions do myths and narratives serve in speechmaking? To what extent, if any, do you believe it is effective for a speaker to use a mythic or narrative structure to build a speech? What if the myth obscures legitimate historical facts?

Using a myth requires the same sense of order of a speaker. It does not free the speaker from adhering to normal structural demands by permitting him or her greater latitude to exaggerate. While it is acceptable to incorporate elements of myth in a speech, a speech must not be in and of itself, a myth.

speaker it would be awkward for you to say "head" before a main idea and "subhead" before supporting points. Instead you must find ways to let your organization reveal itself naturally to your audience members. An effective speech sounds fresh and alive; it sounds as if it were being given for the first time, even though it has been well thought out, well planned, and carefully organized.

Imagine traveling along an interstate highway. The first sign you see reveals that your destination is thirty miles to the south. The next sign indicates that you turn east, while a third sign recommends you make a "U" turn. All of the signs are within a few feet of each other. Would you be confused? Of course you would. Like drivers, listeners look for specific road signs to guide them on the way to your speaking goal. Should you feed them the wrong signals and lead them astray, they will take a detour rather than travel with you.

Just like an essay, a speech needs a clear beginning, middle, and end. In writing a speech, think of the military formula: "Tell them what you are going to tell them. Tell them. Tell them what you told them." This formula works well for many public speakers. When we are speaking in public we simply introduce the topic and let the audience in on what we will be discussing. We then discuss the topic. Finally, we help our listeners remember what we have said by summarizing the main points and tying the presentation together with a concluding statement. U.S. culture created in many of us a preference for such directness. As we shall see later in this chapter, other cultures may not expect speakers to be so explicit.

BUILDING THE SKELETON OF YOUR SPEECH: MAIN POINTS FIRST

IMAGINE YOURSELF WITHOUT A SKELETON. You would simply be a blob of flesh on the floor. It is the skeleton that provides the lifegiving structure to our bodies. The same is true for speeches. We require a speech skeleton on which to hang the ideas contained in our presentations.

The skeleton of your speech is comprised of your **main points.** At the very least, you want your receivers to retain your speech's main points! Otherwise, there would be little reason to have an audience listen to you. For example, if you were speaking on building a business plan for an entrepreneur, you might use the following skeletal structure.

Purpose: To explain the main points of an entrepreneurial business plan

I. The first section of the business plan focuses on the objectives of the business.
II. The second section of the business plan establishes the need for the business.
III. The third section contains the financial projections for the business.

Thus, we have in plain sight the central features of the speech. Because there are three main parts to a business plan, there will be three main points in the speech. Generally, the fewer the main points in your speech (the ideal is between two and five), the easier it is for receivers to comprehend and retain your message. Overload a speech with too many main points and you run the risk of overwhelming your receivers.

There are a variety of **organizational patterns** you can use to structure your speech, including time order, spatial order, cause-and-effect order, problem–solution order, and topical order. Choose the one that lets you arrange your ideas in a way that reflects the nature of your material and also helps you attain your objective.

Time Order: It's Chronological

When you decide to use **time** or **chronological order** to organize the body of your speech, you are explaining to your audience members the order in which events happened. For example, you may want to deal with your topic by taking an historical approach.

Purpose: To inform the audience about the evolution of the right to privacy

Central idea: Americans believe they have a fundamental right to privacy.

I. More than a century ago, Justice Louis D. Brandeis called privacy "the right to be let alone."
II. Within a decade, the courts began to recognize the right to privacy.
III. The Supreme Court relied on a privacy rationale in reaching its famous and controversial decisions on birth control and abortion.
IV. Threats to our privacy abound today.

A speaker giving directions for college computer registration might also choose to use a chronological order.

Purpose: To inform the audience of the computer registration procedures that are being adopted by the college next semester

Central idea: Following three basic steps will facilitate your registration next semester.

I. Registration packets can be picked up from October 10 to 14.
II. During the week of October 17, students will consult with their advisors.
III. Once a schedule is approved the student can use a personal computer to secure a place in his or her chosen classes.

You can see that a chronological organization works best if you are explaining procedures or processes that occur over time. Both historical and how-to topics are usually organized chronologically. Thus, topics like the history of vaudeville, how the Internet developed, or how to make glass lend themselves to this type of organizational format.

A time pattern can be used in a segment of a speech that uses another organizational style as well. For example, a speaker delivering a speech on the problem of institutionalizing the mentally ill might focus during his first main point on how mental institutions developed in this country. Such an organizational tactic would offer receivers a context against which to process those points the speaker will explore during the remainder of the presentation.

Especially useful in informative speaking, a chronological structure is used when you want to organize your main points from earliest to latest or vice versa in order to illustrate a particular progression of thought, as in the following example.

Purpose: To inform the audience about the development of euthanasia

Central idea: Euthanasia has an interesting history.

I. Today euthanasia is considered mercy killing.
II. During the nineteenth century, the concept of euthanasia was associated with the acceleration of the death process.
III. The ancient Greeks were the first to espouse euthanasia as a concept.

A speaker will probably use spatial order when there is something important about the way objects are positioned in space.

Spatial Order: It's Directional

How do things appear in space? If you can observe objects in space they may be candidates for **spatial organization.** The planets, for example, can be discussed in order of proximity to the sun; a speaker may decide to describe the inner workings of an electronic telephone; someone might use a spatial format to describe major plantings in a Japanese garden. Similarily, if you were speaking about the development of the railroads in this country, you could work from East to West. A speech about the "Trail of Tears" could contain ideas developed spatially if the speaker followed the Native American tribes as they were forced to move by foot from various parts of the country into what is now Oklahoma. In each example, main points would proceed from top to bottom (or vice versa), left to right (or vice versa), front to back (or vice versa), north to south (or vice versa), and so forth. Here is an example of how a speaker used a spatial pattern in talking about Stonehenge.

Purpose: To inform the audience of the appearance of the mysterious monuments of Stonehenge

Central idea: The mystery of Stonehenge is revealed in its five circles of stones.

I. The outermost circle of Stonehenge is called the Outer Sarsen Circle.
II. The first circle is called the Outer Bluestone Circle.
III. The second circle is the Inner Sarsen Trilithons.
IV. The third circle is the Inner Bluestone Horseshoe.
V. The innermost circle is the Altar Stone.

Cause-and-Effect Order: It's Relational

When you arrange your main points in the **cause-and-effect order,** you first discuss the causes of a problem and then discuss what should happen. For example, you might use cause-and-effect order when speaking about:

- the causes of glaucoma and its effects,
- the causes of high blood pressure and its effects,
- the causes of Alzheimer's and its impact, or
- the causes of metal fatigue in airplanes and its consequences.

In his speech entitled "Dropping Out," student Deepi Bansi employed cause-and-effect order, at least in part, to help explain the nature of the dropout problem.

. . . what causes students to drop out of high school?

In the Dropout Prevention Handbook, Nancy Mill explores these causes: poor grades and undiagnosed learning needs.

No, the majority of high school dropouts are not hoodlums or drug users or alcoholics. They're students suffering from academic failure. In this nation alone four million students are affected with a learning disability, and of those four million students, nearly 40 percent will drop out of high school because of it.

What are the effects of dropping out for these students, especially if they don't find employment? First of all, unemployment. In Non-college Youth in America, it is noted that 80 percent of our nation's dropouts are without a full time job. Another effect is poverty. Three point four million families in this nation currently are headed by someone under the age of 25 who is a high school dropout, and of these 3.4 million families, nearly one third are living below the poverty level today. Did you know that means their kids have an 80 percent greater chance of growing up in a life of poverty or crime as well?

Speeches arranged in causal order generally contain two main points—one focusing on causes and the other on effects. In other words, a speaker using a causal pattern can proceed from discussing present effects of a problem to discussing pre-

What's the Effect?

1. Whether you decide to use a cause-to-effect or an effect-to-cause arrangement is up to you. Would the following example work equally well if organized in effect-to-cause order? Why or why not?

Purpose: To inform the audience about the causes and effects of homelessness in our major cities

I. Homelessness is caused by three major factors.
   A. People are taken off welfare rolls.
   B. Others do not apply for assistance.
   C. Still others are released from mental health facilities when they are not yet ready to function in society.

II. There are two major effects of homelessness.
   A. There are effects on the homeless themselves.
      1. Homeless people routinely contract a variety of illnesses.
      2. The effects of homelessness on self-concept can be devastating.
   B. Homelessness affects our entire society.
      1. Cities become unsightly.
      2. Sanitation is a major problem associated with homelessness.
      3. Homelessness tends to breed criminal activity.

2. Identify three speech topics that would benefit from an effect-to-cause arrangement and three that would benefit from a cause-to-effect order. Explain your reasons.

ceding causes of the problem; for example, the speaker could start by explaining the effects of high blood pressure and then discuss the causes. A speaker could analyze the effects of illiteracy and then trace the causes. Similarly, the effects of Alzheimer's disease could be presented first, followed by an exploration of its causes.

Problem–Solution Order: It's Workable

Speakers whose purpose is to persuade their audiences to accept their ideas often use a **problem–solution organizational pattern.** When using this structure you reveal first a significant problem that needs a resolution and then a solution to alleviate the problem. Thus, your speech is divided into two main points. For example, a speaker focusing on carjackings in shopping mall parking lots began by referring to the number of carjackings that had occurred recently in local malls. She then discussed a solution that combined increased lighting with additional security patrols.

The next example also illustrates a problem–solution pattern. Notice how the emphasis is on how the problem can best be resolved.

Purpose: To convince my audience that national health insurance can help solve our health care problems

Central idea: National health insurance will solve many of the problems caused by rising health care costs.

I. Rising health care costs have resulted in an uninsured class of people.
II. Implementing national health insurance will solve this problem.

When using a problem–solution format, a speaker may discuss the advantages of the solution as well. When this occurs, the speaker's organization would include three main points:

I. The problem
II. The solution
III. The advantages of adopting the solution

For example, if you were to speak about the problem of ineffective capital punishment methods, you could first discuss the problems that result when antiquated capital punishment systems fail to end a prisoner's life without first producing a great deal of pain and suffering. Second, you could discuss one of the modern electronic devices designed to make capital punishment more humane and efficient. Third, you could discuss the advantages of the modern system.

The next example also presents a pragmatic solution to a problem.

Purpose: To convince my audience that we should act now to revise the way poverty statistics are reported

Central idea: We should act now to solve the problem caused by the way poverty statistics are currently reported.

I. The poverty level is currently understated in order to keep people off welfare rolls.
   A. Poverty levels for families of four are absurdly low.
   B. Poverty levels for single-parent families are even more outrageous.
II. Minimally acceptable income levels must be raised.
   A. Government levels must be raised for families.
   B. Additional help must be given for single parents.

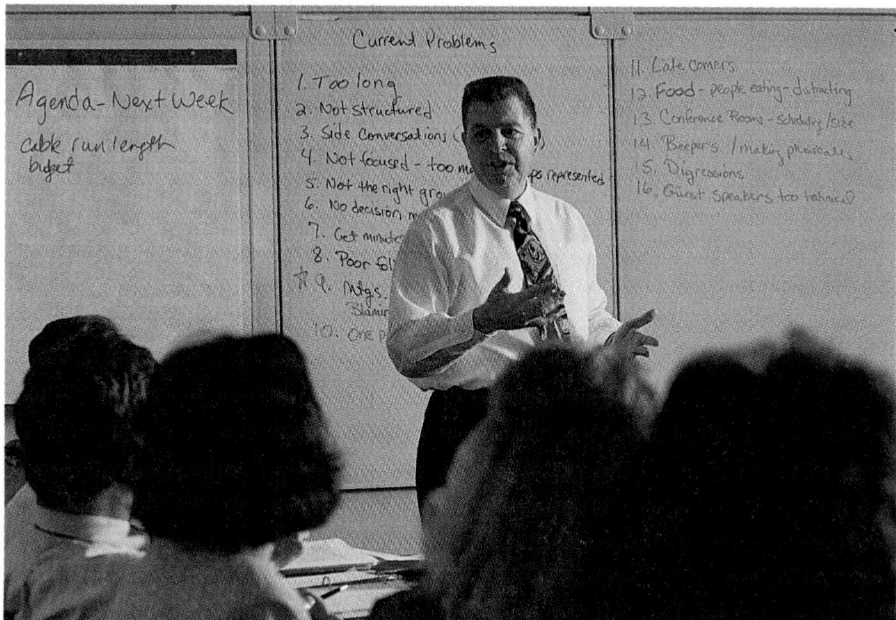

Prior to recommending a solution, the speaker should identify a problem to be solved.

III. These increases will solve some of the problems of the poor.
  A. They will make life easier for families.
  B. Additional aid to single parents will help them help themselves and their children.

Topical Order: It's Part of the Whole

Speakers can also choose to use a **topical order.** Topically organized speeches divide naturally into a number of subdivisions. The subdivisions correspond to different aspects of your topic, or may even serve as a mnemonic (memory trigger) device.

For example, you might consider speaking about the pros and cons of a particular issue confronting your audience; for example, the pros and cons of using animals for medical and product research.

Purpose: To inform my audience of the advantages and disadvantages of using animals for medical and product research

Central idea: Using animals for medical and product research presents both advantages and disadvantages.

I. There are two advantages to using animals as research subjects.
  A. Using animals is more effective than simply using results of test tube experiments.
  B. Using animals is more effective during the early stages of research than using human subjects.

II. There are two disadvantages to using animals in research.
  A. Animals are often mutilated and in pain.
  B. Animals do not respond in precisely the same manner that human subjects do.

You might decide to subdivide your chosen subject into a series of topics that break the material down into units.

Purpose: To inform the audience about the types of nonverbal communication

Central idea: The study of nonverbal communication involves three basic areas.

I. The study of nonverbal communication includes the study of kinesics or body language.

II. The study of nonverbal communication includes the study of paralanguage or vocal qualities.

III. The study of nonverbal communication includes the study of proxemics or space and distance.

Some speakers have even found it helpful to use a memory device that makes it easier for their audience members to recall their main points. Sometimes called gimmick speeches, these presentations are arranged according to a mnemonic. For example, in a speech on speechwriting, one speaker used the word *BRIEF:*

Brainstorm ideas
Research ideas
Interpret ideas
Energize ideas
Finalize ideas

Thus, the word *BRIEF* became the outline for the body of the presentation.

Because it lends itself to almost any subject, topical organization is a very popular organizational format.

"Labels" That Are Easy to Remember

Communication consultant Lani Arredondo tells her clients about mnemonic devices.

Mnemonic devices help people remember. The first letter of each key point . . . spell PRO (Prepare, Relate, Optimize). It's an acronym, a mnemonic device that serves to jog people's memory.

In one presentation on the value of reducing the costs of business, the speaker used the acronym LOW to identify his three key points. The letters stood for Lean and mean, Overtime and Winning edge. That I remember the points months later speaks to the value of acronyms.

Another common mnemonic is to begin each key point with the same letter or word. In one presentation I make, I address the three Cs of customer service: Courtesy, Care and Complaints.

Key points are the highlights of your presentation. You know the audience won't remember everything you say. But if they remember nothing else, you want them to walk away with at least your key points in mind. So take care to select the points that have the most meaning. Arrange them in an order that helps the audience follow them. And if you can label your key points using a mnemonic device, do so if it makes sense; that is, if it reflects the theme of your presentation. . . .

One final factor in determining the sequence of key points is that of impact. Like a symphony, your presentation should build to a crescendo! Arrange your points to lead to an exciting or forceful conclusion.[6]

SPEAKING of ETHICS

Should Audience Education Affect Speech Structure?

Should you present both sides of a topic, or should you present only the side or ideas you are advocating? Before you answer, consider the research findings in this area.

- The two-sided speech is more effective when listeners have at least a high school education and when the weight of the evidence is clearly on one side.
- The one-sided presentation is more effective when listeners have not completed high school.
- The one-sided presentation is more effective when listeners already favor the ideas.
- The two-sided presentation is more effective when listeners are opposed to the speaker's position.
- The two-sided message has an immunizing effect against a speech that follows and is opposed to the main point.

To what extent should access to knowlege depend on how much schooling you have had? Why would people who have at least a high school education be more apt to favor a two-sided presentation than those who did not graduate from high school?

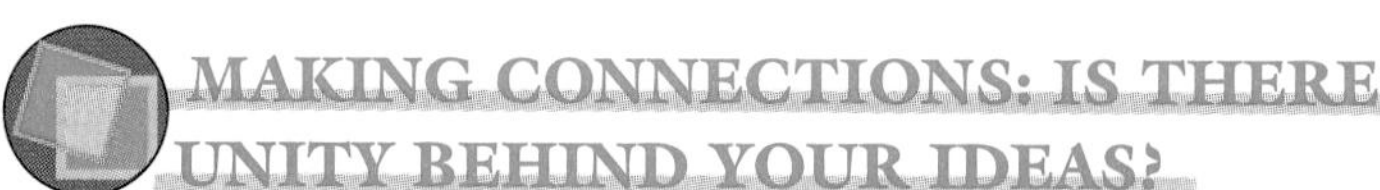

MAKING CONNECTIONS: IS THERE UNITY BEHIND YOUR IDEAS?

YOUR JOB DOES NOT END WHEN YOU HAVE created the basic structure of the presentation. You still need to make sure that the ideas you have included "hang together." That is, you will need to find ways to create a sense of coherence and unity within the presentation. Three devices that effective speakers use to accomplish this are transitions, internal previews, and internal summaries.

Using Transitions

Moving from one main point to the next is very much like getting from one side of a river to the other. In the world of matter, a bridge serves that purpose very nicely. In public speaking, **transitions** work as a bridge from idea to idea. A transition also serves as the mortar or glue to hold the ideas together so that your audience perceives a completed presentation rather than an array of unrelated concepts.

As you work with transitions, remember that they fall into the four *C*s:

Chronological
Contrasting
Causal
Complementary

Chronological transitions help the listener understand the time relationship between the first main point and the one that follows. Words and phrases such as *before,* *after, later, at the same time, while,* and *finally* show what is happening in time order. **Contrasting transitions** include terms such as *but, on the other hand, in contrast,* and *in spite of.* These words show how the idea that follows differs from the one that preceded it. **Causal transitions** are words like *because, therefore,* and *consequently;* causal transitions help show the cause-and-effect relationships between the ideas. **Complementary transitions** help the speaker add one idea to the next. *Also, next, in addition to,* and *likewise* are examples of complementary transitions. Below are some examples of transitions in action.

Chronological

After we completed the first phase of the project . . .
At the same time that we were exploring cultural values . . .
As soon as the Senate passed the new legislation . . .

Contrasting

In spite of the government's attempts to . . .
Although the money was available to build the senior center . . .
On the other hand, we should also consider . . .

Causal

As a result of the ways the members of different cultures define what is "real," "good," and "correct," their interpretations of . . .
Because the maintenance on the bridge was ignored . . .
Consequently, we must now consider how to fund this proposal . . .

Complementary

Next, let's consider the three reasons why we should . . .
Likewise, our experiment was designed to demonstrate that . . .
It is just as important to examine the ways in which animals . . .

Sometimes you can be creative in your use of transitional ideas. For example, you may want to use a flashback to an earlier idea to serve as the transition to the later one. For example, you might say to your audience, "You will remember that earlier I mentioned that location is an extremely important aspect of evaluating real estate."

You can use more than words as a bridge between ideas. Visuals can help you make the transition. Physical movement can illustrate change as well. Walking from one side of the podium to the other as you move to the next main point can serve to show your audience that you are literally changing direction from one idea to the next in your presentation.

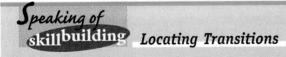

Locating Transitions

Select an article from either *Vital Speeches of the Day,* today's newspaper, or a recent newsmagazine. Circle all of the transitions that the speaker has used and label them chronological, causal, contrasting, or complementary. How effective were the transitions as bridges?

Read a portion of the selection aloud with the transitions. Then read it again, eliminating the transitions. Again, how effective were the transitions in holding the speaker's or writer's ideas together?

Using Internal Previews

An **internal preview** is similar to a transition in that it helps hold your speech together. However, such previews are generally longer than simple transitions. They help prepare audience members to listen and retain the important information that will follow. Let's examine how previews can work for you.

In a presentation on genetic engineering, a speaker told her audience:

We will next consider a technique which allows biologists to transfer a gene from one species to another. It is called recombinant DNA technology.

More than just a transition, this phrase gives the listener a specific indication of what to look for as the speech progresses. While examining the structure of the *Wall Street Journal,* one speaker indicated:

Now I will show you one of the most unique aspects of the Journal—its line drawings.

Another speaker used an internal preview when he said:

Early film comics provided laughter to millions. Today I will show you examples of two of the best: Harold Lloyd and Charlie Chaplin.

You can see how the internal preview might help the audience determine precisely where you are in your presentation and where you are heading.

Using Internal Summaries

The internal preview precedes the information you are discussing; the **internal summary** follows it. Summaries help speakers clarify or emphasize what they have said. For example:

Now that we have discussed the safety hazards to the use of nuclear power, and its cost to society, we can move on to . . .

You can see that it is clear that thousands of teens drive drunk every Friday and Saturday night.

CULTURE'S INFLUENCE ON ORGANIZATION

THE ORGANIZATIONAL PATTERNS WE DISCUSSED in this chapter display a linear logic. They are typical of the ways North American speakers organize and make sense of information. When displaying a **linear logic,** a speaker develops his or her ideas step by step, relying on facts and data to support each main point. Each idea is then linked to another via a series of bridges or transitions. Linear patterns are used predominantly by persons who belong to low-context cultures. Recall that members of low-context cultures characteristically relay the information they want to deliver to others explicitly. They make few assumptions that receivers will understand or intuit what they do not overtly tell them. Because they prefer to make their points directly and quickly, they expect others to do the same. They tend to be rather blunt and outspoken and, as a result, expect others to speak their minds as well. They do not rely solely on emotional appeals and stories to make their points, but offer relevant supporting facts—that is, hard evidence and proof in defense of the positions they take.

Speakers from other cultures and ethnic groups, however, may not find these linear patterns to be as sensible, appropriate, or useful as North Americans.[7] Thus, other speechmaking patterns, most significantly less linear and more configural in form, have also emerged. **Configural organizational formats** are more indirect than linear formats. While direction may be implied in a configural format, it will rarely be explicitly stated in either a speech's introduction or its conclusion. Instead of spelling out key points, the speaker who uses configural thinking relies on examples and stories to carry the crux of his or her message and the audience to decipher the meaning implied in the examples and stories used.[8] Thus indirection and implication, rather than bridges or transitions, are used to circle and connect ideas, establish a main point, and ultimately lead listeners to a conclusion. High-context cultures such as those in Japan, Saudi Arabia, and Latin America, prefer this kind of pattern because they believe the explicit stating of a message is unnecessary. Thus, rather than rely on explicit links to provide a main point, speakers who use a configural pattern devise a series of "stepping stones" that circle a topic but do not hit it head on.

As a result of these differences in orientation, members of high-context cultures may be insulted by the directness and explicitness exhibited in the messages of speakers who belong to low-context cultures. Conversely, members of low-context cultures may perceive the messages delivered by speakers from high-context cultures to be too vague, confusing, illogical, unnecessarily drawn out, filled with digressions, and generally poorly developed.

CONSIDERING DIVERSITY

Indirect Organization

In *The Flight from Ambiguity* researcher David Levine describes the organizational pattern of the Ethiopian Amhara culture. He contrasts it with the typical North American way of organizing information.

> The Amhara's basic manner of communicating is indirect, often secretive. Amharic conversation abounds with general, evasive remarks like Min yeshallal ("What is better?") when the speaker has failed to indicate what issue he or she is referring to. . . . When the speaker is then quizzed about the issue at hand or the object he or she desires, his or her reply still may not reveal what is really on his or her mind; and if it does, his or her interlocutor will likely as not interpret that response as a disguise. . . .
>
> The American way of life, by contrast, affords little room for the cultivation of ambiguity. The dominant American temper calls for clear and direct communication. It expresses itself in such common injunctions as, "Say what you mean," "Don't beat around the bush," and "Get to the point."[9]

- In what ways could people from other cultures have difficulty when communicating with North Americans?
- How could the difficulties be overcome?

When speaking to an audience including people from diverse cultures, effective speakers take steps to adjust their styles of organization to reflect the habitual organizational preferences of their receivers.

According to most intercultural communication theorists, English is primarily a speaker-responsible language, but other languages, including Japanese, Chinese, and Arabic, are more listener-responsible. Native users of speaker-responsible languages typically believe it is up to the speaker to tell the listener exactly what is going to be spoken about and what the speaker wants the listener to know. In contrast, native speakers of listener-responsible languages typically believe that speakers need only indicate indirectly what they are speaking about and what they want the listener to know when they have finished speaking. They believe it is up to the listener and not the speaker to construct the message's meaning.[10]

The following speech outline is organized configurally. Because the speaker does not clearly lay out the speech's main points, the audience will need to participate actively in interpreting what the speaker only implies.

Purpose: To persuade my audience that biological weapons research is a problem.

I. A hypothetical worker, Alan, who works in a lab funded by the defense department, inadvertently infects himself with the biological weapon he is studying.
II. Alan suffers the kind of death that our enemies would suffer were biological weapons used during episodes of warfare.
III. Alan's family suffers with him.
IV. Today, members of Alan's family address Congress, asking, "How can America be involved in something like this?"

Notice the speech's brief outline. While the speaker will neither state a central thesis directly nor preview what is to occur in the speech for receivers, she will elaborate on and embellish each of the ideas identified in the outline during the actual presentation. The speaker will also hint at a solution and encourage receivers to participate actively in its discovery. In effect, it is up to the audience to interpret the meaning of the speaker's narrative from the stories, examples, and testimony she offers. Rather than directly inform receivers of facts and arguments, the speaker who uses a configural pattern of organization implies and suggests, but does not directly state what receivers should think or do. Because the speaker never actually states the thesis of the speech explicitly, the audience bears more responsibility for making sense of the speaker's message, connecting the ideas expressed during the presentation, drawing their own conclusions, and constructing their own solutions to the problem discussed.

SUMMARY

ORGANIZATION IS A CRITICAL FACTOR IN public speaking success. If receivers are to attend to, understand, and retain the ideas of a speaker, they must perceive the speech to be organized. It must have a skeleton on which the speaker can hang key and supporting ideas.

It is also important that the speaker spend time considering how best to organize the speech's content. Among the organizational patterns are: time order, spatial order, cause-and-effect order, problem–solution order, and topical order.

In addition, in order for a speaker to invest his or her ideas with coherence and unity, it may be necessary for him or her to use the following speech connectors: transitions, previews, and internal summaries.

Different cultures display different organizational preferences. Whereas low-context cultures prefer to use highly structured linear thought patterns, high-context cultures prefer more configural patterns.

By following specific organizational precepts, a speaker is able to infuse his or her message with a sense of coherence, more readily share ideas with receivers, and facilitate audience understanding and acceptance.

THE SPEAKER'S STAND

Locate a transcript of a recent speech from *Vital Speeches of the Day,* the *New York Times, Time, Newsweek,* or a local publication. Alone or as a member of a group, analyze the speech by determining:

1. The order of the main points (chronological, spacial, topical, and so forth).
2. The connections transitions, internal previews, and internal summaries.

Discuss these points in detail with your class.

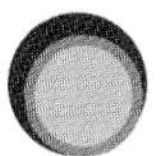

STUDENT FOCUS GROUP REPORT

Take a few minutes to reflect on the various organizational techniques that we have considered in this chapter. In a group of five to seven students, answer the following questions:

1. Revisit the case study at the chapter's opening. Based on what you now understand about speech organization, how would you respond to the questions?
2. Which organizational approach do you prefer? Why?
3. Which organizational approach do you find least useful? Why?
4. In what ways does the selection of a topic influence your choice of organizational format?
5. How might the educational level of your receivers influence your choice of organizational pattern?
6. What tools does the speaker have at his or her disposal to ensure audience members will follow the ideas contained in his or her speech with ease?
7. Summarize the most important information you have learned about speech organization.

Chapter Ten

Introducing and Concluding Your Speech

The Starting Point and the Finish Line

After reading this chapter, you should be able to:

- Explain how the introduction and conclusion affect a speech.
- Describe the purposes served by introductions and conclusions.
- Identify at least five ways of introducing and concluding a speech.
- Identify pitfalls to avoid when creating an introduction and a conclusion.
- Develop introductions that get attention, interest receivers, establish credibility, and preview the body of the speech.
- Develop conclusions that forecast the end of a speech, summarize a speech's main points, provide a sense of closure, and compel receivers to continue thinking about the speech.

CASE STUDY

Where Do I Begin? Where Do I End?

Lauren had just completed the body of her presentation on the dangers of drinking and driving. She had chosen the topic because she had firsthand experience with it. Some years ago, when she was just 14, her brother, a college senior, was killed by a drunk driver. To supplement her personal experience, Lauren conducted extensive research. She interviewed others who had suffered similar losses, law enforcement officials, and representatives from M.A.D.D. (Mothers Against Drunk Driving). She also read numerous articles on the subject and obtained a wealth of statistical data.

Now she felt it was time to concentrate on the next task—how to best craft her presentation's introduction and conclusion. She agonized over which of three possible roads to travel.

(1) She could share her personal experience and relive the horror of her brother's death. (Lauren wondered whether that approach might be too emotional for both her and her audience. Would her receivers stop listening because they would be embarrassed, put off, or alienated by her emotional display?)

(2) She could write her experience into the introduction as if it had happened to someone else. (Lauren asked herself if it would be fair to deceive or mislead her receivers that way.)

(3) She could leave herself out of the speech altogether, and just refer to others who had suffered losses instead. (While selecting choice 2 or 3 would make the story easier for her to relay to others, Lauren couldn't help but feel that neither choice would have the same impact on her audience as choice 1.)

Then she had another idea. "Maybe," Lauren thought to herself, "I could start out with choice 2, but then use the conclusion to reveal that it was not a stranger, but my own brother that I had spoken about during my introduction."

- What advice would you give Lauren about each of her choices? Why?
- Are there any other choices you could recommend to her?
- In what ways does a speaker's revealing his or her emotions get in the way of or facilitate the delivery of a speech's main message?

HOW MIGHT A SPEAKER BEGIN AN EFFECTIVE relationship with an audience? What's a viable way for a speaker to bring that relationship to a close? The speaker–audience relationship is as complex as any of the relationships we share with friends or business associates. For example, friend and business relationships start and terminate daily. Some are productive and allow us to accomplish our goals, while others seem to take us down a dead end. Often, it is how we handle ourselves during a relationship's initial or final stage that determines its ultimate outcome and the effects it will have on those who are party to it. The same may be said of the speaker–audience relationship. The way the speaker introduces and concludes his or her presentation influences the ultimate impact the speech has on those who hear it, and also affects the perception receivers form of the speaker.

Oprah Winfrey gets President's Service Awards Ceremony for Honored Volunteers off to a good start.

During the first few moments of a presentation, the speaker's audience forms an initial impression of both the speaker and the speech. During the last few moments of a presentation, the audience members listen and watch as the speaker lets them know that the speech is about to close and does his or her best to leave them with a favorable impression of both him- or herself and the speech. Therefore, an appropriate beginning and an appropriate ending can make or break both a speech and a speechmaker. They can enhance credibility or destroy it; they can add to or diminish the impact of a presentation; they can help the speaker reach objectives or keep them elusive.

In this chapter we will explore specific speechcrafting techniques you can use to create effective introductions and conclusions for your speeches. We will explore the roles introductions and conclusions perform and we will offer specific guidelines you can follow to ensure you begin and end every one of your speeches as effectively as possible. How to begin and end a relationship with an audience are essential components of the speechmaking process.

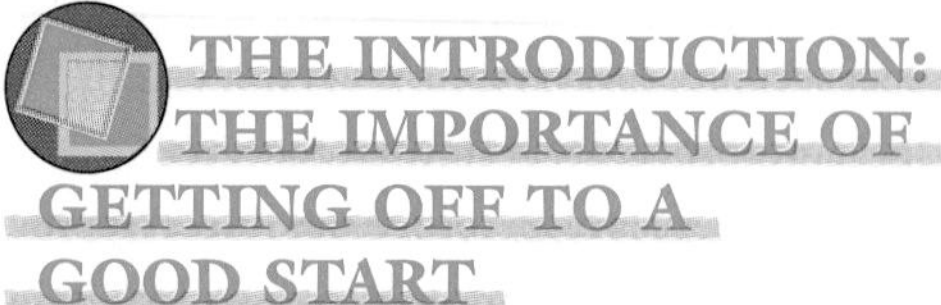

THE INTRODUCTION: THE IMPORTANCE OF GETTING OFF TO A GOOD START

A GOOD BEGINNING is vital to a speechmaker's success. Compare the responses of an interested, receptive, and attentive audience with those of an audience that is uninterested, unreceptive, and alienated. The facial expressions, body postures, and squirm quotients of audience members often tell it all. If the members of your audience are not convinced in the opening seconds of your speech that you and your ideas are worth listening to, their faces will register pain, boredom, or anger; their bodies will lack the tension of attention; and they will tend to fidget. In contrast, if you succeed in your speech's opening seconds in convincing your audience that you and your ideas do merit their consideration, their faces will register appreciation and concentration, their bodies will display interest and concern, and they will sit still.

One of the most difficult challenges facing any speechmaker is how to begin a presentation. Though often the last part of a speech to be written, and usually comprising approximately 10 percent of total available speaking time, the introduction is the first opportunity audience members have to evaluate both the speaker and the speech. As such, if the introduction is to start things off right, it must fulfill certain functions. An effective introduction:

- Builds the speaker's credibility and goodwill.
- Captures the attention and interest of the audience.
- Orients receivers to the organizational development and tone of the speech.

The extent to which you are able to provide audience members with content relevant to these functions helps determine whether audience members respond positively or negatively to you and your speech. Remember, if—and only if—you focus on and fulfill the functions of an effective introduction will you improve the chances that your audience pays careful attention to you.

USE THE INTRODUCTION TO BUILD CREDIBILITY

WHO DO YOU TRUST OR DISTRUST? Whose opinion do you respect or ignore? Who do you really like or dislike? How you answer these questions provides you with clues to your judgments regarding the credibility of specific individuals you know.

Your introduction helps condition your audience to listen to your ideas, and can also convince listeners of your credibility. Thus, if you prepare it effectively, your introduction can put your receivers in a proper frame of mind and enhance their readiness to respond as you hope they will.

An audience is not automatically set to listen to you and react as you wish. Rather, it is your job to motivate audience members to pay attention. It is your role to convince them that you are a knowledgeable, likeable, and believable source. It is your task to prepare them to process the body of your presentation.

Credibility Is in the Ear of the Listener

Credibility is perceptually based. If you perceive an individual to be knowledgeable, trustworthy, and personable, whether the individual actually possesses those qualities is not the issue; in your eyes the individual is someone you believe is competent to offer you advice, has your best interests at heart, and is a person of goodwill.

Credibility can also, of course, be subject based. You may respect your friend's abilities in some areas but not in others. Whatever the situation, however, if you perceive someone to be qualified, sincere, and a person with whom you can identify, your attitude toward that person will be more positive. In your judgment, that person is someone you can believe in and trust, and so you do.

Ideally, the introduction you create goes beyond capturing the attention and interest of your audience. If it is well planned it also shows them that you are qualified to speak on your chosen topic, that you are trustworthy, and that you are likeable. Why should it do all this? Because your ability to influence audience members is related directly to the amount of respect, trust, and goodwill they feel toward you. Audience members form initial impressions of you based on how you look, what you say, and how you speak during your introduction. If, as a result of your introduction, audience members judge you to be qualified to speak on your topic (you convince them that you know what you are talking about), if they are able to identify with you and respond to you (because you were able to establish common ground with them), and if they like and trust you, then you have credibility. In other words, if your audience perceives you to be competent, believable, and likeable, then for them you are a credible speaker. Consequently, if you can build your credibility with your audience early in your presentation, your chances of motivating them to listen to you will increase.

The Issue of Cultural Credibility

If you are of the same sex or ethnic background as the majority of your audience members, you have an obvious "opening advantage." But most speakers can no longer count on having this advantage with most audiences. Again, it is up to you to look analytically at yourself, to weigh your role in relation to major audience factors, and to plan your opening to excite and motivate listeners.

Critics said that President Bill Clinton succeeded in accomplishing this in a speech given to African American leaders on the same site in Memphis where Rev. Martin Luther King, Jr., had delivered what turned out to be his last speech in 1968. The president began his remarks with phrases that reflected the words that King had used nearly three decades earlier. From the outset, Clinton adopted King's voice, words, and style in an effort to establish his own credibility and win over his audience.[1]

Clinton began his address:

I am glad to be here. You have touched my heart. You have brought tears to my eyes and joy to my spirit.[2]

He then continued by referring to the Bible:

The proverb says, "A happy heart doeth good like medicine, but a broken spirit dryeth the bone."[3]

By emulating King's style, Clinton was able to sound a lot like a preacher. He also established himself as a concerned member of the community, one who shared the same interests as his receivers, and on whom they could now look at as more credible. By identifying and sharing the concerns of your receivers you can enhance your cultural credibility as well.

How to Help Your Audience Perceive You as Credible

What can you do so your audience perceives you as credible? First, let's identify the building blocks you have to work with: the preparation that underlies competence; the commitment that underlies trustworthiness; and the confidence that underlies performance. Second, ask yourself the following questions:

Why should audience members listen to *me*?

What have I done or experienced that has prepared or qualified me to speak on the topic?

How personally committed am I to the ideas I am about to share with my audience?

What steps can I take to communicate my concern and enthusiasm to the audience?

How can I use my appearance, attitude, and delivery to help establish my goodwill and make my case?

If you are mindful of the ways listeners perceive you, and if you do whatever you can to increase their motivation to listen to you, then you will find that you use attitude, demeanor, and content to build your credibility in their eyes.

Notice how student Mary Hoffman used her personal experiences to establish her qualifications to speak on her chosen topic, mercury, and to establish common ground with her audience.

Perhaps there is nothing we fear more than a trip to the dentist. While none of us enjoy the poking and scraping that accompany the visit, we all recognize the need for this semi-annual ritual. After leaving the office, we would like nothing better than to be able to say, "Look ma, no cavities," like the kid in the Crest commercial. But I'm willing to bet that didn't happen to any of us very often. Instead, we probably returned a few weeks later and left with numb lips and new fillings. While these fillings may slow the advance of the cavity creeps, they may be causing serious health problems: Silver amalgam, which has been used in dental work for over one hundred and fifty years, was always assumed to be harmless, but new research suggests it may be very dangerous.[4]

William Rodrigues, IBM's general manager for K–12 education, introduced a speech on the topic of improving learning with technology with these words:

There can be no question about the impact of technology on our society over the past fifty years. As we've moved from the post-war era, to the jet age, to the space age, to the information age, technology has taken on an increasingly important role in our daily lives.

Today, it is fair to say that technology touches nearly every aspect of our lives, from commercials sporting web addresses to being able to file your income taxes online.

And the benefits of technology are tangible. It makes our nation's business more productive, it makes our homes safer and more energy efficient, it makes our transportation run more smoothly, and it entertains and informs us.

But are the benefits of technology as tangible for K–12 education?

We certainly know what the promise of technology is for education: better test scores, better student performance, better instruction, overall a more rich and satisfying educational experience for student and teacher alike.

And finally, better educated students, prepared to take their place in a high-technology society.

It is a promise whose realization has been elusive. We all know how to use wide area networks and computers to get cash from ATM machines. The uses of technology to improve education have been less pervasive.[5]

Just as Rodrigues used his IBM credentials to build credibility, student Chris Fleming used both his personal experiences and research he conducted to build credibility with his listeners in a speech entitled "Bring Back the Pony Express." As you read this excerpt, notice how adroitly he communicates his central idea to his receivers.

I've always been a little superstitious when it comes to competition. For example, I had this one suit that I had to wear the final day. It was my lucky suit. Last year I realized a few days before our first tournament that I had not brought my suit to college with me. My mom rushed to the post office and mailed it first class to my dorm on campus but it never arrived. I'm convinced that somewhere, some Saturday night a U.S. postal worker is out on the town, looking sharp and hoping to get lucky in my lucky suit.

But, hey, it could have been worse. Like the woman who dropped her phone bill in the mail, and instead of being delivered uptown, the note landed a month and a half later in Australia. According to a March 24, 1994, Broadcast News Transcript from CNN, this is not just an exception but the rule when it comes to the U.S. Postal System. Mail service continues to get slower, more expensive, and less reliable.[6]

Just as all of these speakers have made their audiences feel good about listening to them, your ability to allow your audience members to sense your concern for them will encourage them to want to listen to you. Both the sincerity of your voice and the commitment portrayed by your facial expressions, eye contact, and gestures can enhance your audience's opinion of you and do much to cement the feeling of goodwill that is so integral to their assessments of your credibility.

If by the time you conclude your introduction your audience perceives you positively, you will find it easier to maintain their interest during the remainder of your speech. If you waste the opportunity offered you to build your credibility in the introduction, you will make it much more difficult to establish a positive image of yourself in the minds of your listeners as you proceed. When your listeners understand how you personally relate to the subject, they are better able to relate to it and to you. If they believe you are genuinely concerned and speaking from your heart, they

SPEAKING of ETHICS

Does It Matter How You Get There?

If the goal of a speaker is worthy in your eyes, does it matter what techniques he or she used to attain his or her goal? For example, in an effort to capture audience attention one student who was delivering a speech on drug abuse claimed that his sister died after taking tainted heroin when in fact she was alive and well and had never even used illegal drugs.

- Is it inappropriate for a speaker to fabricate a story even if doing so will increase listener attention, motivation to respond, or retention?
- Which is more important to you: the content of a speaker's message or the speaker's goal? If, for instance, a speaker succeeds in arousing an audience as the result of an emotionally charged introduction or conclusion but delivers nothing of substance in the body of his or her speech, has the speaker fallen short of his or her goal?
- As a speaker, should you have to prove that the body of your speech contains thoughtful and reasoned discourse prior to using an effective emotional appeal or a hook? Why or why not?

will be more apt to really listen to what you say. You will influence your audience more if they perceive you to be competent, trustworthy, and likeable than you ever will if they judge any of these qualities to be lacking.

USE THE INTRODUCTION TO CAPTURE THE ATTENTION OF RECEIVERS

WE ARE INNUNDATED DAILY with countless messages from other persons—some person to person and some mediated—who attempt to get us to focus on and listen to them. Do we pay attention to all of them? Certainly not. If we did, we wouldn't have a minute to spare. So how do we decide which messages we should focus on and which we should ignore? Usually we focus on those messages that directly involve us, impress us, arouse our curiosity or build suspense, are relevant to our lives, make us laugh, or move us. You can also use techniques like these to gain the attention and interest of listeners at the beginning of a speech.

Just as you form impressions of people you meet quickly, so listeners will form impressions of you and your speech quickly. Unless your speech attracts the attention of your listeners and builds and holds their interest from the outset, whatever you want to communicate to them may be lost simply because they do not want to listen to the body of your speech. Audience interest and speech impact correlate highly. Unless you grab the interest of your audience from the beginning, your effort to share information with them or influence them could be thwarted.

The following techniques, employed individually or in combination, will help you capture and hold the attention and interest of an audience.

Beginning and Ending

Thoughts on Beginnings

According to professional speechwriter Sylvia Simmons, author of *How to Be the Life of the Podium,* "the toughest job a speaker has is breaking the ice and developing some sort of rapport with the audience."[7] Sharon Bower, speech consultant and author of *Painless Public Speaking,* echoes that sentiment: "A good introduction is like a handshake; it introduces you in a friendly way."[8] And according to speech coach Stephen C. Rafe, author of *How to Be Prepared to Speak on Your Feet,* "you have to develop the best possible opening—one that will catch your audience's attention from the first words you speak."[9]

Thoughts on Endings

Simmons notes: "The single worst and most often committed crime against audiences is that of speaking too long."[10] Bower reinforces this when she explains: "Listeners forget long, colorless, and complicated endings . . . a final statement should be short and sweet: short to listen to and sweet to remember."[11] And Rafe advises that you "look over your material and ask yourself, 'What is the most important or logical way to end this communication?' . . . Pick the kind of ending that works best for your audience, your situation, your topic, and your intentions."[12]

Startle or Shock Your Audience

Every once in a while, an introduction appears to compel attention from an audience. The speaker's statement has such an impact that it becomes virtually impossible for the thoughts of audience members to stray from the speech. Student Tara Kubicka used such an approach in opening her speech entitled "Traitorous Transplants: The Enemy Within."

Brian Clark was the kind of son that all parents dream of having, a star football player, junior class president, 3.8 g.p.a. and a devoted brother. Sounds too good to be true, right? Early one afternoon at football practice, Brian collapsed and tests revealed that he had advanced leukemia and the only thing that would help him would be an immediate bone marrow transplant. Against all hope a match was found—Brian received his life-saving transplant. The story doesn't end there, however. You see, the donor died 9 months later of complications stemming from AIDS related pneumonia. Brian's donor had been infected with the HIV virus and now . . . so was Brian.[13]

Such a startling disclosure at the outset of the presentation shocked Tara's audience and piqued their interest. Because the introduction related directly to the subject of her speech, and because she was able to make the members of the audience feel that the message was aimed directly at them, audience members were motivated to listen further.

Another speaker, student Gwen Johnson, used a brief series of startling examples to arouse interest in her audience. Speaking on global dumping, Gwen began:

When Sunday Nana of Koko, Nigeria, agreed to store thousands of leaking and deteriorating metal drums on his land for a mere $100 a month, little did he know he was signing his own and 19 other villagers' death warrants. The drums contained nearly 4,000 tons of toxic waste and caused chemical burns, paralyzation and vomiting of blood by the workers who attempted to clean up the mess.

Downstream from a mercury processing plant in South Africa, Zulu villagers drank from the river with a mercury concentration 1.5 million times the safety standard set by the World Health Organization.

In a Brazilian lead recycling plant, birds that roost in the rafters routinely fall to the floor dead and the workers suffer from headaches, nausea, kidney pains and overpowering weakness; all symptoms of chronic lead poisoning, resulting in massive birth defects and ultimate death.

These are but three examples of the virtual thousands of cases that exist in Third World Nations and were caused by the legal and illegal exportation and dumping practices of American corporations and in some cases our own government.[14]

How might an audience of (1) traditional executives from a multinational corporation, and (2) recent third world immigrants to the United States have interpreted Gwen's opening? Imagine how much less impact Gwen's speech would have had if she had begun by telling her audience members: "Today I am going to speak about global dumping." Instead of paying close attention to her remarks, audience members would probably have tuned out and turned off.

Startling or shocking statements are effective and easy to use. What you need to weigh carefully, however, is how much "heavy dramatization" for shock effect is consistent with an honest treatment of the anecdotal evidence and the audience's credulity. You want to be certain that the materials you use to startle or shock your audience are relevant to your topic, easy for audience members to follow, and trigger

Startling Statements

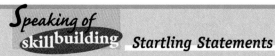

1. Working in teams, prepare hypothetical startling statements you could use to introduce a speech on one of the following topics:
   - Airline safety
   - Native American rights
   - Preparing for final exams
   - Hazards of stereotyping
   - Reducing salt in your diet
2. Spend time carefully watching television advertisements. Describe examples of ads that use startling or shocking openers to capture audience involvement. Then find examples of startling openers that are used by local or national news programs to involve viewers.

interest rather than confusion. If you use an introduction only because it has shock value, but fail to connect it to the crux of your remarks, audience members will become irritated rather than interested, confused rather than intrigued. Startling statements must still be true and supportable.

The introduction used by student Neil Mansharamani in a speech on the effects of handwriting illegibility would be less effective if used in a speech on the treatment of kidney infections.

A 59-year-old woman was admitted to a hospital to receive treatment for a kidney infection, and prescribed the medication Losec. On her 12th day in the hospital, she suffered a heart attack and died. The *Lancet* of May 25, 1991, reports a review of the patient's medical records revealed the reason for her death: the patient received the wrong medication due to an illegibly written prescription. She had been taking Lasix instead of Losec—a medication error that cost her her life. This woman's death was tragic. But the dangers of illegibility are quite common. Recently, in Ohio five people lost their lives when the small plane they were flying in crashed. The *Los Angeles Times* of April 3, 1994, said that an illegibly written barometer reading caused the tragic accident. Illegibility costs lives, not to mention millions of dollars each year. Let's face it. The "writing is on the wall," but we are having a difficult time reading it.[15]

Directly Involve Your Audience

If you can make audience members believe that your topic affects them directly, their motivation to listen will rise. If you can demonstrate that they are personally responsible for or affected by your topic, their interest will increase. We all tend to pay greater attention to things that directly involve us. It is up to you, the speaker, to invite and encourage audience participation in your presentation.

In the very first sentence of the introduction to her speech on the Prozac family of drugs, Kurstin Finch immediately involved her receivers:

Congratulations! You have all been invited to play "Choose Your Own Personality" and take a spin at the Prozac wheel. What will you win? A legitimate cure to chronic depression? A chance at one of a dozen annoying and dangerous side effects? Or maybe a whole new personality![16]

Another speaker, student Brent Wainscott, began his speech, "The Value of Smiles and Laughter," by directly involving his listeners:

Are you . . . tired? Maybe even bored? Come on—you can admit it. Maybe you just feel bad. Maybe? Okay, try this . . . look at someone next to you, and frown at them real hard. Go ahead; you can do it. Give them the look of death. Now laugh at how ugly they look. That's it; now you've got it. Smile at them real big. Good. Now look at me with those big smiles. Well I don't know if you feel better or not, but I sure feel more comfortable standing up here now that you are smiling. Smiles, laughter, humor. They can do many things for us.[17]

Similarly, student Tai Du was able to draw his receivers directly into his speech by asking them a question:

In the sleepy town of Decatur, Illinois, controversy is almost unheard of. Decatur, however, does lay claim to a very industrious inventor, Earl Wright. Throughout the years Earl has invented everything from Corn Silk makeup for women, to tri-colored jello, especially for Bill Cosby. It wasn't until recently, though, that Earl was ecstatic about another invention. Earl invented a life-saving device known simply as the "Sensor Pad." The device helps women detect lumps during self-examination for breast cancer. The pad, composed only of two soft sheets of plastic with silicon inside, helped Mary Gorman of Chevy Chase, Maryland, discover a pea-size lump in her breast . . . that a mammogram missed. Where can you get this miraculous device—NOWHERE—that is in the United States. Why? Because after 9 years and 2 million dollars of research, our federal Food and Drug Adminstration has yet to approve it.[18]

When you directly involve your audience by putting them into the very life of your presentation, you help create a more attentive, more receptive audience.

Arouse Audience Curiosity and Build Suspense

Rhetorical questions—those that require no overt answer or response—are curiosity arousers. "Why?" (we ask rhetorically). Because the first thing receivers usually do when asked a rhetorical question is to think about how they personally would respond. Thus, rhetorical questions provoke the interest of audience members by drawing them into the speech itself. As your listeners try to answer the questions you posed, their participation is ensured.

Iowa State University student Marty Crabbs used a rhetorical question to trigger curiosity in audience members, asking:

Did you know you could buy toxic waste?[19]

Imagine you are part of an audience. How would you respond if asked that same question? You'd probably start thinking about the subject of the speaker's speech, and thus one key purpose of the introduction would be realized. Mentally involved, you would then begin to wonder "Where?" "How?" and "Why?" The speaker can pave a path for you to travel with him or her with a single question.

In similar fashion, student Ben Sutherland used a rhetorical question to generate personal involvement and feed the curiosity of his listeners. As they responded mentally to the question he posed at his speech's outset they involved themselves more fully in his topic, media literacy in the Information Age:

Every time a child we care about sits down with popcorn and a Coca-Cola to watch a Schwarzenegger movie, a tape plays in our mind, "Should I be concerned?"[20]

Once the collective curiosity of an audience is aroused, if a speaker makes audience members wait before satisfying their curiosity, the speaker also succeeds in building suspense. Notice how student Brian Epp used this technique to his advantage. As you read this excerpt from his speech, note the questions you ask yourself repeatedly:

A hidden tax is taking a large bite out of your income. Analysts point out this tax is costing companies between 80 and 300 billion dollars annually while not even officially on the books of the National Treasury.

This hidden tax manifests itself in the products and services we use every day. For example, it accounts for 33 percent of the price of a stepladder and 95 percent of the price you pay for a vaccination. At a time when "no new taxes" is a fervent political refrain, it seems ironic that many of us blithely pay this hidden tax without a question. But what is this tax and where does it come from?[21]

Questions build interest; so does the creation of suspense.

Impress and Interest Your Audience with Quotations

Sometimes a quotation is the most effective technique you can use both to impress your audience and to capture their attention. The words of a well-known figure, a passage from a work of literature, or a familiar phrase may help you communicate information in a more persuasive or comprehensible manner than your words alone could otherwise accomplish.

Student Sarah Nagel opened a speech with the words of a renowned speaker; by doing so, she added credibility to her topic:

When Martin Luther King, Jr., said, "The family is the primary education agency of mankind," he could not have foreseen the steady erosion of parental involvement in our schools. Since the mid-1960s the dominant features of public education have been the centralization of power, the expansion of the educational bureacracy, and the perilous decline in educational quality.[22]

Similarly, student Robert Mattingly used the attention-getting words of a well-known playwright to introduce his speech:

Sleep

Sleep that knits up the raveled sleeve of care,

The death of each day's life, sore labour's bath,

Balm of hurt minds, great natures second course,

Chief nourisher in life's feast.

These words from William Shakespeare's *Macbeth* were written to demonstrate the importance of sleep to our mental and physical well-being. From kings and presidents to persuasive speakers, adequate sleep is needed for peak performance.[23]

Not only the words of famous people have value. The words of "common folk" can also be used when appropriate to arouse greater interest. So can words from walls. Speaking on racial and ethnic relations in American higher education, Michael L. Williams, assistant secretary for Civil Rights, U.S. Department of Education, began his remarks:

On the wall of a church in England there is a sign that reads, "A vision without a task is but a dream, a task without a vision is drudgery, a vision and a task are the hope of the world." My comments this morning concern a vision, a task, and a hope for the future of American higher education.[24]

Even the words from a story can find their way into a speaker's introduction:

It's a scene that is pretty familiar to each one of us. A mother holds her newborn baby in her arms, rocks him back and forth and sings, "I'll love you forever—I'll like you for always—As long as I love—My baby you'll be." Richard Munsch's childhood story *Love You Forever* tells of a mother's love that endures as her little boy grows into a man. One day that man receives a phone call. His mother can no longer care for herself, and now it's her son's turn to care for his mother, and to prove that his love for her also lasts forever.

Today, according to research sponsored by the American Association of Retired Persons, Richard Munsch's childhood story describes the life of over seven million Americans. The fact is, if Mom or Dad lives long enough we'll probably be receiving that phone call.[25]

Make Your Audience Laugh or Smile with You

What can you do to decrease the psychological distance that exists between you, the speaker, and your audience? How can you make your audience feel more at ease so that any psychological barriers separating you are razed and audience members become more willing to listen to your ideas? The answer may lie in humor. When used wisely, appropriately, and with discretion, humor helps precipitate audience attention and at the same time enables audience members to perceive the speaker as a more likeable, friendly person.[26] In many ways humor acts as a bridge to goodwill. Its effect can win you a fair hearing from an audience.

Delivering a speech entitled "Taking Care of Business" before the Economic Club of Detroit, Lee Iacocca, then chairman of the board of the Chrysler Corporation, injected humor into his speech's opening lines. Iacocca began by referring to the man who had introduced him:

Thank you, Joe. It's always good to hear one of your bosses say something nice about you. In fact, these days it's nice to hear anybody say something nice about you! But, Joe has been a member of our board now for about two years, and he has really thrown himself into the car business. Maybe you've noticed—he's even doing his own TV commercials now!

But Joe, I gotta tell you, I think that battery you mentioned is just about dry. I've had a tough four days: A day to fly over, a day to fly back, and in between a brutal schedule of meetings and dinners designed to kill you just in case the jet lag didn't do the job![27]

Humor works best when it is directly related to the content of a speech and not merely "stuck on" for effect or as an afterthought. Speaking on the complex subject of transgenic pharming, student Shawn Harris facilitated understanding and sparked audience interest with humor:

What would you get if you crossed a potato with an antigen? Maybe a new vaccine. Well, what would you get if you crossed a pig with human protein? Quite possibly a new source of organs. OK, what would you get if you crossed a centipede with a parrot? A walkie-talkie.

Well, the answers to the first two questions at least are examples of an amazing new field of technology, that according to *Genetic Engineering News* of October 15, 1995, could possibly double our resources in food production, pest control, and even medicine. And this new technology is called transgenic pharming.[28]

Speaking before the First Annual Intertrade Conference in El Paso, Texas, on global markets and the North American Free Trade Agreement, David E. Moore, president

Humor acts as a bridge to good will. Speakers who use humor that is both relevant and appropriate precipitate audience interest and involvement.

and editorial director of *International Business Magazine,* built rapport with his audience by using humor in his introduction:

> When I first began researching this speech, it suddenly occurred to me that perhaps I might be expected to deliver it in Spanish. And that, in turn, reminded me of a story. The story involves a mother mouse who was leading her baby mice one day out to the field to find something to eat. Suddenly, in the middle of the field, there appeared a very large, very ferocious and very hungry-looking cat. The mother mouse, realizing that she had nowhere to run, stood high on her haunches and said to the cat:
>
> "BOW WOW WOW WOW WOW!"
>
> And the cat, enormously startled, ran away. The mother mouse then turned to her children and said, "Perhaps now, children, you understand the value of a second language."
>
> I expect most of you appreciate the value of Spanish as a second language, because it is going to be increasingly important in tomorrow's global economy.[29]

Remember, the right dose of humor can increase a speaker's likeability. However, to be effective the humor should be relevant to the speaker's message or it will only be an unnecessary distraction. The humor you use should help you make a point and advance your presentation without alienating or offending members of your audience.

Humor. Make sure the joke does not alienate members of a group. If you think the humor you are considering using could offend members of your audience, don't use it. What kind of audience might find the example from David Moore's speech offensive? While United Nations diplomats are sophisticated about language and would see the humor, others might not. What would a group of Cuban-heritage Floridians think? Racist, sexist, ethnic, and off-color jokes and stories are inappropriate and have no place in your presentation.

Richard Weaver, a professor at Bowling Green University, used the following example in a speech he delivered at a staff professional development workshop. Would it offend you? Can you think of any group of people that it might offend?

Speaking of skills and abilities of college graduates, a young man who had been hired by the personnel department of a large supermarket chain reported to work at one of the stores. The manager greeted him with a warm handshake and a smile, handed him a broom and said, "Your first job will be to sweep out the store."

"But," the young man said, "I'm a college graduate."

"Oh, I'm sorry," the manager said, "I didn't know that. Here, give me the broom, and I'll show you how."[30]

Move Your Audience with Stories

When integrated effectively into introductions, stories (illustrations or extended examples) also capture listener attention and hold listener interest. We all enjoy a good story, and if that story is filled with the drama of human interest and is amusing or suspenseful, we enjoy it even more. Of course, the story you use should not only involve the audience, it should also be clearly relevant to the issues you discuss in your speech. The following excerpt from a speech by student Ryan Siskow demonstrates how you can use a story to focus audience attention:

Instead of retiring, 64-year-old Lori Detrick and her 67-year-old husband Norm, have to find new jobs. They had planned for their future by hiring someone to sort through the complexities of financial security and help them create a retirement program. Following the advice of Financial Concepts of Barrington, Illinois, the couple invested their pension fund, which amounted to over $200,000 in a real estate limited partnership. When the couple tried to buy a home in Florida, they found that their money was gone. Like an increasing number of Americans, the Detricks sought assistance in managing their financial affairs, but unfortunately, the Detricks are just one example of a new trend in financial fraud—unethical or incompetent people calling themselves financial planners.[31]

Theresa McGuiness, a student, also used an exemplary story in her introduction to help depict a problem in a way her audience would understand:

Chuck was a sophomore at Alfred University in New York. He was a typical student with goals and dreams, just like yours and mine. He was a student that wanted to be accepted by his peers so badly that he'd do almost anything for his newly found "brothers," including allowing himself to be locked in a car trunk in the middle of winter, and consuming a bottle of wine, a quart of Jack Daniels and a six pack. This pledge's dreams went the way of alcohol poisoning and overexposure.[32]

As you see, a relevant story can serve as an effective opener. In addition, if the story involves you or someone you know personally it can also help establish your experience with the topic. Michael Eisner, CEO and chairman of the Walt Disney Company, used this story to introduce his speech on what it takes to manage a creative organization:

Humbling is something at Disney we encourage. It reminds me of an experience one of our young American Disney executives had when he was opening a new office for us in London and wanted to impress his new British secretary. As she entered his office, he was speaking on the telephone and said, "Why, of course, your majesty, think nothing of it. You can call me any time. See you soon. Regards to Prince Philip."

Then he hung up and said, "Oh, hello, Miss Brown. Did you want to see me?"

"I just wanted to tell, you sir," says the secretary, "that the men are here to hook up your telephone."[33]

SPEAKING of CRITICAL THINKING

Do Feelings Count?

Part of critical thinking involves being able to assess the nature of an emotional appeal in an effort to determine whether it is valid. In a recent column, Boston Globe columnist Susan Trausch complained:

> Our leaders have replaced the handshake with the survey. American businesses are so involved with focus group studies and polls that they wouldn't know a gut reaction if it hit them in the solar plexus. . . .
>
> I think this is particularly true of the newspaper business. . . . I have watched it change from an irreverent, fun, passionate endeavor to a bureaucracy. . . .
>
> We have taken your pulse, gentle reader, and determined that you want "trend pieces," whatever that means. We won't offend you with a strong voice. If a man bites a dog, we'll figure out a way to turn it into a chart.
>
> The same dead center poisons political campaigning and makes for caution instead of creativity from candidates. They are so busy watching the numbers and listening to the spin doctors that they forget they're supposed to care about what they're saying. They forget that the purpose of their speeches is to change the country, not to get a job with perks.[34]

Critics noted that the themes of the 1996 presidential election were poll inspired. The images of the candidates and the issues stressed were crafted based on what the polls revealed the public wanted. Thus, according to former presidential pollster and advisor Dick Morris, President Clinton even took a hiking vacation because polls showed that swing voters liked hiking and the outdoors, even though that activity was not one the president favored.[35]

Is it possible for a speaker to care about what he or she is speaking on if the issue and the stand taken are based on poll results rather than genuine feelings? To what extent should a speaker's true feelings play a role in your evaluation of his or her speech's content? To what degree is your assessment of a speech altered if the feelings expressed by the speaker are diametrically opposed either to what the polls say or to your own feelings?

It is clear that a speaker should use feelings to put an audience in the best frame of mind to receive and respond to a speech. How a speaker expresses his or her feelings influences the audience's evaluation of the speech's content. Even if a receiver's feelings are diametrically opposed to those expressed by the speaker, both the receiver and the speaker have the responsibility to make the effort to understand and empathize with each other. A speaker should not have to echo what society wants to hear just to be given a hearing.

USE THE INTRODUCTION TO PREVIEW SPEECH CONTENT

IN ADDITION TO ATTRACTING ATTENTION and building your credibility, a good introduction previews the content of your speech for your audience. In effect, it raises the curtain on your presentation and sets the scene by preparing audience members for what is to come. From the outset, focus your own eyes on your goal, and your listeners' eyes should follow. The introduction should:

Let the audience know your speech's subject and purpose.

Preview the main ideas that will comprise the body of your speech.

Identify your goals and your expectations for audience responses.

From the very beginning, your audience should have a pretty clear understanding of your intended topic. If your introduction fails to introduce the subject of your speech, audience attention will remain unfocused. Too much of their time will be wasted trying to figure out exactly what it is you are talking about. If, on the other hand, you take the brief time needed to set your agenda so they can easily follow your lead, they will focus more clearly on listening to and understanding your points. Your introduction should clarify and not confuse receivers. It should focus, rather than disperse their attention. Your introduction should alert your audience to what you're going to tell them. It should get them set for what is to come.

Notice how student Alicia Croshal used her brief introduction to prepare the audience for the body of her speech:

Gossip has a bad reputation. It hasn't always had, and it doesn't always deserve it. Allow me to give you the real scoop. It's so juicy that I'm going to develop four main points instead of three! First, I will give you a brief overview of the history of gossip. Then, I'll explain how it fulfills psychological needs, how it functions anthropologically, and finally, how gossip is real news.[36]

In the introduction to his speech on staged auto accidents, student Bond Benton secured audience attention, built his credibility, and lead his listeners into the subject of his speech with ease:

When Joe Smith of Springfield, Massachusetts, left for work that fateful day he had no idea that his life was about to change forever. As he was driving down the street . . . a car traveling the opposite direction to Joe's crashed into his vehicle. He was critically wounded, and as one doctor put it, he was lucky to come out of it alive. The bright promise Joe's life had once offered the world had been snuffed out by this senseless act of fate. Horrible? Yes.

But before you send a sympathy card there's a little something you should know. The car Joe was driving was only traveling five miles an hour at the point of impact and the car Joe struck wasn't even moving. What's more, investigators found that most of Joe's front end damage was probably caused by a baseball bat. The doctor filing the report had a history of falsifying claims and Joe's attorney . . . well, let's just say he made out like a bandit in the whole affair. The entire incident was staged as elaborately as a movie only this show, which billed itself as *Terms of Endearment,* turned out to be *The Sting.*

Joe and his cohorts perpetrated what is commonly called a staged auto accident and those paying the price at this box office include everyone that travels on our nation's roadways. *The Institute for Civil Justice Newsletter* of December 1995 states that staged auto accidents cost the auto insurance industry $18 billion dollars every year. What this means is that every person in this room is paying on average two hundred additional dollars each year on your auto insurance policy. But more alarming than the cost is the fact that these staged auto accidents have deadly consequences for thousands of innocent bystanders each and every year. Clearly, if the problem of staged auto accidents is ignored further the biggest wreck could be the future of safe driving.

To get a better understanding of this problem, however, we will initially take a crash course on the harm staged auto accidents present. We're going to shift gears and examine a few of the costs. And finally, we'll go cruising for some solutions at both the societal and the individual level.[37]

Thus, gaining your audience's attention and building your credibility in their eyes should pave the way for the third function of the introduction, the facilitation of critical thinking and listening via a preview of your speech's content.

THE INTRODUCTION: PITFALLS

A GOOD INTRODUCTION fulfills a trio of functions: It (1) attracts audience attention, (2) builds speaker credibility, and (3) introduces the subject of the speech. These functions exist in a delicate balance with each other. When mixed together in just the right proportions, they form an amalgam of words so powerful that the bridge between speaker and audience is strengthened and the bond between them cemented.

Keep in mind that first impressions cannot be erased. The impression you make during your speech's opening travels with you to your speech's conclusion. To ensure that your initial impression is as positive as possible, avoid the pitfalls to which speakers all too commonly fall prey:

Apologizing for lack of preparation. Lack of preparation is not something audience members readily forgive. All lack of preparation demonstrates is lack of commitment on your part. If you are ill-prepared to present, what you present will be ill-received.

Pretenses can be offensive. Audience members want to know you; they want to know what you think, what you feel, and why. If you pretend to know something when you do not, or pretend to feel something when you do not really care, then in time—usually sooner rather than later, you will be exposed as a fraud. You can enhance your credibility by relying on the knowledge of experts and by researching your topic fully. Be yourself, and your audience will feel comfortable being with you. Attempt to be what you are not, and your audience will soon lose interest in and respect for you.

Rely on relevance, not irrelevant gimmicks. Although gimmicks may gain the attention of your audience, if they are irrelevant to your topic and purpose, that attention will be short lived. Give your listeners the credit they deserve. Treat them as intelligent, and they will give your ideas an intelligent hearing. Treat the audience fairly. If you trick them into paying attention, in the end, their attention will not be paid to you. If an introduction doesn't suit your topic, don't use it.

Long-winded introductions go on and on . . . but an audience does not. Under ordinary circumstances your introduction should comprise approximately 10 to 20 percent of your speech. If you persist in introducing your ideas instead of keeping them relatively brief, you'll find that by the time you get to the body of your speech, your audience will be short on patience and endurance.

The first words you speak should be devised after, not before, the body of your speech. It's a lot easier to make valid judgments regarding the best way to begin your speech after you have prepared the body of your presentation. Do it the other way around, and it may end up being much less effective and fitting.

Remember, although a good introduction is no guarantee that your speech will be successful, if you don't invest time and effort in preparing it, you are almost certainly guaranteed an impenetrable wall between you and your listeners.

THE CONCLUSION: IT'S NOT OVER UNTIL IT'S OVER

A SPEECH CAN'T GO ACCORDING to plan unless you plan where it's going. The destination of a speech is its conclusion. It is during your speech's conclusion that you let the audience know you're ending your presentation, remind them of where you've been, and restate for them where you're going. The final minutes you and your audience are together is the last opportunity you'll have to position your ideas firmly in their minds. It takes great skill to end a speech well. Although you might be tempted to take the easy way out and bring your speech to a close with "That's all folks," "That's the way it is," or "And so it goes," doing so could destroy an otherwise fine presentation. Neither the subject of your speech nor the kind of speech you are delivering matters; what does matter is that you keep the major functions of a conclusion in mind:

- to let your audience know your speech is coming to an end; to forecast your speech's end;
- to focus audience attention on what you have said; to reemphasize your central idea and main points;
- to increase audience understanding of and audience commitment to what you would like receivers to think and/or do as a result of their having experienced your speech; to motivate receivers to respond; and
- to put audience members in a mood conducive to your goals, ending your speech in as memorable a way as you began it so that additional power is added to your presentation; to achieve closure.

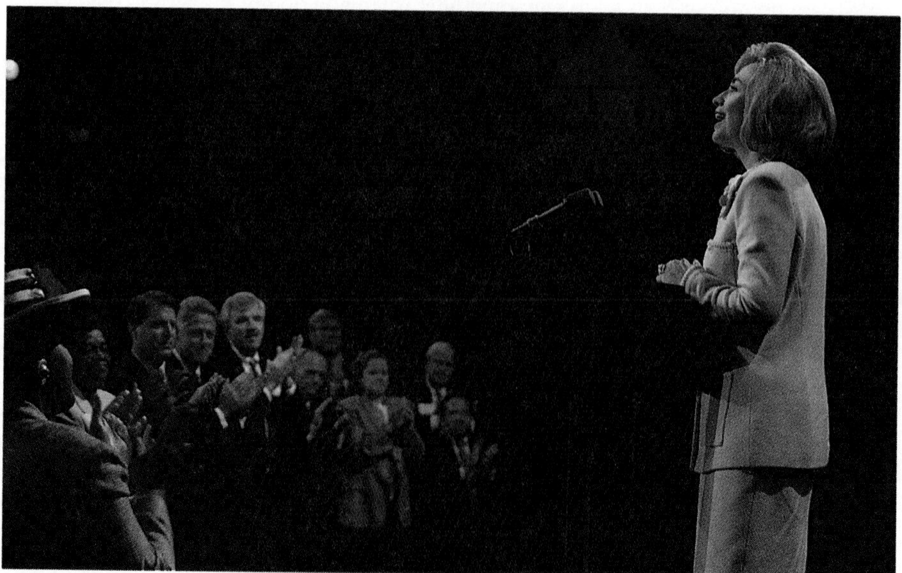

Ending a speech in a memorable way is as important as creating an effective beginning.

A conclusion should not be lengthy; the average conclusion comprises about 5 percent of your speech. However, just as with your introduction, the materials you use in your speech's conclusion must be relevant to your topic, appropriate to the audience and occasion, interesting, and involving. They also need to provide audience members with a sense of completion. The conclusion is your last chance to put the spotlight exactly where you want it to shine.

USE THE CONCLUSION TO FORECAST YOUR SPEECH'S END: SEND A CLEAR SIGNAL

HOW DO YOU BRING a conversation to a close? Do you just stop without warning your partner, turn your back on him or her, and walk away? Probably not. To do so would be construed as rude, and it would be unlikely that your partner would appreciate it. The same holds true for speakers and their listeners.

Conclusions should not take audiences by surprise. It is up to you to signal to your listeners that your speech is coming to an end. The speaker should not walk away from the podium without warning. Instead, you need to give your audience a cue that you're about to stop. You can cue them by your delivery: you might pause, decrease or increase your speaking rate, build momentum, alter your voice tone, or cue them with a transitional phrase. You might, for example, say, "In conclusion," "To review," "In closing," or "Let me end by noting." Such techniques help your audience adjust to the fact that you are approaching the speech's end.

Here is how John Ring, president of the American Medical Association, forecast the conclusion of his speech, "An Alliance of Excellence," for his audience:

> I would like to close with something I read in a *New Yorker* article last summer. In talking about a community fund raising effort, the author commented: "We are not poor as a people. Yet somehow we have become bankrupt as a society."[38]

Another speaker, Talbot D'Alemberte, president of the American Bar Association, signaled the end of a speech on civil justice reform with these words:

> In closing, I want to pay special tribute to lawyers like you who have devoted so much time and energy to our profession. The bar binds us together as a profession uniquely responsible for ensuring justice in our society. Our involvement reminds us that the law is a calling and not simply an occupation or a business.[39]

USE THE CONCLUSION TO REEMPHASIZE YOUR CENTRAL IDEA AND MAIN POINTS

NEW IDEAS SHOULD NOT be introduced in the conclusion to a speech. Instead, those ideas you have already introduced to your audience should be restated, and the main points you want audience members to remember should be reinforced. Think of it this way: you are putting your presentation on "rewind" for a moment; you again have the chance to impress upon your audience key ideas and/or major points and arguments. In effect, you are refocusing the speaker's spotlight on what you have said, reminding your audience what you have covered, and thus putting yourself in a position to make your final appeal. In this phase your goal is to reinforce your audience's understanding of your central idea and their commitment to it. In order to accomplish this goal you can:

1. Repeat your central idea and main points one last time so your audience enjoys an instant replay of your position and your rationale.
2. Use a quotation that summarizes or highlights your point of view.
3. Make a dramatic statement that drives home why audience members should be motivated and committed to respond as you desire.
4. Take them full circle by referring to your introduction.

Whichever techniques you choose to use, remember that your goal is to play back the main ideas of your presentation in as memorable a way as possible so that your purpose is advanced, not stalled.

John F. McDonnell, chairman and CEO of McDonnell Douglas, used the conclusion of a talk entitled "PaxPacifica" to reemphasize his speech's central idea and main points:

> In closing I want to restate the point I made at the outset. There are good and compelling reasons why the U.S. should encourage the export of U.S.-made weapons to friendly nations around the globe. This would serve U.S. strategic interests and it would help shape up the U.S. defense industrial base at a time of declining defense spending. When it is allowed to compete, the U.S. defense industry is not only competitive, but is almost always the first choice of the most knowledgeable customers around the world.[40]

Student Sheri Strickland similarly used her conclusion to summarize her main points:

> Today, we have looked at the problem of repeat child abuse by first looking at the current statistics of child abuse. We then looked at why the child protection agencies that are supposed to be protecting these children are failing, and finally we found some answers to these problems we are facing. Once again we have looked at the numbers and statistics that surround child abuse. We have also looked at several examples of children, who don't care what the numbers and statistics are. They are children. They are the next generation who at this point are powerless to stop the abuse that is being inflicted upon them. How many faces does it take to get us to act? We call them family values. . . . If families truly value what is important and beneficial to the child then we need to support them in every way we can. We cannot continue to fool ourselves with the myth that every family's values demonstrate what is truly valuable.[41]

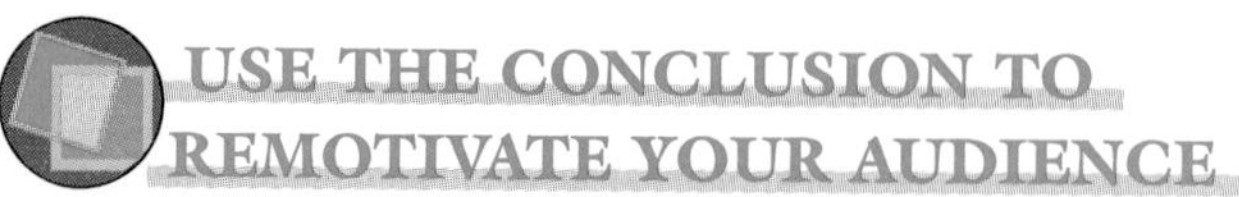

USE THE CONCLUSION TO REMOTIVATE YOUR AUDIENCE

JUST AS YOU NEED an effective introduction to motivate your audience members to listen to your speech, so do you need an effective conclusion to motivate them to respond to your speech as you had hoped. Chances are that unless you end your speech in such a way that audience members feel compelled to remember it, they won't be motivated sufficiently to think or act as you recommend. Your conclusion

CONSIDERING DIVERSITY

From Start to Finish

To what extent can introductions and conclusions serve as communication bridges and help people from diverse backgrounds respond to common content? Consider the following.

During the 1990s Coca-Cola embarked on its first global marketing campaign. Ads for Coke, Diet Coke, Sprite, and Fanta were shown around the world at the same time. By basing their campaign around the unifying themes of joy, laughter, sports, and music, company executives contend they can "achieve more by doing one promotion globally."[42]

In your opinion, would a public speaker be able to accomplish the same thing—that is, could a speech be written so that it would be understood and responded to similarly everywhere in the world? Is it possible that the lessons learned from "global advertising" can also be adopted to faciliate "global speechmaking"?

The advertisement seems to suggest that a simple message for worldwide consumption can be effectively prepared in an American cultural environment, provided it is conveying a general contemporary mood associated with a widely known product. But consider a somewhat more specific worldwide message, such as UNICEF's, which affirms the need to protect children from harm while emphasizing family values and the joy in having children. Would modifications be needed with specific foreign audiences to bridge cultural differences in attitudes toward children?

If the "core content" of such a message could be similar for every cultural setting, could an introduction and conclusion build rapport with different audiences? Consider the tactic adopted by President John F. Kennedy as he stood before the Berlin Wall that threatened both Americans and West Germans. At the conclusion of a reassuring speech in English, he said (in the language of his audience), "Ich bin ein Berliner," thereby identifying his interests and sympathies with those of his audience. Consider the opening or concluding tactics that might be used for the UNICEF message for audiences in a peaceful setting versus those in a civil war setting. In civil war, how might a message's opening or conclusion vary based on an audience in Europe (Bosnia or Chechnya, for example), versus Latin America (Guatemala or San Salvador), Asia (Cambodia), or Africa (Angola or Somalia)?

is no place for you to let down on effort or energy; it certainly is no place for you to let down your audience. Instead, take the time you need to create a striking ending that truly supports and sustains your speech's theme.

Many of the same kinds of materials you used to develop your introduction can help you put the focus where you need it and set a proper concluding mood. For example, speaking before the Foreign Policy Association in New York, U.S. Representative Dave McCurdy integrated a quotation into his concluding remarks:

In 1940, Walter Lippman described challenges facing Americans by saying this:

> You took the good things for granted, now you must earn them today. For every right that you cherish, you have a duty which you must fulfill. For every hope

that you entertain, you have a task that you must perform. For every good that you wish to preserve, you will have to sacrifice your comfort and your ease. There is nothing for nothing any longer.

Those words still hold true today.
I look forward to working with you to provide that leadership.[43]

Student Janeen Rohovit, discussing the need for driver education in a speech entitled "One in Two" motivated her audience with these closing words:

Alan Miller, a regional spokesperson for State Farm Insurance Company, sums up for us by saying, "When drivers are better educated, they are more responsible, they cause less accidents, they cost all of us less money."

Now, you may or may not care about the person sitting next to you and he or she may not care for you. Still, the probability of one in two of us ending up a fatal statistic is eminent. But, by promoting mandatory driver education with regulation from the state and funding from the program itself every driver on the highways of this nation can be traffic and safety literate. A one in two chance. Let's not leave us to fate.[44]

Speaking about how we are endangering the survival of dolphins, student Tara Trainor used personification in her conclusion to motivate her audience:

Yes, he was kind and loving. He always took care of his family and other families too. He travels in wide social circles. In fact, maybe you have met him in his confused, cramped position. He has offered us a tidal wave of love and we have offered him a whirlpool of death. It is time now to put the dolphin in our hearts, not in our fisherman's nets.[45]

Even humor can be used to set an appropriate psychological mood for continued contemplation or action by audience members. In a speech entitled "Rediscovering a Lost Resource: Rethinking Retirement," student Denalie Silha closed with this anecdote:

Listen to Warren Buffet, who has built an investment empire. When asked a few years ago about leaving a woman in charge of one of his companies after celebrating her 94th birthday, he replied, "She is clearly gathering speed and may well reach her full potential in another five or ten years. Therefore, I've persuaded the board to scrap our mandatory-retirement-at-100 policy. My God, good managers are so scarce I can't afford the luxury of letting them go just because they've added a year to their age."[46]

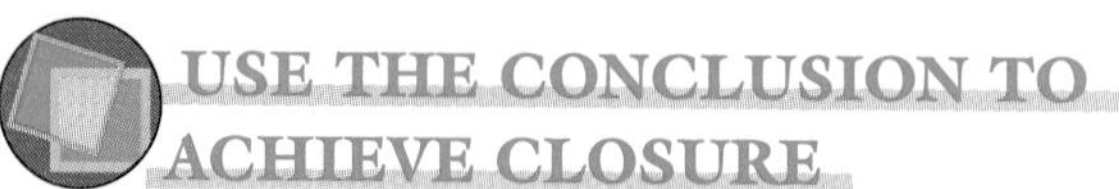

USE THE CONCLUSION TO ACHIEVE CLOSURE

A VERY EFFECTIVE MEANS of giving your speech psychological symmetry or balance is to refer in your conclusion to ideas you explored in your introduction. You might, for example, reuse a theme you introduced at the beginning of your speech, ask or answer the same rhetorical question you used at the outset, refer to an opening story, or restate an initial quotation. Integrating any one of these strategies helps to provide audience members with a desired sense of closure. Because such strategies help your speech sound finished, audience members are not left in a state of wondering whether your speech is actually over. Leave your audience hanging, and your ideas are left hanging. Offer a definite ending to your presentation, an ending that captures the essence of your message, and your audience will end the experience by continuing to talk about what you've said. If your conclusion convinces audience members that you have delivered what you promised in your introduction, then once the speech is over audience members will deliver you the promise of continued consideration.

Speaking on education and learning in the twenty-first century, Future Survey Editor Michael Marien achieved closure with these words:

So I end with the familiar statements where I began. We live in an increasingly complex and changing world. Education in coping with these changes is increasingly important for people of all ages. Continuing education of adults, especially on matters of civic education and the Big Picture, is the most important education of all. I hope that you have an enhanced appreciation of these increasingly heard statements.[47]

Motivational speaker Jeanne Tessier Barone closed her speech entitled "The Sky's No Limit at All" by referring for the second time to a quotation from the poet Rita Dove:

I have no idea what Rita Dove had in mind when she uttered the words we began with: "When the sky's the limit, how can you tell you've gone too far?" But I do know where my attempt to address her question has taken me. By way of conclusion, and in humble tribute to her poetry, let me end this way: The sky is infinite. It is we who make of it a wall. The only way to know is: go.

Standing still is death. And far is never where you are, but where you dream to be. Everything good in life was born in dreams. Be a dreamer.[48]

THE CONCLUSION: PITFALLS

AN EFFECTIVE CONCLUSION LEAVES THE audience fulfilled and in the mood to think about or do what you recommend. Your closing comments are your last chance to make a good impression and fulfill the purpose of your speech. Because by virtue of its placement the conclusion is frequently the part of the speech your audience will remember most clearly, it makes sense to make the final impression audience members have of you as positive as possible.

Don't jar the audience by ending too abruptly. An abrupt ending is an undesirable ending. A conclusion needs to be built carefully or the ideas you've worked so hard to develop will topple like a house of cards.

Long-winded conclusions lose in the end. When you end a speech, you cross the finish line. Hang around that finish line too long without actually crossing it, and your audience could lose interest in you and your ideas at a very critical juncture. Build your conclusion, but keep it tight. Focus attention; don't disperse it.

New ideas belong in a new speech, not in your conclusion to this speech. While restating ideas you've covered in your speech in a fresh way in your conclusion is appropriate, introducing new ideas in the conclusion is not. The conclusion is that part of the speech in which you reinforce what you've already covered; it is your last opportunity to drive home important points, not the time to start making new ones.

End with a bang, not a thud. Devise a conclusion that will stick in the minds of your listeners, not one that will fall flat and have little if any impact on what they retain. Your audience should want to remember you, not yearn to forget you. If you create an ending that has real emotional appeal, you will inspire rather than let down your audience. Your ending should be striking, not count as a strike against you.

SUMMARY

THE WAY A SPEAKER INTRODUCES and concludes a presentation influences the ultimate impact the speech has on receivers and affects receivers' perception of the speaker.

Effective introductions serve three key functions: (1) They build credibility, (2) they capture attention, and (3) they orient receivers to the organizational development and tone of the speech. To fulfill these functions, speakers rely on a number of techniques: they startle or shock receivers, directly involve receivers, arouse curiosity or build suspense, make their listeners smile or laugh with them, or move them with stories. Speakers also use the introduction to demonstrate their qualifications to speak on a topic, and demonstrate that they are trustworthy and likeable, and thereby build their credibility.

Conclusions also have a number of functions to fulfill: (1) Conclusions forecast the end of a speech, (2) reemphasize the central idea of a speech, (3) motivate receivers to respond as a speaker desires, and (4) provide a speech with a sense of closure. To achieve these goals, speakers use cues to help receivers adjust to the fact that a speech is ending, review key points covered, insert quotations or make dramatic statements that reinforce a speech's central idea, and take the audience full circle by referring to the speech's introduction, thereby creating a sense of closure.

THE SPEAKER'S STAND

Develop three different introductions and three different conclusions for a speech on any one of the following subjects, or select a subject of your choice:

- Ageism
- Chemical dependency
- Doing business internationally
- American prisons
- Capital punishment
- Abortion
- The danger posed by comets
- Political correctness
- Greenhouse effect

Present one set of introductions and conclusions to the class. Then ask your classmates to tell you if they found them effective.

In a two- to three-page paper explain the techniques you relied on in each introduction to attract audience attention, build your own credibility, and forecast what is to follow, as well as the techniques used to signal the conclusion, reemphasize your theme and main points, and motivate listeners to respond as you desire. Explain which introduction and conclusion you believe audience members would find most effective and why.

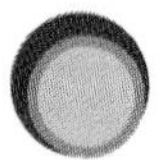

STUDENT FOCUS GROUP REPORT

Now that you have had the opportunity to explore the nature and creation of introductions and conclusions, in a group of five to seven students, respond to the following questions:

1. What choices have you faced or do you see yourself facing as you sought or seek to devise an introduction and a conclusion that fulfills your needs and precipitates the outcomes you desire?

2. Which kinds of introduction or conclusion do you find most effective?
3. Are there any introductory or concluding techniques that you believe a speaker should refrain from using? Which? Why?
4. To what extent, if any, did your topic influence the nature of the introductions and conclusions you created?
5. Summarize the most important information you have learned about the creation and use of speech introductions and conclusions.
6. Revisit the case study at the beginning of this chapter. Based on your understanding of introductions and conclusions, how would you answer the questions?

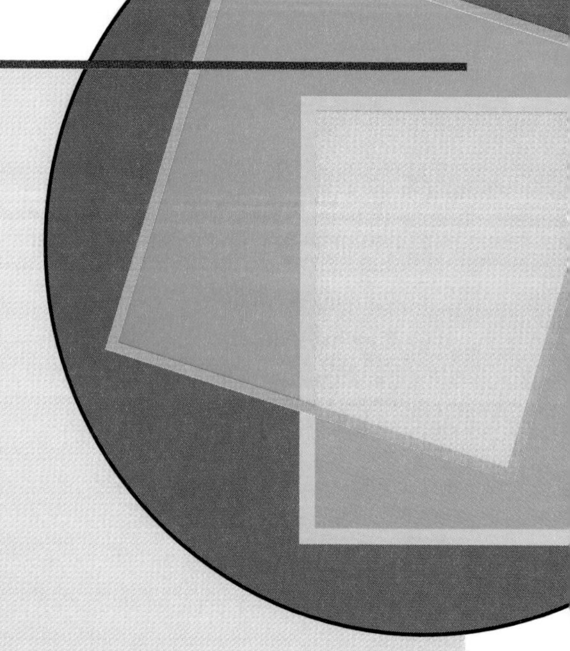

Chapter Eleven

Outlining for Success

After reading this chapter, you should be able to:

- Explain what an outline is.
- Discuss the purposes served by an outline.
- Discuss the process involved in developing an outline.
- Use a planning worksheet.
- Identify as well as compare and contrast the main and supporting points of an outline.
- Describe appropriate outline form and structure.
- Explain why effective outlines are divisions of the whole and exhibit parallel structure.
- Develop an outline of a speech from a speech transcript.
- Develop a formal outline for a speech.
- Prepare speaker's notes from a formal outline.

Is an Outline Really Necessary?

CASE STUDY

Ned was excited. He had been selected to deliver the opening speech at the next meeting of Toastmasters. As the newest member of the group, he was concerned with making a good impression. Although he had been to only a few of the group's meetings, every one of the speeches he had heard had been exemplary, and all the speakers had used only a few notecards to assist them.

But as he considered the challenge facing him, Ned became unnerved. He was an expert on his chosen subject, the importance of play, and had gathered a wealth of information, but he couldn't imagine how he would be able to boil all that he wanted to impart down to just a few notecards. Then it hit him. The first thing he had to do was develop a good working outline—one that illustrated the relationship between his main points and his supporting materials. The working outline was one that could change, and he was certain that it would change a number of times before he actually solidified his plan. As he pondered how to begin, the following thoughts raced through his mind: Should he write the speech out word for word before developing his outline? Should he create a sentence outline or a word outline? Or should he just make a few notes and forget the outline altogether? He couldn't decide.

- If you were in Ned's shoes, how would you proceed?
- Develop an outline that explains the approach you suggest Ned follow.

ONCE YOU HAVE SELECTED the organizational pattern that best supports the subject matter of your speech, you are ready to develop your outline. It is the outline that provides the framework within which you will position your ideas, and it is the outline that helps you analyze the structural integrity of your speech's content much as an engineer inspects the structural integrity of a bridge.

THE OUTLINE'S FUNCTIONS

WHY USE AN OUTLINE? Why not simply research your topic, write out your speech, and then deliver it? By creating a speech without first developing an outline, you have no real way of determining whether your chances of realizing your objective and attaining your speechmaking goals are probable.

An Outline Is a Presentation Roadmap

In many ways, an outline serves as a presentation roadmap. It shows the best speech preparation route for you to follow. It helps you visually determine how the parts of your speech fit together; it helps you ensure that each part of your speech has unity and coherence and that every one of your main points and subpoints is developed logically and supported adequately. The outline is your blueprint for speechmaking success. It lets you assess how your speech holds together before you deliver it to an audience. Therefore, you do need to pay careful attention to it. You need to confirm that your purpose statement and central idea or proposition are clear. You need to critique the construction of your main idea and subpoints. You need to be sure you have identified where you must place transitions or idea connectors. In other words, you need to use the outline to control the development of your material. You need to use it to direct the progress of your speech.

An Outline Facilitates Assessment

An outline can help you organize and clarify your ideas. In the process, it reduces speechmaking uncertainty. It also provides you with a way to package your information so that audience members understand your ideas without becoming lost along the way. In addition, the outline helps you incorporate material that is important and eliminate that which is not. If speakers merely wrote and delivered speeches without first outlining them, time and again audiences would find themselves attempting to decipher series after series of disjointed thoughts. The outline lets the speaker assess the relationships among ideas. By helping the speaker ensure that ideas related to each other are placed together, the outline also better enables the receivers to understand and think critically about the positions the speaker is taking.

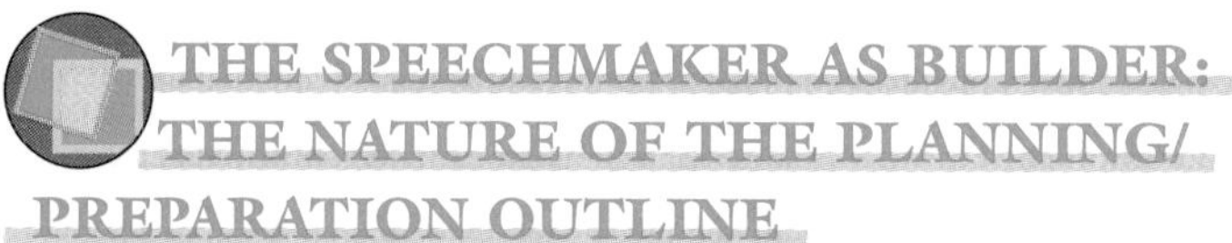

THE SPEECHMAKER AS BUILDER: THE NATURE OF THE PLANNING/PREPARATION OUTLINE

AS SOON AS YOU START WORKING on your presentation, you should begin putting your ideas into outline form. In many ways, the outline you develop will resemble a building that will be constructed using a modular design. Instead of working with building blocks, however, you are working with **idea blocks.** As ideas evolve, you break them down into **main ideas** and **subordinate** or **supporting ideas.** By using this approach, you will be better able both to integrate new ideas and to discard ideas that are extraneous to or beyond the scope of your particular topic, audience, or speechmaking requirements.

If you are very comfortable with the procedures involved in outlining, you may want to proceed directly to preparing a formal outline. However, if you feel you could use some work in outline construction, you may find it helpful to begin your outlining work with a **planning worksheet** similar to the one shown in Figure 11.1.

Using a Planning Worksheet

The planning worksheet gives you the opportunity to practice clustering your ideas into groups so you can more easily see if and how they relate to each other. A planning worksheet also lets you assess whether the topic you have chosen is too large or too small for the time available, as well as identify the areas of your chosen subject that merit additional research and support.

Begin by identifying the purpose of your speech and writing it in the space provided. Next, position two or three main ideas in the top boxes. Then arrange the information you have that supports each of these main ideas in the boxes that follow.

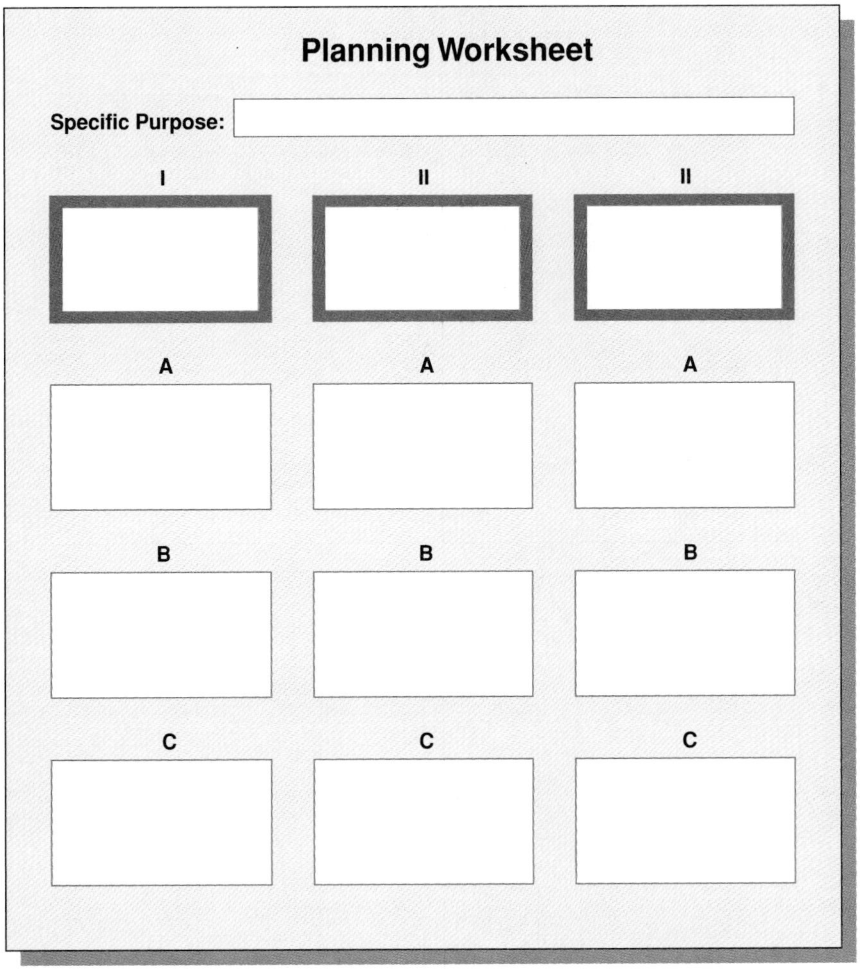

Planning Worksheet

Specific Purpose:

I	II	II
A	A	A
B	B	B
C	C	C

Figure 11.1

A planning worksheet facilitates the development of an outline.

An alternative procedure is to write your main and supporting ideas on index cards and place the cards on a desk or table, moving them around until the best order becomes apparent. For example, one student decided to give an informative presentation on the milestones of the nuclear era. He found that the major work had been done in the areas of bombs, propulsives, and energy. After he conducted research into those areas, the rough planning outline in Figure 11.2 on page 230 evolved. The speaker soon determined that he had gathered far too much material for a five-minute speech. The planning worksheet helped him make the decision to narrow the speech topic to only one area: the development of the nuclear bomb.

Effective Outlines Exhibit Coordination and Consistency

Your outline should consist of **coordinate points.** This simply means that all the main points you discuss should be of equal weight or substance. The main points in an outline are shown as Roman numerals and appear at the left margin. For example,

Figure 11.2

Planning worksheet

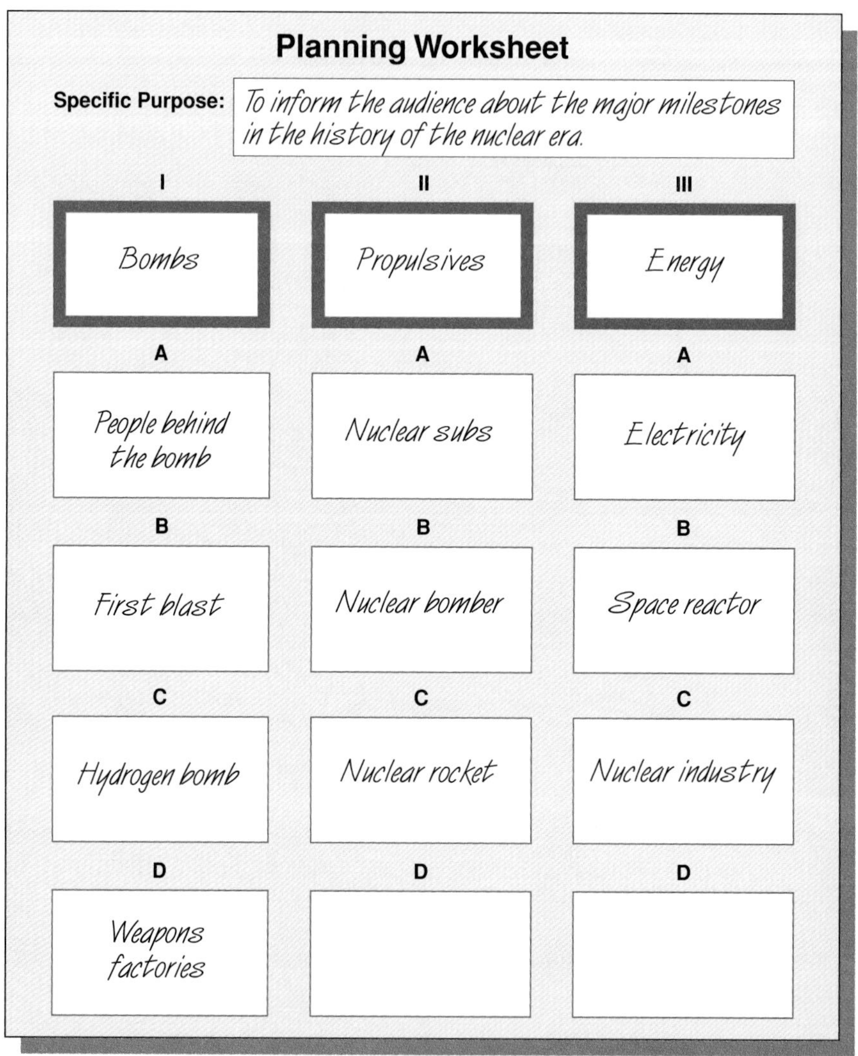

if you were to speak about Mexican customs, you might organize them according to social, business, and religious customs as follows:

I. Understanding the social customs of Mexico can improve Mexican–American relations.
II. Understanding the business customs of Mexico can improve Mexican–American relations.
III. Understanding the religious customs of Mexico can improve Mexican–American relations.

The outline tells us that the speaker plans to spend about the same amount of time discussing the three divisions of Mexican customs. What if the speaker were unable to find much material on religious customs? One solution would be to limit the speech to business and social customs. On the other hand, if there were some religious customs that were essentially social in nature, those elements might be subordinated under the social category.

It is evident that the coordinate points in the speech are the main ideas that you *choose* to develop. These are decisions you make. As a speaker you are ultimately responsible to your audience to ensure that the structure of your speech is developed in as clear and interesting a manner as possible.

Effective Outlines Indent and Subordinate Supporting Ideas

By working with the planning worksheet you have already begun to subordinate ideas. That is, you have started to identify which material is most important. The main ideas or arguments are shown in the Roman numerals of the outline. As you move from a planning outline to the standard outline format, these ideas are entered at the extreme left side of the page. The supporting or subordinate ideas are then indented and labeled with alternating letters and numbers. Below is the basic structure for the body of a speech:

I. Main point #1
   A. Supporting point
      1.
      2.
   B. Supporting point
      1.
      2.
II. Main point #2
   A. Supporting point
      1.
      2.
   B. Supporting point
      1.
      2.

If you had a third main point, it would be developed in exactly the same way, and so on.

When you do fill in the outline, every entry you make will be a **single idea** expressed in a short, complete sentence. By composing an outline that contains only complete sentences, you are better able to think about your ideas, assess their coherence and development, and rehearse your presentation when the time arises.

Group Outlines

Assume that you (or your team) are preparing a speech that describes three majors or areas of concentration available to students at your school. Working together, develop an outline of the body of a speech that includes information about the three.

Recalling the organizational patterns discussed in Chapter 9, describe to the class the organizational pattern you selected. You may wish to write the outline on a handout, an overhead projection transparency, a piece of poster board, or the chalkboard.

Effective Outlines Are Divisions of the Whole

If you are dividing an outline into constituent parts, it must contain at least two subpoints, which are **divisions of the whole** or idea segments. That is, there will be an "A" and a "B," a "1" and a "2," and so forth. Each of the resulting idea segments holds ideas of approximately the same importance. For example, if in your main idea you noted that the death penalty helps control crime, you might divide that idea into these two categories:

I. The death penalty helps reduce crime.
   A. The death penalty hinders criminals who have a fear of death.
   B. The death penalty is the only method that ensures that criminals will not return to the streets.

Of course, there may be times when you want to use only one case or example to support one of your subpoints. The time available to you, the significance of the information you are sharing, or other factors may help you decide that one supporting point is sufficient. These cases are usually exceptions to the division principle cited here and should be used sparingly. In general, your audience will be better informed or persuaded if you give two supporting points rather than just one.

Effective Outlines Exhibit Parallel Structure

The outline must be devised in such a way that the concepts displayed in it exhibit **parallel structure,** that is, ideas must appear to parallel each other or balance with one another. The standard way to accomplish this is to write a short complete sentence for each entry. This technique helps you think through your ideas without writing a complete manuscript.

A Look at Your First Main Point

I. Here is where you put your first main point.
   A. Your first subpoint includes evidence that supports the main point.
      1. The first sub-subpoint gives additional information about subpoint A.
      2. The second sub-subpoint gives additional information about subpoint A.
   B. Your second subpoint includes evidence that supports the main point.

Note that every entry is subdivided into two or more points. The entries all parallel each other and are complete simple sentences.

Effective outlines clearly label all parts, including the introduction, the body, the conclusion, the transitions, and the bibliography.

By handling each of the parts of your speech separately (the body is usually outlined first), and labeling them clearly, you take the steps necessary to ensure you:

1. Prepare an effective introduction and conclusion.
2. Develop an adequate body of material to share.
3. Anticipate how you will get from section to section and point to point.

You thereby improve the chances that you will realize your essential speechmaking objectives. Also, typically included in your outline is your bibliography, highlighting the sources (books, magazines, newspapers, government documents, television programs, interviews, and Internet sites) you consulted during the speech preparation process. The following are two examples of effective outlines.

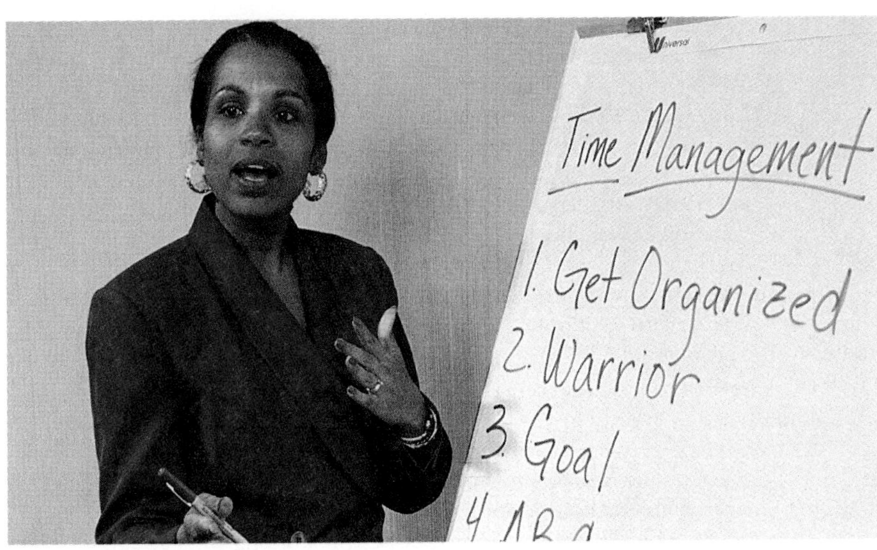

An effective outline is a road map to your speech.

Repetitive Stress Injuries

Specific purpose: To inform the class about the nature of repetitive stress injuries.

Central idea: Repetitive stress injuries are painful injuries caused by a lack of variation in daily work routines.

Introduction

I. Every year repetitive stress injuries strike approximately 185,000 workers.

II. Accounting for over half this country's occupational illnesses, repetitive stress injuries have become a plague on the workplace.

III. Today I want to discuss what I've learned about repetitive stress injuries with you.

(Transition: Let's start with what a repetitive stress injury is.)

Body

I. Repetitive stress injuries are painful occupational ailments.
    A. Repetitive stress injuries are also called cumulative trauma disorders.
        1. Cumulative trauma disorders result from overusing the muscles and tendons of the fingers, hands, arms, and shoulders.
        2. Cumulative trauma disorders result from tugging, pounding, and straining crucial upper body tissues.
    B. Repetitive stress injuries have a number of symptoms.
        1. Initial symptoms tend to be innocuous.
            a. Victims feel tired.
            b. Victims feel old.
        2. Symptoms worsen over time.
            a. The tendons of victims swell.
            b. The muscles of victims are irritated.
            c. Victims experience numbness.
            d. Coordination diminishes in victims.
    C. Carpal tunnel syndrome is an extreme example of a repetitive stress injury.
        1 Tissues in the palmar side of the wrist swell and squeeze a key nerve.
        2. The pain can cripple its victims.

(Transition: Now that you understand what repetitive stress injuries are, let's look at who they affect.)

II. Repetitive stress injuries affect workers in many fields.
  A. Blue-collar workers suffer from repetitive stress injuries.
    1. Meat packers who slice scores of carcasses each day become victims.
    2. Auto workers who drive the same screw hour after hour become victims.
  B. White-collar professionals who use computers suffer from repetitive stress injuries.
    1. Reservationists become victims.
    2. Word processors become victims.
    3. Journalists become victims.

(Transition: We have spent time talking about who is affected by repetitive stress injuries. It's time now to turn our attention to examining how office life today contributes to the problem.)

III. The nature of the modern office contributes to the prevalence of repetitive stress injuries.
  A. Computers may harm workers.
    1. They allow workers to sit with their fingers flying across their keyboards for hours without a break.
    2. The typical hand positions of a person working on a computer contributes to the development of the injury.
  B. Office operations may harm workers.
    1. There is little variation in the daily routine of workers.
    2. Too many workers never even get up from a work station.

IV. The habits and personal traits of workers contribute to their getting repetitive stress injuries.
  A. Heavy people are more susceptible to repetitive stress injuries.
    1. They have to maneuver their arms around their bodies.
    2. They have to contort their arms inward.
  B. Smokers have less risk.
    1. They take periodic cigarette breaks.
    2. They leave their work stations.
  C. Psychological stress adds to the problem.
    1. Insecurity creates additional muscle tension.
    2. Stress decreases oxygen flow.

V. Employers are taking action.
  A. They are redesigning work stations.
    1. They are providing ergonomic chairs.
    2. They are providing wrist supports.
  B. They are trying to break up the daily routine of workers.
    1. They give workers different tasks to perform.
    2. They encourage workers to take breaks.
    3. They provide a stress injury room for training and rehabilitation.
  C. They are using more user-friendly technology.
    1. They are using keyboards with better designs.
    2. They are experimenting with voice-activated computers.

Conclusion

I. Repetitive stress injuries are equal opportunity employers.

II. Repetitive stress injuries debilitate and cripple those unlucky enough to suffer from them.

III. Steps are being taken so you won't be added to the already growing list of repetitive stress injury victims.

Bibliography

Kevin Cobb, "RSI: The New Computer Age Health Assault," *Prevention,* April 1, 1991, pp. 58–64.

Janice M. Horowitz, "Crippled by Computers," *Time Magazine,* October 12, 1992, pp. 70–72.

Gerri Kobren and Charles Hazard, "Body Language: Carpal Tunnel Syndrome," *The Baltimore Sun,* November 2, 1992.

Sara Rimer, "New Reviled College Subject: Computer-Linked Injury," *New York Times,* February 9, 1997, p. 24.

Jim Rosenberg, "Another Newspaper RSI Lawsuit," *Editor & Publisher,* June 8, 1991, pp. 62–66.

Granny Dumping

Specific purpose: To explain why "granny dumping" is on the rise.

Central idea: Increased family stresses and a lack of government assistance are causing families to abandon their older relatives.

Introduction

I. Thirty years ago playwright Edward Albee wrote *The Sandbox,* a play in which a family brings their grandmother to a playground and dumps her in a sandbox.

II. Thirty years ago this idea was labeled as absurd.

III. Now this idea is all too real.

IV. Today, I would like to talk to you about the growing problem of granny dumping.

(Transition: Let's begin by examining the plight of a number of older Americans.)

Body

I. Older Americans are being abandoned by their families.
   - A. John Kingery, 82, was abandoned outside a men's room in Post Falls, Idaho.
     - 1. His clothes were stripped of their labels.
     - 2. An Alzheimer's sufferer, Kingery was not able to remember his name.
   - B. Thousands of older Americans face similiar situations.
     - 1. The American College of Emergency Physicians estimates that 70,000 people are abandoned each year.
     - 2. Most are from families that cannot pay for the necessary care.

(Transition: In addition to the pain that is being inflicted on the elderly, pain is also being afflicted on those who should care for them.)

II. Caregivers are overwhelmed by their responsibilities.
   - A. Millions of Americans carry the burden of caring for one or more older adults.
     - 1. One in five families takes care of an older adult.
     - 2. Caregivers are taxed by bills.
     - 3. Caregivers receive little government assistance.
   - B. Caregivers suffer physical and mental stress.
     - 1. Exhausted caregivers become susceptible to high blood pressure and strokes.
     - 2. Caregivers suffer from depression.
     - 3. Caregivers experience guilt.

(Transition: So much for the problem; what about solutions?)

III. There are a number of solutions.
   - A. Families themselves can work together more effectively.
     - 1. They can avoid placing all of the responsibilities on one person.

2. Relatives can help out with the nonending stack of paperwork required by government agencies.

B. The government needs to do more.
   1. Programs need to be added so that patients can be cared for outside the home at least part of the time.
      a. This would provide variety for the patient.
      b. Such programs would also give a much-needed rest to the family so they could avoid burnout.
   2. An holistic approach to elder care needs to be adopted.
      a. Caregivers need help in coping with the increased stresses that caring for an aged relative creates.
      b. Patients need help so that they are treated with respect.
      c. Both caregivers and patients need help to maintain their dignity.

Conclusion

I. We have seen that there is much that can be done to help people who must help their aging parents.

II. While Albee's *The Sand Box* was labeled as an example of absurdism thirty years ago, granny dumping has become an all too real and all too tragic way of life for tens of thousands of American citizens.

Bibliography

Albee, E., *The Sand Box* (New York: New American Library, 1961).

Rachel Boaz, "Why Do Some Caregivers of Frail Elderly Quit?" *Healthcare Financing Review, 30*(2): Winter 1991, pp. 41–47.

Robert Butler, "Health Care for All: A Crisis and Cost Access," *Geriatrics, 47*(9), September 1992, pp. 34–48.

Paul Krugman, "Does Getting Old Cost Society Too Much?" *New York Times Magazine,* March 9, 1997, pp. 58–60.

"Granny Dumping by the Thousands," *New York Times,* March 29, 1992.

SPEAKING of CRITICAL THINKING

Perceiving a Speech's Structure

In addition to helping you prepare your own presentation, a speech outline also helps you prepare to analyze other's presentations. If, as you listen to a speaker's ideas, you can also picture the structure of his or her ideas, you will be both better able to recall the main points of the speech and more adept at determining whether the support the speaker supplies is adequate. After you develop a clear image of the visual framework of a speech, you are also better equipped to critique the speech and ask the speaker relevant questions.

For practice, read a speech of your choice or one assigned you by your instructor. Working alone or in a group, develop a sentence outline of the main points of the speech's body. Once your outline is complete, answer these questions:

- Is the body of the speech well organized?
- Does the speech exhibit structural integrity?
- How does making an outline of the speech help you answer questions 1 and 2?

CONSIDERING DIVERSITY

Who Is Processing the Speech? What Do They Expect?

William Steere, Jr., chairman and CEO of Pfizer, a pharmaceutical company, delivered a presentation entitled "Plan Globally, Engage Locally: The Public Policy Challenge for Global Corporations" before the Tokyo Chapter of the American Chamber of Commerce when it met in Tokyo, Japan. Read the excerpts on pages 238–239, and then, working either alone or in groups, evaluate the extent to which the speaker's topic and speech structure were or were not appropriate for both the American and the Japanese members of his audience. As you conduct your evaluation, recall from Chapter 9 that Americans have a preference for linear organization, Japanese have a preference for configural organization, and the challenges that such preferences present for speakers.

After reading the speech, answer these questions:

- In your opinion, was the speech well organized?
- To what extent did the speaker discuss a topic that was appropriate for both the American and the Japanese members of his audience?
- To what extent was the structure of the speech appropriate for audience members who prefer that a speech have a linear organizational pattern, in which each idea is linked and moves in a straight line toward the speaker's goal? Explain.

Members of cultural groups display preferences for different organizational patterns. Thus, the organizational pattern used by a speaker may appeal to some receivers and not to others.

(continued)

Considering Diversity *(continued)*

- To what extent was the structure of the speech appropriate for audience members who prefer that a speech have a configural organizational pattern in which the speaker delicately circles a topic, relating ideas to each other indirectly and by implication rather than by specific links? Explain.
- Based on your analysis, how do you think both American and Japanese members of the speaker's audience would have responded to the speech?

PLAN GLOBALLY, ENGAGE LOCALLY: THE PUBLIC POLICY CHALLENGE FOR GLOBAL CORPORATIONS

The speaker establishes a common interest with receivers.

Everyone in this room can count him- or herself part of the growing trend toward a global market. We hear those words, "global market," daily now, and perhaps have grown complacent in our advances, or conversely, frustrated by barriers still in place. . . . If we are to complete the evolution toward borderless industries, I propose to you today that involvement in public policy formation is vital to our interests. Here's an already tired corporate adage: Think globally, act locally.

I'd like to suggest an update that recognizes the integration of corporations within cultures and drives home the need for public policy: Plan globally, engage locally. Conveniently, the pharmaceutical industry and Pfizer's experiences here in Japan make an appropriate model for my talk.

The speaker explains his thesis and previews the two key points he will develop in his speech.

Today, I'll talk about two aspects of public policy: national health care policies and trade policies. . . .

Throughout the world, in developed and developing countries, debates rage about health care costs, the consensus being that they are rising faster than any country could like, and most can afford.

The speaker elaborates on the first main point.

In Japan, the issue has not had the same notoriety, mostly because the public health insurance system has shielded consumer pocketbooks, but there is growing concern. . . . My industry struggles constantly with the widespread belief, both in Japan and elsewhere, that we are overly profitable, and that government price restrictions are a health care cost-cutting solution—with limited pain.

Unfortunately, there is too little recognition that, because they often replace surgery and long hospital stays, pharmaceuticals lower health care costs, even as they relieve patients' suffering. To illustrate what a good value pharmaceuticals are and what a small overall part they play in national health care expenditures, let me give you an example. If all U.S. drug company profits were expropriated each year, that amount would reduce annual U.S. health care expenditures by only one percent. I maintain that pharmaceuticals are a bargain and have been, and will continue to be, part of the solution to rising health care costs. . . .

The speaker uses a transition to switch gears and develops the second main point of the speech.

Let me turn my attention to trade issues. . . . Free trade is a very imporant issue for our business. The health industry must operate in a borderless world if it is to live up to its economic potential and fully serve its mission of improving health. Therefore the reduction and eventual elimination of protectionism is very much in everyone's interest. In fact, the pharmaceutical industry associations of Japan, the U.S. and Europe have recently agreed on a joint request to their respective governments for elimination of all import duties on pharmaceuticals. In addition to calling on governments to lower international trade barriers, we are encouraging governments to harmonize their health-policy regulations, including the drug approval process. . . .

I would like to conclude by emphasizing our responsibilities. Around the world, our generation of business leaders is creating a new world order—blurring national borders by a globalization of corporate activity. Think how evident this trend is already: how many Japanese children assume McDonald's is home grown; and how many of their American counterparts would have any idea that Sony isn't "good old American know-how" in action. Think of how many brands and corporate identities are being instilled into popular culture in hundreds of markets.

The speaker prepares receivers for the conclusion.

The speaker refers to two easy-to-understand examples.

Corporations must take to heart the call to "share the future" of the communities within which they do business. Multinationals are no longer guests in foreign markets—but important influences and I hope visionary leaders. I believe every industry must play an active role in debating and shaping public policy. In doing so we will not only ensure that society gains the maximum benefit from our industries, but we will also ensure the continued success of industry itself.[1]

DEVELOPING SPEAKER'S NOTES: PREPARING TO SPEAK THE SPEECH

ONCE YOU HAVE COMPLETED your formal outline you will want to develop a shortened version of it to use during your presentation itself. We call this shortened version **speaker's notes.** When you are working up your speaker's notes you will want to select **key words** that will help you recall the outline of the speech as you designed it. Researchers and teachers alike have found that speaking from a complete outline causes the speaker to become too tied to a paper instead of concentrating on relating directly to the audience.

Print or type in large block letters when preparing your speaker's notes and use just a key word or two in place of complete sentences to remind you of each of your

SPEAKING of ETHICS

The Organizational Sandwich

Is it appropriate to sandwich less palatable information into the middle of a speech? While the avowed purpose of an outline is to clarify thinking in an effort to facilitate reception, organization can also be used to bury or deemphasize information speakers must reveal but do not want audiences to retain.

In your opinion, is using organization as a means to try and conceal "bad news" ethical? How can developing critical thinking skills help to alleviate the impact of such organizational effects?

According to primary and recency theories of organization, audiences remember better information that is shared with them first or last, and they tend to lose a greater percentage of what is told to them in the middle.[2] This amounts to a reverse cream sandwich cookie: the cream is lost, not relished. Thus, speakers know to put information that could be discomforting or unsettling or with which audiences are apt to disagree in the middle of a presentation, sandwiched between information they will find much more palatable.

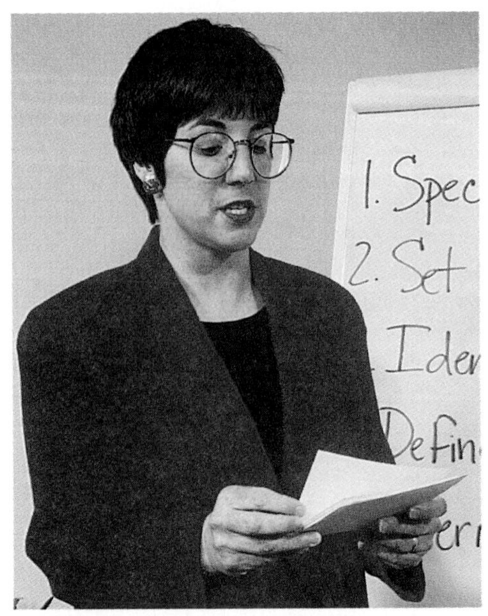

Note cards can help keep a speaker focused on what he or she needs to cover during a speech even when faced with distractions.

main points and subpoints. You will want to lay out your notes on speaker's cards using the same format that you used in the original outline, with Roman numerals and alternating letters and numbers (see Figure 11.3).

As you can see, even when using such brief notes, the speaker is able to identify what he or she has covered and which sections of his or her presentation still need to be covered. Of course, you can also indicate on your notecards exactly where visuals or other forms of support should be integrated and/or displayed. Specific quotations or statistical information can also be written on your cards for easy reference.

Figure 11.3

Sample speaker's notes

I. Smoking is harmful
  A. Animal studies
    (show visual of animal tests)
  B. Human studies
    (show visual of human lungs)

II. Smoking must be banned
    (the surgeon general says...)
  A. Current laws
  B. New laws needed

SUMMARY

An OUTLINE IS A ROADMAP to speechmaking success. By providing a speaker with an overview of the speech, an outline helps the speaker organize his or her thoughts into a meaningful framework characterized by structural integrity.

An outline enables the speaker to test the relative importance of ideas, as well as to see how all the ideas contained in the speech fit together.

Effective outlines exhibit four key characteristics: (1) coordination and consistency (statements that are approximately equal in weight or importance are placed on the same outline level); (2) subordination (supporting ideas are subordinated to main ideas by indenting them); (3) a division of the whole (when divided into constitutent parts, an outline contains at least two subpoints); and (4) parallel structure (concepts displayed in the outline parallel each other).

Once an outline is completed, the speaker then develops speaker's notes (a shortened version of the outline containing key words to use during the presentation).

THE SPEAKER'S STAND

Examine the sample outline that follows and develop key word speaker's notes for a speech. Write your notes on index cards. Compare your keyword notes with those developed by other students in your class.

PRESUMED CONSENT

Specific purpose: To explain to the audience the need for presumed consent to be a law

Central idea: Making presumed consent a law is a means of facilitating organ donation.

Introduction

I. Imagine that you need a new kidney or heart or other organ. You are waiting in a hospital for one to become available. Unfortunately, you cannot wait much longer. You have only a few hours or days to live.

II. Every year 2,000 or more Americans die while waiting for organs to become available.

III. Today, I would like to explain why making presumed consent a law would facilitate organ donation.

(Transition: Let's start with a comparison.)

Body

I. Our bodily organs are like natural resources.
   A. When we think of natural resources, we normally think of trees, water, air, and other environmental elements.
      1. We spend millions conserving and recycling natural elements.
      2. Our bodily parts can also be conserved and recycled.
   B. Our bodily organs can live after we die.
      1. More than 2,000 people die every year waiting for transplants.
      2. Thirty percent of those who need transplants this year will not live long enough to find them.
      3. Tens of thousands of others endure painful and expensive treatments to live with defective organs.
         a. Thousands of people are attached to dialysis machines daily.
         b. Others are attached to machinery to keep defective hearts operating.

(Transition: Now that we understand why we should consider our body a natural resource, let us discuss what presumed consent is and how it can help solve the problems we face.)

II. Presumed consent would enable our organs to be recycled after death.
   A. Presumed consent simply means that a person's organs would be available at the time of his or her death.
      1. There would be no need for anyone to sign a consent form before dying.
      2. Families would not have to give their approval.
   B. Presumed consent is a means of ensuring the human body is treated ethically.

1. Dr. Arthur Caplan of the Center for Biomedical Ethics at the University of Minnesota says, "Presumed consent is the ethically correct thing to do. The decent and humane thing to do is to help people live."
2. People could override presumed consent laws on philosophical or religious grounds.
   a. James Nelson, an ethics specialist with the Communitarian Network, points out that "people could opt not to have their organs removed on religious or philosophical grounds or if they found the idea disturbing."
   b. So, it is not a requirement if the person or person's family chose to object.

(Transition: We have spent a lot of time discussing the ethical basis for presumed consent. It's now time to explore how people feel about it.)

III. People have mixed feelings about making presumed consent the law.
   A. Some people find it difficult to deal with the concept.
      1. Dr. Caplan points out, "There are a lot of people who may support organ donation in the abstract, but when death comes, they don't want to deal with it."
      2. It is difficult for many to talk about their own deaths or the deaths of loved ones.
   B. Others point to the benefits of making presumed consent the law.
      1. They stress that presumed consent will save the lives of thousands every year.
      2. They find solace in the fact that their organs or the organs of those they love would be able to be used to relieve suffering of others who are compelled to live with defective body parts.

Conclusion

I. We can see that presumed consent is sparking and will continue to spark much discussion.
II. It is important for us to listen to this discussion so that we will be in a position to make a decision regarding how we feel about such a law.

Bibliography

Arthur Caplan, *Presumed Consent* (New York: Hasting Center, 1984).

"Routine Donation of Organs Pushed: Ethics Group Seeks 'Presumed Consent,' " Associated Press, December 22, 1992.

Vincente Navarro, "The Unhealth of Our Medical Sector," *Dissent* (New York: Foundation for the Study of Independent Social Ideas, 1987).

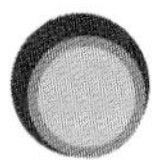

STUDENT FOCUS GROUP REPORT

Now that you have had time to consider the importance of outlining, in a group of five to seven students, answer the following questions:

1. How effective is the use of a key word outline? Would you prefer to read from a manuscript when delivering a speech? Why or why not?
2. How can adequate rehearsal help you bring the key word outline to life?
3. What percentage of your speech preparation time should you allocate to developing your outline? Why?
4. In what ways does the outlining process help you refine your reason for speaking as well as your ideas?
5. To what extent, if any, does having a conception of a speaker's outline influence your perception of the speaker and his or her ideas?
6. In what ways does having a better understanding of the speech organization process enable you to become a more adept consumer of speeches? Explain.
7. Summarize the most important lessons you have learned about outlining.
8. Revisit the case study at the beginning of this chapter. Based on your current understanding of outlining what changes, if any, would you now make in answering the questions?

Chapter Twelve

The Speaker's Words

Language, Thought, and Action

After reading this chapter, you should be able to:

- Explain why word choice plays a critical role in speech development and the realization of a desired effect.
- Define *language.*
- Identify how language can bridge cultural differences.
- Describe why language is a power tool.
- Compare and contrast denotative and connotative meanings.
- Explain the triangle of meaning.
- Compare and contrast how time and place affect meaning.
- Observe the following language guidelines: keep it simple, keep it concrete, keep it appropriate, keep it vivid.
- Describe the differences between oral and written style.

CASE STUDY

Words That Wound[1]

Like many college students, Eden gave little thought to the impact that the words he spoke might have on others. In fact, he was shocked to discover that his uttering of only two words could actually precipitate an incident. One day, when disturbed by a group of students who were socializing loudly beneath his window, Eden yelled, "Shut up, you water buffalo." Though it was later learned that Eden had previously attended a yeshiva where the Hebrew term for "water buffalo" was slang for "foolish person," he was still threatened with prosecution for racial harassment. Eventually, the case died down when the women so addressed by Eden claimed that they were being persecuted by the press, and dropped their charge.[2]

Now consider this. When giving a speech entitled "Campus Sexual Harrassment Policies," a public speaking student, Lindsay (the student's name could indicate a male or female), used a number of hypothetical examples. Featured in Lindsay's examples were two fictional characters by the names Dave Stud[3] and Diane Sex Object. While a number of students laughed when they heard the names, others were offended and objected vocally at the speech's conclusion, noting that the speaker's word choices were sexist.

- What are the possible implications of the epithets and names used in the two scenarios?
- If you were advising Eden and Lindsay, what would you tell them regarding language use?
- To what extent, if any, should colleges concern themselves with issues of political correctness? Be specific in explaining your response.

THE LANGUAGE YOU USE to express your ideas influences audience responses to both you and your speech. In large part, the message you communicate to your audience members and the meaning they extract from that message depends on the words you use.

THE LANGUAGE AND SPEECH CONNECTION

EITHER YOUR LANGUAGE can cause your ideas to live in the minds of audience members long after your speech has ended or, because the language you use angers or alienates receivers or lacks vivid images and impact, it can make listeners wish your speech were over long before it ended. The language you use can either help connect you to your audience or contribute to a speaker–audience disconnection. Only if you select words that appeal to your audience—words that succeed in moving your listeners emotionally and intellectually—will you be able to attain the ultimate goal of your speech.

Choose the right words and you will fulfill your purpose for speaking. Choose the wrong words, words that lack vividness, words that are difficult to understand, words that fail to capture the imaginations of your listeners, and instead of establish-

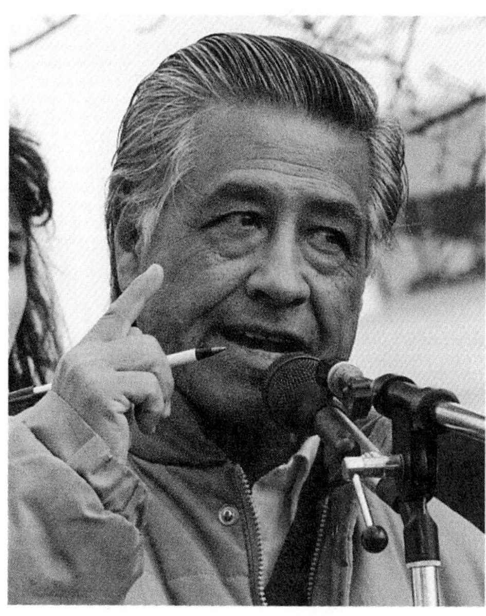

Cesar Chavez uses words that can make ideas live in the minds of receivers long after the speech has ended.

ing communication you might well establish confusion. After all, it is by speaking simply, accurately, and effectively that you increase your chances of making what you say memorable.

Thus, the choice is yours. You can use language that conceals or reveals, is deceptive or expressive, or leads you astray or clears the way for you to share your ideas with an audience. As you will see, words are powerful communication tools. They are the building blocks of every speech you will give. How well you use them, how creatively you work with them to make all the pieces fit, will determine your success as a speaker.

In this chapter we will explore your role as a *word master.* We'll look at how language works and at how the language choices you make can spell the difference between speaking success and failure. Language, in effect, is your speech's control mechanism. If you use words to steer your speech toward your goal you stay in charge; if, on the other hand, you lose control of your words, you take a wrong turn and lose your way. Thus, it is the language choices you make that influence your abilities to control the direction of your speech and to direct your listeners to come to a common understanding with you so they are more apt to respond as you desire.

WHAT IS LANGUAGE?

LANGUAGE IS AN ARBITRARY SYMBOL system composed of words. A **symbol** stands for, or represents, something else. Words, as symbols, represent things or ideas. For language to work, for it to function effectively as our prime message system, there must be a common understanding or basic agreement regarding what the words we are using mean. Only then can members of a language community use language to share meaning and experience.

LANGUAGE AND CULTURAL DIVERSITY

AS A PUBLIC SPEAKER, it is your job to use words to create desired meanings in the minds of your audience members. However, as effective as words are to you in representing and describing your ideas, the meaning of the verbal message you send is neither imprinted on the words you use nor stamped on the words contained in the verbal message your listeners receive. **Meaning does not exist in words,** but in the minds of people who use words. When functioning as a public speaker, your goal in communicating with an audience is to have each of your meanings overlap; only when this occurs will your audience members be able to make sense of your message and comprehend it. Accordingly, one of your prime objectives is to translate the ideas you want to communicate into language your listeners will understand and respond to. Although this sounds easy, far too often problems pop up that turn language into a communication obstacle rather than into a communication facilitator.

Overcoming Communication Obstacles

One of the major obstacles that must be handled when choosing words is the fact that words have both *denotative* and *connotative* meanings. The **denotative meaning** is precise and objective; it is the word's dictionary definition. As a speaker, you need to keep in mind that audience members are not dictionaries; when you use a word they cannot immediately turn to a copy of *Webster's Tenth* to find meaning number four for that word. What audience members do carry with them in their heads is the connotative meanings of words. **Connotative meaning** is variable and subjective in nature. It includes all the feelings and personal associations that a word stimulates in different people. For example, the feelings and personal associations people have for words and phrases such as *home, immigrant, affirmative action,* or *childhood* will differ depending on whether the experiences they associate with each word are good or bad.

If as a speaker you pay attention only to a word's denotative meaning but fail to consider the possible connotative meanings the word could evoke among audience members, you may not be understood as you intended. For this reason, you need to search for words that will likely elicit the meanings and responses you desire from as many audience members as possible. While you know what the words you are using mean to you, the question you must consciously and continually ask yourself is: *What do the words I am using mean to my listeners?* When you put your listeners in the speaker's spotlight, instead of simply speaking the first words that pop into your mind, you take the time needed to identify the best way and the best words to use to evoke a desired audience reaction. A speaker who is sensitive to the way listeners react to words is sensitive to the importance of word choice and capitalizes on the opportunity to establish a strong connection with his or her listeners.

Your ability to choose your words carefully can also help you modify the connotative meanings audience members have for words. Keep in mind that connotative meanings are learned through experience, and you are in a position to add to the experience of your receivers. Understand how your audience responds to words and your audience will better understand and more appropriately interpret what you say. The words you use to share your ideas determine in large part how audience members respond to those ideas.[4]

Cleaning Up Communication Garbage

Speaker and industrial psychologist Michael Brooks believes that although language "is the most necessary component of communication at our disposal," if not handled carefully it can turn into mere "communication garbage."[5] According to Brooks:

Our language—our everyday, garden-variety speaking language—is a wonderful display of our thoughts and intentions. For the most part, it operates well out of the scope of our conscious awareness making it an ideal door from which persuasion can enter and exit. This also explains why we are so very often misunderstood. We labor under the belief system that what one says is what we communicate. Nothing could be farther from the truth. . . .

Most of us never receive any training in communication skills and have married the assumption that talk equals understanding. If you isolate this fact by itself and think about it for a minute, you'll get a glimpse of why our lives are spent continually trying to clean up the mess we make when we "communicate."[6]

- What steps should a public speaker take to avoid making a communication mess?

One of your responsibilities as a speaker is to decide how to best communicate your ideas to your listeners. By choosing the right words with which to encode your ideas, you increase your chances of giving an effective speech. **Strategic word choice** is an essential tool of skilled public speakers. In fact, it may well be their most powerful tool.

Understanding Reasoning and Expression Preferences

Language and the way we use it can become a barrier to speaker–audience understanding.[7] Our language tends to reflect our world view, our interests and concerns, and what we believe to be important. It also reflects reasoning patterns and expression preferences.

People in Western cultures, for example, tend to rely on **inductive reasoning** (reasoning from specific instances or examples) and **deductive reasoning** (reasoning from general principles) to make points and understand those made by others. In contrast, the Arab world relies on emotions. Thus, Westerners may have difficulty locating the main ideas in the speeches of Arabs, and vice versa.[8] Arab speakers, for example, may change course midspeech; to Westerners, it may seem as they have gone off on a tangent as they personalize and emote. As a result, Western receivers listening to an Arab speaker often find themselves working harder to identify the speaker's actual purpose and the speech's main points. Arab speech is also peppered with exaggerations and repetitions. Its stress patterns often confuse Western receivers, causing them to interpret messages as either aggressive or disinterested when that may not be their intent. It is important to remember that culture influences the way we use language.

Asians also differ from Westerners in language use. Whereas North Americans tend to exhibit a frank, direct, sometimes confrontational speechmaking style, Asians, who place a high value on politeness, are more likely to use hints and hidden messages in gestures and euphemisms to convey their message's meaning.[9] For example, whereas Westerners, in general, tend to reveal their personalities openly during their oral presentations, many Asians tend to practice greater subtlety and restraint. Thus, Asians typically neither preview nor identify their speech's purpose or main points for receivers; instead, both are subtly implied or suggested through stories and personal testimony.

Clearly there is more than one way to use language to express ideas. One culture's means of expression is not necessarily better than another culture's. We run into problems when we allow feelings of ethnocentrism to interfere with our ability to process the thoughts of others.

LANGUAGE IS A POWER TOOL

LANGUAGE, AS WE MENTIONED, is your speech's steering mechanism. When you handle it well you are better able to control your audience's perceptions and reactions to you and your speech. Different words used to describe the same event can evoke very different reponses. For example, how do you react to each of the following words or phrases and what kinds of thoughts does each evoke? How do the images you visualize change with the expression used to describe the event?

war *defensive response* *massacre*

While the event itself may be the same, the words used to describe it express how we perceive it and can influence how our audience members respond to it as well. In other words, the impact of our communication is achieved through the words we choose. Our words can help our listeners conceive of the world as we conceive of it. They can help listeners perceive our ideas as we want, and they can also influence listeners' attitudes, values, and actions. The power of words to influence what each of us thinks and how each of us interprets what we experience is part and parcel of how we encounter and react to events. Thus, with language we can control an audience's perceptions, conceptions, and reflections. We can change the way audience members see and think about our subject, and act after our speech. Language can help make an audience feel intensely and it can help audience members overcome apathy. Language helps create the world we want our listeners to inhabit with us. As you will see, when used well, language is a uniter rather than a divider; it evokes fresh, rather than stale, images; and it encourages, rather than discourages, desired attitudes and behaviors.

Language Has the Power to Unite

Through language the speaker and listener may be united and audience members may be stimulated to join together as well. For example, in a speech entitled "The Rainbow Coalition" Jesse Jackson used words to connect himself with his listeners and to bind his listeners to each other:

Tonight we come together bound by our faith in a mighty God, with genuine respect for our country, and inheriting the legacy of a great party—a Democratic Party—which is the best hope for redirecting our nation on a more humane, just and peaceful course.

This is not a perfect party. We are not a perfect people. Yet, we are called to a perfect mission: our mission, to feed the hungry, to clothe the naked, to house the homeless, to teach the illiterate, to provide jobs for the jobless, and to choose the human race over the nuclear race.

We are gathered here this week to nominate a candidate and write a platform which will expand, unify, direct and inspire our party and the nation to fulfill this mission.[10]

Language Has the Power to Evoke Fresh Images

The words you use to describe your subject influence the way your listeners view the world. When you add fresh mental images to your speech, you can trigger new ways of seeing and sensing among receivers. This is what Wilma Scott Heide, former president of the National Organization for Women, tried to do in this excerpt from a speech entitled "Revolution: Tomorrow Is Now!"

Can we wage war like physical atomic giants and consider peace like intellectual midgets equating a partial cease-fire with peace when a fundamental cause of war is the ultimate expression of violence from the masculine mystique and the adoring feminine mystique that sustains it?[11]

Similarly, Sol Trujilo, president and CEO of US West Communication Group, delivered a speech documenting the ways in which the American Hispanic population is reaching new heights and used words to try to evoke fresh ways of seeing among his listeners:

Every time I went out to meet customers I found hard-working Hispanic entrepreneurs, trying to make things work in the world of business.

Some were what I call "Pilgrims"—people just looking for a new way of life. They weren't trying to start the next Hewlett Packard or the next Intel or Netscape. They were just trying to make a better living for themselves and their families, to buy a home, to send their kids to the community college or the university, to take care of their parents because those are the kinds of things that are important to our community.

I also encountered more than a few hard chargers. I call them "Swashbucklers." They were going to change the world, create new markets, get rich. And some I came to know will succeed. I'm sure of that.

So let's really try to understand what is happening in our community. The fact is we are a hard-working people with a culture that values learning, loyalty, performance, and personal responsibility.

Guess what! Those are precisely the qualities that are required to win in the New Economy and that's why our community is doing so well, by any measure, by any standard of comparison. And that is why "Reaching New Heights" is an appropriate theme because we can and we are doing it.[12]

Language Has the Power to Encourage Desired Attitudes and Behaviors

How you describe a subject not only tells how you feel about it, it also influences your listeners' attitudes and behaviors. Your word choices convey your feelings, shape the perceptions of your listeners, and can even move them to action.

When Edwin J. Delattre, dean ad interim of Boston University School of Education, delivered a speech entitled "Condoms and Coercion," he clearly conveyed his attitudes toward his topic to his audience. Delattre used these words to describe what

Because of its power to evoke strong emotion, language often leads to emotional behavior. Can you identify a speaker whose use of language caused you to respond?

he longed to say to both a young child and to all students so that they would understand what was really at stake:

> I want that child to be told the truth.
>
> I want her to learn that her generation, and those a bit older than she, do not have to die in youth. That many of her peers will not die of sexually transmitted diseases; instead they will learn to avoid casual sex because it is incredibly dangerous, and because it diminishes self-respect. . . .
>
> I want them to know that betting your life—or letting someone else bet your life—on a condom is a gamble that only one in eight hundred experts on sexual behavior is willing to risk, and that if our own students behave otherwise, they make a mockery of their stated commitment expressed over and over again in this room, to saving lives.[13]

Thus, depending on your point of view, a condom can be viewed as a valuable weapon in the fight against AIDS or as a "mere balloon" placed "between a healthy body and a deadly disease."[14] The words you choose to use can influence your listeners' opinions and judgments and ultimately perhaps their personal behavior.

People have changed the way they act—at least in part—because of words, and nations have gone to war at least in part because of words. When President Franklin Delano Roosevelt referred to the bombing of Pearl Harbor as "a day that shall live in infamy," he fueled the ire of Americans against the Japanese, and strengthened the resolve of Americans to enter World War II. When President George Bush addressed Congress and the American people on Iraqi aggression in the Persian Gulf, he sought to prepare both for the conflict with these words:

> America and the world must defend common vital interests. And we will.
>
> America and the world must support the rule of law. And we will.
>
> America and the world must stand up to aggression. And we will.

And one thing more. In pursuit of these goals America will not be intimidated.

Vital issues of principle are at stake. Saddam Hussein is literally trying to wipe a country off the face of the earth.

We do not exaggerate.

Nor do we exaggerate when we say: Saddam Hussein will fail.[15]

Well-chosen words can be effective in rallying support for a cause and moving people to action.

MEANING AND THE PEOPLE FACTOR

LET US RETURN TO A KEY PRECEPT of this chapter. The words we use are symbols, nothing more nor less. We should be careful not to confuse words with what they actually represent. For example, the word *homeless* is not the thing "homeless." Words do not automatically convey the same meanings from speaker to listener. Words, instead, are symbols, and as symbols, the only relationship between them and the things they represent exists in our minds.

The Triangle of Meaning

The **Triangle of Meaning,** devised by communication theorists C. K. Ogden and I. A. Richards, provides a model of the tenuous relationships among words, thoughts, and things (see Figure 12.1).

The dotted line connecting a word (a symbol) and an object (a stimulus, also referred to as a referent) indicates that there is no direct connection between the two. Thus, when you use a word like *homeless,* you need to keep in mind that the only connection that exists between the word you are using and what it actually represents is in people's minds (your own, of course, included). Even the presence of the physical thing (an actual homeless person) does not necessarily establish meaning. It is feasible that a number of us could look at the same thing, think entirely different thoughts about it, and thus give it entirely different meanings based on our experiences or lack of experiences with the subject stimulus itself.

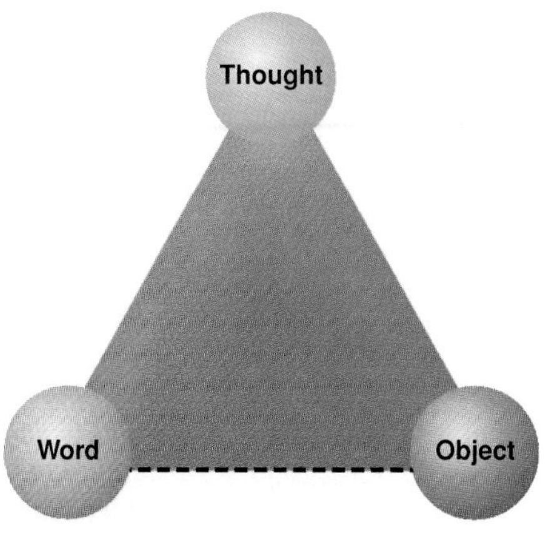

Figure 12.1

The Triangle of Meaning

To become a successful public speaker you need to understand and work with the relationship that exists between words, thoughts, and human behavior. That means that when addressing an audience it is dangerous to assume everyone understands what you mean. Unless you are careful, the words you use to communicate could get in the way. Consider the conversation Lewis Carroll's characters Alice and Humpty Dumpty have in his novel *Through the Looking Glass:*

> "I don't know what you mean by 'glory'," Alice said.
> Humpty Dumpty smiled contemptuously. "Of course you don't—till I tell you. I meant, 'There's a nice knock-down argument for you!' "
> "But 'glory' doesn't mean 'A nice knock-down argument,' " Alice objected.
> "When I use a word, " Humpty Dumpty said in a rather scornful tone, "it means just what I choose it to mean—nothing more nor less."

Can public speakers make words mean whatever they want them to? Not if they want to share their meanings with members of their audiences. Once communication is the goal, we can no longer consider only one meaning for a word. We must also focus on what our words mean to those with whom we are communicating. As we do that we need to carefully consider how time and place could affect the way our listeners process our words.

MEANING AND TIME AND PLACE

EVERY GENERATION EVOLVES new meanings for old words; it's as if we recycle language so it constantly changes. This fact becomes important when you are speaking to audiences composed primarily of persons older or younger than you, or when you are addressing audiences made up of persons of mixed ages. The word "gay," for example, is now an acceptable term for "homosexual," and is well on its way to shedding its past meaning of "happy," "bright," or "merry." Consider, for example, how an audience of your peers, an audience of people in their seventies, and an audience of elementary school-aged children each might interpret any of the following words: *radical, net, surf, rap, gross, red, straight, chill, bite moose, parallel parking, far out, awesome.* Definitions do not necessarily stay with words eternally, and because time can affect a word's meaning, it is important for speakers to be aware of the meaning any given listeners could attach to a word.

The meanings of words change not only through time. Words also change meaning from one section of the country to another. A phosphate, a soda, and an egg cream are all the same drink. Public speakers need to be sensitive to how regional differences affect word meanings or they could find themselves facing a widening communication gap.

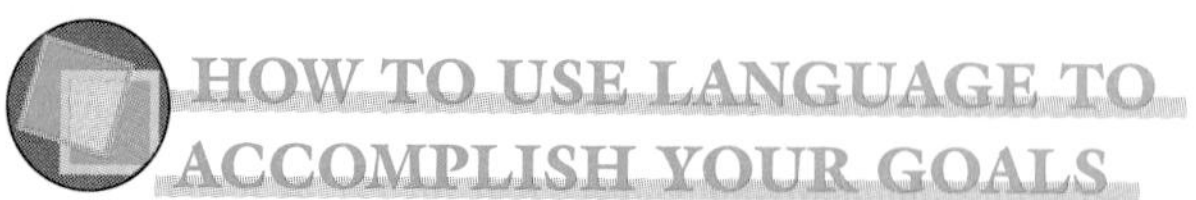

HOW TO USE LANGUAGE TO ACCOMPLISH YOUR GOALS

EVERY PUBLIC SPEAKER faces numerous speechmaking challenges. Among them is the need to choose the right words to communicate a message. Ideally the words you select will help your listeners understand the points you are making. Only if you succeed in having your listeners share the meanings you have in mind will they truly perceive your message accurately. In order to achieve as much sharing of meaning as possible, you need to make strategic language choices—choices that favor the *simple* over the complex, the *concrete* over the abstract, the *appropriate* over the inappropriate, and the *vivid* over the vague. Because we know that language, if not handled carefully, can create problems, it is important that we consider how you can use language to best express your ideas to an audience. Let us explore each of these language options in turn.

Keep It Simple

Whenever you have the choice, you are wise to select the simplest, most familiar word available to you. Never opt to use a lengthy, multisyllabic, less familiar word when a shorter, simpler one will do—the latter is usually more clear to your listeners, and audiences appreciate clarity.

Far too often, speakers who spout unfamiliar words and technological jargon to uninitiated audiences only succeed in communicating their stuffiness and pretentiousness; no real sharing of meaning can occur between such a speaker and his or her audience because the audience has no idea what the speaker is actually talking about.

The following anecdote illustrates how language can obscure meaning, thereby causing it to fail to perform the very function it was designed to fulfill:

> A plumber who had only a limited command of English knew that hydrochloric acid opened clogged drain pipes quickly and effectively. What he didn't know, however, was if it was the right thing to use. So the plumber decided to check with the National Bureau of Standards in Washington, D.C. Seeking confirmation that hydrochloric acid was safe to use in pipes, he wrote the bureau a letter. After processing his letter, a scientist at the bureau wrote back this response: "The efficacy of hydrochloric acid is indisputable, but the corrosive residue is incompatible with metallic surfaces."
>
> The plumber interpreted the scientist's response as a comfirmation and wrote a second letter to the bureau thanking the scientist for the quick reply and for giving him the go-ahead to use hydrochloric acid.
>
> The plumber's thank you really bothered the scientist, who showed it to a superior. His superior decided to write the plumber a second letter. This letter read: "We cannot assume responsibility for the production of toxic and noxious residue which hydrochloric acid can produce; we suggest that you use an alternative procedure."
>
> Though this response left the plumber a bit baffled, he hurriedly sent the bureau a third letter telling them that he was pleased they agreed with him. "The acid was working just fine."
>
> When this letter arrived, the scientist's superior sent it to the head administrator at the bureau. The head administrator ended the confusion by writing a short, simple note to the plumber: "Don't use hydrochloric acid. It eats the hell out of pipes."

To communicate your message's meaning clearly and permit as many members of your audience as possible to share it, you need to make careful word choices—selecting words that leave no doubt about your meaning in the minds of listeners. The more difficult, bloated, and befuddling your language becomes, the more likely your audience—particularly if unspecialized—will have difficulty deciphering its meaning. For this reason, before using the **jargon** of a field remember always to check whether audience members share your specialized vocabulary. Here are some sample word guidelines to keep in mind when speaking before general audiences.

The Issue of Political Correctness

1. Consider the following definitions from *The Official Politically Correct Dictionary and Handbook* by Henry Beard and Christopher Cerf, in which the authors take a humorous look at language that is nonspecific and nonoffensive. In their opinion such language is bland and impedes meaningful communication. What do you think?

Dirty old man—sexually focused chronologically gifted individual
Perverted—sexually dysfunctional
Panhandler—unaffiliated applicant for private-sector funding
Serial killer—person with difficult-to-meet needs
Lazy—motivationally deficient
Fat—horizontally challenged
Dishonest—ethically disoriented
Bald—follicularly challenged
Clumsy—uniquely coordinated
Body odor—nondiscretionary fragrance
Alive—temporarily metabolically abled
Boring—charm free
Airplane crash—controlled flight into terrain
Lie—counterfactual proposition
Drunk—chemically inconvenienced
Looting—nontraditional shopping
Police brutality—inappropriate use of physical force under color of law
Dead—terminally inconvenienced
Worst—least best
Wrong—differently logical
Ugly—cosmetically different
Unemployed—involuntarily leisured
Vagrant—nonspecifically destinationed individual
Spendthrift—negative saver
Ignorant—knowledge base nonpossessor
Solitary confinement—therapeutic segregation
Soft targets—humans or groups of humans selected to be bombed or otherwise militarily attacked.[16]

2. Working in teams, create five interesting culturally sensitive statements by stringing together a number of politically correct definitions. For example, "He was a sexually dysfunctional unaffiliated applicant for private-sector funding" versus the more blunt. "He was a perverted panhandler."

3. What problems does politically correct communication pose for speakers and listeners? How can listeners keep from being abused by speakers who manipulate them via word choice, whether deliberately or unintentionally?

4. Cite examples of how poor word choice can contribute to one being perceived as insensitive, a racist, or a bigot.

Choose	*Don't Use*
try	endeavor
begin	commence
fight	altercation
view	vista
avoid	eschew
building	edifice
pay	remunerate
rain	precipitation

Former Secretary of State and Chief of Staff Alexander Haig mastered the art of confusing audiences by endowing his addresses with a multitude of unintelligible and obscure phrases like "epistemologicallywise," and "subsumed in the vortex of criticality."[17] What was Haig's rationale for speaking this way? Who knows? What we do know is that the words he chose impeded rather than facilitated, confused rather than clarified.

Attempting to impress an audience by using four-, five- or six-syllable words when one-, two-, or three-syllable words work just as well usually backfires. Although you may impress the uninitiated for a brief period with unfamiliar words, in the end you'll lose them.

Keep It Concrete

Using concrete rather than abstract language helps your audience members picture what you want them to. The more abstract you are, the less likely it is that your listeners will share the image you intended for them to visualize. Choosing a more general word to carry meaning instead of selecting a more precise one only invites confusion and misunderstanding. Your job as a speaker is to select words that help create clear pictures in the minds of listeners. Doing this will leave no doubt about your meaning and it will help prevent possible misinterpretation of your message.

Remember, the more abstract the word, the more meanings people will have for it. To reduce ambiguity, enhance concreteness. Concrete words let listeners form clearer mental pictures of your referent, and are also easier for them to recall. The more concrete your language, the more precise your communication. So when you have a choice, follow the guidelines set by these examples:

Choose	*Don't Use*
Mercedes Benz	expensive car
help the American car manufacturer	help the manufacturer
cattle	livestock
pit bull terrior	dog
employee participation	sound business principles
$1,000,000	a bundle
use the same grading standard for all	fair
volunteer at a soup kitchen	help the homeless
aerobics	physical activity

Frequently, instead of using concrete and direct language, speakers choose to use less jarring, more abstract words. Such substitutions, called **euphemisms,** make it easier for speakers to handle unpleasant subjects, but often also make it harder for audiences to develop a clear and accurate perception of what the speaker is saying. Thus, the euphemism can mask a speaker's meaning and change an audience's reaction to what the speaker is talking about simply by changing the word used. Notice how your reactions are changed by the words used in the following word trios:

third-world	underdeveloped	backward
corpse	dead body	loved one
coffin	casket	slumber chamber
heavy	overweight	obese
handkerchief	cloth tissue	nose rag
laying off	firing	downsizing
handicapped	disabled	physically challenged

Concrete words evoke more precise meanings. If you make a conscious effort to be more specific and less general, the speeches you deliver will become clearer, more interesting, and easier to remember.

Keep It Appropriate

The language you use should be appropriate to both you and your audience. Your speech should be phrased in words that suit you (words you understand and are comfortable with), and words your audience will also understand, accept, and respond to. Obscene, racist, or sexist remarks are usually judged offensive by audiences. Thus, common sense must prevail. Although we may use certain terms when conversing with our close friends, such expressions may be inappropriate and unwise when used in a speech. For example, although normally an excellent motivational and persuasive speaker, Jesse Jackson alienated many Jews in New York by referring to their city as "hymie town." One-time presidential aspirant billionaire Ross Perot made a similar gaffe when he delivered an address before the NAACP convention in Nashville and referred to African Americans as "you people."

Of necessity, public speakers must make choices that demonstrate they understand how the situation, the time, and the place affect their use of language. It is up to you to decide what is proper. However, if you offend an audience by using inappropriate language, you risk undermining your credibility and effectiveness as a speaker.

The Issue of Political Correctness. The term **political correctness,** like so many words, means different things to different people; the words themselves have different connotations for each of us. For some of us, being politically correct means using words that convey respect for and sensitivity to the needs and interests of different groups. Thus, when we find ourselves speaking about various issues to audiences composed of persons who are culturally different from us, we may also find ourselves adapting our language so that it demonstrates our sensitivity to the perspectives and interests of our audience. For others, however, political correctness means that we feel compelled by societal pressures not to use some words in our speeches for fear that doing so would cause members of our audience to perceive us as either racist or sexist. Thus, we might opt to clothe our words in politically correct attire in an effort to do whatever is necessary to avoid offending anyone. Still others view political correctness as a very real danger to free speech. Which of these three views comes closest to representing your own?

The Implications of Sexist, Racist, and Ageist Language. Language can be used to demean groups of people. We can show our respect with words, but we can also use words to signal our lack of respect or contempt.

Sexist language suggests that the two sexes are unequal, and that one gender has more status and value and is more capable than the other. For example, in past decades, masculine words were used to include both males and females. Thus, the use of the generic "he" (for he or she) or "man" (for man or woman) in written and spoken discourse virtually excluded females by ignoring them. A sexist language practice called **spotlighting** was also used to reinforce the notion that men, and not women, set the standard. Whereas we rarely hear the following combinations, male physician, male lawyer, male physicist, terms such as woman doctor and female mathematician do tend to be more widely used. Today, however, we are somewhat more apt to substitute gender-inclusive terms such as "chairperson," and "spokesperson," and to use language that equalizes rather than highlights the treatment of sex.

Racist language is another form of discriminatory language. When using racist language an individual displays bigoted views about a person or persons from another group, based on his or her ideas of that individual's race. Racist language dehumanizes the members of the group being attacked. It is the deliberate, purposeful, and hurtful use of words intended to oppress someone of a different color.[18]

Considering Diversity

The Debate over Ebonics

Actor Bill Cosby wrote a column criticizing the endorsment of ebonics as an urbanized version of the English language. He began this way:

> I remember one day 15 years ago, a friend of mine told me a racist joke.
> *Question:* Do you know what Toys "R" Us is called in Harlem?
> *Answer:* We Be Toys.[19]

Cosby went on to discuss the problems of legitimizing the use of ebonics in schools and ended with this thought:

> . . . legitimizing the street in the classroom is backwards. We should be working hard to legitimize the classroom—and English—in the street. On the other hand, we could jes letem do wha ever they wanna. Either way, Ima go over hearh an learn some maffa matics an then ge-sum 'n tee an' then I'll be witchya.[20]

According to Montclair State University Professor Dierdre Glenn Paul, ebonics, or black English, would "most appropriately, be classified as a dialect by linguists. A dialect is defined as the collective linguistic patterns of a subgroup of the speakers of a language. . . . Further, black English is part and parcel of the American lexicon and literary tradition."[21]

In contrast, columnist Jack E. White reminds us not to paint all Afrocentrics with the same brush. He observes that while African American speech patterns are, to a degree, influenced by African roots, "that never stopped orators like Frederick Douglass, Martin Luther King, Jr., and even some of the young rappers from speaking English far better than most white folks do."[22]

Offering another viewpoint, columnist Louis Menand believes that ebonics is an unfortunate idea because it associates language with skin color, and "smacks of cultural separatism."[23]

Bill Cosby has entered the fray on whether or not to legitimize Ebonics. Where do you stand on this issue?

(continued)

Considering Diversity *(continued)*

Much of the furor over ebonics was the result of a resolution passed by officials of the Oakland Unified School District to treat black English as a second language in its classrooms. After a month of national debate, however, the Oakland schools task force issued a new resolution that instead merely called for the recognition of language differences among African American students in order to improve their proficiency in English.[24]

- Is failing to legitimize the use of ebonics in schools, including public speaking classes, racist? Explain your position.
- To what extent, if any, would legitimizing the use of ebonics promote literacy rather than the misuse of language and actually facilitate communication between cultural groups? Explain.

Ageist language discriminates on the basis of age. Unlike Asian cultures, which place a great deal of value on age, U.S. culture tends to disparage the eldery and exalt the youthful. Negative stereotypes such as "She's an old hag," "She's set in her ways," or "He's losing his mind" abound. Ageism is often based on a distaste for and fear of growing older.[25] Decategorizing individuals and changing our expectations will be necessary if we are to improve our communication effectiveness with persons of all ages.[26]

SPEAKING of CRITICAL THINKING

The Language of Approval and Disapproval

A key component of critical thinking involves being able to maintain an open mind even when opinions being expressed are diametrically opposed to your own. Consider the following:

According to former Supreme Court Justice Oliver Wendell Holmes, Jr., "If there is any principle of the Constitution that more imperatively calls for attachment than any other it is the principle of free thought—not free thought for those who agree with us but freedom for the thought we hate."[27]

When a speaker delivers a speech containing ideas we dislike; omitting details we believe are relevant; and referring to persons, places, or things in ways we consider unfair, we are apt to say, "Look how poorly he or she has handled the topic." When we do this, however, what are we actually criticizing? And what steps must we take to look at the speaker's subject from his or her point of view before reacting negatively to it?

A speaker's word choice plays a role in our reaction to his or her speech. Because a speaker's choice of words for the same referent may differ from our own, it could alter the opinion we have of the speaker. For example, the words *janitor* and *sanitary engineer* both mean *custodian.* Yet we associate very different connotations with each term. In fact, we frequently react to the words the speaker uses instead of what the words the speaker uses actually refer to. Receivers need to work hard to prevent a speaker's words from blinding them to what those words represent.

Keep It Vivid

Speech that is vivid contains **figurative language,** which enables listeners to picture the speaker's meaning, and a sound and rhythm that allows them both to sense the speaker's intensity and more fully internalize the impact of the speaker's words.

Behind every vivid speaker is a vivid thinker. You need to see a vivid mental picture in your mind's eye before you can "pass it on" to your audience. You must hear the cadence of your words and sense the rhythm of your speech's movement before you can expect others to be able to do so. To achieve vividness you first must give yourself the freedom to think imaginatively; next you must make a conscious effort to use figures of speech and selected sound patterns that add more force to your thoughts. Doing this will help you gain and sustain the attention of your audience.

Use Figures of Speech. You can make your speeches more vivid by using figures of speech. Because they precipitate striking mental images in listeners, the novel use of figures of speech adds freshness and vitality to a speech.

Among the most commonly used figures of speech are *similes* and *metaphors.* A **simile** is a direct comparison of dissimilar things usually with the words "like" or "as." Because a simile explicitly compares things that are essentially different and are not usually paired with each other, it increases memorability and helps your listeners better understand the meaning of your message. Jesse Jackson's "Rainbow Coalition" speech contained a number of powerful figures of speech, including the following simile:

America is not like a blanket—one piece of unbroken cloth, the same color, the same texture, the same size. America is more like a quilt—many patches, many pieces, many sizes, and woven and held together by a common thread.[28]

In a speech on teaching virtue, Todd G. Buchholz of the Economic Policy Council also relied on a simile to communicate with his receivers when he told listeners:

This combination of right and responsibility helped sew our country together. I fear that today our fabric is being picked at and pawed at like the discount rack at Filene's Basement. [29]

Chief Seattle, a Native American leader, used effective similes to make his point:

The white people are many. They are like the grass that covers vast prairies. My people are few. They resemble the scattering trees of a storm-swept plain.[30]

Notice in these examples how the simile used can improve or worsen an audience's impression of the speaker's subject.

In contrast to a simile, which builds a direct *comparison,* a **metaphor** builds a direct *identification* by omitting the words "like" or "as." Thus in a metaphor the comparison between two things not usually considered alike is implied rather than explicit.

In his "Civil Rights Message, President John F. Kennedy used an effective metaphor when he said:

The fires of frustration and discord are burning in every city, North and South, where legal remedies are not at hand.[31]

And in his renowned "I Have a Dream" speech, Martin Luther King, Jr., added force to the words he spoke with this metaphor:

In a sense we have come to our nation's Capitol to cash a check. When the architects of our republic wrote the magnificent words of the Constitution and the Declaration of Independence, they were signing a promissory note to which every American was to fall heir.[32]

Former New York City Police Commissioner Lee P. Brown also used a metaphor when he told his FBI conference audience:

We have tough gun control laws in New York. Other states don't. The way to control guns in New York is to "drain the swamps" that surround us. And that can be accomplished only through tough federal gun control.[33]

Writer and feminist Gloria Steinem relied on the metaphor to explain the nature of self-esteem:

Self-esteem is not a zero-sum game: by definition, there is exactly enough to go around. By making the circle the organizing image in our minds, a prison of lines and limits will gradually disappear.[34]

In each of these examples, the metaphor used helped give concreteness to a more abstract concept. Every metaphor enhanced the audience's ability to visualize the speaker's message.

Use Sound and Rhythm. Sound and rhythmic patterns can also help empower a speech. Among the sound and rhythmic tools widely used are *parallelism, alliteration,* and *antithesis.*

Parallelism enhances vividness by creating verbal balance through the repetition of words, phrases, or sentences. Jean Otto, founder of the First Amendment Congress and associate editor of the *Rocky Mountain News,* used parallelism to reinforce her message:

Either our liberties exist in the way we live, or what we believe, in the tolerance and acceptance of our fellow human being, or they do not exist at all. Either they inspire us to respect and tolerate, even to welcome, those ideas and those people who are not clones of ourselves, or we reject the entire premise of "created equal." Either we accept the responsibility of freedom, or we forfeit those liberties we assume to be ours by birthright, whether we have earned them or not.[35]

In the same "Civil Rights Message" quoted previously, Kennedy similarly relied on parallelism to help carry his message:

We face, therefore, a moral crisis as a country and as a people. It cannot be met by repressive police action. It cannot be left to increased demonstrations in the streets. It cannot be quieted by token moves or talk.[36]

In the same vein, in his speech accepting the Democratic nomination for president Bill Clinton used parallelism as he told his listeners:

So if you're sick and tired of a government that doesn't work to create jobs, if you're sick and tired of a tax system that's stacked against you, if you're sick and tired of exploding debt and reduced investments in our future, if like the late Civil Rights pioneer Fannie Lou Hamer said you're just plain sick and tired of being sick and tired, then join with us, work with us, win with us.[37]

In his "I Have a Dream" speech King buttressed the forcefulness of his message by adding parallelism and figures of speech to it:

One hundred years later, we must face the tragic fact that the Negro is still not free. One hundred years later, the life of the Negro is still sadly crippled by the manacles of segregation and the chains of discrimination. One hundred years later, the Negro lives in a lonely island of poverty in the midst of a vast ocean of material prosperity. One hundred years later, the Negro is still languished in the corners of American society and finds himself an exile in his own land.[38]

Later in the same speech King uttered words that are now among the most widely cited examples of parallelism:

I say to you today, my friends, that in spite of the difficulties and frustrations of the moment I still have a dream. It is a dream deeply rooted in the American dream.

I have a dream that one day this nation will rise up and live out the true meaning of its creed: "We hold these truths to be self-evident; that all men are created equal."

I have a dream that one day on the red hills of Georgia the sons of former slaves and the sons of former slaveowners will be able to sit down together at the table of brotherhood.

I have a dream that one day even the state of Mississippi, a desert state sweltering with the heat of injustice and oppression, will be transformed into an oasis of freedom and justice.

I have a dream that my four little children will one day live in a nation where they will not be judged by the color of their skin but by the content of their character.

I have a dream today.

I have a dream that one day the state of Alabama, whose governor's lips are presently dripping with the words of interposition and nullification, will be transformed into a situation where little black boys and black girls will be able to join hands with little white boys and white girls and walk together as sisters and brothers.

I have a dream today.

I have a dream that one day every valley shall be exalted, every hill and mountain shall be made low, the rough places will be made plain, and the crooked places will be made straight, and the glory of the Lord shall be revealed, and all flesh shall see it together.[39]

Alliteration involves the repetition of initial consonant sounds in words adjoining or close to each other. When Jesse Jackson referred to his constituents as "the damned, disinherited, disrespected and the depressed,"[40] he used alliteration to add rhythm to his thought, and thereby succeeded in increasing the sentence's memorability and impact. In a keynote speech delivered to delegates of the Democratic national convention, Senator Bill Bradley said: "For too long, American leadership has waffled and wiggled and wavered." Bradley returned to the theme a number of times, often combining it with a rhetorical question like the following:

Tonight in America, wages are flat, unemployment is up, the deficit grows, and health care and college costs skyrocket. What did you do about it, George Bush? You waffled and wiggled and wavered.[41]

Speaking about the future of newspapers, the editorial vice president of the *Philadelphia Inquirer,* Maxwell E. P. King, used alliteration when he said: "Another phenomenon of the mid to late 80s: some papers became gimmicky, glitzy, simpler and shorter. In some cases simplicity turned to simplemindedness."[42] Highlighting the sounds of words in this manner helps capture and sustain listeners' attention.

Antithesis, another means of adding vividness to a speech, achieves its objective by presenting opposites within the same or adjoining sentences. By juxtaposing contrasting ideas, the speaker can sharpen the message and clarify a rhetorical point. Bill Clinton used antithesis when he noted in his second inaugural address:

The promise we sought in a new land we will find again in a land of new promise.[43]

Some years earlier, Clinton had also used antithesis in a foreign policy address:

. . . we must look forward, not backward. I seek not to be the last president of the 20th century, but the first president of the 21st century.[44]

Similarly, Urban League spokesperson Whitney M. Young, Jr., relied on antithesis to carry his message to his audience:

We seek not to weaken America but to strengthen it; not to decry America, but to purify it; not to separate America but to become part of it.[45]

And one of the most widely quoted examples of antithesis in action comes from Kennedy's inaugural address:

And so, my fellow Americans: ask not what your country can do for you—ask what you can do for your country.[46]

Antithesis clearly increases the dramatic impact of a speaker's message.

Hyperbole is the use of extreme exaggeration for effect. One speaker, for example, in discussing the problems of the obese, used hyperbole when he noted that one subject who suffered from obesity felt so hungry that he believed that he could eat a whale. Another speaker used exaggeration to indicate the impact of corporate downsizing: "If we don't stop it," she noted, "everyone will be unemployed." While use of hyperbole can make it easier for a speaker to make his or her point, some criticize its use, believing that such exaggeration can cause receivers to perceive a speaker as inaccurate or even a liar.

When not overused, each of these speechmaking devices can make your message more striking, your ideas more intense, and your presentation more vivid. So remember, choose your words carefully and arrange your phrases and sentences creatively, and you will bring your speech to life.

ORAL VERSUS WRITTEN STYLE

WHEN YOU CREATE A SPEECH you write it to be heard, not read. Therefore, you should use an oral rather than a written style. Written and oral styles differ from each other in a number of important ways—much like formal wear differs from casual wear.

First, an oral style is more *personal* than a written style. When delivering a speech you are able to talk directly to your audience, invite participation, and adapt to reactions in ways a writer and a reader cannot. Second, an oral style is more *repetitive* than a written style. Because listeners cannot rehear or readily replay what you have said as they are able to reread a page of print, idea repetition and reinforcement become staples of the effective speaker. By repeating and restating important ideas, the speaker lets listeners know what is important and what needs to be remembered. Third, an oral style is usually much *less formal* than a written style. While written discourse often contains abstract ideas, complex phraseology, and a sophisticated vocabulary, simpler sentences and shorter words and phrases characterize the oral style.

The language of public speaking is less like the language of an essayist and more like the language of a skilled conversationalist. Listeners are able to better retain and more easily recall a speech if it is filled with everyday colloquial expressions, clear transitions, personal pronouns, and questions that invite participation than if it is invested with abstract language, complex sentences, and impersonal references. If there is a speech inside you and you want to make your points so audience members remember them, make your listeners feel more comfortable by using an oral style. A speech is not mailed to an audience; it is delivered aloud.

SUMMARY

THE LANGUAGE A SPEAKER USES to express ideas influences the way the audience responds to both the speech and the speaker. Both the message a speaker communicates to an audience and the meaning audience members extract from that message are a result of the words used by the speaker. Language can bridge or create barriers between a speaker and an audience.

Speakers need to work to be word masters. They need to understand what language is, how it functions, and what they must do to use language effectively.

Language is a symbol system composed of words. For language to function effectively, there must be basic agreement between speaker and receivers regarding what the words being used mean. Because receivers are not dictionaries, speakers must pay careful attention to the possible connotative meanings the words they are using could evoke.

When language is handled well, the speaker is better able to control audience reactions to the speech. When language is used well it unites speaker and receivers rather than creating a gulf between them; it embellishes a speech with fresh mental images that trigger new ways of seeing and sensing among receivers. Language used well evokes desired attitudes and behaviors in receivers.

In order to use language to help you attain your speechmaking goals, keep your choice of words simple, concrete, appropriate, and vivid and recognize the key differences between oral and written discourse.

THE SPEAKER'S STAND

Choose a controversial subject. Develop two two-minute speeches that espouse very different positions—the first containing words and figures of speech that are likely to bias listeners in favor of the subject, the second containing words and figures of speech that are likely to bias them against it.

Deliver both speeches to class. Ask class members which version they found more effective and why.

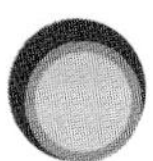

STUDENT FOCUS GROUP REPORT

Now that you have had the opportunity to consider the role played by a speaker's words in the success or failure of a speech, in groups of five to seven students, respond to the following questions:

1. What can a speaker do to ensure that the language of his or her speech functions as a facilitator of communication?
2. What obstacles to understanding must a speaker overcome if a speech is to be understood as intended?
3. In what ways can a speaker use language to steer a speech to a successful conclusion?
4. Of what value is an understanding of the "Triangle of Meaning" to public speakers?
5. For what reasons should speakers strive to keep their language simple, concrete, appropriate, vivid, and reflective of an oral style?
6. Summarize the most significant information you have learned about language.
7. Revisit the case study at this chapter's beginning. Based on what you now understand about language and its impact, in what ways, if any, would you revise your answers?

Select a group member to report your conclusions to the class.

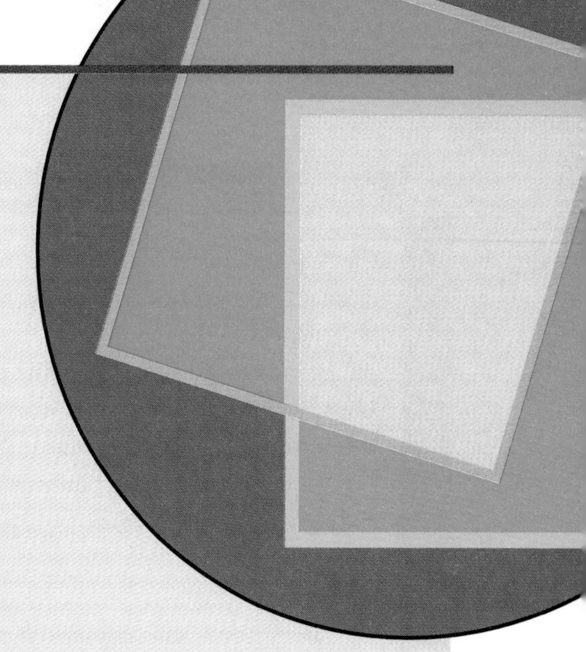

Chapter Thirteen

The Speaker's Delivery

Style, Voice, and Body Language

After reading this chapter, you should be able to:

- Describe how a speaker's voice, body, and delivery style can enhance or detract from his or her message.
- Explain the components of good delivery.
- Distinguish between the following methods of delivery: memorization, manuscript, extemporaneous, impromptu, and sound bite.
- Identify and illustrate how the following cues can help speakers communicate with receivers: pitch, volume, rate, articulation, and pronunciation.
- Identify and illustrate how the following kinetic cues can help speakers communicate with receivers: gestures, body movements, facial expressions, eye contact, and posture.
- Explain how culture affects the use and interpretation of nonverbal cues.
- Identify and illustrate how appearance affects the reception given a speaker.
- Describe how to rehearse a speech.

CASE STUDY

Must You Believe Your Own Words?

Casey was a United States citizen whose job required that she register as a lobbyist for a foreign government. As part of her responsibilities, Casey did what was necessary to ensure that the interests of her client were served. Often, this required that she speak before various legislative committees or public interest groups in an effort to persuade them to support positions of importance to her client. Usually, this task posed little if any problem for Casey. She was a fine speaker who found herself at ease addressing small, informal groups as well as large, formal ones. This time was different, though.

Casey's client had just informed her that she needed to deliver a speech defending a practice that she personally opposed: the genital mutilation of women. Casey told herself that she was just the messenger hired to deliver a message. After all, if she didn't deliver it, for a hefty price, someone else would.

Casey wrote and rehearsed the speech, attempting to make her words sound convincing. As the time for the presentation grew closer, she again agonized over the fact that her message could have an impact on the lives of tens of thousands of people. While giving an effective speech would surely allow her to continue in her very lucrative position, she wondered if her audience would be able to detect her lack of sincerity and commitment to the position she was now advocating.

- If you were Casey, would you have written such a speech? If not, why not? If so, would you have delivered such a speech? Why or why not?
- Have you ever doubted a speaker's commitment to his or her topic? What verbal and nonverbal behaviors did he or she display that contributed to your doubt?

THE MESSAGE of public communication is more than just the words used; the public communicator, too, is the message. This means that when you communicate with an audience, it is not merely the words you use that comprise the message you send. Before, during, and after you speak, you also send your audience signals that reveal to them your state of mind, your feelings, and your attitudes. Your posture, facial expression, eye contact, gestures, vocal inflection, volume, and rate of speaking are just a few of a kaleidoscope of nonverbal cues that add to or detract from the impact of your words.[1] Audience members are affected not only by what you say, but by what you do, and by how you sound.[2]

Your delivery affects your credibility as a speaker. Poor delivery can kill good ideas. For that reason, having something to say is only half the battle. You also need to master how to present those ideas to others.

In this chapter we will focus on the speaker's delivery—what audience members see and hear when a speaker communicates. Our focus is switching from what you say to how you say it, for your words alone will rarely, if ever, make others want to listen to you. Take away effective delivery, and your ideas lose much of their power; their communicative potential remains unfulfilled. By taking the time to explore how a speaker can use noverbal cues (paralinguistics—voice, kinetics—body language, and proxemics—space and distance) to enhance the understanding and acceptance of ideas by audience members, you take another step toward expanding your ability to process and deliver spoken messages effectively.

The body talks during the delivery of a speech, revealing to receivers what speakers think about themselves and their topics.

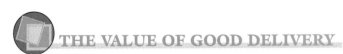

THE VALUE OF GOOD DELIVERY

GOOD DELIVERY TELLS YOUR AUDIENCE that you really care about both your topic and your listeners. Good delivery supports the content of your message. It helps your audience interpret your message appropriately, and it helps close whatever gap may exist between you and your listeners. Because good delivery feels natural to you, and because it is conversational in tone, it also sounds as if you are talking with rather than at your audience members. In other words, good delivery sounds spontaneous, as though you were speaking the words in your presentation for the very first time.

Audiences Respond to Nonverbal Cues

When listening to an effective presentation, the audience senses the speaker's energy, feels the forcefulness in the speaker's ideas, and responds to the speaker's enthusiasm and sense of communication. Neither the body language nor the voice of the accomplished speaker calls attention to itself. When audience members are not distracted by what you do or how you sound, they are better able to free themselves to concentrate on what you have to say—that is, the content of your speech.

Researchers have discovered that more than 65 percent of a message's social-emotional meaning is communicated via its nonverbal delivery. Thus, less than 35 percent of a message's social-emotional meaning is communicated by words.[3]

Audiences Believe Nonverbal Cues

Audiences tend to believe nonverbal communication. Deliver your speech honestly and effectively, and your audience members are likely to believe you. In the minds of your audience members, effective delivery and effective public speaking are partners. A speaker who is judged to be enthusiastic, who looks at his or her listeners directly, who sounds conversational and appears to be communicating with spontaneity helps to precipitate an increase in audience member interest, attention, and confidence in the speaker. In contrast, a decrease in any of these charactertisics virtually guarantees

Read My Eyes, Not My Lips

Two-time Peabody Award winner, writer, speaker, and broadcast anchor Charles Osgood offers advice to speakers in his essay "Read My Eyes, Not My Lips." Have you ever listened to a speaker whose words and facial expressions contradicted each other? Which message channel did you believe?

This is the age of "your lips tell me *yes, yes,* but there's *no, no* in your eyes."

Just think about it. You used to be able to tell what people were thinking by listening to what they say. Nowadays, for one reason or another, many people will tell you one thing when they are thinking exactly the opposite.

You ask the boss for a raise or a promotion, for example, giving him the full sales pitch about how long it's been and how much you've been contributing these days.

And what he tells you is that the home office has put a freeze on raises and promotions just now, but that as soon as the right opportunity presents itself, he'll do everything he can to see that you get what you've got coming.

While he is saying this, however, his face and tone of voice are saying:

"You know what I hate about this job? It's having to listen to whiners like you. Why don't you just go back and do your job and stop complaining. Go away and leave me alone!"

We are trained not to say unpleasant things to each other, so the words may come out sounding polite and civilized enough. But watch the face.

"I'd love to go out with you tonight, George," says Cybil, "but I have to wash my hair."

Meanwhile her face and tone of voice are saying: "Get out of my life, creep. I wouldn't go out with you if you were the last man on earth."

Three classic lines are:

"You're looking great!"

"It was swell running into you!"

"Let's have lunch!"

Meanwhile, the face and eyes are saying:

"God, she looks like death warmed over."

"Just my luck to run into this turkey when I'm running late."

"Let me out of here!"

It's almost as if one believed that someday a higher court would be reading a transcript of the conversation, in which all the words would be taken at face value, and the facial expressions and tone of voice completely removed.

"See, Your Honor? I did *not* tell the plaintiff to 'go stuff it.' All I told him to do was to 'have a nice day.' "

It's not what you say, but the way that you say it.

If you are such an accomplished dissembler that you can think one thing and say another with your words and voice and facial expressions all at the same time, then I would say there is only one vocation for you—and I am not referring to the used-car or aluminum-siding business.

A person with your gifts and inclinations is ideally suited for the U.S. Congress.[4]

a decrease in audience member interest, attention, and confidence. That means that you will do well to concentrate on steps you can take to maintain an enthusiastic demeanor, eye contact with your listeners, and a sense of spontaneity, as well as on what you can do to avoid distracting your listeners with nonverbal mannerisms that impede effective communication. Your voice and your body language should be appropriate to your material and the size of your audience. They should help you share your content, not interfere with that sharing.

You will be listened to more carefully if you look and sound enthusiastic, display good eye contact with your listeners, and appear spontaneous. If you are listened to more carefully, the audience will remember more of what you say. And isn't that a big part of your reason for speaking?

DELIVERY STYLES: A POTPOURRI OF METHODS

AN EFFECTIVE SPEAKER IS ABLE to identify the most appropriate delivery style or method to use when presenting a speech. The speaker's choice is based on an analysis of several factors including the nature of the speaking occasion, the purpose of the presentation, and the speaker's own strengths and abilities. Thus, when asked to deliver a speech, ask yourself these questions. Would you do best to:

deliver your speech from memory?
read it from a manuscript?
speak extemporaneously?
make a few impromptu remarks?
present a sound bite for media consumption?

Answering these questions will help you decide whether your presentation style should be:

memorized,
a manuscript delivery,
impromptu,
extemporaneous, or
a succinct sound bite.

Whichever method you select should not call attention to itself. Listeners must be free to concentrate on your ideas, not on your style of delivery. Each of these styles is appropriate for different topics, audiences, and situations. How, then, do you decide which delivery method to use? Although extemporaneous speaking is the method preferred by most speech teachers and is usually emphasized in speech courses primarily because it unites careful planning with a seemingly spontaneous delivery style, it is still useful to understand all five styles and the situations that could provide you with a good rationale for selecting to use any one of them.

Speaking from Memorization

When you write your speech out in full, commit it to memory, and then recite it for an audience without using a manuscript, an outline, or speaker's notes, you are

speaking from memorization. Speaking from memorization requires considerable skill and speaking expertise. For one thing, the pressures brought about by the actual presentation could cause you to draw a blank at any point during your speech. When that happens, instead of listening to you speak, your audience is left with a stunning silence, and you're left to grope for the words you lost. When you speak from memory, you attempt to deliver your speech word for word, and that makes it even more difficult for you to recover if you make a mistake.

Far too frequently, speakers who speak from memory expend too much of their time and energy remembering, and too little of their time and energy concentrating on establishing a communicative relationship with their audience. Imagine how uncomfortable it must feel to be giving a speech and not have a clue as to what to say next, and then to have to search awkwardly for words to use while standing in front of a room or auditorium filled with people. That's the risk you face if you become unduly nervous when speaking from memorization.

The tension you feel when delivering a memorized speech could affect your delivery in other ways as well. When speaking from memory your delivery could come off as stiff, stilted, and unnatural rather than flexible, friendly, and relaxed. Your ability to respond easily to audience feedback might also be inhibited. Because you are afraid to deviate from your memorized text for fear you would forget an entire segment of your presentation, you are less able to clarify, amplify, or adapt to the immediate reactions of your listeners.

This is not to suggest that memorizing a speech does not offer certain advantages, because it does. It is much easier to establish and sustain eye contact with your listeners when you don't have to continually look down at a manuscript or notes. Your hands, not constrained by holding papers or your place, are thus freer to gesture and support the meaning of your message.

While there certainly are a number of speaking occasions that lend themselves to speaking from memorization, including toasts and testimonials, acceptance speeches, speeches of introduction, and eulogies, the bulk of your speechmaking experiences will be a composite of the remaining delivery methods.

Manuscript Reading

Like speaking from memorization, **manuscript reading** requires that a manuscript be written out in full and delivered word for word. The speaker, however, need not commit the text to memory. On the other hand, because reading aloud well requires every bit as much skill as mastering a script and delivering it expressively, manuscript reading is not as easy as it sounds. In fact, if you do not invest a lot of time practicing reading your manuscript aloud, you could end up *eye-tied* to your manuscript, and thus deprive your audience of meaningful eye contact. That means that instead of eyeing your audience, establishing a mental bond with them, and adapting to their feedback, you are stuck to your script.

How do you like listening to a speech that is read to you when the speaker does not read it well? It's not very satisfying for the audience. Lack of familiarity with your manuscript and lack of ability to transmit it with fluency and ease contribute to a lack of audience awareness and interest. To be sure, it is a challenge to bring the printed page to life for listeners. Doing so requires that you take your eyes off the manuscript and use them instead to close the communicative gap that exists between you and your listeners. If you read in a monotone, if your delivery sounds mechanical you will bore your listeners. Thus, the reading of your speech needs to sound like conversation to your listeners; it needs to sound as though it was meant to be spoken rather than read, or it will not have the impact you desire.

Certain occasions necessitate the delivery of a manuscript speech. Among these are presidential, foreign policy, and political addresses; official proclamations; and presentations at business, trade, and stockholder meetings. Any time a speaker needs to be especially careful about the phrasing of a problem or policy, or when time is limited, a manuscript speech is probably in order. The key to effective delivery of a manuscript speech, however, is to sound and appear as if you are not reading. It is one thing to rely on a manuscript to help you avoid making a misstatement, committing a slip of the tongue, or otherwise distorting the wording of your message. It is another thing to be able to focus not only on your manuscript, but also on your audience. For a manuscript speech to achieve maximum impact, the speaker must be able to do just that.

Impromptu Speaking

How did you feel the last time you were put on the spot and asked to say a few words? Perhaps someone asked you to describe yourself in an interview, answer a question in class, or explain your position during a meeting. Were you ready to respond without extensive time to plan, prepare, or practice? Were you able to maintain direct eye contact with your listeners while you clearly announced the question you were answering, stated the points you wished to make, supported your points with appropriate examples, and summarized or restated your primary response for your listeners? Whether you realize it, you are likely to give at least one, if not many, impromptu speeches daily, and many of the presentations you will deliver during your business life will probably be impromptu.[5]

Unlike memorization and manuscript reading, both of which allow for and even demand extensive preparation time, in **impromptu speaking** a speech is delivered "off the cuff" and with little, if any, prior notice to or preparation by the speaker. Meaning "in readiness" and literally delivered by you on the spur of the moment, impromptu

Many of the presentations we deliver on the job will be impromptu ones. Have you ever been called on to deliver an impromptu speech at work? What messages did your body broadcast about you to receivers?

speaking requires that you be able to think on your feet. All you really have to rely on when delivering an impromptu talk is your knowledge and previous experience.

If you are adept at gathering your thoughts quickly and summarizing them succinctly, then whenever the opportunity presents itself to you, you will be prepared to deliver an impromptu speech. It is important to realize that all the lessons learned delivering planned speeches can be applied to the impromptu situation and vice versa. The principles of effective structure, support, and delivery cut across these methodologies. While unplanned speaking may seem unnatural or awkward to you, it offers you both flexibility and the opportunity to demonstrate your speaking versatility. Perhaps more than any other speechmaking style, delivering an impromptu speech helps you reveal to others what you are like and what genuinely concerns you.

Speaking Extemporaneously

- Preparation—not memorization.
- Conversation—not verbatim.

These words describe the characteristics of the extemporaneous speech. Let's consider them.

When a speech is prepared and practiced in advance but is neither written out word for word nor memorized, it is most likely an example of **speaking extemporaneously.** The extemporaneous speaker delivers his or her speech using only an outline or speaker's notes to refer to in order to jog his or her memory. Partly because the exact words to be spoken are selected by the speaker virtually at the moment of their delivery, the language he or she uses seems more natural and spontaneous. The lack of memorization also helps precipitate a more conversational quality and generous eye contact, and allows the speaker to monitor audience reactions and adjust to the feedback received. This ready-response ability of the extemporaneous speaker gives the audience the impression that the speech is being created right before their eyes and ears. Freed from the need to follow a written manuscript word for word, the speaker is better able to establish a more direct connection with audience members.

The emphasis in extemporaneous speaking is on communication, not recitation or memorization. It requires that the speaker be flexible enough to adapt to the audience and demands extensive planning, organization, and practice; however, it is one thing to be knowledgable about a topic and quite another to have your mind ordered and prepared to present that knowledge to others. Because it sounds spontaneous and because it builds speaker confidence, extemporaneous speaking is the method prefered by most public speaking teachers and experienced speakers alike.

Sound Bite Speaking

According to political media advisor and communications consultant Roger Ailes, today's speakers inhabit a "headline society."[6] As Ailes sees it, "In today's society, long-winded people will soon be as extinct as the dinosaur."[7]

Because media audiences (like audiences in general) are impatient for information, speakers need to be able to distill their messages effectively. Notice how speakers can lose or hold attention by the way they package a thought:[8]

SPEAKING of ETHICS

Is It Style over Matter?

Mark Twain once noted, "It usally takes more than three weeks to prepare a good impromptu speech."

Is it ever ethical for a speaker to pass off memorized or even extemporaneous remarks as impromptu? Should audiences know that they are the recipients of a "stump" speech or canned presentation? How might the audience's perceptions of the amount of time and effort a speaker devoted to formulating a speech (however brief) influence their response to the speaker and his or her message?

Who has more talent or skill: a speaker who can utter remarks on the spur of the moment and make them sound planned, prepared, and practiced, or a speaker who carefully plans, prepares, and practices his or her remarks but can make them sound unrehearsed and spontaneous? Should the "reality" of the speaking style be of concern to an audience?

Dull	*Interesting*
The two leading ways to achieve success are improving upon existing technology and larger obligation.	The two leading recipes for success are building a better mousetrap and finding a bigger loophole. —Edgar A. Schoaff
To construct an amalgam, you have to be willing to split open its component parts.	To make an omelet, you have to be willing to break a few eggs. —Robert Penn Warren
Capital will not produce great pleasure, but it will remunerate a large research staff to examine the questions proposed for a solution.	Money won't buy happiness, but it will pay the salaries of a large research staff to study the problem. —Bill Vaughan

Having something to say is only part of the speaking equation. The other part is being able to get it across to an audience in a way that is fresh, attention grabbing, and memorable. It is essential in today's mediated, sound bite society that you be able to adjust and focus your statements to fit the limited time available to you; then, when time permits, you can amplify those statements with examples, statistics, quotations, and so forth. Thus, when delivering a sound bite, your goal is to be able to capture the essence of your subject succinctly, conversationally, and memorably.

THE SPEAKER'S VOICE: THE SOUND OF SPEECH

HOW EFFECTIVE ARE YOU AT voicing your thoughts? Does your voice turn you into a winner, or does it turn you into a victim, making it difficult for you to re-

Speaking of skillbuilding: Distill That Thought

1. Choose a subject that interests you. Then select a partner and without preparation, and constrained by a 60-second time limit, share your knowledge of that subject with your partner in the most effective way you can.
2. Choose another subject and this time plan what you are going to say—take a couple of minutes and distill your thoughts, packaging them so they fit neatly into the 60-second time limit. Choose another partner and make your presentation to him or her.
3. Ask each of your partners to evaluate what they grasped from your presentation and why.

late your ideas and feelings to others? Does your voice control you or do you control your voice, thereby also better controlling the meaning you transmit to an audience?

Nonverbal communication researcher Albert Mehrabian tells us that 38 percent of the meaning of a message delivered by a speaker is carried by the voice.[9] For this reason, how you say your speech can in large part determine how it will come across to your receivers. Your vocal cues play an important role in the formulation of your audience's response to your speech and their reaction to you.[10] Your credibility as a speaker and your ability to communicate with and influence others is affected by the adequacy of your voice.

With this in mind, answer these questions honestly:

Does my voice help me convey the meaning of my speech clearly, or does it add to listener confusion and doubt?

If I were in my audience, would I want to listen to me for an extended period of time?

Does my voice enhance or detract from the impression I make?

A number of **paralinguistic** (vocal) **cues** play a part in creating the impression you make on an audience: among these are pitch, volume, rate, and articulation and pronunciation.

Pitch: High versus Low

Pitch is the highness or lowness of your voice on a tonal scale; it is your voice's upward or downward inflection. We vary pitch when speaking to avoid talking in a monotone and to add expressiveness to the message. A speaker who talks on "one note" frequently is characterized as monotonous by an audience and contributes to the assessment of him or her as lacking in commitment, bored, and therefore boring. In contrast, a speaker who varies his or her pitch contributes to the audience's assessment of him or her as lively, animated, and interested. How would you rather be perceived?

Our **habitual pitch,** which is the level at which we speak most often, may or may not be our optimum pitch, which is that level at which our voice functions best and the level that allows us extensive vocal variation up and down the scale. In order to speak with variety, you need to vary your pitch. If your voice is consistently pitched much too high—yielding fragile, unsupported tones—or much too low—yielding overly deep, extended tones—it will distract listeners and prevent them from paying as much attention to your ideas as they might otherwise.

Audiences do tend to stereotype speakers on the basis of their voices. Lower-pitched voices are stereotyped as more mature, sexier, and stronger than are higher-pitched voices, which are frequently associated with helplessness, nervousness, and tension.

It is your pitch that reveals to your audience whether you are making a statement or asking a question, expressing concern or conviction. It is your pitch that conveys your emotion and can make you sound angry or annoyed when you think you are expressing patience and tolerance instead. Many Arabic speakers tend to exhibit a higher pitch, which conveys a more emotional tone than is characteristically conveyed by English speakers. Speakers who are able to vary their pitch to reflect the mood they are expressing are more effective at giving interpretation to their ideas and more persuasive than those who exhibit an hypnotically repetitive pitch pattern.[11]

In contrast to English, many Asian languages are tonal. Depending on the tone used, the same words when said with a different tone or pitch will convey vastly different meanings. For example, depending on the tone a speaker used, the meaning of the word *Ma* could change from "mother" to "horse."

Volume: Loud versus Soft

Volume, the loudness or softness of the voice, is the second vocal characteristic affecting a speaker's meaning. If your audience is unable to hear you, you cannot expect them to understand you. On the other hand, if your voice is too loud, it could alienate audience members, causing them to turn you off in an effort to turn you down. Your goal is to speak with enough force that you will be heard by everyone in attendance. This means that you do not want to speak so softly that you underwhelm your receivers or so loudly that you overwhelm them. Good breath control will let you vary your volume as needed.

Speakers should regulate volume to reflect the size and acoustics of the room, the size of the audience, and any competing background noises. In addition, increasing your volume at particular points can help you stress and emphasize specific words and ideas and add emotional intensity to your delivery and energy to the room. In contrast, decreasing your volume can also help you gain and/or sustain audience attention, convey a contrasting emotion, or add suspense.

In general, Latinos and Arabs tend to speak more loudly than Americans.[12] For Arabs, loudness connotes strength and sincerity, whereas speaking too softly implies that one lacks confidence or is timid.[13] In contrast, many Asians speak so softly that sometimes they sound to Americans as if they are whispering. For Asians, a gentle, soothing voice is reflective of good manners.[14]

If you speak too loudly you run the risk of being stereotyped as overbearing and aggressive. If you speak too softly, however, you could be stereotyped as timid and scared. To be perceived as an effective speaker, you must vary your volume to control your meaning. The volume at which you speak should enhance, not distort, the sound of your speech.

Rate: Fast versus Slow

Rate is the speed at which you speak. Most of us speak between 125 and 175 words per minute, with 150 words per minute average. A speaker who speaks too quickly communicates a desire to get his or her speaking over in record time; audience members find it difficult to keep up with him or her and become increasingly upset at not having the time to process the speaker's message adequately. A speaker who speaks too slowly communicates tentativeness and lack of confidence; frequently, the overly deliberate pace makes the audience unresponsive, uninterested, and bored. So if you do not want to be known as the hare or the turtle of the speaking circuit, don't abuse rate, but do use it to add variety to your delivery.

Since speaking rate can be used to change a speech's mood, speakers should slow down when relaying serious and complex material and pick up the pace when heading toward a climax or when sharing lighter contents. For example, Martin Luther King began his "I Have a Dream" speech uttering words at approximately 92 words per minute; he finished it at a rate of approximately 145 words per minute. King's rate of speech quickened as he headed toward his speech's emotional climax. Thus, adept speakers know how to use rate to convey an emotional intensity that is reflective of the speech's content. The trick is to use a rate appropriate to the ideas you are expressing. Think of rate as the pulse of your speech; it should quicken to convey agitation, excitement, and happiness and fall to convey seriousness of purpose, serenity, or sadness. Your rate of speaking should suit your speech.

A device used to slow the rate of speech is the *pause*. Knowing when to pause is a skill you need to master if you are to communicate effectively in public. For example, you can pause to emphasize meaning, to underscore the importance of an idea, to lend dramatic impact to a statement, to give your listeners time to digest or reflect on what you have said, and to signal the end of a thought. It is your pauses that help control your message's rate and rhythm. In fact, according to *60 Minutes* producer Don Hewett "the pauses tell the story. They are as important to us as commas and periods are to the *New York Times*."[15] Thus, one thing you do not want to do is fill a meaningful pause with meaningless sounds and phrases such as "er," "uh," "um," "okay," or "you know." Such vocalized pauses or fillers are nonfluencies and only succeed in disrupting the natural flow of your presentation. Nonfluencies transform the functional pause into a dysfunctional and annoying interruption, which in the process diminishes your credibility.

In general, Arabs, Hispanics, and Italians tend to speak at a faster rate than do native speakers of English.

Articulation and Pronunciation

Do you have lazy or loose lips that make it difficult for you to articulate and pronounce the words you use? If you answer "yes," it's not your lips that are lazy or loose; it's you.

Articulation is the way you pronounce individual sounds. Ideally you speak the sounds of speech sharply and distinctly. When you fail to utter a final sound (a final *t* or *d*, for example); fail to produce the sounds of words properly; or voice a sound in an unclear, imprecise, or incorrect way (*come wimme, dem, idear*), then you are guilty of faulty articulation. As a speaker, your responsibility is to say your words so your audience can understand them. If your listeners can't understand you, they can't respond appropriately, and they may simply conclude you either don't know what you are talking about or are an inept speaker.

While the focus of articulation is on the production of speech sounds, the focus of **pronunciation** is on whether the words themselves are said correctly. When you mispronounce a word you are apt to suffer a loss in credibility. Speakers sometimes mispronounce words by adding unnecessary sounds, omitting necessary sounds, reversing sounds, or misplacing an accent. Thus, they mistakenly say:

chick for chic (sheek),
nucular for nuclear,
prespiration for perspiration,
Febuary for February,
PO · lice for po · LICE,
athalete for athlete, or
libary for library.

Your goal as a speaker is to pronounce words clearly so that audience comprehension is maximized, not diminished. If your pronunciation of a word confuses your listeners, understanding suffers. If there is any question in your mind whether you are pronouncing a word correctly, look up its correct pronunciation in a dictionary. If you are too lazy to look it up, you not only have lazy lips and loose lips, you have lazy fingers, and that's one sign of a weak speaker. Don't wait for a listener to point out a pronunciation error to you—check yourself first. That's smarter speaking.

Dialects and Regionalisms

The standards of speech differ as you travel from region to region and from cultural group to cultural group. People who live in different parts of the country or who belong to different cultural or ethnic groups often speak different dialects. A **dialect** is a speech pattern characteristic of a particular area or group. While there is no one area or group whose dialect is absolutely right or wrong, people do have preferences and hold preconceptions regarding the appropriate use of language. In fact, some go so far as to stereotype others on the basis of their dialects. Thus, people in the Northeast may be perceived by people in the South as brusque and abrasive whereas Southerners may be perceived by Northeasterners as slow and surface-sweet. Midwestern speech patterns, in contrast, are frequently held up as a standard to emulate, and characterize the dialects exhibited by many television news anchors. Most people have grown accustomed to Midwestern speech, and prefer to listen either to it or to someone who sounds just like they themselves do. Thus, the aesthetic preferences for a dialect held by audience members could influence the reception given you as a speaker.

The only time you really have to worry about your dialect is if it interferes with effective communication. Keep in mind the following quotation from John Steinbeck's *The Grapes of Wrath:*

> "Everybody says words different," said Ivy. "Arkansas folks say 'em different, and Oklahoma folks says 'em different. And we seen a lady from Massachusetts, an she said 'em differentest of all. Couldn't hardly make out what she was sayin.' "

The question you need to ask yourself when preparing to address an audience is: Will the dialect I use get in the way and block the development of a sound relationship and understanding with the members of my audience? If the answer is no, then there is probably no reason for concern. However, if the answer is yes, then you will want to take some action to overcome the prejudices listeners hold about your dialect.

THE SPEAKER'S BODY LANGUAGE: RIGHT BEFORE YOUR EYES

A PUBLIC SPEAKER DOESN'T STOP sending messages simply because he or she stops speaking. Even when the speaker's mouth is silent, his or her appearance, facial expression, eyes, posture, and movements continue talking to the audience, suggesting to them what the speaker is thinking and feeling. The speaker's body talks before, during, and after a speech, and its message can either supplement or contradict the meaning inherent in the words the speaker uses.

The study of **kinetics,** or body language, includes a consideration of gestures, body movements, facial expressions, eye behavior, and posture. Consequently, the way a speaker uses his or her hands, the surprised look in the speaker's eyes, the speaker's draping him- or herself over the podium, the sarcastic smirk on the speaker's face, and the way the speaker walks to and away from the speaker's stand are all part of the speaker's use of kinetics. The point is that in addition to what you say, what you do and how you look when you do it tell a great deal about you and are important. In fact, your body language affects your audience's judgments of your credibility.[16] Based on body language, audiences form opinions regarding your believability, competence, and likeability. For this reason, an adept public communicator knows how to use body language effectively—so it adds to rather than weakens impact.

If your body language is listless, you may leave your audience listless as well. If your body language is active and meaningful, you will help encourage an active and meaningful audience response. Your goal is to be an effective visual aid, to project an image of vitality, so that you command attention. The speaker who conveys a postive speaker's image to an audience is the speaker who earns a more positive response from that audience. While appearance is not a substitute for performance, your visible nonverbal behavior does make an impression on audience members and can cement or weaken the speaker–audience relationship. Let us explore a number of behaviors you can exhibit to enhance your use of body language.

The Role of Body Action: Dos and Don'ts of Movement

Your physical behavior carries meaning. The meaning your receivers give it affects their reception of your speech.[17]

Approaching the Audience. A Chinese proverb can serve to remind us of how body language can reveal a speaker's personality to an audience: "Let me see you walk and I'll tell you what you're like." Even as you approach the speaker's stand, you are sending nonverbal messages to your audience. You have not yet spoken a word, yet by your rate of moving, the amount of forcefulness in your step, the way you carry yourself and move your arms, the directness or indirectness of your gaze, and the way you stand before them, listeners form opinions of you. For your body language to be effective, what you do from the outset needs to reinforce what you say during your presentation.

During Your Presentation. Throughout the delivery of your speech, your body and your words should say the same thing. If they don't—if what you do is inconsistent with what you say—your listeners will tend to believe your body language rather than your words. And they are right to do so, because that's probably where the truth lies. Thus, among your goals are the following: to use nonverbal cues to make it easier, not harder, for your listeners to believe you are sincere and to make it easier, not harder, for them to listen to you.

In addition, the body movements you exhibit should be purposeful. **Purposeless movements** distract from what you say. Continually pacing like a caged lion, moving randomly or perpetually like a wind-up toy, or standing rigid and expressionless like a statue are attention distractors; by calling undue attention to a speaker's movement, they act to subvert the speaker's message. **Purposeful movements,** on the other hand, allow your audience to focus on what you are saying, rather than what you are doing. Thus, the movements you use must make sense—otherwise it is better for you to stay still.

Let us look more closely at how to use effective gestures, eye contact, and appearance to gain an advantage.

Gestures Speak, Too. If you consider the interpersonal contacts you have, both you and the person with whom you are interacting use gestures to clarify, support, and emphasize the points you are making or the ideas you are expressing. The same is true of public speakers. They, too, use voluntary and visible bodily actions—**gestures**—to both reinforce and illustrate their feelings and ideas. Gestures, if used meaningfully, can help a speaker accentuate a thought, build redundancy into the message, and generally animate the speech.

A speaker who gestures effectively may be perceived by audience members as natural, relaxed, and in touch with his or her thoughts. A speaker whose gestures are stiff and unnatural may be perceived by audience members as uptight, undynamic, and unsure. So if you don't know what to do with your arms and hands and legs and feet when you speak, consider this: How do you want your audience to perceive you? Do you want them to see you as:

nervous and uptight—clutch one arm with the other or stand in a fig leaf pose;
a wooden soldier—hold your hands stiffly at your sides;
distant and closed off—cross your arms and legs in front of you;
combative and in charge—place your hands on your hips;
overly confident and self-assured—clasp your hands behind your back;
relaxed and composed—let your arms hang naturally and loosely at your sides.

It is important to remember that the meaning of a gesture may differ across cultures. For example, in the United States, making a circle with the thumb and index finger while extending the others represents "okay," in Japan and Korea it symbolizes "money," and among Arabs, when accompanied by a baring of teeth, it signifies extreme hostility.[18]

While African Americans, persons from Mediterranean cultures, Middle Easterners, and South Americans tend to be animated and expressive speakers, members of many Asian cultures tend to equate vigorous gestural action with poor manners and a lack of personal restraint; thus, they are apt to use fewer gestures and speak in a less lively and more subdued manner.[19]

Timing is crucial for effective gesturing. Your job is to concentrate on the message you wish to communicate and to free your hands to help emphasize and reinforce your points. Your gestures shxould flow naturally with your words. If you gesture too early or too late, you and your message will appear artificial and contrived. Under most conditions, gestures should coincide with, not precede or follow, verbal content. If your gestures are appropriate (adapted to your audience), natural (appear spontaneous), and consistent (supportive of your message), then they will enhance the delivery of your speech. Of course, if they draw attention to themselves, if they upstage both you and your ideas, then they distract the audience and defeat you. Keep your gestures unobtrusive, and they will help you speak volumes.

Posture: General Conclusions. The slouching speaker versus the speaker who stands erect. The speaker who drapes him- or herself over the lectern versus the speaker who stands straight, head held high. Each posture sends a different message to audience members. The way you hold your physical self is a nonverbal broadcast transmitting information your listeners will use to evaluate you and your presentation.

Audiences have expectations regarding the postures they expect speakers to exhibit.[20] A speaker who stands tall, with shoulders squared, sends a message of strength to audiences, whereas a speaker whose shoulders are either raised or stooped sends a message of stress or submissiveness, respectively. A speaker who leans toward an audience is usually perceived more positively than one who leans away or appears to withdraw from contact with the audience. Thus, a slight forward tip of the speaker's upper body can convey interest and concern to listeners.

Face and Eye Power. The speaker's face is his or her main means of communicating emotion. Audience members rely on a speaker's facial cues to reveal what is being communicated to them in the speaker's words. The face can either reinforce or contradict the speaker's verbal message.

When you speak, the facial cues you provide enable your listeners to interpret the meaning of your message. At times speakers attempt to guide their listeners through this process by either intensifying, deintensifying, neutralizing, or attempting to mask an emotion they are feeling. When you *intensify* an emotion you exaggerate your facial expressions to reflect the degree of expression you believe audience members expect you to exhibit. For example, you may communicate more excitement than you actually feel in an effort to generate excitement among listeners. When you *deintensify* an emotion, you diminish your facial expressions so that audience members will judge your behavior as more acceptable. Thus, you may downplay the rage you feel in an effort to temper audience member reactions. When you *neutralize* an emotion, you suppress your real feelings so as to suggest greater inner strength and resilience to listeners. Thus, you attempt to hide any fears, nerves, or sadness. And when you *mask* an emotion, you try to replace one emotion with another to which you believe audience members will respond more favorably. You might, for example, choose to conceal feelings of outrage, anger, jealousy, or anxiety if you believed audience members would find them unacceptable.

Certainly, inappropriate facial expressions can undermine a speaker's efforts. If a speaker smiles, for instance, when discussing a serious issue, that behavior contradicts the verbal message being sent by the speaker and will diminish whatever bonding between speaker and audience occurred to that point. The fact is your face plays a key role in revealing your thoughts and emotions to your listeners. The audience sees your

CONSIDERING DIVERSITY

Do the "Eyes" Have It?

According to some researchers, the amount of eye contact a person habitually displays is, at least in part, culturally determined. This means that the frequency of looking at any audience member and the duration of such gazes varies across cultural groups.[21]

Does this fact give speakers from one cultural group either an unfair advantage or a serious disadvantage when addressing a primarily homogeneous audience composed of an ethnic or a cultural group different from their own? Part of a public speaker's education should include an orientation to the nonverbal preferences and behaviors of a variety of cultures. For example, knowing that Arabs, Latin Americans, and Southern Europeans tend to look directly into the face of the person they are communicating with, while Japanese, Chinese, Northern Europeans, and Pakistanis tend to avoid focusing on the faces of those they interact with could affect both a speaker and a listener. Not knowing that African Americans tend to use more eye contact when speaking than White Americans do, but that the opposite is true when listening could precipitate serious misinterpretations of reaction.

What steps, if any, do you suggest speaker and listener take to alleviate the problems caused by a culture's different use of nonverbal cues? Speakers from one cultural group cannot hope to establish their credibility and clearly communicate their meaning to the members of another cultural group when their use of eye contact is sending a message that could be misconstrued.

Yasser Arafat's cultural background may influence his use of facial cues including eye contact.

face; it is visible for their constant inspection. If it is expressionless, it will work against you. If it fails to support your interest in your audience and your involvement in your topic, it will also fail to communicate your goodwill and sincerity. Your facial cues can do much to establish or destroy your credibility.

There are cultural differences in the use of facial cues. For example, in many Mediterranean cultures people tend to exaggerate facial signs of unhappiness. In contrast, Asians tend not to show emotion readily, preferring to mask expressions of sorrow, sometimes even with laughter.[22]

Of all the facial cues you exhibit, none does more to affect the relationship with your audience than the presence or absence of eye contact. Establishing effective eye contact with an audience serves a number of important functions. First, it signals that the lines of communication are open between speaker and listeners. For some reason, it is easier for audience members to not listen to a speaker who has not established eye contact with them. Second, it psychologically reduces the distance between speaker and listeners and helps to cement the bond between them. Third, it allows the speaker to obtain valuable feedback from audience members regarding how the speech is coming across, enabling the speaker to adjust his or her delivery as needed. And fourth, it communicates the speaker's confidence, conviction, concern, and interest.

What happens to the speaker–audience relationship if eye contact is missing or deficient? Audience members may question the speaker's openness, honesty, or integrity. They may conclude that the speaker is trying to hide something or conceal feelings. Audience members may also interpret a lack of eye contact as speaker boredom or disinterest, or even as an indication of the speaker's unfriendliness, lack of knowledge, or inexperience.

Eye contact allows for a sharing between speaker and listener. Take it away, the sharing suffers. If you think about it, you start a face-to-face conversation with a friend, associate, or acquaintance by making eye contact, and you end it by terminating eye contact. Eye contact says "I care about what you think and I have something to tell you." When either your eye contact or your partner's eye contact is poor, one of you may conclude that it's due to nervousness, hostility, dishonesty, or lack of interest and concern. At best, the individual who lacks eye contact will be perceived as ill at ease. What is true of a conversation between two people is also true of the public speaker–audience relationship. Thus, you would do well to keep these guidelines in mind when speaking to an audience:

Begin by looking audience members in the eye.

Eliminate eye dart—the tendency for your eyes to jump around the room like a scared rabbit. Instead, keep your gaze steady and personal as you distribute it evenly about the room or auditorium; in this way you visually demonstrate your interest in everyone present.

Do not stare blankly. A blank stare can be mistaken for a hostile glower or it can be construed as a sign of a blank mind.

Maintain eye contact with your listeners for at least three seconds after you conclude your speech. Don't close the eye-door before your final words have had a chance to sink in. Do not rush from the lectern. Doing that sends the wrong message and diminishes your message's staying power as well.

The Appearance Factor

Your clothing and grooming are important in creating a first impression with your audience members and in influencing their perceptions of your competence and trust-

SPEAKING of CRITICAL THINKING

Should We Be Focusing on How Instead of What or Vice Versa?

According to James A. Herrick, author of *Critical Thinking: The Analysis of Arguments,* "A source who stands neither to lose nor gain if his or her testimony is accepted as true is called an *unbiased source.*"[23] In contast, Herrick notes that a source who stands to lose if his or her testimony is accepted as true is a *reluctant source,* and a source who stands to gain if his or her testimony is accepted as true is a *biased source.*[24]

If a public speaker is functioning as a source and is adept at using nonverbal signals to create impressions of credibility in his or her receivers, what must an audience do to determine which type of source the speaker is? That is, what means can audiences use to make intelligent guesses about their speaker? Asking questions like these prior to hearing a speaker can help audience members more adequately assess a speaker's remarks. In other words, speakers are not the only parties to a speech who should conduct research; audiences also need to research speakers.

worthiness.[25] Because you want audience members to accept and retain your message, you need to present yourself as positively as possible. This means that your appearance, like your gestures (and unless specifically used as a visual aid), should be unobtrusive rather than distracting and should not isolate you from your receivers. Your words should not have to compete with your appearance for the attention of your listeners. The way you dress will help make both you and your message more appealing to listeners if you keep in mind that your physical appearance needs to reflect both the occasion and the nature of your speech. For instance, if you were giving a speech on surfing, it might be fitting for you to wear "jams" or a T-shirt, while a suit would be most appropriate to wear when giving a business speech.

CULTURE AND NONVERBAL DELIVERY

THE NORMS FOR NONVERBAL behavior vary from culture to culture. To a great degree, our cultural conditioning determines both our nonverbal repertoire and our interpretation of observed nonverbal cues.

To summarize, when it comes to eye contact, for example, we know that many persons of Arabic, Latino, and Southern European descent tend to look directly into the faces of their receivers, while Chinese, Japanese, Northern Europeans, and Pakistanis are more apt to avoid focusing directly on the faces of their receivers. African Americans tend to use more eye contact than White Americans do when performing speaking roles, but less when functioning as receivers.[26]

Cultural norms also govern the intensity of the nonverbal behavior displayed. Peoples from Mediterranean cultures, for instance, may tend to exaggerate or amplify an emotional appeal, while Asians may conceal the intensity of emotion by masking it with a smile.[27] Asians also make less use of their arms and hands to emphasize points than do Westerners. Similarly, Asians use a lower voice to express emphasis rather than a louder one. As the importance of a speaker's point increases, Asian speakers often decrease speaking volume instead of increasing it, as Westerners might do.[28]

Cultural norms regulate gestures used as well. While in the West, a speaker placing his or her hands on his or her hips may suggest confidence, among Asians such a gesture reflects obstinacy. Another arm gesture that may send the wrong message to an audience of Asians is the folding of one's arms across one's chest; they may interpret such a gesture as arrogant. Keeping one's hands in one's pockets is also frowned on by Asians. Meaningless gestures can cause problems as well. Whereas in the United States scratching one's lip may mean it itches, in China scratching one's lip is an invitation to sexual intimacy.[29]

Emblems are nonverbal symbols that have a direct verbal translation and are widely understood by the members of a culture. In the United States commonly understood emblems include making a circle with one's thumb and index finger—the okay sign—and the two-fingered peace symbol. Yet, as we have discussed, these do not necessarily transfer well to other cultures.

Vocal cues vary from culture to culture as well. For example, the higher pitch and intonation pattern used by Arabic speakers tend to convey extreme emotion to North Americans. As a result, North Americans may believe that the Arabic speaker is angry or agitated when he or she is neither. In like fashion, the constrained use of nonverbal cues by Asians may convey uninvolvement when that is not the case. For similar reasons, an Arabic receiver may interpret the speech pattern and emotion displayed by a North American to indicate that she or he is weak and uncommitted to the position taken.[30]

It is important to understand that a member of one cultural group may be less apt to establish his or her credibility as a speaker with members of another cultural group when cultural conditioning leads him or her to send nonverbal cues that are likely to be misconstrued by members of that group. Thus, it becomes important to both speakers and receivers to recognize when they are sending nonverbal messages that members of another culture might misinterpret or consider inappropriate.

REHEARSAL: THE PRACTICE PROMISE

"IF I'M SUPPOSED TO SOUND spontaneous and natural, and as if I'm giving my speech for the first time, why do I need to rehearse it?" asks the novice speechmaker. There are several answers to this question:

First, since we usually engage in conversation, not speechmaking, speechmaking is not our most frequent means of communicating with others. Thus, for us to sound "natural" when delivering a speech, we ought to practice.

Second, just as actors in a play rehearse their parts until the role becomes a part of them, so a speechmaker needs to rehearse his or her part until it becomes "one" with him or her. For the actor, every night of the play is opening night; so, too, for the speechmaker with every presentation of a speech. It is the dress rehearsals and practice periods that get both to that point.

Third, athletes practice in scrimmage sessions, pilots practice flying in simulations, even physicians role-play treating patients. Like these professions, the speaker, too, must prepare to meet an audience.

Finally, the old adage has merit: Practice makes perfect—that is, if you practice correctly.

What is the right way to practice? Although rehearsal is a highly individual matter, we can provide you with some basic guidelines.

- Begin your rehearsal by reading through your outline or manuscript a number of times. Then, if you are delivering a manuscript speech or a speech from memory, continue to rehearse with a triple-spaced manuscript that you have marked so you can easily tell which words and phrases to stress, where to speed up and slow down, and where to pause. If you are delivering an extemporaneous speech, as you rehearse develop a list of key words and phrases from that outline on note cards. From then on use these notes to spark your memory. Be sure to type or print quotations and statistics in large letters on separate cards.
- Be sure you verbalize every example and illustration, recite every quotation, and say aloud every statistic you plan to use. Familiarity begets clarity when it comes to public speaking.
- If you will be using visual or audio aids, work with them during your practice sessions.
- Do your best to mirror the conditions and setting you will experience when actually delivering your speech.
- Audio- or videotape your rehearsal and play it back for self-evaluation, or attain feedback from people who watched your rehearsal.
- As you review your tape, ask yourself whether you are expressing your ideas as clearly as you would like to. Specifically: Do you have an attention-getting step? Is the language contained in the body of your speech understandable to audience members? Is your support adequate? Is the organization easy to follow? Does your conclusion contain both a summary and a psychological appeal?
- Time your presentation in an effort to determine whether it is too long; this is the time to cut out nonessential information. If it is too short, this is the time to make it more substantial.
- Pay attention to your use of nonverbal cues during rehearsals as well. Again, obtain constructive feedback that lets you know if you make enough eye contact, employ meaningful gestures, and use your voice and appearance to advantage.

Practicing lets you revise and improve your presentation prior to delivering your speech. Spreading your practice time over at least three to five rehearsal sessions will work better than if you try to cram your practice into one drawn-out session. One extended practice session will not afford you the time you need to polish your speech and delivery to the degree that distributed practice sessions will. Distribute rehearsals and speech delivery day will be more rewarding for you.

Preparing for the Q & A Session

Knowing how to handle yourself during a question-and-answer session is just as important as preparing yourself to deliver the speech. Because you worked hard to come across as a credible speechmaker, you also want to be certain that that perception is not affected by the Q & A session that follows. Because last impressions, like first impressions, influence audience reactions, how can you prepare yourself so that you don't blow it during this phase? You can:

- Anticipate some of the questions audience members will ask, and prepare answers to them in advance.

- Have someone rehearse you by asking you the potential questions you've brainstormed as well as others designed to unnerve you.
- Repeat a question aloud, if it is phrased in a neutral manner, before answering it; if needed, you can rephrase it to remove any venomous or loaded words.
- Practice saying "I don't know," if you don't know. You still have time to find out the answers prior to the actual delivery day. And if you have to answer a question with an "I don't know" on delivery day, promise to find out the answer and get back to the person who posed the question.
- Remember, you don't need to answer more than is asked. If you wonder, why not, consider this example provided by communication professional Bob Boylan:

> Johnny, 7 years old, comes to his mother and says, "Where did I come from?"
>
> The mother gulps and asks, "What did you say?"
>
> Johnny repeats, "Where did I come from?"
>
> The mother is ready this time. "Well, it's about time you ask that question. Dad and I have been thinking you would. You see, Johnny, your dad and mom love each other a lot. Because of that, we sometimes lie close to each other and something called a sperm passed between Daddy and Mommy. It happened about 8 years ago and you were conceived. You started to grow in Mommy's tummy and Mommy's tummy got bigger every month. I went to see Dr. Brown. He checked my tummy every month to make sure you were growing okay. My tummy got bigger and bigger for 9 months. And then I went to the hospital. Daddy and Dr. Brown were there. Johnny, you know where you came from? You came out of Mommy's tummy—that's where you came from!"
>
> Johnny's expression was one of great puzzlement. "Wow!" he said. "That's the most incredible story I've ever heard. Frank, my friend, comes from Boston and I was just wondering where I came from!"[31]

Remember, answer only the question. If the questioner wants more information, he or she will ask more questions.

SUMMARY

THE SPEAKER'S DELIVERY ADDS to or detracts from the impact of a speaker's words. How a speaker sounds and what a speaker does when delivering a speech affects the audience's perception of him or her. By taking time to explore how to use nonverbal cues, a speaker can work to enhance the understanding and acceptance of ideas by audience members. In the minds of receivers, effective delivery and effective public speaking are partners. A speaker who is enthusiastic, has good eye contact, sounds conversational, communicates with spontaneity, and does not distract listeners with ineffective nonverbal mannerisms is usually evaluated more positively by receivers.

A speaker is not tied to using one speaking style. Among the five presentation styles from which speakers may choose are the memorized speech, the manuscript speech, the extemporaneous speech, the impromptu speech, and the sound bite. The extemporaneous style is the method preferred by most speech teachers; it is useful to understand and be able to use each delivery option.

A critical factor in delivery is the speaker's voice. A speaker who uses his or her voice effectively is able to use pitch, volume, rate, articulation, and pronunciation to advantage.

The body language exhibited by a speaker is also a critical factor in delivery. If a speaker displays effective movements, gestures, posture, facial expressions, and eye contact, then it is easier for the speaker to create a good relationship with receivers. A speaker's clothing and grooming are also critical in helping the speaker create a good first impression with audience members.

Of course, every speaker needs to rehearse a speech adequately prior to presenting it.

THE SPEAKER'S STAND

Napoleon once said, "To involve a person, you must speak to his eyes." Prepare a two- to three-minute speech on one of the following topics or on a topic of your choice of which your instructor approves:

- the strengths (or weaknesses) of the welfare system
- how to choose a major
- dangers of secondhand smoke
- censorship of the Internet
- the horror of horror movies
- date rape
- silly superstitions
- how to work your way through college
- how to handle a job interview
- how to buy a personal computer
- how people dream
- the symptoms of chronic fatigue syndrome

During your presentation, picture each member of your audience as an individual, and one at a time, have five seconds of sustained eye contact with each one while you speak. At the end of your presentation, ask audience members to assess how your eye contact made them feel. Also ask them to critique other aspects of your delivery including your use of voice, gestures, and movement.

STUDENT FOCUS GROUP REPORT

Now that you have had the opportunity to explore nonverbal cues during the delivery of a presentation, in a group of five to seven students, answer the following questions:

1. Which nonverbal cue do you find is easiest to control? Why?
2. Which nonverbal cue poses the greatest challenge to you? Why?
3. What techniques do you use to successfully support the words of your speech nonverbally?
4. How can nonverbal behavior make the public speaker's job easier or harder?
5. What kinds of questions should audience members ask themselves when processing a speaker's verbal and nonverbal messages?
6. Summarize the most significant information you have learned about the speech delivery process and nonverbal communication.
7. Revisit the case study at the beginning of the chapter. Based on your current knowledge of delivery, in what ways, if any, would you now revise your answers to the questions?

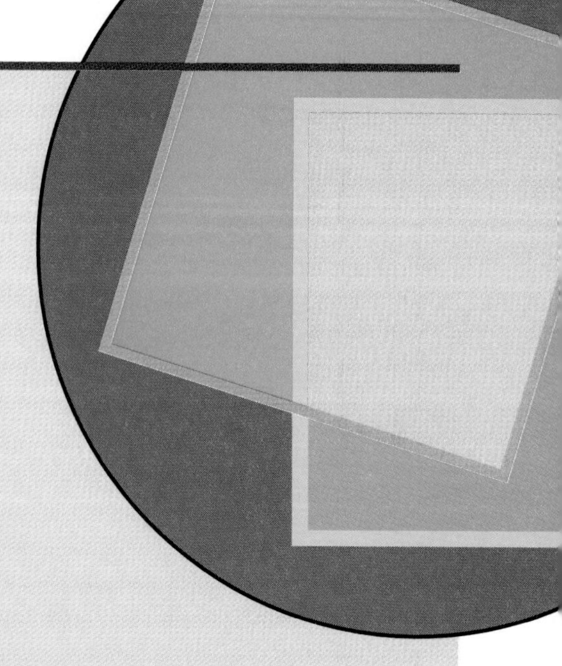

Chapter Fourteen

Speaking with Visual Aids

After reading this chapter, you should be able to:

- Explain why a speech often benefits from the incorporation of one or more visual aids.
- Discuss the functions served by visual aids.
- Assess the strengths of the following kinds of visual aids: real people; objects and models; photographs; graphs; charts, drawings, and maps; slides, videotapes, and overhead transparencies; computer-generated graphics; and electronic presentations.
- Identify criteria to use when selecting visual aids.
- Enumerate the dos and don'ts of preparing and using visual aids.
- Integrate one or more visual aids into a speech you deliver.

CASE STUDY

Seeing Is Believing

Kelly paced the floor. This was the first case she was trying on her own, and she was nervous. She rehearsed and rerehearsed her closing statement to the jury. This was the last chance she would have to cement whatever rapport she had been able to establish with jurors, review the key facts of the case with them, and convince them that they must find for her client. She longed for a visual image that she could use to make the jurors understand exactly what had happened to her client to leave him in such wanting physical condition.

Kelly's client had broken his neck while diving into a shallow swimming pool. His head had slammed into the pool's concrete bottom, leaving him a quadriplegic.

After much searching, Kelly found a wooden artist's doll that clearly showed the base of the skull and the neck. She decided to use the doll to demonstrate visually the damage done to her client's body. She had secured the one prop she believed would tie her presentation together—a prop she could manipulate and hold up at will before the jury. Kelly stopped pacing, and started rehearsing with the doll.

- Did Kelly need such a visual? Why or why not?
- What other visuals, if any, might Kelly have used during her closing argument to add impact to her presentation?

"SPEAK THE SPEECH," said Shakespeare's Hamlet. And we do. In fact, many of us think of a public speech as filled with words—word after word after word. Too few of us, however, conceive of it as potentially rich in visuals. Yet, visuals, like words, can be powerful tools and the speaker's ally. This is not a new idea. Consider this observation by presidential advisor and communication and media relations specialist Merrie Spaeth:

> When Moses came down from the mountain with clay tablets bearing the Ten Commandments, it was perhaps history's first example of a speaker using props to reinforce his message. It wouldn't have had the same impact if Moses had simply announced: "God just told me 10 things, and I'm going to relay them to you."[1]

The old adage "a picture is worth a thousand words" is more true today than ever before. We live in an increasingly visual age in which the average American either watches television or surfs the Internet for about one quarter of his or her waking hours.[2] It is a world filled with billboards, films, VCRs, and computer screens. In addition, the rapid emergence of electronic imaging and computerized presentations is contributing to making visual communication an increasingly important part of the speechmaking process. The odds are that you will use visual aids when you deliver presentations in the future. In fact, virtually any speech you deliver will benefit from the incorporation of one or more relevant visual aids.

Today's audiences are more attuned to messages that appeal to their eyes than to those that appeal solely to their ears. Thus, speakers who tailor their presentations to appeal to both the eyes and the ears of their listeners will attain greater speechmaking success than those who insist on appealing to the ears alone.

The effective integration of visual materials into a speech can make a significant difference in the way an audience responds to a speaker. "Show and Tell" did not die in kindergarten. The politicans and professional speakers of today use a plethora of props, pictures, and illustrative objects to make their points come alive for receivers. Both Bill Clinton and Ronald Reagan have produced a number of memorable visual aids during speeches. Clinton once held up a prop—a dummied-up universal-coverage ID card—during a health care speech. Reagan once literally dropped 43 pounds of federal budget documents with a thud to emphasize that he would never approve such spending. Similarly, a CEO used two unique visual aids to demonstrate his commitment to change. The CEO, the head of a large insurance company, began a speech to 250 agents by discussing how the insurance industry had changed. First he held up a McDonald's bag, noting that the fast food industry, which didn't exist until a few decades ago, thrives today because it meets customer needs. Then he talked about new technology and what it would mean for each agent in his audience. He then dragged a trash can to center stage, filling it with a pile of receipts and bookkeeping forms. The agents in his audience gave him a standing ovation.[3] As we see, today's speakers are transforming the old show and tell, enriching their speeches with both simple and sophisticated visual aids that help them explain, describe, or prove a point.

In this chapter we will explore how **visual aids**—stimuli that rely on sight to make a point and support a speech or a speaker—can make it easier for you to communicate your ideas with greater clarity and impact. We will look at how the use of a wide range of compelling visual evidence can make your speech more interesting, vivid, and involving for your receivers, and help you speak with greater confidence so you can achieve your speechmaking goals.

WHY USE VISUAL AIDS? GAINING THE SPEAKER'S ADVANTAGE

VISUAL AIDS ARE OFTEN CLEARER than speech itself. Able to heighten attention with a single picture, speed comprehension with a single graph, reinforce main points with a single chart, and enhance recall and memorability with a vivid display of visual evidence, today's speakers are capitalizing on the basic lessons taught us by the newspaper *USA Today:* graphics attract audiences—pictures, drawings, graphs, charts, and color can add interest and impact to the presentation of information. In other words, if audiences can *see,* not just hear, what you are communicating, they may understand it better, and thus they may retain more of it. Since members of today's visual society are for the most part more influenced by what they see than by what they hear, the careful speaker will use visual aids to reinforce, not replace, a spoken message.

Visuals Facilitate the Speaker's Job

Visuals facilitate the speaker's job by increasing listener understanding, enhancing receiver memory and recall, clarifying the presentation's organizational format, helping

Visual aids, in this case Johnnie Cochran wearing a knit cap, can increase the impact of a speaker's words. Are you more persuaded by what you see or what you hear?

the speaker control the attention and interest of receivers, and enhancing the presentation's impact and the speaker's credibility.

Visuals Increase Receiver Comprehension. Charts and graphs, for example, can be used to help clarify complex statistical information for receivers. Because more than 80 percent of all information we receive is processed through our sense of sight, a variety of visual aids help supply the "show me" dimension expected and even required by many of today's listeners.[4]

Visuals Enhance Memory and Recall. When a spoken message is reinforced visually, memory and retention of the message increase. Researchers tell us that we remember only 10 percent of what we read, 20 percent of what we hear, and 30 percent of what we see, but they also tell us that we remember over 50 percent of what we see and hear simultaneously. Figure 14.1 illustrates how a visual aid affects the retention of a message.[5]

Visuals Facilitate Organization. By displaying main ideas on a computerized projection, chart, poster, overhead transparency, or slide, you help your listeners follow your presentation. As a result, you are better able to stress your key points and they are better able to perceive your speech's basic plan, structure, or design. While you

	After Three Hours	*After Three Days*
Speech Alone	70%	10%
Visual Alone	72%	20%
Speech and Visual	85%	65%

Figure 14.1

When combined with speech, visual aids enhance the retention of a message.

Claudyne Wilder

Claudyne Wilder is president of Wilder Management Services, a management consulting firm, and has coached thousands of executives into becoming dynamic public speakers. In this excerpt from The Presentations Kit, *Wilder offers advice on working with visuals.*

Which Guide Do You Want? Which Guide Are You Now?

Guide 1: You are seated in the back row of a large conference room. You came to see a slide show on a mountaineering trip you have always wanted to take. The speaker holds up materials, but you cannot see them since the room is too dark. She then begins a 10-minute slide show introducing you to the climbing area. She stands slightly in front of the screen, making it impossible for you to see the complete picture. When she points to the route of ascent, instead of a long pointer, she uses her finger, thus covering up the exact region to which she is referring. She has given each person a map, but in the darkened room, it is impossible to follow the climbing route she is explaining.

Guide 2: Your guide begins by telling you the story of the man who took the slides. She then takes a pointer, dims the lights, but leaves enough light so you can write notes on the handout. As you sit

can verbally state your speech's main points and integrate internal summaries that reiterate them, your receivers will still benefit from additional visual support.

Visuals Help Control the Attention and Interest of Receivers. By providing the audience with something more concrete to focus on than words alone, whether a dramatic photograph, object, or graph, you directly center their attention on the point you want to make. Most listeners require a speaker's help to maintain their attention and interest, and visual aids, often clearer than the words they reinforce, meet that need more quickly, more vividly, and more compellingly than words alone. By carefully selecting visuals that help you manage your audience's attention, you subtly move your audience with you as you progress toward your conclusion. In effect, visual aids offer you an additional control mechanism, and a speaker who is able to control an audience's attention is better able to control an audience's reaction.

Visuals Add Impact. Visual aids increase your personal persuasiveness by enhancing the impact of your message. In fact, a study undertaken by the 3M Corporation indicated that speakers who made visuals an inherent part of their presentations were 43 percent more likely to persuade their audiences than were speakers who relied exclusively on spoken words.[6] It appears that visual support also adds to a speaker's credibility by causing audiences to perceive the speaker as a better communicator—one who is more clear, more concise, more interesting, more prepared, more professional, more believable, and thus more persuasive.

Visuals Enhance Speaker Credibility. Well-planned and well-conceived visuals can enhance your credibility in the eyes of your receivers. Audiences rate speakers who use visuals during presentations as more prepared, persuasive, and believable in the back row, you clearly see the details on the screen as pointed out by the guide. She uses a pointer to pinpoint the exact area that she is discussing. You can feel yourself get excited as she talks. Once you have written down the facts you need, she turns off the slide projector. She shares a few anecdotes about people who have previously hiked up this mountain. She then turns the projector back on, showing some beautiful pictures. She ends by having you visualize yourself on the top of the mountain. The last slide you see shows the top of the mountain with the words at the bottom of the slide, *I climbed it.*

Guide 1 needs help in learning how to use visuals to enhance her presentation. Guide 2 uses her visuals to keep people interested and to communicate and educate.

Our society has become more and more picture-oriented. Most of us watch television, go to the movies, and patronize the home video business. Airline emergency procedures are now in picture form; instructions come with diagrams; newspaper ads usually have pictures in them. We are living in an era where visual stimulation occupies more and more of our daily lives. People can recite entire scenes from movies and plays, yet do not remember a word of the dialogue. This is not surprising if we recognize that, as children, many people spent hours in front of the television. The fact that we have developed from a culture whose orientation was predominantly auditory to one whose orientation is primarily visual is of critical significance to the modern day presenter. The "language" that most people understand and expect these days is not just oral but a combination of oral and visual. Use visuals to enhance your talk and the retention of your group.[10]

than speakers who fail to use visuals.[7] For example, one speaker, a banker, used a visual aid to demonstate his business acumen. The banker, speaking before an audience of potential clients—all company treasurers—regarding his bank's expertise in foreign exchange, held up an array of different foreign bills, some familiar to his receivers and some new to them. Because he was able to identify such unfamiliar currencies from countries as Liberia and Turkmenistan, the speaker impressed his listeners with his specialized knowledge. His credibility grew, in their eyes.[8]

To summarize, visuals are the icing on your presentation cake. Their very presence can put you ahead of the pack. As Robert W. Pittman, AOL executive, MTV creator, and former Time Warner executive, notes:

> Generations who grew up with TV communicate differently than previous generations. . . . The TV babies . . . seem to be happy processing information from different sources almost simultaneously. . . . Because of TV, perhaps, TV babies seem to perceive visual messages better; that is, through sense impressions. They can 'read' a picture or understand body language at a glance.[9]

Consequently, to speak the language of today's audiences, speakers need to talk with more than words; they also need to talk with visuals.

KINDS OF VISUAL AIDS

VISUAL AIDS COME IN ALL SHAPES AND SIZES. They can be animate or inanimate; two dimensional or three dimensional; they can range from people, models, and objects to photographs, graphs, charts, drawings, slides, videotapes, and computer-generated materials. Visual aids are limited only by the speaker's imagination, resources, and budget. The two key questions a speaker needs to ask when planning on integrating visuals are:

1. What can I do to bring my presentation visually alive for my listeners?
2. What types of visual aids should I use?

Real People

A **human being** can make an effective visual aid, that is, if his or her use is well planned, tailored to meet the needs of the presentation, and not allowed to distract audience members by running away with the show. One student delivering a speech on self-defense brought along two other people skilled in the art of self-defense to simulate "the attacker" and "the victim"; by so doing the speaker was able to demonstrate each of the basic moves a victim could use to get him- or herself out of a threatening situation. Another student used a number of male and female student models to illustrate the right and wrong ways to dress for a job interview.

When using *living* visual aids, keep several guidelines in mind.

1. Be sure your "human visuals" are willing and committed to helping you accomplish your objectives.

2. Be sure to rehearse with your "aids" prior to the big day. Relying on "spur-of-the-moment" volunteers can be a risky proposition and can inhibit the smooth integration of the visual aids into your presentation.

3. Do not have your "aids" share the speaker's area with you until their services are required. Instead, introduce them to your audience only when you are ready to use them. Once you have used them to help convey your message, have them step out of the speaker's spotlight by moving them back into the audience or out of sight. The rule is: "Put the visual away when you are finished with it," even if it is a living, breathing human being. Keep in mind that your human visual aids are your tools; they are subordinate to your speech. You need to maintain control of them.

4. Finally, be aware that you too serve as a visual aid. In addition to illustrating the main points in your presentation, for example, you might show how to give an insulin injection, demonstrate the proper stance for fencing, or model the dress of your native country or the special attire worn by a baseball catcher. You also add vitality to your presentation simply by the way you look, stand, and move before your audience (see Chapter 13).

Objects and Models

Objects and **models** can also be used to enliven a presentation. Both can effectively add clarity, interest, and drama to your ideas. Let us explore each in turn.

An actual object is useful when you want to show audience members exactly what it is you are speaking about. It is "the real thing," so the actual object has the power to compel listeners to focus their attention on your message, and by so doing can help them better understand your subject. To be used effectively, however, the object must be large enough to be seen by everyone in your audience but small enough so you can carry it to your presentation and handle it with ease. For example, a tennis racquet, a Civil War sword, a native costume, a musical instrument, food, a toy, and so forth, can be used to show your listeners what you are talking about or to demonstrate how to do something. Again, the visual aids you incorporate should be kept out of sight until needed. If you keep the object in the audience's sight before you are ready to show or use it, you risk losing your audience's attention. Instead of concentrating on you, your listeners may focus on the object, speculating about what it is, what you are going to do with it, or how you are going to use it. When this happens, it moves to the forefront of their attention and you, upstaged by an object, move to the background. Objects need to be attractions, not distractions. Remember to conceal them before you reveal them, and they will be able to fulfill that function better.

Keep this in mind too: unless you are certain you can control them, inanimate objects make better visual aids than animate objects. It is also important that all animate props be stored and treated humanely prior to, during, and after the speech. One student presented a speech on the proper way to handle a snake. During one demonstration she placed the snake on a display table at the front of the room; much to her surprise, as she was turning to make a point, the snake slithered out of her reach and was on its way into the audience when it was finally recaptured by the now nervous speaker. Before using an animate visual aid, consider in advance the kinds of problems it could create for you and your listeners. Remember, you use the visual aid to add credibility and drama to your presentation, not to create chaos.

Another speaker used an animate visual aid during a business presentation in a way that allowed him to fully control its presentation. In an effort to convince his associates that they weren't adapting quickly enough to change, the speaker used a live lobster as a prop. Holding up the lobster, the speaker said: "When the colonists arrived here, lobsters were plentiful. They no longer are." The speaker then made the point that while the environment had changed, lobsters hadn't. As the audience members leaned forward in their seats, the speaker plopped the lobster into a pot of boiling water. Then, pacing up and down the stage, he spoke of the changing business environment—being sure to periodically check the pot. At his speech's conclusion, the speaker held up the cooked lobster and said that companies and people who resist change are sure to become someone's lunch. "But we will change," he said, making his point quite dramatically.[11] Such visual depictions make presentations more interesting and entertaining than they would be if the speaker presented his or her ideas with words alone.

If you conclude that your visual aid is too large to bring to your presentation; too small to be seen; or too dangerous, valuable, or fragile to carry around, then you might opt to use a model in its place. One student who delivered a speech on the human heart used a larger-than-life replica of a heart that opened to reveal the inner workings of its chambers. Another student who delivered a speech on CPR brought "Resusci Annie," a life-sized model used for practice in CPR courses.

Speakers use models all the time when delivering informative or persuasive talks. Probably each of us is familiar with models of the solar systems used in science classes, models of buildings and communities used in architectural presentations, models of airplanes or ships used to plan war games, models of teeth used by dentists and hygienists to demonstrate proper brushing techniques, and models of babies used by health care professionals when instructing prospective or new parents on how to care for an infant. Three-dimensional models can be quite useful to speakers who use them appropriately. Because they represent the object being discussed—sometimes better than the object itself—they serve as useful substitute objects, or surrogates.

Speaking of skillbuilding: Evaluating the Objects Used as Visual Aids

Jim Eae added both credibility and drama to his speech entitled "Equality" by using four apples as visual aids in both the introduction of his speech and segments of its body, and then a stone as a visual aid during the speech's conclusion. Selected excerpts of his speech appear below. Read them and then answer the questions that follow.

[*From the introduction*] Four apples—similar by their outer appearance, almost identical by their insides, and yet their flavors are worlds apart. This one right here, it's a sweet one, really sweet. This one right here, it's kind of sour. This one is bitter, and the last is a combination of all. Four apples—two red and two green—similar, but very different.

I'm not just talking about the differences between apples. I'm also talking about the differences between people. Color you may say is only skin deep, but it is much more than that. It determines where you come from. It determines what you believe in. It determines where your social interests lie. It even determines who you fall in love with. Your color helps determine your uniquess and your individuality. It helps mold you into the person you are and the person you hope to become.

[*From the body*] George F. Snyder, author of *Black No More,* imagined a world where everyone was the same color. The front cover of his book reads, "A Negro doctor discovers how to turn black skin white. All blacks in America turn white, whiter than white, so white the whites have to turn out white to show that they rank those damn white niggers." Could you imagine this world if everyone was the same color? I could, and I would hate it.

The hope some have of a color blind society brings up the question: If everyone conformed and became the same, which culture would we adapt to? Would the Japanese society of respect and hard work be dominant? Would everyone choose to have the strength and endurance of the African Americans? Would the conquering attitude of the Caucasian American reign supreme? . . .

My favorite apple is this green one right here. It is colored but not too colored. It is sweet, yet still sour, but best of all, it is different from every other apple. If someone were to come up with the perfect medium for the taste and color of apples, I would object because I would not have the variety to choose from anymore. I would have to settle for a bland color and a bland taste. I pray this never happens.

A great man once said, "If any of you are without fault, then let he be the first to cast a stone." It is time we stop casting stones and accept people for who they are, color and all. . . .

[*From the conclusion*] Let the man without any fault cast the first stone. During the civil rights era even police were casting stones at peaceful protesters. I, myself, have been hit with several stones of a color blind society. For example, there were times when I wanted to speak up as a black man and not just a human, but I have to forfeit my thoughts, my ideas, and my feelings for you. Equality—that's the solution.

Alexander Kremble, a black nationalist who spent twenty years as a missionary in Liberia and founded the first organization for African American intellectuals, said the race problem is a moral one, and like all other great battles of humanity, its solution will be fought with weapons of truth. Here it is, the first stone of equality, and I cast it to you. Not because I am without fault, but because I know it is the best solution for both you and me. The solution is equality, and now the solution is no longer in my hands, but yours. So I ask, "What are you going to do it with?"

- ☐ In your opinion, to what extent were the speaker's use of visual aids effective? Explain.
- ☐ Do you believe audience members would find the visual aids distracting or helpful? Why?
- ☐ If you were the speaker, would you have thrown a stone at your audience? Why or why not?

Photographs or Color Copies

Photographs or **color copies** (when enlarged so everyone can see them) also make effective visual aids. Rather than uttering the all-too-common apology, "I know you can't see this well, but, . . ." your job when you use a photo or color copy is to make sure audience members *can* see it well. The rules to keep in mind are:

Select your photos or copies with care.
Enlarge them sufficiently.
Control them capably.

Whenever possible, photographs should not be passed around the room because doing so diverts attention from you. In effect, the person waiting to look at the photograph, the person looking at it, and the person who has just looked at it are not with you because they are concentrating on something else.

When used properly, however, photos can add realism, drama, and impact to your presentation. For example, during the civil suit against OJ Simpson, lawyers for the plaintiffs displayed numerous photos of Simpson wearing Bruno Magli shoes in an effort to damage Simpson's credibility after he testified under oath that he never owned such "ugly" shoes. In an effort to help students visualize the horrors created by the civil war in Nigeria, a student used a photo showing starving children and appealed to his classmates to contribute to relief efforts. Another student talking about emergency rescue procedures used a photo of a burning aircraft from which all on board had escaped to drive home the message of the value of rigorous training in rescue techniques.

Color pictures are usually more effective than black-and-white photos, but it is most important in terms of visibility that the photo's central features contrast clearly with the background.

SPEAKING of ETHICS

Visuals and Perception

What ethical question regarding the use and misuse of visuals do these excerpts from Walter Goodman's article "How Bad Is War? It Depends on the TV Pictures" prompt you to ask?

> Television, as Karl von Clausewitz neglected to mention, is war and politics by other means. But what means exactly? Its use in the war in the Persian Gulf and the politicking before and since reveal the sort of weapon it is.
>
> While it was storming the desert, the Pentagon kept news cameras at bay and transmitted its own high-up high-tech photographs of pinpoint strikes. On the Iraqi side, the looting of Kuwait was closed even to Peter Arnett, but cameras were invited to record the Iraqi ruler patting children's heads, and Western correspondents were encouraged to take pictures of what was apparently a bombed

(continued)

Speaking of Ethics *(continued)*

air raid shelter in Baghdad. ("We never quite got ahead of the story about the bomb shelter," concedes Richard N. Haass, a special assistant to the President.)

When the war was over, Washington became friendlier to television news, welcoming coverage of homecomings and victory parades; the Pentagon and the President even cooperated in a hurray-for-our-side docudrama. Critics of the war meanwhile have been bringing back pictures of the sufferings of Iraqi civilians. It all depends on which way you point the lens and whether you take off the cap.

A few weeks ago Mr. Haass, who is attached to the National Security Council and participated in planning the war, gave a talk about the impact of television to journalists and officials brought together in Washington by the Annenberg Washington Program and the Johns Hopkins Foreign Policy Institute. He said there was no impact worthy of the word until the actual attack on Iraq in January.

But even before that, he said, television served the Administration as "our chief tool" in developing domestic and international support, that is, "selling our policy." "The Administration," he added, wanted "to get out there with something that is very black and white in terms of where you stand, that can be explained very quickly." A CNN debate, he observed, does not invite nuance. . . .

Once the war was on, he allowed that the way it might come across on the tube did enter into the extraordinary care taken by the military to avoid "collateral damage." "A decision was made that it was just not worth the political fallout that would obviously accrue if innocents were hurt," he said. Particularly if they were hurt on screen. For similar reasons television constrained Washington from continuing the ground war and moving toward Baghdad. The Administration, he said, was especially concerned about how the sight of Americans piling on Iraq would play in Arab countries.

Although Mr. Haass emphasized that television did not change "the moral calculation" against more fighting, he granted that it sharpened that calculation. So at least a little credit or blame must go to television for the abrupt end to hostilities that left President Saddam Hussein of Iraq in power and his forces largely intact.

The sorts of pictures that worried Pentagon planners could be seen last week in a "Frontline" documentary titled "The War We Left Behind." It focused on civilians, particularly children going without milk and medicine as a result of those smart-bomb strikes on power stations and the continuing United Nations sanctions.

Since the program was made by Leslie and Andrew Cockburn, viewers cannot have been astonished by the underlying animus against the Administration. But aside from the political slant, their documentary demonstrates that if you turn the camera in the direction of the victims, you can make any notion of a just war seem like camouflage for barbarity. . . .

The politics of the camera lies in such pictures. The Pentagon paid tribute to their power when it kept journalists away from the human beings at the other end of its bomb sights. Mr. Haass put it this way: "The impact of television seems to be greatest when it has images." No revelation there, but he may have been hinting that if the networks had not carried pictures of the Kurdish refugees night after night, the Administration might have been better able to subdue its humanitarian impulses.

Paul D. Wolfowitz, an Undersecretary of Defense, told the Washington meeting that watching the debate in Congress on the war against Iraq must have strengthened Saddam Hussein's "conviction that we wouldn't do anything, and if we ever did anything, we wouldn't do it decisively." . . .

The plight of Kurdish refugees when brought home by television, moved the nation sufficiently to compel Washington to send aid and then to set up a security zone. But suppose, as some urged, that the United States had gone further and unleashed troops against the Iraqi attackers, resulting in more casualties among civilians? Somebody's camera would assuredly have been there, on the ground, in the hospitals, and pity for the Kurds would have turned to revulsion against the cruelties committed in saving them. The only good war, as the Pentagon controllers understood, is one where the cameras are miles away from the targets.

Is any cause worth certain death and destruction, when they can be seen in the living room?

So here is the Clausewitzian doctrine for the video age: When focused on distant pinpoint hits, military briefings, parades and enemy aggression, the camera can rally a spirit of combat. But when it turns toward the down and dirty consequences of war, it becomes the super weapon of pacifism. And like other weapons, it can be put to the service of defenders or aggressors, democrats or dictators.[12]

Give an example of how the presence or absence of visual support influenced your attitude toward a subject. If you were a speaker advocating a particular policy, would you use only visuals that supported your side? For instance, if you were advocating the continuance of welfare how would the visuals you chose to use compare or contrast with those you would employ if you were advocating the elimination of welfare and the substitution of workfare in its place?

Graphs

Speakers integrate **graphs** into their presentations in an effort to help their listeners better understand statistical data. Well-designed graphic formats can help speakers communicate statistical information, illustrate trends, and vivify patterns. Among the graphs most commonly used by speakers are line graphs, bar graphs, pie graphs, and pictographs.[13]

Speakers rely on **line graphs** to help them show trends over time. Figure 14.2 is one such graph used by a student in a speech on abortion. The speaker chose the graph to support her contention that abortions are on the decline. Referring to the graph the speaker said:

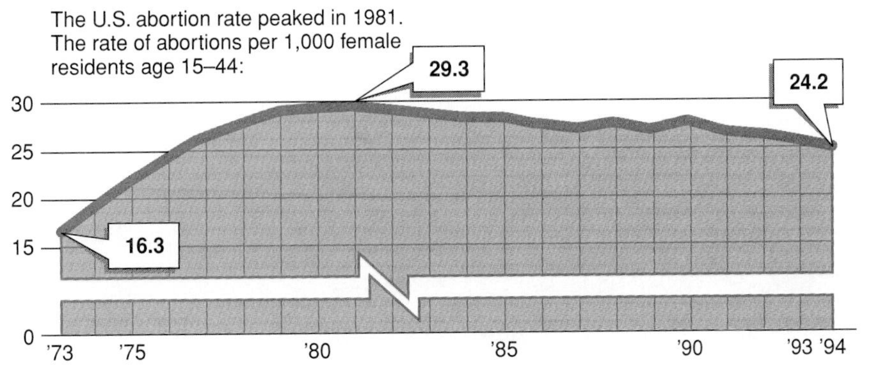

Figure 14.2

> As you can see from the graph derived from information in the August 8, 1996, issue of *USA TODAY*, abortions have declined from the peak year of 1981.[14]

By incorporating these words, the speaker helped her listeners interpret the graph. By describing the course revealed by the statistical data, she was able to substantiate the apparent trend.

A line graph can also be used to make comparisons by adding two or more lines to it. In Figure 14.3 comparisons are made between the percentages of Hispanics, African Americans, and Asians in Bergen and Passaic counties in New Jersey. The lines are color coded for clarity.

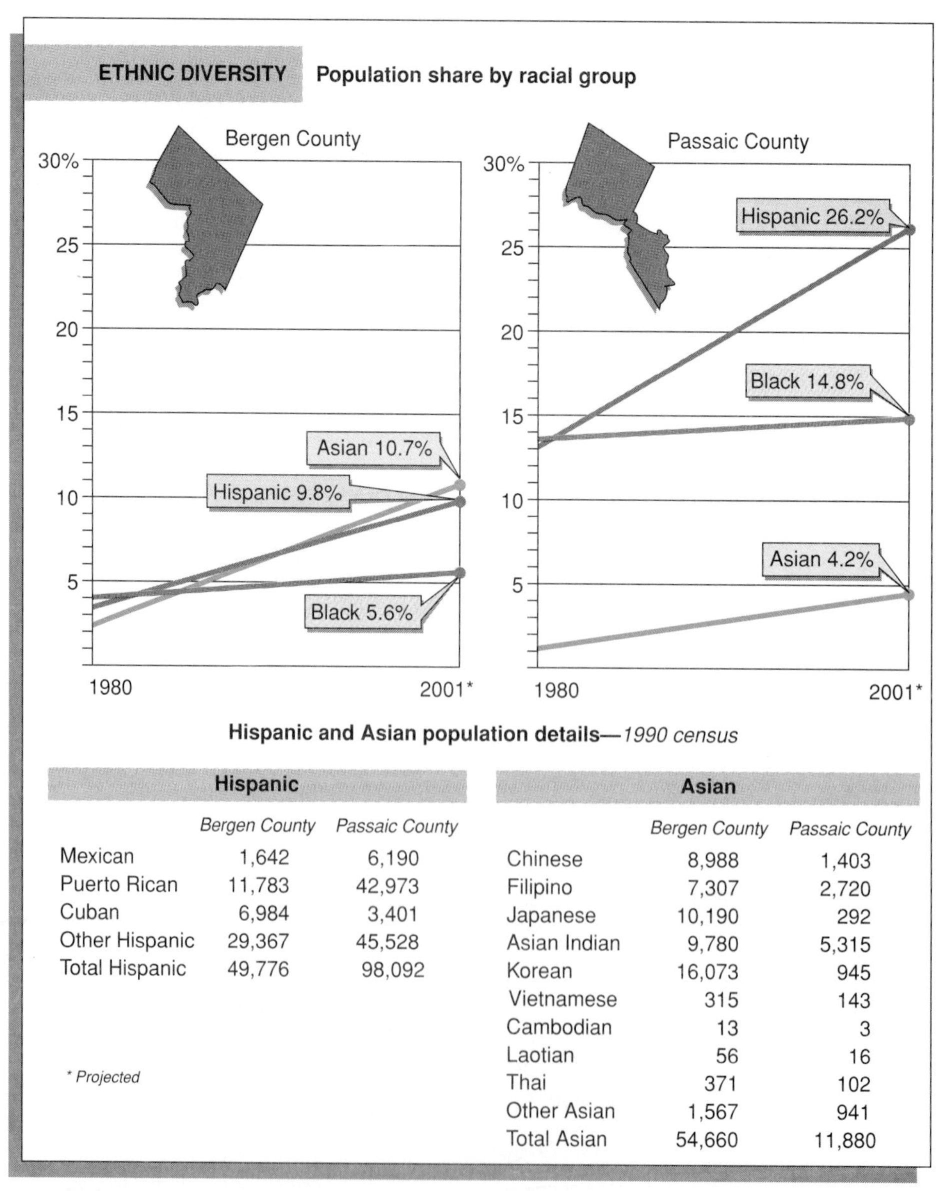

Hispanic	Bergen County	Passaic County
Mexican	1,642	6,190
Puerto Rican	11,783	42,973
Cuban	6,984	3,401
Other Hispanic	29,367	45,528
Total Hispanic	49,776	98,092

Asian	Bergen County	Passaic County
Chinese	8,988	1,403
Filipino	7,307	2,720
Japanese	10,190	292
Asian Indian	9,780	5,315
Korean	16,073	945
Vietnamese	315	143
Cambodian	13	3
Laotian	56	16
Thai	371	102
Other Asian	1,567	941
Total Asian	54,660	11,880

** Projected*

Figure 14.3

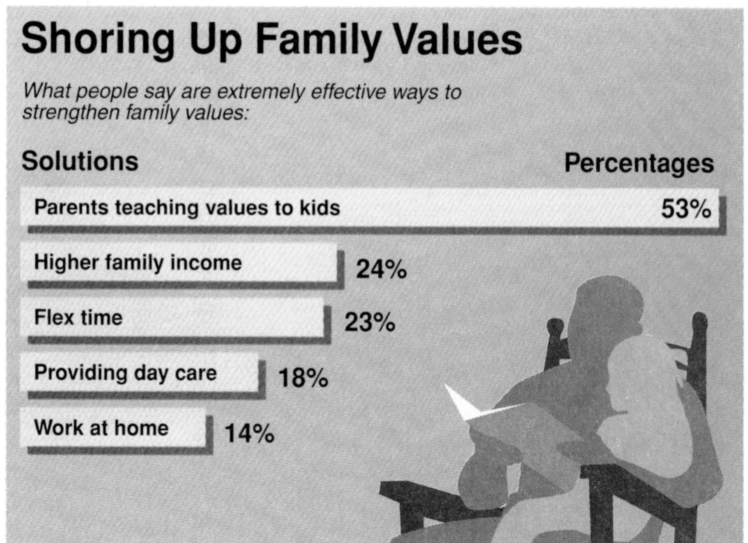

Figure 14.4

Bar graphs enable speakers to compare and/or contrast two or more items or groups.

The **bar graph,** like the line graph, is useful for comparing or contrasting two or more items or groups. Figure 14.4 is a bar graph that shows opinions on the strengthening of family values.

Figure 14.5 is another color-coded bar graph, this one used in a speech on telecommuters (a term meaning employees who work outside of the company office) to show the growth in the number of people who work in their own homes.

By referring to each bar of the graph the speaker made his case that there has been and probably will continue to be a steady increase in the number of people who

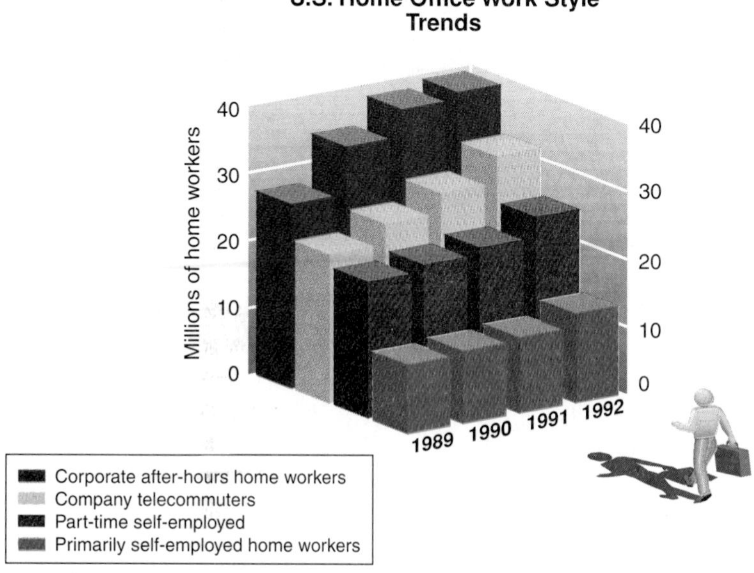

Figure 14.5

When color coded, bar graphs facilitate comprehension.

Figure 14.6

Bar graphs can show growth over time.

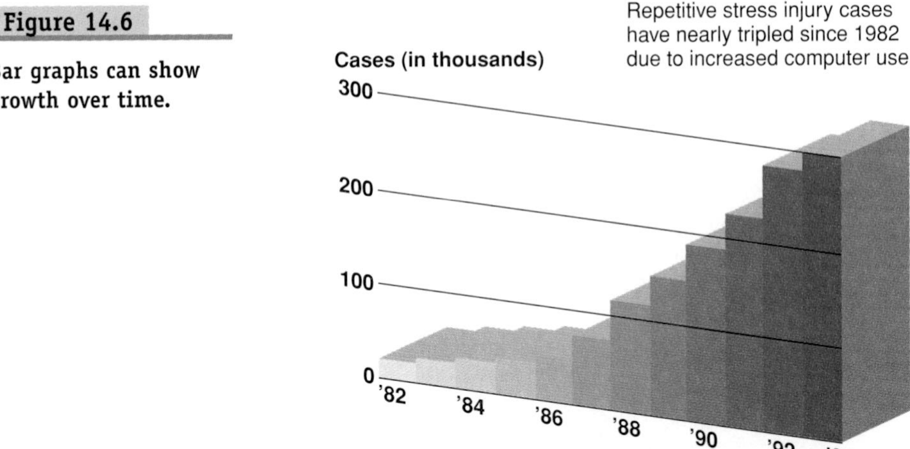

work at home. "In total," the speaker noted, referring to the graph, "39 million Americans or 31.4 percent of the adult work force labor in a home office at least part time. The largest segment, 12.1 million, consists mainly of the self-employed."

Similarly, the bar graph in Figure 14.6 was used by a speaker advocating that stricter measures be taken to prevent repetitive stress injuries. The graph dramatically illustrates the rise in repetitive stress injuries due to increased computer use.

Bar graphs can be either horizontal or vertical. But even while varying in length, the bars should be kept the same width. When prepared properly the bar graph is usually easy for the uninitiated to read and interpret. While speakers could transmit the statistical information contained in bar graphs verbally, referring to the bar graphs helps make those data more meaningful and dramatic for receivers.

In contrast to line and bar graphs, **pie graphs** are good for illustrating either percentages of a whole or distribution patterns. Also referred to as circle graphs, pie graphs indicate and dramatize the size of a subject's parts relative to each other and to the whole. Ideally, for purposes of clarity, pie graphs should contain from two to five "slices" or divisions, and should be clearly labeled. Pie graphs are the simplest way of graphically representing percentages available to a speaker. Figure 14.7 shows a pie graph used by a speaker discussing the types of radio stations His-

Figure 14.7

Simple pie graphs speed comprehension.

Hispanics 12 years old and up listen to radio an average 25 hours 15 minutes a week – more than the U.S. average of 22 hours. Types of stations Hispanics listen to:

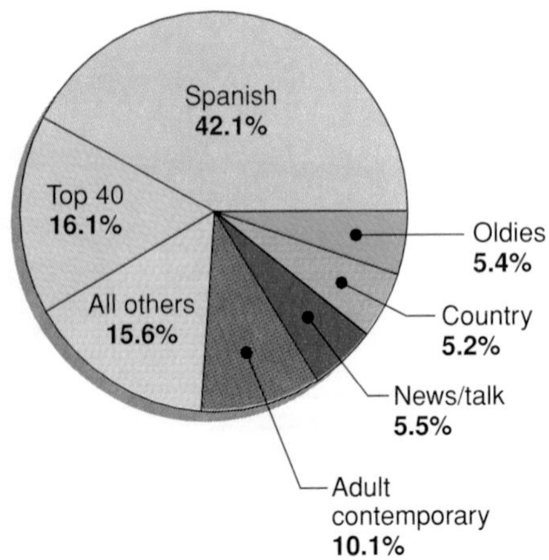

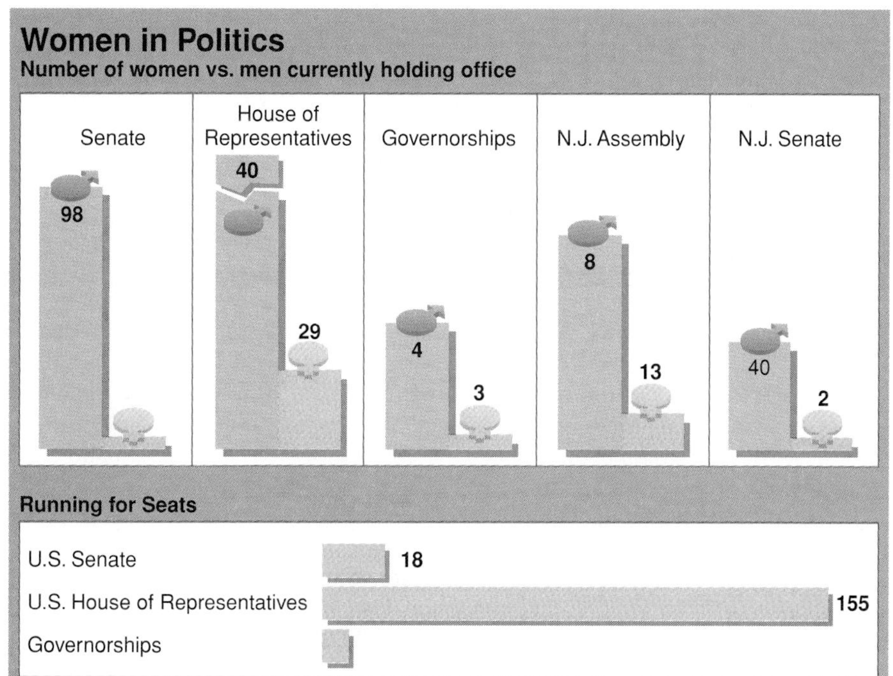

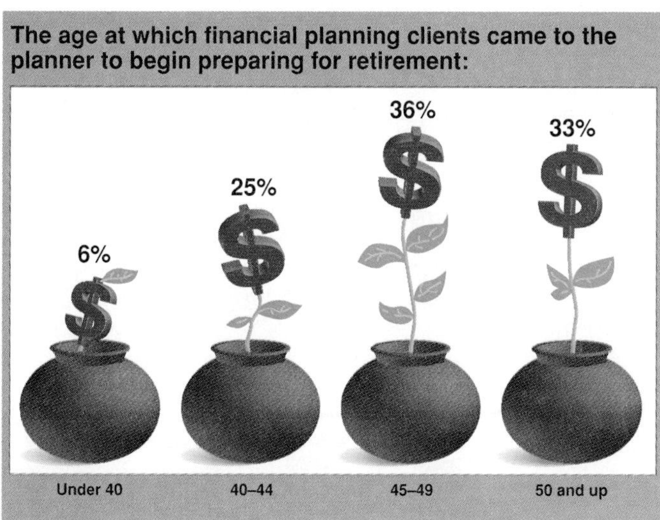

Figure 14.8

Pictographs are less formal and add interest.

panics listen to. Notice that the graph contains seven main divisions. Any more cuts in the pie would have made the graph too cluttered.

Pictographs include pictorial representations of the graph's subject. For example, the graphs in Figure 14.8, describing the number of women in politics compared to men and when people consult financial planners, appear somewhat less formal than bar graphs and thus may be even more interesting for receivers.

Whatever types of graphs you use, keep in mind the following guidelines.

- Keep the graph as simple as possible. Graph overload—too many graphs or too much information on a single graph—contributes to information overload and can overwhelm receivers.

- Help receivers with the interpretation process. Don't assume they will read the graph the way you expect them to read it.
- Make sure the graph is large enough for the audience to see everything written on it. Poor graph visibility decreases speaker intelligibility. Clear graphs facilitate clear speech.

SPEAKING of CRITICAL THINKING

Evaluating What You See

Consider this: Is there more to the graph in Figure 14.9 displaying the average scores of four English classes on an achievement test than meets the eye?[15]

While the graph pictured in Figure 14.10 shows the same information as the previous graph, why are we led to perceive the results differently? Why does showing the bars full length instead of cut short as in Figure 14.9 change our impression of the information?[16]

Speakers who use visual aids can derive a lesson from these examples. A speaker should never present information in such a way that it seems to mean one thing but on closer inspection is determined to mean something else.

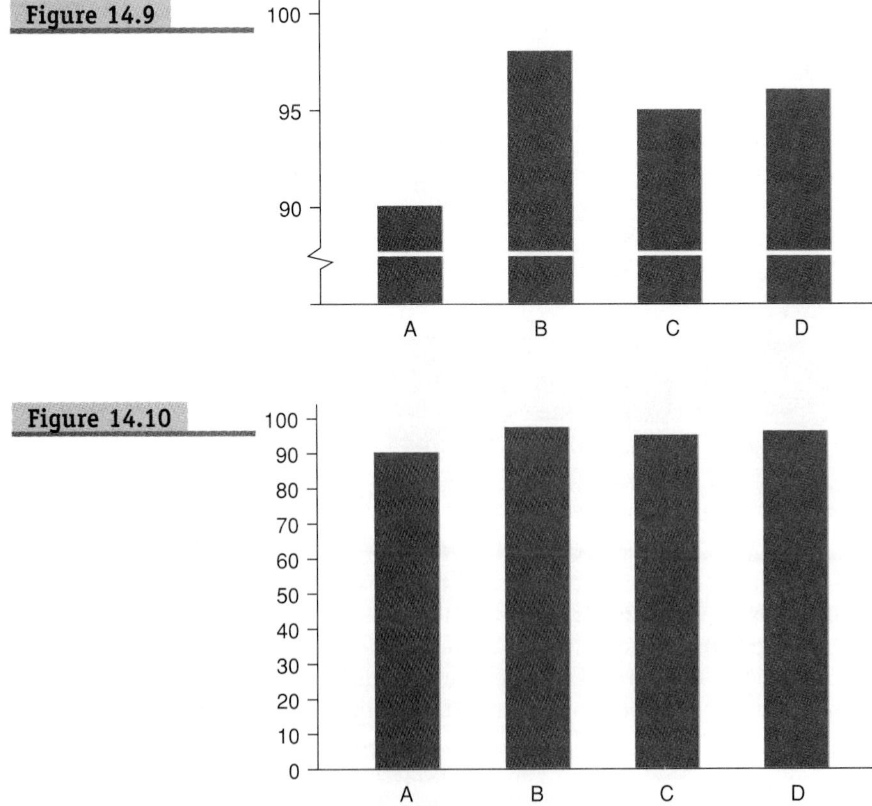

Figure 14.9

Figure 14.10

Vanilla
25.2%
Chocolate
8.8%
Neapolitan
6.1%
Strawberry
5.1%
Peach
4.5%
Top-selling flavors
Cookie Dough
Apple
Cheesecake
Brownie
Caramel combinations
Fast-growing flavors
Share of ice cream sales (in dollar terms)
Recently introduced flavors whose sales grew most

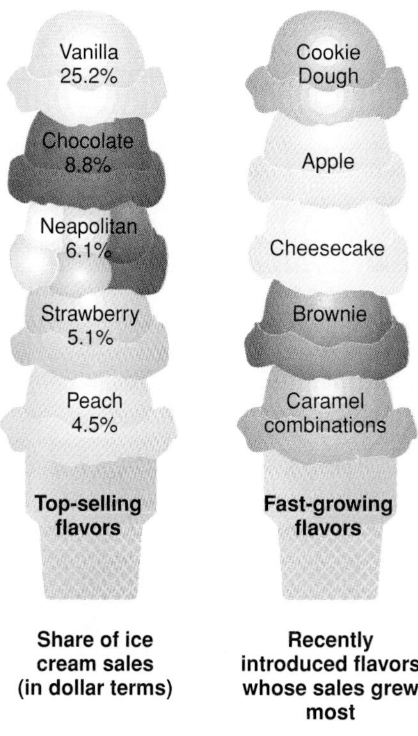

Figure 14.11

The word chart is the most commonly used chart.

Charts, Drawings, and Maps

Speakers use **charts** to help them compress or summarize large amounts of information. By enabling listeners to organize their own thoughts and follow your speech's progress, charts also simplify note taking and facilitate retention. The most commonly used is a word chart like the one pictured in Figure 14.11.

To vivify the information in a chart and give it more eye appeal, the speaker can use a drawing that enhances key words, as shown in Figure 14.12.

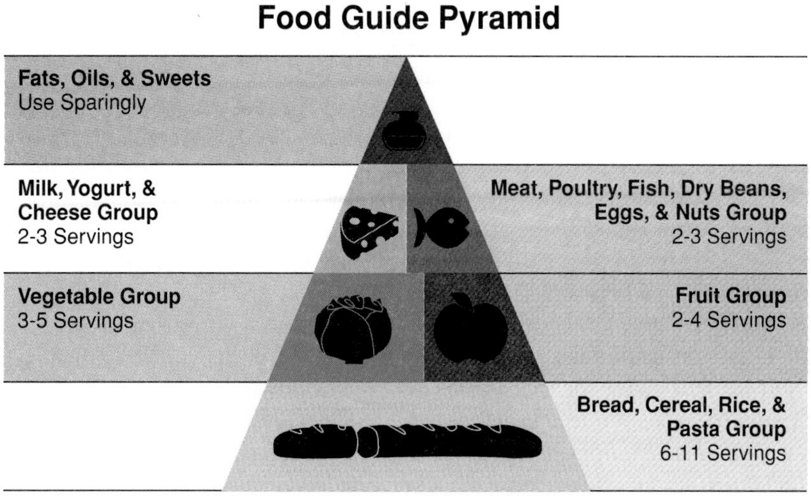

Food Guide Pyramid
Fats, Oils, & Sweets
Use Sparingly
Milk, Yogurt, &
Cheese Group
2-3 Servings
Meat, Poultry, Fish, Dry Beans,
Eggs, & Nuts Group
2-3 Servings
Vegetable Group
3-5 Servings
Fruit Group
2-4 Servings
Bread, Cereal, Rice, &
Pasta Group
6-11 Servings

Figure 14.12

Drawings or sketches enhance the meaning of key words.

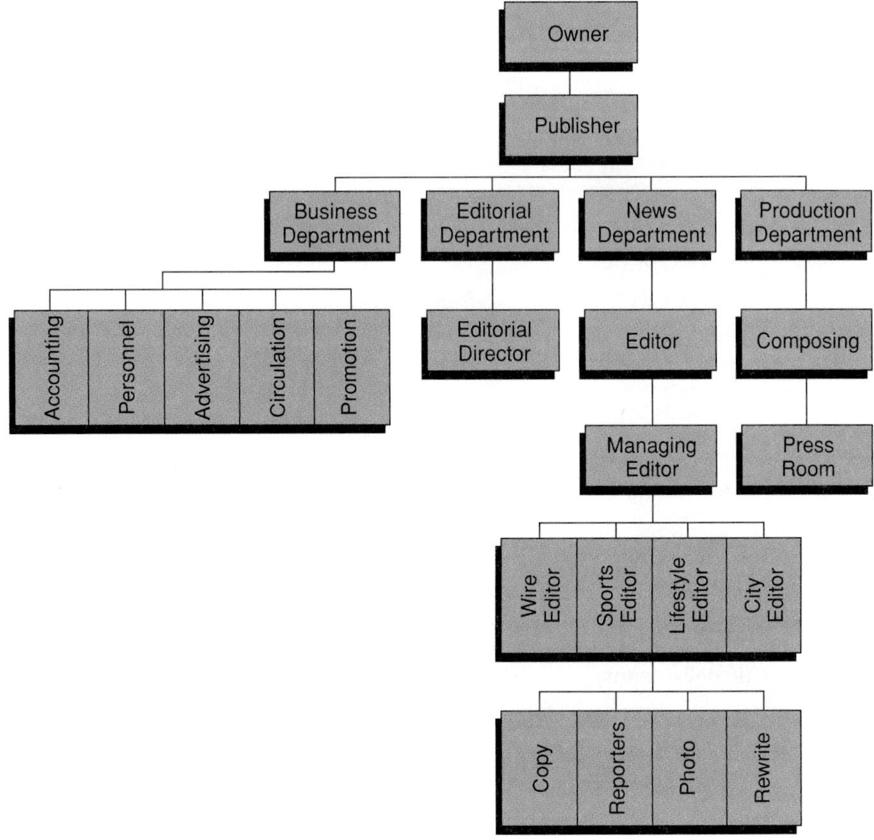

Figure 14.13

Organizational charts reveal chains of command.

The chart is also particularly useful for speakers who want to discuss a process, an organization schema, channels of communication, or chains of command as Figure 14.13 exemplifies. Most commonly displayed on a flipchart, a poster, or an overhead projector, charts are versatile and adaptable speech aids.

Like charts, **drawings and maps** can also be customized by the speaker to help him or her illustrate specific speech points. Drawings and maps help translate complex information into a visual format that receivers usually grasp more readily. A speaker who sought to compare and contrast different swim strokes used the drawing depicted in Figure 14.14 to facilitate her task. This visual made it easier for the speaker to refer to and explain each swimmer's arm and leg movements in turn. Initially, only that portion of the drawing the speaker was referring to was visible to the audience; remaining sections were covered until mentioned by the speaker.

The drawings in Figure 14.15 enabled the speaker to accurately describe the differences between four kinds of broken bones: simple fractures, compound fractures, complete fractures, and incomplete fractures, just as the drawing in Figure 14.16 on page 308 made it easier for the speaker to explain how rabies spreads.

Maps also make versatile visual aids. One speaker used the map in Figure 14.17 on page 308 as visual support when delivering a speech on tornadoes. As you can see, the U.S. Plains states, which consume a key portion of the visual aid, are a prime tornado target.

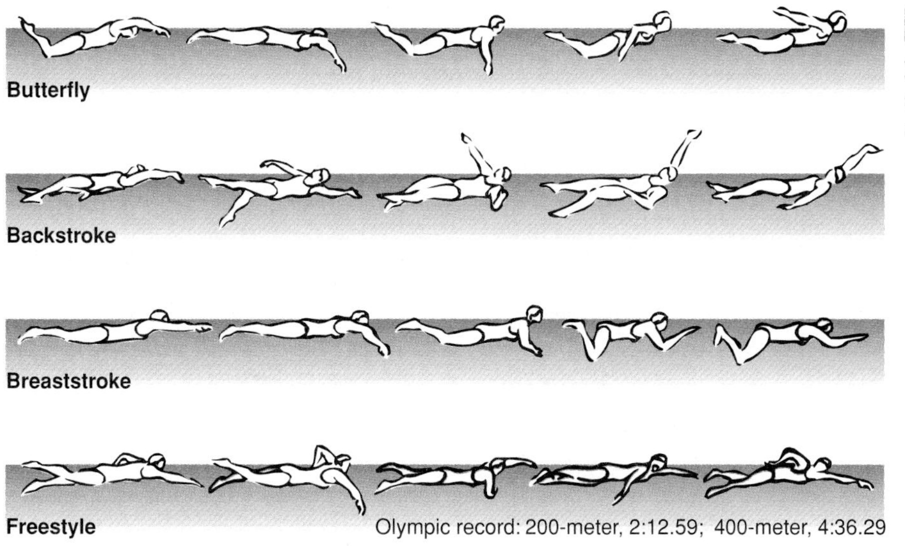

Figure 14.14

Drawings facilitate the sharing of key message aspects.

Although you do not need to be an artist, drawings and maps should be prepared in advance, not produced on the spur of the moment. Attempting to generate them while your audience is watching can consume valuable speaking time, cause audience members to lose patience with you, produce art that is less than suitable for use, and obscure rather than clarify the points you hope to convey.

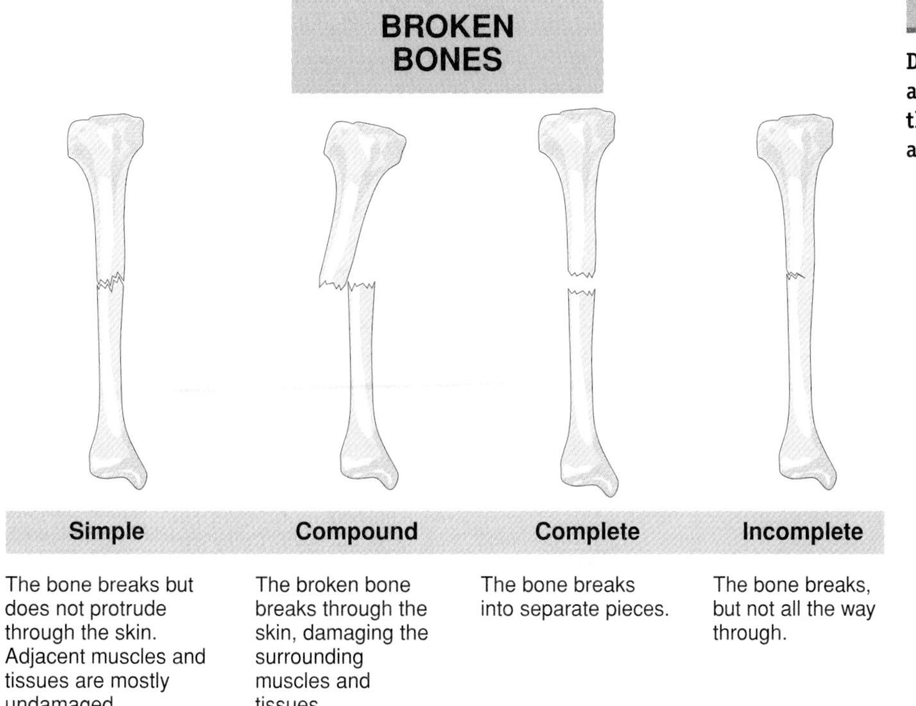

Figure 14.15

Drawings can help the audience to understand the technical points of a speaker's message.

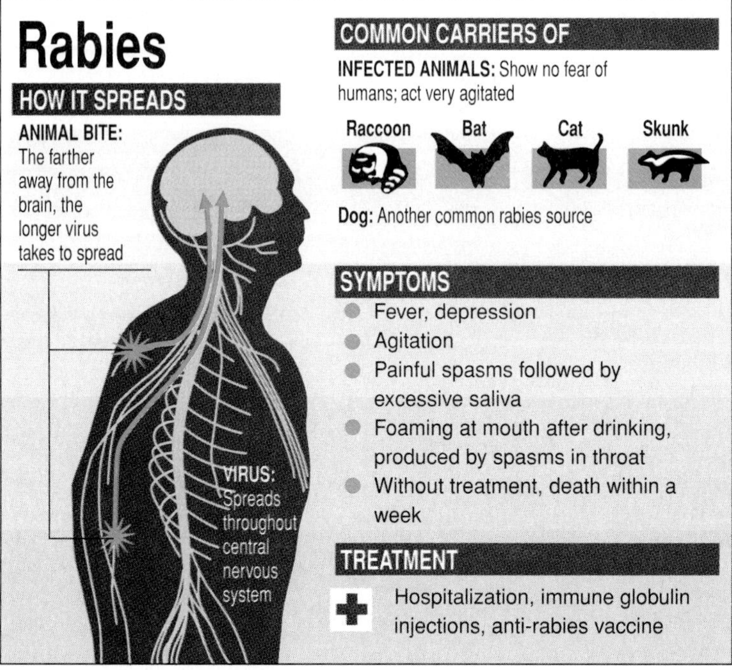

Figure 14.16

Drawings can relate complex ideas.

Whether you make your own drawings and maps, have someone make them for you, or use some that were published previously, the feature you are going to discuss should be easy to see.

Slides, Videotapes, and Overhead Transparencies

Requiring more preparation time and the use of special equipment, **slides, videotapes,** and **overhead transparencies,** are used extensively in business and professional settings. Each of these visual aids can help make a speech more dynamic, involving, and exciting for receivers. Because they allow a speaker to custom design more sophisti-

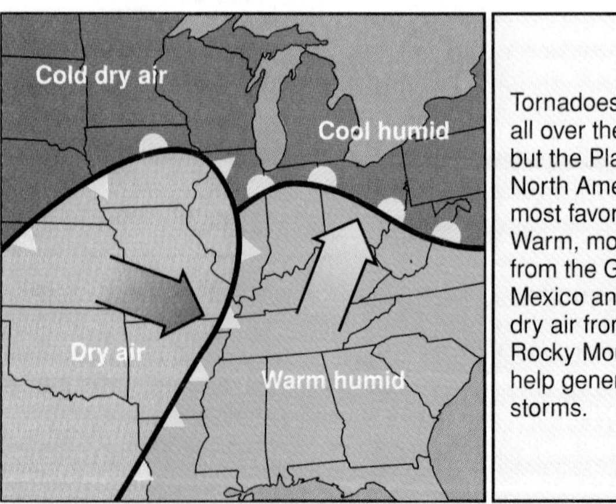

Figure 14.17

Maps can show movement as well as location.

cated examples of visual support, they can be extremely effective tools to use with today's media-wise audiences.

Though these visual aids do require that speakers familiarize themselves with more complicated equipment and usually necessitate more money for preparation and more time for rehearsal and set-up, the vividness and reinforcement these visuals provide is difficult to beat. Still, they should not be used unless the presenter or an assistant is well versed in their use and adept at coordinating the presentation with the showing of the visuals.

Computer-Generated Graphics

Because they are professional looking, easy to create, and easy to enlarge or convert to transparencies for presentation, **computer-generated graphics** can add contemporary flair, a sense of real drama, professionalism, and credibility to a speech.[17] When produced by a computer, graphics are usually crisper, clearer, more readable, and more visually appealing than those produced freehand.

Speakers can use computer-generated graphics to enhance the environment (hanging a welcoming banner or sign) or to supplement the content of their speech (computer-generated graphics can be used as transparencies, slides, charts, graphs, or drawings and can be integrated at relevant points in a presentation). Like desktop publishing, "desktop speaking" is taking off. While you do need to know how to operate a computer and a graphics program (or have access to someone who has these skills), you do not have to have artistic talent to create the visuals themselves. With the advent of computer graphics, technology is helping transform ordinary presentations into extraordinary speechmaking events. Figure 14.18 is an example of a successful computer-generated graphic.

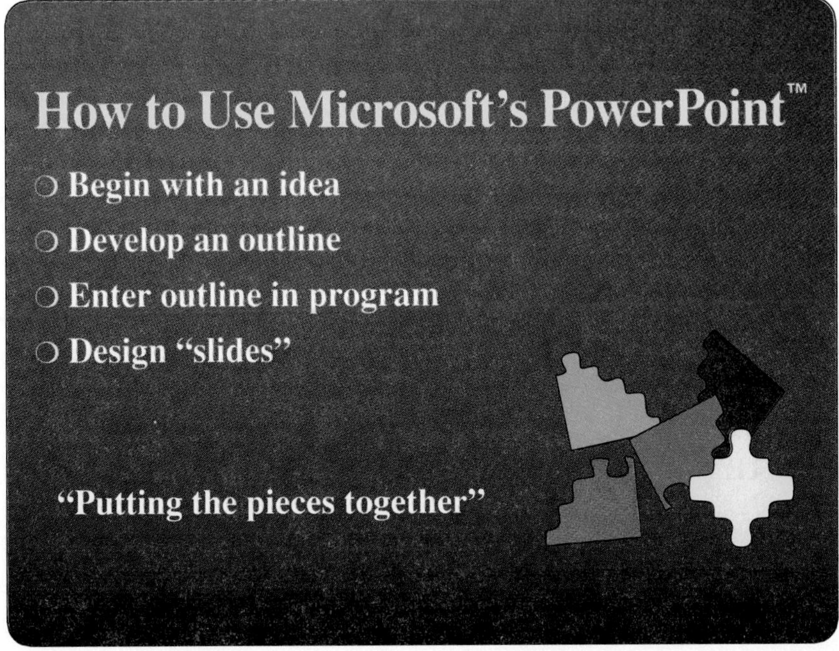

Figure 14.18

Through the use of new technology, a speaker can transform a presentation into an electronic screen show.

Electronic Presentations

With the widespread use of personal computers, LCD projectors, and presentation software such as PowerPoint, Persuasion, Harvard Graphics, Word Perfect Presentation, and Adobe Director, it is now possible to deliver speeches that are more like electronic screen shows. The portability of electronic visuals allows multiple visuals to be contained on a single diskette while enabling the speaker to instantly revise or change visuals. In addition, with electronics the speaker can change from one visual to the next more quickly and with ease.

Electronic presentations enable you to make your presentation in either a linear or a nonlinear fashion. A number of presentation graphic software programs enable you to jump to or insert other visuals during an electronic presentation. For example, with Lotus Freelance Graphics for Windows you can create hyperbuttons that allow you to jump to any specified visual in your electronic screen show presentation. Hyperbuttons enable you to plan a series of presentation options in anticipation of or in response to different reactions from your audience.

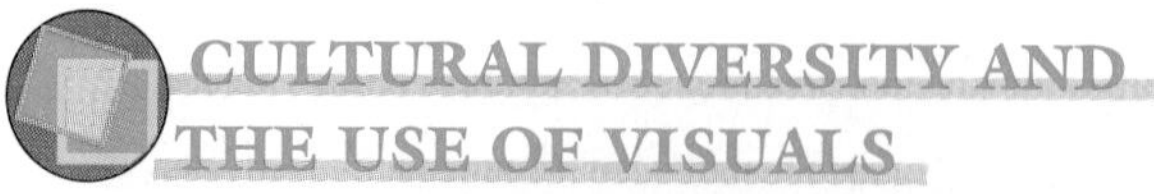

CULTURAL DIVERSITY AND THE USE OF VISUALS

VISUAL AIDS ARE DESIGNED TO FACILITATE the sharing of meaning between speaker and receivers. When joined together with the speaker's words, the visual aid becomes an integral part of the package of symbols used to convey the speaker's message. What speakers and creators of visual resources need to keep in

Considering Diversity

Visuality

In the cartoon in Figure 14.19, male advertising executives are looking at an advertising visual that "tested well on women." Though humorous, the cartoon hints at a more serious question: Are there some visuals that would be more appropriate for speakers to use with men than with women or vice versa? Should a speaker adjust the visuals he or she uses depending on the sexual composition of his or her audience? Factors such as sex, age, ethnic group, or race can also influence the selection and use of visuals by a speaker.

Next, consider this textbook as well as others you are using this semester. To what extent do you think factors like those mentioned above influenced the selection of visuals used to support textual content?

Figure 14.19

"We've checked, and it's fine with women."

mind, however, is that visuals, like words and nonverbal cues, will be interpreted by others based on their own cultures and life experiences.

As a result of our sharing the words of persons different from us and processing the visuals they supply to augment those words, we may in time widen our perceptual base of understanding and learn to see as they do. As Johnetta B. Cole notes in *Conversations:*

> Meeting the world is not just a joyride and source of personal insight and enlightenment. As we reach out and acquaint ourselves with the world, we will not only think globally but, hopefully, feel globally as well. Thinking globally will instill in us the capacity for empathy—that honest concern for others that sees the connections between the yearning for freedom and equality in an East German in Leipzig, a South African in Johannesburg, and an African American in Atlanta; we see the ties that bind a physician in a small African village, a nurse in the hills above

> Port-au-Prince, and a doctor in rural Mississippi. As it increasingly registers that we are all of the same human species, we will come to know that a homeless child in Palestine is no less deserving of our prayers and concern than a homeless child in Harlem.[18]

By noting the differences in the ways people from other cultures use visual aids to accomplish their speechmaking goals, we can learn more about how they seek to accomplish their objectives in general. Are they subtle and abstract or literal and direct?

Visuals can also be used to help address language differences. Imagine having to listen to a presentation that is not in your native language. Simple visuals can help increase both your understanding and your comfort level.[19]

ATTAINING THE VISUAL ADVANTAGE: HOW TO GET THE MOST FROM YOUR VISUAL AIDS

ONE SIGNER of the Declaration of Independence, John Hancock, envisioned his signature as a potent visual message to the King of England; thus Hancock made sure to sign his name large enough to be "seen by the King of England without his glasses." Like Hancock, you want to ensure that your visuals are large enough, clear enough, and dramatic enough to be attended to by audience members and have the impact you desire. As we see, if you follow specific guidelines, you can prepare and use visual materials that enhance the informative and persuasive power of your presentations. As with any other skill, however, mastering how to select, design, integrate, and use visuals takes patience, persistence, and practice. So before deciding whether to use a visual, ask and answer these four questions:

Can the point I am making be strengthened by a visual aid?

Can a visual make it easier for the members of my audience to understand and accept what I am saying?

Will a visual aid add credibility to my ideas and to me?

Might anyone in my audience find the visuals I am thinking of using inappropriate or distracting?

Guidelines for Preparing Visuals

In order to use a visual, you have to choose a visual, a choice that may not be as simple as you'd expect. Three key criteria should be used to weigh the potential power of a visual:

Is it worth its cost?
Will the amount of time and effort you expend preparing the visual pay off in audience interest and response? Your goal is to use visual aids that are cost effective.

Does it talk to receivers?

Will the visual facilitate your task by saving you words? Will your listeners be able to understand and relate to the visual? Your goal is to use visual aids that speak directly to the experiences of your receivers.

Are you skilled enough and equipped to use it effectively?

Is equipment on site? Will you have the opportunity to practice with the equipment? While your goal is to increase your skill at working with equipment, having unrealistic expectations regarding the time it will take you to master using a piece of equipment could eat into valuable speech rehearsal time. Remember, using visuals well takes practice too.

When selecting a visual, always keep the objectives of your speech uppermost in your mind, and limit each visual to one main point. Data dumping, or cluttering a visual with too much information, should be avoided; simplicity should lead the way. Remember, every visual you choose to use should be:

Clear and concise.
Large and legible.
Simple and straightforward.

It is important that the typefaces you use in your visuals be consistent because too much typeface variety increases distractability. Thus:

DO	*DON'T*
Print in big block letters.	Write in cursive.
Use as few words as possible.	Dump data.
Check all equipment.	Assume equipment will be in working order.
Rehearse with your visuals.	Let your unfamiliarity with visual usage impede receiver reception.

It is equally important that visuals be succinct rather than verbose. Don Keough of the Coca-Cola Company said it best: "Some pictures may be worth a thousand words, but a picture of a thousand words isn't worth much."[20]

When possible, try to use visuals in color. Audiences respond to color and increasingly expect speakers to use color in their presentations. Research finds that color enhances readership, receptivity, and retention.[21] It enhances content by helping your message stand out. Color can also be used to convey mood. For example, red is frequently used to symbolize anger, energy, danger, or a crisis, and can be used to excite or agitate receivers, while blue is usually more calming, and green commonly signifies growth.[22]

The Dos and Don'ts of Using Visuals

Following simple guidelines will also facilitate your use of visuals during your presentation. Visuals, like speeches, need to be introduced, presented, interpreted, and concluded. Visuals that are left to audience members to detect and decode die without fulfilling a purpose. Visuals can add strength to your presentation but won't if you take them for granted, fail to explain them, or keep them in sight when you are finished referring to them.

Bearing in mind these dos and don'ts will keep you and your visuals on the right track:

DO	*DON'T*
Be sure your visuals are in place before starting.	Rely on others to position visuals.
Present and explain each visual.	Take receiving skills of listeners for granted.
Stand to one side of the visual and talk to the audience, making sure everyone can see the visual.	Rely on receivers to provide their own interpretations.
Keep physical possession and control of your visuals.	Maintain eye contact with your visual instead of with your receivers.
Put the visual away when you are finished referring to it; you take center stage.	Pass visuals around the room.
	Keep the visual before the audience after using it or it will upstage you.

Following these "dos and don'ts" will enable your visuals to reinforce your verbal message. Remember, visuals do not replace speakers. Visuals are there to help speakers stimulate listener interest and understanding. Visuals don't make decisions regarding a speaker's success; listeners do.

SUMMARY

THE CAREFUL INTEGRATION of visual aids into a speech makes a significant difference in the way an audience responds to a speaker. By enabling a speaker to communicate his or her ideas with greater clarity and impact, visual aids enhance the speaker's effectiveness.

Visual aids serve five key functions: they help increase listener understanding; they enhance memory and recall; they facilitate message organization; they help the speaker control audience attention and interest; and they increase the personal persuasiveness of the speaker and his or her message.

The speaker has a variety of visual aids from which to choose. The visuals a speaker employs can be animate or inanimate, two or three dimensional, and range from people, models, and objects to photographs, graphs, charts, drawings, slides, videotapes, computer-generated materials, and electronic presentations.

By taking the time to see that the visuals they use are adapted to the audience, setting, and subject, speakers are better able to attain a real visual advantage.

THE SPEAKER'S STAND

Select a speech from *Vital Speeches of the Day* and describe how one or more visual aids could be used to clarify or amplify the speaker's message.

Next, prepare a three- to five-minute presentation on a subject approved by your instructor and in which you use at least two visual aids to support your verbal content. Be creative in selecting and preparing your visuals and be sure to follow the guidlines stressed in this chapter.

STUDENT FOCUS GROUP REPORT

Now that you have had the opportunity to explore the ways visual aids are used by speechmakers, in a group of five to seven students, answer the following questions. As you do, remember that this is your opportunity to discuss what you have learned about the use of visual aids and to speculate on how you can put this knowledge to work in future presentations you deliver.

1. What are the main challenges you will face or have faced as you seek to (or sought to) integrate visual aids into your speechmaking?
2. What kinds of information more readily lend themselves to visual depiction? What kinds of information appear to resist visual depiction?
3. Are there any kinds of visual aids that you think speakers should refrain from using? Explain.
4. By what criteria should speakers and their audiences judge visual aids?
5. What kinds of visual aids do you find most effective?
6. Summarize the most significant information you have learned about visual aids.
7. Reexamine the case study at the beginning of this chapter. In what ways—if any—would you revise any of your responses to the questions?

Select a team member to report your conclusions to the class.

Chapter Fifteen

Speaking to Inform

After reading this chapter, you should be able to:

- Discuss the functions of informative speaking.
- Compare and contrast the following informative speeches: a speech about objects; a speech about events/people; a speech about processes/procedures; a speech about ideas/concepts.
- List and explain the principles for developing an effective informative speech.
- Demonstrate your ability to develop a message that creates information hunger in your receivers.
- Demonstrate your ability to develop a message that relates your ideas directly to your receivers.
- Demonstrate your ability to develop a message that exhibits clarity, simplicity, and concreteness.
- Design and deliver an informative speech.

CASE STUDY

The Power of Information

Raul had been on the job for about a year. He had attended all the company orientation and training sessions and had finally settled down to the day-to-day routine of his job as a group manager. Every morning Raul diligently checked his E-mail, which this morning included a series of bombshells from the vice president for human resources:

Bombshell 1: Raul's division was going to be "rightsized."

Bombshell 2: A "rightsizing" task force had been formed.

Bombshell 3: Every group manager was being asked to prepare and deliver a seven-minute presentation to that task force that defined the nature of the person's responsibilities, revealed his or her thoughts about the organizational needs being served by his or her specific job, and demonstrated the significance that his or her continuation and departure would have for the company.

Reality stared Raul in the face. The amount of information that he was able to provide the "rightsizing" task force about the nature of his job and its effect on the organization as a whole might well determine whether he would be retained.

Raul asked himself an important question: How can I best explain to the task force what it is that I do? I need to help them understand how my job fits into the company's mission so that they fully realize and comprehend my value here, he reasoned.

- How would you suggest Raul organize the information he provides the task force members?
- What can he do to arouse and maintain the interest and attention of his receivers?
- Which speechmaking techniques can he use to help set him apart from other presenters who will appear before the task force?

HOW DO WE COME to know what we know? Where does all the information we possess come from? Actually, we derive a large percentage of what we know from other people who are willing to share their knowledge with us. It is the sharing of knowledge, the transfer of information, that helps us better understand our world and our place in it. The dissemination of accurate information enables us to interpret experience, act on it, and make reasonably valid decisions.

It is only because others are willing to teach us what they know that we are able to live better and grow. To be sure, we all benefit from the willingness of others to add to our information storehouses. We benefit from the coach who instructs us in a sport and from the physician who explains an illness to us. We learn from the teacher who lectures us in class and from the boss who defines a company's objectives. If people are skilled in expressing the knowledge they possess, they can make a positive difference in our lives. Without such people, we might wander around in a state of confusion rather than a state of clarity; we would be continually frustrated rather than enlightened.

Consequently, being able to convey information to others is one of the most useful skills you can acquire. Once you have that skill, you, too, will be equipped to use your knowledge to increase someone else's understanding. You will be in a position to use your knowledge to enable others to learn what they need to know, what you think they would benefit from knowing, or what they simply desire to know.

It has been said that we live in the age of information. Even as you read this page, the sum of human knowledge is growing at an unprecedented rate. We have more to tell others today than ever before in our history, and tomorrow there will be even more information to impart. Are you ready to do your share so others who listen to you can add to their knowledge and enhance their understanding? Are you ready to shape, assemble, and deliver what you know in forms others will be able to comprehend easily? That's what this chapter prepares you to do—to share information you have with people who lack it but need it, or who possess it but don't fully understand it.

ADDRESSING DIVERSITY: SPEAKING OF DIFFERENCES

AS YOU PROCEED THROUGH this chapter, you will discover why the sharing of knowledge is effective if it is planned, adapted to the diverse backgrounds of receivers, and related to the needs and interests they possess. Because the old maxim "listen and learn" is as valid today as it was in days past, the main objective of this chapter is to give you an opportunity to familiarize yourself with a prime means of sharing what you know with others—the informative speech. As we discuss this topic, we also address the speaker's need to recognize diversity and adapt to difference.

In the speech that follows, student Andi Lane addresses a diversity issue when she shares her understanding of what it means to be hearing impaired. Notice how she uses her own experiences as a starting point.

Information can be shared in diverse ways with diverse audiences. For the hearing impaired, signing is a crucial means of sharing information.

WHAT IT MEANS TO BE DEAF

At the beginning of this year I moved into an apartment. When I arrived at my new place, my roommate was there to greet me, and she saw my stereo. She got really excited, and she said, "Great you have a stereo for us to listen to." I laughed and told her that was a pretty funny joke, as I turned and ran up the stairs. But Sarah never knew I said that. You see, Sarah is profoundly deaf and relies upon lip reading as her primary source of communication. Living with Sarah has taught me many things, but I've also become more aware of the problems which the deaf and hearing impaired face on a daily basis. My interest in the subject has led me to take a course on basic sign language and communication with the hearing impaired.

Beginning with this personal anecdote is a fine way to start. The speaker builds credibility and audience interest simultaneously.

Today I'd like to talk to you about three aspects of being hearing impaired: the deaf culture, communication with the deaf, and acceptance of the deaf.

The speaker reveals her subject and previews the content.

"What exactly is deaf culture?" you might ask. This is a legitimate question, since even those who are deaf and involved in the deaf culture have a difficult time explaining it. In his book, *Sign Language and the Deaf Community,* William Stokes says that there are several characteristics which can help us define the deaf culture. The deaf culture is closed and limited to only those who are deaf. Members have a common language which they share and common beliefs about others who are deaf and also those who are hearing. They also have shared goals; one of their primary goals is a goal of acceptance—acceptance in employment, politics, and every aspect of life.

The speaker moves into the first main point of her speech. She defines deaf culture for receivers; because she has only limited experience with the subject, the use of an authoritative source enhances her credibility.

It's also interesting to compare the hearing world to the deaf culture. In deaf culture there's less emphasis on personal space; people have to be close together in order to read each other's signs. There's also less importance placed on time. People are not always punctual; there's a more relaxed feeling in the deaf culture.

Eye contact is lengthy, necessary, and polite in the deaf culture. Also when you do introductions—we usually greet each other; we meet each other; we exchange first names. In the deaf culture, you exchange first names, last names, and where you attended school.

And my final point, the difference between the hearing world and the deaf culture, is that the hearing world is more reserved where the deaf culture is more tactile. An illustration of this is that in the hearing world we shake hands. In the deaf culture—usually they exchange hugs. These are just some of the more important differences that were pointed out by Dr. Kenya Taylor, who is an audiologist.

The speaker introduces her second main point and uses comparison and contrast to help clarify the differences in communication among members of the deaf and hearing cultures for audience members. The use of specific examples adds understandability and interest.

Daily life is, of course, very different for those who have a hearing problem. Communication is the main distinguishing factor. Sign language is usually taught to children at a very early age to provide them with a sense of vocabulary—a way to communicate their thoughts and ideas.

There are many different types of sign language, and these vary from area to area much as spoken language does, much like a dialect. The two most common types are signed English and the American sign language. Sign language, basic sign, is usually taught to beginners and follows the main sentence structure as spoken English does. ASL is used by those who are hearing impaired. It's a shortened, more abbreviated form. While the same signs are used, it's the format which differs according to Greenburg in his book, *Endless Sign.*

The speaker continues her discussion of the second main point by explaining the nature of sign language. Again she is careful to identify the source of her information.

As mentioned before, children are usually taught sign language at a very early age. It is later that they acquire lip reading or speech skills, if they acquire them at all. Most deaf people can lip read to some extent. Now, of course, this presents special problems to the person. They must always be alert and aware of what's going on. And imagine being in a dimly lit room or trying to talk to a person who has a

The speaker's use of specific instances is designed to clarify the problems faced by the hearing impaired and the hearing as they attempt to communicate with each other.

habit of looking away. Also, when you are talking to a deaf person they can't hear sarcasm in your voice; you need to say what you mean.

The speaker draws on her personal experiences to make a point. Notice how doing this adds credibility to her presentation.

Nonverbals are important; they pick up information from any way that they can get it. It's funny, because now I have a habit of when I get in my car at night, I flip on the interior light. This is because I'm accustomed to riding with Sarah. Even when she's not in the car, the light's on, because it's impossible to communicate without the interior light on.

The speaker uses a hypothetical illustration or narrative to involve receivers directly, increase their interest, and facilitate their understanding.

Right now, I'm going to paint for you all a hypothetical situation, and I would like for you to put yourself in it. And it's a situation where you will be trying to communicate with a deaf person. Let's say you're at a restaurant; you're working there. It's a real busy place, the most popular place in town. One night a man comes in, alone, and is seated in the back corner, which is dimly lit. You're in a rush, and you go over to him, and you pour his water. And as you're pouring his water, you say: "May I take your order?" And you look up, and he doesn't say anything. First of all, he doesn't know you are addressing him, and second of all, he has no idea what you said. So you repeat yourself, "May I take your order?" And the man says, "I am deaf." But you don't know what that is; you don't know sign language. He speaks, and you can't understand him, and you're about to panic. In this situation, what you don't need to do is panic. You need to remember that the only difference between you and him is that you can hear and he can't. Communication is always possible, even if you have to point at the menu or write notes.

A transition at the start of this paragraph paves the way for the speaker to introduce her final main point.

Which leads me into my final point, the importance of accepting those with hearing problems. The more aware we are of the problems faced by the deaf and the greater our understanding, the less predjudiced we are going to be. The main difference, the only difference, in fact, between us—those who can hear—and people who can't hear is that we hear sounds with our ears, while they hear words and expressions with their eyes. And they feel with their hearts just like we do. We can't measure a person's intelligence by the degree of a hearing loss or the way that they speak. They are our equals.

Notice how the speaker cites an authoritative source prior to offering tips.

I have a few tips from *The Hearing Instruments,* Volume 36, that will help us become more sensitive when we're talking to a deaf person. First of all, you talk in a normal fashion; don't shout at them because they can't hear you anyway. Try to keep your hands away from your mouth, because, of course, if they're trying to read your lips and your hands are over your mouth, they're not going to be able to understand you. Chewing, eating and smoking are considered rude. You want to get the person's attention before you begin to talk to them, and it's perfectly acceptable to lightly touch their arm, wrist—somewhere along there. And finally, make sure that the hearing impaired person is not facing the light. That's something that we probably wouldn't think of. But if they're facing the light, they're not going to be able to concentrate on communication.

The speaker summarizes her message. In addition, by again using personal experiences as well as reviewing what she's learned from them, she gives her speech a sense of closure.

Today I've shared with you some background information about the deaf culture, ways in which deaf people are able to communicate, and the importance of accepting deaf people for who they are. In the short time I've lived with Sarah, I've learned so much. I learned that you don't talk to her when your back is turned or when you're in another room. I've learned that I can scream as loud as I want to in the apartment, and it wouldn't make any difference at all. I can achieve the same end result by just telling her I'm upset. And I've learned that one of my most dear friends has a profound hearing loss, but I still love her.

As Andi Lane's speech coach, answer these questions:

1. Think about the speech's introduction and its conclusion. To what extent, if any, did the introduction succeed in getting your attention? To what extent was the speaker successful in tying her introduction and conclusion together?

2. What means did the speaker use to establish and maintain her credibility? What kinds of information were most useful? most memorable? Which were most effective in building her credibility?

3. Are you now able to understand what it means to be deaf? If so, what did the speaker do to help you internalize such an understanding? If not, what could the speaker have done to promote better understanding?

4. Were the speaker's use of supporting materials effective? How many different kinds of supporting materials did the speaker use? In what ways did they facilitate your understanding? Your emotional involvement?

5. Focus on the speaker's use of transitions. How effectively did the speaker move from one point to the next? To what extent was it easy to identify the speaker's main points?

6. What did the speaker do to help widen receiver appreciation of diversity issues?

7. Finally, what might the speaker change or add to enhance her presentation?

TYPES OF INFORMATIVE SPEAKING

THERE ARE A WIDE VARIETY of topics about which we can share information and develop understanding. We can speak about ideas and objects, about processes and procedures, and about people and events. Though this list is far from exhaustive, the categories on it represent a number of the most common ways speakers package their information for delivery to others.

When speaking about an object, the speaker's goal is to paint an accurate picture of it in the minds of receivers. What techniques might this speaker use to accomplish this goal?

Speaking about Objects

Objects provide speakers with a wide variety of valid subjects on which to speak. Speeches about objects can cover anything tangible—such as a machine (the operation of a dialysis machine); a building, a structure or a place (the design of the White House, the mystery of Stonehenge); or a thing or a phenomenon (the human heart, quicksand, a black hole, a comet, an asteroid). Objects may be animate or inanimate, moving or still, visible to the naked eye or beyond its scope. Whatever the object you choose to focus on, however, your goal remains the same: to paint an accurate, interesting, and informative picture of it.

More examples of objects that could form the basis of an effective informative speech are:

compact disc players
volcanos
the Great Wall of China
the rainforests
the World Bank
the ozone layer
condoms
the Blarney Stone
the Loch Ness monster
dolphins
a Japanese garden

Once you select an object for a topic, your next step is to create a specific purpose that identifies the aspect of the object you will focus on. The following are sample purpose statements for informative speeches about objects:

to inform my audience about Australia's Outback
to inform my audience about the anatomy of the liver
to inform my audience about the design of the pyramids
to inform my audience about prehistoric cave paintings

Speeches on objects lend themselves to chronological, spatial, or topical organizational formats. A chronological design would be most appropriate if you were going to stress how a design or a phenomenon had evolved over time (for example, the formation of the Hawaiian Islands). In contrast, a spatial or physical framework would enable you to discuss one major component of the object at a time, as you might do when discussing the entrance, antechamber, and burial chambers of the Egyptian pyramids. Finally, a topical format would allow you to divide your subject into groups or major categories, as you would be apt to do when speaking about volcanos, focusing first on extinct volcanoes, second on dormant volcanos, and third on active volcanos.

Following is a sample outline for a speech on rainforests that is organized topically.

Specific purpose: To inform my audience about the major purposes served by tropical rainforests.

Central idea: Tropical rainforests help fulfill biological diversity, medicinal, and weather-control functions.

Main points:

I. Tropical rainforests house and comprise one-half to three-quarters of all living species.

II. Tropical rainforests are important sources of medicines.

III. Tropical rainforests help maintain the Earth's weather systems.

The next outline is organized spatially.

Specific purpose: To inform my audience about the design of a motorized skateboard

Central idea: A motorized skateboard includes three main parts (the steering mechanism, the platform, and the motor) that contribute to its effective operation.

Main points:

I. The 0.5 horsepower motor, mounted on the rear, drives the skateboard.

II. The three-foot platform is the central component of the vehicle.

III. The steering mechanism, located at the front of the platform, makes the vehicle both versatile and portable.

If, on the other hand, your specific purpose is to explain the evolution or history of your chosen subject, then you might use a chronological format like the one a student used when speaking about the history of prisons.

Specific purpose: To inform my audience about the history of prisons in America.

Central idea: Although prisons in America originally fulfilled a revenge function, prisons evolved into centers for correction and rehabilitation.

Main points:

I. In colonial America the main purpose of prisons was revenge.

II. At the turn of the 1800s, correction became a goal of prisons.

III. By the 1900s, prisons became centers for rehabilitation.

Whatever the organizational method you choose to use, be sure to adhere to the guidelines, discussed in greater detail in Chapter 9.

Speaking about Events/People

What happened? To whom did it happen? What makes a person remarkable? What makes an event significant? Most of us are intrigued by interesting people and fascinated by compelling events; as such, people and events also make fine informative speech topics.

A speech about an event focuses on something that happens regularly (a holiday, a birthday), or something that happened (Pearl Harbor, the first manned trip to the moon), something that marks our lives (graduations, funerals), or something that left us with a lasting impression (the *Challenger* space shuttle disaster, the assassination of a public figure). The event you discuss might be one you personally witnessed (a political rally), or one you choose to research (the significance of the Declaration of Independence, the importance of the Million Man March). Whatever your topic, your goal is to bring the event to life so your audience can visualize and experience it. The following events skim the surface of potential speech topics:

the Oklahoma City bombing

the Holocaust

the crash of TWA flight 800

the disintegration of the Soviet Union
the Glorious Revolution
the Olympic games
Halloween
Chinese New Year

If instead of telling about an event you tell about the life of a person—someone famous or someone you know personally, someone living or dead, someone admired by or abhorrent to all—your goal is to make that person live in your audience members' minds, to enable them to appreciate the person's unique qualities, and to help them understand the impact the individual has or had. Why is the person worthy of our attention? The following are just a few of the figures who would make interesting informative speech topics:

Enrico Fermi
Clare Boothe Luce
Cochise
Anita Hill
Lee Harvey Oswald
Adolph Eichmann
Nelson Mandela
Eleanor Roosevelt
Charlie Chaplin

For instance, a speech on Adolph Eichmann would become interesting if the speaker used it to explore the mind of a mass murderer. A speech on Charlie Chaplin could develop an understanding of comedic genius, and a speech on Anita Hill could help audiences comprehend the nature of sexual harassment.

Speeches on events and people lend themselves to a variety of organizational approaches; speakers find chronological, topical, and causal patterns especially useful. For example, if your speech is to explain the history of an event or person you would probably choose to use a chronological sequence.

Specific purpose: To inform my audience of major milestones during the presidency of John F. Kennedy.

Central idea: The administration of President John F. Kennedy was marked by four major milestones that affected the course of history.

Main points:

I. First, the inauguration of John F. Kennedy offered the dream of a new Camelot.
II. Then the Bay of Pigs invasion brought the administration into conflict with Cuba.
III. Next, the Cuban Missile Crisis brought the world to the brink of disaster.
IV. Finally, the assassination of John F. Kennedy brought the dream of Camelot to a close.

On the other hand, a topical organization would allow you to approach your subject from a different angle.

Specific purpose: To inform my audience about the life of Martin Luther King, Jr.

Central idea: Martin Luther King, Jr., was a minister, an adherent of passive resistance, and a social activist.

Main points:

I. Martin Luther King, Jr., was a minister whose sermons became famous speeches.

II. King, an adherent of passive resistance, modified Gandhi's concepts to fit the American civil rights movement.

III. King was a social activist who sought to establish equality for all races.

If instead of using a chronological or topical pattern of organization you choose to use a causal order, then you are also in a good position to recount the reasons for an occurrence or outcome.

Specific purpose: To inform my audience why the *Challenger* space shuttle disaster occurred.

Central idea: Ineffective decision making caused the destruction of *Challenger* and its crew.

Main points:

I. There were two major causes for the poor decision making that precipitated the *Challenger* disaster.
   A. NASA was under great pressure to launch the vehicle.
   B. Morton Thiokol engineers fell victim to groupthink.

II. The effects of ineffective decision making were calamitous.
   A. The O-rings melted.
   B. The rocket exploded.

The point is that either an event or a person can form the basis of an effective informative speech and afford you the opportunity to enlarge the scope of audience member knowledge.

Speaking about Processes/Procedures

How do you do that? Why does this work? Can I make one too? Much of our time is spent asking or answering questions like these as we either seek to acquire new understandings or seek to share our understandings about how to do something, how something works, how to make something, or why something happens with others. What we are really looking at, however, when we participate in such exchanges are those processes and procedures that produce particular results—that lead either to our having new information or to our developing new skills.

Here are examples of purpose statements about processes/procedures:

to inform my audience how tornadoes develop;
to inform my audience how to prevent groupthink;
to inform my audience how to write a resume;
to inform my audience how to perform the Heimlich Maneuver;
to inform my audience how to lose weight safely;
to inform my audience how the electoral college works;
to inform my audience how an atomic reactor functions;
to inform my audience how the futures market works;
to inform my audience how to dress for success; or
to inform my audience members how to protect themselves from the flu.

If you are delivering a "how" speech, then your primary goal is audience understanding of your subject:

how the AIDS virus spreads;
how colleges select students;
how tsunamis develop; or
how the greenhouse effect works.

If, on the other hand, you are delivering a "how-to" speech, then your primary goal is to communicate not just information but specific skills so audience members can learn how to do something:

how to avoid contracting the AIDS virus;
how to write an effective essay;
how to buy a used car; or
how to lobby your legislators.

There is virtually no end to the list of processes and procedures about which you can speak. What is important is that you are able to use an array of effective verbal and nonverbal messages to explain and illustrate the process or procedure to others, and that you have a sincere desire to explain the process or procedure so someone else will be able to understand, describe, and apply what you have shared.

When delivering a speech that focuses on a process or procedure, you will probably find it most useful to arrange your ideas in either chronological or topical order. Chronological order works well because it naturally reflects the sequence, approach, or series of steps used from start to finish in making or doing something. Topical order works well because sometimes, instead of taking listeners step by step through a process or procedure, you might find it more useful to discuss the major principles, techniques, or methods listeners need to understand to master the process or procedure. Let us next explore how these two approaches differ from each other.

Specific purpose: To inform my audience how scientists will save Earth from colliding with a comet in the future.

Central idea: There are four major steps scientists will use to save Earth from colliding with a comet in the future: identify which comet is on a collision course with Earth, determine the date contact will occur, send a spacecraft to intercept the intruder, and detonate nuclear warheads on the comet's surface.

Main points:

I. First, scientists need to identify which comet is on a collision course with Earth.
II. Scientists next need to determine the date the comet will hit the Earth.
III. Scientists then send a spacecraft to intercept the comet.
IV. Finally, nuclear warheads will be detonated on the comet's surface to change its course.

In the preceding example, the speaker used a chronological format to explain the scientists' procedure sequentially. However, she could have also organized her speech topically as follows:

Specific purpose: To inform my audience of the methods used by scientists to deflect a comet from colliding with Earth.

Central idea: Scientists use two key strategies to prepare for comets that could strike Earth: they study the past and they attempt to forecast the future.

Main points:

I. Scientists study the past to determine the effects of previous comet–Earth impacts.

II. The Central Bureau for Astronomical Telegrams of the International Astronomical Union works with scientists to forecast future comet–Earth impacts.

Organizational compactness keeps speeches about processes and procedures clearer and more comprehensible than they would be if a discussion of the steps or sequence involved were not packaged into meaningful units. A speech containing too many main points or step after step after step with no logical categorization effort is usually too difficult for receivers to interpret and remember. Therefore, it's unlikely that listeners will be able to follow what you are sharing with them. Keep the units of information (your main points) manageable, and you'll facilitate better listener management of the process or procedure as well.

Speaking about Ideas: Concepts and Definitions

What does the word "love" mean? What exactly is "pornography"? How do we define the term "child abuse"? What does "boasting" mean? How about "chi"? How can we explain what an "existentialist" is? What do we need to do to clarify the nature of "common law," "double jeopardy," or an "iatrogenic injury"? The answer to each of these queries lies in the development of an informative speech about the idea in question.

Your goal when speaking about a particular idea is to explain it in such a way that audience members agree that defining the idea has relevance and importance for them, and because of this they are motivated to seek clarification or elaboration from you regarding your ideas on the topic.

What kinds of ideas make the best topics for extended concept speeches or speeches of definition? The answer is general or abstract—ideas that allow for creative analysis and interpretation conveyed in words that give you leeway in theorizing about them. For example, any of the following topics would be appropriate for a speech about an idea:

the meaning of shyness;
the fundamentals of Confucianism;
muscular dystrophy: The disease;
the nature of a liberal education;
the grief cycle;
the nature of workfare in a post-welfare society; or
the Islamic justice system.

Often the concepts or words you choose to define have meanings that differ depending on one's experience with them. This is particularly likely for nontangible topics such as prejudice, wealth, and responsible citizenship. In contrast, tangible topics such as chemical warfare or depression are less apt to evoke such diverse interpretations.

Let's look at a few of the general topics we've identified above and create some specific purpose statements that could each be developed into a speech about the idea:

to inform my audience about the meaning of prejudice;
to inform my audience about different philosophies of wealth; or
to inform my audience about the basic tenets of responsible citizenship.

A speech about an idea can easily be developed by using a topical order in which key aspects of the idea are enumerated and discussed in turn. A good example of this came from a student speech on racism.

Specific purpose: To inform my audience about the nature of racial prejudice.

Central idea: Racial prejudice is a system of oppression that operates to limit its victims economically, politically, and socially.

Main points:

I. Racism is a form of economic oppression.
II. Racism is a form of political oppression.
III. Racism is a form of social oppression.

Another student speech explained the nature of chemical dependency by analyzing competing theories on the subject.

Specific purpose: To inform my audience about four major theories accounting for chemical dependency.

Central idea: The four major theories accounting for chemical dependency vary according to their emphasis on biological or environmental factors.

Main points:

I. One theory says chemical dependency is a result of an instinctual drive.
II. A second theory says chemical dependency can be traced to a person's attitudes and beliefs.
III. A third theory says chemical dependency is due to a moral weakness.
IV. A fourth theory says chemical dependency is attributed to an addictive personality.

SPEAKING of ETHICS

Inside the Definition

If the purpose of a speech of definition is to clarify the meaning of a term, then is it appropriate for a speaker to use a definition that conceals the impact of the word's actual meaning? For example, it has been reported that in corporate America we no longer "lay off" or "fire" employees. Here is how various company spokespersons have defined the attempts to "rightsize" each of their companies:

Strengthening global effectiveness (Proctor & Gamble)

Lean concept of Synchronous Organization Structures (General Motors of Canada)

Reducing duplication, or focused reduction (Tandy Computer)

Career transition programs (General Motors)

Reshaping (National Semiconductor)

A release of resources (Bank of America)

A normal payroll adjustment (Walmart)

Involuntarily separated from the payroll (Bell Labs)[1]

Is it ethical for a speechmaker to make words mean whatever he or she chooses them to mean? Explain your response.

In addition to being organized topically, speeches about ideas also lend themselves to chronological development. The following student example illustrates this.

Specific purpose: To inform the audience about the nature of sexual harassment.

Central idea: The meaning of sexual harassment has become broader through the years.

Main ideas:

I. The concept of sexual harassment in colonial times was limited to sexual violence against women.

II. During the nineteenth century, sexual harassment also took the form of psychological abuse.

III. Today sexual harassment includes verbal abuse as well.

As you can see, speeches about ideas are particularly challenging, primarily because they tend to deal with concepts for which we could all have varied interpretations, making it doubly difficult to explain the meaning of our ideas so audiences understand them.

THE INFORMATIVE SPEAKER SPEAKS: GOALS AND PURPOSES

AT THE HEART of an informative speech is the sharing of information. When you share information, you transfer an idea you have or a skill you have mastered to others. Through this transfer, you hope to accomplish at least one of the following goals: (1) to expand what others know by adding to their knowledge, or (2) to clarify what they know by reducing their confusion or uncertainty. Knowledge is power, so by fulfilling either or both of these goals, you also empower your receivers.

To empower your receivers, you need to transmit your information to them in ways that make it not only possible but also probable that they will understand your message and work to retain it. Because audience members can only learn what they focus on or listen to, you also need to discover ways to present your information so your receivers' motivation to know is aroused and sustained. To accomplish this, the message you deliver must be: (1) clear and accurate, (2) involving and interesting, and (3) meaningful and memorable. Let us explore each of these qualities in turn.

Be Clear and Accurate

When is a message clear? A message is clear if it is easy for others to follow and understand. Unclear messages confuse and confound their receivers with unfamiliar language, sentence structures that are convoluted and difficult to follow, and supporting materials that don't illustrate the ideas the speaker is trying to express. Clear messages are free of jargon, reinforced by supporting materials that illustrate the speaker's ideas, and expressed in easy-to-follow sentence patterns. Clear messages do not need to be translated to be recognizable; they are not puzzles to be solved. Rather, they are accurate expressions of a speaker's intent. As such, they help to remove questions from the minds of receivers.

Clarity and accuracy go hand in hand. If your message contains inaccurate or vague facts and figures, is based on rumor or hearsay, and is not supported by either

Speaking of skillbuilding ***Huh? (Unclear) versus Aha! (Clear)***

Following are a number of "unclear" words or phrases that would probably need to be translated to be transformed into "clear" words or phrases that audiences readily understand.

Unclear	*Clear*
cephalagia	headache
agrypnia	insomnia
precipitous	steep
nil desperandum	"It ain't over till it's over."

Based on your understanding of unclear and clear words, select a recent issue of *Vital Speeches of the Day* and locate five examples of words used by speakers that merit translation in order to enhance clarity.

primary or secondary research, then your receivers have every right to question your honesty and integrity. In today's audiences, many listeners relish assuming the role of fact checker and enjoy playing trip the speaker! Rather than risk losing your credibility by feeding such people vague information, make it your business to do your own fact checking prior to delivering your message. Take the time you need to verify all the facts and figures you intend to share with receivers; take the time you need to base your message on a solid foundation of well-documented research.

Be Involving and Interest Arousing

The more vivid and interesting you make a message, the easier it becomes for your receiver to listen to it. An audience that doesn't perceive a reason or feel a need to listen to your remarks is an audience that probably won't learn from you either. Thus, it is up to you to present your information in a way that promotes and sustains audience member attention. Most subjects can be made interesting if they are well adapted to the audience. From the outset receivers need to believe that your speech will benefit them—whether because you are about to add to their knowledge, satisfy their curiosity, or show them how what you know can help them enjoy or improve their lives. For example, if you were talking to a group of career women about the management styles of women and men, your speech would probably interest them because of its potential to affect them directly, as well as to enhance their understanding of similarities between them and their male counterparts. Similarly, if you addressed a heterogeneous audience on how the changes in demographics in the United States will affect the workforce in the twenty-first century, your speech would also interest your listeners because it would add to their knowledge and better prepare them to respond to changing times.

Messages that speak to the needs and concerns of audience members do not leave audience members behind, but rather take them along on an informative trip of the speaker's design. What matters to the speaker must also matter to the speaker's audience or it won't matter at all that the speaker sought to share it with them. Remember, people only want you to share something if it is something they want. If they don't want it, your wanting to share it with them, while generous, is unnecessary.

Be Meaningful and Memorable

What is meaningful to audience members is information that they perceive to have relevance and applicability to their lives. Listeners must see a reason to retain the information you share with them—either because they believe they may need to apply it at a future point in time or because they believe just knowing it could prove useful to them.

In order for your speech to remain with your audience after you have finished speaking, you must convey the same enthusiasm you have for your subject to your listeners, and you must transmit it in a way that nourishes their memory processes. To do this, you can: (1) let them know what you think is important for them to retain, and (2) stress those points via verbal and nonverbal means; that is, use repetition, pauses, vocal emphasis, and gestures to reinforce content. In addition, if you allow an audience to use the information you have given them during or immediately following your speech whether by building in audience participation or seeking some behavioral response from your receivers, then their chances of actually assimilating and using the information you provide them with are increased. You too will benefit in the process because you'll have developed a better feel for what your audience is able and willing to do with what you have shared.

Interest or Entertainment?

Dr. Ruth Westheimer is a psychologist who has also been both a popular television and radio talk-show host and guest, as well as a sought-after speaker.

> I don't start out to be funny. But if it comes out that way, I use it. If they call me an entertainer, I say that's great. When a professor teaches with a sense of humor, people walk away remembering.[2]

Echoing Dr. Westheimer, author, professor, and speaker Neil Postman notes that elementary, high school, and college teaching; religious training; talk shows; and political debates are also mixed with entertainment to increase their palatability to receivers:

> What all this means is that our culture has moved toward a new way of conducting business, especially its important business. The nature of its discourse is changing as the demarcation line between what is show business and what is not becomes harder to see each passing day. Our priests and presidents, our surgeons and lawyers, our educators and newscasters need worry less about satisfying the demands of their discipline than the demands of good showmanship.[3]

After considering these two statements and reflecting on your own experiences, decide whether audiences today expect the informative speaker to entertain them. Is it possible for a speaker to sustain audience interest without being entertaining? Explain your position.

SPEAKING of CRITICAL THINKING

Challenge Your Topic, Your Listeners, and Yourself

You cannot begin to share information with an audience until you identify the information you want to share. To decide what that is, you need to think more critically about your subject—that is, you need to reflect on your subject and ask questions about it rather than merely take it for granted. Then you can weigh the options open to you and choose those you will develop.

Begin by identifying your topic.

TOPIC: ____

An example topic is: news coverage of women.

Reflect on your topic by jotting down at least five questions you might need to answer to help your receivers think about your topic. What would they be curious about? One way to awaken your own curiosity is to ask the old reporter's questions, who, what, why, when, where, and how. For instance, in regard to news coverage of women, you might ask: How does the definition of news affect the coverage of women? Why are there more references to males than to females in the news? When females are covered in the news why are they sometimes demonized? Where in the news were women given prominance? What damage, if any, is done by the way the news covers women?

Next, ask your peers for questions about your subject not already on your list that they would like answers to. Add the questions to your list of compiled questions. For example, if you were speaking on news coverage of women in 1997, they might also ask you to discuss why you thought women appeared to be relatively invisible when compared to men, how you felt the media needed to change, as well as what you learned from your study of the subject.

Start by challenging yourself with some good questions. What do you want to know about? Should you change to a more challenging topic? If you are not genuinely interested in your subject, it will be hard for you to ask good questions about it. Further, your audience won't be interested in your subject either. It makes sense to work persistently and carefully to fill your mind with questions about your subject because a mind is like a car; it doesn't run on empty.

TECHNIQUES THAT INCREASE YOUR EFFECTIVENESS IN SPEAKING TO DIVERSE AUDIENCES

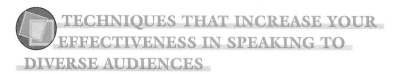

WHY IS IT THAT some instructors are more able than others to make it easier for students to learn new material? Why are some more interesting and involving? Why do some instructors succeed in motivating students to remember more of the information they share than do others? Perhaps it is because they have a talent for transmitting information and ideas. They can communicate their messages clearly, have a system for organizing or clustering their ideas, possess a means of connecting the ideas they transmit to ideas with which we are already familiar, and have a means of motivating people to pay attention and to consider and apply what they have taught. Because they do not ignore our needs, they do not bore us. Because their manner tells us that they are committed to teaching us, we take their invitation to learn more seriously.

Effective teachers and effective informative speakers have much in common. The central goal of the informative speaker, like the central goal of the teacher, is to share knowledge and precipitate listener understanding. Like the teacher, the informative speaker aims to arouse the interests of listeners, sustain their attention, and encourage them to retain and master the information being shared.

Of course, the very best informative speakers apply all the techniques and strategies we have discussed thus far—techniques and strategies that acknowledge: (1) the importance of audience analysis and motivation, (2) the value of support and research, (3) the significance of sentence structure and word choice, (4) the need to organize and outline ideas, and (5) how effective delivery can help us accomplish our goals. Now let us look at how to apply these strategies in informative speeches.

Create Information Hunger in Your Listeners

So you want your listeners to learn a new body of content. How will you motivate them to want to do that? It won't be by boring them, and it certainly won't be by putting them to sleep. In order for your listeners to want to learn what you want to share with them, you must show them how your information will benefit them. If you are delivering a speech on how to be a good friend, for example, could what you are sharing with them make them happier? If you are delivering a speech on how to eat a balanced diet, could your ideas make them healthier? If you are delivering a speech on how to nurture your self-esteem, might your speech make them feel better about themselves? To what extent will listening to you talk about how to invest safely in stocks make them wealthier?

Audiences get hungry for information when you link your ideas with their individual interests or goals. The audience's appetite for new knowledge increases as you satisfy their personal need fulfillment. Thus, since receivers look for information that affects them personally, to create information hunger in your receivers you need to convince them that they have a personal need to know what you are about to convey. If you succeed in showing the audience that the content of your speech is somehow vital to them, then they are much more likely to listen carefully to you and learn from you and, what's more, they will work hard to do it. For your receivers to want to work hard, however, you must capture and sustain their interest. The information hunger that you create during the introduction to your speech (your speech's appetizer) must be sustained during the body of your speech (its main course) and enhanced further during your conclusion (your speech's dessert). If you stop putting your listeners into your speech at any point or if, at any point, you fail to talk about your topic in terms they will respond to, their information hunger will drop, and because their appetite has been satiated rather than sustained, your effectiveness as a speaker will drop too. In other words, *relevance plus originality equals interest.* Always keep this equation in mind.

Speakers create information hunger among receivers by linking their ideas directly to the interests and goals of receivers.

Avoid Information Overload or Underload

What makes a speech informative? A speech is informative if it informs listeners, facilitates their understanding, or helps them acquire new information or new ways of perceiving or interpreting data—that is, if it helps them to develop fresh insights. A speech that fails to meet these critieria is uninformative.

There are two key reasons why a speech is judged to be uninformative: either it underloads the audience—that is, it lacks enough that is new so receivers fail to gain from experiencing it—or it overloads the audience—that is, it overwhelms listeners with so much new information and so many new insights that they are unable to process the speaker's message in a meaningful fashion. You can take steps to avoid overloading or underloading receivers.

Pace, Don't Race. Your job as an informative speaker is to communicate your ideas so listeners understand them, not to race to see how much new material you can cram into their brains during five or ten minutes. Thus, the informative speaker paces the information he or she passes out during a speech. Present your information too slowly, and you'll lose your listeners; present your information too quickly, or present too much new information, and you'll also lose your listeners as they strain to keep up and ultimately give up as you unwittingly leave them behind. The speaker who tries to show off how much he or she knows to the audience, the speaker who fails to allow the audience the time they need to process new information, the speaker who fails to build redundancy into the delivery of new information because "there is just too much to cover and too little time to cover it" is just as uninformative as the speaker who adds nothing new to what the audience already knows. Thus, the real challenge facing the informative speaker is to know not only what to include, but to be able to judge what *not* to include as well.

Take Knowledge for Granted, and No New Ideas Will Be Planted. Neither underestimate nor overestimate the knowledge and skills of your receivers. Instead, your job as an informative speaker is to work to communicate even the most sophisticated ideas as simply and clearly as possible. The more you assume your listeners know, the larger and fuller you imagine their storehouses of information to be, the greater your chances of being misunderstood. Instead, respect the intelligence of your receivers, but work hard to identify how you can clarify the complex and make the unfamiliar familiar.

You can clarify the complex by reducing the amount of jargon and technospeak you use, choosing instead to use language that those who are not as knowledgable about your subject will also readily comprehend. You can make the unfamiliar familiar by showing your listeners how you are building or adding on to what they already know. When you relate new information to old, when you use creative analogies to help listeners make connections, you will attract listener attention rather than deflect it.

Repeat, But Don't Retreat. Informative speakers also help their listeners process the content of their speeches by using **repetition** (saying the same thing again) as well as **restatement** (saying the same thing in another way by using other words). Informative speakers strike a delicate balance between repetition and newness. They are careful that they do not become overly repetitious because this would cause their speech to go into a retreat mode. At the same time, they realize that a certain amount of repetition and creative redundancy are needed if listeners are to understand and retain the speech's main points.

Relate Your Ideas Directly to Your Audience

A speech needs to involve listeners. Listeners who are not moved by a speaker to sit up and pay attention usually suffer as the speaker unintentionally puts them to sleep. Because a speech is judged by the way the members of an audience respond to it, to precipitate as positive an audience reaction as possible you need to capture audience interest at the start, maintain it during the speech's body, and hold it until the speech's conclusion. In other words, while delivering new information and insights to your audience is critical for you, the informative speaker, unless your audience members are convinced that your presentation has relevance for them, all the new information in the world you have to offer them will fall on deaf ears.

You can use all the materials we considered in Chapter 5 to help you customize your content for your particular audience. For example, you can use stories to make your facts more vivid, pose questions to arouse curiosity, draw analogies, integrate humor, and create visual aids to help you bring your ideas home to your audience and show them why what you are sharing is relevant to their lives. If you become overconfident and assume the audience members are aware of a connection between themselves and your subject, you could lose the opportunity to tie them to your topic. Instead, put yourself in their place, and seek to answer this question as honestly as you can: "If I were a member of my audience, what could the speaker say that would connect me to his or her ideas and draw me closer and involve me rather than make me want to pull away?" Remember, the ties that bind listeners to speakers are relevance, interest, and involvement.

Achieve Clarity, Simplicity, and Concreteness

Receivers resist overworking to get a speaker's point. Consequently, the message that succeeds in informing receivers is the message that gets through to them, and the

CONSIDERING DIVERSITY

Who Is Interested in What Information? Does Information Change with a New Audience?

An African proverb says: "The earth is a beehive; we all enter by the same door, but live in different cells," meaning that people share a basic capacity to look at the same world of ideas (a hive), focus on a particular topic (a door), and strive for a similar goal (a cell). Yet in spite of similar access to the same information, people are individually motivated and they head for different destinations. The same information can take a different course when delivered to several audiences.

Consider an informative topic such as how to avoid contracting AIDS. The scientific and social information on this topic are the same everywhere in the world, yet no two groups will have the same approach to hearing such information. Some will not want to hear it in any form; others will want to focus on an immediate problem they have to solve. Some people will have very distorted preconceptions on the subject, and some may even feel the subject is of no concern to them. How would you characterize cultural conditions contributing to different audience expectations on the topic?

For example, an informative talk on this subject as addressed to a group of prison inmates would be aimed at specific remedies for a high-risk group. (The talk might consist of very basic biological data as applied to a discussion of channels of transmission and specific physical methods of preventing exposure.) The same talk addressed to a group of apprehensive parents in a middle-class suburb would be focused on the effects of presenting such basic information to children at various ages. A talk on this subject to a group of Japanese businessmen visiting the United States would be aimed at their concerns for minimizing the impact of this disease in their country.

Each of these cultural groups will have special concerns and levels of readiness to deal with certain aspects of the basic topic of AIDS prevention. It is your task as a speaker to anticipate these cultural concerns, to test your material in view of what diverse audiences might want to know, and to select and organize your speech to fit the culture and audience.

What can speakers do to communicate with each culture cell in an audience? To what extent should speakers overtly acknowledge the presence of diverse cultures? Should speeches be global mosaics that cut laterally across group cells and develop common understandings, or should speakers who belong to specific racial or ethnic groups speak only to the interests of their own group? In other words, should speakers include in their speeches only content that attracts the many, or should they provide content that identifies and reinforces distinctions between audience groups? Discuss the advantages and disadvantages of each approach.

message that gets through to them is a message that is easy for them to comprehend. It is up to the speaker to: (1) clarify exactly what the audience should understand after receiving a speech, (2) simplify content so receivers are able to process the central idea and main points of the speech with minimal effort, and (3) offer receivers concrete support (specific facts and examples) as well as speak concretely (use language receivers are familiar with and words that are strong in specific details and evoke specific images).

Clarity Overcomes Confusion. When your ideas are organized, you don't attempt to cover too many points, you connect the points you do cover to each other via effective transitions, and you use a vocabulary that expresses the ideas you want to express without your becoming overly technical, then your speech has clarity.

Despite how accurately your words express your ideas, if your receivers fail to understand and follow you, you cannot hope to inform them. Presentations that have clear structures, that group together related facts, and that use oral signposts to help receivers follow the progression of ideas usually better enable listeners to grasp a speaker's message. Once your audience members understand and are able to follow the organization of your speech, they find it easier to grasp the ideas of your speech. For example, a speaker discussing the nature of passive smoke would be more effective if he or she organized the main ideas around a clear definition and a discussion of key effects than if he or she confused the issue by intermingling the effects that smoking and passive smoking have on health care costs. Speakers who use an organizational structure that makes sense to receivers usually find their speech makes sense to receivers too.

If the purpose of your speech is clear and announced early in your presentation, if the main points you develop are previewed in your introduction and then developed with an organizational format that supports your purpose, if you use language and visual aids to reinforce your message, if you review what you have covered in your conclusion, then your listeners' ability to comprehend your message will increase. Receivers simply are able to learn more from a speech that is organized than from one that is disorganized. Whereas a disorganized speech creates mind puzzles, an organized speech solves them.

Simplicity Overpowers Complexity. For listeners to grasp your message's meaning it must be clear not only in structure, but also in the language that embellishes that structure. You can do all the previewing, presenting, and reviewing you'd like, but if receivers do not understand the words you are previewing, presenting, and reviewing, they won't understand your ideas, let alone remember them.

Therefore, you need to define unfamiliar words and concepts for receivers, use everyday, nontechnical language, and compare new information you are trying to convey with information already familiar to them whenever possible. For example, if you used the word *sabadella* in a speech on insecticides, you would need to point out that sabadella is a Mexican plant of the lily family that chemical companies use to make a variety of insecticides. If you select and explain your words carefully, then your receivers will elect to listen and learn from you.

Concreteness Eliminates Misinterpretation. Speakers who come down to Earth and who talk to receivers rather than letting their ideas hover somewhere between the heads of their listeners and the heavens are less likely to be misinterpreted by their receivers. If you use concrete words, if you enhance your message with sufficient specificity and detail for listeners to form clear mental pictures, if you ground your ideas in particular rather than vague references or abstractions, then you put your subject where it belongs—directly into the minds of your receivers.

Personalize Your Ideas

Remember, although your goal may be to share ideas, people are interested in people. Thus, nothing enhances the communication of ideas more than the integration of personal anecdotes, examples, and illustrations. It is the drama of human interest that makes a speaker's facts come alive. So if you have a choice between just expressing your ideas and expressing your ideas creatively and with emotional impact, choose the latter. Your success as a speaker will increase to the extent that you are able to bring your topic to life for your receivers.

OUR BODIES ARE LIKE MACHINES

BY ROSHAMA HAZEL

The speaker introduces the speech with an interesting extended analogy that captures the attention of receivers.

Our bodies are like machines. We fuel them, tune them up now and then, and we use them so they don't rust. If we notice a problem, we put them in the shop for repair, just like our cars. Most of us believe that the similarity ends there because we trust our medical system more than our mechanics. After all, mechanics make mistakes. "The clamp came off," your mechanic tells you. "Our mistake," he says. "We'll fix it for you free of charge."

The speaker continues the introduction by citing statistical evidence from a respected source to add credibility and segue to the purpose statement.

But some things can't be fixed free of charge—and tragically some things can't be fixed at all. According to a study at Harvard University School of Public Health, "1.3 million Americans may suffer unexpected, disabling injuries in hospitals each year, and 198,000 may die as a result." It becomes painfully obvious that a costly stay in an American hospital may result in illness, injury, or even death.

Because it is likely that one of us or someone we love will need medical attention in a hospital, we need to diagnose the threatening problem known as iatrogenic injuries or adverse effects.

The speaker previews the speech.

We will do this by examining the scope and types of iatrogenic injuries. Then we can learn ways to protect ourselves and others who may become victims of our own cures.

The speaker introduces the first main point.

First, let's define and examine the scope of iatrogenic injuries.

According to Dr. Lucien Leape, director of the Harvard University School of Public Health study, "medical injury is indeed a hidden epidemic." So hidden that most of us have never heard the term.

The speaker defines "iatropic injury" clearly for receivers.

Webster's *New World Dictionary* defines the word iatrogenic as "anything caused by medical treatment." So, if you are the victim of an iatrogenic injury, it means that while you were being medically treated by a physician or hospital, you had something else happen to you because of the treatment.

The irony of the situation could be humorous if it were not for the tragic results.

Expert testimony is used to add credibility.

Iatrogenic injuries are frequent and sometimes deadly. The Harvard study reports that they cause four times the annual fatalities as highway accidents. This is not a new phenomenon. It is just well hidden. According to Dr. Leape, "Hundreds of mistakes occur every day in a major hospital," many of them going "unreported, unrecognized, uninvestigated, and unknown."

The speaker continues the discussion of the first main point by using both expert testimony and statistical evidence.

If injuries are uncovered and reported, hospitals attempt to minimize them. When asked about the problem, Jon Ross, a spokesman for the American Hospital Association, responded that "community hospitals around the country make 31 million admissions annually." He contends that the impact of 1.3 million injuries shrinks when viewed among so many patients treated each year.

When we consider that seven out of ten iatrogenic injuries studied by the Harvard group were preventable and nearly one third resulted from negligence, the impact of Mr. Ross's comment shrinks. Is he saying, "Everybody makes mistakes?" Is he implying that the 198,000 potentially unnecessary fatalities are part of business as usual? His response becomes unacceptable when we analyze the consequences.

The speaker's use of questions involves receivers in critically assessing the information.

The human costs of iatrogenic injuries are evident throughout the medical system. Let's examine the types most frequently found. Infections top the list. According to a report issued by the Centers for Disease Control there is a "strong rise in the incidence of hospital-induced infections in the last two decades. The most common injury is wound infections, easily 90 percent of which are preventable." The Harvard study reports that infections due to surgery account for 48 percent of the iatrogenic injuries. Invasive technologies, such as urinary catheters, are another cause of hospital-induced infections. These technologies "are overused and often used only for the convenience of hospital staff," says Dr. Robert Haley, at the University of Texas Southwestern Medical Center. Eugene Robin stated in his book *Matters of Life and Death,* in 1991, the problem with infections is so pervasive that doctors call them nosocomial infections so they can be discussed without the patient knowing it was induced because of their hospital stay.

The speaker introduces the second main point. Statistical evidence and testimony from respected sources are used to explain the nature of the problem.

Next, and perhaps more deadly, is the incorrect dispensing of medication. The February 1993 issue of the *AARP Bulletin* tells us about a woman named Martha who entered a New York hospital to receive one of her last chemotherapy treatments. She was beating cancer and she looked forward to her long struggle being over. Unfortunately, it was over much sooner than she thought. She received the wrong drug, which was far more powerful than what was prescribed. A few days later, she died.

The speaker's use of a series of illustrations humanizes the problem and helps make the unfamiliar more familiar.

On February 5, 1995, the *Baltimore Sun* reported a serious case at an Annapolis hospital. Morphine was given to four newborns instead of the prescribed hepron solution. None of the babies died but medical experts fear that consequences may result later. After investigation, two things were discovered. First, morphine, which is a controlled substance, should have been under lock and key. Instead, the morphine and the hepron were sitting side by side in a closet. The pharmacist reached for the wrong one. Second, the pharmacist was working under an expired license. These two examples are part of the 20 percent of the errors studied by Harvard that involved the use of drugs.

The last area of hospital-induced injuries, but certainly not least, is the performance of incorrect surgery.

The speaker uses the words "The last area" to signal a transition.

A 56-year-old woman was admitted to a suburban hospital for a routine D and C. A hospital clerk incorrectly scheduled her for a full hysterectomy. "Everybody makes mistakes?" "We'll fix it for you free of charge?" Luckily, the error was recognized and the surgeon performed the correct surgery. But others are not as fortunate. Willie King was scheduled to have his right leg amputated below the knee. According to the *Baltimore Sun,* February 20, 1995, during surgery, the surgeon incorrectly amputated his left leg instead. These results are tragic.

The speaker uses a series of examples to dramatize this point.

We can continue to trust our doctors more than our mechanics and put ourselves in increased risk of injury or death, or we can become informed and listen to some good advice.

Here the speaker makes the transition to the third main point.

Lowell Levin, professor of public health at Yale University School of Medicine, warns us that "medical care, like so many other things, is problematic; it's not a

The speaker again uses expert testimony as support.

sure thing. Patients must understand that hospitals are hazardous and medical care is a dangerous enterprise."

The speaker cites specific steps receivers can take to protect themselves.

We don't have to put ourselves at risk because we lack understanding. In his article, "When Hospitals Make You Sick . . . or Worse," William Barnhill gives us ways to protect ourselves.

Try to stay out of the hospital. You can do this by getting a second opinion. Surgery is often unnecessary. If you must be admitted to the hospital, be assertive. Ask questions and don't be afraid of hurting someone's feelings. When medication is prescribed, ask your doctor to spell the name, write it down, and write down the dosage you should be taking. When a nurse brings you the medication, make sure you're getting the right product before you take it. Don't sign away your rights by allowing the hospitals to use substitute surgeons or physicians.

The speaker uses an internal summary to facilitate receiver understanding.

The use of a rhetorical question further involves receivers.

With one in 25 hospital patients suffering from iatrogenic injuries, and with more than two-thirds of them preventable, the authors of the Harvard study suggest that "it is time for the medical profession to become as concerned about safety as about cure." The medical community knows about the problem and now, so do we. We understand the nature of iatrogenic injuries and the physical consequences they bring. We also know that we can and should become aggressive when it comes to our health care especially when we consider that, according to *Personnel,* 1991, as Americans we spend over 400 billion dollars a year on hospital stays. That accounts for two-thirds of the total amount of money we spend on health care. Do we need to add to that costs because of unnecessary and preventable injuries?

By relating the conclusion to the introduction, the speaker provides the speech with a sense of closure.

Remember the Ford commercial that asked, "Would you like your car fixed by someone named Earl or Bud?" I'd like to ask a similar question. Do they become any more conscientious and risk free because they are Drs. Earl and Bud? Take care of your machine by demanding the same from health care professionals as you would from your mechanic. Not everything can be fixed free of charge.[4]

SUMMARY

INFORMATIVE SPEAKING INVOLVES the sharing or transfer of information from speaker to receivers. As a result of an informative speech, the speaker expands or clarifies what receivers know by adding to their knowledge or reducing their confusion.

In order to fulfill his or her goal, an informative speaker must realize a number of objectives: (1) the informative speaker needs to make his or her message clear and accurate (his or her message needs to be easy for others to follow and understand); (2) the speaker needs to support his or her message with primary or secondary research; (3) the speaker needs to make his or her message involving and interesting; and (4) the speaker needs to make his or her message meaningful and memorable.

Informative speakers have four main types of informative speeches from which to choose. They can speak about (1) objects, (2) events/people, (3) processes/procedures, and (4) ideas/concepts.

It is as a result of learning how to create information hunger in receivers; relate ideas directly to receivers; and achieve clarity, simplicity, and concreteness that an informative speaker improves his or her ability to design and deliver a successful informative speech.

THE SPEAKER'S STAND

Prepare and deliver a five- to seven-minute informative speech. Be sure to integrate research and supporting materials that bring your presentation alive for your audience and use both an organizational format and language that facilitates audience understanding. Also, prepare an outline and include a bibliography of the sources you consulted.

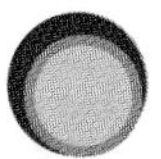

STUDENT FOCUS GROUP REPORT

Now that you have had the opportunity to consider the nature and functions of informative speaking, in a group of five to seven students, answer the following questions.

1. What are the greatest challenges facing you as an informative speaker? How do these compare to those that you face as a member of an informative speaker's audience?
2. Which type of informative speaking poses the fewest challenges? Which type poses the most challenges?
3. Which speechmaker attitudes facilitate the delivery of an informative speech? Which attitudes impede effective informative speech delivery?
4. How might cultural diversity or ethnic sensitivity affect our abilities to deliver and/or receive informative discourse?
5. What factors differentiate between informative and uninformative speaking?
6. Summarize the most important information you have learned about informative speaking.
7. Revisit the case study at the beginning of the chapter. Based on what you now know about informative speaking, what advice would you now offer Raul?

Chapter Sixteen

Speaking to Persuade

After reading this chapter, you should be able to:

- Define *persuasion.*
- Explain consistency theory, inoculation theory, and social judgment theory.
- Describe how culture can influence persuasive style and persuasiveness.
- Define and distinguish among attitudes, beliefs, and values.
- Identify four kinds of persuasive goals.
- Compare and contrast the following types of persuasive speaking: speaking on a question of fact; speaking on a question of value; and speaking on a question of policy.
- Explain Monroe's Motivated Sequence.
- Define *evidence* and discuss how facts, statistics, examples, illustrations, and testimony function as support.
- Identify the three essential facets of effective reasoning.
- Compare and contrast the following: deductive reasoning, inductive reasoning, causal reasoning, and reasoning from analogy.
- Identify the following fallacies: hasty generalization, post hoc ergo propter hoc, slippery slope, red herring, false division, argument ad hominem, appeal to popular opinion, appeal to tradition, and appeal to authority.
- Target audience needs and fears and arouse the emotions of receivers.
- Design and deliver a persuasive speech.

CASE STUDY

Both Sides

As he searched the Internet for potential speech topics, Ian stared at what appeared before him on his computer screen: the image of a sheep named Dolly. The sheep interested him because it was an exact genetic copy of another sheep. Scientists had accomplished this feat for the first time by slipping genes from a 6-year-old ewe into an egg and then inseminating another sheep with the egg. Ian pondered the meaning of what research scientists had accomplished. By using DNA from the ewe's udder cells, they had proved that mature mammal cells specialized for something other than reproduction could be used to regenerate an entire animal. No one had thought that was possible. The technique fascinated Ian. He had recently seen the film *Multiplicity,* in which Michael Keaton's character allows a scientist to clone him in an effort to reduce the amount of stress in his life. Ian felt similar stress. A full-time college student who also worked 30 hours a week and supported a family, Ian often wished that he, too, could clone himself so that he could be two places at one time. Hmmm, he thought, This is a great topic for my next persuasive speech. I'll talk about why we should support the cloning of a human being. With that, he continued his research on the topic.

At another computer sat a student from Ian's class. Interestingly enough, she, too, was focused on the image and story of the cloned sheep. Only her reaction was not nearly as accepting as Ian's. Unlike Ian, Janice was outraged. Who are we to play God? she thought to herself. She remembered viewing the film *The Boys from Brazil,* in which latter-day Nazis conspire to produce 94 clones of Adolf Hitler. What made her nervous was her realization that in the United States there existed no laws or regulations banning human cloning research. "That's it," she murmured, "I'll give my speech on why Congress must pass a law banning human cloning research."

Imagine that you are in Ian and Janice's class.

- Where do you stand on the issue of cloning?
- What could Janice and Ian say to convince you to support their respective positions?
- What kinds of arguments and appeals would you find most effective?
- What persuasive strategies could each use to try to persuade you to change your current way of thinking?

VOTE FOR STAN JONES FOR COUNCIL. Vote for Sharon Smythe for assembly. Buy tickets to see the No Doubt or Jewel concert. Buy tickets to attend a political rally. Petition for a scholarship. Petition to protect freedom of speech on the Internet. Support a woman's right to choose. Support the right to life movement. March against capital punishment. March for the death penalty. Give money to help fund Amnesty International. Give money to help fund Greenpeace. Which way do you go? Which way do you turn? Countless choices. Countless advocates.

PERSUASION IN ACTION

NUMEROUS INDUSTRIES AND INSTITUTIONS including advertising, public relations, politics, and religion have as their key task to attempt to persuade you.[1]

In fact, efforts to influence you happen hundreds of times daily. It is estimated that approximately once every two and one half minutes, someone makes the effort to persuade you.[2]

Persuasion, the attempt to change or reinforce attitudes, beliefs, values, or behaviors, permeates our lives. Sometimes we are aware of it, sometimes not. Sometimes we are the target of the persuasive attempt; other times we are the persuader taking aim at the target.

You cannot avoid being persuaded by others or doing the persuading yourself. Every day persuaders bombard you with messages in an effort to influence your opinions, beliefs, attitudes, values, and behaviors. Every day you similarly formulate a barrage of persuasive messages in an attempt to do the same to others. Sometimes persuasion works, other times it doesn't. Sometimes the persuader succeeds in obtaining commitments from us. Other times he or she falls short of the goal or fails to move us at all.

This chapter explores the persuasive process and the understandings and skills you must master if you are to function as an effective and ethical advocate and succeed in changing the minds or behaviors of persons listening to you. Because persuasive speakers must be able to communicate information clearly, because they must be able to analyze their audiences and customize their presentations based on their understanding, because word choice and organization matter, and because persuasive

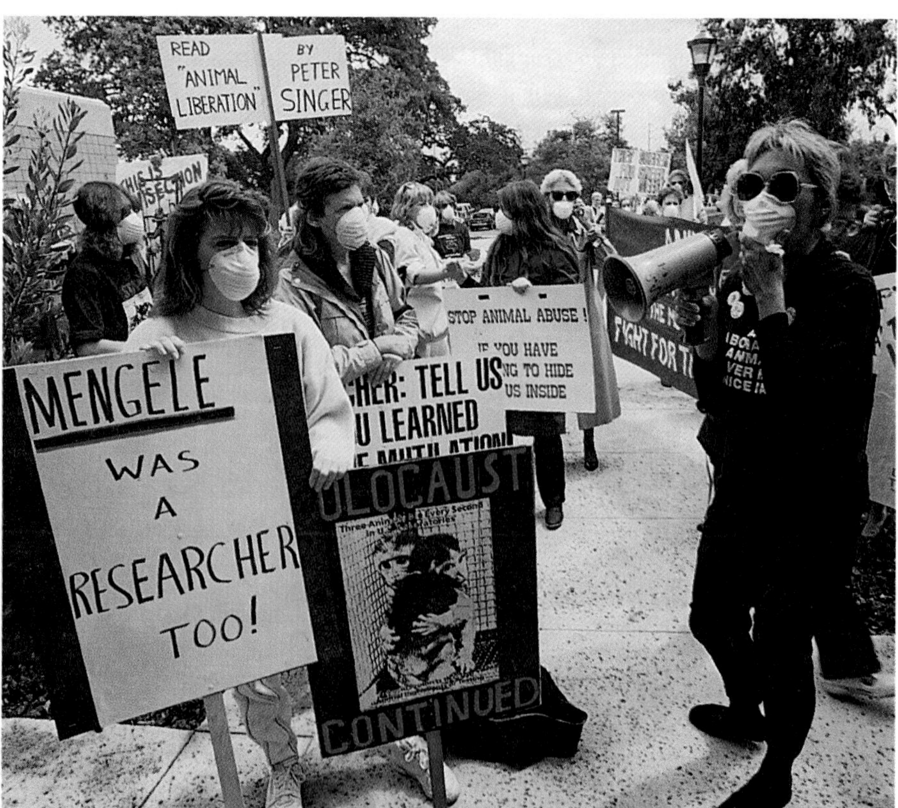

Advocates of countless causes attempt to persuade groups of people to support their ideals. To which appeals have you recently responded?

speakers also use all the skills used in informative speaking, this chapter asks you to use and build on all the elements considered to this point.

Your goal, however, is an ambitious one. Rather than simply conveying information, you are now also interested in influencing and affecting the opinions, beliefs, values, and actions of others. Your goal is to persuade your listeners to agree with you and, at times, to support their agreement with action. How much of your goal, if any, you are able to realize will depend on your skills, your audience, and the nature of your objective.

Let's explore a number of theories that help explain the persuasive process: how cultural diversity may influence the persuasion preferences of advocates and receivers; what a persuader needs to understand about attitudes, beliefs, and values; the various types of persuasive speeches and organizational designs; and the qualities of persuasive discourse that set one speaker apart from another and give one a more persuasive edge.

THREE THEORIES OF PERSUASION

THERE ARE A PLETHORA OF persuasive theories that focus on how and why we are able to persuade others. We will focus on the three that are most useful to public speakers.

Consistency Theory

Consistency theory tells us that we tend to seek out messages that are consistent with the values and beliefs that we and those with whom we interact hold. It also tells us that we are likely to attempt to protect our existing views by avoiding messages that contradict or challenge them.

According to consistency theory, our beliefs are related either in a state of **consonance** (consistency) or **dissonance** (inconsistency). The premise behind the theory is that it bothers us and we experience mental discomfort if something we believe turns out to be inconsistent with what we or others we value think. Thus, consistency theory proposes that the more uncomfortable we actually feel, the more motivated we become to change something so that we will be able to feel more comfortable or more psychologically balanced once again. In other words, it is imbalance that moves us to want to change. Imbalance functions as our potential persuader or motivator.

The more tightly held the beliefs or attitudes of individuals, the harder it is for persuaders to get those persons to consider opposing points of view. Only if persuaders are able to introduce a sense of psychological imbalance in the minds of receivers and confront them with information they might have otherwise ignored can persuaders hope to motivate receivers to respond as they desire. According to consistency theory, if no inconsistency is aroused, there will be no persuasion. Thus, to persuade receivers you must first upset them or knock them off balance.[3]

Inoculation Theory

What if you want to prevent receivers from being influenced by others who come after you? What if your goal is to help others resist changing the way they think or act once they accept your persuasive message? **Inoculation theory** uses a medical analogy that suggests that you can prevent persuasion just as you prevent disease. We inoculate the body with a small dose of a weakened form of a disease-producing virus, causing the body to develop antibodies to the disease; so too can we inoculate a person's cognitive system with persuasive antibodies (a defense or a refutation) in case he or she is "exposed" to opposing persuasive messages.

Inoculation theory suggests that persuaders must take opposing arguments into consideration. In fact, it confirms that to be most effective, persuaders should present their receivers with the arguments of the opposing point of view as well as a refutation to those arguments. That way, when the other side does expose the receivers to those arguments, they will be less effective or not work at all because the receivers will have heard them already, will be armed with effective counterarguments, and thus will be in a better position to resist them and defend themselves against them.[4]

Social Judgment Theory

According to **social judgment theory,** the instant we hear a message we immediately decide where it should be placed on the attitude scale or continuum that we carry around in our minds. Researchers Carolyn Sherif, Muzafer Sherif, and Roger Nebergall explain that an attitude is an amalgam of three zones: the **latitude of acceptance** (opinions we find acceptable), the **latitude of rejection** (opinions we find unacceptable), and the **latitude of noncommitment** (opinions about which we are undecided and thus find neither acceptable nor unacceptable).[5] (See Figure 16.1.)

The greater the ego involvement of receivers, the more the established position serves them as an anchor, the greater their latitude of rejection, and the more difficult it becomes to persuade them to move that anchor and alter their position. On the other hand, people who are less ego involved or who care less strongly will have much larger latitudes of noncommitment.

When it comes to persuasion, social judgment theory reminds us that conversion from one end of the attitude continuum to its other end is a rarity. Thus, the greater the change a persuader wants to produce in receivers, the more difficult the task becomes. Persuasion is usually not a one-step affair. The only way for a persuader to accomplish significant change is through a series of small, gradual, successive steps. Typically, a persuasive speech is but a single step in a persuasive campaign. Consequently, persuaders are generally more effective when they strive for small changes over a period of time.[6]

Figure 16.1

Attitude is an amalgam of three zones.

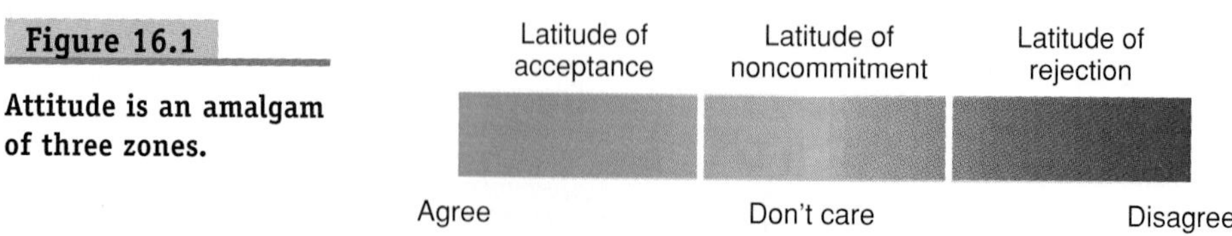

CULTURAL DIVERSITY AND THE PERSUASIVE PROCESS

INDIVIDUALS FROM DIFFERENT cultures do not necessarily respond in the same way to persuasive attempts or persuasive styles.[7] Both the reasons people use for finding credible specific information and individuals and the means they use to try to persuade others vary from culture to culture. For example, many Muslims use parables, especially from the Koran, as evidence. They assume that those with whom they share a story will find its message persuasive. Similarly, the oral tradition from which African American speakers draw also leads them to prefer an **analogical speaking style,** which relies on the telling of an analogy, story, or parable from which receivers can derive an implicit or explicit moral. This pattern is often emotional and dramatic in tone as shown in this excerpt from a speech by Jesse Jackson:

Thirty-three years ago tonight, a young preacher about the same age as my son was putting the final touches on one of the great prophetic messages of our age.

On August 28, 1963, Dr. King projected a vision of peace and equality that could heal our nation, and a troubled world.

His vision touched America's conscience. The Republicans in San Diego put forward the image, the vision, of a big tent. . . .

What is our vision tonight? Just look around.

This publicly financed United Center is a new Chicago mountain top. To the South, Comiskey Park, another mountain. To the west, Cook County Jail, with its 11,000 mostly youthful inmates.

Between these three mountains lies the canyon.

Once Campbell's Soup was in this canyon. Sears was there, and Zenith, Sunbeam, the stockyards. There were jobs and industry where now there is a canyon of welfare and despair.

This canyon exists in virtually every city in America.

As we gather here tonight:

one-fifth of all American children will go to bed in poverty;

one-half of all African-American children, growing up amidst broken sidewalks, broken families, broken cities, broken dreams;

the No. 1 growth industry in urban America, jails;

one-half of all the public housing built in this nation during the last decade, jails;

the top 1 percent wealthiest Americans own as much as the bottom 95 percent—the greatest inequality since the 1920's.

As corporations downsize jobs, outsource contracts, scab on workers' rights, a class crisis emerges as a race problem. The strawberry pickers in California, the chicken workers in North Carolina, deserve a hearing and justice.

We must seek a new moral center.[8]

In contrast, members of White American culture view explicit "facts" or physical evidence rather than analogies or stories as the highest form of evidence. As such, they prefer to use a **quasilogical style** that relies more directly on statistics and expert testimony to prove a conclusion. We see this style at work in a speech delivered on December 4, 1991, by banking executive Janet Martin before members of the North Toronto Business and Professional Women's Club:

Careers are limited by a glass ceiling that enables women to glimpse but not grasp top executive positions. While the barriers are invisible, they are there nonetheless. In a poll conducted by *Business Week* and Louis Harris Poll, 60 percent of management women in large corporations identified "a male-dominated corporate culture" as an obstacle to women's success.

. . . Might the glass ceiling exist because the personal trade-offs and sacrifices women must make are greater than those their male counterparts face? John Kenneth Galbraith once told writer Michael Bliss that, "In the modern world, women's liberation consists of submerging a personality to a corporation rather than a husband." Harsh as Galbraith's view may be, he does have a point. Reports published from the *Wall Street Journal* a few years ago revealed that while 94 percent of male executives were married, only 41 percent of their female counterparts were. Ninety-five percent of male executives had children, compared to 39 percent for women. A very small percentage of men were divorced or never married. For women executives, the number was 45 percent.[9]

Augmenting these two styles is the **presentational style,** which emphasizes and appeals directly to the emotions of receivers rather than to logic. Speakers who use this style rely on the rhythmic, sensory, and emotional qualities of words to increase the vividness of their message and arouse receivers to believe and act as they want them to. For example, former Senator Eugene McCarthy used this style of speaking in a speech denouncing the Vietnam War.

The message from the administration today is a message of apprehension, a message of fear, yes—even a message of fear.

This is not the real spirit of America. I do not believe that it is. This is a time to test the mood and spirit:

To offer in place of doubt—trust.
In place of expediency—right judgment.
In place of ghettos, let us have neighborhoods and communities.
In place of incredibility—integrity.
In place of murmuring, let us have clear speech; let us again hear America singing.[10]

Cultures also vary regarding views of the value of testimony and who they perceive as authorities. In various African cultures, for instance, the words of a witness hold little, if any, weight because the people assume that if you speak up about what you have seen, you are doing so because you hope to gain something personally. Thus, unlike North Americans, those peoples believe that no one is an objective or credible observer of events.

Cultures also differ regarding the communication techniques they judge to be reasonable, and consequently they disagree as to what persuasive strategies they find most appropriate and persuasive. Some North Americans, for example, find the persuasive speaking style of Mexicans overly emotional, dramatic, and deficient when it comes to accuracy. Remember that many North Americans tend to prefer a more logical style, one that relies on statistics and expert testimony rather than drama and intuition to make the truthfulness of the argument apparent to receivers.

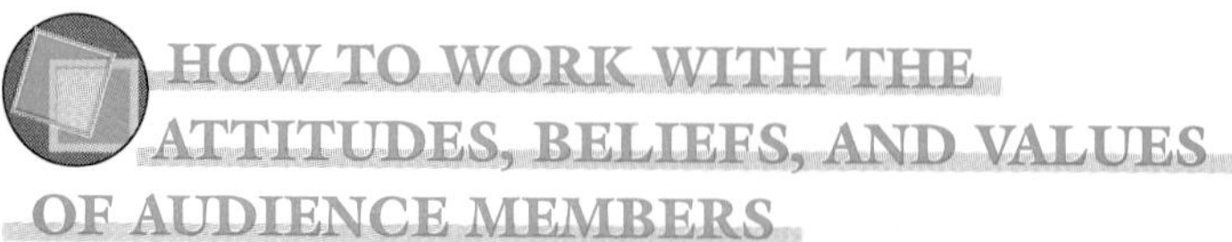

HOW TO WORK WITH THE ATTITUDES, BELIEFS, AND VALUES OF AUDIENCE MEMBERS

WHEN YOU CHANGE or reinforce someone's attitudes, beliefs, or values (without coercing or manipulating them), you are practicing persuasion successfully. Let us now focus more closely on attitudes, beliefs, and values and their relation to persuasion as we look at how you can use them to achieve greater persuasive impact.

What Are Attitudes?

An **attitude** is a mental set or a predisposition that both you and your audience members have about stimuli (people, places, things, events) that cause you to respond to or evaluate them in positive or negative ways. Attitudes reflect your likes and dislikes; they indicate of what you do or do not approve. Your attitudes toward any stimulus can be classified along a continuum that ranges from positive to negative, with neutrality or indifference at its midpoint.

The more you know about your listeners' attitudes and why they feel as they do, the better your ability to tailor your message so it speaks directly to them. If you and your listeners share a similar attitude toward your topic, then your task is simplified. If your attitudes are very different, however, your task becomes somewhat more complex. Fortunately, audience attitudes tend to congregate at a particular point along the attitudinal continuum. Thus, if you are able to identify where that point is—that is, what the general audience attitude is—then you can build an approach that takes that attitude into consideration. For example, if most people in your audience are neutral toward your topic, perhaps because they know nothing or very little about it or because they have not yet been moved by anyone to care about it, then you know that your primary need is to supply them with reasons to care and evidence with which to substantiate a position. If, on the other hand, most people oppose your proposition, the nature of your task changes; you now need to offer arguments that reduce hostility or negativity and provide information that can redirect audience attitudes. Similarly, if most people are in favor of your proposition, then your main task is to provide information and arguments that give listeners reason to reaffirm their stance, and if appropriate, act on it.

As a speaker you have the potential to instill, change, or intensify an attitude. Attitudes differ not only in **direction** (are they positive or negative?) and **intensity** (how positive or negative are they?), but in **salience,** or the importance and relevance an attitude has for its holders. For example, while listeners may have a positive attitude toward affirmative action programs and may feel strongly about the need to correct previous inequities, the attitude they hold may not be salient for them if they do not believe it affects them now or could affect them in the future.

Among the forces shaping one's attitudes are family, religion, schooling, social class, and culture. These forces also shape our beliefs.[11]

What Are Beliefs?

Whereas attitudes are measured along a favorable–unfavorable continuum, beliefs are measured along a probable–improbable continuum. It is your beliefs that determine whether you accept something as true or false. Your upbringing and past experiences and evidence presented work together to convince you of the truthfulness or falsity inherent in statements of belief.

Attitudes and beliefs work together. If you have a positive attitude toward someone or something, you are more likely to believe good things about the object of your attention. If, on the other hand, you have a negative attitude toward someone or something, you are more apt to believe the worst. The process, as we see, goes both ways. Thus, if you believe that television encourages laziness in children, precipitates reading problems in young learners, and contributes to children being overweight, then you would be more apt to have a negative attitude toward television. In contrast, if you start out with a positive attitude toward television, then you are more apt to believe that such views are exaggerated or untrue.

What Are Values?

In contrast to attitudes and beliefs, **values** are more enduring, more deeply ingrained indicators of what we each feel is good or bad, right or wrong. Were you to value intangible assets rather than wealth, or honesty rather than deception, for example, you would classify intangible assets and honesty as desirable. If, however, you did not value them, you would classify them as undesirable or unnecessary. In other words, values motivate behavior. They guide our conduct by reminding us of what we find most important. They also help us decide what is worth trying to change or influence.

Among the top five values identified by Americans in one Gallup report were good family life, good self-image, being healthy, having a sense of accomplishment, and working for a better America.[12] Since behavior is at least in part value based, speakers can use those findings as a means to relate what they are advocating with one or more of these values. Thus, you can use values, beliefs, and attitudes to move your receivers closer to your goal. Any time you move a receiver even a little bit closer to the position that you advocate, persuasion is in process, and you are making progress.

THE PERSUASIVE SPEAKER: GOALS AND PURPOSES

PERSUASIVE SPEAKERS SEEK CHANGE that usually involves one of the following:

1. reinforcement of a position,
2. shift in a position,
3. adoption of a behavior, or
4. elimination of a behavior.

Identify the Type of Response Desired

The intent of the persuasive speaker is not simply to increase the knowledge base of receivers, as is the case for an informative speaker. Rather, the intent of the persuasive speaker is to influence audience response so that in addition to gaining knowledge, receivers also feel differently, think differently, or act differently than they did before listening to the speech.

To succeed, the persuasive speaker must be able to identify his or her speech making objectives succinctly and specifically. To this end, the speaker must answer two questions:

1. What exactly am I trying to reinforce or change in my receivers?
2. How must the members of my audience alter their beliefs, attitudes, values, or behaviors if they are to respond as I desire?

"Why bother?" you ask. "What difference can one persuasive speaker make?" The answer is simple. Any time one of us affects the nature and quality of the lives of others around us, we make a significant difference. Any time one of us succeeds in helping another make a choice from among competing options, we make a significant difference. Everyone reading this chapter can make a difference.

> A young daughter and her father were walking on the beach early one morning. A bad storm the night before had washed thousands of starfish up on the shore. Many of them were still alive. As the two walked along, the father would bend down, pick up a single starfish and toss it back into the ocean. The daughter watched him do this for some time. Then she asked, "Dad, why are you throwing those starfish back in? There are thousands of them. What difference can it make?" The father didn't respond right away. He looked at the starfish in his hand, tossed it back into the ocean and said, "It made a big difference to that one."[13]

To the extent that you change the ideas and behaviors of one or more of your receivers, to the extent you obtain a commitment or elicit a desired action from them, you are persuasive, and you are changing your world—presumably for the better. If you fail to bring about such desired change, if you fail to influence anyone, you simply have been unpersuasive—for the moment.

Define the Specific Aims of the Speech

Once you establish your overall persuasive goal, whether to convince your audience members to change (1) their way of thinking, or (2) their way of acting, your next challenge is to decide on the type and direction of the change you seek and to motivate your audience to respond appropriately. You must define the specific aims of your speech. Specifically, do you want audience members to:

- **Adopt** a new way of thinking or behaving?
- **Sustain or reinforce** a way of thinking or behaving?
- **Discontinue or extinguish** a way of thinking or behaving?
- **Avoid** a particular way of thinking or behaving?

For example, if your goal were to persuade receivers to adopt a new way of thinking or behaving, you might want them to:

> Donate money to help establish an adult literacy program.
>
> Support the legalization of prostitution in all 50 states.
>
> Support the establishment of a college recycling program.
>
> Write their legislators to support a law advocating strict gun control.

If, on the other hand, your goal were to persuade receivers to sustain or reinforce their current way of thinking or behaving, you might work to have them:

> Reaffirm their belief in freedom of the press.
>
> Strengthen their willingness to participate actively in student government.
>
> Intensify their belief that a women's college prepares a woman for leadership better than a coed college.
>
> Reaffirm their belief that every American has a responsibility to vote in every election.

If your goal were to persuade receivers to *extinguish* a current way of thinking or behaving, you might express that goal by seeking to have them:

Persuasive speakers try to motivate receivers to intensify, revise, or extinguish their existing beliefs, attitudes, or behaviors. Which of your beliefs, values, or attitudes have you altered after listening to a speaker?

Stop smoking.
Refrain from sitting in the sun.
Change their attitudes toward homework.
Reassess their attitudes toward math and science courses.
Limit the amount of time they spend viewing television.

Finally, if you seek to *deter* listeners from (or have them avoid) starting to think or act in a particular way, then your aim might be to have them:

Not use or try fad diets.
Not think of school as a waste of time.
Not remove asbestos unless qualified and licensed to do so.
Not allow the cloning of a human being.

The ethical obligations assumed by those who persuade are substantial. It is up to you to ensure that any changes you request are sound and in the best interests of your receivers. It is up to you to find ways to stimulate your receivers to think (change an attitude or belief) or do (perform some act) as you desire without harming them or the public. While you may want something from your receivers, you owe them something, too. In effect, you as persuader and your receivers as persuadees make commitments to each other.

To summarize, persuaders work to either reinforce, extinguish, strengthen, or discourage existing ways of thinking or behaving, as well as to instill or deter new ways of thinking or behaving. Whatever your persuasive goal, chances are someone disagrees with you as to its merits, or there would be no need for you to pursue it in an effort to lead listeners to alter their perceptions and/or actions.

As a persuader, you function as more than an instructor; you are a leader. Thus you have the opportunity to do more than inform; you have the opportunity to shape thought and change behavior. For this reason, besides informing your receivers of the facts of a situation and discussing with them different ways of viewing a situation, you also suggest to them which option is best for them to pursue.

What understandings must you have and what strategies can you use to achieve your persuasive goals?

TYPES OF PERSUASIVE SPEAKING

As A PERSUADER, you seek to influence receivers by moving them closer to the position you advocate. Any time you succeed, however small that movement may be, you have exerted influence and exercised your persuasive power. Whereas the informative speechmaker aims to increase what the audience *knows*, the persuasive speechmaker aims to change what an audience *thinks* or *does*. In addition to categorization by whether the persuader aims to establish, intensify, extinguish, or deter a way of thinking or behaving in receivers, the persuasive speech can also be categorized according to whether it focuses on a **question of fact** (past, present, or future), a **question of value** (an evaluation of a person, event, situation, or action), or a **question of policy** (what you think should be done).

Defining the nature of the "question in question" is among the first issues you must face, because how you answer it affects both the content and the design of your presentation. Ask yourself: "Am I going to make a claim about what is or what is not, how good or bad something is, or that something ought to be?" Whatever your response, your claim represents your **proposition,** that is, the relationship you wish to establish between accepted facts and your desired conclusions. Each proposition you formulate requires that you uncover and use particular kinds of evidence, motivational appeals, and methods of organization.

Speaking on a Question of Fact

Propositions of fact are conclusions asserting that something does or does not exist, is or is not true, is or is not valid. Propositions of fact affirm or deny the existence of something, the occurrence of something, or the relationship between two or more things. The following are typical propositions of fact:

Extrasensory perception exists.
Increasing taxes on alcohol will reduce alcohol consumption.
A high-fiber diet prevents cancer.
Sustained exposure to lead paint poses substantial health risks.
The harmfulness of high cholesterol is exaggerated.
IQ tests discriminate against racial and ethnic minorities.
The federal deficit is a threat to our economic security.
Air travel poses fewer risks than travel by rail or by car.
Helium balloons kill animals.

In each case the goal of the speaker is to persuade receivers as to the factual nature of the statement. How can you, the idea advocate, do this? The answer is with an array of evidence and arguments that convince receivers that your interpretation of a situation is valid, and thus that the statement you are making is true and accu-

Persuasion

In this excerpt from Persuasion in Practice, *author Kathleen Kelly Reardon defines and differentiates persuasion from two other means of influence—manipulation and coercion.*

. . . [P]ersuasion is a form of communication in which every person who ventures forth into the company of others must participate. Persuasion is necessitated by the single fact that all of us differ in our goals and the means by which we achieve them. . . .

Whether persuasion is intended to improve the state of the persuadee or merely to further the goals of the persuader, it does differ from manipulation and coercion. Manipulation involves furthering the goals of the manipulator at the expense of the person being manipulated. It essentially involves "pulling the wool over the eyes" of others. The people being manipulated are not encouraged to reason about the situation, but are entranced by false promises, deceived by insincere verbal or nonverbal behaviors, or "set up" in the sense that the situation is contrived

rate. What you attempt to do when speaking on a question of fact is to persuade your listeners that the conclusion you have drawn is undeniable. Thus, a proposition of fact centers on receiver belief regarding the truthfulness or falsity inherent in your statement.

In this excerpt from a speech, student Brad Braddy focuses on a proposition of fact. His proposition was that violence in the workplace threatens the security of the American workforce.

> Workplace violence ranges from physical assault, shootings or stabbings, to homicide. The February 1994 issue of *Human Resources Focus,* published by the American Management Association, reported that over half of those violent acts are committed by an employee toward another employee and 13 percent pit an employee against a supervisor. Although fist fights are the most prevalent form of workplace violence, *H.R. Focus* found that 17 percent of the episodes involved shootings. And the Florida Department of Labor reported that more workers died of gunshot wounds last year than from any other occupational injury.
>
> Which brings us to homicide. The July 29, 1994, *Morbidity & Mortality Weekly Report,* published by the Department of Health & Human Resources, defines occupational homicide as "a fatality resulting from an intentional nonself-inflicted injury that occurs in a work setting." Last year, there were 1,216 occupational homicides throughout the United States, which is up 32 percent over the average of the 1980s.
>
> On a national level, occupational homicide is now the number one cause of job-related deaths among female workers and the second leading cause of job-related deaths overall. At the state level, occupational homicide is the number one work-related killer in South Carolina, Alabama, Connecticut, California, Mayland, Michigan, and Washington D.C.[14]

Organizing the Question of Fact Speech. When speaking on a proposition of fact, part of the challenge revolves around your ability to convince listeners that your conclusion is based on objective evidence. At the same time, in order for listeners to be converted to your point of view you need to present the facts as persuasively as to limit their choices. Manipulation differs from persuasion in that it does not involve up-front reasoning with others. . . .

Coercion is another means of influencing behavior that does not involve up-front reasoning. Coercion involves physical force or some form of threat . . . [and] is less likely than persuasion to lead to long-term changes in behavior because the persuadee has not *chosen* to adopt the new behavior and thus is not committed to retaining it. . . .

Persuasion involves guiding people toward the adoption of some behavior, belief, or attitude preferred by the persuader through reasoning or emotional appeals. It does not rob people of their ability to choose. . . . It does not use force or threat and does not limit the options of others by deceit. Persuasion is not always in the best interests of the persuadee. Even the persuader with good intentions may lead persuadees to do what might not be in their best interests. In all cases, however, persuasion does not deprive persuadees of their choices by deceit or force. . . .

The goal of persuasion is to change someone's attitudes and/or behavior. Since most people are naturally protective of their views and their behaviors, this intention, if not properly presented, can encourage people to close their minds to change.[15]

- What can the persuader do to keep the minds of persuadees from closing, without resorting to manipulation or coercion?

possible. It is common for persuasive speeches on questions of fact to be organized topically, as Brad's speech was. Each point Brad mentioned in support of his proposition of fact offered listeners a reason why they should agree with him. You can do the same as you work to convince your listeners to accept your point of view. The next example demonstrates how:

Specific purpose: To persuade my audience that the homeless are lacking the resources to regain a place in American society.

Proposition: The homeless are lacking the resources to regain a place in American society.

Main points:

I. The homeless do not have permanent residences, so they are forced to drift from place to place.

II. The homeless have no place in the economic system.

III. The homeless suffer from conditions of hunger, disease, and mental health.

Again, each main point represents a reason you provide your receivers in the hope that they will be influenced to accept your point of view or proposition.

Suppose you sought to persuade receivers of the following: "American voters are subjected to unfair persuasion." In this case, your specific purpose, your proposition, and the main points of your speech might read like this:

Specific purpose: To persuade my audience that American voters are subjected to unfair persuasion.

Proposition: Abuses of persuasive techniques bombard the American voter during elections.

Main points:

I. American voters are exposed to too many attack ads.

II. American voters are exposed to too many big lies.

III. American voters are exposed to too many one-sided arguments.

Keep in mind that when you speak on a proposition of fact, your goal is to convince your audience to accept your perception of the facts, even though your version of them is open to question. If you are going to convince listeners of the correctness of your point of view, your reasons and your evidence must also be convincing. Thus, you will need to provide receivers with support drawn from: (1) recent sources, (2) experts who agree with you, and (3) particular instances that reinforce your proposition.

Speaking on a Question of Value

Our values are our guides. Deep-seated beliefs, they serve as standards for evaluation. In your opinion, what is good? What is bad? What is proper? What is improper? What is right? What is wrong? What is moral? What is immoral? A proposition of value provides an answer to questions just like these; as such, a proposition of value represents your assertion of a statement's worth; it represents a conclusion or claim regarding the judgment expressed in a statement.

When speaking on a proposition of value your speechmaking goal is to convince your audience of the validity of your evaluation. Your task is to justify your belief or opinion so that your receivers accept it too. The following statements are propositions of value:

Testing products on animals is improper.
Euthanasia is wrong.
Walking is the best exercise.
Fetal tissue research is morally justifiable.
The death penalty is cruel and unusual punishment.
Subliminal advertising is wrong.
A fetus's right to life is more important than a woman's right to choose.
It is wrong to pay a man more than a woman for similar work.
It is immoral to clone a human being.

In each case, how could you convince your listeners to arrive at the same conclusion you have? You could do it by offering information, evidence, and appeals, as well as by establishing standards or criteria that you would hope would compel audience agreement with your value judgment. In order to analyze a proposition of value, you must do two things: (1) Define the object of evaluation and support that definition; (2) provide value criteria for determining what the evaluative term means, that is, how do you define what is "proper," what is "wrong," or what is "immoral?"

In this example a student talks about why it is wrong for prisons to dehumanize their occupants. By quoting directly from an issue of *California Prisoner,* the student is buttressing support for her assessment:

> Probably the most pernicious consequence of the modern warehouse prison is that so many prisoners now "stagnate." That is, for the duration of their prison terms, they make no progress toward being equipped to live a non-criminal life on the outside; in fact they become less equipped. This is particularly regrettable because most prisoners are relatively poorly educated, vocationally unskilled, and some have serious physical and psychological problems when they go to prison. In addition, most express some desire to better themselves during their prison sentence.[16]

In the next example, the speaker explains why she believes it is immoral to fund researchers who seek to clone human beings. By referring to the work of Father Richard A. McCormick, a professor of Christian ethics at the University of Notre Dame, she hopes to build support for her stance.

Cloning would tempt people to try to create humans with certain physical or intellectual characteristics. It would elevate mere aspects of human beings above what University of Notre Dame Reverend Richard A. McCormick says is the "beautiful whole that is the human person."[17] But who among us should decide what the desirable traits are, what the acceptable traits are? Might this practice lead to the enslavement of humans by humans?

Organizing the Question of Value Speech. Speakers use a variety of organizational formats when preparing speeches on propositions of value. A **reasons approach,** for example, works well if listeners are either neutral on or only slightly acquainted with the speaker's subject. With each reason presented as a main point, the speaker offers a rationale designed to justify the speech's goal. One student used a "reasons" outline to express her position that "dehumanizing prison inmates is proper."

Specific purpose: To convince my listeners that it is proper for prisons to dehumanize inmates.

Proposition: It is proper for prisons to dehumanize inmates because punishment must encourage contrition and learning, and must fit the crime.

Main points:

I. The system must make prisoners contrite.
II. Pain and suffering encourage learning.
III. The punishment should fit the crime.

Another student used a similar approach to describe why she believed allowing white families to adopt black children was morally wrong.

Specific purpose: To convince my audience that allowing white families to adopt black children is morally wrong.

Proposition: It is morally wrong for white families to adopt black children because such adoptions violate the child's ethnic identity, foster feelings of rejection, and fail to deal with the racism problem.

Main points:

I. Being adopted by a white family destroys the black child's sense of ethnic identity.
II. Too many black children adopted by white families are returned to foster care, thereby fostering a sense of rejection in the children.
III. Having white families adopt black children fails to address fully the problem of racism.

After hearing that speech, another student was motivated to deliver one espousing an opposing set of values. The following outline uses a refutational strategy that summarizes this speaker's assessment of the practice. When arguing against a previously espoused position, you first note the stance being refuted, state your position, support it, and demonstrate vividly why your position undermines the one previously stated.

Specific purpose: To convince my audience that allowing white families to adopt black children is morally right.

Proposition: It is morally right for white families to adopt black children because such adoptions do not damage ethnic identity, but foster sensitivity and tolerance and build cultural bridges.

Main points:

I. Being adopted by a white family does not damage a black child's sense of ethnic identity.

II. When white families adopt black children greater sensitivity and tolerance are acquired by parents and the children.

III. Transracial adoption builds cultural bridges.

Even though speeches on questions of value do not ask listeners to do anything, they frequently precipitate action on the part of receivers. Receivers who are persuaded of the rightness or wrongness, morality or immorality of a particular belief are simply more apt to exhibit behaviors in support of or in opposition to that belief in the future.

Speaking on a Question of Policy

What should be done? What action should be taken? Your answer lies in the formulation of a proposition of policy. A proposition of policy suggests that some action or some change in policy be effected to remedy an existing situation or solve a perceived problem. When you speak on a question of policy, you recommend a change (or no change), and your goal is to earn either audience members' approval of the policy you are advocating or their overt participation in an action program.

You can probably identify countless instances in which someone to whom you were listening advocated the acceptance and/or implementation of a specific course of action. When a legislator recommends the passage or rejection of a balanced budget bill, when a social activist urges the elimination of discriminatory wage practices, or when a political strategist campaigns for the adoption of a constitutional amendment abolishing the electoral college, each is petitioning for a particular policy because he or she believes it is both needed and desirable; hence the traditional inclusion of the word "should" in the phrasing of the proposition itself.

Speeches on propositions of policy are given for a number of different reasons. In addition to speakers who urge the adoption of a new course of action, there are also those who speak to defend the existence of a specific policy (abortion should remain legal, for example) as well as those who speak to deter acceptance of a proposed change in policy (prayer should not be allowed in public schools, for instance).

When speaking on a question of policy, your job is to convince your listeners that your stance is the right one. That is accomplished first with reasons, and second by proposing practical action or a solution. Propositions of policy usually involve and build on both propositions of fact and propositions of value. Thus, in order for you to persuade your audience that action is merited, you first have to establish in their minds a proposition of fact as well as have them accept a proposition of value.

Unless you believe you can show a need for the policy you are advocating, there is no point in defending or arguing for it. Once you demonstrate that a need exists, it is then incumbent on you to suggest a solution and illustrate how that solution would help alleviate the problem.

The following are typical propositions for policy speeches:

A culturally literate student should study America's multicultural reality.

Congress should pass a national health insurance law.

College athletes should have to maintain a minimum C average to compete in sports.

The use of drugs should be decriminalized.

The death penalty should be abolished.

Creationism should not be taught in schools.

We should support the hospice movement.

Grade inflation should be ended.

The cloning of human beings should be illegal.

Let's look more closely at the first example. If you were to speak on this proposition, you might determine that your responsibilities included convincing your receivers of three things: (1) that there was a problem with the way culture is taught in our schools now, (2) that our education system is overly eurocentric, and (3) that existing curricula need to be modified to include courses in other cultures and courses in race in America.[18]

Organizing the Policy Speech: Diverse Concerns. A speech on a proposition of policy naturally divides into a **problem–causes–solution** organizational framework. The first main point depicts the nature and seriousness of the problem, the second main point explains the causes of the problem, and the third main point proposes the solution and describes its practicality and its benefits.

Specific purpose: To persuade my audience that a culturally literate student should study America's multicultural reality.

Proposition: A culturally literate student should study America's multicultural reality.

Main ideas:

I. Cultural illiteracy among students has become a serious problem on campus.
   A. American students still perceive Asian, African American, Chicano/Latino, and Native American students as strangers.
   B. Racial slurs and ethnic violence on campuses are increasing.

II. College curricula contribute to cultural illiteracy among students.
   A. Courses are taught from an overly Eurocentric perspective.
   B. Students are rarely required to take ethnic studies.

III. The problem can be solved by defining an educated person as one who has an awareness of multicultural reality.
   A. Students need to know the origins and histories of cultures they will interact with during and after college.
   B. Faculty members can be trained in ethnic studies in order to strengthen ethnic studies programs.
   C. The need for greater cultural diversity will not go away.

Individuals often agree about the facts surrounding an issue, and may even share a similiar value orientation; despite these agreements, however, they may disagree about what should be done. For example, an entire community may agree that homelessness among children is a serious problem, and they may share a value that stresses that we are responsible for all children, not just our own flesh and blood; yet they may disagree regarding what should be done to improve the lives of homeless children. Some, for instance, may argue that homeless children should be placed in foster homes; others may propose that more money should be spent on housing the homeless; still others may contend that homelessness should be viewed as a natural disaster so that a mammoth effort could be made to rid society of homelessness altogether.

Other times disagreements about policy revolve not just around solutions, but also around what the relevant facts and/or values are. The issue of whether public high school students should be given condoms to fight the spread of AIDS is typical of the kinds of disagreements in facts and values that characterize policy disputes. Opponents of condom distribution argue that artificial forms of birth control are unethical and not valid as a means of AIDS prevention. Proponents point out that if a condom saves a human life, it cannot be considered immoral or unethical, and the facts show that condoms help control the spread of AIDS. Of course, those opposed to condom distribution counter that abstinence is even more effective. Thus we see that policy disagreements revolve around values, facts, and courses of action.

Whatever the nature of the policy disagreement, there are four aspects of any controversy that advocates usually address:

1. Is there a problem with the status quo?
2. Is it fixable—are the causes rectifiable?
3. Will the proposed solution work?
4. Will the costs of fixing the problem outweigh the benefits of fixing the problem—that is, will the proposed solution help, or will it create new and more serious problems?[19]

The amount of time you need to spend discussing your proposition's causes, plan, or practicality depends on a number of factors including your topic and your audience's knowledge, attitudes, beliefs, and opinions. Should your audience be unfamiliar with your topic and unaware of a need for a change, then you would be wise to spend extra time covering need before discussing either your plan or its practicality. In contrast, if your listeners were aware of the problem you were discussing and were convinced of a need for action, then you would be in a position to review quickly the need for change and move on to a consideration of your plan and its viability. When this is the case, you might organize your presentation by using a **comparative advantages** order. In lieu of spending a great deal of time exploring why there is a problem, you would instead spend more of your time explaining why the solution you propose is better than other proposed solutions.

Specific purpose: To persuade my audience why women should learn the art of self-defense as a means of preventing date rape rather than dressing differently, denying their romantic desires, or talking firmly.

Proposition: Learning the art of self-defense is more beneficial to a woman as a means to protect herself against date rape than is either dressing demurely, refraining from dating, or talking firmly.

Main points:

I. Learning the art of self-defense costs less in the end and is more effective than purchasing an all-new wardrobe to prevent date rape.

II. Learning the art of self-defense is more effective than is refraining from dating as a means to prevent date rape.

III. Learning the art of self-defense is more practical than is talking firmly to prevent date rape.

Whichever part of your proposal generates the most controversy or disagreement among receivers is where you need to concentrate your persuasive efforts. Thus, if you were to propose that pornographic movie houses be banned from operating in your town, you would probably want to devote much of your time to a discussion of the effects of pornography as well as an analysis of how doing so would not interfere with the First Amendment right of freedom of speech.[20] If, on the other hand, you opposed the banning of pornographic movie houses, one of your major points might be to stress that taking such an action would create more problems than it would remedy, especially when it comes to First Amendment rights.

Speaking of Critical Thinking

Side-Wise

In an essay entitled "Corn-pone Opinions," Mark Twain noted:

> Men think they think upon the great political questions, and they do, but they think with their party, not independently; they read its literature, but not that of the other side.

Now consider this excerpt from the book *Age of Propaganda* by psychologists Anthony Pratkanis and Eliot Aronson:

> Suppose you are about to make a speech attempting to persuade your audience that more spending on education is necessary or that the budget deficit should be reduced through cuts in domestic spending. Would you persuade more people if you stated your view and ignored the arguments against your position, or would you be more persuasive if you discussed the opposing arguments and attempted to refute them?
>
> Before trying to answer this question, let's look closely at the factors involved. If a communicator mentions the opposition's arguments, it might indicate that he or she is an objective, fair minded person; this could enhance the speaker's trustworthiness and thus increase his or her effectiveness. On the other hand, if a communicator so much as mentions the arguments on the other side of the issue, it might suggest to the audience that the issue is a controversial one; this could confuse members of the audience, make them vacillate, induce them to search for counterarguments, and ultimately reduce the persuasiveness of the communication.
>
> With these possibilities in mind, it should not come as a surprise to the reader that there is no simple relation between one-sided arguments and the effectiveness of communication. It depends to some extent upon how well informed the audience is and on the audience's initial opinions on the issue.
>
> Research generally finds that the more well-informed the members of the audience are, the less likely they are to be persuaded by a one-sided argument and the more likely they are to be persuaded by an argument that brings out the important opposing arguments and then attempts to refute them. This makes sense: A well-informed person is more likely to know some of the counterarguments; when the communicator avoids mentioning these, the knowledgeable members of the audience are likely to conclude that the communicator is either unfair or is unable to refute such arguments. On the other hand, an uninformed person is less apt to know of the existence of opposing arguments. If the counter-argument is ignored, the less-informed members of the audience are persuaded; if the counterargument is presented, they might get confused.[21]

- Carefully weigh the insights offered by Twain and Pratkanis and Aronson. Then consider this question: When a speaker limits his or her discussion to one side of an issue, what judgment, if any, is the speaker making about your intelligence, and how do you feel about that?

AN ORGANIZING FRAMEWORK FOR A PERSUASIVE SPEECH

MANY SPEAKERS HAVE FOUND one organizational framework particularly effective in motivating receivers to act: this preferred pattern is called **Monroe's Motivated Sequence** and was developed more than three decades ago by Alan Monroe, a professor of speech at Purdue University. Based on the psychology of persuasion, Monroe's Motivated Sequence is comprised of five key phases that sequentially move listeners toward accepting and acting on a proposition of policy.

Phase One—Attention. It is at the outset of a speech (Chapter 10) that you work to gain the attention of your audience. In this phase it is up to you to whet the collective appetite of receivers and increase their interest in your proposal.

Phase Two—Need. During this part of the speech you show your receivers that there is a serious problem with a present situation. By explicitly stating the need and illustrating it with an array of supporting materials and by showing audience members what's wrong and relating it to their interests and desires, you prepare them for your solution.

Phase Three—Satisfaction. You have shown your audience that there is a need, and now you satisfy their desire for a solution. In this phase you present your plan and explain it fully to audience members. Help them understand that alleviating the problem will also satisfy their interests and desires.

Phase Four—Visualization. You "drive your plan home" by visualizing its benefits for your receivers, by visualizing how things will be different and better when your plan is put into action. In other words, you need to demonstrate for receivers how what you are proposing will benefit them and improve the situation as well.

Phase Five—Action. As soon as your audience is persuaded that your policy is the right one, you are ready to ask them to support it and act on it. Tell audience members specifically what you would like them to do, and conclude (as discussed in Chapter 8) with an appeal that reinforces their commitment and desire to respond as you ask.

As one theorist suggested, "Rhetoric is the process of adjusting ideas to people and people to ideas."[22] The diversity inherent in ideas is matched only by the diversity of viewpoints that people have about them.

The next outline illustrates how one speaker used the motivational sequence to help her design a presentation advocating the rejection of ethnocentrism in public schools.

INTRODUCTION

Phase One: ATTENTION

I. In Eastern Europe, where nationalism and ethnicity are on the rise, racial, ethnic, and religious tensions are also on the rise.

II. In the United States, we are also preoccupied with tensions about race and ethnicity.

III. Unlike Eastern Europe, we are not going to disintegrate.

IV. Today I would like to explain to you why our greatest concern as educators should be to promote multiculturalism in our schools.

BODY

Phase Two: NEED

I. The need to promote multiculturalism in schools can no longer be ignored.
   A. Children in American classrooms represent all the world's races, religious, and ethnic groups.

- B. We must educate all children so they can enjoy productive lives as American citizens.

II. These problems could be alleviated by promoting a curriculum that is pluralistic rather than ethnocentric. *Phase Three: SATISFACTION*
- A. The pluralist approach prepares children to live in a world of competing ideas and values, to be able to live and work with people from different backgrounds, and to learn to examine their own beliefs.
  1. Pluralism teaches children that they are part of a multiracial, multiethnic world.
  2. Pluralism teaches we are all part of a cultural mosaic.
  3. Pluralism stresses critical thinking.
- B. The ethnocentric approach to American culture insists that we must identify only with people who have the same skin color or ethnicity.
  1. Ethnocentrism immerses children in a prideful version of their own race and ethnicity.
  2. Ethnocentrism teaches children to respect only those who are part of their own group.
  3. Ethnocentrism teaches children not to raise doubts.

III. The public schools must prepare the younger generation to live in a world of differences. *Phase Four: VISUALIZATION*
- A. Imagine the history curriculum not as a tool to build ethnic pride, but as a subject in which we learn about our society.
- B. Imagine if differences were not grounds for hatred, but grounds for respect.

IV. A program on multiculturalism has been proposed to the school board. *Phase Five: ACTION*
- A. You can help ensure its passage by circulating petitions I will give you after my speech.
- B. If we all support these changes, we can build a better-balanced school curriculum.

CONCLUSION

I. I urge you to help rid our schools of ethnocentrism.

II. It is time to teach respect for those who are different.[23]

PERSUASIVE SPEAKING AND AUDIENCE DIVERSITY: STRATEGIES THAT ENHANCE PERSUASIVE SPEAKING EFFECTIVENESS

WHO HAVE YOU RECENTLY attempted to persuade, and who do you hope to persuade in the future? What do the targets of your efforts think of you? How do they feel about your subjects? What do they think is your motivation for speaking before them? Your answers to these questions affect the way you put your persuasive presentation together; your answers also influence your overall persuasiveness. The strategies you choose depend on the unique demands of your particular speaking situation, as well as your ability to integrate and apply them persuasively.

Move Closer to Your Goals

By understanding your audience's knowledge base, interests, and attitudes toward your goal, you move closer to your goal. When you equip yourself with reasons and a solid body of evidence supporting your speech goal and tailor them to the interests and concerns of receivers, you move closer to your goal. When you find ways to explain to receivers why they should accept your proposition as true, you move closer to your goal. When you position your material in an organizational framework reflective of your assessment of your audience's attitude, you move closer to your goal. When you use language that arouses the interests and concerns of your receivers, you move closer to your goal. When you convince your listeners that they should view you as a credible source, you move closer to your goal. And finally, by developing a dynamic and effective delivery style, you move closer to your goal. Whether you are speaking on a question of fact, value, or policy, it is the ability to customize and adjust (not distort or sacrifice) your messages to suit the needs of a particular audience that makes it more feasible for you to realize your goal.

No matter how proficient a persuader you become, no matter how skilled you become at applying techniques of persuasion, you will probably be unable to persuade all the people to accept all of your messages all of the time (see Figure 16.2). Some of your listeners, for example, will take a position diametrically opposed to yours and you will most likely have little, if any, chance of totally changing their minds. You may, however, be able to move them a step closer to your goal, and that's a step in the right direction. Others may already accept your stance, and while you may not have to persuade them to accept your point of view, you still need to motivate them to stay with you as you work to bring others in line with them and inch closer to your goal. And then there are the undecided or the uncommitted; provide these listeners with reasons to care, solid evidence, and the right appeals, and you'll move them a lot closer to your goal too. Can you move everyone in your audience to the goal post? No. Some you will, others you will move closer, and some, their feet firmly entrenched, will stay right where they are—for the moment, anyway.

When you select that portion of the audience you most want to move closer to your goal with any one speech, you have selected a **target audience.** It is this segment of your audience that you need to keep uppermost in your mind; it is their needs, their values, their concerns, and their interests that you consider as you design your presentation. Selecting a target audience, however, does not give you the right

Figure 16.2

Speakers rarely succeed in persuading their receivers to agree with everything they say.

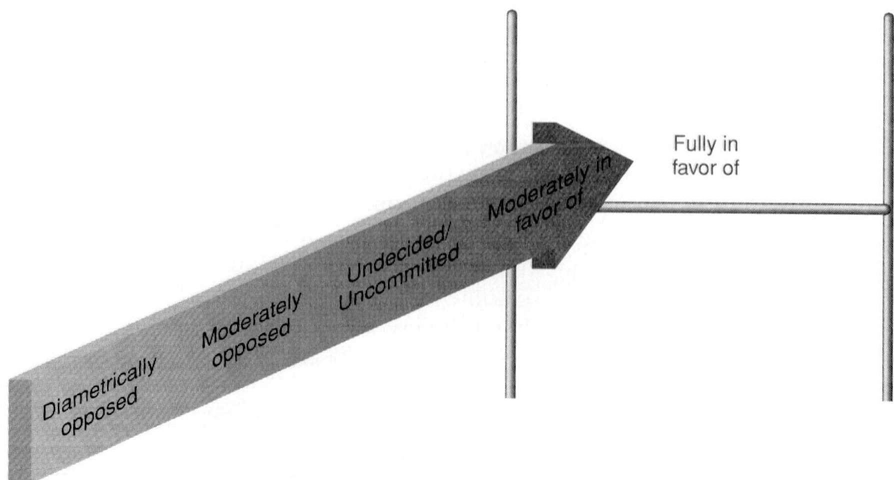

to ignore or discount the importance of the remainder of your audience; after all, you are speaking before them as well, and they, too, may be swayed by appropriately chosen facts, opinions, and examples. However, if you are a sensible speaker, you will decide which segment of the audience you most want to reach right now, and then aim your message and supporting materials directly at them. To succeed at this, you also need to consider how you should structure your speech to produce the desired persuasive effects.

For example, a politician starting a campaign for public office may speak before an audience containing avid supporters, curious uncommitteds, and ardent opponents. While the major thrust of the politician's appeal will be targeted to those she expects will work in her behalf, she is careful not to alienate other segments of the audience and, indeed, hopes that her remarks will move them toward her end of the support continuum.

Your practice of persuasion will improve your ability to hit the target. As you learn how to enchance your credibility in the eyes of your receivers, as you find ways to win over receivers with evidence, as you improve your ability to use reasoning to convince and language to touch, you become a more adept persuader, and you move even closer to your goal.

Build Credibility

A credible source is one who is perceived as qualified to address an audience on a particular subject. Who do you view as a highly credible source? What about yourself? Do you have credibility in your own eyes? Some people who are well-respected by others and are believed by those who know them to have credibility do not view themselves as credible. Suffering from an affliction called the "Imposter Phenomenon," such individuals do not believe they deserve the respect they get. Instead, they view themselves as frauds, each thinking that his or her reputation has surpassed its reality. Source credibility is a fluid phenomenon; it varies with the perceiver. With public speaking it is the audience, not the speaker, that determines whether a speaker has credibility.

The amount of source credibility you have for your receivers influences how they evaluate your message. The higher the credibility they perceive you to have, the more apt they are to believe what you say, and the more likely they are to do as you advocate.

Your credibility in their eyes is affected by three major factors: (1) their perceptions of your **competence;** (2) their perception of your **character,** and (3) whether they think you are dynamic or possess **charisma.** In addition, your credibility can also be divided into three constituent parts: **initial credibility** (how your receivers perceive you before you speak); **derived credibility** (how they perceive you while you are speaking); and **terminal credibility** (how they perceive you after your speech). Having high initial credibility can have a hidden advantage for you. If at the very start of your persuasive speech your listeners believe you know your subject and are well informed, that you are honest and concerned for their well-being, as well as energetic and committed to your point of view, then they will be more apt to give your ideas a receptive hearing. This is not to say that speakers with high initial credibility do not sometimes end their presentations with low terminal credibility; that can and does occur. But so does the opposite situation. Thus, your initial credibility can be enhanced or weakened by the contents of your message and your delivery style. Additionally, the opinions audience members have of you at the end of one speech could affect the way they view you at the beginning of another speech. You are only as credible as your receivers perceive you to be—at the moment. For example, the maker of a new brand of ice cream would need to more clearly demonstrate his or her knowledge of ice cream manufacturing, retailing, and distribution when speaking before an audience of representatives from major food store chains than would the maker of an established ice cream. On the other hand, overconfidence might cause someone from a major corporation to exhibit a lack of concern for the needs of receivers and a lack of familiarity with product innovations, and he or she might thereby lose credibility.

Because your audience will decide whether to think or do as you advocate based on how competent, trustworthy, and dynamic they judge you to be, you would be wise to provide them with the fuel they need to ignite a positive judgment. To establish your competence, share how your background and experience qualify you to speak on your chosen subject, document your ideas, and cite the sources you use. To promote confidence and trust in your receivers do not lie, exaggerate, or distort the facts or engage in name calling or other unethical practices. Indicate why you are concerned with the well-being of your receivers, and whenever possible demonstrate how you are putting your concerns for them above your own personal interests. By practicing and refining delivery techniques, by speaking your words enthusiastically and convincingly, you will enhance judgments of charisma. Thus, you can improve your credibility by planning your speech thoroughly, researching it carefully, organizing and phrasing your ideas appropriately, establishing common ground with your listeners, and delivering your ideas dynamically. When your receivers perceive you to be the kind of person they like and admire, when you include in your speech the words and thoughts of persons audience members like and admire, when you demonstrate that you share a number of attitudes, beliefs, and values with your receivers, then both your credibility and their persuasibility will increase.

As helpful as perceived credibility (**ethos**) is to the realization of your persuasive goal, only when credibility is united with evidence and reasoning (**logos**) will your message achieve more lasting impact.

Use Evidence

Evidence is the supporting materials used for persuasive purposes. The kinds of supporting materials we looked at in Chapter 8 can all be used to enhance your effectiveness as a persuader. For example, you can use specific **facts and statistics** to lay the groundwork for persuasion and validate the conclusions you are asking receivers to accept. Similarly, you can use more detailed **examples** or **illustrations** both to create human interest and to motivate receivers to respond as desired and/or become involved. In like fashion, **expert testimony** from sources that receivers respect can be used to add credence and confirmation to the positions you advocate. By relying on evidence that is substantial, relevant, and recent, you move your listeners closer to your goal. In contrast, if the conclusions you want your receivers to draw are based not on strong evidence but on weak, insufficient, or dated evidence, you will lack persuasive power. Because today's listeners have learned to be skeptical of unsupported generalizations, it is essential that you make a commitment to support your positions with strong evidence. Let us look once more at the key types of evidence and establish guide posts you can use to test the strength and validity of each form of support.

Facts. A **fact** is a statement that can be proven true or false based on direct observation. Which U.S. president sent troops to Bosnia? When did TWA flight 800 fall from the sky? The answers to these questions are absolute. Facts, once proven, are noncontroversial and can be verified on demand. However, for a number of reasons, their use often precipitates controversy. For instance, there may not be enough information to label a statement a fact. We do not know for sure that cellular phones cause cancer or that oat bran reduces cholesterol levels. Still, people try to convince others that the statements they are making are true. Without direct substantiation of a fact's truth, however, we can only make an inference.

An **inference** is a conclusion we draw based on a fact. You know that as a persuader it will be neccessary for you to draw inferences, to infer from what has been observed, but you will want to be able to assess the validity of your inferences—to ensure that they have a high probability of being true.

Antonia C. Novello, former surgeon general of the United States, used facts to support her proposition that young people must have the health information they need to make vital, healthy choices. In a speech entitled "Health Priorities for the Nineties" delivered in Los Angeles, she told the members of her audience:

> Illegal, underage drinking is one issue which I have identified to be a cornerstone of my agenda as Surgeon General. . . .
>
> I have been working on this issue since September, 1990, when I launched a "fact finding" mission on this issue. I toured the country talking to community leaders, to teachers, and to young people about the problem of illegal underage drinking.
>
> I learned that this issue is *more pervasive than I originally realized*—and that it is truly the mainstream drug abuse issue plaguing most communities and families in America today.
>
> I also learned that, in order to realize any success, we need to strengthen our prevention efforts—I've learned that *prevention works best if the message* the young person gets at home is the one he or she gets at school, and at church, and is the one *reinforced by his community and his peers. . . .*
>
> In June 1991, I released *Youth and Alcohol: Drinking Habits, Access, Attitudes and Knowledge* and *Do They Know What They Are Drinking?*
>
> The studies show that:
>
> • At least 8 million American teenagers use alcohol every week, and almost half a million go on a weekly binge (or five drinks in a row)—confirming earlier studies by the National Institute on Drug Abuse. . . .
>
> • Many teenagers who drink are using alcohol to handle stress and boredom. And many of them drink alone, breaking the old stereotype of party drinking.
>
> • Labeling is a big problem. Two out of three teenagers cannot distinguish alcoholic from non-alcoholic beverages because they appear similar on the store shelves.
>
> • Teenagers lack essential knowledge about alcohol . . . close to two million do not even know a law exists pertaining to illegal underage drinking.[24]

To confirm the validity of the facts and inferences you use in support of a persuasive argument, ask yourself if the following guide post statements can be answered *true:*

- ❑ There is little, if any, controversy regarding whether the statement made is true.
- ❑ The statement is based on a report by someone who directly observed the situation or the event.

Statistics. Statistics are numbers used to summarize a group of observations. They are helpful in showing contrasts and comparisons in observed data and in emphasizing and magnifying distinctive patterns and significant differences. As with facts, you need to verify the accuracy and the validity of the statistics you use. Eddie Williams, president of the Joint Center for Political and Economic Studies, used the following statistical evidence in a speech delivered before the Public Affairs Council of Pomona, California, titled "The Future of Black Politics: From the Margin to the Mainstream."

The inevitability of demographic change, as well as some of the implications of that change, was underscored in the Hudson Institute's report for the Labor Department on Workforce 2000. By the beginning of the next century, four out of every five people entering the American workforce will be minorities, women and immigrants. One in every three Americans will be a racial minority. In fact, in the next century the phrase "racial minority" may become less meaningful because no racial, ethnic or color group will comprise an absolute majority of Americans. In many political jurisdictions today we already find a majority of minorities, and it is clear that the nation as a whole is headed in that direction.[25]

Test your statistics by seeing if you can label these guide post statements as *true:*

- ❑ The statistics I am using are recent.
- ❑ The statistics are from an unbiased and reliable source.
- ❑ The statistics are noncontroversial.
- ❑ The statistics are drawn from a sample representative of the entire population.

Examples and Illustrations. Examples and illustrations are used to vivify and develop facts. As noted in Chapter 8, speakers use the following kinds of examples: specific instances and real or hypothetical illustrations or narratives.

Speakers use a series of **specific instances** (brief examples, usually no longer than a sentence or two) to support points they want accepted by receivers. They use **illustrations** or **narratives** (extended examples) to add more drama and emotional involvement to their messages. Specific and extended examples, when *real,* are used by speakers to build their cases and to encourage audiences to draw desired conclusions. On the other hand, while speakers also use hypothetical examples (examples invented to make a point) to enhance interest and further audience identification with their topics, they should not use them to encourage receivers to draw conclusions. In "Pesticides Speech," Cesar Chávez, president of the United Farm Workers of America, used an example to add emotional impact to his proposition that pesticides sprayed on table grapes are killing America's children:

. . . The children who live in towns like McFarland are surrounded by the grape fields that employ their parents. The children contact the poisons when they play outside, when they drink the water and when they hug their parents returning from the fields. And the children are dying. They are dying slow, painful, cruel deaths in towns called cancer clusters. In cancer clusters like McFarland, where the childhood cancer rate is 800 percent above normal.

A few months ago, the parents of a brave little girl in the agricultural community of Earlimart came to the United Farm Workers to ask for our help. Their four year old daughter, Natalie Ramirez, has lost one kidney to cancer and is threatened with the loss of another. The Ramirez family knew about our protests in nearby McFarland and thought there might be a similar problem in their home town. Our union members went door to door in Earlimart and found that the Ramirez family's worst fears were true. There are at least four other children suffering from cancer and/or diseases which the experts believe were caused by pesticides in the little town of Earlimart, a rate 1200 percent above normal. In Earlimart, little Jimmy Caudillo died recently from leukemia at the age of three.[26]

You can validate your examples and illustrations by determining if you can label each of the following four guide post statements as *true:*

- ❑ The example is typical; it is representative of what actually occurs.
- ❑ The example is significant; it shows clearly that a number of things are influenced by it.
- ❑ There is little if any controversy regarding the veracity of the example.
- ❑ The example comes from a reliable source, one perceived to be an authority.

Testimony. The opinions of respected individuals are used by speakers to add credence to the conclusions they draw. In a speech titled "Diversity: The Key to Quality Business," John E. Cleghorn, president and COO of the Royal Bank of Canada, used testimony to reinforce his point that ethnic, racial, and cultural differences should be viewed as building blocks rather than impediments:

This is the age of the individual. People are less willing to be assimilated, even if it's only for the working part of their day. As leading U.S. diversity expert Roosevelt Thomas, Jr., puts it, prospective employees are saying: "I'm different, and proud of what makes me so. I can help your team, and I would like to join you, but only if I can do so without compromising my uniqueness."[27]

If you can respond to the following guide post statements with *true,* then the testimony you are using is probably fair, unbiased, and appropriate.

- ❑ The source being quoted is a recognized expert.
- ❑ The source has no personal stake in the issue being presented.
- ❑ The source's statement is consistent with the statements of other experts.
- ❑ The source's statement is not contrary to what the source has said in the past—that is, the source is not waffling.

Although all of these kinds of evidence can be of aid to you as you build your speech, ask yourself which kinds your audience will expect and respond to most favorably. Keep in mind that in addition to helping you prove the validity of your proposition, evidence can also be used to help "inoculate" your receivers against arguments made by those who disagree with you by applying counterpersuasion efforts.[28] Evidence that is most persuasive is that which the audience was not aware of, evidence that makes each listener question his or her position if it's different from yours, evidence that anticipates the questions and doubts of receivers and puts them firmly to rest. While finding such evidence is not easy, it is well worth the effort if it helps prove your proposition.

Appeal to Reason

Effective persuasive speakers reason with their audiences by presenting evidence and arguments that help move their receivers closer to the desired goal of their speech. Effective reasoning depends on these three essential facets working together:

1. Evidence—the bases for your conclusion
2. Conclusion—the inferences you draw, which you need to substantiate with evidence
3. Warrant—a statement (uttered or implied) that explains the relationship between the evidence and your conclusion; that is, warrants contain the information that establishes a link between your data and your claim.[29]

It is the warrant that connects what you know (your evidence) to the proposition you want your receivers to accept (your conclusion).

Persuaders rely on four key methods of reasoning to move receivers toward affirming and/or acting on their goal: (1) deductive reasoning, (2) inductive reasoning, (3) causal reasoning, and (4) analogical reasoning.

Deductive Reasoning. When you use **deductive reasoning,** you move from the general to the specific. You offer general evidence that leads to a specific conclusion.

Deductive reasons take the form of **syllogisms,** which are used in persuasion to structure arguments. A syllogism is composed of three parts: a major premise (that is, a general statement or truth; for example, *plastic litter kills animals*); a minor premise (a more specific statement that describes a claim made about a related object; for example, *birds, turtles, sea lions, and an array of mammals have died from ingesting plastic litter*); and a conclusion (derived from both the major premise and the minor premise; for example, *we must keep plastic litter away from animals*). The next examples also illustrate how syllogisms work:

MAJOR PREMISE: We must condemn speech that precipitates violence.
MINOR PREMISE: A speech by the grand wizard of the Ku Klux Klan in our state will precipitate violence.
CONCLUSION: Therefore, we must condemn this speech.

MAJOR PREMISE: Persons who go on fad diets instead of changing eating habits permanently usually gain back the weight they have lost.
MINOR PREMISE: You want to maintain weight loss.
CONCLUSION: Therefore you should avoid fad diets.

You can evaluate examples of deductive reason by asking and answering two questions that examine a deductive argument's validity:

1. Are both the major premise and the minor premise true?
2. Does the conclusion follow logically from the premises?

When you use deductive reasoning you introduce your receivers to your general claim first. One of the potential disadvantages of the deductive approach is that *receivers who oppose your claim may tune out and not pay attention to the specifics you offer.* Instead of giving you the opportunity to provide reasons for them to accept your conclusion, they may be too busy rebutting your initial contention in their own minds. Of course, if you are addressing an audience that is not hostile to your proposal but favors it and merely needs reinforcing, then deductive reasoning will work better.

In this example from a speech entitled "Sacred Rights: Preserving Reproductive Freedom," Faye Wattleton, president of Planned Parenthood, defends legal protection for reproductive choice. Notice how she uses deductive reasoning to make a point:

We've already seen some bizarre legal outcomes of this religious definition of human life. Lawsuits have cropped up claiming fetuses as dependents for tax purposes—or charging "illegal imprisonment" of the fetuses of pregnant inmates—or seeking to reclassify juvenile offenders as adults by tacking an extra nine months onto their age![30]

Inductive Reasoning. When you use **inductive reasoning,** you progress from a series of specific observations to a more general claim or conclusion. You offer audience members particular reasons why they should support your generalization. For example:

FACT 1:	The divorce rate is at an historically high figure.
FACT 2:	It is estimated that 60 percent of today's five-year-olds will live in a single-parent family before they are eighteen.
FACT 3:	About three million children between five and thirteen have no adult supervision after school and are more likely to use drugs.
CONCLUSION:	There is widespread family instability in American society.[31]

Reasoning from specifics to a generalization is common practice. The next example is also illustrative of this pattern.

FACT 1:	The standard of living for most American familes has declined.
FACT 2:	Home ownership opportunities have declined.
FACT 3:	Opportunities for high school graduates to attend college have declined.
CONCLUSION:	This is the first generation in American history to have more downward than upward social mobility.

When we utter statements like "College graduates earn more than high school graduates," "Fad diets do not produce long-lasting results," or "Racial tension is increasing in major cities," audience members have a right to know that we are basing our conclusions on particular observations or occurrences. It is essential that the facts we present support the conclusions that we draw.

FACT 1:	One of every three children violates the "no drinking before the age 21" law by the age of 12.
FACT 2:	Businesses benefit from violating the "no drinking before the age of 21" law.
FACT 3:	Parents commonly violate the "no drinking before the age of 21" law.
CONCLUSION:	"The no drinking before the age of 21" law is widely disregarded in our society.

In the last example of inductive reasoning the speaker provided three ways the "no drinking before the age of 21" law is violated regularly and then drew a conclusion. The speaker could also have chosen to work backward by starting with a conclusion and then providing facts to support it. You can evaluate whether a speaker's use of inductive reasoning is effective by asking and answering these two questions:

1. Is the sample of specific reasons of a substantial size to justify the conclusion drawn?
2. Are the instances cited typical and respresentative?

In effective inductive reasoning, generalizations flow logically from the specific evidence you offer.

Causal Reasoning. When using **causal reasoning**—that is, reasoning that unites two or more events to prove that one or more of them caused the other—a speaker either cites observed causes and infers effects or cites observed effects and infers causes. We use causal reasoning daily. Something takes place and we ask: "Why?" Similarly, we hypothesize about the effects of certain actions. The next series of statements illustrates causal reasoning:

The stereotype of the successful minority hurts Asian Americans.

Focusing on averages and success stories hurts Asian Americans.

The fact that many organizations no longer consider Asians a disadvantaged minority hurts Asian Americans.

The problems faced by the majority of Asian Americans are not being taken seriously enough.

Passive smoking causes respiratory disease among nonsmokers.

Passive smoking causes cancer among nonsmokers.

Passive smoking causes heart disease among nonsmokers.

Cigarette smoking is hazardous to the health of nonsmokers and should be banned from public places.

In this excerpt from a speech by Dr. Bernice Sandler, senior scholar in residence, National Association for Women in Education, in Washington, D.C., titled "Men and Women Getting Along: These Are the Times That Try Men's Souls," Sandler uses causal reasoning to make a point:

Peer harrassment makes women feel less than equal. They may feel uncomfortable and annoyed. They may feel embarrassed, humiliated or degraded. They may feel disgusted, they may feel helpless, angry, unsure of how to respond. They may feel insulted, and they may be fearful of violence. They may also feel guilty and blame themselves, as if *they* did something that caused the men to act so badly. The cumulative effect of repeated harassment can be devastating. It reinforces self-doubt, and affects a woman's self-esteem, and even her academic experience. It makes co-education less equal for women. It makes some women angry at men, and it may make it more difficult for some women to trust men.

Peer harassment also affects men. Peer harrassment teaches men that relationships based on power are better than those based on intimacy and friendship. It makes it difficult for a man to form a healthy and satisfying relationship with a woman because it is hard to be committed to someone for whom he and others have so little respect. When men view women as objects to be demeaned and scorned, men find it difficult to relate to women as equal human beings—much less as friends or potential romantic partners or as co-workers. Even a man's friendship with other men will be shallow if the way to friendship with his brothers is to ridicule women rather than (build) a friendship based on shared feelings.[32]

You can evaluate the soundness of causal reasoning by asking and answering two questions:

1. Is the cause cited real or actual?
2. Is the cause cited an oversimplification?

Remember, causal reasoning associates events that precede with events that follow; it shows us that antecedents lead to consequences.

Reasoning from Analogy. Finally, when **reasoning from analogy,** we compare like things and conclude that because they are comparable in a number of ways, they are also comparable in another, until now, unexplored respect. For instance, if you proposed that the strategies used to decrease welfare fraud in a major city would also work in your city, you would first have to establish that your city was like the other city in a number of important ways—perhaps the number of persons on welfare, the number of social service workers, and its financial resources. If you could convince audience members that the two cities were alike or paralleled each other, except for the fact that your city did not yet have such a system in place and that the number of cases of welfare fraud was consequently higher in your city than in the other city, then you would be reasoning by analogy. Reasoning by analogy suggests that if two things are similar, then what is true of one should be true for the other. Something we are familiar with or aware of can be used to demonstrate something unfamiliar or unknown. In a speech entitled "Reshaping Political Values in the Information Age: The Power of the Media" Lawrence K. Grossman, former president of both PBS and NBC News, used an analogy to buttress his argument:

> For the first 150 years of the Republic, Congressmen, once they were in Washington, had little contact with their constituents. Members of Congress had to exercise their own independent judgment on most issues. Political theorists from Thomas Hobbes to Edmund Burke had debated the classic question, "How much should elected representatives directly reflect the opinion of their constituents back home?" But that debate took place in a world in which many groups couldn't vote, news was scarce and hard to come by, and no one really knew how to measure public opinion other than in an election. The difficulties of travel and irregularity of mail delivery made communication between constituents and Congress problematic in the extreme. Thomas Jefferson bought the Louisiana Purchase from France, doubling the size of the nation, without telling a soul about it until more than a year later. Most people in the country didn't know the War of 1812 had ended until many months after the peace treaty was signed. And the nation was much smaller then.
>
> Today, things have swung to the opposite extreme. Daily polling, e-mail, 800 numbers, faxes, the internet and call-in shows have exponentially increased the daily contact that representatives have with their constituents. The Orwellian nightmare of a tyrannical government holding all citizens under constant electronic surveillance, "Big brother is watching you," has been stood on its head. Instead of big brother watching every citizen, in the telecommunications era every citizen now can keep the nation's political leaders under constant electronic surveillance. The president's private life has become a public spectacle.[33]

Use these two questions to check the validity of the analogy you devise:

1. Are the objects of comparison alike in essential respects? That is, are they more alike than they are different?
2. Are the differences that exist significant?

The best speakers combine several kinds of reasoning in an effort to justify the position they are taking. Thus, your reasoning options are open. If you are going to speak ethically, however, you do not have the option of becoming unreasonable—that is, of using an argument that has only the facade but not the substance of valid reasoning.

THE ETHICS OF SENSEMAKING: REASONING WITHOUT LOGICAL FALLACIES

A FALLACY IS A FLAWED REASON. It is unreasonable to offer audience members patterns of reasoning that have been marred by the inclusion of one or more fallacies. Among the reasoning fallacies you should be aware of are the hasty generalization, post hoc ergo propter hoc, the slippery slope, the red herring, the false division, the argument ad hominem, the appeal to popular opinion, the appeal to tradition, and the appeal to authority. In addition to not using these kinds of fallacious reasons yourself, you will also want to be able to spot them when they are used by others. Effective reasoning and effective thinking go hand in hand. When you attempt to persuade with inadequate evidence or inappropriate arguments, you abuse the practice of critical thinking and you misuse the reasoning process. When reasoning becomes a mirage, the validity of the persuasive process suffers. Let's explore how.

Avoid Hasty Generalizations

You make a **hasty generalization** when you are too quick to draw an inference and thus jump to a conclusion that is based on too little evidence. To avoid inflicting your presentation with this reasoning defect, you need to be sure to have reviewed enough typical cases to validate your claim. Urging the recall of a sleeping pill because a few people have suffered adverse personality changes attributed to it, or the closure of a food chain because of one case of salmonella are examples of hasty generalizations.

Avoid Post Hoc Ergo Propter Hoc

Post hoc ergo propter hoc is translated literally as "after this, therefore, because of this." Reasoning suffers from this malady when you assume inappropriately that because one event preceded another, the first event caused the second event to happen. Because an event may have more than one cause or be preceded by an event that had absolutely nothing to do with it, this line of thinking adds confusion rather than clarity. What this fallacy reminds us is that correlation is not equivalent to causation. Just because one event happens subsequent to another does not necessarily mean that it was caused by the first event. The collapse of the Soviet Union is not necessarily due to the presidency of George Bush, just as the rain storm did not occur because you washed your car, and a friend's pregnancy did not occur because she ate Chinese food. Determining the relationship that exists between two things can be complicated, so tread lightly.

Avoid the Slippery Slope

You find yourself on a **slippery slope** when you assert that one action will precipitate or set in motion a chain of actions. This kind of suspect reasoning was used to justify United States involvement in Vietnam and in that instance at least has come to be known as the "Domino Theory"; adherents argued that if Vietnam fell to the Communists, then Laos, Thailand, Cambodia, and eventually all of Asia would fall to the Communists as well. As we now know, Asia did not fall entirely into Communist hands.

Similarly, arguing that if our government assumed responsibility for health care and initiated a national health insurance program then before we knew it, we would be living under socialism, is another example of a slippery slope argument in free fall; the argument is weak and subject to question.

Avoid the Red Herring

When you put a **red herring** in your speech you attempt to send the members of your audience on a wild goose chase. By leading them to consider an irrelevant issue, you stop them from considering the subject actually under discussion. The term "red herring" is attributed to an act performed during an English fox hunt in which the hunt master would drag a red herring across a trail in an attempt to divert the dogs from chasing the fox. When you distract your audience from concentrating on real issues by injecting an irrelevant issue into your speech, you deflect their attention from the meaningful issue. For example, in an effort to defend the right of individuals to smoke in public places, one speaker attempted to deflect his listener's concern by focusing instead on the dangers of automobile emissions.

Avoid the False Division

When you infect your speech with a **false division** (also referred to as a "false dilemma" or "false dichotomy"), you inappropriately require the members of your audience to choose between two options (usually polar extremes) when in reality there are many options in between. "America: Love it or leave it," "Live free or die, " When guns are outlawed, only outlaws will have guns," "If you are not part of the solution, you are part of the problem," "If you're not for it, you're against it," and "Either you served in the armed services or you are unpatriotic," are examples of the false division at work.

Avoid Argument Ad Hominem

When you present your audience with an **argument ad hominem** (literally, an argument against the man), you inject name calling into your speech. In effect, you ask members of your audience to reject an idea because of a flaw in a person associated with that idea. Whenever a speaker attacks a person's character instead of his or her stand on a particular issue, an attempt is being made by the persuader to infuse "ad hominem" venom into the receptors of persuadees. "She's just a member of generation X." "He's a baby boomer with baby boomer ideas." "Social security is a liberal plot to undermine our financial stability." Each of these is an example of name calling—an unreasonable response to a situation that demands reason.

Avoid Other Inappropriate Appeals to the Audience

Like the argument ad hominem, the appeals to popular opinion, tradition, and misplaced authority also ask audience members to act unreasonably and reject or accept an idea without actually considering the idea itself. Also known as the "bandwagon fallacy," the **appeal to popular opinion** tells receivers that because "everyone is doing it" or "supporting it," they should too. Just because many believe something, however, does not necessarily make it true. False notions can be widely held. Just as ideas should not be rejected because of a person connected with them, so ideas should not be accepted because "everyone thinks it's great."

The **appeal to tradition** is similar. When you appeal to tradition, you ask the members of your audience to accept your idea or plan because that's the way it's always been done, or to reject a new idea because the old way of doing things is better. By discouraging the reexamination of established ways of doing things, appeals to tradition reinforce the status quo simply because "that's the way it is." But because it was or is that way today does not necessarily make it better or best. Women didn't always have the right to vote, nonwhites weren't always guaranteed equal rights, and the handicapped didn't always have equal access.

Appeals to misplaced authority also rely for their impact on a lack of critical thinking on the part of receivers. When we are asked to endorse an idea because a well-liked personality who knows little or nothing about the idea's value and is not an expert on the subject endorses it, we are face to face with an unreason, and we should question it critically. What we must keep in mind is that name recognition does not necessarily equal expertise. While Arnold Schwarzenegger may be an expert when it comes to talking about what makes an adventure or science fiction film work, he has little if any expertise in foreign relations; thus, his opinion on the foreign policy of the United States would probably be less valued by a discerning audience than would that of a former secretary of state.

As you get better at reasoning, you also get better at both detecting examples of unreasoning and evaluating critically the unreasonableness exhibited by the speaker.

TARGET AUDIENCE NEEDS AND FEARS AND AROUSE THE EMOTIONS OF RECEIVERS

WE THINK. WE REASON. WE ALSO FEEL. And we tend to react most strongly when we feel angry, anxious, excited, concerned, or guilty. When speakers arouse such feelings in us, when they use **pathos** or appeals to our emotions to enhance the arguments they are making to support their claims, they hope to instill in us appropriate attitudes and beliefs and elicit from us desired actions.

Emotional appeals are effective at eliciting a wide array of human feelings. When effective, they help convince us to think or behave differently. In fact, it is often only with an emotional appeal that a speaker can succeed in motivating audience members to respond as desired. By eliminating complacency or passivity in receivers, by making it impossible for receivers to be bored or unaffected by a speech's content, emotional appeals move listeners closer to a speaker's goal. Thus the strongest arguments—and therefore the strongest speeches—are amalgams of logic and passion.

The greater your understanding of what your audience needs, fears, and aspires to achieve, the greater your chances of gaining their attention, sustaining their interest, and ultimately persuading them to accept what you are advocating or follow through on what you are asking them to do.

The classic theory of needs looked to again and again as a means of explaining human motivation was developed by a psychologist named Abraham Maslow and is now referred to as **Maslow's Hierarchy of Needs.**[34] Maslow depicted motivation as

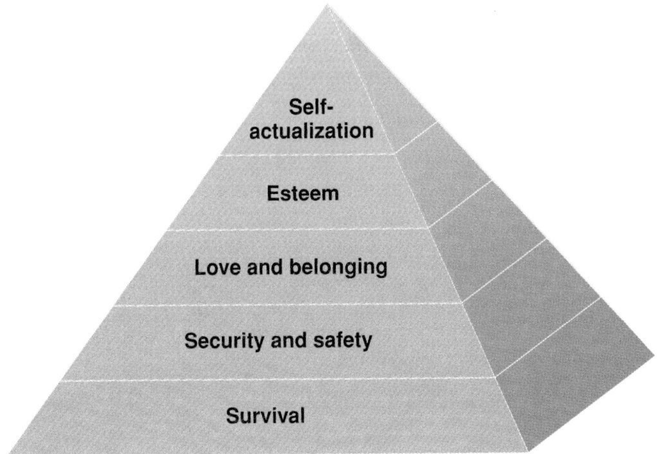

Figure 16.3

Depicting motivation as a pyramid, Maslow's Hierarchy of Needs helps speakers focus on appeals they can use to facilitate attention, involvement, and receptivity among receivers.

a pyramid; our most basic needs are at the pyramid's base and our most sophisticated needs are at its apex (see Figure 16.3).

According to Maslow, among our survival needs are the basic necessities of life: air, shelter, food, water, and procreation. Safety needs include the need for security and the need to know that our survival needs are being satisfied. We have a need to feel safe and secure, and to know that those we care about are protected as well. Our need for love and belonging is located at the third level of the hierarchy; there also lies our needs for social contact and to fit into a group. The fourth tier focuses on esteem needs—represented by our need for self-respect, and our need to feel that others respect and value us. Finally, situated at the pyramid's apex is our need for self-realization, defined as our need to realize our full potential and to accomplish everything we are capable of. By focusing on audience members' relevant need levels, speakers have in their possession the keys needed to unlock audience attention, in-

Like many contemporary speakers, Nelson Mandela tries to relate his ideas to the needs and interests of audience members.

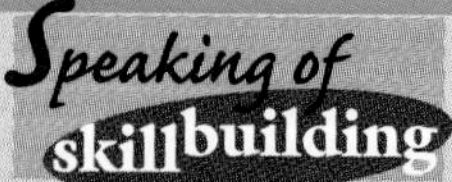

How to Handle the Hierarchy of Needs

Use Maslow's Hierarchy of Needs to target the types of needs you will appeal to when attempting to persuade receivers to believe or behave as you desire in the following situations.

1. You want to persuade an audience of high school seniors not to drink and drive.
2. You want to convince the police that foot patrols in a major city are in the best interests of all.
3. You want to persuade an audience of college students to donate blood.
4. You want to convince an audience of veterans that flag burning should be a criminal act.
5. You want to convince Congress that a law should be passed prohibiting members of any president's cabinet from ever becoming lobbyists.

volvement, and receptivity. As a persuader you should realize that unless audience members have their physiological needs met, they will rarely be motivated by appeals to other needs.

One means of persuading audience members to respond as you desire is to create fear in them, to encourage them to draw in their minds a vivid picture of serious or dire consequences that could arise, were they to refrain from taking certain actions. Threats to loved ones are particularly effective motivators—more effective than fear appeals directed at your listeners themselves. In order for a fear appeal to work as successfully as possible, however, audience members must believe:

- You are a credible source.
- The threat you describe is real.
- Taking action to remove the threat will restore them to a state of balance.

Considering Diversity

Are the Same Things Important to All?

Compile three different lists: of attitudes, beliefs, or values: one list that could cause you to argue vehemently for the attitude, belief, or value; one that could cause you to argue vehemently against the attitude, belief, or value; one that could cause you to display little if any interest in the attitude, belief, or value. Share your lists with other students in an effort to identify the attitudes, beliefs, and values people felt were most important and to which they were most and least committed.

To what extent, if any, were similar attitudes, beliefs, and values shared by persons of similar ethnic, racial, economic, or social backgrounds? To what extent, if any, were they different?

Effective speakers use their knowledge of such similarities and differences to develop appeals and arguments that succeed in moving receivers closer to their desired goals.

When the message you design succeeds in generating fear among receivers, both your persuasiveness and their persuasability increase.[35] Keep in mind, however, that only if the message you present reveals to receivers how the threat can be removed will the fear you produce be effective in changing their attitudes or behaviors. If you know what audience members fear most, if you understand what they absolutely do not want to give up or lose, if you can locate and/or create vivid examples that arouse fear in them, then you have the means to move them closer to the position you are advocating. Remember, however, that once you do induce fear in them, you have an ethical responsibility to explain how what you are asking them to think or do will free them of the fear you have induced.

PUT THREE TENETS OF PERSUASION INTO PRACTICE

WOULDN'T LIFE BE SIMPLE if just by following an equation or a formula you could attain your persuasive goals? "X + Y = Z!" However, persuasion is not a pure science, and no such equation exists. On the other hand, there are a number of principles you can use to guide you as you prepare to deliver a persuasive speech to a group.

Think Small to Avoid a Big Fall

A common error among speakers is to expect a dramatic conversion in the way listeners view their proposals. Instant conversions and dramatic changes are the exception; they are not the rule. Persuasion is traditionally a step-by-step process; if you try to skip too many steps at one time, if you expect too much from your receivers as a result of your one speech, then your persuasive attempt becomes clumsy and you precipitate your own failure. Your receivers will be much more apt to change their way of thinking and/or behaving if the change you request requires smaller rather than larger changes. Keep in mind, however, that you can expect more change from receivers who have not taken a position on an issue of controversy than from those who are already committed to an opposing position.

Use the Desire for Consistency

If you use the present attitudes, beliefs, and values of receivers as a base and build your suggested changes on top of them, then you show how what you are advocating is consistent with the way audience members think and behave. We are more comfortable if we are shown that there is consistency among our attitudes, beliefs, values and behavior. When we feel that what someone is asking us to believe, think, or do contradicts our current beliefs, we will be less apt to be persuaded by them. However, if someone can show us why what we currently believe, think or do is in opposition to, out of sync with, or dissonant with attitudes or beliefs we hold or what we value, then to restore balance, consistency, and comfort or a feeling of well-being to our world, we will change as requested. Thus, one way to convince listeners to accept or act on your proposition is to demonstrate for them that a current situation has created an imbalance in their lives and that you can help them restore their lives to a balanced state.

Don't Put the Best in the Middle

Experts on persuasive placement advise speakers to use both primacy and recency theories as guides when positioning key persuasive points. Consequently, your goal is either to put your strongest point up front in an effort to win listeners to your side early in your presentation or to put your strongest argument last in an effort to build momentum for change and acceptance among listeners toward the end of your speech. Whether you choose to use a primacy or a recency approach to speech design, keep in mind that the middle position is weaker than either one. Thus, your best and strongest argument certainly does not belong there. By positioning your arguments appropriately, you can enhance receiver persuasibility.

MEDICAL PRIVACY—REALITY OR FICTION

by Tina Campbell

The speaker uses an illustration to add human interest and to immediately involve receivers in considering the problem she wants to address.

Jim Gatten, a land developer, visited his doctor for a routine checkup. His doctor asked him several common questions, such as how much alcohol do you drink? Gatten responded that he drank approximately two six packs of beer a month. Jim never thought that comment could turn his life upside down. However, a few months later Gatten was denied health insurance. And the reason? His medical records had been released to the insurance company—and even more amazing—with inaccurate information. Jim Gatten was denied insurance because his medical records stated he drank two six packs of beer a day rather than a month. Mr. Gatten learned what most Americans don't realize—there is no such thing as medical privacy anymore.

By explaining the problem and how it affects the audience, the speaker enhances audience involvement.

The use of statistics adds importance to the subject.

The speaker clearly states her proposition and previews the content of the speech.

Medical information that has been made public has had devastating effects. It has cost people their jobs, ruined their standing in the community, and, in extreme cases, pushed people to end their own lives. The unauthorized disclosure of the medical records of ordinary citizens has become a growing concern for each of us. The *Atlanta Journal and Constitution* of August 19, 1994, informs its readers that survey results confirmed two out of three people are concerned about the protection of their medical records—and rightly so. These findings suggest that as we move toward national health care reform, there is a strong need for more active steps to be taken to protect medical privacy. First, let's diagnose the significance of this problem. Then we'll turn to the causes, and finally I'll offer a prescription to protect our medical privacy.

The speaker introduces the first main point.

The speaker uses a variety of authoritative sources to demonstrate the seriousness of the problem and the consequences of inaction.

First, as we diagnose this problem we can turn to the *Gannett News Service* of November 1, 1994, to see that the days of patient confidentiality are over. Between insurance companies, careless medical professionals, and confusing release forms, insurers can find medical secrets about a patient and use the information any way they see fit, with or without your knowledge. And in this case, what you don't know can hurt you. A study released last year by the National Academy of Sciences' Institute of Medicine concluded that threats to medical privacy are "real and not numerically trivial." For example, a 1993 Harris poll showed that of those surveyed, 27 percent of the public—representing fifty million American adults—report that an organization to which they had given their medical information had disclosed it to others without their permission. And as we turn to the October 1994 issue of *Consumer Reports,* we learn that medical information is often sold or traded. Drug companies and mailing-list brokers use the information to support giant medical mailing lists that let them target patients with specific health problems. As the health care profession becomes more and more competitive, patient medical records aren't just gathering dust anymore. For example, a computerized medical record can easily be accessed by people outside the physican's office. The Physician Computer Network, which is partially owned by IBM, has computer access to the patient records of 41,000 doctors. This means that the records of one out of every ten office-based doctors in the U.S. are a general network that can be accessed by any of its many subscribers. Dr. Jeanne Kasslen writes in her 1994 book *Bitter Medicine* that the protection of medical records is at best sporadic in the private sector. And amazingly, often what leaks out is not even correct. The Massachusetts-based Medical Information Bureau, or MIB, maintains medical records on approximately fifty million people for insurance companies. If you have ever filled out an application for insurance, most likely that company turned to the MIB to get a medical history on you. MIB President Neil Day admits that 3 to 4 percent of the database is incorrect. This may not sound very significant, but it means that the records of roughly a half a million people are inaccurate. Insurance underwriters making decisions based solely on MIB reports could wrongly reject or overcharge many thousands of consumers every year. With all of these possible case scenarios the American public is becoming afraid to confide in their doctors. Sadly, these are the individuals who most need all the information we can provide so that they can do their jobs.

The speaker directly addresses receivers, drawing them into the speech.

Now that we have a clear picture of how this lack of medical privacy can affect each of us, let's examine three main reasons why our medical privacy is at risk—inadequate governmental involvement, minimal precautions taken by the medical community, and lack of individual knowledge. The *Times-Picayune* reports on March 30, 1994, that the right to confidentiality concerning personal medical histories and health records has been eroding over the past several years. In agreement, *The National Law Journal* of May 30, 1994, provides insight into our government's neglect. There are no federal laws to protect medical privacy. Each state has different levels of legal protection. Beyond this, no one has a clue which rules apply when medical records cross state lines for insurance purposes. It becomes a complicated guessing game in which there are no clear winners. Alan Westin, professor of law and government at Columbia University, stressed in the *Daily Labor Report* of August 19, 1994, that most state laws enacted to protect medical privacy rights are much too narrow in scope and are for this reason ineffective in dealing with this situation.

The speaker segues into the next part of the speech.

The speaker again employs a wide array of authoritative sources, testimony, and examples to buttress the case being made.

Of course our government can't shoulder all of the blame. According to the *Newswire* of February 21, 1995, the medical community, by computerizing records, has set itself up for failure. Industrial officials stated in the February 21, 1995, *Business Wire* that computer programs designed for the medical profession can be just as safe for storage of records as the doctor's office itself. However, these programs must not only be used correctly, they must also include such precautions as passwords and data encryption so that computer hackers can't just sit down at a terminal and extract data. Of course, the previously mentioned book *Bitter Medicine* stresses that these computer hackers are not as significant a threat as insider fraudulence. Insiders obtain the information for anyone wanting to buy it—and sell your privacy for the right price. This is really easier than you think, according to a *20/20* transcript from September 30, 1994. To see just how easy it is to tap into someone's medical records, *20/20* hired a private investigator, gave him the name of a woman, and asked him to find out everything he could about her medical history. By just picking up the telephone, calling a few local hospitals and claiming to be with an insurance company he was allowed access to privileged information.

Beyond industry failure, a lack of public knowledge about our medical privacy has also allowed this erosion of our rights. Many of us are under the impression that if someone wants access to our records that we will be contacted before any information is released. This is not normally the case—very seldom are patients no-

The speaker directly involves receivers in a consideration of the issue by addressing a common misconception.

By anticipating a prospective audience concern, the speaker adapts to audience needs.

The speaker segues into the solution phase of the speech.

By drawing on respected sources, the speaker adds credibility to the plan put forth.

The speaker personalizes the plan of action for receivers.

The speaker reviews the speech and refers back to the example used in the introduction, thereby achieving closure.

tified if someone accesses their records. We tend to have enough trust in our physicans not to ask questions. Even those who are aware that their records have been misused are often reluctant to come forward and stop this from happening to others, explains *Consumer Reports* of 1994. Recognizing the three reasons that led to the erosion of our medical privacy, let's see how we can regain what we never should have lost in the first place. Any solutions enacted must include governmental and medical community action. Additionally, each of us must get involved.

First, the government needs to be more involved with the issue of medical privacy. Turning to the December 1994 issue of *Money* we are told that stronger federal laws should take the place of all state laws. The American Hospitals Association and other industry groups support one uniform law. This would ensure that each state had the same restrictions placed on the protection of medical records and it would also answer the question of whose laws to follow when medical information must be transferred across state lines. Representative Gary Condit of California, chairman of a House subcommittee that oversees information issues, is in the process of drafting a health privacy bill. The heart of this bill will be uniform legal protection on the federal level so that our privacy is no longer in the hands of individual states. The *Daily Labor Report* of January 13, 1995, explains that the privacy issue is more likely to take center stage in reform legislation because it has grown more controversial through increased scrutiny. We must let our elected officials know that we support such laws.

However, federal legislation alone won't be enough. The medical community needs to do its part in the protection of medical privacy. This can be accomplished by simply setting up and monitoring specific guidelines to handle medical information. The *Canada Newswire* of May 31, 1994, spells out areas of focus. First, designate all personal medical information as sensitive and penalize those who release unauthorized information. Next, state exactly who has access to the medical records and what information they can obtain. Third, provide each individual the right to access his or her own medical records in the system. And very importantly, hire data-processing organizations based on their record of providing confidentiality and security standards.

Until such laws are created there are many steps that we can take to protect ourselves. Whenever you as a consumer deal with an insurance company make sure that you read the statement that authorizes the release of your medical information. If the authorization is vague, modify it and initial the changes. Make sure that these changes set limits on the type of information that can be collected as well as how long that information can be used. Don't be afraid to question your insurance company. They are there for your benefit, not vice versa.

More important, each of us must become aware and knowledgeable about our own medical records. Speak to your physician, and ask him to let you read your medical records. It is a good idea to obtain a copy of your own MIB record by just simply writing to them so that you can check for any errors. I do have copies of their address and would be more than happy to give it to anyone who is interested at the conclusion of my speech. If we as consumers make an effort to protect our privacy, sooner or later Congress will get the message, and this issue will become as important to them as it is to each of us.

Today, I've shown you how the lack of medical privacy in the U.S. has serious effects on each of our lives. Our lack of knowledge about this issue, along with governmental and medical community inadequacies, have allowed this problem to flourish. Don't forget the solutions I have provided and remember to be an active consumer so that we can change this state of emergency. Finally, remember the problems Jim Gatten endured because of one simple comment. No one, including the ones we love, should ever be forced to deal with this breach of confidentiality. Our medical records must remain private. It's a nonnegotiable issue.[36]

SUMMARY

PERSUASIVE ATTEMPTS TO CHANGE or reinforce attitudes, beliefs, values, and behaviors permeate our lives. In contrast to an informative speaker, a persuasive speaker calls on receivers to make choices among ways of thinking and behaving. A persuasive speaker usually seeks to accomplish one of the following: reinforcement of a position, shift in a position, or adoption or elimination of a behavior.

Persuasive speeches can be categorized according to whether they focus on a question of fact, value, or policy. The specific claim the persuasive speaker makes represents his or her proposition, that is, the conclusion the speaker wants receivers to draw.

While there are a number of organizational formats available to persuasive speakers, Monroe's Motivated Sequence has been singled out as particularly effective. It is composed of the following five key phases: attention, need, satisfaction, visualization, and action. The framework was designed to move receivers toward accepting and acting on a proposition of policy.

Persuasive speakers who learn to use a number of effective persuasive strategies are better able to move receivers closer to their goals. Once a persuasive speaker knows how to build his or her credibility, use a variety of types of evidence, use a variety of types of reasoning, reason without becoming unreasonable, and apply key principles of persuasion, he or she has a better chance of attaining his or her specific speechmaking objectives.

THE SPEAKER'S STAND

Deliver a five- to seven-minute persuasive speech. Be sure to buttress your presentation with evidence and reasons designed to convince your audience that your claim is sensible, as well as with emotional appeals that arouse their desire to respond as you request.

In addition, prepare an outline and include a bibliography of at least five sources you consulted.

STUDENT FOCUS GROUP REPORT

Now that you have had the opportunity to consider the requirements of persuasive speaking, in a group of five to seven students, answer the following questions:

1. What are the main challenges facing you as: (a) a persuasive speaker and (b) a member of an audience listening to a persuasive speech?
2. Which type of persuasive speaking presents you with the fewest problems? Which type poses the most problems for you?
3. Which speechmaker attitudes and abilities would facilitate the design and delivery of an effective persuasive speech? Which attitudes and behaviors would impede effective speech design and delivery?
4. How might a culturally diverse audience complicate and/or simplify a persuasive speaker's task?
5. What factors differentiate persuasive speaking from speaking that turns out to be unpersuasive?
6. To what ethical principles should persuasive speakers adhere?
7. Summarize the most important information you have learned about persuasive speaking
8. Revisit the case study at the chapter's opening. Based on what you now know, how would you revise your original answers?

Chapter Seventeen

Speaking on Special Occasions

After reading this chapter, you should be able to:

- Explain why speakers give special occasion speeches.
- Compare and contrast the goals and functions of various kinds of special occasion speaking.
- Define and distinguish between the following types of ceremonial speaking: the speech of introduction, the speech of presentation; the speech of acceptance; the commencement address; the keynote address; the speech of tribute; and the after-dinner speech.
- Prepare and deliver a ceremonial speech.

CASE STUDY

Graduation Speech

It had been almost a quarter of a century since Maria Delgado graduated from college. Now a successful businessperson and a benefactor of her alma mater, Maria had felt honored when the president of the school called and asked if she would deliver the commencement address at this year's graduation. Maria quickly accepted the invitation.

As the day approached, she became increasingly pensive. While she had enjoyed her years at the school and believed they had prepared her for graduate school and the world of work, she wondered what, if anything, she had in common with its present graduating class. In addition to the fact that the campus had become much more diverse than it had been when she attended it, these students were also representatives of "generation X," while she was a "baby boomer." What could she say to these students at graduation that would enable her to bridge the gap she perceived existed between them? How could her words help prepare them for their future?

- Put yourself in Maria's place.

1. What factors would you consider as you prepared the speech?
2. What would you do to build rapport with your receivers?
3. What would you speak about?
4. What effect would you want your speech to have?

"FOUR SCORE AND SEVEN YEARS AGO," begins one of the most famous special occasion speeches ever delivered in the history of the United States. Abraham Lincoln's address at the dedication of the national cemetery at Gettysburg was designed to reflect the needs of a very special occasion. When delivering that speech, now referred to as the "Gettysburg Address," Lincoln's purpose was not only to pay tribute to those who died during the Civil War, but also to help bring the nation together. As a special occasion speaker, you too may be called on to mark an event that is important to a particular group or community, to celebrate, commemorate, entertain, or inspire an audience.

Why do we give special occasion speeches? The ritualistic nature of certain occasions seems to call for them. People are born, married, retire, and die. Some people receive awards for sales productivity; others receive awards for athletic prowess. Groundbreakings are held for buildings. The openings of museums, theaters, or other public locations are cause for celebration.

In many ways, special occasions are the punctuation marks of life. They are the rituals that draw us together in celebration of some person or event. Right now, somewhere, there are individuals receiving or presenting awards, speaking to commemorate deeds well done, paying tribute to the memories of friends now departed, extolling the importance of a holiday, inspiring others to achieve greatness, or entertaining at banquets.

Special occasions are just that—they stand out from the routine because of their uniqueness. They are extraordinary, and they enrich our lives with their aura of specialness. Speeches delivered to help mark these occasions can be distinguished from

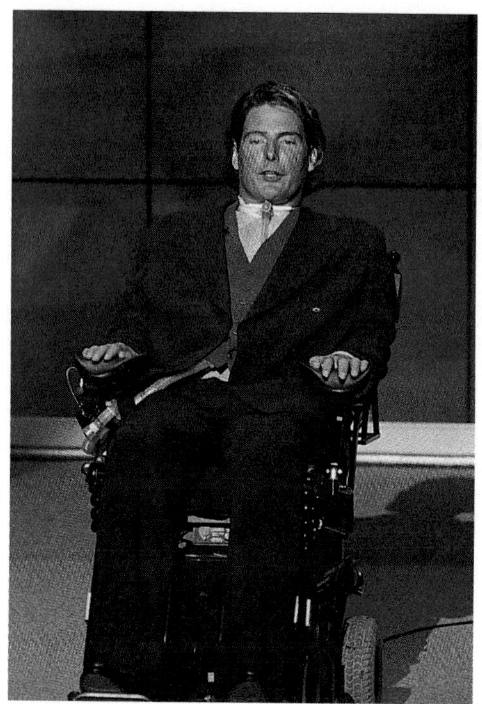

Unlike Christopher Reeve, you may never have the opportunity to make an Academy Award presentation. However, you may very well be asked to speak at another equally meaningful occasion.

other kinds of speeches we have considered thus far by the purposes they are designed to serve. While they may also inform and/or persuade, this is rarely, if ever, their prime function. Rather, their aim is to reflect the nature and needs of the special occasions that brought them about in the first place. By stressing the importance and the significance of a person or event, by stressing values that bind people together, and by playing a key role in a ritual, a special occasion speech also helps mark the specialness of the celebration.

THE CEREMONIAL SPEAKER: GOALS AND FUNCTIONS

THE INDIVIDUALS WHO SERVE as the speechmakers on special occasions serve a number of important functions. First, they are there to help magnify the significance of the event or person being honored, and second, they are there to help unify the audience by affirming the common values exhibited through the celebration of this person or event. To accomplish these objectives, the speaker must fully understand both the nature of the special occasion and the role he or she is to play in it.

For example, commencement speakers frequently reinforce the value of education and try to spur on graduates to achieve greatness. Those who deliver tributes or eulogies recognize shared values and achievements and acknowledge how the individual being honored contributed to the richness of the lives of those he or she touched. Whatever the special occasion, it is the speaker's obligation to deliver a speech ap-

Speaking of Critical Thinking

The Power of Words in Ceremonial Discourse

According to speechwriter Peggy Noonan, if the Gettysburg Address were to be delivered today, it would likely be edited by various political staffers as follows:[1]

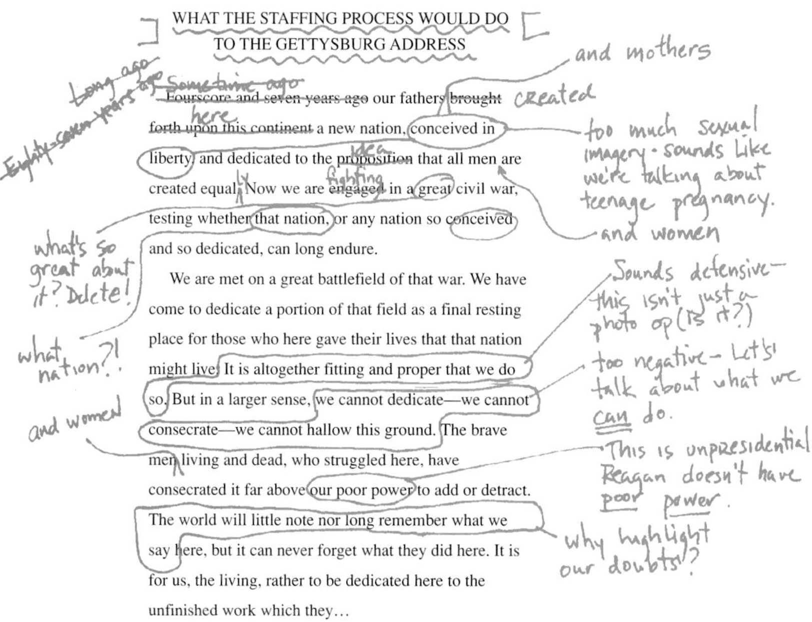

WHAT THE STAFFING PROCESS WOULD DO TO THE GETTYSBURG ADDRESS

~~Fourscore and seven years ago~~ our fathers ~~brought forth upon this continent~~ a new nation, conceived in liberty, and dedicated to the ~~proposition~~ that all men are created equal. Now we are ~~engaged~~ in a great civil war, testing whether that nation, or any nation so conceived and so dedicated, can long endure.

We are met on a great battlefield of that war. We have come to dedicate a portion of that field as a final resting place for those who here gave their lives that that nation might live. It is altogether fitting and proper that we do so. But in a larger sense, we cannot dedicate—we cannot consecrate—we cannot hallow this ground. The brave men living and dead, who struggled here, have consecrated it far above our poor power to add or detract. The world will little note nor long remember what we say here, but it can never forget what they did here. It is for us, the living, rather to be dedicated here to the unfinished work which they…

What do the suggested revisions reveal about the following: (1) the fear people have of words, and (2) the perceived power they attribute to words? To what extent, if any, would the changes indicated have altered the meaning of the original speech's text? Be specific.

propriate to that specific situation. Audiences come to such events with particular expectations, and the speaker's success depends on his or her ability to conform to established norms.

This is not to suggest that you become robot-like when delivering a special occasion speech. Far from it! As a special occasion speaker you have a real opportunity to show yourself as a warm, caring person. You are no longer speaking just for yourself; though the words you use are your own and the feelings you express are sincere, you are now speaking as a representative of a group. You are speaking to reflect the group's sentiments, to add a special texture to the fabric of someone's accomplishments or life, and to wrap the occasion in language and symbolism to which everyone present will be able to respond appropriately. The greater your knowledge of the people or events that precipitated the celebration, the more effective your speechmaking becomes. Though the spotlight may seem to be on you, your job is to refocus its beam onto the person or event that is the subject of the occasion and thus your speech.

TYPES OF CEREMONIAL SPEAKING

IN THE YEARS AHEAD IT IS likely you will be part of a number of special occasions that may require you to deliver a ceremonial speech. In this chapter we will explore those kinds of special occasion speeches you will be most apt to give. Among the types of ceremonial speeches we will explore are the speech of introduction, the award presentation and acceptance, the keynote address, the commencement address, the tribute, and the after-dinner speech.

The Speech of Introduction

When you deliver a **speech of introduction,** your task is to create a desire among audience members to listen to the featured speaker. By serving in effect as a "warm-up" or "advance agent" for the main speaker, you pave the way and psychologically prepare receivers for that speaker's presentation.

Your Responsibilities as an Introducer. During your brief introductory remarks, your goal is to: (1) establish the nature of the occasion (why the speaker is to speak); (2) enhance the speaker's credibility with receivers (foster perceptions of the speaker's competence); and (3) encourage audience members to focus on the speech's content (stress the importance and the timeliness of the speech). Though your speech of introduction should be short, lasting no more than two to three minutes, during that time it is your job to give receivers the information they need to comprehend who will be adressing them, what the subject of that person's speech will be, and why they should pay careful attention to it. Your role, while limited in scope (after all, you are not presenting the featured speech yourself) is nonetheless very important. The way you introduce the speaker—the nature of the background material you offer receivers about the speaker and why he or she was invited to speak, plus the context you provide for the speech to follow—will affect the reception given the speaker by members of the audience. For this reason, rather than merely offering a recitation of a resume, you want to use your speaking time to truly celebrate the person you are introducing. You are the bridge between the featured speaker and the audience, and it is up to you to establish the mood for his or her presentation.

If the bridge you build between speaker and audience is to be sturdy and secure, you need to be sure that the remarks you deliver are in keeping with the tone the main speaker will set. If you arouse the curiosity of receivers, if you create in them a real desire to listen to the speaker, if you avoid creating expectations the speaker will be unable to fulfill but you succeed in focusing the spotlight on the speaker and his or her topic in such a way that receivers are enthusiastic about listening to him or her, then you will have built a bridge that the anticipation of audience members will sustain.

The more well known the featured speaker is, the briefer the introduction you need to supply. For example, all that is usually said when introducing the president of the United States is: "Ladies and gentlemen, the president of the United States." Few of us, however, will have such an opportunity. In any case, your purpose is not to offer a detailed chronology of events in the speaker's life. Your job is simply to let receivers know that following you is a speaker they will both enjoy and profit from listening to, and why.

A Sample Speech of Introduction. The following speech of introduction was used by the chairperson of a sales organization's education committee to introduce motivational speaker Allan Dalton to an audience of real estate sales people.

INTRODUCING MR. MARKETING

During the past 14 years Allan Dalton has made a significant impact on the real estate industry in North America, and has consulted with real estate companies in all 50 states and Canada. His marketing management workshops and seminars have changed the lives of real estate agents and revolutionized entire companies. Allan has created four national real estate systems that are seen regularly on network television, and his video training programs can be found in more real estate offices in North America than probably any other.

The introducer enhances the speaker's credibility.

A former member of the Boston Celtics, Allan is now on an industrywide mission to help real estate salespeople like yourselves dramatically increase their income by helping consumers strengthen their security through real estate.

Ladies and gentlemen, I am pleased to present Mr. Marketing himself, Allan Dalton.

The introducer establishes the nature of the occasion and stresses what receivers will gain from the speaker's presentation.

The Speech of Presentation

The **speech of presentation** is another common form of ceremonial speaking. The event that precipitates this kind of speech is the presentation of an award such as the Nobel Prize, the Congressional Medal of Honor, or the Heisman trophy. Like the speech of introduction, the speech of presentation is usually brief; however, it often contains a somewhat more formal accolade.

Your Responsibilities as a Presenter. When delivering a speech of presentation, you are not just recognizing an individual, you are also honoring an ideal, and to this end you have three goals to achieve: (1) to summarize the purpose of the award or gift, including its history, its sponsor, the ideals it represents, and the stringent criteria used to select the receipient; (2) to discuss the accomplishments of the person being honored, including what the individual specifically did to achieve the award; and (3) to introduce and present the award winner to the audience (when possible, leave this to the very end; it adds drama to the announcement).

When you make a speech of presentation you shine the spotlight on an individual chosen to receive special honors or recognition. During your speech you acknowledge what the recipient did to achieve the award, and you discuss him or her in a way that enhances the significance of his or her achievements to audience members. As with the speech of introduction, you are not the star of the occasion; the audience did not come to listen to you, but rather to celebrate the winner.

When delivering a speech of presentation, avoid overpraising the recipient. What you want to do instead is to express sincere appreciation to the awardee for his or her

How would you have worded a speech of presentation for Tiger Woods after his success in the 1997 Masters?

accomplishments and to highlight the behavior, values, and ideals exhibited by the recipient that led to his or her receiving the award. After listening to your speech, there should be no question among audience members that the individual being honored deserves the award. For example, in presenting the Nobel Peace Prize to Elie Wiesel, the Nobel Committee noted that in a time of "violence, repression, and racism," Elie Wiesel spoke for "peace, atonement, and dignity." The committee went on to cite him as "one of the most important spiritual leaders and guides" of our time.[2]

A Sample Speech of Presentation. Actor Gregory Peck delivered the following speech of presentation when he awarded actor Danny Kaye the Jean Hersholt Humanitarian Award. Notice how by focusing on the special contributions Kaye made, Peck also explains the reasons for bestowing the award on Kaye.

GREGORY PECK PRESENTS AWARD TO DANNY KAYE

The speaker discusses the myriad accomplishments of the honoree.

It's a long trip from Brooklyn to Buckingham Palace, and it's a far piece from Beverly Hills to an obscure village in Bangladesh. Danny Kaye has made both journeys, sustained by his remarkable gifts, his grace, and his intelligence. He has been a star of the first magnitude since his remarkable talent exploded on the Broadway stage in *Lady in the Dark* in 1941, and one who has had a high sense of priority: His wife, Sylvia, his daughter, Dena, have always come first in his life—and then, in no special order, his work, the world's children, and great music.

For UNICEF (United Nations International Children's Emergency Fund), he continues to travel the world, bringing joy and hope to children on all the continents, and initiating programs to save them from hunger and give them a better chance in life. He has been doing this for years, with no pay and without fanfare. No trumpets. No headlines. His reward, the laughter of children.

As forbearing and skillful as he is with children, so he is with symphony orchestras, groups of seventy or eighty highly disciplined artists. He cannot read music, yet he has conducted major orchestras all over the world with musicianship that is sensitive, completely serious, and, at times, likely to veer off alarmingly into the hilarious. Danny's irrepressible *joie de vivre* makes his concerts joyous occasions for musicians and audiences alike. Bach and Mozart have no better friend. Nor have the orchestras and their pension funds. Nor have we.

And thus, for his prodigious labors for the children of the world, for the wondrous people who make music, the Board of Governors proudly gives the Jean Hersholt Humanitarian Award to a "Citizen of the World" who does honor to our profession—Mr. Danny Kaye.[3]

The speaker summarizes the purpose of the award and presents the award winner to the audience.

The Speech of Acceptance

The **speech of acceptance** is given in response to a speech of presentation. It is usually brief and and gives the person being recognized the opportunity to formally accept the award or praise being given to him or her.

Your Responsibilities during an Acceptance Speech. In an acceptance speech the recipient thanks, recognizes, and gives credit to both those who bestowed the honor and those who helped him or her attain it; reflects on the values represented by the award; explains, in particular, what the award means to him or her; and accepts it graciously. Speeches of acceptance, though also usually brief, are often inspirational in tone, and when well done also leave no doubt in the minds of audience members that the award was given to the right person.

A Sample Acceptance Speech. In the following acceptance speech excerpts, notice how Elie Wiesel, upon receiving the Nobel Peace Prize, helped receivers understand the meaning of the award and the ideals it honors. By pledging to continue his efforts and by using language in keeping with the dignity of the occasion, Wiesel also communicated the deeper meaning inherent in the award.

ELIE WIESEL ACCEPTS AWARD

It is with a profound sense of humility that I accept the honor you have chosen to bestow upon me. I know: your choice transcends me. This both frightens and pleases me.

The speaker accepts the award.

It frightens me because I wonder: do I have the right to represent the multitudes who have perished? Do I have the right to accept this great honor on their behalf? I do not. That would be presumptuous. No one may speak for the dead, no one may interpret their mutilated dreams and visions.

It pleases me because I may say that this honor belongs to all the survivors and their children, and through us, to the Jewish people with whose destiny I have always identified.

The speaker credits those who helped him attain the award, and through an extended narrative reflects on the values the award represents.

I remember: It happened yesterday or eternities ago. A young Jewish boy discovered the kingdom of the night. I remember his bewilderment, I remember his anguish. It all happened so fast. The ghetto. The deportation. The sealed cattle car. The fiery altar upon which the history of our people and the future of mankind were meant to be sacrificed.

I remember: He asked his father, "Can this be true? This is the 20th century, not the Middle Ages. Who would allow such crimes to be committed? How could the world remain silent?"

And now the boy is turning to me: "Tell me," he asks, "what have you done with my future? What have you done with your life?"

And I tell him that I have tried. That I have tried to keep memory alive, that I have tried to fight those who would forget. Because if we forget, we are guilty, we are accomplices.

And then I explained to him how naive we were, that the world did know and remained silent. And that is why I swore never to be silent whenever and wherever human beings endure suffering and humiliation. We must always take sides. Neutrality helps the oppressor, never the victim. Silence encourages the tormentor, never the tormented. . . .

The speaker explains the personal meaning the award has for him.

Of course, since I am a Jew profoundly rooted in my people's memory and tradition, my first reponse is to Jewish fears, Jewish needs, Jewish crises. For I belong to a traumatized generation, one that experienced the abandonment and solitude of our people. It would be unnatural for me not to make Jewish priorities my own, Israel, Soviet Jewry, Jews in Arab lands.

But there are others as important to me. Apartheid is, in my view, as abhorrent as anti-Semitism. To me, Andrei Sakharov's isolation is as much of a disgrace as Juset Begun's imprisonment. As is the denial of Solidarity and its leader Lech Walesa's right to dissent. And Nelson Mandela's interminable imprisonment.

There is so much injustice and suffering crying out for our attention: victims of hunger, or racism and political persecution, writers and poets, prisoners in so many lands governed by the left and by the right. Human rights are being violated on every continent. More people are oppressed than are free.

And then, too, there are the Palestinians to whose plight I am sensitive but whose methods I deplore. Violence and terrorism are not the answer. Something must be done about their suffering, and soon. I trust Israel, I have faith in the Jewish people. Let Israel be given a chance, let hatred and danger be removed from her horizons, and there will be peace in and around the Holy Land.

Yes, I have faith. Faith in God and even in His creation. Without it no action would be possible. And action is the only remedy to indifference: the most insidious danger of all. Isn't this the meaning of Alfred Nobel's legacy? Wasn't his fear of a war shield against war?

There is much to be done, there is much that can be done. One person—a Raoul Wallenberg, an Albert Schweitzer, one person of integrity, can make a difference, a difference of life and death. As long as one dissident is in prison, our freedom will not be true. As long as one child is hungry, our lives will be filled with anguish and shame. . . .

This is what I say to the young Jewish boy wondering what I have done with his years. It is in his name that I speak to you and that I express to you my deepest gratitude. No one is as capable of gratitude as one who has emerged from the kingdom of the night.

The speaker accepts the award graciously and with humility.

We know that every moment is a moment of grace, every hour an offering; not to share them would mean to betray them. Our lives no longer belong to us alone; they belong to all those who need us desperately.

Thank you Chairman Aarvik. Thank you, members of the Nobel Committee. Thank you, people of Norway, for declaring on this singular occasion that our survival has a meaning for mankind.[4]

The Commencement Address

The speaker of a **commencement address** praises and congratulates a graduating class. Commencement addresses are delivered by all sorts of people including politicians, distinguished alumni, actors and actresses, esteemed educators, and notable citizens.

Your Responsibilities as a Commencement Speaker. Because the commencement audience usually includes predominantly the families and friends of the graduates, people who want to hear glowing statements of praise about just one person—their relative or friend—it is incumbent upon the speaker to give them what they want. Usually, however, commencement speakers acknowledge how both the graduates and members of the audience contributed to the success being recognized that day.

Most commencement addresses do not stop with celebrating the recent achievements of graduates, however; they also challenge the graduates to focus on the future and the roles they will play in the months and years ahead. Commencement addresses that avoid cliches while emphasizng the accomplishments and promise of the graduates are the most effective.

A Sample Commencement Address. The following excerpted commencement address by Johnetta B. Cole, the president of Spelman College, was delivered to a graduating class of the College of New Rochelle.

JOHNETTA B. COLE ADDRESSES GRADUATES

The speaker congratulates the graduates and the other members of the audience.

You are absolutely wonderful. I have never been at a commencement quite like this. My sister, Sister Dorothy Ann, colleagues and staff of the College of New Rochelle, and distinguished members of this platform party, and most important of all this afternoon, the righteous class of 1991, let's greet our families and friends, because you know, as I know, without them you would not be here, at this, your commencement.

I want to talk about us women folk. I will do this without ignoring the men, who are no less a part of this ceremony. I do so convinced that our lives are so intertwined as women and men that as Martin Luther King once put it: "Until all of us are free, none of us is free." This address is about women, but it is addressed to and for both the women and men of this class of 1991 of the College of New Rochelle.

Now, clearly we women folk have made enormous progress. The job of securing equality for us is not yet done. To those who suggest that the job is done, I ask a series of questions:

The speaker identifies a series of problems and challenges that graduates will need to overcome as they make their way into the future.

Why are women and children the majority of those living in poverty?

Why do women college graduates of all racial and ethnic groups earn less than men with high school diplomas?

Why do women professionals still earn 68 percent of what male colleagues with comparable experience earn?

Why do us women folk comprise fewer than 16 percent of all state legislators and less than 6 percent of Congress? Don't folks know that we belong in the House and Senate, too?

Why is adequate child care seen as a woman's issue?

As a rule, why do girls emerge from adolescence with poor self-images, lower expections, and much less self-confidence than boys?

The last of this series of questions: Why is it that less than a dozen of the 6400 top ranking CEOs are women?

The inevitable answer is quite simply, sexism is alive and well in our nation. But I didn't have to come from Atlanta, Georgia, to tell you that. Perhaps I did have to come from Spelman—a great women's college—to discuss what to do about it. What do we do about the forms of discrimination against women in our society?

My answer, my sisters and brothers, is very simple. We must organize and we must act. In terms of sexism that is aimed at women, we women folk along with men must call it when we see it. Whether it is in our workplaces, in the public arena, or in our own homes. . . .

It seems to me that in all institutions in our society—schools, churches, synagogues, and workplaces—we must monitor matters on a daily basis so that we women get our fair share.

In terms of the struggle against sexism, we can say that the gains of women since the second wave of the women's movement are substantial. But unless we are vigilant, they will be taken away from us by those who refuse to understand that we women folk own half of the stock.

The last few years have seen an assault on hard earned women's rights. What is called for by many would define our place as only in the kitchen. And when we exit, "to the rear," we are told, and 2, 3, 4 steps behind our men folk. Now it seems to me that the problem with a woman walking behind her man is she can't see where she's going.

My sisters and my brothers. Let us remember that not all discrimination is a result of men victimizing women. It is possible that some women use differences as the basis for domination and exploitation. Yes. Do I mean the possibility of racism among women? I sure do! Do I mean intellectual elitism on the part of some women as they look down on less educated women? Yes. Do I mean the exploitation of women who work for women by the women for whom they work? Yes!

The point is this. Privilege can and will coexist with oppression. And being the victim of one form of oppression does not make one immune from turning around and victimizing somebody else.

What is to be done about the exploitation of women by us women? It seems to me that clearly we must follow those examples of women and men who have created and sustained the struggle for justice in our land. I mean the women and men who have countered the existence of racism and sexism in our country. . . .

So, my sisters, it seems to me that it takes constant vigilance for us to deal with racism and ethnic chauvanism among us women folk. . . .

Now, Sister Dorothy Ann told me I had a matter of minutes, and it is about those minutes. But as I bring closure on this, your graduation address, I want to end with the words of one of my sheroes, an African American woman whose very name stands in opposition to racial and gender inequality. These then are the words of Sojourner Truth, the great 19th century Christian soldier in the battle for the rights of Black people and the battle for the rights of women. Listen to them:

The speaker uses the words of Sojourner Truth to motivate graduates to take the lead and assert themselves in their efforts to realize their potential.

> My friends, I rejoice that you are Black. But I don't know how you're gonna feel when I get through. I come here from another field—a country in slavery. They got their liberty. So much good luck to have slavery partly destroyed—not entirely. But I want its root and grass destroyed. Then we're gonna be free, indeed. I feel that I have to answer for deeds done in my body as much as a man. Now, there is a great stir going on about colored men getting their rights. But not a word about the colored women. And if colored men get their rights, but the colored women don't get theirs, you see the colored men will be the masters over the women, and it will be just as bad as it was before. So, I'm for getting going while things is stirring, because if we wait until things is still, it's gonna take a great while to get it going again. And I want women to have their rights.
>
> Now, that little man back there in black. He says women can't have as much rights as men because Christ wasn't a woman. I want to ask you—where did Christ come from? Where did your Christ come from? He came from a woman. Man ain't had nothin' to do with it.
>
> Now if the first woman God ever made was strong enough to turn the world upside down, then these women here ought to be able to turn it back and get it right side up again.

> Now the men better let them. And a final message, sisters. I ain't clear what you be active about. If women want rights they ain't got, why don't they just take them and stop talking about it!

And so my sisters and brothers, of this graduating class, I wish for you the courage to insist upon your rights and the will and determination in securing those rights.

And I wish you the very best.

The Keynote Address

The purpose of the **keynote address** is to get a meeting off to a good start by establishing the right tone or mood. Whereas the commencement speaker is like a coach who is congratulating a team for a job well done, in many ways the keynote speaker is more like a cheerleader whose task it is to push listeners in the right direction and to inspire and motivate them to take appropriate action.

Your Responsibilities as the Presenter of a Keynote Speech. The functions of the keynoter vary. Some keynote speeches challenge receivers to act or achieve a goal while others outline a problem or series of problems for them to solve. Some keynote speeches are designed to generate enthusiasm and commitment, while others are designed to demonstrate the importance of a theme or outcome.

The best keynote speakers are adept at focusing audience attention on common goals, skilled at communicating the central focus of those gathered, and proficient in setting a tone that arouses interest and encourages commitment.

A Sample Keynote Speech. The functions of the keynote speech are well illustrated in a keynote address delivered by the late Representative Barbara Jordan, which is excerpted here.

BARBARA JORDAN, KEYNOTER

One hundred and fourty-four years ago, members of the Democratic Party first met in convention to select a Presidential candidate. Since that time, Democrats have continued to convene once every four years and draft a party platform and nominate a Presidential candidate. And our meeting this week is a continuation of that tradition.

The speaker establishes the significance of the occasion.

But there is something different about tonight. There is something special about tonight. What is different? What is special? I, Barbara Jordan, am a keynote speaker.

A lot of years passed since 1832, and during that time it would have been most unusual for any national party to ask that a Barbara Jordan deliver a keynote address . . . but tonight here I am. And I feel that notwithstanding the past that my presence here is one additional bit of evidence that the American Dream need not forever be deferred.

Now that I have this grand distinction what in the world am I supposed to say?

I could easily spend this time praising the accomplishments of this party and attacking the Republicans, but I don't choose to do that. . . .

The citizens of America expect more. They deserve and they want more than a recital of problems.

The speaker focuses the audience's attention on common goals and problems.

We are a people in a quandary about the present. We are a people in search of our future. We are a people in search of a national community. . . .

Throughout our history, when people have looked for new ways to solve their problems, and to uphold the principles of this nation, many times they have turned to political parties. They have often turned to the Democratic Party.

What is it, what is it about the Democratic Party that makes it the instrument that people use when they search for ways to shape their future? Well I believe the answer to that question lies in our concept of governing. Our concept of governing is derived from our view of people. It is a concept deeply rooted in a set of beliefs firmly etched in the national conscience of all of us.

Now what are these beliefs?

The speaker motivates receivers to remember their values and to take action based on them.

First, we believe in equality for all and privileges for none. This is a belief that each American regardless of background has equal standing in the public forum, all of us. Because we believe this idea so firmly, we are an inclusive rather than an exclusive party. Let everybody come.

I think it no accident that most of those emigrating to America in the 19th century identified with the Democratic party. We are a heterogeneous party made up of Americans of diverse backgrounds. . . .

We believe that the government which represents the authority of all the people, not just one interest group, but all the people has an obligation to actively, underscore actively, seek to remove those obstacles which would block individual achievement . . . obstacles emanating from race, sex, economic condition. The government must seek to remove them.

We are a party of innovation. We do not reject our traditions, but we are willing to adapt to changing circumstances, when change we must. We are willing to suffer the discomfort of change in order to achieve a better future.

We have a positive vision of the future founded on the belief that the gap between the promise and reality of America can one day be finally closed. We believe that.

This, my friends, is the bedrock of our concept of governing. This is a part of the reason why Americans have turned to the Democratic Party. These are the foundations upon which a national community can be built. . . .

In other times, I could stand here and give this kind of exposition on the beliefs of the Democratic Party and that would be enough. But today that is not enough. People want more. That is not sufficient reason for the majority of the people of this country to vote Democratic. We have made mistakes. In our haste to do all things for all people, we did not foresee the full consequences of our actions. And when the people raised their voices, we didn't hear. But our deafness was only a temporary condition, and not an irreversible condition. . . .

And now we must look to the future. Let us heed the voice of the people and recognize their common sense. If we do not, we not only blaspheme our political heritage, we ignore the common ties that bind all Americans.

Many fear the future. Many are distrustful of their leaders, and believe that their voices are never heard. Many seek only to satisfy their private work wants. To satisfy their private interests.

But this is the great danger America faces. That we will cease to be one nation and become instead a collection of interest groups: city against suburb, region against region, individual against individual. Each seeking to satisfy private wants.

If that happens, who then will speak for America?

Who then will speak for the common good?

This is the question which must be answered . . .

Are we to be one people bound together by common spirit sharing in a common endeavor or will we become a divided nation?

For all of its uncertainty, we cannot flee the future. We must not become the new puritans and reject our society. We must address and master the future together. It can be done if we restore the belief that we share a sense of national community, that we share a common national endeavor. It can be done. . . .

As a first step, we must restore our belief in ourselves. We are a generous people so why can't we be generous with each other? We need to take to heart the words spoken by Thomas Jefferson: "Let us restore to social intercourse that harmony and that affection without which liberty and even life are but dreary things."

The speaker's inspirational tone encourages receiver commitment.

A nation is formed by the willingness of each of us to share in the responsibility for upholding the common good.

A government is invigorated when each of us is willing to participate in shaping the future of this nation.

In this election year we must define the common good and begin again to shape a common future. Let each person do his or her part. If one citizen is unwilling to participate, all of us are going to suffer. For the American idea, though it is shared by all of us, is realized by each one of us.

And now, what are those of us who are elected public officials supposed to do? We call ourselves public servants but I'll tell you this: we as public servants must set an example for the rest of the nation. . . .

If we promise as public officials, we must deliver. If we as public officials propose, we must produce. If we say to the American people it is time for you to be sacrificial; sacrifice. If the public official says that, we (public officials) must be the first to give. We must be. And again, if we make mistakes, we must be willing to admit them. We have to do that. What we have to do is strike a balance between the idea that government should do everything and the idea, the belief, that government ought to do nothing. Strike a balance.

Let there be no illusions about the difficulty of forming this kind of a national community. It's tough, difficult, not easy. But a spirit of harmony will survive in America only if each of us remembers that we share a common destiny. If each of us remembers, when self-interest and bitterness seem to prevail, that we share a common destiny.

I have confidence that we can form this kind of national community.

I have confidence that the Democratic Party can lead the way. I have that confidence. We cannot improve on the system of government handed down to us by the founders of the Republic, there is no way to improve upon that. But what we can do is to find new ways to implement that system and realize our destiny.

Now, I began this speech by commenting to you on the uniqueness of a Barbara Jordan making the keynote address. Well I am going to close my speech by quoting a Republican president and I ask you that as you listen to these words of Abraham Lincoln, relate them to the concept of a national community in which every last one of us participates: "As I would not be slave, so I would not be master. This expresses my idea of Democracy. Whatever differs from this, to the extent of the difference, is no Democracy."[5]

The Speech of Tribute

Whether delivered to honor a living or dead person or an event, the purpose of the **speech of tribute** is to acknowledge and praise the honoree.

Your Responsibilities as Presenter of a Tribute Speech. The tribute speaker's job is to inform the audience of the accomplishments of a person or the importance of an event, but it is also to heighten the audience's awareness of and appreciation for the contributions achieved by the person or the outcomes or values of the event being commemorated.

To achieve this, the tribute speaker needs to involve the audience members by making the contributions of the person or the outcomes or values of the event relevant to their lives. He or she also needs to clearly explain why the individual or event is being celebrated or recognized, tell stories that make the accomplishments of the person or outcomes or values of the event live in the minds of receivers, and praise the honoree without engaging in gross exaggerations that cause the tribute to become unbelievable or even dishonest.

Three main features characterize the speech of tribute: (1) a section that describes what makes the subject of the speech worthy of praise and special recognition (the reasons for the recognition); (2) a section that explains in more depth what the subject actually accomplished; and (3) a section urging the audience to let the past accomplishments of the subject inspire them to make the values underlying the subject's accomplishments their own, so that they will seek new and greater goals.

A Sample Speech of Tribute. Although sometimes the subject of a tribute speech is a well-known figure, the person being singled out for special recognition does not need to be famous. In fact, each of us probably can think of one or more individuals who are neither famous nor public figures, but who still deserve special praise, as did student Dolores Bandow. In her speech, "A Bird Outside Your Window," Bandow pays tribute to her daughter Elizabeth, who was born with a genetic anomaly.

"A BIRD OUTSIDE YOUR WINDOW"—A TRIBUTE TO ELIZABETH

The speaker introduces receivers to the subject of the tribute.

I am here today to celebrate life. I am here to celebrate a particular life which began nine years ago this month. The day I gave birth to our third child, November 2, 1977, I thought was the bleakest day one could experience. My hopes for a healthy baby were sniffed away. Of two children born at the hospital that hour, both had birth defects. The other child died. For one dreadful, fleeting moment, I thought it would be easier if ours had.

To admit such a transient thought and regret such a thought is sobering. How selfish; how self-pitying; how wrong I was. I had wanted a "perfect" baby. But by shattering our illusion of perfection with her birth, she has been perfecting our reality with her life.

The speaker explores what the tribute's subject taught her and explains how the subject's achievements helped her realize the value of life.

Elizabeth's life has taught me compassion, unconditional love, humility; and has set me on a path to wisdom. The Greek philosophers said, "Wisdom begins when you realize that you don't know what you thought you knew." I thought I knew sadness; I hadn't. I thought I knew happiness; I thought I knew love; not all kinds. I thought I knew compassion; I thought I knew humility; I hadn't. In her book, Judith Viorst views life as a series of *Necessary Losses* that people must give up in order to grow up. Here was one of those losses—the loss of an ideal that was being traded for humanity.

As I lay in the hospital bed those days following her birth, reading medical genetics textbooks instead of Dr. Spock, I learned that humans need 46 chromosomes—precisely. Any more or any fewer can result in abnormalities of every cell. Overwhelmed by the data, unable to sleep, I would steal down to the nursery in the wee hours of the morning where I had to scrub my arms and hands with betadine and don a surgical gown and mask before entering. Elizabeth was caged in an isolet with tubes and wires reaching out from every orifice like guy wires holding her down. Electronic blips marched across oscilloscopes. Rapid, high-pitched beeps competed with babies' cries for attention. But when my hands found their way through the maze to stroke her face, she nuzzled against me in her suckling instinct. At that moment, I saw her not as a syndrome but as my infant daughter. She made me peer beyond the "accidentals" to the "essence" of human life.

Later, at the age of seven months, Elizabeth was in heart failure, fighting for life. Before I took her to the hospital for heart surgery, I prepared to say "good bye" to her. Unable to make myself cross the threshold with her, I turned around and saw the flowers. I carried her over and let her breathe the fragrance. I pointed up to the clouds; I lifted her up to the trees and told her to look at it all—see it. But it was I who was seeing it as never before.

The stories that the speaker shares vivify the subject's triumphs for receivers.

Standing there I remembered a poem I had heard over and over in my childhood from an old family phonograph record. The poem included the words of a sad old Negro preacher addressing a couple in Savannah who were mourning their child. He said, "Now, Father didn't give you that baby by a hundred thousand miles. He just thinks you need some sunshine and he lent him for a while. And he let you love and keep him till your hearts were bigger grown. And these silver tears you're sheddin' are just interest on a loan. . . ." Sunshine is indeed what Elizabeth brought us in the form of illumination and enlightenment. She still casts her light.

Recently I've been grumpy over turning 40. When I was bemoaning my greying hair, sagging skin, and aching joints, Elizabeth said, "Mom, you should be glad to be living a long, long time. Celebrate!" With that piece of advice, once again she helped me peer beyond the superficial to realize the privilege of a healthy life despite sagging jowls and greying hair.

Elizabeth has been to me the bird that sings too early outside your window and rouses you from that dream state—she sang her song. Like that uninvited bird that sings incessantly, while you wish it would whistle its tune outside someone else's window—she sang her song to me. And like that bird's tune, I harked, heard, and hummed it back.

My song is this: keep in mind that children with birth anomalies are not the pitiful. Not they, but we with our attitude, ignorance, and insensitivities are pitiful. Just consider, "There but for the grace of God go I."

Yes, there was a brief moment at her birth when her unwelcome song jarred me awake. Sometimes the thing we welcome least is a blessing which, disguised, knocks boldly on our door; then rejected, sneaks quietly in the back door of the heart and establishes residence before being recognized—quietly working magic—quietly transforming.

So Elizabeth, I thank you for singing your song outside my window and forcing me to look through that window beyond the "accidentals" to the "essence." Thank you for allowing me to glimpse through that window and see the flowers through your eyes. Thank you for showing me my reflection in that window—for making me realize that the alternative to growing old is not being alive. And thank you, Elizabeth, for making growing old worthwhile.

To you, Elizabeth:
L'Chaim[6]

Your success in delivering a tribute speech will depend on whether you are able to use words effectively to convey the thoughts and emotions inherent in the occasion. The keys to delivery of a successful tribute speech are sincerity and knowledge. Sincerity is important because exaggeration has no place in a speech of tribute; in addition to being potentially embarrassing, exaggeration makes the information you are sharing less believable. Instead, you need to focus on creating vivid, specific im-

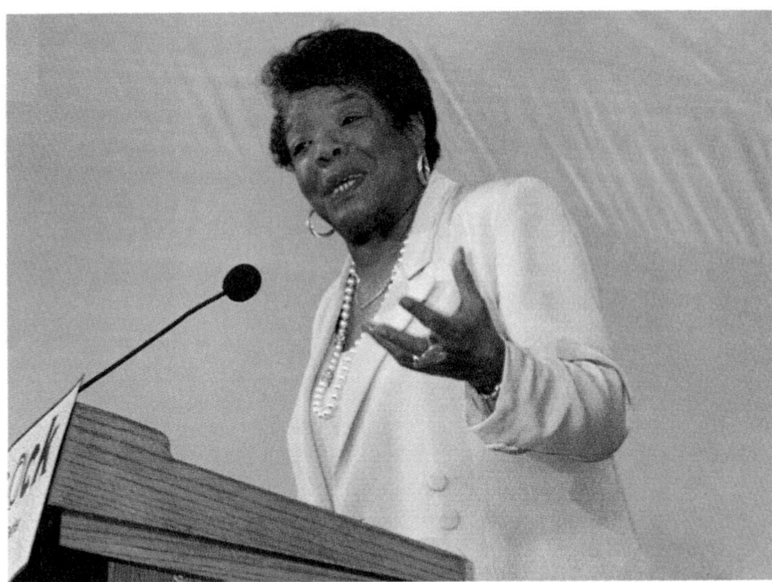

Dr. Maya Angleou's poetry and prose inspire, pay tribute to, and celebrate the value of the individual.

ages of accomplishment that in themselves demonstrate the influence and importance of the honoree. In addition, by possessing the background information that lets you tell stories that illustrate and give life and meaning to what the honoree has attained, you also stir the sentiments of receivers and reveal to them why they should join with you in paying tribute to the individual.

The Eulogy

A special form of tribute speech is the **eulogy.** When delivering a eulogy, you pay tribute to a person who has died. A eulogy is usually presented graveside or at a memorial service. While some are very brief, perhaps lasting only a minute or two, others are more lengthy, lasting ten or twenty minutes.

Eulogies

According to speech writer Peggy Noonan, eulogies deserve special attention.

I love eulogies. They are the most moving kind of speech because they attempt to pluck meaning from the fog, and on short order, when the emotions are still ragged and raw and susceptible to traps. It is a challenge to look at a life and organize our thoughts about it and try to explain to ourselves what it meant, and that most moving part is the element of implicit celebration. Most people aren't appreciated enough, and the bravest things we do in our lives are usually known only to ourselves. No one throws ticker tape on the man who chose to be faithful to his wife, or the lawyers who didn't take the drug money, or the daughter who held her tongue again and again. All this anonymous heroism. A eulogy gives a chance to celebrate it.[7]

SPEAKING of ETHICS

Should We Give Speeches of Tribute or Deliver Eulogies Only for Those We Have Known Personally?

A number of speech practitioners caution that speeches of tribute, including eulogies, should only be given by speakers who: (1) are very familiar with the person who is the subject of the speech, and (2) are able to contain and control their own emotions during the delivery of the speech.

If a speaker genuinely believes that his or her life was affected by the subject of the tribute, and he or she is willing to do in-depth research and conduct interviews to develop an effective speech of tribute, does he or she have as much a right to deliver the speech as someone who knew the subject well? Would it be unethical or unsuitable to have the tribute speech made by someone who never even met the deceased?

Your Responsibilities When Delivering a Eulogy. When delivering a eulogy, your goal is to comfort the members of your audience without letting your own grief overwhelm you. This sometimes becomes difficult because of the emotional nature of the speech. The following qualities characterize the eulogy:

1. The speaker begins by acknowledging the special loss suffered by the family of the deceased.
2. The speaker celebrates the life of the deceased by acknowledging the legacy the individual leaves to humanity.
3. By interspersing honest emotion together with anecdotes, personal recollections, and quotations from others, the speaker emphasizes the uniqueness or essence of the subject and succeeds in bringing the group together to share and ease their sense of loss by transcending their sorrow and concentrating instead on how fortunate they were to have known the deceased.

A Sample Eulogy. This eulogy was delivered by the ninth Earl Spencer at the London funeral of his sister, Diana, September 6, 1997. The tribute was viewed by millions of people throughout the world.

A BROTHER'S TRIBUTE

I stand before you today the representative of a family in grief, in a country in mourning before a world in shock. We are all united not only in our desire to pay our respects to Diana, but rather in our need to do so.

The speaker begins by acknowledging the loss experienced by the family, country, and world.

For such was her extraordinary appeal that the tens of millions of people taking part in this service all over the world via television and radio who never actually met her, feel that they, too, lost someone close to them in the early hours of Sunday morning. It is a more remarkable tribute to Diana than I can ever hope to offer her today.

Diana was the very essence of compassion, of duty, of style, of beauty. All over the world she was a symbol of selfless humanity, a standard-bearer for the rights of the truly downtrodden, a truly British girl who transcended nationality, someone with a natural nobility who was classless, who proved in the last year that she needed no royal title to continue to generate her particular brand of magic.

The speaker celebrates the life of the deceased by providing examples of her legacy to humanity.

Today is our chance to say "thank you" for the way you brightened our lives, even though God granted you but half a life. We will all feel cheated that you were taken from us so young, and yet we must learn to be grateful that you came along at all.

Only now that you are gone do we truly appreciate what we are now without, and we want you to know that life without you is very, very difficult.

We have all despaired at our loss over the past week, and only the strength of the message you gave us through your years of giving has afforded us the strength to move forward.

The speaker refuses to engage in hyperbole.

There is a temptation to rush to canonize your memory. There is no need to do so. You stand tall enough as a human being of unique qualities not to need to be seen as a saint. Indeed, to sanctify your memory would be to miss out on the very core of your being, your wonderfully mischievous sense of humor with the laugh that bent you double, your joy for life transmitted wherever you took your smile, and the sparkle in those unforgettable eyes, your boundless energy which you could barely contain.

But your greatest gift was your intuition, and it was a gift you used wisely. This is what underpinned all your wonderful attributes. And if we look to analyze what it was about you that had such a wide appeal, we find it in your instinctive feel for what was really important in all our lives.

The speaker describes the qualities that distinguished and set the deceased apart.

Without your God-given sensitivity, we would be immersed in greater ignorance at the anguish of AIDS and HIV sufferers, the plight of the homeless, the isolation of lepers, the random destruction of land mines. Diana explained to me once that it was her innermost feelings of suffering that made it possible for her to connect with her constituency of the rejected.

The speaker humanizes the deceased by noting her vulnerabilities.

And here we come to another truth about her. For all the status, the glamour, the applause, Diana remained throughout a very insecure person at heart, almost childlike in her desire to do good for others so she could release herself from deep feelings of unworthiness, of which her eating disorders were merely a symptom.

The world sensed this part of her character and cherished her for her vulnerability, whilst admiring her for her honesty. The last time I saw Diana was on July the first, her birthday, in London, when typically she was not taking time to celebrate her special day with friends but was guest of honor at a charity fund-raising evening.

The speaker's personal insights into the life of the deceased, his use of specific examples, and his expressions of honest emotion vivify his portrayal of her.

She sparkled, of course, but I would rather cherish the days I spent with her in March when she came to visit me and my children in our home in South Africa. I am proud of the fact that apart from when she was on public display meeting President Mandela, we managed to contrive to stop the ever-present paparazzi from getting a single picture of her.

That meant a lot to her.

These are days I will always treasure. It was as if we'd been transported back to our childhood, when we spent such an enormous amount of time together, the two youngest in the family.

Fundamentally, she hadn't changed at all from the big sister who mothered me as a baby, fought with me at school, and endured those long train journeys between our parents' homes with me at weekends. It is a tribute to her level-headedness and strength that despite the most bizarre life imaginable after her childhood, she remained intact, true to herself.

The speaker criticizes those who misunderstood, misrepresented, and mistreated the deceased during her life. (In your opinion, do these comments belong in this eulogy?)

There is no doubt that she was looking for a new direction in her life at this time. She talked endlessly of getting away from England, mainly because of the treatment she received at the hands of the newspapers.

I don't think she ever understood why her genuinely good intentions were sneered at by the media, why there appeared to be a permanent quest on their behalf to bring her down. It is baffling. My own, and only explanation is that genuine goodness is threatened to those at the opposite end of the moral spectrum.

It is a point to remember that of all the ironies about Diana, perhaps the greatest is this: that a girl given the name of the ancient goddess of hunting was, in the end, the most hunted person of the modern age.

She would want us today to pledge ourselves to protecting her beloved boys, William and Harry, from a similar fate. And I do this here, Diana, on your behalf. We will not allow them to suffer the anguish that used regularly to drive you to tearful despair.

The speaker encourages us to make the objectives and dreams of the deceased our own.

Beyond that, on behalf of your mother and sisters, I pledge that we, your blood family, will do all we can to continue the imaginative and loving way in which you were steering these two exceptional young men, so that their souls are not simply immersed by duty and tradition but can sing openly as you planned.

The speaker promises to work to fulfill the wishes of the deceased.

We fully respect the heritage into which they have both been born, and will always respect and encourage them in their royal role. But we, like you, recognize the need for them to experience as many different aspects of life as possible, to arm them spiritually and emotionally for the years ahead. I know you would have expected nothing less from us.

William and Harry, we all care desperately for you today. We are all chewed up with sadness at the loss of a woman who wasn't even our mother. How great your suffering is we cannot even imagine.

The speaker directly addresses the family, reemphasizes the uniqueness and special qualities of the deceased, and reiterates how fortunate her family, the country, and the world were to have had her.

I would like to end by thanking God for the small mercies he has shown us at this dreadful time: for taking Diana at her most beautiful and radiant, and when she had so much joy in her private life.

Above all, we give thanks for the life of a woman I am so proud to be able to call my sister: the unique, the complex, the extraordinary and irreplaceable Diana, whose beauty, both internal and external, will never be extinguished from our minds.

The After-Dinner Speech

Generally designed to be entertaining, the **after-dinner speech** is a prevalent form of public address. Neither overly technical nor filled with ponderous details or complex information, the after-dinner speech is usually lighthearted and takes a good-natured, sometimes humourous, whimsical, or mildly satirical look at a topic of interest and relevance to the audience.

Your Responsibilities as an After-Dinner Speaker. If you are asked to give an after-dinner speech you'll probably want to choose a topic that is nontechnical and that allows you to approach it in a lighthearted way and to interject humor into your presentation. Humor, when used appropriately, helps relieve tension and relax receivers. It also enables receivers to remember your presentation more easily.[8] However, humor should not be forced; rather, it should be functional, develop out of the situation you are sharing, and be used to help you make a point.

Even as it makes a point, the after-dinner speech also depends on your ability to organize your speech's content in an imaginative, creative, lighthearted, and stimulating way while maintaining a sense of decorum and good taste. Remember, after-dinner speeches are usually delivered on occasions when audience members are in a mood for being entertained, and therefore, must be easy to digest . . . as desserts usually are.

A Sample After-Dinner Speech. The following excerpted after-dinner speech was prepared by Joel Schwartzberg.

AN AFTER-DINNER SPEECH

The speaker sets a light-hearted tone.

Okay, here we go, okay, I'm sorry. I'm just a little nervous right now. A lot of tension, don't know what I could do about it, but wait a minute. You know, I was rifling through Eastern Michigan's extemp file this morning *(laughter)* and I found this article that says if you stare into a fish tank for a while, it will relax you. Of course the fish will later seek therapy, but that's okay. *(laughter)* [Speaker displays a cardboard fish tank.] This will work just perfectly. Now we're really in business. All right, this will just take a few minutes, ten max. Ah. *(laughter)* Dee-dee. Now you're probably saying, "What is he doing? These aren't real fish, it's a piece of cardboard. It's two-dimensional!" *(laughter)* Well, first, I think it's pretty rude to be talking during my speech. *(laughter)* Second, accepting a two-dimensional image as reality is something our society is very accustomed to doing. By the time I'm finished with my speech today, hopefully we will understand the scope of the two-dimensionalization of the world, how we can stop it, and how to pronounce it properly. *(laughter)* Now, in order to get an understanding of this issue, we will first look at different forms of two-dimensionalization around the world and how we have allowed them to fester in our society. Second, we will see how society likes to categorize itself by these two-dimensional ideas, and third, we will look at some ways to try to focus on our own vision to break down these cardboard visions. Finally, we'll do the hokey-pokey and turn ourselves around *(laughter)* because hey, that's what it's all about. *(laughter)*

The speaker's topic lends itself to humor.

The speaker is both whimsical and satirical as he explores his topic.

Now, two-dimensionality in our society often comes from stereotypes. Stereotypes, say, that Jews are money hungry, that blondes are dumb, that Hispanics are lazy, that public speakers think that everything in life can be explained in three points. *(laughter)* Well, all of this is truly ridiculous because first, *(laughter)* we all come from different backgrounds. Second, you can't generalize about someone just because of the way he or she appears. And third, hey, I lent someone a whole quarter yesterday, and I want it back tomorrow or else the interest goes up. *(laughter)* Now, the stereotypes in turn come from two-dimensional representations in our society, often as seen through television. . . .

The speaker's good nature helps receivers consider an array of absurdities.

In today's society things are a lot different, but not altogether much better. Through television, we're still exposed to a world where there are few, if any Hispanics, Asians or elderly people. Also, while we as adults are able to distinguish reality from television, our children are less likely to be critical and more likely to believe what they see. And what do they see? Cardboard. Robbie Jayson, a writer and producer for two kid-oriented productions so diverse as *Different Strokes* and *Webster* *(laughter)* told me that the entire biographical background for the major character of Willis Jackson on *Different Strokes* consisted of only four words: he likes roller boogie. Three if you use a hypen. *(laughter)* Now, we must understand television is not the only villain in this quest to reverse Christopher Columbus' theory of a three-dimensional Earth. Nope, the evil lurks in the seemingly most innocent places. Song lyrics. "Her name was Lola, she was a show girl *(laughter)* with *(laughter)* yellow feathers in her hair and a dress cut down to there." *(laughter)* You know the rest, fisticuffs, gunplay, Lola goes nuts. *(laughter)* But what do we really know about Lola? What's her last name? Weren't they hiring at McDonald's? *(laughter)* What does she look for in a good pimp? *(laughter)* We can also see a glaring two-dimensionalization in the world of literature. I picked up this book today in the Mankato State University Bookstore: *(unintelligible)*, "Night Shadows," in search of two-dimensional people, places and situations. "Knight leaned close, his face but a breath away from hers. I'm going to kiss you now and you'll want me, just as you did that night in the carriage." *(laughter)* We can also see a growing two-dimensionalization in the world of film, where people, places and events, sometimes even true historical events, are rearranged by cardboard all the time. Steven Spielberg presents Woody Allen in a Spike Lee film. A Vietnam Vet returns home as a ghost *(laughter)* to help his widow build a small pizzeria in Brooklyn. Co-starring Dennis Hopper as the Vietnam War. *(laughter)*

One thing is for sure, we are all living in an increasingly two-dimensional world, with the exception of Shirley MacLaine, who's living in several two-dimensional worlds. *(laughter)* . . . Cardboard imagery is most blantantly used when we try to categorize people by two-dimensional standards. This is a subscription form to the CBS Columbia Music Club. Among other things, it asks you to check a box which includes your favorite type of music. Here they give you hard rock: Van Halen, U2. Easy Listening: Johnny Mathis, Barry Manilow. And, black music: Freddy Jackson, Luther Vandross. Now, does black music mean the performers are black? Does it mean the listeners are black? Who are they talking about? I mean, think about it. Hi, I like Spanish music because I'm from Spain. Hi, I like black music because I'm from Black. *(laughter)* This labeling in fact often comes from very unexpected places. A two-year study by the Center for Women's Studies in 1989 branded the Scholastic Aptitude Test as being "in favor of males." Ray Retchie, of the *Miami Herald,* polled a local high school and found that most of the girls there were insulted that the center would deem an analogy question that began "dividends is to stockholders" as being quote, "unfamiliar territory for women."

The humor the speaker employs is functional and appropriate.

Now, whenever we label someone a minority, talented, liberal, cool, nerd, extemper, *(laughter)* there are limitations and expectations set on that person that either they can't achieve, or sometimes surpass to the point of disbelief. Sometimes it's not so much a matter of living up to these cardboard ideals as it is paying for them. Now we are all categorized when we get insurance. Men, for example, pay higher auto insurance than women because stereotypically, we drive faster. These people have obviously never seen my mother on "double coupons" day. In fact, blacks pay higher life insurance than whites because they are more likely to die young. . . .

Now, there are some things we can do to overcome the progression of such narrow-minded areas. First, we can't take everything we see and hear at face value. Take it for granted like a Joel Siegel movie review. *Turner and Hooch?* I loved it. *Karate Turtles?* I loved it. *Citizen Kane?* It was a little slow. *(laughter)* Second, we must try to resist society's temptation to label us as being one way or another because of race, religion, background, calling, sex, no sex. *(laughter)* Okay, but then you're out of here. *(laughter)* Finally, we can overcome two-dimensionality by taking in that media which presents cardboard personalities of people and minorities in a positive, realistic and three-dimensional light. Which doesn't mean you have to go out and buy *Warmed by Love,* but try to stay away from that which tries to categorize, to cardboardize you or your society.

So we have seen cardboardization, categorization, labelization, made a realization about the elimination of the proliferationalization of two-dimensionalization in our nation, *(laughter)* not to mention the emancipation proclamation, and so without further hesitation I'd like to say thank you very much and have a three-dimensional day.[9]

CEREMONIAL SPEAKING AND CULTURAL DIVERSITY

CULTURAL FACTORS MAY AFFECT an audience's response to a speech. Thus, just as we ought to take cultural factors into account when we develop informative and persuasive speeches, so should we take them into account when we develop special occasion speeches. That way we can also show our respect for the cultures of the persons to whom we are speaking by adapting our ceremonial speeches to reflect their cultural assumptions and practices. Doing this allows us to achieve cultural inclusion and can help make our speechmaking as effective as possible.

Because culture is pervasive, one's culture may influence what kinds of events and persons we consider important enough to be the subject of a ceremonial speech. Culture also may influence who is recognized during a speech and who is thanked when such recognition is received. For example, while individualistic cultures might be more apt to single out a person based on his or her individual achievements, collectivist cultures might recognize a person's contributions to a group. Similarly, when accepting an award, a member of an individualist culture might be more likely to accept sole credit for the contribution and bask in the individual praise given him or her than would a member of a collectivist culture, who would probably praise others in lieu of taking credit.

CONSIDERING DIVERSITY

Who Is Introducing or Honoring Whom?

Should speeches introducing or honoring a member of a particular cultural or ethnic group—when that is the focus of the speech—be delivered only by a member of that same group, or does the recognition being given the honoree attain even more significance if remarks are made by someone who does not share the cultural or ethnic background of the subject, or does it matter at all?

For example, should the speech of introduction made for Elie Wiesel be delivered by a Jew? Should African American journalist Charlene Hunter Galt deliver the commencement address to an all-white graduating class? Could Mother Hale be eulogized by any minister as effectively as by an African American preacher? Should a person from a collectivist culture make an award to a person whose culture is more individualist?

To what extent do the following remarks made by African American football player Gayle Sayers of cancer-stricken White teammate Brian Piccolo during Sayers's acceptance of an award for most courageous football player of the year alter your thoughts about the way questions like these should be answered?

> He has the heart of a giant and that rare form of courage that allows him to kid himself and his opponent, cancer. He has the mental attitude that makes me proud to have a friend who spells out the word courage twenty-four hours a day.
>
> You flatter me by giving me this award but I tell you here and now that I accept it for Brian Piccolo. Brian Piccolo is the man of courage who should receive the George S. Halas award. It is mine tonight, it is Brian Piccolo's tomorrow. . . . I love Brian Piccolo and I'd like all of you to love him too.
>
> Tonight, when you hit your knees, please ask God to love him.[10]

Similar guidelines are at work for other special occasion speech forms, including the tribute speech. For example, an audience whose members have a collectivist orientation would probably expect the speaker to focus on the person's group-related achievements, whereas an audience whose members have more of an individualist orientation would probably expect the speaker to highlight the person's individual achievements instead.

SUMMARY

SPECIAL OCCASION SPEECHES help punctuate the high-water marks of our lives. They are part of the rituals that draw us together. Speeches of celebration are designed to reflect the nature and needs of the occasions that prompted their delivery.

Special occasion speakers help magnify the significance of the event or person being recognized at the same time that they help unify the audience by affirming the common values exhibited through the celebration of the person or the event.

Today's speechmakers need to be comfortable with a variety of types of ceremonial speaking including the speech of introduction, the speech of presentation, the speech of acceptance, the commencement address, the keynote address, the speech of tribute, and the after-dinner speech.

THE SPEAKER'S STAND

Prepare and deliver either an award presentation, a commencement address, a speech of tribute, or an after-dinner speech on a subject of your choice. Remember to follow the specific criteria suggested for whichever format you choose.

STUDENT FOCUS GROUP REPORT

By this point you have had the opportunity to consider and experience the unique requirements of speaking on a special occasion; in a group of five to seven students, answer the following questions.

1. To what extent, if any, does speaking on a special occasion differ from more traditional speechmaking?
2. How might your ethnic or cultural background as well as your sense of ethics influence a decision regarding whether you are the right person to deliver a special occasion speech?
3. Which types of special occasion speeches pose the greatest number of challenges for speechmakers? Which types pose the fewest challenges? Explain.
4. In what ways do the expectations of audience members affect the special occasion speaker? Give specific examples.
5. What unique qualities, if any, should a special occasion speaker possess?
6. Do public figures make better special occasion speakers than private citizens? Explain.
7. Summarize the most important information you have learned about speaking on special occasions.
8. Revisit the case study at the beginning of this chapter. In what ways, if any, would you now change your answers?

Select a spokesperson to report the group's conclusions to your class.

Chapter Eighteen

Speaking in the Small Group

After reading this chapter, you should be able to:

- Define and identify the characteristics of a small group.
- Compare and contrast speaking in public with speaking in a small group.
- Compare and contrast how group leaders and members can contribute to or detract from a group's effectiveness.
- Explain the Reflective Thinking Sequence.
- Define and list the characteristics of *groupthink.*
- Discuss specific techniques you can use to facilitate group problem solving.
- Participate in a group discussion.
- Demonstrate how the results of a group's efforts can be communicated beyond the group.

CASE STUDY

The Group

Janice was part of a campus group responsible for studying the challenges that student diversity presented for her college. As the student body had increased in diversity, curricular changes had been made, new student interest groups created, and minority faculty members hired. The group studying diversity was composed of seven individuals from a number of different cultures: one Asian, one African American, one Hispanic American, one Arab American, one Native American, one Indian, and one White American. Among the tasks the group had to complete was the following:

> Imagine that you are from another planet. Your job is to develop a description of a typical student from this college to take back home with you.

- What problems do you think the group might have fulfilling the assignment?
- How would you suggest they work together to facilitate its accomplishment?
- How should they present their findings?

Until now we have concentrated on equipping you, the individual speaker, with the skills you need to address a public audience. In this chapter our focus changes somewhat, as we explore first, the kinds of communication behavior exhibited in groups; second, how you function and relate to the members of a group; third, a structure that facilitates the operation of a group; and finally, how the results of your efforts can be communicated to others who have a stake in your group's work—perhaps an employer, the board of directors, or even the public at large.

Small groups abound in society. Just for fun, compile a list of all the groups to which you now either belong or aspire to belong. Chances are, you either are a member of or would like to join a number of committees or task forces, one or more clubs, a team or two, and, of course, a group of friends and a family group. According to small-group researchers, groups surround us; in fact, there are more groups in society than there are people.[1]

Consequently, you probably have had—and will continue to have—numerous opportunities to participate as the member of a group. Most likely, a significant percentage of the speaking you will do will also occur in a group setting. Some businesspeople spend more than 700 hours a year interacting in groups. In fact, according to researchers, most of the average manager's time is spent in group meetings of one kind or another.[2] Because it is done a lot, however, does not mean it is done very well. Unfortunately, far too few of us have had any training in communicating in small groups; thus, much of our group meeting time is wasted. According to authors Roger Mosvick and Robert Nelson, today's companies lose the equivalent of thirty days or 240 hours a year for every person who participates in work groups.[3]

In this chapter our goal is to provide you with the skills and knowledge you need to ensure that the time you spend in groups is not wasted. Because group work consumes between 35 percent and 60 percent of a typical manager's work day, it makes sense to learn how to do it effectively. If members of a group learn to work together

How many groups do you currently belong to? What purposes do these groups fulfill? What can members of a group do to facilitate the group's success?

well, they can almost always solve a problem or make a decision better than can an individual working alone. There is indeed strength in numbers, if the strength is harnessed.[4]

WHAT IS A SMALL GROUP?

A **SMALL GROUP** can be defined as a limited number of people (often as few as three) who communicate over a period of time and usually face to face to make decisions and accomplish particular goals. Groups composed of five to seven people appear to function best because this size enables members to communicate with each other as they interact to reach a goal, but it is not uncommon for some work groups to contain as many as fifteen people. All individuals in the group have the potential to influence each other and are expected to function as both speaker and listener. Because members can respond virtually immediately to the verbal and nonverbal messages of others in the group, groups are often characterized by spontaneous interactions between members—interactions that ultimately lead to the group's success or failure.

Because group members share a common objective, random assemblages of individuals do not ordinarily constitute groups. Thus, we do not usually think of people waiting for an elevator or waiting to cross the street as a group. Instead, we expect members of a group to occupy certain roles with respect to one another, and to work with each other—to *cooperate*—to achieve a desired end. As group members do this, they develop certain attitudes toward each other and ordinarily derive a sense of satisfaction from belonging to and participating in the group. We also expect the members of a group to adhere to the group's norms—the "dos and don'ts" that groups establish to regulate the behavior of their members and make it possible for them to attain their goals.

Every group defines its own objectives, establishes its own norms, and by so doing, sets its own operating climate. Ultimately, it is the way members relate to each other, the roles they assume, and how they exchange information and resolve communication problems that pop up that determines whether the work of the group will be effective. It is the way members interact—*what they say and how they say it*—that determines both the health and the long-term viability of the group. According to theorist Charles Redding, a **healthy group** exhibits five characteristics:

1. Supportiveness
2. Participative decision making
3. Trust among group members
4. Openness and candor
5. High performance goals[5]

Groups lacking these characteristics suffer and may ultimately cease to exist because they fail to provide members with needed rewards.

In this chapter we will focus on two key kinds of problem-solving groups:

1. The **fact-finding group,** whose members attempt to share thoughts and information in an effort to enhance understanding and learning; and
2. The **decision-making group,** whose members seek a consensus regarding what the group should or should not do.

Whatever the specific nature of your group's task, knowing how to operate and interact effectively in the group setting is vital for personal and professional success.

CULTURE AND GROUP INTERACTION

JUST AS POPULATION diversity can influence the makeup of audiences so can it influence the nature of group participation. In addition, cultural differences can affect the way individuals interact with each other when they find themselves in a group.

Cultural clashes may make it difficult for members of groups to establish working relationships. For example, when the Corning Corporation, an American firm, and Vitro, a Mexican firm, tried to develop an alliance, their efforts were sabotaged by cultural confusion. Business analysts note that problems between representatives of the two firms surfaced because of the stereotypes each held of the other's approach to decision making, and because of conflicts in their work styles. For example, the Mexicans perceived the Americans' communication style as too direct, while the Americans viewed the Mexican style as too timid. Mexicans displayed an unwillingness to criticize, which also troubled the more outspoken Americans. The Americans were used to eating during meetings, but the Mexicans preferred to go out for leisurely meals. The Mexicans liked to work late into the evening and thus wanted to conduct business meetings at hours when the Americans expected to be finished working. The decision-making approaches practiced by the two companies, however, created the greatest hurdle: Because Mexican businesses tend to be significantly more hierarchial than American companies, the decision making proceeded more slowly than the Americans could tolerate.[6]

The Japanese decision-making style also differs from the American style. Again, Americans value openness in groups, but the Japanese value face-saving and the preservation of harmony. Whereas Americans stress the value of the individual and individ-

CONSIDERING DIVERSITY

Contrasting Perceptions of the Group

According to researchers Dolores and Robert Cathcart, concepts of *group* are "cultural variants rather than universal theories."[7] For the Japanese, groups are a natural setting for human interaction. Because in general the Japanese want to avoid being singled out for praise or blame, blending into a group is the preferred alternative. The Japanese expression that translates as "the nail that sticks up is hit" exemplifies this attitude perfectly.[8] In contrast to the American perception that a group is a "collection" of individuals in which a person is free to select roles to perform and even free to choose whether to affiliate with the group at all, the Japanese believe that the self is subordinate to the group, and that individuals must display a strong loyalty, not to themselves, but to the group. In Japan, if you were to leave a group, you would also run the risk of losing your identity.

As another example, Native Americans do not like to compete publicly with others for fear they would embarrass one of their group. Winning is far less important than the potential damage that could be done if a "loser" felt humiliated.

- How can you use such differences in perception to improve the operation of a group?
- How can a group use the different styles, values, and customs of its members to its advantage?

ual responsibility, the Japanese stress the value of the group and collective responsibility. The Japanese submerge the individual within the group, merging the identity of one with the other, whereas Americans, even when in a group, tend to retain a sense of individuality and personal identity.[9] Clearly, when interacting in groups, it is wise to consider how cultural factors may affect the communication experience of the group's members.

HOW DOES SPEAKING CHANGE WHEN THE PUBLIC YOU'RE SPEAKING TO SHRINKS?

WHEN YOU PARTICIPATE in small group communication, you need to make a number of skill adaptations. First, you need to focus your attention on the interaction among multiple speakers and listeners, rather than on the single speaker who is addressing a much larger group of receivers.

In addition, the formality of the situation changes. Instead of standing before a group and delivering a speech, you are now a group member whose function it still is to express a point of view, but in a way that allows virtually everyone listening to you to participate as well. In a group there are a number of people doing the discussing, not just one. Group members speak and listen to each other. Third, whereas when you speak before an audience the time you have to present your point of view is usually very limited, when you interact with a group there can be free discussion of the topic until group members reach an impasse or can commit themselves to supporting a conclusion.

When you function as a public speaker you may well be unaware of audience disagreement with your position, either because audience members suppress them or because no forum for such expression is provided to them. In small groups, however, disagreements among members may be expressed often. The reasons for the disagreements are generally explored by members, and an effort is made by the group to resolve them.

Finally, when you address an audience as a speaker, you express your point of view, and it is up to your receivers to accept or reject your ideas. When interacting in a group, however, decisions will be reached by you and other group members together, ideally, by consensus.

Not everything changes, however, when the shift is made from public to group comunication. The following requirements remain the same:

1. You need to have a command of the subject.
2. You need to be able to support your comments with research.
3. You need to organize your ideas effectively.
4. You need to pay attention to the way your ideas affect others.
5. You need to be aware of the needs and concerns of receivers.
6. You need to use language that others will understand and respond to appropriately.

The Advantages of Group Decision Making

Compared to individual decision making, the problem-solving group offers certain advantages. First, it facilitates the pooling of resources. Instead of only one contributor, a number of people with different information and contrasting viewpoints are able to contribute to the decision-making process. Because a broader array of knowledge is applied to finding a solution to a problem, it is likely that a more effective solution will emerge.

Second, the act of participating in decision making strengthens the commitment individuals are willing to make to implementing the decision. Participation and motivation are effective problem-solving partners. When working in a group, members are more willing to examine differences openly and to explore compromises.

Third, costly errors are often filtered out by the group before they do any damage. In other words, by focusing the eyes of a number of persons on potential solutions to a problem, weaknesses that would often by missed by one are detected. Thus, groups can foster superior decision making and be better at controlling error.

Fourth, a decision made by a group is usually received better than a decision suggested by an individual. The persons to whom the decision is reported usually respect the fact that a number of people working cooperatively reached a particular conclusion.

Fifth, reaching a decision in a group can be more fulfilling and personally reinforcing than reaching a decision alone. The feeling of belonging makes a difference.

The Disadvantages of Group Decision Making

There are certain potential disadvantages inherent in group decision making. Unless the group's norms establish that the following behaviors will not be tolerated, each could impede effective group functioning.

First, sometimes we enter a group with personal objectives that are at odds with the group's objectives; as a result, the group's objectives may be sacrificed or sabotaged as we undermine them in an effort to achieve our personal goals.

Second, there can be too much comfort in numbers. When we know that there are other people available to assume our responsibilities if we slack off, we may opt to do just that. By maintaining a low profile we can coast along and be carried by the efforts of other group members.

Third, one or more very vocal, forceful, or powerful members can dominate the group, preventing others from exerting their fair share of influence; by steamrolling over others, these individuals make it less likely that all members will participate fully or even make their true feelings known. This can precipitate **groupthink**—the development of a single, uncritical "groupmind" that seeks to avoid conflict and leads ultimately to the making of inferior and problematic decisions.

Fourth, the intransigence of one or more members may make it impossible for the group to reach a consensus; if a group member comes to the group unwilling to listen to other points of view or to compromise, the decision-making process will likely become deadlocked.

Fifth, the group experiences a **risky shift;** it makes a decision that is riskier than an individual working alone would have been comfortable making.

Finally, it takes longer for most groups to make decisions than it does individuals. Whether the potential advantages of working in groups outweigh the potential disadvantages depends on how effectively the group is able to perform its tasks.

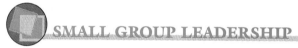

SMALL GROUP LEADERSHIP

MORE SUCCESSFUL GROUPS have a major attribute that helps distinguish them—effective leadership.

What Is Leadership?

Normally when we think of a group leader we think of someone who is in an appointed or elected position. However, it is not always so. Leadership is not the exclusive possession of any one group member, and a group need not have a designated leader to have leadership. Indeed, groups in which every member feels prepared to share leadership often work best. After all, to lead a group is to influence the group. When influence is positive the group is led toward the realization of its goal. When leadership is negative, the group is inhibited from attaining its goal. Thus, every member can be thought of as a potential leader, and while a group may not need to have a specific leader to reach its goal, it always requires leadership.[10]

What Functions Do Small Group Leaders Serve?

Effective leaders exhibit role versatility; they perform combinations of task and maintenance functions designed to move the group closer to its goal. **Task leadership be-**

haviors include establishing an agenda, giving and soliciting information and opinions, offering internal summaries that describe the group's progress, helping to keep the group on track, and helping the group to analyze and evaluate issues and reach a consensus. **Maintenance leadership behaviors** include the expression of agreement and support, the reduction and release of group tensions, the resolution of differences of opinion and group conflicts, and the ability to enhance morale and increase member satisfaction.

It is the leader who establishes a group climate that both encourages and stimulates meaningful interaction among group members. It is the leader who must fully comprehend the group's goals and have a clear vision of how to reach them.

How Do Leaders Contribute to or Detract from Group Effectiveness?

Although ideally every group member should be prepared to assume a leadership role when necessary, this is not always the case. Sometimes the leader who emerges in a group is not the most effective leader, but simply the loudest and most forceful member. Sometimes interpersonal difficulties preoccupy members and overpower the group, making it difficult for members to focus on the task objective.

The assumptions that individuals bring to a group regarding how people work also influences the leadership style they will exhibit. According to management expert Douglas McGregor, the assumptions we make tend to divide us into **type X leaders** and **type Y leaders.**[11] To find out which category you lean toward, read the following eight assumptions that a leader might make about how and why people work. Review them and select four that you believe best exemplify your perception.

Depending on his or her style, a leader can contribute to or detract from a group's effectiveness. What are the qualities you most admire in the leader of a small group? Which of these qualities do you possess?

1. The average group member will avoid working if he or she can.
2. The average group member views work as a natural activity.
3. The typical group member must be forced to work and must be closely supervised.
4. The typical group member is self-directed when it comes to meeting performance standards and realizing group objectives.
5. A group member should be threatened with punishment to get him or her to put forth an adequate effort.
6. A group member's commitment to objectives is related not to punishment but to rewards.
7. The average person prefers to avoid responsibility and would rather be led.
8. The average person not only can learn to accept responsibility but actually seeks responsibility.

If you chose mostly odd-numbered items, McGregor categorizes you as a type X leader; if you chose mostly even-numbered items, you are a type Y leader. Type Y

Judith B. Rosener

In this excerpt from "(Wo)men at Work" Bettijane Levine compares Rosener's findings about the leadership styles of men and women.

Women, take heart. Men, take note.

A new groundbreaking study shows that the two sexes differ dramatically when it comes to leadership—and that the feminine approach may be the wave of the future.

Male executives tend to lead the traditional way; by command and control, according to the study, conducted by Judith B. Rosener of the University of California, Irvine. Men give an order, explain the reward for a job that's well done, and pretty much keep their power and knowledge to themselves.

Female executives, on the other hand, tend to lead in non-traditional ways: by sharing information and power. They inspire good work by interacting with the staff, by encouraging employee participation, and by showing how employees' personal goals can be reached as they meet organizational ones.

The findings were based on the responses of 355 women and 101 men, matched for their position and for the type and size of organization.

The "female" style of leadership may be especially appropriate for the corporate climate of the Nineties and may be one reason that more women will quickly achieve positions of great power in the next few years, explains Rosener, a professor in UC Irvine's graduate school of management.

The International Women's Forum commissioned the study.

"The male leadership model of command and control is not necessarily better or worse than the female model," Rosener says. "If there is a fire, for example, you need a command-control-type leader to order everyone out, with no questions asked."

In fact, for years the traditional male leadership style has been the only style at top corporations. No other style was thought to exist. Rosener says it's still in place "at most Fortune 500-type" companies, where strict hierarchial structure means that all orders flow from the top, with everyone below following them.

But the hierarchial structure is starting to look anachronistic in a world where corporations have international headquarters and where decision making is required at lower levels, Rosener says.

It does not function as well in a global economy of multi-national companies, service industries, and leaders are greater risk takers than type X leaders, and they are also more willing to work to help members realize their full potential. Type Y leaders delegate more responsibility to group members than do type X leaders, and are also more apt to focus on helping members develop a personal sense of achievement.

The assumptions made by leaders affect both the climate and the operation of a group. Assumptions have consequences, both positive and negative. So do preferred leadership styles. Your preferred leadership style—that is, whether you exhibit a pattern of behavior that establishes you as an *autocratic, laissez-faire,* or *democratic* leader—exerts an influence on your group, and sets the tone for its operation.

Authoritarian or **autocratic leaders** assume positions of superiority in groups; convinced that they are "the boss," they dominate the groups they are in by organizing all group activities and giving orders to other members. Although such a style is usually highly efficient, the efficiency is characteristically offset by low group satisfaction.

In contrast, the **laissez-faire leadership style** is characterized by a "do your own thing" approach. The leader does little, if anything, to actively help the group achieve

fast-changing technology businesses, where it's impractical to have only a few top people from whom all planning and orders flow.

The structure could actually be harmful to corporations in which far-flung, lower-level employees need to make quick, accurate decisions, backed by knowledge and power to make the decisions.

The female tendency to share knowledge, power, and responsibility may be what's needed next, Rosener says. The trouble is, most executives at top companies would still consider these to be non-managerial skills, not qualifications for the top job.

Why? Until now, there has been little research and no proof to document the existence and efficacy of leadership techniques.

Indeed, says Rosener, studies had found that there was little or no difference between leadership styles of men and women who make it to the top.

"That's because researchers always looked at Fortune 500-type companies, where there are no women," Rosener says. "And any woman who made it in a firm like that would have to do so by emulating the male management style."

She says that other studies focus on mid-level management, giving no clue about how women really function once at the top.

Rosener says her study also found that women "are enthusiastic about work" and "think it is fun,'" whereas "men describe work as work."

Other significant findings:

- Top executive women earn about the same as men. The mean income for women studied is $140,000 per year; the mean for men is $136,000. This contradicts most other studies saying that women are paid less then men.
- Sixty-eight percent of the women studied were married. This is inconsistent with previous findings, which indicate that top executive women sacrifice their personal lives in pursuit of success.

Rosener says the good news from this study is that high-achieving women can have it all. They can marry, earn as much as men, use a leadership style that comes naturally, and still ascend to the top spot.

But to do all that, they'll have to find a company that appreciates the female leadership style—or start a company of their own.[12]

■ How do you think the change in leadership style will affect the current imbalance in the number of power positions occupied by men and women? How might it affect the way groups are run in organizations?

its goal, preferring instead to simply let things happen as they will. Far too often, members of a laissez-faire group are frustrated due to a lack of guidance from their leader, lose direction, and are left to struggle on their own. As a result, they are distracted from the task at hand, and the quality of work they produce suffers.

It is the **democratic leadership style** that has been shown to be most effective in facilitating the development of a functional group. The democratic leader involves the group fully in the decision-making process. By neither dominating nor abandoning the group, but participating in the group and encouraging the democratic process, the democratic leader is able to guide the group toward its objective. Under democratic leadership, the group carries out both task and maintenance functions, establishes operating procedures, and draws its own conclusions. Because morale and motivation to participate improve under democratic leadership, most people prefer to work in a group with a democratic leader.

Of course, the leadership style that emerges in a group depends ultimately on the group task, the conditions under which the group must operate, and the relationships among members.

SMALL GROUP MEMBERSHIP

EFFECTIVE LEADERSHIP is essential for group success, but so is effective membership. For membership to be effective, all must participate fully and actively in the life of the group. Every member must assume and fulfill certain responsibilities and be cognizant of how his or her performance contributes to or detracts from the group's attaining its goal. Thus, in order for your behavior to contribute to goal realization, you need to display communication relevant to your group's effort. You need to be willing to acquire and share information and opinions, and you need to be sensitive to the feelings and needs of others in your group. You need to put the group's interests above your personal interests and do your best to listen attentively to all viewpoints, especially those in opposition to your own, plus analyze evidence, carefully keeping a watchful eye out for examples of faulty reasoning or incorrect information. As researchers note, a key difference between effective and ineffective groups lies in the ability of the former to examine and evaluate the validity of evidence offered.[13]

More productive groups have more productive members. Let us next examine specific roles you can perform that will contribute to your group's chances for success.

The Roles and Responsibilities of Membership

A group role is a particular type of behavior exhibited by a group member. Specific roles do not belong to specific members; rather, they are performed by members and a number of roles may be performed by either the same or different members of a group. It is the roles members perform that influence the progress of the group. Positive group roles accomplish both task and maintenance functions. They both help meet the group's goal and contribute to how group members interact with each other as they work toward that goal. The roles members perform can improve task performance, help the group maintain itself by fostering a concern for the needs and feelings of group members, or inhibit group performance by revealing an overriding concern for self and minimal concern for group success. The options are open; the choices are yours.

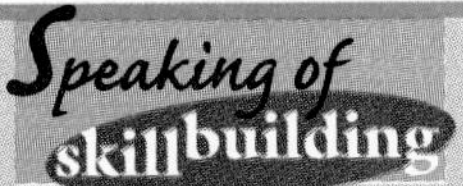

Group Role Call

What kind of group member are you? Consider the assets and the liabilities you bring to a group experience by indicating which of the following roles you characteristically perform in a group and noting specific instances of how your behavior either contributed to or detracted from the success of your last group.[14]

Task-Oriented Roles Performed in the Group:

- ❑ *Initiating.* You defined a problem; suggested methods, goals, and procedures; and started the group moving along new paths or in different directions by offering a plan.
- ❑ *Information Seeking.* You asked for facts and opinions and sought relevant information about the problem.
- ❑ *Information Giving.* You offered ideas, suggestions, personal experiences, and/or factual data.
- ❑ *Opinion Giving.* You supplied opinions, values, beliefs, and revealed your feelings regarding what was being discussed.
- ❑ *Clarifying.* You elaborated on or paraphrased the ideas of others, offered examples or illustrations, or tried to increase clarity by decreasing confusion.
- ❑ *Coordinating.* You summarized ideas and tried to draw various contributions together constructively.
- ❑ *Evaluating.* You evaluated the group's decisions or proposed solutions and helped establish criteria that solutions should meet.
- ❑ *Consensus Testing.* You tested the state of agreement among members to see if the group was approaching a decision.

Maintenance-Oriented Roles Performed:

- ❑ *Encouraging.* You responded warmly, receptively, and supportively to others and their ideas.
- ❑ *Gatekeeping.* You sought to keep channels of communication open by helping reticient members contribute to the group and/or by working to prevent one or two members from dominating the group.
- ❑ *Harmonizing.* You mediated differences between members, reconciled disagreements, and sought to reduce tension by injecting humor or other forms of relief at appropriate opportunities.
- ❑ *Compromising.* You exhibited a willingness to compromise to maintain group cohesion; you were willing to modify your stance or admit an error when appropriate.
- ❑ *Standard Setting.* You assessed the state of member satisfaction with group procedures and indicated the criteria set for evaluating group functioning.

Self-Serving Roles Performed:

- ❑ *Blocking.* You were disagreeable and digressed so that nothing was accomplished.
- ❑ *Aggressor.* You criticized or blamed others and sought to deflate the egos of other members as a means of enhancing your own status in the group.
- ❑ *Recognition Seeking.* You made yourself the center of attention; you focused attention on yourself rather than the task; you spoke loudly and exhibited unusual or outlandish behavior.
- ❑ *Withdrawing.* You stopped contributing, appeared indifferent to group efforts, daydreamed, or sulked.
- ❑ *Dominating.* You insisted on getting your own way; you interrupted others; you sought to impose your ideas and run the group.
- ❑ *Joking.* You engaged in horseplay or exhibited other inappropriate behaviors.
- ❑ *Self-Confessing.* You revealed personal feelings irrelevant to the work of the group.
- ❑ *Help-Seeking.* You played on and tried to elicit the sympathies of other group members.

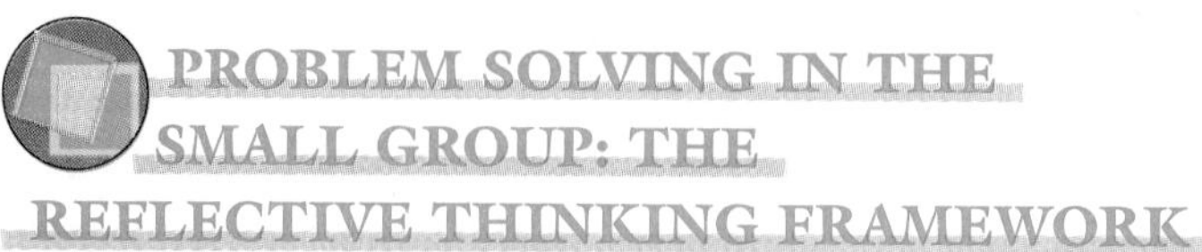

PROBLEM SOLVING IN THE SMALL GROUP: THE REFLECTIVE THINKING FRAMEWORK

THE QUALITY OF A GROUP'S decision making depends on both its leadership and its membership, but it also depends on the nature of the decision-making system used by the group. One method of organizing the decision-making process that has been effective in improving problem-solving effectiveness is derived from the writings of philosopher and educator John Dewey and is called the **Reflective Thinking Framework.**[15]

The Reflective Thinking Framework consists of six basic steps and offers a logical system for group discussion.

STEP ONE. Define the Problem. Is the problem phrased as a clear and specific question that is not slanted and thus will not arouse defensivesness? Is it phrased so as to allow a wide variety of answers rather than a simple yes or no? (For example, "What should the government's policy be toward gun control?" instead of "Should the government rip the guns out of the hands of law-abiding citizens?")

STEP TWO. Analyze the Problem. What are the facts of the situation? What are its causes? What is its history? How severe is it? Who is affected and how?

STEP THREE. Establish Criteria for Solutions. What criteria must an acceptable solution fulfill? By what objective standards should we evaluate a solution? What requirements must a solution meet? How critical is each criterion?

STEP FOUR. Generate Potential Solutions. How will each possible solution remedy the problem? How well does each solution meet the established criteria? What advantages or disadvantages does each solution present?

STEP FIVE. Select the Best Solution. How would you rank each solution? Which solution offers the greatest number of advantages and the fewest disadvantages? How can we combine solutions to produce an even better one?

STEP SIX. Suggest Strategies for Implementation. How can the solution be implemented? What steps should we take to put the solution into effect?

By systematically working its way through this framework and suspending judgment as it does so, your group can both keep the discussion on track and improve the quality of its decision making. The Reflective Thinking Framework helps group members avoid "early concurrence"—the tendency to conclude discussion prematurely. By causing members to explore all data and evaluate alternative courses of action methodically, and by opening them to new information rather than enouraging them to base decisions on what they know at the moment, the system also helps guard against "groupthink"—the tendency to let the desire for consensus override careful analysis and reasoned decision making.[16]

In order for the Reflective Thinking Framework to function effectively for your group, ask yourself the following questions as you work your way through it:

To what degree are the resources of all group members being well used?

To what degree is the group using its time wisely?

To what degree is the group emphasizing fact finding and inquiry?

To what degree are members listening to and respecting the ideas and feelings of other members?

To what degree is pressure to conform deemphasized and pressure to search for diverse viewpoints stressed?

To what degree is the group's atmosphere supportive, trusting, and cooperative?

SPEAKING of CRITICAL THINKING

The Groupthink Fiasco

Dr. Irving Janis, author of *Victims of Group Think,* notes that groups have the ability to precipitate the worst as well as the best in human decision making. Janis's research confirmed that when groups let the desire for consensus override the group's responsibility to conduct a thorough analysis of the problem in question, the group becomes dysfunctional and potentially destructive. According to Janis, the following behaviors characteristic of groups in the throes of groupthink cause the group to sacrifice reasoned decision making:

1. The group feels so secure that members ignore all warning signs that the decision they are making is wrong.
2. Group members rationalize in order to justify the group's decision.
3. Group members defend their decision by noting its inherent morality.
4. Group members adopt a "we versus they" mindset and depict any opposed to their decision in simplistic and stereotypical ways.
5. Group members censor their comments because they do not want to destroy the group's sense of unanimity.
6. The leader and/or the members of the group apply direct pressure to dissenting members in an effort to persuade them to adhere to the group's will.
7. Group members function as "mind-guards" in an effort to keep outside ideas or opinions from becoming known and destroying the group's cohesiveness.
8. The silence of any group members is interpreted as agreement.

- Choose one of the following events and explain the extent to which a group think mentality could have contributed to its outcome:

  the Bay of Pigs invasion;

  the explosion of the space shuttle *Challenger;*

  the stock market crash of 1929;

  Watergate; or

  an event of your choosing.

Decision-making effectiveness depends on the degree that group members feel free to speak up, maintain open minds, and exhibit a willingness to search for new information.

Considerations That Facilitate Problem Solving

Both the statement of the problem for discussion (the content of the decision making) and the ability to brainstorm correctly can faciliate the group's goal attainment. Let's explore how.

Establishing the Question for Decision Making. The content of most of the group discussions you will participate in will revolve around three kinds of questions: questions of fact, questions of value, and questions of policy. It is important that you be able to recognize and formulate each.

Questions of fact focus on the truth of an assertion. Because either inconsistent or contradictory information exists, group members are asked to discover the truth. Questions such as What is the likelihood that global warming is changing the earth's climate? What evidence supports the guilt or innocence of Lee Harvey Oswald? or What are the effects of exercise on blood pressure? require the group to analyze and interpret available data and evidence carefully.

Questions of value focus on subjective judgments of quality. The following are questions of value: Is it better for a woman to attend a women's college than a coed institution? How desirable is national health insurance? To what extent is it acceptable for a physican to assist in a patient's suicide?

Questions of policy focus on whether future action should be taken. The key word in a question of policy is "should." What should we do to lower the suicide rate among teenagers? What should be the federal policy regarding intervention in the internal disputes of a foreign country? What should colleges do to increase student diversity?

Brainstorming: The Raw Material of Ideas. Fresh ideas can help solve both old and new problems. Fresh ideas come from freeing frozen thought patterns and encouraging new avenues of thought. **Brainstorming,** a system devised by Alex Osborn, allows this to happen.[17]

It has long been recognized that the best way to develop a good idea is to first have lots of ideas. To do this, however, a problem solver cannot grasp at the first solution that arises, but instead must suspend judgment, giving ideas enough time to surface and develop freely. Although brainstorming is most frequently incorporated into the solution phase of the Reflective Thinking Framework, it can be used to prompt creative inquiry during any stage of the problem-solving process.

To ensure a successful brainstorming session, follow these guidelines:

1. *Suspend judgment.* Brainstorming is not the time to evaluate or criticize ideas.
2. *Encourage freewheeling.* Brainstorming is not the time to consider an idea's practicality. In fact, the wilder the idea, the better. You can tame or tone down ideas later if necessary.
3. *Aim for quantity of ideas.* Brainstorming is not the time to concentrate on idea quality, nor is it the time to censor any of your ideas. The more ideas you generate, the greater your chances of coming up with a good one.

SPEAKING of ETHICS

How Equal Is Equal?

If groups truly are to pool their resources in an effort to make the best decisions possible, then every member must feel free to contribute and have equal access to influence all other members. When it comes to equal participation for men and women, however, this is apparently not the case. Even though the perception may be that women do more talking, according to researchers Barbara and Gene Eakins, in mixed sex groups men speak more frequently and for longer than women.[18] In fact, the longest speaking turns of women failed to equal even the shortest turns of men.

Is it ethical for men to monopolize discussions this way? Should they be doing more to encourage women to exert greater influence in an effort to change the status quo, or is it up to women to turn things around? What problems could a group encounter if its work depended more on the input provided from one subgroup than on input from all participants?

4. *Record all ideas.* Brainstorming is not the time to evaluate or eliminate possibilities. You'll need all the ideas you can come up with.
5. *Evaluation occurs only when brainstorming is concluded.* Only after the brainstorming session is over should you evaluate the ideas you proposed for usefulness and applicability.

PRESENTING THE OUTCOMES OF GROUP DISCUSSION

SO YOUR GROUP works its way through the reflective thinking framework and comes to a decision. Probably the problem solving you did occurred for the most part in private meetings and without the presence of an audience; in few instances, however, does your group's work end there. Usually your group is then asked to go public and report its findings to another audience (perhaps to your class, the head of your division at work, or even the organization's president) either to inform them of the group's decision or to advocate for the adoption of the group's proposals, or both. Most often the group's findings or its recommendations are presented to this other audience through an oral report, a panel discussion, a symposium, or a forum. Let us explore each of these formats in turn.

The Oral Report

When delivering an oral report of your group's deliberations and conclusions, your job is to inform or persuade an audience. The group's leader or a chosen spokesperson prepares a speech that describes the group's goals, discusses how the group analyzed the problem, reviews suggested solutions, summarizes the strengths and weaknesses of each solution, and offers the group's decision.

You approach the oral report of group work as you would any other speech. This means your report should contain an introduction (in which you explain your purpose, interest your audience in your results, and provide an overview of your main points), a body (in which you describe the problem, explain your criteria for a solution, and your reasons for choosing the solution you did), and a conclusion (your opportunity to summarize what you have accomplished and urge the acceptance of your group's decision or the adoption of your recommendation).

As with any speech, in addition to being well organized, your report must be adapted to reflect the needs, concerns, and interests of the people you are addressing, contain an array of supporting materials and evidence (including visual aids, if appropriate), use language that accurately and effectively communicates its content, and, of course, be rehearsed.

The Panel Discussion

A panel discussion requires group members to conduct a discussion in front of an audience. The positive and negative aspects of the issues involved in the discussion are debated for the benefit of audience members, although usually without their direct involvement. Thus the group replays in public the problem-solving discussion it had in private. In effect, during a panel discussion the audience eavesdrops on exchanges between group members as they discuss the issues. Neither memorized nor scripted, the panel discussion topic is researched and carefully planned so that all group members will be able to discuss major issues intelligently.

The Symposium

A symposium is a discussion in which a number of individuals present individual speeches of approximately the same length on a central subject before the same audience. Because a symposium's speakers address members of the audience directly, there usually is little, if any, interaction among the speakers during their actual presentations; however, after the delivery of the planned speeches, participants may discuss their reactions with each other as well as field questions from the audience.

Symposiums are designed to (1) shed light on or explore different aspects of a problem, (2) provide material for subsequent discussion, or (3) review different steps covered during a group's problem-solving experience. Ideally, each speaker is aware of what others will present so that duplication of information is avoided.

The Forum Presentation

Unlike the other formats, a forum is a discussion that requires full audience participation. After a moderator and/or each speaker makes a brief opening statement, audience members are free to question the participants, who answer their queries with brief impromptu responses. A town meeting is one example of the forum in action.

A forum works best when there is a moderator to introduce the program and the speakers, as well as to clarify and summarize the program's progress as needed. It also helps when group members are aware which issues will be discussed during the forum because they can then prepare themselves to respond to questions quickly and thoroughly.

The town meeting forum involves full audience participation. The effectiveness of this format depends, at least in part however, on the skills of the moderator.

SUMMARY

IN ADDITION TO ADDRESSING a public audience, speakers also need to be prepared to speak in a variety of group settings. Because small groups abound, you probably have had and will continue to have numerous opportunities to participate as a group member or leader.

A small group is a limited number of people who communicate with each other over a period of time, usually face to face, to make decisions and accomplish specific goals. All members of a group have the potential to influence all other members and are expected to function as both speaker and receiver.

Every group defines its own objectives, norms, and operating climate. More successful groups have a number of major attributes that distinguish them: in particular, these are effective leadership, effective membership, and the nature of the decision-making system used by the group.

In many instances, after a decision is reached or a problem solved, the findings of a group are presented to others through an oral report, a panel discussion, a symposium, or a forum.

THE SPEAKER'S STAND

Your instructor will divide you into small groups. Your assignment is to identify and formulate a question of fact, value, or policy for your group to discuss. Then conduct a group discussion on your chosen question using the reflective thinking framework. Be sure to outline exactly what you hope to accomplish during each stage of the sequence.

After you complete your discussion, prepare a brief paper explaining your group's accomplishments and identifying obstacles you needed to overcome as you sought to complete your task. Also analyze the qualities of leadership, membership, and decision-making experienced by your group.

Finally, your instructor will ask you to use one or more of the following formats to present your findings to the class: a panel discussion, an oral report, a symposium, or a forum presentation.

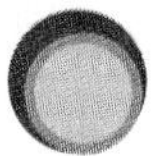

STUDENT FOCUS GROUP REPORT

Now that you have had the opportunity to consider and experience what it is like to be part of a decision-making group, in a group of five to seven students, answer the following questions.

1. What are the greatest challenges facing you as a participant in a decision-making group? How do these compare and contrast with the challenges you face as a public speaker?
2. How can group members facilitate or impede the functioning of a group?
3. How might an individual's sense of ethics affect his or her performance in a small group?
4. How could cultural diversity influence the operation of a small group?
5. Is it more important to be an effective group leader or an effective group member? Explain.
6. Summarize the most important information you learned about speaking in the small group.
7. Revisit the case study at the beginning of this chapter. Based on your understanding of the small group, in what ways, if any, would you now revise your answers?

Select a spokesperson to report your group's conclusions to the class.

Notes

CHAPTER 1

1. Louis Menand, "Everybody Else's College Education," *New York Times Magazine,* April 20, 1997, pp. 48–49.
2. Richard Brislin, *Understanding Culture's Influence on Behavior* (New York: Harcourt Brace Jovanovich College Publishers, 1993), p. v.
3. For a discussion of how cultural diversity enriches us, see H. Ned Seelye and Jacqueline Howell Wasilewski, *Between Cultures* (Lincolnwood, IL: NTC Publishing Group, 1996), p. 16.
4. See Anthony Pratkanis and Elliot Aronson, *Age of Propaganda* (New York: W. H. Freeman, 1992).
5. Lee Iacocca, *An Autobiography* (New York: Bantam, 1984), p. 16.
6. Dan B. Cortes, Jerry L. Winsor, and Ronald D. Stephen, "National Preferences in Business and Communication Education," *Communication Education,* 1989, pp. 6–14.
7. See Richard Whately, *Elements of Rhetoric,* 7th ed. (London: John W. Parker, 1946), p. 10.
8. See Elizabeth M. Fowler, "Training 21st Century Executives," *New York Times,* June 20, 1989, p. D13.
9. Patricia Ward Brash, "Beyond Giving a Speech," *Vital Speeches of the Day,* November 15, 1992, pp. 83–86.
10. Gary Blonston, "A More Diverse U.S. Looms," *The Record,* December 4, 1992, pp. A1, A14.
11. For a book that facilitates such preparation, see Richard D. Lewis, *When Cultures Collide* (London: Nicholas Brealey Publishing, 1996).
12. See Allan R. Cohen and David L. Bradford, *Influence without Authority* (New York: Wiley, 1990), p. ix.
13. Deborah Tannen, *That's Not What I Meant* (New York: William Morrow, 1986).
14. In Robert Boostrom, *Developing Creative and Critical Thinking* (Lincolnwood, IL: National Textbook Company, 1992), p. 239.

CHAPTER 2

1. Judy Keen, "Fitzwater Weighs Anchor," *USA Today,* December 4, 1992, p. 2A.
2. David Wallechinsky, Irving Wallace, and Amy Wallace, *The Book of Lists* (New York: William Morrow, 1977), p. 469.
3. Joe Ayres, "Perception of Speaking Ability: An Explanation for Speech Fright," *Communication Education,* July 1986, pp. 275–287.
4. See for example, Bernardo J. Carducci with Philip G. Zimbardo, "Are You Shy?" *Psychology Today,* 28: November/December 1995, pp. 34–41, 64–70, 78–82.
5. For a summary of these studies, see D. W. Klopf, "Cross Cultural Apprehension Research: A Summary of Pacific Basin Studies," in J. A. Daly & J. A. McCroskey, eds., *Avoiding Communication: Shyness, Reticence, and Communication Apprehension,* (Beverly Hills, CA: Sage, 1984) (pp. 157–169); D. W. Klopf and R. E. Cambra, "Communication Apprehension among College Students in America, Australia, Japan and Korea," *The Journal of Psychology,* 102; 1979, pp. 27–31; and S. M. Ralston, R. Ambler, and J. N. Scudder, "Reconsidering the Impact of Racial Differences in the College Public Speaking Classroom on Minority Student Communication Anxiety," *Communication Reports,* 4: 1991, pp. 43–50.
6. James C. McCroskey, "Oral Communication Apprehension: A Summary of Recent Theory and Research," *Human Communication Research, 4:* 1977, p. 78.
7. For information on work in neurolinguistic programming, see Richard Bandler and John Grinder, *Frogs into Princes* (Moab, UT: Real People Press, 1979); and Genie Z. Laborde, *Influencing with Integrity* (Palo Alto, CA: Syntony Publishing, 1984).
8. Virginia P. Richmond and James P. McCroskey, *Communication: Apprehension, Avoidance, and Effectiveness,* 3rd ed. (Scottsdale, AZ: Gorsuch Scarisbrick, 1992).
9. See Barbara G. Markway, Charyl N. Carmin, C. Alex Pollard, and Teresa Flynn, *Dying of Embarrassment: Help For Social Anxiety and Phobia* (Oakland, CA: New Harbinger Publications, 1992).
10. See, for example, L. Kelly, "Social Skills Training as a Mode of Treatment for Social Communication Problems," in J. A. Daly and J. C. McCroskey, eds., *Avoiding Communication: Shyness, Reticence, and Communication Apprehension* (Beverly Hills, CA: Sage, 1984), pp. 189–207; and G. M. Phillips, "Rhetoritherapy versus the Medical Model: Dealing with Reticence," *Communication Education, 26:* 1977, pp. 34–43.
11. Theodore Clevenger, Jr., "A Synthesis of Experimental Research in Stage Fright," *Quarterly Journal of Speech, 45:* April 1959, p. 136.

12. J. A. Daly, A. L. Vangelisti, H. L. Neel, and P. D. Cavanaugh, "Pre-Performance Concerns Associated with Public Speaking Anxiety," *Communication Quarterly, 37:* 1989, pp. 39–53.
13. Virginia P. Richmond and James C. McCroskey, *Communication Apprehension, Avoidance, and Effectiveness,* 4th ed. (Scottsdale, AZ: Gorsuch Scarisbrick, 1996).

CHAPTER 3

1. Louis A. Day, *Ethics in Media Communications: Cases and Controversies,* (Belmont, CA: Wadsworth, 1991), p. 2.
2. Cicero, *De Inventione* (Cambridge, MA: Loeb Classics, 1949), p. 3.
3. Charles E. Little, ed., *The Institutio Oratoria,* Vol. 2 (Nashville, TN: George Peabody College for Teachers, 1951), pp. 223–224.
4. James A. Jaska and Michael S. Pritchard, *Communication Ethics: Methods of Analysis* (Belmont, CA: Wadsworth, 1988).
5. "Do You Believe What Newspeople Tell You?" *Parade Magazine,* March 2, 1997, pp. 3–6.
6. Anthony R. Pratkanis and Eliot Aronson, *Age of Propaganda,* (New York: W.H. Freeman, 1991), p. 11.
7. Alison Mitchell, "Consult Polls. Choose Phrase. Repeat." *New York Times,* December 3, 1995, p. E3.
8. Sissela Bok, *Lying: Moral Choice in Public and Private Life* (New York: Knopf, 1989).
9. See Sissela Bok, *Lying* (New York: Pantheon, 1978); Sissela Bok, *Secrets* (New York: Random House, 1989); and Steven A. McCormack and Timothy R. Levine, "When Lies Are Uncovered: Emotional and Relational Outcomes of Discovered Deception," *Communication Monographs, 57,* June 1990, p. 119.
10. Adetokunbo F. Knowles-Borishade, "Paradigm for Classical African Orature," in Christine Kelly et al. (eds.), *Diversity in Public Communication: A Reader.* (Dubuque, IA: Kendall-Hunt, 1995), p. 100.
11. "The Texaco Tapes," *The Record,* November 8, 1996, p. L10.
12. Khalid Abdul Muhammad, "The Secret Relationship Between Blacks and Jews," Speech transcript, November 29, 1993.
13. Ibid.
14. See Barbara Warnick and Edward S. Inch, *Critical Thinking and Communication* (New York: Macmillan, 1994), p. 11.
15. See Renee Blank and Sandra Slipp, *Voices of Diversity* (New York: Amacom, 1994).
16. J. Holmes and J. Rempel, "Trust in Close Relationships," in C. Hendrick, ed., *Close Relationships* (Newbury Park, CA: Sage, 1989).
17. Holger Kluge, "Reflections on Diversity," *Vital Speeches of the Day,* January 1, 1997, p. 171.

CHAPTER 4

1. Paul Rankin, "The Measurement of the Ability to Understand Speaker Language," (Ph.D. Dissertation, University of Michigan, 1926), p. 43; and L. Barker, R. Edwards, C. Gaines, K. Gladney, and F. Hailey, "An Investigation of Proportional Time Spent in Various Communication Activities by College Students," *Journal of Applied Communication Research, 8:* 1980, pp. 101–109.
2. For a thorough discussion see Ralph G. Nichols and Leonard R. Stevens, *Are You Listening?* (New York: McGraw-Hill, 1957).
3. See Arthur Robertson, *The Language of Effective Listening* (Carmel, IN: Scott Foresman Professional Books, 1991), pp. 44–45.
4. See E. D. Hirsch, Jr., *Cultural Literacy* (Boston: Houghton Mifflin, 1987); and Blaine Goss, "Listening as Information Processing," *Communication Quarterly, 30:* Fall 1982, pp. 304–307.
5. See Lyman K. Steil, Joanne Summerfield, and George deMare, *Listening: It Can Change Your Life* (New York: Wiley, 1983).
6. Richard D. Lewis, *When Cultures Collide* (London: Nicholas Brealey Publishing, 1996), pp. 48–49.
7. See Richard Paul, *Critical Thinking: What Every Person Needs to Survive in a Rapidly Changing World* (Rohnert Park, CA: Center for Critical Thinking, 1990).
8. See Steil et al., pp. 18–20.
9. Walter Pauk, *How to Study in College* (Boston: Houghton Mifflin, 1989), pp. 121–133.
10. Charles Osgood, "Hello, Is Anybody There?" in *The Osgood Files* (New York: G. P. Putnam's Sons, 1991), pp. 37–39.
11. Peter F. Drucker, "Behind Japan's Success," *Harvard Business Review,* January–February 1980.
12. For more information on the relationship between notetaking and listening see Robert Bostrom and D. Bruce Searle, "Encoding, Media, Affect and Gender" in Robert Bostrom, ed., *Listening Behavior: Measurement and Application* (New York: Guilford Press, 1990), pp. 28–30; and Florence L. Wolff, Nadine C. Marsnik, William Tacey, and Ralph Nichols, *Perceptive Listening* (Englewood Cliffs, NJ: Prentice-Hall, 1983), pp. 88–97.
13. Paul Higday, "Ferrofluids," in *Allyn & Bacon Student Videos, 1996,* pp. 19–21.

CHAPTER 5

1. *Cephalgia* and *kwashiorkor* mean headache and malnutrition, respectively.
2. For a detailed discussion of this see Cindy Jenefsky, "Public Speaking as Empowerment at Visionary University," *Communication Education, 45:* October 1996, pp. 343–355.
3. Lane Cooper, *The Rhetoric of Aristotle: An Expanded Translation with Supplementary Examples for Students of Composition and Public Speaking* (New York: Appleton-Century Crofts, 1960), p. 136.
4. See, for example, Jonathan R. Alger, "The Educational Value of Diversity," *Academe,* January–February 1997, pp. 20–22.
5. Peggy Noonan, *What I Saw at the Revolution* (New York: Ivy Books, 1990), pp. 70–72.

6. Jean Otto, "Freedom to Speak and Write," *Vital Speeches of the Day,* January 1, 1992, pp. 187–188.
7. James A. Baker III, "America and the Collapse of the Soviet Empire," *Vital Speeches of the Day,* January 1, 1992: p. 162.
8. James R. Houghton, "Leadership," *Vital Speeches of the Day,* July 1, 1996, pp. 571–572.
9. See William McGuire, "Attitudes and Attitude Change," in Gardner Lindszly and Eliot Aronson eds., *The Handbook of Social Psychology,* Vol. 2 (New York: Random House, 1985), pp. 287–288.
10. Nancy W. Dickey, "Our Sisters' Sicknesses, Our Sisters' Satchels: The Past, Present and Future of Women and Medicine," *Vital Speeches of the Day,* July 15, 1996, pp. 582–583.
11. Deborah Tannen, *You Just Don't Understand* (New York: Ballantine Books, 1992), p. 42.
12. Kathleen Kelly Reardon, *Persuasion in Practice* (Newbury Park, CA: Sage, 1991), p. 88.
13. Ibid.
14. Ibid.
15. Ibid., p. 89.
16. See Hovland, Janis, and Kelley, *Communication and Persuasion* (New Haven, CT: Yale University Press, 1961), p. 183.
17. See William J. McGuire, "Persuasion, Resistance and Attitude Change," in I. Pool et al. eds., *Handbook of Communication* (Skokie, IL: Rand McNally, 1973), pp. 216–252.
18. See William A. Henry III, "Beyond the Melting Pot," *Time,* April 9, 1990, p. 29.
19. For detailed discussions of how cultures differ based on whether they are individualist or collectivist, high or low context, tolerant or intolerant of uncertainty, and high or low power, see Edward T. Hall, *Beyond Culture* (Garden City, NY: Anchor, 1977); Geert Hofstede, *Culture's Consequences: International Differences in Work-Related Values* (Beverly Hills, CA: Sage, 1980); Geert Hofstede, *Cultures and Organizations: Software of the Mind* (London: McGraw-Hill, 1991); and Terence Brake and Danielle Walker, *Doing Business Internationally* (Princeton, NJ: Princeton Training Press, 1995).
20. Ray Halbritter, "Indian Economic Futures: Governance and Taxation," *Vital Speeches of the Day,* December 15, 1996, pp. 153–154.
21. See Yu Kuang Chu, "Some Suggestions for Learning about Peoples and Cultures," in Seymour Fresh ed. (Evanston, IL: McDougal and Littell, 1974), p. 52.
22. Valerie Lynch Lee (ed.), *Faces of Culture* (Huntington Beach, CA: KOCE, TV Foundation, 1983), p. 69.
23. *Newsweek,* February 3, 1992, p. 17.
24. David E. Sanger, "Japan Premier Joins Critics of America's Work Habits," *New York Times,* February 4, 1992, p. A10.
25. "Japanese Leaders Export More Barbs," *The Record,* February 4, 1992, p. A27.
26. From a speech by Dan Quayle delivered before the Commonwealth Club of California, May 19, 1992.
27. Bill Clinton, "Acceptance Speech," Democratic National Convention, July 16, 1992.
28. Kenneth L. Woodward, "The Elite, and How to Avoid It," *Newsweek,* July 20, 1992, p. 55.
29. Anthony Lewis, "The Two Nations," *New York Times,* February 13, 1992, p. A27.
30. Senator Al Gore, "Acceptance Speech," Democratic National Convention, July 16, 1992.
31. See Gregory Beals, "A Crucial Messenger," *The Record,* November 10, 1991, p. A29, and Ira Berkow, "Magic Johnson's Legacy" *New York Times,* November 8, 1991.
32. *The Record,* November 8, 1991, p. A29.
33. Bill Pennington, "The Extraordinary Ervin," *The Record,* November 8, 1991.
34. See Edwin Diamone, "Magic and the Media," *New York,* December 2, 1991.
35. Roger Ailes, *You Are the Message* (New York: Doubleday, 1988), p. 51.
36. Ibid.

CHAPTER 6

1. For a discussion of *kibun,* or personal harmony, see Myron W. Lustig and Jolene Koester, *Intercultural Competence,* 2nd ed. (New York: HarperCollins, 1996), pp. 296–297.
2. For an analysis of topics used in speeches by leaders of the largest corporations in the United States, see Robert J. Meyers and Martha Stout Kessler, "Business Speeches: A Study of the Themes in Speeches by America's Corporate Leaders," *Journal of Business Communication, 17,* (3): 1980, pp. 5–17.
3. For a discussion on brainstorming by a key developer of the process see Alex F. Osborn, *Applied Imagination* (New York: Scribner's, 1962).
4. For a variation on this technique see R. R. Allen and Ray E. McKerron, *The Pragmatics of Public Communication,* 3rd ed. (Dubuque, IA: Kendall-Hunt, 1985), pp. 42–44.
5. See Don Aslett, *Is There a Speech Inside You?* (Cincinnati, OH: Writer's Digest Books, 1989), pp. 18–19, 30.
6. Roger E. Axtell, ed., *Do's and Taboos around the World,* 3rd ed. (New York: Wiley, 1993).
7. See also Richard D. Lewis, *When Cultures Collide* (London: Nicholas Brealey Publishing, 1996).
8. Marshall R. Singer, "Culture: A Perceptual Approach," in Larry Samover and Richard Porter eds., *Intercultural Communication: A Reader,* 4th ed. (Belmont, CA: Wadsworth, 1985), p. 67.
9. See Roger Hart, *The Sound of Leadership* (Chicago: University of Chicago Press, 1987).
10. See Anthony Pratkanis and Eliot Aronson, *Age of Propaganda* (New York: W.H. Freeman, 1991), p. 55.
11. Patricia Ann Compos, "Tissue Engineering," in Karla Kay Jensen, ed., *Allyn & Bacon/AFA Student Speeches Video I* (1996), pp. 14–16.

CHAPTER 7

1. We would like to thank the reference librarians at both the College of New Rochelle and the New York Institute of Technology for their invaluable input for this section.

2. Ted Spencer, "The Internet Comes of Age for 1997," *Spectra,* January 1997, p. 5.
3. Randy Reddick and Elliot King, *The OnLine Student* (Fort Worth, TX: Harcourt, Brace College Publishers, 1996), p. 3. For particularly valuable information on conducting research, see pages 161–179.
4. Patrick McGeehan, "Playing the Numbers, Sometimes for Laughs: Demographic Duo," *The Record,* December 13, 1992, pp. B1–2.

CHAPTER 8

1. D. J. O'Keefe, *Persuasion: Theory and Research.* (Newbury Park, CA: Sage, 1990), pp. 168–169.
2. Eliot Aronson, *The Social Animal,* 6th ed. (New York: W.H. Freeman, 1992), p. 88.
3. Claudette Mackay-Lassonde, "Let's Stop Fooling Ourselves," *Vital Speeches of the Day,* July 1, 1996, pp. 569–571.
4. Kellie Rider, "Happily Ever After?" In *Winning Orations, 1990* (Mancato, MN: Interstate Oratorical Association, 1990), p. 95.
5. Brian Swenson, "Gun Safety and Children." In *Winning Orations, 1991* (Mancato, MN: Interstate Oratorical Assocation, 1991), p. 101.
6. Kurstin Finch, "Are the Stakes Too High?" In *Winning Orations, 1995* (Mancato, MN: Interstate Oratorical Association, 1995), p. 88.
7. Pam Espinoza, "Medical Testing: A Prescription for Error." In *Winning Orations, 1989* (Mancato, MN: Interstate Oratorical Association, 1989), p. 11.
8. H. Hinds, "Testing Prescription Drugs for the Elderly." In *Winning Orations, 1989* (Mancato, MN: Interstate Oratorical Association, 1989), p. 53.
9. P. A. Sullivan, "Women's Discourse and Political Communication: A Case Study of Congressperson Patricia Schroeder," *Western Journal of Communication, 57,* 1993, pp. 530–545.
10. Sheila Wellington, "Women Are in the Wrong Conduits," *Vital Speeches of the Day,* December 15, 1996, pp. 148–150.
11. Terrika Scott, "Curing Crisis with Community." In *Winning Orations, 1995.* (Mancato, MN: Interstate Oratorical Association, 1995), p. 12.
12. Ann Lorentson, "Seeking Alternatives to Traditional Plastics: Is It Time for a Change?" In *Winning Orations, 1989* (Mancato, MN: Interstate Oratorical Association, 1989), p. 33.
13. Greg Robinson, "The Canine Frankenstein." In *Winning Orations, 1988.* (Mancato, MN: Interstate Oratorical Association, 1988), p. 71.
14. Luther Lasure, "Heads We Win, Tails We Lose." In *Winning Orations, 1988* (Mancato, MN: Interstate Oratorical Association, 1988), p. 114.
15. Joan Didion, "Why I Write," *New York Times Book Review,* April 27, 1976.
16. E., Bliss, ed. *In Search of Light: The Broadcasts of Edward R. Murrow, 1938–1961* (New York: Knopf, 1967).
17. Jocelyn So, "Liquid Bone." In Karla Kay Jensen, ed., *Video User's Guide for the Allyn & Bacon/AFA Student Speeches Video I,* 1995, p. 38.
18. Laura Oster, "Deforestation: A Time for Action." In *Winning Orations, 1990* (Mancato, MN: Interstate Oratorical Association, 1990), p. 80.
19. Lori M. Hawkins, "Critical Thinking: An Ancient Philosophy for Modern Times." In *Winning Orations, 1988* (Mancato, MN: Interstate Oratorical Association, 1988), p. 46.
20. Lisa Reinhack, "In Pursuit of the Not So Trivial." In *Winning Orations, 1988* (Mancato, MN: Interstate Oratorical Association, 1988), p. 121.
21. Shannon Dyer, "The Dilemma of Whistleblowers." In *Winning Orations, 1989* (Mancato, MN: Interstate Oratorical Association, 1989), pp. 63–64.
22. Kelly Campbell, "The Decoy Virus Vaccine." In Karla Kay Jensen, ed., *Video User's Guide for the Allyn & Bacon/AFA Student Speeches Video I,* 1996, p. 24.
23. Doug Wehage, "Title Unknown." In *Winning Orations, 1990* (Mancato, MN: Interstate Oratorical Association, 1991), p. 90.
24. Tracy A. Shario, "Discrimination in Defense." In *Winning Orations, 1991* (Mancato, MN: Interstate Oratorical Association, 1991), p. 84.
25. See D. Huff, *How to Lie with Statistics* (and J. A. Paulos, 1988); *Innumeracy: Mathematical Illiteracy and Its Consequences.* (New York: Hill and Wang, 1988).
26. Jorge L. Carro, "Capital Punishment from a Global Perspective: The Death Penalty: Right or Wrong?" *Vital Speeches of the Day,* August 1, 1996, p. 630.
27. Nancy Shaver, "A Family Disease." In *Winning Orations, 1990* (Mancato, MN: Interstate Oratorical Association, 1990), p. 79.
28. Bob Moore, "Emergency Room Physicians: America's Prime-time Crisis." In *Winning Orations, 1995* (Northfield, MN: Interstate Oratorical Association, 1995).
29. G. Cowley, "Can Sunshine Save Your Life?" *Newsweek,* December 30, 1991, p. 56.
30. Terrika Scott, "Curing Crisis with Community." In *Winning Orations, 1995* (Northfield, MN: Interstate Oratorical Association, 1995), p. 11.
31. See O'Keefe, pp. 135–136; [Reinhold, *Persuasive Effects of Evidence,* pp. 34–39.]
32. Ben Lohman, "Fiberglass Insulation." In Karla Kay Jensen, ed., *Video User's Guide for the Allyn & Bacon/AFA Student Speeches Video I,* 1996, p. 53.
33. Theresa McGuiness, "Greeks in Crises." In *Winning Orations, 1990* (Mancato, MN: Interstate Oratorical Association, 1990), p. 75.
34. Becky McKay, "Homeless Children: A National Crisis." In *Winning Orations, 1990* (Mancato, MN: Interstate Oratorical Association, 1990), p. 42.

CHAPTER 9

1. For a scholarly discussion of what we can learn about organization from an orderly universe, see Margaret J. Wheatley, *Leadership and the New Science* (San Francisco: Berrett-Koehler Publishers, 1994).

2. Christopher Spicer and Ronald Bassett, "The Effect of Organization Learning from an Informative Message," *Southern Speech Communication Journal, 41:* Spring 1976, pp. 290–299.
3. Todd S. Purdum, "The Speech: Verdict: No Bridge to the History Books," *New York Times,* January 21, 1997, p. A14.
4. Janice Hocker Rushing, "Ronald Reagan's 'Star Wars' Address: Mythic Containment of Technical Reasoning," *Quarterly Journal of Speech, 72:* 1986, pp. 415–433.
5. Ibid.
6. Lani Arredondo, *How to Present Like a Pro* (New York: McGraw-Hill, 1991), pp. 28–29.
7. See also Deborah A. Lieberman, *Public Speaking in the Multicultural Environment* (Englewood Cliffs, NJ: Prentice-Hall, 1994).
8. See, for example, the section on organization preferences in Myron W. Lustig and Jolene Koester, *Intercultural Competence,* 2nd ed. (New York: HarperCollins, 1996).
9. David Levine, *The Flight from Ambiguity* (Chicago: University of Chicago Press, 1985), pp. 25–28.
10. See, for example, J. Hinds, "Reader versus Writer Responsibility: A New Typology," *Writing across Languages: Analysis of L2 Written Text,* Ulla Connor and Robert B. Kaplan, eds. (Reading, MA: Addison-Wesley, 1986), pp. 141–152; and Lustig and Koester.

CHAPTER 10

1. John M. Murphy, "Inventing Authority: Bill Clinton, Martin Luther King, Jr., and the Orchestration of Rhetorical Traditions," *Quarterly Journal of Speech, 83;* 1997, pp. 71–89.
2. William J. Clinton, "Remarks to the Eighth Annual Holy Convocation of the Church of God in Christ." In *Selected Speeches of President William Jefferson Clinton* (Document No. PR: 42:2: Sp 3) (Washington, DC: President of the United States, 199), p. 21.
3. Ibid.
4. Mary Hoffman, "Mercury: Nothing to Smile About." In *Winning Orations, 1991,* (Mancato, MN: Interstate Oratorical Association, 1991), p. 55.
5. William E. Rodrigues, "Raising the Bar, Lowering the Barriers," *Vital Speeches of the Day,* April 1, 1997, p. 375.
6. Chris Fleming, "Bring Back the Pony Express." In *Winning Orations, 1995,* (Northfield, MN: Interstate Oratorical Association, 1995), p. 37.
7. Sylvia Simmons, *How to Be the Life of the Podium* (New York: Amacom Books, 1991), p. 5.
8. Sharon Bower, *Painless Public Speaking* (London: Thorsons Publishers Limited, 1990), p. 58.
9. Stephen C. Rafe, *How to Be Prepared to Speak on Your Feet* (New York: Harper Business Publications, 1990), p. 89.
10. Simmons, p. 220.
11. Bower, pp. 96–97.
12. Rafe, p. 78.
13. Tara Kubicka, "Traitorous Transplants: The Enemy Within." In *Winning Orations, 1995* (Northfield, MN: Interstate Oratorical Association, 1995), p. 52.
14. Gwen Johnson, "Global Dumping." In *Winning Orations, 1991* (Mancato, MN: Interstate Oratorical Association, 1991), p. 69.
15. Neil Mansharamani, "The Writing on the Wall." In *Winning Orations, 1995* (Northfield, MN: Interstate Oratorical Association, 1995), p. 52.
16. Kurstin Finch, "Are the Stakes Too High?" In *Winning Orations, 1995* (Northfield, MN: Interstate Oratorical Association, 1995), p. 88.
17. Brent Wainscott, "The Value of Smiles and Laughter." In *Winning Orations, 1990* (Mancato, MN: Interstate Oratorical Association, 1990), pp. 70–71.
18. Tai Du, "Death by Federal Mandate." In *Winning Orations, 1995* (Northfield, MN: Interstate Oratorical Association, 1995), p. 77.
19. Marty Crabbs, "Toxic Trafficking: How the Defense Department Is Selling Toxic Waste." In *Winning Orations, 1990* (Mancato, MN: Interstate Oratorical Association, 1990), p. 33.
20. Ben Sutherland, "Terminator 101: Media Literacy in the Information Age." In *Winning Orations, 1995* (Northfield, MN: Interstate Oratorical Association, 1995), p. 33.
21. Brian D. Epp, "The Hidden Tax: Anarchy in America's Tort Liability System," in *Winning Orations, 1990* (Mancato, MN: Interstate Oratorical Association, 1990), p. 37.
22. Sarah Nagel, "An Educational Choice." In *Winning Orations, 1990* (Mancato, MN: Interstate Oratorical Association, 1990), p. 54.
23. Robert Mattingly, "Rock around the Clock." In *Winning Orations, 1995* (Northfield, MN: Interstate Oratorial Association, 1995), p. 35.
24. Michael L. Williams, "Racial and Ethnic Relations in American Higher Education," *Vital Speeches of the Day,* January 1, 1992, p. 174.
25. A. McCallen, "Eldercare—The New Employee Benefit." In *Winning Orations, 1991* (Mancato, MN: Interstate Oratorical Association, 1991), p. 93.
26. See Charles R. Gruner, "Advice to the Beginning Speaker on Using Humor—What the Research Tells Us," *Communication Education 34:* April, 1988, pp. 142–147.
27. Lee Iacocca, "Taking Care of Business." *Vital Speeches of the Day,* March 1, 1992, p. 295.
28. Shawn Harris, "Transgenic Pharming," in Karla Kay Jensen, ed., *Allyn & Bacon Student Speech Video I,* 1996, p. 33.
29. David E. Moore, "Global Markets and the North American Free Trade Agreement," *Vital Speeches of the Day,* February 1, 1992, p. 243.
30. Richard L. Weaver II, "Motivating the Motivators," *Vital Speeches of the Day,* May 15, 1996, p. 466.
31. Ryan T. Siskow, "The Name Game: This Time It's Financial Planners." In *Winning Orations, 1990* (Mancato: MN: Interstate Oratorical Association, 1990), p. 30.
32. Theresa McGuiness, "Greeks in Crisis." In *Winning Orations, 1991* (Mancato, MN: Interstate Oratorical Association, 1991), p. 73.

33. Michael Eisner, "Managing a Creative Organization," *Vital Speeches of the Day,* June 1, 1996, p. 502.
34. Susan Trausch, "A Once Proud America Is Sinking into the Middle Ground," *The Record,* January 17, 1992, p. B7.
35. Dick Morris, *Behind the Oval Office: Winning the Presidency in the Nineties* (New York: Random House, 1997).
36. Alicia Croshal, "Gossip: It's Worth Talking About." In *Winning Orations, 1991* (Mancato: MN: Interstate Oratorical Association, 1991), p. 1.
37. Bond Benton, "Staged Auto Accidents," in Karla Kay Jensen, ed., *Allyn & Bacon, Student Speeches Video I, 1996,* pp. 66–67.
38. John Ring, "An Alliance of Excellence," *Vital Speeches of the Day,* April 1, 1992, p. 368.
39. Talbot D'Alemberte, "Civil Justice Reform," *Vital Speeches of the Day,* March 1, 1992, p. 308.
40. John F. McDonnell, "PaxPacifica," *Vital Speeches of the Day,* April 1, 1992, p. 372.
41. Sheri Strickland, "Title Unknown," *Winning Orations, 1995,* (Mancato, MN: Interstate Oratorical Association, 1995), p. 22.
42. See Roger Cohen, "For Coke, World Is Its Oyster," *New York Times,* November 21, 1991, p. D5; and Michael Lev, "Advertisers Seek Global Messages" *New York Times,* November 18, 1991.
43. Dave McCurdy, "Foreign Policy Today," *Vital Speeches of the Day,* April 1, 1992, pp. 375–376.
44. Janeen Rohovit, "One in Two." In *Winning Orations, 1990* (Mancato, MN: Interstate Oratorical Association, 1990), p. 11.
45. Tara Trainor, "A Loyal Friend." In *Winning Orations, 1990* (Mancato, MN: Interstate Oratorical Association, 1990), pp. 53–54.
46. Denalie Silha, "Rediscovering a Lost Resource." In *Winning Orations, 1991,* (Mancato, MN: Interstate Oratorical Association, 1991), p. 81.
47. Michael Marien, "Education and Learning in the 21st Century," *Vital Speeches of the Day,* March 15, 1991, p. 344.
48. Jeanne Tessier Barone, "The Sky's No Limit at All," *Vital Speeches of the Day,* October 1, 1996, p. 752.

CHAPTER 11

1. William Steere, "Plan Globally, Engage Locally: The Public Policy Challenge for Global Corporations," *Vital Speeches of the Day,* December 1, 1992.
2. Dominic A. Infante, Andrew S. Rancer, and Deanna F. Womack, *Building Communication Theory,* 3rd ed. (Prospect Heights, Il: Waveland Press, 1997), p. 521.

CHAPTER 12

1. A similar case study appears in Teri Gamble and Michael Gamble, *Contacts* (Boston, MA: Allyn & Bacon, 1998).
2. This case is also discussed in Lynne V. Cheney, *Telling the Truth* (New York: Simon & Schuster, 1995), p. 63.
3. The name "Dave Stud" was suggested by an incident reported in Cheney, p. 56.
4. See John McCrone, *The Ape That Spoke: Language and the Evolution of the Human Mind* (New York: Marroni, 1991).
5. See Michael Brooks, *The Power of Business Rapport* (New York: HarperCollins, 1991), pp. 123–124.
6. Ibid.
7. Richard Breslin and Tomoko Yoshida, *Intercultural Communication Training: An Introduction* (Thousand Oaks, CA: Sage Publications, 1994).
8. Larry A. Samovar and Richard E. Porter, *Communication between Cultures* (Belmont, CA: Wadsworth, 1991), p. 152.
9. Christopher Engholm, *When Business East Meets Business West* (New York: Wiley, 1991), p. 106.
10. Jesse Jackson, "Rainbow Coalition," presented to the Democratic National Convention, July 17, 1984.
11. Wilma Scott Heide, "Revolution: Tomorrow Is Now," presented to the National Organization for Women Convention, February 17, 1973.
12. Sol Trujilo, "American Hispanic Population," *Vital Speeches of the Day,* December 1, 1996, p. 124.
13. Edwin J. Delattre, "Condoms and Coercion: The Maturity of Self-Determination." *Vital Speeches of the Day,* April 15, 1992, p. 416.
14. Delattre, p. 414.
15. George Bush, "Iraqi Aggression in the Persian Gulf," address to a joint session of Congress, September 11, 1990.
16. Definitions from Henry Beard and Christopher Cerf, *The Politically Correct Dictionary and Handbook* (New York: Villard Books, 1992).
17. See Morris K. Udall, "Stalking the Elusive Malaprop," *Saturday Evening Post,* October 1988, p.40.
18. See, for example, David Schuman and Dick Olufs, *Diversity on Campus* (Boston, M: Allyn & Bacon, 1995).
19. Bill Cosby, "Elements of Igno-Ebonics Style," *Wall Street Journal,* January 10, 1997.
20. Ibid.
21. Dierdre Glenn Paul, "Despite Media's Attitude, Ebonics Decision Makes Sense," *The Record,* January 9, 1997, p. L9.
22. Jack E. White, "Ebonics According to Buckwheat," *Time,* January 13, 1997, p. 62.
23. Louis Menand, "Johnny Be Good: Ebonics and the Language of Cultural Separatism," *The New Yorker,* January 13, 1997, p. 4.
24. Tim Golden, "Oakland Scratches Plan to Teach Black English," *New York Times,* January 14, 1997, p. A10.
25. For a discussion of age discrimination in the workplace see Marianne Lavelle, "On the Edge of Age Discrimination," *New York Times Magazine,* March 9, 1997, pp. 66–69.
26. William B. Gudykunst, *Bridging Differences* (Thousand Oaks, CA: Sage, 1994).
27. Jean Otto, "Freedom to Speak and Write," *Vital Speeches of the Day,* January 1, 1992, p. 191.
28. Jackson.

29. Todd G. Buchholz, "Teaching Virtue: The Grimm Attack on American Tales," *Vital Speeches of the Day,* April 15, 1992, p. 397.
30. Chief Seattle, "The Indian's Night Promises to Be Dark," in *Indian Oratory: Famous Speeches by Noted Indian Chieftains,* W.C. Vanderwerth, (Norman: University of Oklahoma Press, 1971).
31. John F. Kennedy, "Civil Rights Message," June 11, 1963.
32. Martin Luther King, Jr., "I Have a Dream," August 28, 1963.
33. Lee P. Brown, *Vital Speeches of the Day,* January 1, 1992, p. 183.
34. Gloria Steinem, *Revolution from Within* (Boston: Little, Brown, 1992), p. 190.
35. Otto, p. 189.
36. Kennedy.
37. Bill Clinton, "Acceptance Speech before the Democratic National Convention," July 16, 1992.
38. King.
39. King.
40. Jackson.
41. Bill Bradley, "Keynote Speech," presented to the Democratic National Convention, July 13, 1992.
42. Maxwell E. P. King, "The Future of Newspapers," *Vital Speeches of the Day,* April 15, 1992, p. 398.
43. "Text of Bill Clinton's Speech," *The Record,* January 21, 1997, p. A9.
44. Bill Clinton, "A Strategy for Foreign Policy," *Vital Speeches of the Day,* May 1, 1992, p. 421.
45. W. J. Banach, "In Search of an Eloquent Thank You," *Vital Speeches of the Day,* October 15, 1991, p. 63.
46. John F. Kennedy, "Inaugural Address," January 20, 1961.

CHAPTER 13

1. Bert Decker, *You've Got to Be Believed to Be Heard* (New York: St Martin's Press, 1992), p. 31.
2. For an interesting discussion of nonverbal cues, lying, and judgments of speaker credibility, see Paul Ekman, *Telling Lies* (New York: Norton, 1992).
3. See, for example, Ray Birdwhistell, *Kinetics and Context* (Philadelphia: University of Pennsylvania Press, 1970), and Albert Mehrabian, *Silent Messages* (Belmont, CA: Wadsworth, 1971).
4. From Charles Osgood, *The Osgood File* (New York: G.P. Putnam's Sons, 1991), pp. 59–60.
5. See "The Public Course: Is It Preparing Students with Work Related Skills?" *Communication Education, 36:* 1987, pp. 131–137.
6. Roger Ailes, *You Are the Message* (New York: Doubleday, 1989), p. 17.
7. Ibid.
8. Ibid.
9. Mehrabian.
10. R. Geiselman and John Crawley, "Incidental Processing of Speaker Characteristics: Voice as Connotative Information," *Journal of Verbal Learning and Verbal Behavior, 22:* 1983, pp. 15–23.
11. Judith A. Hall, "Voice Tone and Persuasiveness," *Journal of Personality and Social Psychology, 38:* 1980, pp. 924–934.
12. Rosita Daskel Albert and Gayle L. Nelson, "Hispanic/Anglo-American Differences in Attributions to Paralinguistic Behavior," *International Journal of Intercultural Relations 17:* 1993, pp. 19–40.
13. Larry A. Samovar and Richard E. Porter, *Communication between Cultures:* 2nd ed. (Belmont, CA: Wadsworth, 1995), p. 200.
14. Ibid.
15. Leon Fletcher, "Polishing Your Silent Languages," *The Toastmaster:* March 1990, p. 15.
16. For a discussion of what happens when a speaker's body language is inconsistent with his or her words, see James B. Stiff and Gerald R. Miller, "Come to Think of It . . . Interrogative Probes, Deceptive Communication and Deception Detection," *Human Communication Research, 12:* 1986, pp. 339–357.
17. For an exploration of the meaning of human gestures see Desmond Morris, *Body Talk* (New York: Crown, 1994).
18. Robert G. Harper, Arthur N. Wiens, and Joseph D. Matarazzo, *Nonverbal Communication: The State of the Art* (New York: Wiley, 1978), p. 164.
19. See, for example, Min-Sun Kim, "A Comparative Analysis of Nonverbal Expression as Portrayed in Korean and American Print-Media Advertising," *Howard Journal of Communications, 3:* 1992, p. 321; Michael L. Hecht, Mary Jane Collier, and Sidney A. Ribeau, *African American Communication: Ethnic Identity and Cultural Interpretation* (Newbury Park, CA: Sage, 1993), p. 112.
20. See Nancy Henley, *Body Politics* (Englewood Cliffs, NJ: Prentice-Hall, 1977).
21. See, for example, Virginia P. Richmond, James C. McCroskey, and Stephen K. Payne, *Nonverbal Behavior in Interpersonal Relations* (Englewood Cliffs, NJ: Prentice-Hall, 1987), pp. 82–83; and Samovar and Porter.
22. See Kim, p. 321, and Hu Wenzhong and Cornelious L. Grove, *Encountering the Chinese* (Yarmouth, ME: Intercultural Press, 1991), p. 116.
23. James A. Herrick, *Critical Thinking: The Analysis of Arguments* (Scottsdale, AZ: Gorsuch Publishers, 1991), p. 47.
24. Ibid.
25. Shelly Chiden, "Communication of Physical Attractiveness and Persuasion," *Journal of Personality and Social Psychology 37:* 1979, pp. 1387–1397.
26. See Samovar and Porter, p. 195.
27. See, for example, Myron W. Lustig and Jolene Koester, *Intercultural Competence,* 2nd ed. (New York: HarperCollins, 1996), p. 192.
28. Christopher Engholm, *When Business East Meets Business West* (New York: Wiley, 1991), p. 124.
29. H. Ned Seelye and Jacqueline Howell Wasilewski, *Between Cultures,* Lincolnwood, IL: NTC Publishing Group, 1996), p. 46.
30. Lustig and Koester, p. 210.

31. Bob Boylan, *What's Your Point?* (New York: Warner Books, 1990), p. 125.

CHAPTER 14

1. Merrie Spaeth, " 'Prop' Up Your Speaking Skills," *Wall Street Journal,* July 1, 1996, p. A14.
2. See Bill Carter, "Does More Time On-line Mean Reduced TV Time?" *New York Times,* January 31, 1997, p. D5; Steven Levy, "Breathing Is also Addictive," *Newsweek,* December 30, 1996/January 6, 1997, pp. 52–53, and Anne Cronin, "This Is Your Life, Generally Speaking," *New York Times,* July 26, 1992, p. E5.
3. Spaeth, p. A14.
4. See Alan L. Brown, *Power Pitches* (Chicago: Irwin, 1997); and Virginia Johnson, "Picture-Perfect Presentations," *Training and Development Journal,* 43: 1989, p. 45.
5. See Elena P. Zayas-Baya, "Instructional Media in the Total Language Picture," *International Journal of Instructional Media,* 5: 1977–78, pp. 145–150.
6. Donald R. Vogel, Gary W. Dickson, and John A. Lehman, "Persuasion and the Role of Visual Presentation Support: The UM/3M Study," commissioned by Visual Systems Division of 3M, 1986.
7. One early study was "A Research Report on the Effects of the Use of Overhead Transparencies on Business Meetings" (St Paul, MN: 3M Company, 1978).
8. Spaeth.
9. Robert W. Pittman, "We're Talking the Wrong Language to TV Babies," *New York Times,* January 24, 1990, p. A23.
10. Claudyne Wilder, *The Presentations Kit* (New York: Wiley, 1990), pp. 105–106.
11. Spaeth.
12. Walter Goodman, "How Bad Is War? It Depends on the TV Pictures," *New York Times,* November 5, 1991, p. C18.
13. See Tom Mucciolo, "Driving Data with Charts," *Speechwriter's Newsletter,* January 1, 1997, p. 6.
14. "The Statistics on Abortion in the USA," *USA TODAY,* August 8, 1996, p. 4A.
15. From Robert Boostrom, *Developing Creative & Critical Thinking: An Integrated Approach* (Lincolnwood, IL: National Textbook Company, 1992), p. 231.
16. Ibid.
17. See Tom Mucciolo and Rich Mucciolo, *Purpose, Movement, Color: A Strategy for Effective Presentations* (New York: MediaNet, Inc., 1994).
18. Johnetta B. Cole, *Conversations* (New York: Anchor Books, 1993).
19. Spring Asher and Wicke Cambers, *Wooing & Winning Business* (New York: Wiley, 1997), p. 56.
20. Wilder, p. 109.
21. See Virginia Johnson, "Picture Perfect Presentations," *The Toastmaster,* February 1990, p. 7.
22. Tom Mucciolo, "Use the Power of Color," *Speechwriter's Newsletter,* November 15, 1996, p. 6.

CHAPTER 15

1. Chicago Tribune, January 9, 1997.
2. As quoted in the Wisconsin State Journal, August 24, 1983, Section 3, p. 1.
3. Neil Postman, *Amusing Ourselves to Death: Public Discourse in the Age of Show Business* (New York: Penguin Books, 1985), p. 97.
4. Roshama Hazel, "Our Bodies Are Like Machines." *Winning Orations, 1995* (Northfield, MN; Interstate Oratorical Association, 1995), pp. 45–47.

CHAPTER 16

1. Advertising is the prime industry of persuasion; over $180 billion a year is spent on advertising. See, for example, Stuart Elliott, "Advertising: A Sunny Forecast for Ad Spending Grows Even Brighter," *New York Times,* June 14, 1995, p. D9.
2. Noted more than two decades ago by Alvin Toffler, *Future Shock* (New York: Bantam Books, 1970), p. 3.
3. See Dominic A. Infante, Andrew S. Rancer, and Deanna F. Womack, *Building Communication Theory,* 3rd ed. (Prospect Heights, IL: Waveland Press, 1997), pp. 161–164.
4. Infante et al., p. 178.
5. Carolyn Sherif, Muzafer Sherif, and Roger Nebergall, *Attitude and Attitude Change: The Social Judgment-Involvement Approach,* (Philadelphia, PA: W.B. Saunders, 1965).
6. Social judgment theory is explained succinctly in Em Griffin, *A First Look at Communication Theory* (New York: McGraw-Hill, 1994), pp. 220–227.
7. This discussion draws on the work of Myron Lustig and Jolene Koester, *Intercultural Competence: Interpersonal Communication Across Cultures,* 2nd ed. (New York: HarperCollins, 1996), especially pp. 221–228.
8. Jesse Jackson, "We Must Seek a New Moral Center," *Vital Speeches of the Day,* September 15, 1996, pp. 717–718.
9. Janet Martin, "Room at the Top: Women in Banking," in Jack Griffin and Alice Marks, ed., *The Business Speaker's Almanac* (Englewood, Cliffs, NJ: Prentice-Hall, 1994), pp. 321–322.
10. "Senator Eugene McCarthy Crystallizes Dissent by Denouncing the War in Vietnam," in William Safire, ed., *Lend Me Your Ears: Great Speeches in History* (New York: Norton, 1992), p. 143.
11. A framework for understanding both attitudes and beliefs is offered by Martin Fishbein and Icek Ajzen in *Belief, Attitude, Intention and Behavior: An Introduction to Theory and Research* (Reading, MA: Addison-Wesley, 1975).
12. See "Social Values: Public Values Intangible Assets More Than Material Possessions," *The Gallup Report,* March/April 1989, pp. 35–44.
13. Meyera E. Oberndorf, "The Changing Role of Women in the 21st Century," *Vital Speeches of the Day,* October 1, 1992, p. 754.
14. Brad Braddy, "Workplace Violence and the Explosive Employee," *Winning Orations 1995* (Northfield, MN: Interstate Oratorical Association, 1995), p. 14.
15. Kathleen Kelly Reardon, *Persuasion in Practice* (Newbury Park, CA: Sage, 1991), pp. 1–2, 5.

16. John Irvin and Michael Snedeker, "Warehouse Prisons: Life Inside in the Modern Age," *The California Prisoner,* August 1989.
17. See also Gustav Niebuhr, "Suddenly, Religious Ethicists Face a Quandary on Cloning," *New York Times,* March 1, 1997, pp. 1, 10.
18. See, for example, Ronald Takati, "An Educated and Culturally Literate Person Must Study America's Multicultural Reality," *The Chronicle of Higher Education,* March 8, 1989, and Wendy Griswold, *Cultures and Societies in a Changing World,* (Thousand Oaks, CA: Pine Forge Press, 1994).
19. See Martha Cooper, *Analyzing Public Discourse* (Prospect Heights, IL: Waveland Press, 1989), p. 46.
20. See Dominic A. Infante, *Arguing Constructively* (Prospect Heights, IL: Waveland Press, 1988).
21. Anthony Pratkanis and Eliot Aronson, *The Age of Propaganda* (New York: W.H. Freeman, 1991), pp. 154–155.
22. Donald C. Bryant, "Rhetoric: Its Function and Its Scope," *Quarterly Journal of Speech 39:* December 1953, p. 26.
23. This outline is based in part on a speech by Diane Ravitch, delivered on November 2, 1990, entitled "Multiculturalism in the Public Schools." It is included in R. R. Allen and Wil A. Linkugel, *Contemporary American Speeches* (Dubuque, IA: Kendall Hunt, 1992), pp. 257–262.
24. Antonia C. Novello, "Health Priorities for the Nineties," *Vital Speeches,* August 15, 1992, pp. 666–672.
25. Eddie Williams, "The Future of Black Politics: From the Margin to the Mainstream," *Vital Speeches of the Day,* March 15, 1991, pp. 348–350.
26. Text provided by the national headquarters of the United Farm Workers.
27. John E. Cleghorn, "Diversity: The Key to Quality Business," in Jack Griffin and Alice Marks, ed., *The Business Speaker's Almanac* (Englewood Cliffs, NJ: Prentice-Hall, 1994), p. 336.
28. See John C. Reinard, "The Empirical Study of the Persuasive Effects of Evidence: The Status after 50 Years of Research," *Human Communication Research, 15:* 1988, pp. 3–59.
29. See Stephen Toulman, *The Uses of Argument* (Cambridge, UK: Cambridge University Press, 1958).
30. Provided by Planned Parenthood.
31. Based on a speech by Stanley Eilzen, chairman of the department of sociology at Colorado State University, "Problem Students: The Socio-Cultural Roots," *Vital Speeches of the Day,* May 15, 1990, pp. 476–480.
32. See Project on Status & Education of Women.
33. Lawrence K. Grossman, "Reshaping Political Values in the Information Age," *Vital Speeches of the Day,* January 15, 1997, p. 206.
34. See Abraham H. Maslow, *Motivation and Personality,* 2nd ed. (New York: Harper & Row, 1970).
35. See F. J. Boster and P. Mongeau, "Fear Arousing Persuasive Messages," in R. N. Bostrom, ed., *Communication Yearbook* (Beverly Hills, CA: Sage, 1984), pp. 330–375.
36. Tina Campbell, "Medical Privacy—Reality or Fiction," *Winning Orations 1995,* (Northfield, MN: Interstate Oratorical Association, 1995), pp. 100–102.

CHAPTER 17

1. Peggy Noonan, *What I Saw at the Revolution* (New York: Ivy Books, 1990), p. 237.
2. James R. Andrews and David Zarefsky, *Contemporary American Voices* (New York: Longman, 1992), pp. 418–419.
3. Delivered by Gregory Peck at the 1982 awards ceremony of the Academy of Motion Picture Arts and Sciences.
4. Elie Wiesel acceptance of the 1986 Nobel Peace Prize, *New York Times,* December 11, 1986, p. A8.
5. Barbara Jordan, "Democratic Convention Keynote Address," *Vital Speeches of the Day,* August 15, 1976, pp. 645–646.
6. Dolores M. Bandow, "A Bird Outside Your Window," in Richard L. Johannesen et al, *Contemporary American Speeches* (Dubuque, IA: Kendall Hunt, 1992), pp. 402–404. L'Chaim means "to life."
7. Noonan, pp. 261–262.
8. Robert M. Kaplan and Gregory C. Pascoe, "Humorous Lectures and Humorous Examples: Some Effects upon Comprehension and Retention," *Journal of Educational Psychology 69:* 1977, pp. 61–65.
9. In *1990 Championship Debates and Speeches,* Vol. 5, Christina L. Reynolds et al, ed., (Annandale, VA: Speech Communication Association, 1991), pp. 95–98.
10. Gayle Sayers with Al Silverman, *I Am Third* (New York: Viking Press, 1970), p. 77.

CHAPTER 18

1. As far as the authors can tell, Bobby R. Patton and Kim Giffin, authors of *Decision-Making Group Interaction,* 2nd ed. (New York: Harper & Row, 1978), p. 1, were the first to cite this fact.
2. Robert Gebeloff, "Oh No, Not Another Meeting," *The Record,* June 20, 1994, pp. C-1, C-4.
3. Roger K. Mosvick and Rober B. Nelson, *We've Got to Start Meeting Like This!* (Glenview, IL: Scott, 1987), p. 4.
4. See Charles Pavett and Ellen Curtis, *Small Group Discussion: A Theoretical Approach* (Scottsdale, AZ: Gorsuch Scarisbrick, 1990), pp. 25–60.
5. Charles Redding, *Communication within the Organization* (New York: Industrial Communication Council, 1972).
6. Anthony De Palma, "It Takes More Than a Visa to Do Business in Mexico," *New York Times,* June 26, 1994.
7. Dolores Cathcart and Robert Cathcart, "Japanese Social Experience and Concept of Groups," in Larry A. Samover and Richard E. Porter, eds., *Intercultural Communication: A Reader,* 4th ed. (Belmont, CA: Wadsworth, 1985), p. 190. See also Dolores Cathcart and Robert Cathcart, "The Group: A Japanese Context" in Larry A.

Samover and Richard E. Porter, eds., *Intercultural Communication: A Reader,* 7th ed. (Belmont, CA: Wadsworth, 1994), pp. 293–304.

8. Ibid.
9. See Cathcart and Cathcart, 1994.
10. See J. Kevin Barge, "Leadership as Medium: A Leaderless Group Discussion Model," *Communication Quarterly 37(4):* Fall 1989, pp. 237–247.
11. Douglas McGregor, *The Human Side of Enterprise* (New York: McGraw-Hill, 1960).
12. From Bettyjane Levine, "(Wo)men at Work" *Los Angeles Times,* October 29, 1990.
13. See Randy Y. Hirokowa, "Group Communication and Problem Solving Effectiveness: An Investigation of Group Process," *Human Communication Research, 9:* Summer 1983, pp. 291–305.
14. See Kenneth Benne and Paul Sheats, "Functional Roles of Group Members," *Journal of Social Issues, 4:* 1948, pp. 41–49.
15. See John Dewey, *How We Think* (Boston, MA: Heath, 1910).
16. See Irving Janis, *Victims of Groupthink: A Psychological Study of Foreign Policy Decisions and Fiascos* (Boston, MA: Houghton Mifflin, 1972).
17. Alex Osborn, *Applied Imagination* (New York: Scribner, 1957).
18. Barbara Eakins and Gene Eakins, *Sex Differences in Communication* (Boston: Houghton Mifflin, 1978).

Index

Photo Credits

Page 3, Reuters/Gary Cameron/Archive Photos
Page 11, Naum Kazden/New York Times Pictures
Page 15, Topham/The Image Works
Page 25, Mary Kate Denny/Tony Stone Images
Page 28, Tabuteau/The Image Works
Page 34, Rhoda Sidney/The Image Works
Page 42, Reuters/Corbis-Bettmann
Page 45, AP/Wide World Photos
Page 49, Gary Wagner/Stock, Boston
Page 57, Bob Daemmrich/Stock, Boston
Page 62, Charles Gupton/Stock, Boston
Page 63, Joe Sohm/Chromosohm/The Image Works
Page 81, AP/Wide World Photos
Page 83, Francis Apesteguy/Gamma Liaison
Page 95, © Syracuse Newspaper/Kevin Jacobus/The Image Works
Page 108, Richard Pasley/Stock, Boston
Page 114, Gaye Hilsenrath/The Picture Cube
Page 118, Reuters/Jeff Mitchell/Archive Photos
Page 127, Jon Riley/Tony Stone Images
Page 133, Pascal Quittemelle/Stock, Boston
Page 140, Paula Lerner/Woodfin Camp & Associates
Page 159, AP/Wide World Photos
Page 164, Gilles Mingasson/Gamma Liaison
Page 178, AP/Wide World Photos
Page 185, Dion Ogust/The Image Works
Page 189, Hugh Sitton/Tony Stone Images
Page 192, Eric Millette/The Picture Cube
Page 202, AP/Wide World Photos
Page 213, Paula Lerner/The Picture Cube
Page 218, Dirck Halstead/Gamma Liaison
Page 233, Will Hart
Page 237, Don Farber/Woodfin Camp & Associates
Page 240, Will Hart
Page 245, UPI/Corbis-Bettmann
Page 250, Bob Daemmrich/Stock, Boston
Page 257, AP/Wide World Photos
Page 267, Will Hart

Page 271, Robert E. Daemmrich/Tony Stone Images
Page 281, Reuters/Corbis-Bettmann
Page 291, AP/Wide World Photos
Page 310, Doug Mason/Woodfin Camp & Associates
Page 318, Will Hart
Page 321, Will Hart
Page 334, Will & Demi McIntyre/Photo Researchers
Page 344, Chuck Nacke/Woodfin Camp & Associates
Page 352, Mark Reinstein/The Image Works
Page 377, AP/Wide World Photos
Page 386, Bob Strong/The Image Works
Page 390, AP/Wide World Photos
Page 400, AP/Wide World Photos
Page 410, Robert Harbison
Page 415, Walter Bibikow/The Picture Cube
Page 425, Paula Lerner/The Picture Cube

Text Credits

Chapter 1

Professional Insight box, p. 7, excerpted from Patricia Ward Brash, "Beyond Giving a Speech," presented to a meeting of Women in Communication, Milwaukee, Wisconsin; in *Vital Speeches of the Day,* November 15, 1992, pp. 83–86. Reprinted by permission of *Vital Speeches of the Day* and Miller Brewing Company.

Chapter 3

Professional Insight box, pp. 52–53, excerpted from Holger Kluge, "Reflections on Diversity," presented to the Diversity Network, Calgary, Alberta, Canada, October 28, 1996; in *Vital Speeches of the Day,* January 1, 1997, p. 171. Reprinted by permission of *Vital Speeches of the Day* and Canadian Imperial Bank of Commerce (CIBC).

Chapter 4

Professional Insight box, pp. 66–67, reprinted by permission of The Putnam Publishing Group from "Hello, Is Anybody There?" in *The Osgood Files* by Charles Osgood, pp. 37–39. Copyright © 1991 by Charles Osgood.

Considering Diversity, pp. 68–69, excerpted from "Behind Japan's Success" by Peter F. Drucker; *Harvard Business Review,* January–February 1980. Copyright Peter F. Drucker 1980; reprinted by permission from the author.

Student speech, pp. 75–77, by Paul Higday, "Ferrofluids," in Karla Kay Jensen, ed., *Video User's Guide for the Allyn & Bacon/AFA Student Speeches Video I* (Needham Heights, Mass.: Allyn & Bacon, 1996), pp. 19–21. Reprinted by permission.

Chapter 5

Professional Insight box, pp. 84–85, from *What I Saw at the Revolution* by Peggy Noonan, pp. 70–72. Copyright © 1989 by Peggy Noonan. Reprinted by permission of Random House, Inc.

Speech, pp. 87–88, excerpted from Jean Otto, "Freedom to Speak and Write," speech presented before the First Amendment Congress in Richmond, Virginia; in *Vital Speeches of the Day,* January 1, 1992, pp. 187–188. Reprinted by permission of *Vital Speeches of the Day* and Jean Otto, Associate Editor, *Rocky Mountain News.*

Speech, p. 88, excerpted from James A. Baker III speech presented at Princeton University; in *Vital Speeches of the Day,* January 1, 1992, p. 162. Reprinted by permission of *Vital Speeches of the Day.*

Speech, pp. 88–89, excerpted from James R. Houghton, "Leadership," speech presented at a leadership conference; in *Vital Speeches of the Day,* July 1, 1996, pp. 571–572. Reprinted by permission of *Vital Speeches of the Day* and Corning Inc.

Speech, p. 89, excerpted from Nancy W. Dickey, "Our Sisters' Sicknesses, Our Sisters' Satchels: The Past, Present, and Future of Women and Medicine," speech delivered to the Simmons College Graduate School of Management Alumnae Association, 17th Annual Professional Development Conference for Women, Women 2000: Into the New Millennium, Boston, May 4, 1996; in *Vital Speeches of the Day,* July 15, 1996, pp. 582–583. Reprinted by permission of *Vital Speeches of the Day* and the American Medical Association.

Speech, p. 92, excerpted from Ray Halbritter, "Indian Economic Futures: Governance and Taxation," delivered at Cornell University; in *Vital Speeches of the Day,* December 15, 1996, pp. 153–154. Reprinted by permission of *Vital Speeches of the Day* and Ray Halbritter, Oneida Indian Nation.

Speech, p. 97, excerpted from Senator Al Gore, vice-presidential acceptance speech delivered before the Democratic National Convention, July 16, 1992.

Chapter 6

Professional Insight box, pp. 110–111, from Don Aslett, *Is There a Speech Inside You?* (Cincinnati, Ohio: Writer's Digest Books, 1989), pp. 18–19, 30. Reprinted by permission of Exley Publications Ltd.

Student speech, pp. 120–122, by Patricia Ann Compos, "Tissue Engineering," in Karla Kay Jensen, ed., *Video User's Guide for the Allyn & Bacon/AFA Student Speeches Video I* (Needham Heights, Mass.: Allyn & Bacon, 1996), pp. 14–16. Reprinted by permission.

Chapter 7

Figure 7.2, p. 138, printout from the Bergen County (New Jersey) Public Library's computerized catalogue system.

Figure 7.6, p. 146, used with the permission of CompuServe Incorporated.

Professional Insight box, pp. 150–151, excerpted by permission from Patrick McGeehan, "Playing the Numbers, Sometimes for Laughs: Demographic Duo," *The Record,* Hackensack, N.J., December 13, 1992, pp. B1–B2.

Student speech, pp. 151–154, by Suzi Kim, "Dry Cleaning," in Karla Kay Jensen, ed., *Video User's Guide for the Allyn & Bacon/AFA Student Speeches Video I* (Needham Heights, Mass.: Allyn & Bacon, 1996), pp. 62–64. Reprinted by permission.

Chapter 8

Student speeches attributed in the endnotes to various editions of *Winning Orations* are reprinted by permission of the Interstate Oratorical Association.

Speech, pp. 160–161, excerpted from Claudette Mackay-Lassonde, "Let's Stop Fooling Ourselves"; in *Vital Speeches of the Day,* July 1, 1996, pp. 569–571. Reprinted by permission of *Vital Speeches of the Day,* Angela Christopoulos, and Claudette Mackay-Lassonde.

Speech, pp. 163–164, excerpted from Sheila Wellington, President of Catalyst, "Women Are in the Wrong Conduits," in *Vital Speeches of the Day,* December 15, 1996, pp. 148–150. Reprinted by permission of *Vital Speeches of the Day* and Catalyst.

Student speech, p. 170, excerpted from Kelly Campbell, "The Decoy Virus Vaccine," in Karla Kay Jensen, ed., *Video User's Guide for the Allyn & Bacon/AFA Student Speeches Video I* (Needham Heights, Mass.: Allyn & Bacon, 1996), p. 24.

Speech, p. 172, excerpted from Jorge L. Carro, "Capital Punishment from a Global Perspective: The Death Penalty—Right or Wrong?" In *Vital Speeches of the Day,* August 1, 1996, p. 630. Reprinted by permission of *Vital Speeches of the Day* and Jorge L. Carro, Professor of Law, Emeritus, University of Cincinnati.

Figure 8.1, p. 173, "Deaths from Breast Cancer," *Newsweek,* December 30, 1991, p. 56. Newsweek–Frank Garland. © 1991, Newsweek, Inc. All rights reserved. Reprinted by permission.

Professional Insight box, pp. 174–175, from George F. Will, "Playing with Numbers," *The Record,* January 5, 1992. © 1992, Washington Post Writers Group. Reprinted with permission.

Student speech, p. 178, excerpted from Ben Lohman, "Fiberglass Insulation," in Karla Kay Jensen, ed., *Video User's Guide for the Allyn & Bacon/AFA Student Speeches Video I* (Needham Heights, Mass.: Allyn & Bacon, 1996), p. 53. Reprinted by permission.

Chapter 9

Professional Insight box, p. 193, excerpted from Lani Arrredondo, *How to Present Like a Pro* (New York: McGraw-Hill, 1991), pp. 28–29.

Chapter 10

Student speeches attributed in the endnotes to various editions of *Winning Orations* are reprinted by permission of the Interstate Oratorical Association.

Speech, p. 205, from *Vital Speeches of the Day,* April 1, 1997, p. 375. Reprinted by permission of *Vital Speeches of the Day* and IBM K–12 Education: William E. Rodrigues, General Manager; James E. Schnitz, Ph.D., Director of Solutions Strategy; Raymond J. Cadmus, Jr., Communications Manager; and Linda L. VanCott, Research Associate. Copyright 1997 IBM Corporation.

Speech, p. 215, excerpted from Susan Trausch. "A Once Proud America Is Sinking into the Middle Ground," *The Record,* January 17, 1992, p. B-7. Reprinted courtesy of *The Boston Globe.*

Student speech, pp. 216–217, excerpted from Bond Benton, "Staged Auto Accidents." In Karla Kay Jensen, ed., *Video User's Guide for the Allyn & Bacon/AFA Student Speeches Video I* (Needham Heights, Mass.: Allyn & Bacon, 1996), pp. 66–67. Reprinted by permission.

Chapter 11

Speech, pp. 238–239, excerpted from William Steare, "Plan Globally, Engage Locally: The Public Policy Challenge for Global Corporations," in *Vital Speeches of the Day,* December 1, 1992. Reprinted by permission of *Vital Speeches of the Day* and William Steare, Pfizer Inc.

Chapter 12

Speech, p. 249, excerpted from Sol Trujilo, "American Hispanic Population," *Vital Speeches of the Day,* December 1, 1996, p. 124. Reprinted by permission of *Vital Speeches of the Day* and the Center for the New West.

Speaking of Skillbuilding box, p. 254, "Solitary confinement" and "soft targets" from Hugh Rawson, *A Dictionary of Euphemisms and Other Doubletalk* by Hugh Rawson (New York: Crown, 1981); other definitions from Henry Beard and Chris Cerf, *The Official Politically Correct Dictionary and Handbook* (New York: Villard Books, Random House, 1992).

Speech, p. 260, excerpted from Jean Otto, "Freedom to Speak and Write," speech presented before the First Amendment Congress in Richmond, Virginia; in *Vital Speeches of the Day,* January 1, 1992, p. 189. Reprinted by permission of *Vital Speeches of the Day* and Jean Otto, Associate Editor, *Rocky Mountain News.*

Speech, p. 261, excerpted from Martin Luther King, "I Have a Dream," August 28, 1963. Reprinted by arrangement with The Heirs to the Estate of Martin Luther King, Jr., c/o Writers House, Inc., as agent for the proprietor. Copyright 1963 by Martin Luther King, Jr., copyright renewed 1991 by Coretta Scott King.

Chapter 13

Professional Insight box, p. 268, reprinted by permission of The Putnam Publishing Group from "Read My Eyes, Not My Lips," in *The Osgood Files* by Charles Osgood, pp. 59–60. Copyright © 1991 by Charles Osgood.

Chapter 14

Professional Insight box, pp. 292–293, from Claudyne Wilder, *The Presentations Kit,* pp. 105–106. Copyright © 1990 by John Wiley & Sons, Inc. Reprinted by permission of John Wiley & Sons, Inc.

Speaking of Ethics box, pp. 297–299, excerpted from Walter Goodman, "How Bad Is War? It Depends on the TV Pictures," *New York Times,* November 5, 1991, p. C18. Copyright © 1991 by The New York Times Company. Reprinted by permission.

Figure 14.2, p. 299, data courtesy of The Alan Guttmacher Institute; graph from *USA Today,* August 8, 1996, p. 4A. Copyright 1996, *USA Today.* Reprinted with permission.

Figure 14.3, p. 300, from "Ethnic Diversity: Population Share by Racial Group," *The Record,* January 1, 1997. Reprinted with permission of *The Record* of Hackensack, N.J.

Figure 14.4, p. 301, from "Shoring Up Family Values," *USA Today,* July 29, 1992, p. D1. Copyright 1992, *USA Today.* Reprinted with permission.

Figure 14.5, p. 301, adapted from "U.S. Home Office Work Style Trends," *The Record,* July 19, 1991, p. B1. Drawing by Milton Melendez/The Record. Reprinted with permission of *The Record* of Hackensack, N.J.

Figure 14.6, p. 302, data from Bureau of Labor Statistics. In "Casualties of the Information Age," *Time,* June 26, 1995, p. 23.

Figure 14.7, p. 302, from "Hispanics Tuning In," *USA Today,* November 17, 1995. Drawing by Anne R. Carey and Gary Visgaitis, *USA Today.* Copyright 1995, *USA Today.* Reprinted with permission. Data from Interep Research.

Figure 14.8a, p. 303, from "Women in Politics: Number of Women vs. Men Currently Holding Office," *The Record,* August 2, 1992.

Figure 14.8b, p. 303, from "Better Late than Never," *USA Today,* January 13, 1997. Drawing by Cindy Hall and Suzy Parker. Copyright 1997, *USA Today.* Reprinted with permission. Data from National Endowment for Financial Education.

Figure 14.11, p. 305, from "Top-Selling Flavors/Fast-Growing Flavors," *New York Times,* August 2, 1992. Copyright © 1992 by The New York Times Company. Reprinted by permission.

Figure 14.12, p. 305, Food Guide Pyramid, in *The Sunday Record,* August 2, 1992, p. F1.

Figure 14.14, p. 307, from "Olympic Record," *Newsweek,* July 27, 1992, p. 51. Newsweek–Blumrich. © 1992, Newsweek, Inc. All rights reserved. Reprinted by permission.

Figure 14.15, p. 307, from *The Record,* August 3, 1992.

Figure 14.16, p. 308, from "Rabies: How It Spreads," *The Record,* May 10, 1995. Data from *The World Book Medical Encyclopedia.* Reprinted with permission of Knight-Ridder/Tribune In-formation Services.

Figure 14.17, p. 308, from "Where Do Tornadoes Occur?" *The Record,* May 5, 1995. Information from "Florida Weather," "Weather," "Severe and Unusual Weather,"

World Book Encyclopedia; "Violent Storms," Tornadoes," *The Weather Almanac.* Reprinted with permission of Knight-Ridder/Tribune Information Services.

Figure 14.18, p. 309, reprinted by permission from Steven A. Beebe and Susan J. Beebe, *Public Speaking: An Audience Centered Approach,* 3d ed. (Needham Heights, MA: Allyn & Bacon, 1997), p. A18.

Chapter 15

Student speech, pp. 338–340, by Rosharna Hazel, "Our Bodies Are Like Machines," *Winning Orations,* 1995, pp. 45–47, by permission of the Interstate Oratorical Association.

Chapter 16

Student speeches attributed in the endnotes to various editions of *Winning Orations* are reprinted by permission of the Interstate Oratorical Association.

Speech, p. 347, excerpted from Jesse Jackson, "We Must Seek a New Moral Center," *Vital Speeches of the Day,* September 15, 1996, pp. 717–718. Reprinted by permission of *Vital Speeches of the Day* and Rev. Jesse L. Jackson, Sr., Founder and President, Rainbow PUSH Coalition, Inc.

Speech, pp. 347–348, excerpted from Janet Martin, "Room at the Top: Women in Banking," speech delivered to the North Toronto Business and Professional Women's Club, Toronto, Ontario, Canada, December 4, 1991. In Jack Griffin and Alice Marks, eds., *The Business Speaker's Almanac* (Englewood Cliffs, N.J.: Prentice-Hall, 1994), pp. 321–322.

Professional Insight box, pp. 354–355, excerpted from Kathleen Kelly Reardon, *Persuasion in Practice,* pp. 1–2, 5. Copyright © 1991 by Sage Publications, Inc. Reprinted by permission of Sage Publications, Inc.

Speaking of Critical Thinking box, p. 361, from *The Age of Propaganda,* pp. 154–155, by Anthony Pratkanis and Eliot Aronson. © 1992 by W. H. Freeman and Company. Used with permission.

Speech, p. 367, excerpted from Antonia C. Novello, "Health Priorities for the Nineties," *Vital Speeches of the Day,* August 15, 1992, pp. 666–672. Reprinted by permission of *Vital Speeches of the Day.*

Speech, pp. 367–368, excerpted from César Chávez "Pesticides" speech, by permission of the César E. Chávez Foundation, P.O. Box 62, La Paz, Keene, CA 93531 (tel. 805/822-5571, ext 230; fax 805/822-6103).

Speech, p. 372, excerpted by permission of the author from Dr. Bernice Sandler, "Men and Women Getting Along: These Are the Times That Try Men's Souls."

Speech, p. 373, excerpted from Lawrence K. Grossman, "Reshaping Political Values in the Information Age: The Power of the Media," in *Vital Speeches of the Day,* January 15, 1997, p. 206. Reprinted by permission of *Vital Speeches of the Day* and

Lawrence K. Grossman, author of *The Electronic Republic: Reshaping Democracy in the Information Age,* and former president of PBS and NBC News.

Figure 16.3, p. 377, from Abraham H. Maslow, *Toward a Psychology of Being* (New York: Van Nostrand Reinhold, 1968), Figure 14.2. Reprinted by permission.

Chapter 17

Speech, p. 387, from Peggy Noonan, *What I Saw at the Revolution* (New York: Ivy Books, 1990), p. 237.

Speech, pp. 390–391, Gregory Peck's speech of presentation of the Jean Hersholt Humanitarian Award to Danny Kaye at the 1981 Academy Awards. Copyright © Academy of Motion Picture Arts and Sciences, 1982.

Speech, pp. 391–392, Elie Wiesel, Nobel Prize acceptance speech, delivered December 10, 1986. Reprinted by permission of Nobelstiftelsen (The Nobel Foundation).

Speech, pp. 393–395, from commencement address delivered by Johnetta B. Cole, the president of Spellman College, to the 1991 graduating class of the College of New Rochelle. Reprinted by permission of Marie Brown Associates. Copyright © 1991 Johnetta B. Cole.

Speech, pp. 395–397, excerpted from Barbara Jordan, "Democratic Convention Keynote Address," in *Vital Speeches of the Day,* August 15, 1976, pp. 645–646. Reprinted by permission of *Vital Speeches of the Day.*

Speech, pp. 398–399, from Dolores M. Bandow, "A Bird Outside Your Window," in Richard L. Johannesen, R. R. Allen, and Wil A. Linkugel, compilers, *Contemporary American Speeches* (Dubuque, Iowa: Kendall/Hunt Publishing, 1992), pp. 402–404. Copyright © 1992 Dolores M. Bandow. Reprinted by permission of Dolores M. Bandow.

Professional Insight box, p. 400, from Peggy Noonan, *What I Saw at the Revolution* (New York: Ivy Books, 1989), pp. 261–262.

Eulogy, pp. 404–405, for Diana, Princess of Wales, by her brother, Charles Spencer, 9th Earl Spencer, at Westminster Abbey on September 6, 1997.

Speech, pp. 404–405, by Joel Schwartzberg, Emerson College, after-dinner speech, in Christine Reynolds, Larry G. Schnoor, and James R. Brey, eds., *1990 Championship Debates and Speeches,* vol. 5 (Annandale, Va.: Speech Communication Association, 1991), pp. 95–98. Used by permission of the Speech Communication Association and the author.

Chapter 18

Professional Insight box, pp. 416–417, from Bettijane Levine, "(Wo)men at Work," *Los Angeles Times,* October 29, 1990. Copyright, 1990, Los Angeles Times. Reprinted by permission.